£24.95

Innovation, Economics and Evolution

book

R

Innovation, Economics and Evolution

Theoretical Perspectives on Changing Technology in Economic Systems

Peter Hall

HARVESTER WHEATSHEAF

New York · London · Toronto · Sydney · Tokyo · Singapore

First published 1994 by
Harvester Wheatsheaf
Campus 400, Maylands Avenue
Hemel Hempstead
Hertfordshire, HP2 7EZ
A division of
Simon & Schuster International Group

Typeset in 10/12 pt Times
by PPS Limited, Amesbury, Wiltshire

Printed and bound in Great Britain by
Redwood Books, Trowbridge, Wiltshire

British Library Cataloguing in Publication Data

A catalogue record for this book is available from
the British Library

ISBN 0-7450-1251-5

1 2 3 4 5   98 97 96 95 94

For Jenny, Christopher and Bronwyn

Contents

Acknowledgements

I am indebted to a number of good friends for their support at various stages in the preparation and writing of this book – in particular Stan Metcalfe, Malcolm Treadgold, Peter Drake, Paul Robertson and Stefan Markowski. I wish to thank the University of New South Wales for providing me with time, as part of a Special Studies Program in 1989, to get the project under way and the Department of Economics, Research School of Pacific Studies, Australian National University for providing me as a Visiting Fellow with space, stimulation and secretarial assistance at that time.

I am also most grateful to Mrs Jill Kenna who worked assiduously and cheerfully to process and reprocess most of the words in this book. Without her input, the manuscript would never have been completed. Mrs Jean Considine also gave a helping hand.

Finally, my wife Jenny and children Christopher and Bronwyn had to take second place too often to the preparation of the manuscript for this book. I deeply appreciate their support and understanding.

Peter H. Hall   March 1993

1

Innovation, systems and evolution

Aims

The aims of this book are first, to explain the impact of technological change on economic activity, magnitudes and structures and second, to explain the determinants, particularly from an economic perspective, of technological change – its direction and its rate.

An underlying theme throughout the book is that economic and technological change are causally intertwined. At any given moment, the uses to which scarce resources are put in an economy depend heavily on the current technology. But some of those resources will be devoted to changing the current technology – in turn, influencing the structure of the economy and, as a result, the conditions bearing on decisions about the next round of technological changes. Technological and economic development are inextricably linked. The complex and subtle relationships involved here continue to fascinate and often defeat analysis. But this book aims to provide some idea, largely from the viewpoint of economics, of what has so far been achieved.

Technology and innovation

In a classic source (Schmookler, 1966) **technology** is defined as the 'social pool of knowledge of the industrial arts' (p. 1) and **technological change** as changes in this stock of knowledge. But 'technology' as a concept has been given both narrower and broader meanings than this (Enos, 1989). They range from the technical information contained in patents alone, to that more generally communicable in written form, on to include the artefact dimension of machines and then to encompass the technical know-how of humans (engineers, managers, machine operators, etc.) which may often be neither documented nor communicable. Broader definitions still include the **institutions** which facilitate employment of technical knowledge (including firms and the ways in which they organise themselves), and the **socio-political** and **legal**

environments which influence the direction and rate of transfer of technical knowledge and its associated artefacts.

Depending on the context and the definition therefore, technological change may relate not only to changes in knowledge which in principle all potential users could easily obtain, but also to the on-the-job experience and learning of individuals and developments in the machines with which they work. It could also apply to organisational development and socio-cultural change. Where such change involves any sort of improvement in terms of an agreed criterion, we talk of technological progress or advance.

We shall focus in this book on changes in knowledge, know-how and machines, but by no means ignore the important facilitating role of organisational change. In some analytical work, 'technical' change is distinguished from 'technological' change by defining the first to comprise the *effects* of the latter (Kennedy and Thirlwall, 1972). Thus technical progress includes the increased quantity of output which changes in technology make it possible to produce from given quantities of inputs, the improved quality of existing products which an advance in technology might generate and the new products resulting from new technology, assuming they are regarded as socially beneficial. However, this distinction is not easy to maintain. A new or improved product, for example, may well be a machine or intermediate input in the production process which comprises part of the technology (as defined above to include artefacts). Surely the product change is as much a part of technological change as an element of technical progress.

Examples which blur the distinction are numerous, which probably helps to explain why it is usually ignored. We prefer to take the position that, given the breadth of meanings which 'technology' has acquired, it is better to allow the notion of technological change to encompass both changes in technological knowledge and the effects that new knowledge has on production processes and products, i.e. to subsume technical change within technological change.

That said, technological and technical change require innovation. Like 'technology', 'innovation' has broad and narrow meanings. The overall **process of innovation** encompasses the entire range of activities which contribute to producing new goods and services and producing in new ways. In a narrower meaning, innovation occurs when a new good, service or production method is put into commercial use for the first time, usually meant as first in the economy, but sometimes as a first for a firm, or first in the world. When a given product is produced in a new way, **process innovation** occurs; when the product is altered or a new product is introduced, **product innovation** takes place but as noted above, some product innovations are also process innovations.

In general terms, the book covers the economics of technological and technical change or, alternatively, the economics of innovation.

Economics and systems

Economics may be viewed as the study of those branches of human behaviour in which the relative values of commodities (broadly defined) are determined. Or, to use another definition, it is about how society makes use of its scarce resources. The framework within which economics analyses these questions is well known. Individuals, assumed to know their own best interests, line up on opposite sides of markets for each commodity, including materials, labour and other inputs into the production process. On the **demand side** are potential buyers, on the **supply side** potential sellers. As individuals on either side of the market make decisions which they believe will best serve their interests, **trades** are agreed upon: quantities to be exchanged at stated prices. Values are thus determined and resources allocated among uses and users as a result of trading relationships. But how are these relationships and the connections among markets as well as within them to be analysed?

The answer is that economic activity is envisaged to take place within **systems**, connected and interdependent sets of relationships among the entities under study. Economics amounts to investigating how trading systems work, bearing in mind that much trade involves resources used in production, so the amounts traded reflect how production is itself undertaken, i.e. the technology. Often, economists talk about 'models', sets of relationships written down mathematically in a way designed to offer a simplified description of a more complex reality. Formally, an economy is a mathematical model of a system dedicated to economic activity. In this chapter, we prefer to talk in terms of the unifying idea of the system, since we want to draw attention to themes which arise both within and beyond economics.[1]

Crucial to the application of system thinking is defining appropriate **boundaries**. The analytical importance of such boundaries is that certain events, decisions and processes are placed outside and thus beyond the explanatory realm of the set of principles assumed to govern the relationships within the system. Such things are described as **exogenous** to the system, but may have important implications for the system if they occur. By contrast, changes which can be explained solely by reference to the relationships comprising the system are described as **endogenous**.

In the case of economies, boundaries may take a number of forms. Geographical boundaries separate economic relationships within a given nation or region from events elsewhere. Sectoral boundaries separate economic relationships within a given industry from activity in other parts of the economy. Corporate legal boundaries separate economic relationships within the system called 'the firm' from events beyond. And, central to our needs in this book, a functional form of boundary separates activity identified as economic from other activity viewed as non-economic. Examples of 'non-economic' activity might be political, astronomical, literary or sexual.

Often implicitly included on such a list are **scientific** and **technological** activities. The first can be defined as 'the creation, discovery, verification, collation, reorganisation and dissemination of knowledge about physical, biological and social nature' (Kline and Rosenberg, 1986: 287). This is a very general definition, but emphasises that scientific activity is about the search for and communication of knowlege about how the world works. The 'scientific method' used in such a search is traditionally viewed as an application of the **inductive approach**, looking for general principles or 'laws' which 'explain' particular events we observe.

As a counterpoint, technological activity is often viewed as employing the **deductive approach**, seeking particular applications of general principles which science has uncovered. As we noted previously, technological change involves expanding our knowledge of the industrial arts, increasing our knowledge of how to make artefacts and more generally how to satisfy material wants with either goods or services. Conceptually, technological activity may at times overlap scientific, but its emphasis is very much upon putting scientific principles to use.

The distinction between scientific and technological activity is clearly worth bearing in mind in a book like this. At this stage, however, the point to bring out is that both scientific and technological activities employ resources which could be put to alternative use and this implies that decisions with economic content have to be made to undertake them.

The reason it is important to make this point at the outset is that much economic analysis takes as its basic data natural resources, consumer preferences and the state of technology. Another way of putting this is to say that the boundaries of economic systems are defined to exclude analysis of what determines natural resource availability, likes and dislikes and knowledge of how to undertake production. These data are taken to be exogenous. Analytically, this is very convenient. It makes it possible to focus sharply on the effects of these factors (and changes in them) without having ttto clutter or complicate the analysis with discussion of what might have caused them to be as they are. The procedure can be defended by arguing that such factors (and changes in them) are, in some sense, 'beyond economics'. Yet if these data are even only partially explicable in economic terms, that defence is flawed. This book is principally concerned with changes in technological data but also takes into account changes in consumer preferences. I wish to argue that viewing the technology (and changes in it) as exogenous is strategically useful for getting us into the analysis, but ultimately indefensible given the interactions between economic and technological factors. Let us expand on that a little.

Technological change and economic systems

Important elements of economic change arise from technological change, but some economic change is not technology-driven. Important elements of technological change are motivated by economic considerations, but some technological change is independent of economics. When we view technological change as wholly exogenous to the economic system, we are implicitly saying it has no connection with economics. When we view it as wholly endogenous, we commit ourselves to the position that all technological change is economically driven. It would be difficult to defend either extreme convincingly. If therefore we wish to focus on the economic change which does arise from technological change, we must expect to take account of both exogenous and endogenous change in the technological data. Some of the relationships which change technology and its uses will thus be incorporated within economic systems (i.e. endogenised), but allowance will also have to be made for changes in technological knowledge and applications which arise independently of economic factors and cannot therefore be explained within any system of economic relationships.

We now make two further related points about systems. First, a set of relationships can only comprise a system if the relationships are all in some way causally related to each other. This is a somewhat stronger statement than that a relationship belongs to a system if it lies on one side of a boundary rather than another. Defining some boundary does not imply that all that lies within it comprises a causally linked set of relationships. It is a platitude in economics that 'everything depends on everything else', which confirms the relevance of thinking in terms of systems when considering economic analysis. But the statement is usually taken to mean that outcomes in one market affect outcomes in others, assuming given technology. For our purposes, however, a further question is how the technology used in an economic system might itself be endogenously shaped by economic pressures.

When parts of an economic system are defined in terms of exogenously given technological determinants, system change reflecting the impact of technological change can be relatively simply represented as changes in technological parameters, such as the capital and labour required to produce a unit of a given output. Because such parameters contribute to defining the structure of the system, we note that changes in them will often change relationships within and among economic variables, but that the explanation for such economic change must be limited to analysing the impact of events which have occurred outside the system. Once technology is endogenised, however, there is a dramatic qualitative change in what is being attempted. The technological parameters which provide a description of production methods become sensitive to events elsewhere in the system. This offers the possibility of seeing how a system might be able to change its own structure, how it might go about **self-organisation** (Prigogine and Stengers, 1985).

A second point has to do with **connections between levels**. Every system comprises relationships between entities or groups of entities. The entities chosen decide the level at which relationships within the system offer an explanation. In physics, for example, one might operate at the subatomic level, taking as entities the parts of an atom which together make up the system which is an atom. Or one might operate at the level of observable physical objects made up of atoms and ignore whatever might be happening at the atomic and subatomic levels. An obvious example of a system comprising such objects would be the solar system. In biology, one might look at individual organisms, or at species, or at the ecological level at which species compete. The classic example of a biological system would be a population of some organism in its natural environment. Similarly, in economics, we may look at individual decision-making units (households, firms, governments), multiples of firms and households in industries and markets and economy-wide aggregates of the activity of these units. Again, a complete description of an economic system would have to include references to the economic environment in which the unit or aggregate of units was operating.

Ideally, the accounts we give of how 'macro' level systems work should be consistent with the accounts we give of their 'micro' level components. Physics searches for such consistency in the form of a Unified Field Theory which could reconcile the findings of quantum mechanics with general relativity and gravity. Analogously, economics continues to search for analytical structures which put microfoundations under robust macroeconomic propositions, or build up macroeconomic predictions from a microeconomic base. This sort of quest is much like that for the Holy Grail and, as yet, we have no wholly satisfactory multilevel accounts in either the physical, biological or social sciences.[2] Understanding has to be acquired in a more piecemeal fashion, however, with an eye to linking levels wherever possible. To understand how technological and economic relationships are intertwined therefore, we shall look for relationships at a number of levels. But what we learn from the operation of microlevel systems will also contribute to an understanding of how macrolevel systems might work.

Explaining system change

Two approaches to system change

At any given moment, we can describe a system in terms of its **state**. In turn, the state of the system can be defined by reference to the values taken at that moment by the **state variables**, those variables whose paths through time describe changes in the state of the system. To say how the system changes, we must acquire an understanding of how the state variables come to take the values they do at any moment. Explaining how the sequence of states arises is an explanation of the process of change. Economics has taken from science two fundamentally different ways of looking at this question. One, taken from physics, views changes in the state of systems as determined by externally given natural laws. System change according to such laws is described as **mechanical**. The other, taken from the biological sciences, views system change as being generated by forces working within the system itself. This is described as the **evolutionary** approach.

We shall characterise the mechanical approach as the Two-T way of thinking: one 'T' to stand for typological and the other for timeless laws. The evolutionary approach we shall characterise as the Two-P way of thinking: one 'P' for population and the other for path dependence.

Mechanical

Under the mechanical approach, complex reality is simplified by assuming that basic units of analysis are either identical, or that some description of a single unit can be adopted which captures the essence of all. Such a unit is said to be **representative**. The physical sciences take entities such as atoms as their basic unit. In economics we find the representative firm and the representative household. This is the typological aspect of mechanical thinking. As Mayr (1982) puts it, variation in this view is merely a nuisance, attributable to the 'imperfect manifestation of the underlying essences', a distraction from the *typical* in which clues to the laws of the universe are to be found (p. 38).

The assumption is then made that mechanical systems obey fundamental laws of nature which determine the state of the system at each moment. Perhaps the most famous of such principles are Newton's Laws, upon which classical mechanics was built. These relate to the effect of applying forces to objects in a frictionless world and have been used, for example, to explain the motion of the planets in the Solar System. Such laws are timeless in the sense that they hold in all places at all times. Given their existence, the motion of the system is always predictable and the operation of the system said to be deterministic. If one knows the laws (and scientists see it as their job to uncover them), one can predict what will happen next and what must have happened in the past. However, the language of 'past' and 'future' is somewhat misleading in this connection. Possible states must be compatible with the laws but since the laws are immutable, the whole system could run equally well in any direction compatible with the laws, and no logical distinction described in terms of 'backwards' or 'forwards' can be made. Mechanical systems are in this sense 'reversible'. The laws operate independently of time, and hence are timeless in a very fundamental sense.

It is precisely this style of thinking which pervades much economic analysis. And that is deliberate. When Adam Smith and David Hume were shaping the theoretical concept of an economic system which economists today have inherited, 'the economic regularities and laws which were sought after were dominated by [an] equilibrium concept ... considered applicable *regardless of time and place*' (Pribram, 1983: 616). [My italics]

Evolutionary

The two Ps of evolutionary thinking provide a stark contrast with with the two Ts of mechanical thinking. In population thinking, explicit account is taken of the observation that all members of a population (e.g. a species of plant or animal) are different from each other. Analysis recognises this variation because it is seen as a central means of explaining how systems change. Rather than appealing to externally given natural laws, evolutionists seek mechanisms generated within the system arising from the inherent variety it contains as explanations for change. Rather than seeking general principles of unknown origin about how a system functions, evolutionists delve into how observed states come into being and give rise to other states. These are questions about creative forces rather than pure functioning. In this endeavour, the diversity of experience is viewed as central to understanding, not as a nuisance which gets in its way. The notion of diversity is obviously relevant to economics once it is recognised that no two firms in an industry are identical, that their performance varies widely and that their products are often different. Much variation arises because of deliberate or unintended innovation.

The other P, path dependence, points to the essential historicity, or contingent nature of the evolutionary approach. In a mechanical vision of the world, every state is determined by the immutable laws which co-determine all states: there is nothing in any one state which independently influences any other state. But in the evolutionary way of thinking, events in the state at $(t + 2)$ depend (partly) on events specific to the state at $(t + 1)$, and those at $(t + 1)$ to events at t. Outcomes at any given moment depend on how the system got there, i.e. the path it took. Thus a major change in climatic conditions between t and $(t + 1)$ will imply that in the new environment very different biological and botanical characteristics will be required of flora and fauna if they are to survive. We can predict, according to general principles, what these characteristics will need to be, but the particular physical forms in which these characteristics will appear can only be developments and adaptations of forms which already exist. There is no external mechanism for starting afresh to craft perfect designs for each environment. In practice, Nature starts with the forms already there.

While this puts constraints on what is possible, the precise forms of potential adaptations to the new environment will be very numerous. The material in species' gene pools will offer many possible alternatives. The actual direction taken must to a significant degree be a matter of chance. Crucially, this adds a third P to the evolutionary perspective on system change; it is probabilistic, by way of contrast with the deterministic nature of the mechanical approach.

One purpose of this book is to see how economics might draw upon evolutionary modes of analysis to acquire a deeper understanding of innovation-related change. In the next section, therefore, we look further into the nature of evolutionary reasoning.

Evolutionary reasoning

Natural selection

It is a defining characteristic of any analysis we identify as 'evolutionary' that randomness or unpredicability have an essential role to play in explanations about the transition from one state to another. As Philippe Van Parijs (1981) has observed: the 'evolutionary perspective ... focuses on mechanisms of *filtering* or *trial and error*, i.e. on mechanisms of selection between actual ... alternatives. ... [The] variation on which the selection operates ... must be *blind* ...' (pp 51–2). But equally, the great contribution of evolutionary biology has been to point to mechanisms which nonetheless shape and structure history, but offering a form of 'explanantion' different from that offered in the 'law-based' mechanical approach of classical physics. 'At the first step, the production of genetic variability, accident ... reigns supreme. However, the ordering of genetic variability by *selection* at the second step is anything but a chance process' (Mayr, 1982: 520). [My italics].

In its most basic form, the Darwinian evolutionary process can be represented as the operation of three principles: variation, heredity and selection (Metcalfe, 1989). Variation calls for the population comprising a species to vary from specimen to specimen in at least one physical characteristic of significance for its capacity to survive and reproduce. An economic analogue would be interfirm differences in productive efficiency or capability. Heredity supposes the existence of 'copying' mechanisms by which the species may retain stability of form, continuously for some substantial period of time. We know that DNA contains and transmits the relevant genetic information from one generation to the next. Heredity which transmits information illustrates the relevance of analogous mechanisms in economic systems for transmitting technology as information from one generation to another, i.e. education and training. These mechanisms allow 'organisational genes' to persist and be made subject to selection. They also form a basis for 'corporate culture'. In natural selection, some forms are better able to survive and reproduce in their environment (i.e. they are better *fitted* to it) and thus become dominant, relative to other forms. Put succinctly, natural selection is 'the differential reproduction of individuals that differ uniquely in their adaptive superiority' (Mayr, 1982: 57). While firms do not reproduce, the corporate strategies and behaviour patterns of some fit them better to survive and prosper in a given economic environment than those of others.

As we pointed out in the previous section, evolutionary mechanisms must build on diverse populations. In the absence of variety there is no scope for selection. And since selection shapes the direction of change, absence of variety means selection mechanisms have no role to play in explaining how change occurs. Variety ensures scope for selection at any given moment; heredity introduces enough inertia into the system to ensure that, even if selection proceeds relatively slowly, forms are sufficiently stable to allow it to do its job.[3]

Evolutionary explanation and other forms of explanation

Explanation in the framework of Darwinian natural selection links species change to developments in characteristics which serve individual organisms best in their quest to reproduce. As we have said, this is a proposition about populations. At the heart of natural selection is a competition among individuals making up a population. The distribution of characteristics over the population reflects which have served individuals best and worst, in the struggle to survive and reproduce in a given environment. Those characteristics which allow individuals to compete most success-fully for scarce resources allow them to live longer and reproduce more. Given heredity, these characteristics come to dominate within the population. When the environment changes, the characteristics which allow most success in the competition for resources will also change: the species adapts.

The biologist's so-called 'functional' type of explanation thus 'explains' observed characteristics in terms of a purpose they must, under some environmental pressure, have served in enabling organisms to survive longer and reproduce more effectively. Such explanation is qualitatively quite different from explanations found in classical physics with its emphasis on timeless, 'law-based' relationships between objects and the forces working on them. On the other hand, neither form of explanation takes account of intentional, purposeful or goal-directed activity which occurs in social organisations. In the presence of such activity, it is possible to 'explain' an event by reference to the intentions or goals of the person(s) taking part in the activity. For example, if the event to be explained is 'Ms Smith went to the theatre last night', we could offer the explanation that Ms Smith had wanted to see the play being performed at the theatre. There is no physical law which required Ms Smith to be at the theatre last night, though various laws might be invoked to explain the physics of how she got there. It might also be possible to show that her attendance at the theatre (a 'behaviour' rather than a physical characteristic on this occasion) was entirely irrelevant to her reproductive prospects. Nonetheless, we have a perfectly respectable – in this case intentional – explanation for the event.[4]

What this tells us, among other things, is that when modes of reasoning familiar in the physical and biological sciences are transferred to a social context, great caution is in order. We must recall that many innovation events are influenced by intentional or purposeful activity. This implies that the purely probabilistic selection mechanisms of evolutionary biology must be modified or augmented to allow for search and learning activity directed to innovating. As Nelson and Winter (1982) put it: 'It is neither difficult nor implausible to develop models of firm behavior that interweave "blind" and deliberate processes. Indeed, in human problem solving itself, both elements are involved and difficult to disentangle' (p. 11). This leads them to appeal openly to analogies to the Lamarckian evolutionary mechanism of so-called 'soft inheritance', i.e. the inheritance of acquired characteristics, now widely discredited in evolutionary biology itself.

Historicity and path-dependence

This brings us back to a point we made earlier about the essentially historical nature of evolutionary models – their 'historicity'. What happens next is always heavily constrained by what has already happened; the future can only ever be built upon the past. Thus, in nature, species-wide changes in form can only take place by means of altering forms which already exist. Most biologists would argue that the characteristics of organisms we see at any moment are a 'patchwork of features that were specifically selected for a particular function ... and others that are the by-product of the genotype as a whole and are simply tolerated by selection' (Mayr, 1982: 590).[5] While modern biologists talk about evolution as an 'optimisation' process, therefore, it is crucial to realise that they do not have in mind the emergence of forms which are the best possible, but rather the opportunistic way in which natural selection makes use of that part of available variation which leads most easily to needed adaptations (Mayr, 1982: 590). This must involve building on the way in which history has already taken a species and explains how path dependence arises.

While Lamarck is widely discredited in biology, his notion of acquiring inherited characteristics has a similar role to play in social systems. Technology we use today has much in common with that used in the recent past. That is no coincidence.

Technology is a body of ideas which solves production problems. To a large extent, the way we go about solving those problems draws upon what we have learned in the past about how to solve them. For that reason, technological knowledge is cumulative.

Gradual evolution versus *punctuated equilibrium*

Whether we appeal to Darwinian natural selection or Lamarkian soft inheritance to give direction to the process of evolution, there is a strong commitment in such explanations to gradual change. If economic theory were to draw on this tradition to deal with technological change, therefore, it would have to be on the implicit assumption that most of, if not all, such change was indeed gradual.

It is now widely accepted that much technological change is incremental and gradual. But there is also a tradition in economics flowing from Schumpeter (1934) which stresses the importance of sudden, discontinuous 'quantum leaps' in technology which give birth to new industries and reshape old ones. Consider, for example, the impact of the silicon chip. In this context, it is relevant to consider punctuated equilibrium, an alternative view of the long-term dynamics of system change which in biology has been advanced by Eldredge and Gould (1972) but which also appears in the physical sciences (Prigogine and Stengers, 1985), the history of science (Kuhn, 1970) and in work on human development (Levinson, 1978), group dynamics (Gersick, 1991) and organisational change (Tushman and Romanelli, 1985).

The essential difference between the two approaches is that gradualism emphasises the potential for a high degree of adaptability, given sufficient time for a series of small changes to yield optimal adjustments, while punctuated equilibrium stresses that large changes occur rapidly in periods of 'revolution' when 'growth rules' are determined according to which the system then operates for a protracted period of time.

One way of understanding the force of the punctuated equilibrium perspective is to recognise that every system has 'deep structure' (Gersick, 1991: 13). In several versions of the approach, deep structure takes the various forms of genetic programmes (biology), order parameters (physical sciences), paradigm (history of science), life structure (individuals) framework (groups) and strategic orientation (organisations). Deep structure is the set of fundamental 'choices' a system has made of the basic parts into which its units will be organised, and the basic activity patterns that will maintain its existence. Deep structures are highly stable because of the many options they rule out, despite the large variety of particular choices they define as available (Gersick, 1991: 14–16).

Deep structure provides the 'design of the playing field' and 'rules of the game' according to which system operates during the period of 'equilibrium'. During equilibrium, adjustments made to changes in the environment are successfully achieved without displacing the deep structure. But the deep structure is also kept in place in social systems by inertia, based on individuals' limited awareness of alternatives, lack of motivation to change and personal obligations to maintain the status quo. By contrast, changes made in the punctuations to equilibrium – the revolutions – do upset the deep structure, leaving the system temporarily disorganised. Then a subset of the system's old pieces, along with some new ones, can be put back together in a new configuration, which operates according to a new set of rules (Gersick, 1991: 19).

This theme appears in the book in connection with the emergence of so-called 'technological paradigms' (see Chapter 2) and the discussion of radical innovation and its economy-wide effects (see Chapters 2 and 7). It clearly offers a complementary, if not competing vision to gradualism. We emphasised the role of 'blindness' or unpredictability in the gradualist account and should recognise that that alone makes the processes it describes irreversible and hence at odds with the mechanical vision of change described earlier. But on the punctuationist account, the irreversibility of detailed changes to form is not of prime importance; it is the principles combined in the deep structure which really matter. Given the metamorphic nature of revolutionary change when it occurs, that too is clearly irreversible. But since deep structure brings long periods of subsequent 'order, coherence and organisation' (despite the superficial changes which characterise 'equilibrium'), those same episodes of irreversibility may punctuate long periods in which the mechanical style of analysis may after all, be a reasonable approximation (Prigogine and Stengers, 1985: 15).

Scientific metaphor in economics

It may be wondered why a book about the economics of innovation has devoted so much space to a discussion of science. The answer to that question is that a very large part of economics has drawn on metaphors from the sort of physics we have described as providing an essentially mechanical view of how systems work.

This point has been taken up at great length by Mirowski (1986, 1988, 1989). He argues that the mathematical 'box of tools' which dominates the prevailing 'neo-classical' approach to economics is so small that it deserves to be called only a pouch or a purse containing nothing more than the techniques of constrained optimisation. But his principal grumble is not that economics draws on a narrow range of techniques, *per se*. It is rather that the mathematics used was appropriated from physics by economists in the late nineteenth century at a time when physical laws were thought, by definition, to be perfectly reversible in time. This, in turn, he suggests is to blame for giving neoclassical economics its 'stubbornly ahistorical bias' (Mirowski, 1986: 189).

This is and Mirowski means it to be a rather general criticism of economic methodology: ' ... not one neoclassical economist in over one hundred years has seen fit to discuss the appropriateness or inappropriateness of the adoption of the mathematical metaphor of energy in a prerelativistic gravitational field in order to discuss the preferences and price formation of transactors in the marketplace' (1986: 187).

Now while physics has certainly changed since those prerelativistic, pre-entropic days, the possibility remains that outdated, misunderstood and even erroneous ideas in one sphere might nonetheless be useful as metaphors for enhancing understanding in another (Pullen, 1990: 32) In fact, our position would be that drawing on analogies is always potentially dangerous, but also potentially useful if it helps us formulate well-defined questions.

In the case of economics, the way in which questions have often been formulated reflects the considerable debt the discipline owes to the mechanical view of the world described above. The success economists have had in interpreting the world around them has repaid this debt many times over. But the suspicions aroused in science by the findings of quantum mechanics, and the work on entropy and dissipative structures, for example (Prigogine and Stengers, 1985), should also signal to us the potential value of alternative approaches.

It is accepted here that the mechanical approach has proved immensely fruitful in providing insights into problems relating to the static allocation of resources and to dynamic problems in which systems expand along smooth, continuous trajectories. But where the economic system is changing in its qualitative character – and occasionally, even, in its 'deep structure' – and we want to know how and why, we would argue that an alternative approach and other metaphors might be more useful. We do not mean that 'conventional' (neoclassical) economics has failed to shed light upon issues related to innovation. Far from it, as much of later chapters attest. What we mean is that economists became so accustomed to setting up their research programmes in a mode derived from the mechanical metaphor of physics that they tended to ignore the possibility that questions might usefully be asked in a different way.

In particular, there was a strong inclination, first, to focus on equilibrium states of the system, i.e. states from which the system would have no tendency to depart unless subjected to an exogenous shock. Second, when technological change is considered, it has often been in terms of such an exogenous shock, making it impossible to consider its origins. Third and in line with the methods of statics developed in nineteenth century physics, there has tended to be less emphasis on the path of adjustment between equilibrium states than on comparing the states themselves.

More recent developments in economics have, without abandonning 'neoclassical' methods, made significant efforts to endogenise technological change and also dealt with adjustment mechanisms operating between equilibrium states. However, it is unclear that such efforts, which will be addressed in Chapters 5, 6 and 7, have been able to establish the uniquely powerful claims to explanatory success which tended to accompany the analysis of multimarket, general equilibrium analysis in the absence of technological change (Arrow and Hahn, 1971).

One reason for this has already been noted: innovation changes the very nature of the framework in which market analysis is couched. It changes both production possibilities and the goods and services produced. Once technological change is recognised to be continuous, it is possible to respond with a modelling strategy which links together sequences of equilibrium states as an approximation of what is happening. But that presupposes relatively rapid adjustment to equilibrium in all markets, an assumption which remains controversial. Admitting the possibility that adjustments might be so slow that equilibrium is the exception rather than the rule, equilibrium analysis loses its claim to logical superiority. This at once suggests that the search for alternatives is a perfectly defensible and legitimate activity – and particularly the search for alternatives which deal with changing conditions out of equilibrium.

Secondly, the endogenisation of technological change in economic systems would be relatively straightforward (and indeed, mathematically trivial) if all new knowledge and innovation-related goods and services were traded in markets under conditions identical to those for, say, apples or flapjacks. The mechanical analogy is at its best in cases like this, when modelling trade in divisible and undifferentiated commodities, where information is good and equally good on both sides of the market and where firms are 'atomistic', small relative to the market and all using the same well-defined technology to produce a single good. Assuming only that firms on the supply side maximise profit and households on the demand side utility, we need no specific knowledge of the machinery of price determination, or detailed knowledge about the transactors to be able to predict equilibrium prices and quantities. It can be shown that the market will work to generate an equilibrium price at which the quantities suppliers wish to produce will exactly meet the quantities demanded (Koopmans, 1957, is a classic reference).

On the other hand, if new knowledge or artefacts embodying it are involved, the conditions for trade diverge substantially from those described in the last paragraph. (A seminal paper here is Arrow, 1962, who raises in a slightly different context most of the points made below.) First, innovators may be unable to acquire the legal right to appropriate all or any of the benefits generated by their idea. Second, generating new knowledge may require a large scale of operation or the deliberate coordination of effort over several smaller operations. Third, uncertainty of outcome implies a need for risk-sharing. But while risk-sharing is the function of insurance markets, insurance against the possible failure of innovations cannot usually be taken out. Another aspect of uncertainty is that users of new technology do not and cannot know all about it. To represent them as well informed and able to maximise profit is thus potentially misleading.

When these (and sometimes other) factors are at work, the market may not be able to operate at all. Suppose, for example, we knew objectively that an individual inventor's new gadget would be of great value to certain users. The gadget might nonetheless not be traded if uncertainty about prospects on the side of the users discouraged them from offering the inventor much for it, and the nature of the gadget made it difficult for the inventor to protect it with a patent. The inventor would be unable to demonstrate the value of the gadget without revealing so much about it that its tradeable value would substantially fall. Knowing this, the inventor might well refuse to demonstrate it. But then, of course, potential buyers could not be convinced to pay enough to make the inventor part with it. Here, the market would simply fail to operate.

More often, however, the market will work, but not as well as it might and certainly not as predictably as suggested by the model of simple, atomistic firms. One way or another, it becomes unavoidable to ask more about how trade is arranged, to inquire into the processes which influence the generation, development and transfer of new technology and to see what implications these aspects of innovation have for economic magnitudes.

The evolutionary approach in economics is one response to this challenge, for it de-emphasises equilibrium states in favour of examining the processes of change, as they relate to both the generation and adoption of new technology. It also puts to one side notions of perfect knowledge and substitutes learning and search in its place. Where the market model of atomistic firms explores the characteristics of so-called competitive equilibrium states, the evolutionary approach looks instead at how firms compete, the dynamic process of competition itself.

Evolutionary modelling is however only one of a number of approaches taken to coping with the difficulties posed by technological change for understanding how economic systems might work. At different points in the book, we shall also encounter the contributions of transactions cost theorists and game theory. The former have looked at the range of institutional arrangements (governance alternatives) which might evolve in response to the difficulties posed for market-based transactions when innovation is present. The latter appeals to its own brand of equilibrium concepts to frame analysis of interdependent and strategic behaviour when innovation is used as a competitive weapon among only a few (and often only two) firms. Each has its own insights to offer, but the area is so rich in possibilities that none can yet claim to be a general theory of the economics of innovation.

Notes

1. See von Bertalanffy (1962) for an introduction to general systems theory.
2. In terms of purely static analysis, and given restrictive assumptions, general equilibrium analysis (Arrow and Hahn, 1971) is one of the more ambitious attempts at this made by economists. Chapter 7 of this book contains examples of attempts to give microfoundations to growth models of the aggregate economy. Interested readers might also follow up the work of Eliasson (1986) and his school.
3. This point is explored by Matthews (1984). See also Mayr (1982: 594–5), especially the references to Haldane (1957) and the responses of Mayr himself, and Lewontin (1974).
4. These matters are considered at length in Elster (1983) especially Part 1.
5. The 'genotype' is the total genetic constitution of an organism, to which DNA importantly contributes, to be contrasted with the 'phenotype' which is the totality of characteristics of an organism (Mayr, 1982: 958–9).

References

Arrow, K. (1962) 'Economic welfare and the allocation of resources for invention', in R. Nelson (ed.) *The Rate and Direction of Inventive Activity*, Princeton, NJ: Princeton University Press.

Arrow, K.J. and F. Hahn (1971) *General Competitive Analysis*, Edinburgh: Oliver and Boyd.

Eldredge, N. and S.J. Gould (1972) 'Punctuated equilibria: An alternative to phyletic gradualism', in T. Schopf (ed.) *Models in Paleobiology*, San Francisco: Freeman, Cooper 82–115.

Eliasson, G. (1986) 'Micro heterogeneity of firms and the stability of industrial growth, in R.H. Day and G. Eliasson (eds) *The Dynamics of Market Economies*, Amsterdam: Elsevier Science Publishers, ch. 4, 79–104.

Elster, J. (1983) *Explaining Technical Change: A Case Study in the Philosophy of Science*, Cambridge: Cambridge University Press.

Enos, J.L. (1989) 'Transfer of technology', *Asian-Pacific Economic Literature* 3(1), 3–37.

Gersick, C.J.G. (1991) 'Revolutionary change theories: A multilevel exploration of the punctuated equilibrium paradigm', *Academy of Management Review* 16(1), 10–36.

Haldane, J.B.S. (1957) 'The cost of natural selection', *Journal of Genetics*, 55, 511–24.

Kennedy, C. and A.P. Thirlwall (1972) 'Technical progress: A survey', *Economic Journal*, 82, 11–72.

Kline, S.J. and N. Rosenberg (1986) 'An overview of innovation', in R. Landau and N. Rosenberg (eds) *The Positive Sum Strategy: Harnessing Technology for Economic Growth*, Washington, DC: National Academy Press, 275–305.

Koopmans, T. (1957) *Three Essays on the State of Economic Science*, New York: McGraw-Hill.

Kuhn, T.S. (1970) *The Structure of Scientific Revolutions* 2nd edn, Chicago: University of Chicago Press.

Levinson, D.J. (1978) *The Seasons of a Man's Life*, New York. Knopf.

Lewontin, R.C. (1974) *The Genetic Basis of Evolutionary Change*, New York: Columbia University Press.

Matthews, R.C.O. (1984) 'Darwinism and economic change', *Oxford Economic Papers 36* (Supplement) 91–117.

Mayr, E. (1982) *The Growth of Biological Thought: Diversity, Evolution and Inheritance*, Harvard: Belknap Press.

Metcalfe, J.S. (1989), 'Evolution and economic change', in Z.A. Silberston (ed.) *Technology and Economic Progress*, London: Macmillan, ch. 4, 54–85.

Mirowski, P. (1986) 'Mathematical formalism and economic explanation', in P. Mirowski (ed.) *The Reconstruction of Economic Theory*, Boston: Kluwer-Nijhoff, ch. 6, 179–240.

Mirowski, P. (1988) *Against Mechanism*, Totawa: Rowman and Littlefield.

Mirowski, P. (1989) *More Heat than Light*, New York: Cambridge University Press.

Nelson, R.R. and S. Winter (1982) *An Evolutionary Theory of Economic Change*, Cambridge, MA: Belknap Press of Harvard University Press.

Pribram, K. (1983) *A History of Economic Reasoning*, Baltimore: Johns Hopkins.

Prigogine, I. and I. Stengers (1985) *Order Out of Chaos: Man's New Dialogue With Nature*, London: Collins.

Pullen, J.M.P. (1990) 'Metaphorical economics; or, The metaphor is the message', *HETSA Bulletin*, 14, 29–51.

Schmookler, J. (1966) *Invention and Economic Growth*, Cambridge, MA: Harvard University Press.

Schumpeter, J.A. (1934) *The Theory of Economic Development*, Cambridge, MA: Harvard University Press.

Tushman, M. and E. Romanelli (1985) 'Organisational evolution: A metamorphosis model of convergence and reorientation', in L. Cummings and B. Staw (eds) *Research in Organisational Behavior*, Vol. 7, Greenwich, CT: JAI Press, 171–222.

Van Parijs, P. (1981) *Evolutionary Explanation in the Social Sciences: An Emerging Paradigm*, London: Tavistock Publishers.

von Bertalanffy, L. (1962) 'General system theory: A critical review', *General Systems*, 7, 1–20.

2

Perspectives on innovation

Introduction

The purpose of this chapter is to provide an overview of major perspectives which have been taken on innovation. We start with a general definition of the process of innovation, consider its relationship to national innovation systems, analyse its components and lay the foundations for tracing the subtle and complex causal connections which drive the process. In the second part of the chapter, we focus on specific economic concepts associated with innovation.

Economists can contribute much to an understanding of the economic motivations for innovation and the impact of innovation on economic systems. But it must also be acknowledged that not all explanations for innovation are economic. The study of innovation has long attracted the attention of business management analysts and historians and valuable contributions are also being made by sociologists, political scientists, geographers, psychologists, physicists, biochemists and engineers. Insights from the broader field of innovation studies, to which these scholars have contributed, provide a setting for the economic focus.

The process of innovation defined

In his path-breaking work, Jacob Schmookler (1966) defines innovation in the following terms.'When an enterprise produces a good or service or uses a method or input that is new to it, it makes a technical change. The first enterprise to make a given technical change is an innovator. Its action is innovation.' Notice three things about this definition. First, innovation is regarded as a business activity, it is in enterprises that innovation occurs. Second, whenever *any* firm does something it has not done before, its actions are viewed as contributing to technical change. But only if a firm is the *first* to do it in the economy is its achievement regarded as innovation. Firms which subsequently do the same thing are defined to be imitators adopting the innovation in the ensuing process of diffusion. Third, the definition uses the term technical rather than technological change.

All of these points are controversial. First, while it is true that the decisions of business firms are crucial to an understanding of technical change, other types of institution are also importantly involved in various aspects of innovation. In particular we could point to universities and other educational institutions, not for profit research organisations, government bodies and backyard inventors. An essential point here, however, is that institutions such as these rarely have either competence or interest in commercial production in the sense of putting their findings to work themselves, as envisaged in Schmookler's definition. Increasingly, however, there is a tendency for them to try to sell their ideas and even to hire their expertise in giving advice on how other, i.e. commercial, units should go about using new technology.

Within any country, the range of institutions which contribute to innovation and the linkages among them comprise the **national innovation system** (Lundvall, 1992; Nelson, 1993). Nationally, the innovation process takes place within this system and the behaviour of its components and the nature of the links among them constitute an important aspect of understanding why specific features of the innovation process vary from one country to another. It is also important to note that elements of the national innovation system will have international connections. For example, firms which innovate nationally are likely these days to be parts of multinational enterprises. And researchers in universities and research institutions must regard one of their roles to be aware of global developments in their areas of expertise, will travel internationally to conferences to expose themselves to new ideas and are increasingly part of a community on the move.

All such institutions and the individuals who serve them contribute to innovation, but some much less directly than others, with much less immediate effect on commercial production and with the pressure of reduced economic incentive. Where market signals (relative prices) seem unlikely to encourage enough innovation in certain parts of the system, government is usually perceived to have a role in either undertaking the activity itself, or providing grants, tax concessions and subsidies, or using its purchasing power to encourage such activity.

Second, note that the distinction between innovating and imitating firms is often unclear. In their attempts to imitate, firms often do things differently (unintentionally or by design) from the way they were done by the first firm, becoming innovators in their own right. The sharp division between innovation and imitation thus becomes blurred.

Third, we acknowledge a tradition of distinguishing between technological and technical change; the former has been taken to refer to an increase in the stock of knowledge itself, while the latter has been applied to the effects of expanding the knowledge base (Kennedy and Thirlwall, 1972). Such effects include higher productivity, the production of new goods or the improvement of existing ones. But very often, new knowlege is generated as an integral part of the whole learning process in which higher productivity is achieved or better-quality goods are produced. And much of the new knowledge is highly specific, in the sense of being relevant only (or principally) to the particular production processes or goods for which it was discovered. This makes it less useful to distinguish between technical and technological change than to make other types of distinction developed later. In this book, the term technological change will be used to cover changes in the knowledge (both documented and carried around in peoples' heads) associated with producing goods and services of economic value, in artefacts which embody and reflect the use of new knowledge and in the organisation of production. If we want to identify effects separately, we shall specify changes in productivity or the performance characteristics of goods and services.

We thus accept Schmookler's view that technological change must encompass not only changed methods of producing existing goods, but also changes in the goods themselves. Futhermore, technological change may also be allowed to include reference to the list of 'new combinations' discussed by Schumpeter (1934) including new markets and marketing methods, new forms of business organisation and new legal and regulatory conditions. In this book, however, we deliberately have little to say about policy issues and hence largely put the last of these to one side.[1]

We shall define the process of innovation to include **all of the activities which bring about technological change and the dynamic interactions among them**. Notice, however, that the process of innovation may well include activities which in themselves involve little or no novelty. Deploying existing technology on a repeated basis to meet a market need in itself implies little that is novel. Yet it is only by serving a market for an extended period that suppliers learn how they could change the technology to meet market needs more effectively. Such learning is of the essence in the innovation process. Again, it may be impossible to invest in new machines without obtaining finance. Yet from the viewpoint of the financing institution, the financing operation may appear largely routine. The innovation process, therefore, in principle includes aspects of all economic activity, not simply the activities (like research and development) which are exclusively directed to changing the technology.

Elements of the innovation process

The core elements of the innovation process have conventionally been represented in one of two ways: either as a set of research and development activities or as a sequence of stages.

Research and development activities

In the first approach, the aim is to define and distinguish between different types of research and development activity (OECD, 1981; National Science Board, 1983; Irvine and Martin, 1984). The main criterion used for making the distinctions is the purpose for which the activity is undertaken.

Research is usually divided into two broad categories, **basic** and **applied**. In each case, the activity involves original investigation, but with basic research the main aim is to obtain a more complete understanding of the subjects under study, whereas applied (sometimes called 'mission-oriented') research is directed primarily towards a specific practical aim, or for finding possible uses for the existing findings of basic research. As Irvine has pointed out, however, the usual definitions of basic research fail to allow for a further distinction within that category which is widely recognised and of considerable relevance to policy decisions about the allocation of resources to R&D activity. Basic research may be either **pure curiosity-oriented** or **strategic**. The first corresponds to the idea of academic research carried out with the aim of producing new knowledge primarily for its own sake. Strategic research, on the other hand, is carried out with the expectation that it will produce a broad base of knowledge likely to form the background to the solution of recognised current or future practical problems (Irvine and Martin, 1984: 4).[2]

The **development** element of R&D (often described as experimental development) involves systematic but non-routine technical work directed towards producing new or improved materials, products and services, including the design and development of processes and prototypes.

It has to be said that ambiguity is always likely to surround the application of all of these terms in practice. Obvious reasons for this are that research never intending to be immediately 'useful' can sometimes turn out to have strategic value in the sense defined above. On the other hand, work designed with a specific practical objective in mind may nonetheless generate new insight into more general and sometimes unrelated questions. Once we know the outcome of the activity, therefore, we might well be inclined to describe the research or development in somewhat different terms from those applied at the outset.

Notice also that the resources absorbed by these activities vary considerably. It is a truism, for example, that where business innovation is concerned, research costs tend to be systematically much lower than development costs. This issue is considered at greater length in Chapter 4.

Finally, the activities defined previously can be anchored to the notion of the national innovation system if we ask where they are usually performed (Irvine and Martin, 1984: 3–5 offer a useful summary). Pure, curiosity-oriented research is normally a major function of the university-based research system and funded on the basis of peer review to judge its intrinsic merit. The same system also undertakes strategic research, but shares this task with government-funded research agencies and the laboratories of the larger science-based companies. In a general way, the resources devoted to strategic research will ultimately be linked to some perception of its potential economic or social value, beyond that of advancing knowledge *per se*. Applied research is mostly carried out by industry and the laboratories of mission-oriented government agencies but may also be undertaken, under contract, within academic institutions. Finally, almost all experimental development occurs in industry and mission-oriented government agencies.

One implication of this is that innovation-related activity is sometimes likely to be concentrated at particular nodes within the broader system and sometimes occurs as the result of interaction among several or many institutions. We have what the OECD has described as 'a maze of overlapping networks' (OECD 1992, 77). These range from the tightly knit but highly specialised and rather narrow networks among scientists in a subdiscipline of the natural sciences and among production engineers in a narrow group of firms in the same industry, to looser and wider networks involving firms as corporate entities and linkages to government and academic institutions. One dimension of the analysis of innovation explores the nature of such networks and their linkages (OECD, 1992: ch. 3), but as yet we are far from having anything like a fully fledged theory of networks. So while it is important to acknowledge the potential importance of the emerging theory of networks, we shall later focus on theory based on the more traditional institutional structures of the firm and the market.

Stages in the innovation process

We turn now to the stages of innovation approach, which divides the innovation process into three steps: invention, innovation and imitation or diffusion. Following Kennedy and Thirlwall (1972), we may first define **invention** as 'the devising of new ways of attaining given ends ... [embracing] both the creation of things previously non-existent, using either new or existing knowledge, and the "creation" of things which have existed all the time (e.g. penicillin)' (p. 51). The keyword in connection with invention is **creation**. Inventive activity requires inputs and research effort may be one of them, though as the definition suggests, much invention merely involves using existing knowledge in a novel way. Inventions themselves may be **patented**, i.e. the inventor is invested with a property right which entitles him or her to claim a financial reward from any commercial use of the invention. Inventions are inputs into the development of innovations, but by no means all inventions have the potential for commercial (or even technological) success.

In this approach, 'innovation is the commercial application of inventions for the first time' (Kennedy and Thirlwall, 1972: 56). Where invention involves conceiving ideas, an act of creation, innovation implies putting ideas to use.

The final stage, **imitation**, comprises the post-innovation adoption of new technology and is an important mechanism by which diffusion of new technology occurs. Imitation (if successful) implies diffusion, but more widespread use of a new element of technology could occur in the absence of imitation if two or more firms independently developed the same idea at the same time. This is by no means unusual.

This view of the innovation process as a three-stage sequence has been widely used but must be treated with considerable care. First, it may be difficult to allocate all of the events in the innovation process unambiguously to one stage or another. We have noted, for example, that imitative activity often involves elements of innovation. As another example, applying one set of new ideas (innovation) may simultaneously stimulate creativity (invention) on the job. Second, there is a difference between arguing for a three-way division and a three-stage sequence. In other words, we might accept the analytical usefulness of having three conceptual 'boxes' without accepting that each one must occur only before or after others. Clearly the idea of a unidirectional flow through time (invention > innovation > imitation) is upset when attempts at imitation are a precursor to innovation. But more generally, appealing to the notion of unidirectional flow implies a belief in causal mechanisms in which the whole innovation process is led and triggered by invention. Very often, however, creative, inventive research effort is a problem-solving response to some perceived need, either in the market or in firms' production processes (Marquis, 1988).

'Science-push' and 'market-driven' innovation

The argument developed in the last paragraph may also be applied to the view of innovation which is implicit in the R&D activities approach outlined earlier. There has traditionally been a view especially among scientists that technological innovation is driven or pushed by science and, in particular, by pure scientific research. As is noted in Ronayne (1984) and Irvine and Martin (1984), this view was expounded most explicitly and influentially by the leading American scientist, Vannevar Bush (1945) in his book *Science the Endless Frontier*. A quotation indicates his position: 'New products and processes are founded on new principles and conceptions which, in turn, are developed by research in the purest realms of science' (p. 19).

The science-push model is also known as the **linear** model of innovation, with causation originating in science and flowing forward unidirectionally to technology and commercial use. It is now recognised that to represent the innovation process as linear and science-driven is hopelessly innaccurate and simplistic. One of the great contemporary names in the study of innovation, Nathan Rosenberg, has said 'Everyone knows that the linear model is dead'. A rather more general framework for innovation analysis is presented in the next section. But first consider for a moment innovation at the level of the corporation to understand why the linear model must be abandoned.

Technology changes within firms as the result of a number of processes; individuals and teams learn from their experience of production processes how they and the artefacts they use must adapt if efficiency is to be raised; process- and product-related technical problems raised by users are attacked and often resolved by firms' production engineers; mission-oriented research departments in large corporations broaden the base of general knowledge about how the natural world works; changes in science stimulate research into developing new technology. Of these, only the last fits well into the linear model.

One response to the increasingly obvious deficiencies of the linear, science-push model was to offer the counter-claim that market demand almost exclusively determined what applied research was undertaken and the experimental development to which it led. The market-led hypothesis appeared in its most influential form in the work of Schmookler (1966) and remains important in any discussion of the subject which incorporates economic influences.

Yet while economists often preferred the market-pull approach to that of science-push, it gradually became clear that, as in all situations analysed in economics, *both* demand-and supply-side factors needed to be incorporated and, linked. This point was made most forcefully by Mowery and Rosenberg (1982). Contemporary frameworks for the analysis of innovation are attempting to respond to this challenge. But as yet, no map of the whole process has emerged which commands universal assent. In what follows, we review what has so far been achieved.

Links, chains and feedbacks

From the discussion so far, we can now begin to appreciate that the innovation process comprises a set of linked activites which may, occur in a variety of sequences and sometimes simultaneously. The output of many of the activities in the process is a flow of information which constitutes an addition to the knowledge base of the economic unit in which the activity takes place and the overall knowledge base of the community. To say that activities are linked, therefore, often amounts to saying that information or new knowledge flows between them.

The knowledge is sometimes embodied in machines. But often it is carried mainly in the heads of individuals, so that linkages require individuals in different elements of the process to communicate with one another or to move from one activity to another with their knowledge. If the knowledge can be articulated and documented so clearly that potential users can 'work off the blueprint' directly, the linkage merely requires the document itself to be transferred, quite possibly as the result of a market transaction. But this mode of transfer often gives rise to difficulties associated with the problem of writing down all the procedures necessary to get a production process up and running. To convince yourself of this proposition, consider the difficulties of learning relatively straightforward word-processing from a manufacturer's manual.

These considerations alert us to the idea that the speed and direction of innovation are likely to be related to the quantity of technological knowledge extant at any moment and to the issues surrounding the ease or difficulty of transferring it successfully. This will depend on the characteristics of the knowledge itself, the skills and competencies of those attempting both to communicate and absorb it and the incentives and threats bearing upon potential suppliers and users of technology throughout the system.

A framework within which, issues like these could be investigated has been supplied by Kline and Rosenberg (1986). In a model designed to move away completely from single-cause explanations of innovation and unidirectional flows within the process, they emphasise the central role of **feedback** in innovation (which can also be thought of as learning) and emphasise that far from feeding on science, technological development often stimulates scientific research. Problems encountered during development may require new scientific advances if they are to be solved. For example, much of the pressure to create new materials results from feedback from problems encountered in developing steam turbines, jet engines, semiconductors and solar energy cells.

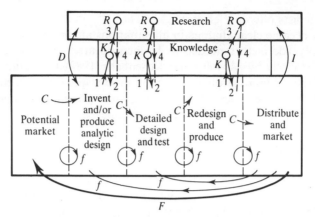

Symbols on arrows: C = central-chain-of-innovation; f = feedback loops; F = particularly important feedback. $K - R$: Links through knowledge to research and return paths. If problem solved at node K, link 3 to R not activated. Return from research (link 4) is problematic – therefore dashed line. D: direct link to and from research from problems in invention and design. I: support of scientific research by instruments, machines, tools and procedures of technology

Figure 2.1 Chain–Link model showing flow path of information and cooperation. (Reprinted with permission from *The Positive Sum Strategy: Harnessing Technology for Economic Growth*. Copyright 1986 by the National Academy of Sciences. Courtesy of the National Academy Press, Washington, DC.)

These considerations led Kline and Rosenberg to propose what they call the **chain-linked** model of innovation. This identifies five sorts of path along which information flows might occur (Figure 2.1). The first is called the **central chain of innovation** (marked by arrows labelled *C*) and starts with the 'design' for a new process associated with either a product innovation or producing an existing product at a more competitive price. The new design is seen as arising from a market need identified in a potential market and the central chain takes it through development and production to marketing and distribution. If successful, the innovation will change conditions in the market.

A second 'path' (in fact there is a set of them) focuses on feedbacks, each of which is labelled with an *F*. Of these, the most important is from existing and potential users, for it is now widely recognised that the condition most likely to generate success for an innovation is the existence of unmet market needs. It is common sense that unmet market need should be a necessary condition for successful innovation, though it is clearly not sufficient. Making product changes are likely to have market appeal relies on feedback from existing and potential users.[3] In fact, the stimulus for product improvement might come from many angles including top managers and marketing departments, competitors and suppliers, and customers (Twiss, 1987: 12). Such feedback may influence fundamental design principles (analytic design changes requiring invention), or the way components fit together to make a system which functions more or less well (changes in the detail of system design), or the way manufacture is organised (for example, changes in physical production aimed at reducing cost). As noted previously, feedback also occurs from production to development and within development itself. Problems of production and opportunities for improvement spotted on the factory floor, constitute information which is fed back to those working on development and perhaps even research issues. Problems associated with efforts to accommodate a new component in the course of adapting an existing production set-up may ultimately indicate opportunities for using entirely different basic principles for design. In fact, the game of looking for feedbacks is almost inexhaustible.

The third and fourth types of path link the central chain to scientific knowledge. Recall from Chapter 1 that the Kline and Rosenberg (1986) definition of science is 'the creation, discovery, verification, collation, reorganisation, and dissemination of knowledge about physical, biological and social nature' (p. 287). Research output in any year is defined as the additions and corrections to science over that period, but the main component of science always remains 'the current totality of stored human knowledge about nature'. In relation to innovation, Kline and Rosenberg's main point is that most innovation is done with knowledge already in the heads of the people in the organisation doing the work and to a lesser extent with other information readily accessible to them. 'It is only when those sources of information fall short of solving the problem that there is a need for research in order to complete a given innovation' (p. 288).

Kline and Rosenberg acknowledge (path three, arrow *D*), that there can be direct links between research and the creation of ideas which lead to innovation. This is most likely to be the case in so-called **science-based** industries which, by definition, rely much more than others on rapid advances in science as a feedstock for their development. In the last two or three decades, electronics and computing have been a leading example, but pharmaceuticals and biotechnology are other current instances. But they emphasise that most innovation will rely more heavily on the use of existing scientific knowledge (path four, arrows marked *K*). This is particularly likely to be true of what Pavitt (1984) calls **specialist supplier** industries (such as those producing machine tools and scientific instruments) and **scale intensive** industries (like glass and cement manufacture), both of which draw heavily on existing science to make incremental, evolutionary advances in the technology they either supply to others or use themselves.

Different elements of scientific knowledge are likely to be most relevant for different aspects of innovation. At the invention stage, principles of pure science will be most apposite; during development, scientific knowledge about the working of systems; during production, knowledge about processing. Only when existing knowledge, indicated by nodes in the knowledge 'box', fail to solve problems thrown up in the central chain of innovation will workers then resort to seeking extensions to knowledge through research. The return arrows from research (where nodes are labelled *R*) are dashed to indicate that it is always uncertain whether knowledge can in fact be extended in a way which will solve given problems.

The remaining path (marked *I*) is in the nature of another feedback. It indicates that the products of innovation may support the extension of scientific knowledge. Examples here might be the microscope (with its impact on modern medical research) and the telescope (with its impact on astronomy).

The chain-link depiction of the innovation process is much more sastisfactory than the linear view. It explictly recognises that all innovation results from both technological opportunity on the one hand, arising from invention, research and development activities and market need on the other. The two are analytically separable and we regard the distinction as too useful to dispense with. But we should also keep at the back of our mind the reality that they are themselves linked. As Kline and Rosenberg (1986) put it: 'A perceived market need will be filled only if the technical problems can be solved, and a perceived performance gain will be put into use only if there is a realizable market use.' This, in turn implies that arguments about the relative importance of market pressure and the 'push' from new science and technology are in a sense artificial, since 'each market need entering the innovation cycle leads in time to a new design, and every successful new design, in time, leads to new market conditions' (pp. 289–90).

The depiction is also useful for prompting important analytical questions which a 'map' like this cannot, answer. First, what is the organisational infrastructure which enables and facilitates the flows of information shown here? When activities generate outputs of value, we usually assume that markets or other institutions exist to organise transactions and determine the terms and conditions under which such outputs will be traded. But information and knowledge goods create rather special problems for market trading; difficulties of appropriating the rewards of invention, meeting the challenge of indivisibilities in some necessarily large-scale research projects, overcoming opportunistic behaviour by users and potential users and dealing with uncertainty, all impede the smooth operation of competitive, atomistic markets.

There may be reasons why firms will choose to do their own R&D, rather than contract it out to specialist laboratories. Firms may also choose to set up joint research ventures, strategic alliances and networks. Which arrangements are chosen may affect how much R&D is ultimately done and which. This sort of issue has been raised (see pp. 206–12) in economic analysis which concentrates on the nature of transactions between trading units (pioneered by Williamson, 1975), and in work on complementary assets (Teece, 1986) and conglomerate firms. Kline and Rosenberg's picture establishes the technological linkages which should be considered. But in an essentially technological picture, the linkages mainly amount to information flows occurring in an institutional vacuum and driven by casually described economic motivation. Bearing in mind that innovation is importantly motivated by economic considerations, much of this book will assume (either explicitly or implicitly) the existence of economic institutions capable of organising technology flows. On the other hand, how firms organise themselves to deal with changing technology, what influence this might have upon the path of change and how different forms of market structure influence innovation are central issues to be discussed.

A second question raised by the chain-link depiction: is What **unit of analysis** is being used as the basis for the picture? Are we looking at a particular innovation, or all the technological innovation occurring throughout all or part of the innovation system, or a single corporate entity and its suppliers or an industry? Part of the problem is that in the economics of innovation, a source of potential confusion lies in the failure of much work to distinguish explicitly between analysis based on a technological unit – a technology – and that based on an economic unit, the industry. If industries were defined in terms of their technology, and if each industry could be characterised unambiguously by a unique technology, this would present no problem. But industries are usually defined by their output and distinguished from each other by reference to the observation that some outputs are much better substitutes for each other in market demand than are others. Production units which make goods that are close substitutes for each other are said to belong to the same industry. Any pair of production units which made goods that were poor substitutes would be defined as belonging to different industries. In practice, the criterion of 'close' substitutability is not always easy to apply, but the conceptual basis for it is reasonably clear and has a ready intuitive foundation.

To analyse innovation, however, defining industries in this way presents certain problems arising partly from the fact that a technology is not defined by output but rather by reference to the nature of a production process which might yield outputs which are in no way substitutes for each other in the market. For example, metal-casting technology has been used by the same production unit to make both car components and guns. To confuse matters further, there are many instances in which a given good can be produced with qualitatively very different technologies. For example, a telephone call identical from the viewpoint of the consumer can be facilitated by copper cables, optical fibres, radio signals or transmissions through a satellite, with switching devices which are manually operated or automatic, mechanical or electronic. There is no one-to-one correspondence between specific sorts of technology and specific industries.

Where a given technology may serve several or many industries, it is defined to be **generic**. This means first that technological units of analysis (technologies) and economic units of analysis (firms and industries) may often cut across each other. This complicates analysis. Second, technological innovation may cut across many industries in its effects and over time it can blur and then reshape industry boundaries altogether. The 'convergence' of the computer and telecommunications industries is a familiar example. The role of technological innovation in generating structural change is too important to ignore. Though the non-coincidence of technological and economic units makes analysis much more difficult, the cross-cutting must be acknowledged rather than assumed away.

But this leaves unanswered the question of how we are to regard the chain-linked depiction of Kline and Rosenberg. Is it a picture of an industry or a technology? We said above that the picture was essentially technological. If that is the case, the activities shown in the picture could be confined to a single industry, comprising one or many firms, but might also depict activities being undertaken in a number of industries, all using similar processing methods. Whichever is the case, the activities might each be performed by separate specialist firms, or various sets of the activities might be performed by the same firm. Interfirm and interindustry economic patterns of behaviour are crucial to understanding the dynamics of the process of innovation and need to be incorporated in the bare framework.

If we see the picture as that of an industry, we need to recognise that the output defining a given industry can be produced by different technologies, the relationship(s) between which are not explicit in the picture. We also need to take account of the fact that R&D activity directed towards solving the technological problems of one industry can be relevant in others. Understanding the influence of innovation on changing industry structures require us also to make explicit what sorts of technology serve each industry and how changing technology redefines industrial boundaries.

Paradigms, trajectories and the 'inner logic' of innovation

One way of characterising the chain-link model of innovation is to say that it locates technological change in its scientific and market environment, indicating the many ways in which the technology may both influence and be influenced by that environment. However, not only does it lack institutional content, it also emphasises cross-system relationships at the expense of bringing out the path-dependent nature of much technological change. The cumulative dynamics of innovation are, however, stressed elsewhere by Rosenberg, particularly when he takes on claims that all innovation can be explained by economic pressures and incentives.

> The ultimate incentives are economic in nature; but economic incentives to reduce cost always exist in business operations and precisely because such incentives are so diffuse and general, they do not explain much in terms of the particular sequence and timing of innovative activity . . . .Technology is much more of a cumulative and self-generating process than the economist generally recognises. (1976: 110)

In this section, we look at the broad concepts which have developed around the perception that technological development does up to a point have a life of its own which governs its evolution. This is not the same as arguing for technological determinism, which suggests that all social, economic and political change can be explained by antecedent changes in technology. Rather, it merely suggests that the specific path of technological change at any moment is significantly determined by existing technology – and to that extent is independent of non-technological factors. Such a view follows naturally from a perspective which views development in any context as being guided for long periods of time by 'deep structure' (see Chapter 1).

The characterisation offered here takes the notion of a **paradigm**, found in the history of science (Kuhn, 1970) and transfers it to the study of technology. Technological change occurs within paradigms and is associated with changes in paradigms themselves. In science, a paradigm can be thought of as a way of looking at the world (or part of it) which enables problems to be defined and research to be given pattern and structure. The mechanical and evolutionary approaches to thinking about change in the natural universe discussed in Chapter 1 offer examples of counterposed scientific paradigms. Analogously, Dosi (1988: 1127) defines a **techno-logical paradigm** as a 'pattern' of solutions to selected techno-economic problems, based on selected principles derived from the natural sciences, and specific rules aimed at acquiring new knowledge. Examples include the internal combustion engine, oil-based synthetic chemistry and semiconductors. Each paradigm has both an artefact dimension (the motor car, plastics, the integrated circuit) and the dimension of a set of heuristics (aids to answering questions like 'Where do we search next?', and 'What sort of knowledge should we draw on?')

The latter dimension is emphasised in the terminology of Sahal (1985), who talks about technological guideposts. This concept is very much like the dominant design of Abernethy and Clark (1985), and the optimal recipe (Bjorn-Anderson, *et al.*, 1982). While there are differences in flavour, all these concepts are associated with the emergence of a common and durable approach to design, embodied in artefacts, which resolves a given technological problem. The motor car (in its many guises) solves the problem of transporting people with a high degree of flexibility. The farm tractor offers a solution to performing a wide range of agricultural operations with one machine. The semiconductor solves the problem of performing large numbers of arithmetic operations quickly and with a minimum of tedium.

The emergence of such dominant designs constitutes revolutionary innovation. Sahal suggests that it requires the symbiotic combinations of technology: innovation in which complementary technologies are brought together to create new ways of doing things. Consider the jet aircraft. This combined the jet engine with titanium-based alloys and swept wings. But at any moment, the potential opportunities for knitting technologies together like this may be numerous and in some cases not at all obvious. There is an inevitable element of chance or uncertainty associated with knowing in advance which technologies will be combined to yield a dominant design and how they will be combined in practice.

Once a technological paradigm is in place and has given rise to a dominant design, further innovation tends to be evolutionary, modifying step by step the dominant design by giving better answers to questions shaped by the existing paradigm, rather than seeking fundamentally different designs by asking different questions. The technology then evolves along a **technological trajectory** (Dosi, 1988: 1128, 1137) defined as 'the activity of technological progress along the economic and technological trade-offs defined by a paradigm'. More concretely, such trajectories often arise from what Rosenberg calls 'technological imperatives'; bottlenecks in connected processes and obvious weak spots in products (Rosenberg, 1969). Nelson and Winter (1982: 258–9) found their concept of a **technological regime** (which is much like a technological paradigm) on technicians' beliefs about what is feasible, or at least worth attempting, so that trajectories are seen as the result of following these beliefs up. 'In some cases a few directions seem much more compelling of attention than others. Particularly in industries where technological advance is very rapid, advance seems to follow advance in a way that appears almost inevitable', (p. 258). This 'inevitability' leads them to talk of *natural* technological trajectories. While natural trajectories are specific to particular paradigms, a strong family likeness may appear among the natural trajectories found in particular eras. Progressive exploitation of latent economies of scale across a wide range of technologies offers one example (Hughes, 1971). Miniaturisation might be another (Braun and MacDonald, (1978).

Sahal, who offers the alternative term **innovation avenue**, describes the trajectory for aircraft in terms of improved trade-offs among horsepower, gross take-off weight, cruising speed, wing loading and range. He argues that if the evolution of technology can be characterised by fixed mathematical relationships between such performance variables, despite changes in the scale of the technology, then 'it can be justifiably concluded that technical progress is governed by an *inner* logic or law of its own' (Sahal, 1985: 71). As an example, he finds that between 1928 and 1957, aircraft cruising speed (CS) could be linked to average gross take-off weight (W) by the equation:

$$\log CS = 2.37 + 0.293 \log W$$

where R-squared, the coefficient of determination, is 0.88 and the standard error 0.14. As an associated instance, he finds that the parameter:

$$[(\text{Wing loading} \times \text{cruising speed})/(\text{passenger capacity})]$$

can be given a precise value (285.6) which is almost entirely independent of scale. It should be noted, however, that his results for an alternative example, tractor technology, offer much less clear results and in general it is hard to believe that all technological change could be resolved into such sharply defined 'avenues' of development.

While Dosi specifically mentions technological and economic trade-offs in his definition of a trajectory, the major emphasis of this approach is that trajectories arise from the dynamics of technological problem solving. The impression that the cumulative causation involved here is envisaged as a technological phenomenon with a life of its own. To what extent the direction of problem solving – search – is truly independent of economic motivations will always be an issue. But as this section should have made clear, it does appear that from technological considerations alone we can glean some important insights about the dynamics of innovation.

We note in closing that the notions of diffusion and technological trajectory are closely related. On the one hand, imitation is rarely perfect and contains elements of innovation. On the other, trajectories by definition involve advances which build on what has already been achieved in a given paradigm or regime. The often imperfect imitation that constitutes a substantial part of diffusion is thus also a major vehicle for taking a technology along a trajectory. An analytical model which exploits this connection (Silverberg, *et al.*, 1988) is discussed in Chapter 6.

The impact of technological change

As we have already noted, innovation may have an impact on processes of production, products and the nature of the production system overall. In this section, we characterise those changes in greater detail. We should note, however, that assessing the impact of innovation is an enterprise full of pitfalls. First, advances of significant novelty may have limited economic value because potential consumers attach little importance to the improved services provided by the innovation. Second, socio-economic value should not be equated or confused with the level of technical sophistication: technologically simple changes may yield massive returns (e.g. containerisation), while highly complex innovations may attract no market interest. Added to the problem that innovations have no obvious or uniform size, these factors imply that there can be no generally agreed way of measuring their importance or impact (Kline and Rosenberg, 1986: 278–82). Nonetheless, it is useful to acquire a repertoire of concepts to think about such questions.

Impact on production processes

To measure the impact of a process innovation, the standard methods are to look at either **productivity** or **unit costs**.[4] Productivity is a measure of what can be produced as output from what is put into production as input. Partial measures of productivity link output to inputs of a given factor of production. The most commonly measure encountered here is **labour productivity**: output per unit (hour) of labour input. Labour productivity has enjoyed popularity derived from the relative ease of its calculation, but suffers from the serious logical flaw that production generally involves at least two factors of production. For this reason it is preferable where possible to use a **total** measure of productivity, defined as output per unit of all inputs (usually capital and labour) combined.

It might appear that the appropriate measure of output in productivity measures should be the real value of sales or turnover of a firm, industry or economy. But it is usually preferable to use real value-added, which is the result of subtracting from sales the real value of intermediate inputs, energy and materials. The resulting measure of productivity thus abstracts from the impact of factors which have added value in supplier industries, domestically or abroad.

If that approach is taken to labour productivity, the appropriate measure is real value-added per hour of labour; as a result, **growth** in productivity will be the amount by which the growth rate in value-added exceeds that in employment (in terms of hours). Labour productivity may grow, either because investment in new capital enhances the capacity of labour to contribute to growing output, or for a variety of reasons more directly to do with innovation. First, existing technology might come to be more efficiently used as the result of on-the-job learning by those directly engaged in the production process, formal training and education to raise the quality of labour inputs, and/or improvements in the organisation and management of production; in this case, technical efficiency increases. Second, new production methods might be introduced, either through purchasing capital of new design or other innovational intermediate inputs, or undertaking changes based on R&D undertaken within the industry or firm. Industries which do little of their own R&D

but remain technologically 'state of the art' by buying in recently developed machines and materials have been described as **supplier dominated** in a technological sense (Pavitt, 1984). In this case it is technological innovation which is driving productivity up. Finally, existing technology, used at a given level of technical efficiency, may contribute to raised productivity if operated on a larger scale. This will be the case when the technology itself is characterised by **economies of scale**. At the macro-economic level, productivity may also rise as the result of moving productive resources from relatively low-return uses to higher return employment.

Conceptually, the last two of these can and do occur independently of innovation (i.e. with existing technology), but may also affect and be affected by innovation. This is one reason why it is hard to sort out the quantitative effects of innovation from other productivity-raising factors. Further, even when the focus is on value-added, productivity increases measured in one sector may still reflect productivity advance elsewhere, and the spill-over effects of innovation which took place elsewhere may prove impossible to separate out.

Total factor productivity (TFP) can only be measured if some device is used to assign weights to each of the inputs used in production. In a two-input world, the arithmetic measure of TFP (T) is:

$$T = Q/(aK + bL)$$

where Q, K and L are, respectively, indices of output, capital and labour. The inputs are weighted by a and b, the shares of capital and labour in output, where $(a + b) = 1$. Usually, the weights are measured as output shares in the base year from which measures of change are taken. But logically unresolvable problems, in the area of index numbers, surround the question of whether this procedure should be adopted in preference to using current-year weights.

A geometrical measure is based on the device used in economics to define the technical relationship between inputs and output in production, the **production function**. The production function is discussed in detail in the next section, but at this point it is sufficient to note that one of the commonest specific forms taken by the production function is:

$$Q(t) = T(t)K^a(t)L^b(t) \tag{2.1}$$

which by logarithmic differentiation with respect to time t yields a useful expression for the rate of change in TFP:

$$(dT/dt)/T = (dQ/dt)/Q - a(dK/dt)/K - b(dL/dt)/L \tag{2.2}$$

In other words, if there are two inputs (labour and capital), TFP growth is equal to the rate of output growth minus the output share weighted contributions of labour and capital input growth. From this expression, it can be seen why TFP growth is often referred to as the 'residual' in explaining output growth rates; it is what remains after quantitative increases in labour and capital inputs have already been accounted for. As before, enhanced technical efficiency, technological advance and scale effects contribute to TFP growth. The growth rate of labour productivity equals the sum of TFP growth and the growth in capital per unit of labour weighted by the capital's output share.

While productivity analysis can be performed at the level of the firm, industry or economy, it should be noted that working at higher levels of aggregation raises problems of its own. First, it makes sense to relate inputs to output through a production function such as (2.1) at the level of the firm, or in an industry in which all firms are using more or less the same methods of production to produce similar output. But the status of the relationship is clearly somewhat different if it subsumes a myriad of subrelationships among microlevel production activities. Second, the aggregates cover a heterogeneous collection of labour inputs (by skill and experience), capital inputs (by type and age) and outputs. Particularly fierce debates have raged over the permissibility of thinking in terms of a capital aggregate and in connection with technological progress it has always been a worry that simpler models take 'advance' to affect all ages of capital goods on an equal basis.

It is, however, possible to argue that, in general, greater flows of output (with given technology) will always require greater flows of input (as implied by (2.1)), and that, even if microlevel production functions are different, they can be aggregated if the costs of producing an extra unit of output in every industry are equal to the price charged for that unit in the market. This latter condition is often violated in practice; for example, price will exceed this 'marginal' production cost in certain types of monopoly. But, as with other conditions necessary for aggregation, the real question is how badly the prospect of obtaining meaningful conclusions is affected when they fail to hold. There is no simple answer to that question, but the importance of determining the influence of productivity growth means that empirical work continues to be done on the implicit assumption that distortions are not ruinous.

Table 2.1 reproduces the findings of an OECD study of TFP growth showing how productivity growth in member countries was high in the post-war era to the early 1970s but has since declined. The authors of the study (Englander and Mittelstadt, 1988) suggest a slow-down in technological advance, reduced scope for closing the gap on US technology, an end to scale-related productivity rises associated with post-war reconstruction and changes in the composition of the labour force as explanations.

There are, practical problems in separating out the purely quantitative changes in inputs from the qualitative changes which contribute to TFP growth. One way around this difficulty at the micro-level is simply to look at how far production costs fall as the result of innovation. Relatively small falls are associated with run-of-the-mill innovation, larger falls with radical innovation. In the context of the economic theory of the firm, 'small' and 'large' can be given precise conceptual content (see Chapter 4, especially references to Arrow). On the other hand, such definitions are only useful when we assume to start with that innovation is the only reason for which production costs have fallen.

Table 2.1   Productivity growth in OECD countries: average percentage change per annum

	OECD (Average)	USA	Japan	West Germany	France	UK	Canada	Sweden
1960s–1973								
Labour productivity	4.1	2.2	8.6	4.9	5.9	3.3	2.9	3.1
Capital productivity	−0.4	0.3	−2.4	−1.1	0.6	−0.7	1.1	−1.7
TFP	2.8	1.5	6.1	2.8	4.3	2.0	2.2	1.4
1973–79								
Labour productivity	1.6	0.3	3.2	3.4	3.5	1.3	2.0	2.2
Capital productivity	−1.4	−0.9	−3.0	−1.1	−1.2	−1.9	−0.3	−1.8
TFP	0.7	−0.1	1.8	1.8	2.1	0.2	1.1	0.8
1979–86								
Labour productivity	1.4	0.6	2.8	2.0	2.5	1.9	1.1	1.2
Capital productivity	−1.3	−1.0	−2.0	−1.3	−1.4	−0.8	−2.6	−1.9
TFP	0.6	0.0	1.7	0.8	1.3	1.1	−0.3	0.1

(Source: Englander and Mittelstadt, (1988)

Impact on products

An alternative way to view the impact of innovation relates to qualitative changes in the objects generated by production. In this connection Sahal (1985) notes that all such objects might be considered as systems, the simplest of which would contain only one part, but most of which comprise several or many components. As the scale of the object changes, three sorts of qualitative change may also occur: first, **structural** innovations which arise if the overall system and its component parts grow (or shrink) at different rates; second, **material** innovations which arise if the stuff from which the system is built changes, which it may have to if performance is to be maintained when systems grow to a larger (or are reduced to a smaller) scale; third, **systems** innovations which arise when different sets of design principles are combined to yield entirely new structural forms. Using the example of the jet plane, the jet engine was a systems innovation, replacing a reciprocating mechanism with a rotating one, the titanium-based alloys necessary to withstand high temperatures were material innovations and the swept wings needed to counteract metal fatigue associated with increased engine power were a structural innovation.

Impact on competitive structures

We conclude with a characterisation, devised by Abernathy and Clark which draws together many of the strands already discussed. The purpose of the approach is not just to categorise innovations but to analyse the varied role they play in competition. Impact is determined by reference to the extent that innovation affects relative advantages of actual and potential competitors. Technological competition will interest us throughout this book and as a background to much of the economic analysis of this topic, it is useful to have this more general (and specifically economic) approach.

Table 2.2 shows all the ways in which a firm might compete through innovation and all of the impacts innovation might have. Notice here that Abernathy and Clark use as a central organising principle the distinction between impacts on the supply side – production and technology – and impacts on demand, i.e. markets and

Table 2.2 Innovation and firm competence

Domain of innovative activity	*Range of impact of innovation*	
I. *Technology/production*		
Design/embodiment of technology	Improves/perfects established design	Offers new design/radical departure from past embodiment
Production systems/ organisation	Strengthens existing structure	Makes existing structure obsolete demands new system, procedures, organisation
Skills (labour, managerial, technical)	Extends viability of existing skills	destroys value of existing expertise
Materials/supplier relations	Reinforces application of current materials/suppliers	Extensive material substitution; opening new relations with new vendors
Capital equipment	Extends existing capital	Extensive replacement of existing capital with new types of equipment
Knowledge and experience base	Builds on an reinforces applicability of existing knowledge	Establishes links to whole new scientific discipline/destroys value of existing knowledge base
II. *Market/customer*		
Relationship with customer base	Strengthens ties with established customers	Attracts extensive new customer group/creates new market
Customer applications	Improves service in established application	Creates new set of applications/ new set of customer needs
Channels of distribution and service	Builds on and enhances the effectiveness of established distribution network/service organisation	Requires new channels of distribution/new service, after market support
Customer knowledge	Uses and extends customer knowledge and experience in established product	Intensive new knowledge demand of customer; destroys value of customer experience
Modes of customer communication	Reinforce existing modes/methods of communication	Totally new modes of communication required (e.g. field sales engineers)

The left-hand column divides the competitive ingredients of a firm's innovative activity into those determining its capabilities in technology and production and those affecting its markets and linkages to customers. Innovation in each area has impacts shown in the two columns to the right. Impacts range from 'conservative' shown in the middle column to 'radical' shown on the far right. Double headed arrows represent the idea that impacts range between these extremes. Conservative impacts enhance the firm's existing competence; radical impacts disrupt and destroy it.

(Source: Abernathy and Clark, 1985. Reprinted with permission from W.J. Abernathy and K.B. Clark (1985): 'Innovation; mapping the winds of creative destruction', *Research Policy* 14, published by Elsevier Science Publishers)

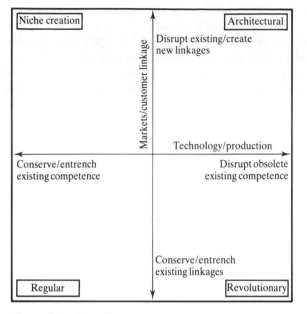

Figure 2.2 Transilience map (Source: Abernathy and Clark, 1985). (Reprinted with permission from W.J. Abernathy and K.B. Clark (1985) 'Innovation: mapping the winds of creative destruction', *Research Policy* 14, published by Elsevier Science Publishers.)

customers. Part I, the top half, brings together in the first column the factors that determine the capabilities of the firm in technology and production. The list includes elements found traditionally as inputs into the production function and others which are not. In the right-hand top quandrant of the table we show the impact which innovation might have if it occurred in relation to any of these elements. Impacts which conserve and enhance the firm's competence in its existing general form are shown in the first of two columns in the quadrant. Impacts which disrupt and destroy existing competence, and hence reduce its value or render it obsolete, are shown in the second column. These are extremes between which a spectrum will usually exist.

In the bottom half of the table, the corresponding list in the first column relates to markets and linkages to customers. In the bottom right quadrant we show the effects which innovation might have on these elements, again divided according to the conserving or destructive implications which innovation might bring.

The spectra between conservation and disruption are now used in Figure 2.2 to provide what Abernathy and Clark call a 'transilience map', transilience being a term of their own invention to describe the capacity of innovation for influencing a firm's resources, skills and knowlege. At the western edge of the map are innovations which do most to enhance and conserve firms' existing technological and production competence. At the eastern edge, innovations which are most disruptive for such competence. Along the southern edge, we find innovations which strongly entrench existing markets and linkages to customers, on the northern edge, innovations which most undermine existing markets but are most favourable to opening new ones.

Assuming the existence of a spectrum between the extremes in both competence and market linkages, the map can be divided into quadrants. First, in the north-east quadrant are innovations which disrupt existing production methods and market linkages, those which Schumpeter had in mind when he spoke of the 'creative destruction' needed to bring about economic growth. Such innovation by definition creates new industries because it creates new markets with product innovations and redefines the boundaries of existing ones. Abernathy and Clark describe such innovation as **architectural**, it 'defines the basic configuration of product and process, and establishes the technical and marketing agendas that will guide subsequent development'. Their prime example is the Model T Ford – 'a creative act of adapting and applying latent technologies to previously unarticulated user needs'.

Second it is at the architectural stage that Dosi's technological paradigm is established, but a dominant design or technological guidepost may not emerge until the transition to **revolutionary** innovation, shown in the south-eastern quandrant. Such innovation contrasts with evolutionary advance in technology in that, like architectural innovation, it disrupts and renders established technical and production competence obsolete. Nonetheless, it is applied to markets which by this stage have a well-defined structure, e.g. the passenger aeroplane market which existed before jet aircraft displaced propeller-driven craft. Third, when existing technology is used to open new markets, as shown in the north-west quadrant, we have innovation which takes the form of **market niche creation**. A good example of this is the Sony Walkman which combines lightweight earphones and a portable radio or casette player to create a new niche in personal audio-electronics. Such innovation is the essence of most of what economists call product differentiation.

Finally, and closest to what we have generally described as 'evolutionary' innovation, is what Abernathy and Clark describe as **regular** innovation. This is found in the south-western quadrant and involves change that builds on established technical and production competence and that is applied to existing markets and customers. It is this sort of innovation Mensch (1979) seems to have in mind when he talks of 'improvement innovations', and Marquis (1988) when he identifies 'nuts and bolts' innovation. The cumulative effect of regular innovation on costs and performance can be enormous.

Production, technological progress and the language of economics

To discuss technological change in the context of economic analysis, it is necessary to become more familiar with distinctions used in the discipline. A small number of very general distinctions require no prior knowledge of economics at all. These will be presented first. But many distinctions about technological change which economists make are based on concepts and tools which structure almost of all their analytical work. These receive separate treatment.

General distinctions

Exogenous *versus* endogenous advance

As noted in Chapter 1 technological progress is described as exogenous if it occurs outside the economic system and hence independently of economic variables. It is endogenous if it occurs within the system and is hence subject to economic influences.

This sort of distinction is one of purely analytical convenience, based on where boundaries have been drawn to define the limits of the 'economic' domain.

Embodied and disembodied advance

This distinction relates to *how* new technological ideas enter production. Technological progress is said to be **disembodied** when it has the effect of raising the productivity of all machines **of all ages**. While such progress may appear implausible, it should be remembered improvements in the organisation of work can indeed increase the productivity of all machines and might be regarded as a source of disembodied progress. On the other hand, progress is described as **embodied** if it enters the production process by being built into the design of new machines, i.e. machines constructed after the new technological idea was hatched.

The construction date of capital is called its **vintage**, and much analysis of economic growth which has adopted the embodiment assumption weights the most recent vintages of capital in the overall capital stock most heavily, because of the assumption that new technological knowledge can only be embodied in new machines. Embodied technological progress is often treated as exogenous. But some of the most interesting work on technological progress in economics makes it both endogenous to the economic system and embodied in machines. These concepts are discussed in major survey articles by Hahn and Matthews (1964) and Kennedy Thirlwall (1972).

The economic approach to production

Much of the economic analysis of technological progress takes place in the area of production theory. Distinctions relating to technological progress in economics are therefore often shaped by the economic analysis of production itself. A brief summary of the simple foundations of that theory is provided before an economic taxonomy of technological progress is presented. This section may readily be omitted by readers already familiar with economics.

Production can be defined as a value-adding process which involves transforming or converting inputs (such as the services of labour, capital, materials and energy) into outputs. Exactly how inputs generate outputs is described by the technology, defined as the body of ideas which tells how to undertake production. Production is often thought of as a **material** transformation, applying energy to change the shape of a sheet of steel or the chemical composition of a pharmaceutical, But it may equally well be a **spatial** transformation, applying energy to transport goods to market, for example. And it may also involve a **temporal** transformation, applying energy to keep goods cool in storage, for instance, until they are required. Many examples of production in the service industries involve transforming information.

Varied and complex as real-world production actually is, economists represent it in a particularly simple way, arguing that it is not their business to be interested in production methods *per se*, which are really the concern of engineers. They instead aim to capture the essence of production through a general and rather abstract account of relationships between inputs and outputs found in the production function (which was introduced briefly above).

The production function shows which inputs and how many units of each would be required making best use of existing technological knowledge to produce specified quantities of a given sort of output per period. If $Q(t)$ is the flow of output at period t, and $X_1(t)$, $X_2(t)$, ... $X_n(t)$ are flows of inputs 1, 2, ... n at the same period, the production function can be written in the general form:

$$Q(t) = F(X_1(t), X_2(t) \ldots X_n(t)) \tag{2.3}$$

in which F contains the technological information telling how the inputs can be transformed into output.

It is usually assumed that if any input increases while all others are constant, output will increase, but that repeated additional ('marginal') doses of any given input will at some point start to bring increasingly small additions to output if the remaining inputs are held constant. Mathematically, all first partial derivatives $dQ(t)/dX_1(t)$, ..., $dQ(t)/dX_n(t)$) are positive and all second partial derivatives eventually become negative. Since the output generated by an additional unit of input is called the **marginal product** of that input, we say that production functions are usually assumed to be characterised by the (eventually) **diminshing marginal product** of all inputs.

For expositional convenience, much economic analysis reduces the list of inputs to two: capital $K(t)$, and labour, $L(t)$. The production function can then be represented diagrammatically. In Figure 2.3 quantities of capital and labour are represented by distances from the origin along the y and x axes, respectively. The line drawn in the quadrant formed by the axes is called an **isoquant**. It represents all the pairs of capital and labour quantities required to produce a specified quantity of output, say $Q_0(t)$. This line is usually assumed to bow inwards towards the origin, because economists argue that if one unit of capital after another were withdrawn from production, increasing additional quantities of labour would on each occasion be required to prevent any decline in output. The slope of the isoquant at any given point (which can be found by inspecting the slope of a tangent to that point) shows how much

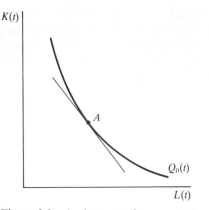

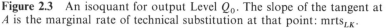

Figure 2.3   An isoquant for output Level Q_0. The slope of the tangent at *A* is the marginal rate of technical substitution at that point: mrts_{LK}.

extra labour must be employed when one unit of capital is removed. This is called the **marginal rate of technical substitution** between capital and labour (mrts $_{L,K}$). It is measured by the ratio $dK(t):dL(t)$, which must be negative. Its absolute value falls for movements down the isoquant, since $dL(t)$ continually rises for equal reductions in $K(t)$. The jargon used to describe this feature of the isoquant is **diminishing marginal rate of technical substitution**. The diminishing of the mrts is meant to capture the idea that inputs into production are not perfect substitutes for one another. And the less labour is a substitute for capital, the more additional labour will be required to compensate for the withdrawal of successive units of capital, making the isoquant more sharply curved.

For any given level of output, particular ratios of capital and labour, represented by the slope of a ray to a point on an isoquant, may be described as techniques of production. When isoquants are continuous and smooth, the implication is that the technology offers an infinitely wide range of such techniques. If there is only a limited number of techniques, as in Figure 2.4, the isoquant is no longer smooth. Single points will represent the combinations of capital and labour required to produce the given flow of output under each of the 'few' techniques available, were any one of them to be used exclusively. Straight lines will join these points if the techniques can be used in varying combinations to produce the same output flow. The isoquant is then 'kinked'. An the limit, there may be only one technique available. The isoquant then shrinks to a single point, representing a **fixed coefficient** technology, where the 'coefficient' is the unique capital:labour ratio.

Since more output will flow from the application of more of both inputs, any point to the north-east of another must lie on an isoquant associated with a higher level of output. The production function for a given type of output is represented by the set of all isoquants (the isoquant map) relating to that output. An example is given in Figure 2.5. The technology defines the shapes and positions of the isoquants.

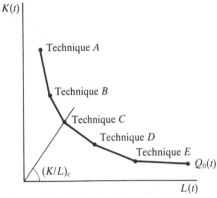

Figure 2.4   A kinked isoquant based on a restricted range of techniques.

The isoquant and isoquant map are fundamental tools in the theory of production. From the isoquant map can be derived the **total product curve** (**TPC**). The TPC is found by assuming that one input (usually taken to be capital) cannot be varied immediately in response to changed conditions. What will happen to output if the remaining input is varied? The answer can be found by reading across the isoquant map along a horizontal line whose level is determined by the fixed level of capital inputs. See for example the line *ABCDE*, drawn in Figure 2.6 in relation to capital level $K_0(t)$. Along that line can be found a set of values linking labour inputs (measured on the horizontal axis) to flows of output (found by inspecting the labels on each isoquant). These pairs of values are then represented on the TPC. It will be seen that the TPC has a positive but diminishing slope. Since the slope of the TPC shows by how much output rises when labour input rises by a small amount, holding capital

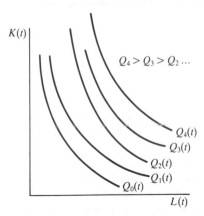

Figure 2.5   An isoquant map: a diagrammatic representation of the production function.

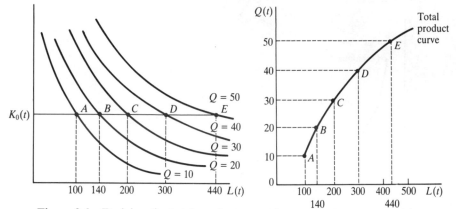

Figure 2.6 Deriving the total product curve from an isoquant map with fixed capital ($K_0(t)$) and variable labour inputs.

inputs constant, this merely reflects the property of diminishing marginal product for any input, in this case the marginal product of labour.

An important feature of the production function is now identified: **returns to scale**. To understand this characteristic, perform the following mental experiment: Suppose *all* inputs increase by a given multiple, say two. What will then happen to the flow of output? If output rises by more than the given multiple (in our example, it more than doubles), there are **increasing returns to scale** over the range of input and output quantities for which we performed the experiment. If output rises by less than the given multiple, there are **decreasing returns to scale**. If output rises by exactly the same multiple, there are **constant returns to scale**.

Representing technological change

It is now time to put this conceptual apparatus to work. Let us focus on the unit isoquant, the isoquant, associated with a flow of one unit of output per period. It is part of the definition of the production function, and all isoquants that they should relate only to technology which makes minimum use of inputs. Methods which fail this test in producing a unit of output can be represented by points to the north-east of the unit isoquant, representing the same output but greater quantities of inputs. All such points are technically inefficient.

A technological change is an addition to the set of ways in which production could be effected, and can be represented as a point somewhere on the isoquant diagram. If the new 'blueprint' is associated with a point to the north-east of the existing unit isoquant, such as *R* in Figure 2.7, the new way of making a unit of output uses more inputs than other known methods. But if the new method were represented by a point like *P*, the unit of output could be made with fewer units of input than before.

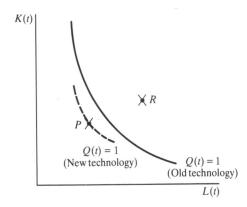

Figure 2.7 Changing technology and the shifting unit isoquant.

Here there has been a technological advance. To be consistent with the definition of the production function, the isoquant must now be redrawn to pass through this point. Technological advance is therefore represented by a shift in the isoquant.

Notice two points. First, technological advance may allow all or only part of an isoquant to shift. If only a narrow range of techniques is affected, only part of the isoquant shifts. If many or all are affected, the whole curve must shift. Second, although the previous exposition was conducted in terms of the single-unit isoquant, technological change will usually affect input requirements at many or all levels of output. The whole isoquant map will shift towards the origin.

In terms of the TPC, technological advance is represented by an upward shift of the curve, because producing given output with fewer inputs is logically equivalent to producing more output with the same quantity of inputs. Again, technological progress may not affect the whole TPC, merely a segment.

The production function also underlies the analysis of costs, which in turn is also influenced by technological progress. In the economic analysis of production, it is assumed that the choice of technique minimises production costs, given prevailing input prices. This calls for technical efficiency but also implies an important element of economic efficiency – requiring input users to combine scarce inputs in proportions which reflect their relative scarcity. Illustrating this calls for using the **isocost line**, a device showing all the combinations of labour and capital which can be bought for the same expenditure. To derive it, note that total expenditure, E, must comprise the sum of the total costs of capital and labour services:

$$E = rK + wL \qquad (2.4)$$

where r is the hiring or rental cost per unit of capital and w the wage rate. By a simple rearrangement of (2.4):

$$K = E/r - (w/r)L \qquad (2.4')$$

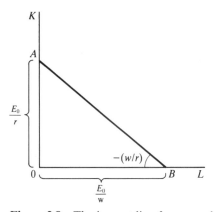

Figure 2.8 The isocost line for expenditure level E_0

For given values of r and w, (2.4′) can be solved to show all of the combinations of K and L which can be purchased for a total expenditure level, indicated by a specific value of E, say E_0. In Figure 2.8, OA shows the amount of K, E_0/r, which would be bought if all expenditure were on K. OB is the maximum amount of L, E_0/w, that the same expenditure could obtain. If one unit of labour were hired, $L = 1$ in (4′), and the amount of capital which could now be hired with $E = E_0$ would fall by (w/r). Every time one further unit of labour was hired, the amount of capital which could be hired without changing total expenditure would again fall by (w/r). Repeated application of this procedure generates the isocost line shown in Figure 2.8. Its slope represents the ratio $-(w/r)$, the **wage: rent ratio**, and is steeper the higher w is relative to r. Its position is determined by the level of E; higher isocost lines represent higher levels of total expenditure.

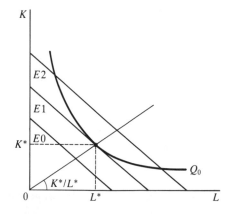

Figure 2.9 The cost minimising choice of inputs to produce output level Q_0.

For economic efficiency, the technique which minimises total expenditure has to be used. To illustrate this, assume that we wish to find the cost minimising technique for output level Q_0 in Figure 2.9. Expenditure will be minimised when the point on the isoquant is found (the technique chosen) which touches the isocost line nearest to the origin. In Figure 2.9, the isocost line nearest the origin which allows output level Q_0 to be reached is labelled $E1$. Any expenditure less than this (such as $E0$) would not buy enough inputs to produce Q_0. Any expenditure greater than this (such as $E2$) would buy more inputs than are needed and would not be cost minimising. For expenditure $E1$, the amounts of inputs purchased are K^* and L^*, and the technique used is characterised by the ratio K^*/L^*.

It should at once be apparent that technological progress, which shifts the isoquant towards the origin, will enable the same amount of output to be produced on a lower isocost line. Technological progress thus leads to cost reductions.

Classification of biases

Factor augmentation

If technological progress is disembodied and exogenous, it was shown earlier that it could be represented by upward shifts in the TPC, or inward shifts in isoquants. Algebraically, the simplest way of capturing progress of this kind is to incorporate the shift factor into the production function:

$$Q(t) = F(X_1(t), \ldots X_n(t), t); \ \mathrm{d}F/\mathrm{d}t > 0 \tag{2.5}$$

All this says is that, even if all inputs remained constant, output would still rise as a result of the increasing stock of technological knowledge over time t.

Even retaining the simple disembodied, exogenous view of progress, however, it can be argued that certain changes in knowledge will increase the efficiency of some inputs more than others. This has led economists to think of advance in terms of **factor augmentation**.

Technological progress then implies that a greater flow of output $Q(t)$ can be generated by the same amounts of input $K(t)$ and $L(t)$ It is as if the inputs, or factors of production, had been increased, or augmented. To capture the implications of technological progress, therefore, multiplicative terms are often applied to $K(t)$ and $L(t)$, and the values taken by these multipliers used to indicate the impact technological change would have on production if the new techniques were put to use. A form of the production function which captures this idea is:

$$Q(t) = F(A(t)K(t), B(t)L(t)) \tag{2.6}$$

It should be noted that the production function in the context of this analysis, and the discussion of factor-saving biases in the next section, related to *aggregate* output and inputs. The terms $A(t)K(t)$ and $B(t)L(t)$ are called, the flow of effective capital services and the flow of effective labour services. Even if $K(t)$ and $L(t)$ – the actual flows – remain constant, their effective contribution to production increases if $A(t)$ and $B(t)$ increase. It is important to note that augmentation of a given factor does not require that there has been any change in that factor. Solow (1970) gives the example in this connection of a typist whose performance in terms of contribution to output is raised by the improved design of the machine. The typist is neither stronger nor more accomplished, and does not work longer hours, but because the machine works better, the effect is to 'give one secretary the strength of 1.04 secretaries after a year has gone by'. Table 2.3 summarises the distinctions most often made.

Table 2.3   Capital- and labour-augmentation coefficients from the production function and the classification of technological progress

Values of multipliers	Type of progress
$A(t)$ rising; $B(t) = 1$	Pure capital augmenting
$A(t) = 1$; $B(t)$ rising	Pure labour augmenting
$A(t)$ and $B(t)$ rising at the same proportionate rate per period	Equally capital and labour augmenting

It is worth noting that this classification focuses on what might be considered special cases; nothing is said about the plausible range of cases in which both $A(t)$ and $B(t)$ might be rising, but at *different* rates. Furthermore, the use that is made of this classification often limits the analysis yet further; it is usually assumed that if $A(t)$ and/or $B(t)$ are rising, they do so at a *constant* proportional rate. There is no reason to expect this to be the case. Rather, this is a good example of a case in which economists have sought assumptions which make for tractable analysis (i.e. yield well-defined conclusions), which also yield conclusions consistent with observed data.

In this case, if a pure labour augmenting progress is assumed, there is a possible explanation for the apparent constant labour share in aggregate income over long periods of apparently turbulent economic history (see Chapter 7).

Factor-saving biases and concepts of neutral progress

One important aspect of technological progress is that it is often **biased**. In particular, it is often said to be either 'labour-saving' or 'capital-saving'. These are common expressions. The purpose of this section is see what they might mean, to point out that each might have several meanings and to see how the systems of classification which give rise to such expressions can be linked to the notion of augmentation.

The intuition behind bias is that if there is labour-saving advance, isoquants will shift more towards the labour axis than the capital axis. While progress may allow savings in both inputs, proportionately more labour than capital is saved for all techniques. If advance is capital-saving, proportionately more capital than labour is saved.

The problem with this simple intuitive approach is that it is impossible to make it analytically operational unless more structure is introduced. The production function comprises the entire map of isoquants and when the whole production function shifts, it is unclear which points on each set of old- and new-technology isoquants should be compared with each other for the purposes of identifying bias. There is no unique way of performing this task and economists have adopted differing strategies.

We consider schemes of classification offered by Hicks, Harrod and Solow.[5] In the definitions proposed by Hicks (1963), bias is measured along a given **capital:labour** ratio; in those of Harrod (1948), a given **capital:output** ratio; and in those of Solow (1963), a given **labour:output** ratio.

Each of the strategies has something in common, however. This is the idea that technological progress can be viewed as factor-saving in terms of a given input if advance results in a fall in the income share of that input relative to the others. Remember that we are dealing with aggregates here so it makes sense to talk about income shares. Note, though, that if output is growing, the total income earned by the factor may rise, even though its share falls. If the total incomes received by all inputs are constant, or rise or fall at the same percentage rate, the relative shares will be constant and technological progress is described as **neutral**. Changes in the relative factor shares are thus taken to show non-neutral progress, advance characterised by factor share bias.

In Hicks' schema, technological progress is defined to be **labour-saving** if the marginal product of capital (dQ/dK) rises relative to that of labour (dQ/dL), **capital-saving** if dQ/dK falls relative to dQ/dL, and neutral if the ratio of the marginal products is constant. To understand this definition, note first that the ratio of the marginal products is also dL/dK, which if we focus only on absolute values is the reciprocal of the mrts, since the mrts shows by how much capital inputs may fall without loss of output when labour inputs rise by a small amount. A rise in dQ/dK relative to dQ/dL, therefore, implies a fall in the mrts, a fall in the ratio implies a rise in the mrts, and a constant ratio implies an invariant mrts. Since technological progress involves a shift in the production function, the Hicks schema requires us to compare the mrts at points on the old- and new-technology isoquants. The points for comparison lie on any ray representing a given capital:labour ratio.

Hicks' schema is illustrated in Figures 2.10–2.12 where a new-technology unit isoquant Q_N must be compared with the corresponding old-technology unit isoquant, Q_O. In Figure 2.10, the technological progress illustrated is Hicks labour-saving. To see why, focus first on the capital-labour ratio $(K/L)_a$. The slopes of the isoquants at A and A' represent the $mrts_{L,K}$ at each of these points, and in Figure 2.10 the mrts at A' is less than that at A. Comparing B' with B, a similar conclusion is reached for the shift down $(K/L)_b$ and, as drawn, would also hold for any other capital:labour ratio.

In Figure 2.11 we show an example of Hicksian capital-saving technological progress. Here the mrts at A' is greater than that at A, and that at B' exceeds that at B. In Figure 2.12, the mrts at A is the same as that at A', and that at B the same

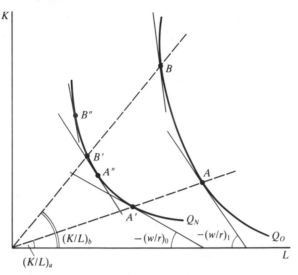

Figure 2.10   Hicks labour-saving progress.

as that at B'. The progress shown there must be **Hicks-neutral**. It is worth noting that Hicks-neutral progress is also equivalent to progress described earlier as equally capital and labour augmenting (Uzawa, 1960/1).

To link this to factor shares, recall first that the share of capital in output is rK/Q and the share of labour wL/Q. The factor shares ratio may be written rK/wL. Now make two assumptions found very widely in economics. First, all firms hire their inputs under competitive conditions. We may then invoke a well-known result from economic theory that in equilibrium the return or rental rate on capital, r, is equal to its marginal product, dQ/dK, and the wage rate, w, is equal to the marginal product of labour, dQ/dL. Second, the production function is characterised by constant returns to scale. This means we can use Euler's theorem which states that if all inputs are rewarded at the rate of their marginal products, the total value of output will be exactly exhausted in paying them.

Under the first of these assumptions, labour-saving progress, reflected as a rise in the ratio of dQ/dK to dQ/dL will be associated with a rise in r/w. For any given level of K/L, this means the relative shares ratio must also rise, since the second assumption guarantees that all income generated in production must be distributed between capital and labour. By the same token, r/w will fall under capital-saving technological progress and so will the relative shares ratio. When progress is Hicks-neutral, r/w will be constant for any given K/L, so the factor shares ratio will not change.

In Figure 2.10–2.12, isocost lines of the appropriate slope have been drawn tangent to each of the pairs of points A and A' to show the w/r ratios associated with cost-minimising production at those points. In Figure 2.10, the ratio falls from a numerical value of $(w/r)_1$ to $(w/r)_0$, implying that if progress is labour-saving, labour

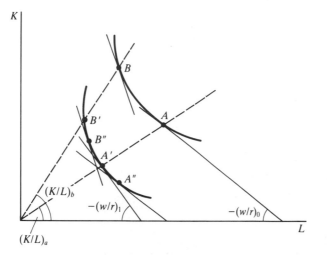

Figure 2.11 Hicks capital – saving progress. Here the numerical value of $(w/r)_1$ exceeds $(w/r)_0$.

in effect becomes less scarce compared with capital and so commands less of a return relative to that of capital. The minus sign before each (w/r) in the diagrams is there to remind us that, at the given factor prices, any increase in capital use for a given total outlay must imply a reduction in labour use.

In Harrod's schema, (K/Q) is held constant in comparing old with new isoquants. If the marginal product of capital (equal to r under competitive conditions) is unchanged when the shift occurs, then capital's share is constant. Assuming also that

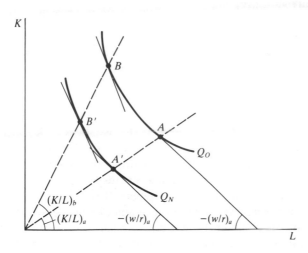

Figure 2.12 Hicks-neutral progress.

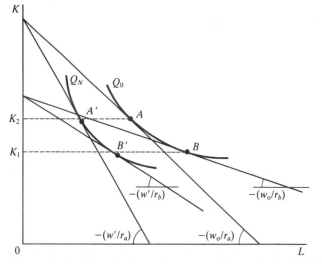

Figure 2.13 Harrod-neutral progress. (Figures 2.13–2.15 build with permission a diagrammatic device in G. Hacche (1979) *The Theory of Economic Growth: An Introduction*, Chapter 8, p. 122, published by Macmillan: London.)

there are just two inputs, capital and labour, a constant capital share together with constant returns to scale implies a constant labour share and hence unchanging relative shares. Technological progress at a given capital:output ratio which leaves the return on capital unchanged also preserves the relative share ratio and such advance is defined as **Harrod-neutral**.

Harrod-neutral progress is illustrated in Figure 2.13, which draws on Hacche (1979: 120–5). As before, Q_O and Q_N are unit isoquants for 'old' and 'new' technology. Since each represents the same output level, any movement along a horizontal line towards the vertical K axis implies a shift at a given capital-output ratio. If r is constant throughout any comparative exercise, the isocost line will be anchored at a given vertical intercept.

In Figure 2.13, a given level of r is preserved when the unit isoquant shifts either from A to A' with capital input of K_2 or from B to B', where $K = K_1$. Thus the technological progress reflected in the shift is Harrod-neutral. Relative shares are kept constant by two forces operating in different directions; the capital:labour ratio rises (the slopes of rays OA' and OB' would be steeper, respectively, than rays OA and OB), but (r/w) falls (the isocost line becomes steeper). It can also be shown that Harrod-neutral progress is equivalent to pure labour-augmenting progress (Robinson, 1937/8). Why this is so can be seen from Figure 2.13 the same amount of output is produced with the same amount of capital, so it is as if labour has become more efficient in using the capital to produce output.

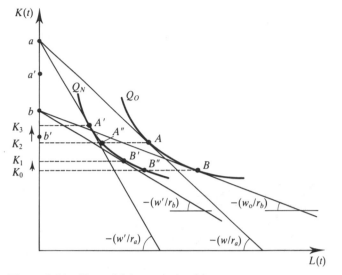

Figure 2.14   Harrod labour-saving bias.

Harrod labour-saving progress is illustrated in Figure 2.14. Comparing A with A', r has been held constant, but under cost-minimising conditions, the capital : output ratio rises. Alternatively, if A is compared with A'', the capital : output ratio remains constant but r must have risen (since the isocost line tangent to A'' would have a vertical intercept a'). Similar arguments apply between B, B' and B''. In each case, rK/Q increases and, given the Euler condition, wL/Q falls, so the relative shares ratio rises – the sign of labour-saving progress. **Harrod capital-saving** progress is illustrated in Figure 2.15.

In Solow's system, L/Q (or its reciprocal, output per head) is held constant. *Solow-neutral* technological progress occurs when the real wage rate w, is constant under shifts of the production function, with the consequence that constant relative shares are again observed. Solow-neutral technological progress is equivalent to pure capital-augmenting advance. As in the other cases, a labour-saving bias is reflected in a rise in capital's share relative to labour's and a capital-saving bias in a fall in the relative shares ratio.

It may be asked why one schema is not enough. The answer is that different schemes of classification have been found useful in different contexts. For example, growth theory (discussed in Chapter 7) indicates that the capital : labour ratio is very likely to change over time so that to use a measure which by construction holds K/L constant may not be very helpful in that context. Harrod's approach has been particularly favoured in growth analysis and Solow devised an alternative schema to deal with issues arising in the context of vintage capital models.

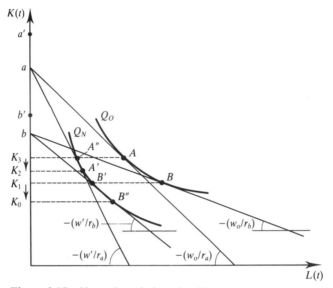

Figure 2.15   Harrod capital-saving bias.

Hicks and Harrod compared

It should by now be clear that the systems of classification used by Hicks and Harrod are quite different from each other and not related to each other in any clear way. This can be shown by stating the following proposition: *There is only one form of the production function under which technological progress can be both Hicks- and Harrod-neutral. This form is the Cobb-Douglas production function* (which appeared earlier as equation (2.1)). This implies first, that with other forms of the production function, Harrod-neutral progress could be either Hicks labour- or capital-saving; and second, that under the one form where progress is neutral according to both classifications it is, by definition, labour-augmenting in one case and equally labour- and capital-augmenting in the other (Layard and Walters, 1978: 292).

The isoquant map for the Cobb-Douglas production function is shown in Figure 2.16. At every point at which any ray from the origin crosses isoquants for successively higher levels of output (e.g. *A*, *B*, *C* and *D*), the mrts at that point is the same. Understanding the proposition in the previous paragraph also requires familiarity with another economic concept, the **elasticity of substitution**.

Moving downwards along an isoquant, first the capital : labour ratio becomes lower; second, the $mrts_{L,K}$ becomes smaller and, under competitive conditions, production at any given point implies a lower value of w/r, or higher r/w. The elasticity of substitution is a number which measures the relationship between proportional changes in these ratios:

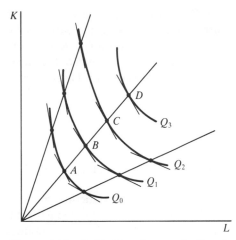

Figure 2.16 Cobb-Douglas production function.

$$\text{Elasticity of substitution} = \text{MINUS } \frac{\% \ \text{Change in } K/L}{\% \ \text{Change in } (r/w)} \tag{2.7}$$

Since a rise in (r/w) will always be associated with a fall in the capital:labour ratio, this ratio will always be negative, and is conventionally preceded by a minus sign to convert it into a positive number. When a given percentage rise in (r/w) is associated with a smaller (larger) percentage fall in the capital:labour ratio, the elasticity of substitution will have a value less than (greater than) one. The intuition here is that when a given change in relative input prices brings about only a small amount of substitution between the inputs, it must be because they are not easy to substitute for each other. This is reflected in a relatively 'small' value of the elasticity (less than one). When the technology permits ready substitution between inputs, the same change in input prices induces a much larger amount of substitution, reflected in a 'high' value of the elasticity.

In an intermediate case, a given percentage rise in (r/w) is associated with an identical fall in the capital:labour ratio and the elasticity of substitution is equal to one. The implications for relative shares are immediate: if K/L falls by a smaller (larger) proportion than r/w rises, then the relative shares ratio (rK/wL) will rise (fall). When the elasticity takes a value of one, however, any given percentage rise in (r/w) will be associated with an equal percentage fall in K/L, and the relative shares will be unchanged.

Now it is a characteristic of the Cobb-Douglas production function that its elasticity of substitution is always equal to one. In terms of isoquants Q_O and Q_N, Hicks- and Harrod-neutrality involve comparing the same point on Q_O with different points on Q_N. This means that on Q_N, the capital:labour ratios will differ. In order for each capital:labour ratio to be associated with the same relative shares ratio, the proportional difference between the two K/L ratios must be exactly offset by a proportional difference in the opposite direction in (r/w). In other words, as we move along Q_N between the two points of comparison with that on Q_O, K/L and r/w must move in counterbalancing opposite directions. But this can happen only if the isoquant has unitary elasticity of substitution, i.e. if it is part of a Cobb-Douglas production function.

Other dimensions of bias

While bias on technological progress is usually taken to apply to factor saving, it might also apply to **scale, substitutability** or **scope**.

In the case of scale, advances relevant to large-scale production but technically inapplicable to smaller scales sometimes take place. It was suggested earlier that one highly visible technological trajectory was the exploitation of scale economies across many types of production and this implies that less attention was paid to increasing productivity at smaller scales. Only the high-output isoquants in the production function would have benefited from technological progress.

Turning to substitutability, it has been noted that technological change may sometimes influence only a segment of any given isoquant. This would reflect an advance in relation to only a narrow range of capital:output ratios, usually those associated with economically efficient production when relative input prices remain stable over a long period of time. Such progress will have the effect of sharpening the curvature of isoquants in the locality of this range of techniques, implying that less and less capital-labour substitution would take place in response to a given change in relative input prices. In the limit, progress might focus on a single capital:labour ratio, with the result that isoquants would become L-shaped and the elasticity of substitution equal to zero.

It is tempting to describe technological progress which reduces the elasticity of substitution as 'flexibility decreasing'. But that would imply that flexibility in production is defined only by substitutability among inputs. While this makes sense when there is single-output production, it abstracts from other dimensions in which flexibility might be varied under multioutput production. Later in the book it will be noted that firms and economies usually produce more than one output, in which case it is possible to achieve economies of scope, cost reductions associated with increasing the range of outputs produced. Technological change might favour increased jointness in production and if so could be viewed as scope-enhancing.

Sources of innovation

When technological progress is endogenous, either its rate or bias or both, are explained as part of the working of the economic system. In this section, we have so far concentrated on economists' descriptions of the sorts of shift which might occur in the production function, irrespective of what causes the shift. But any classification focusing on the endogeneity of progress must relate to *why* the shift occurs in the first place.

One of the foundation stones of this book is that we may look to economic motivations for at least a significant fraction of the explanation for technological and technical change. That proposition might be taken to mean that the economically explained portion of technological advance all rests on decision-makers' conscious and deliberate weighing of benefits and costs, i.e. on explicit optimising procedures. For some innovation this is undoubtedly true, but in other cases, progress arises almost automatically as a 'spin-off' from efforts to achieve technical and economic efficiency. On the other hand, it creates a false dichotomy to say there is a clear division between innovation flowing from decisions made with full cognisance of potential consequences and that arising more or less spontaneously from efficient production. There is a spectrum. While the general point must therefore be made, we will not use it as the basis for classification.

An alternative way of classifying endogenous change, and one which we ought to expect from economists more than anyone, might differentiate between **demand-induced** and **supply-driven** innovation. The demand/supply distinction is widely exploited in the literature, but it is important to recognise that, in relation to any innovation, both demand- and supply-side factors are invariably at work, so we ought not to talk as if innovations can be classified as resulting exclusively from either 'demand-pull' or 'supply-push'. The appropriate perspective is that innovation results from an interaction between the two sets of factors (Mowery and Rosenberg, 1982).

The subtlety of the supply/demand distinction is reflected in Pavitt's (1984) attempt to characterise the pattern of intersectoral differences in innovation sourcing and experience. **Supplier-dominated** sectors were referred to earlier and typically include, for example, agriculture, wood and paper products and construction. Firms in these sectors typically devote few resources to developing their own innovations and rely heavily on suppliers of equipment and materials to provide them with the process innovations which form the bulk of their new technology. Their technological trajectories are shaped mainly by cost-cutting efforts, so the price and performance of exogenously developed capital goods is important.

Science-based firms, on the other hand, engage in substantial R&D to take technological and commercial advantage of new scientific knowledge developed in universities and other research institutions. Leading current examples of sectors containing such firms are electronics and chemicals. But as we noted in the work of Abernathy and Clark (1985) shifting currents in scientific knowledge itself will, over time, give rise to changes in the sectors which should be identified as science-based.

Pavitt's third category is what he calls **production intensive**, but this includes two rather different types of firm. First, there are those which are specialist suppliers – firms which provide equipment and instrumentation and whose focus is on product innovation to meet the needs of their customers. Some new technology they develop for themselves; users often provide operating experience, testing facilities and design and development resources. Second, there are scale-intensive firms which produce bulk materials like steel and glass or are major assemblers. They again undertake some of their own innovation work, but in this case it is usually directed to solving production problems and their production engineering departments are an important source of their new technology.

Notice that while the focus here has been the sources of innovation, interaction between supplier and user is either implicit or explicit in every case. Supplier-dominated firms can indirectly exert pressure on suppliers by the purchasing choices they make. Science-based firms interested in staying in business will research the market and new science to determine where development is likely to be most profitable. And the relationship between specialist suppliers and users is complementary, almost symbiotic.

Having focused on intersectoral differences in innovation sourcing, this chapter concludes by adjusting the lens to identify, at a more general level the ways in which economists have said technological progress comes about. A feature of each of this list is that in all cases **investment** in new capital is a prerequisite for progress. Without at this stage labouring the point, we note that Kaldor (1957), Kaldor and Mirrlees (1962) and Scott (1989) have been among those to emphasise the difficulty of separating technological progress from investment in new capital, of distinguishing between shifts *of* the production function and shifts *along* it brought about by increasing the capital:labour ratio. Kaldor's technical progress function and Scott's investment programme contour map were both constructed to provide theories of growth with endogenous technological progress meant to circumvent this problem.

Many other theories, however, put this problem to one side and proceed, conceptually at least, on the understanding that it is possible to separate out generic sources of and contributions to technological progress. These in turn are incorporated in the working of the economic system and elements of progress it endogenises. This topic is treated at length in Chapter 7, but here we present with little further comment the ways in which the speed and/or bias of technical progress might be explained. These are: through research and development, (R&D); learning-by-doing, (LBD), training and education, intra-firm diffusion, through inter-firm diffusion and responses to changes in relative input prices.

Each of these sources of advance has given rise to its own subprogramme of research in economics. The last is associated with a famous debate on induced bias, flowing from Hicks' concern to explain whether progress would tend to be labour-saving if the wage:rent ratio rose over the long run. Hicks (1963) argued that as labour became relatively more expensive, it should be expected that successive choices of innovation would be guided by the aim of achieving labour-saving progress. Hicks' conclusion has been shown to be valid (Ahmad, 1966) if basic research is assumed to be unaffected by economic influences, and has Hicks-neutral implications for an innovation possibility curve, an envelope of all unit isoquants representing all of the possible innovations among which firms might choose. But Rosenberg (1982) has questioned the true exogeneity of basic research that this account presupposes. As the earlier part of this chapter suggests, even the generation of new technological possibilities may be linked to economic conditions, which throws doubt on the structure of the Ahmad analysis.

Moreover, current innovation choices are guided by past developments to such a large extent that, if it has been profit maximising increasingly to concentrate on labour-saving technology for a long period, we should expect that to have shaped the trajectories of technological change which most firms would be following. It is not so much that firms are systematically induced to choose labour-saving innovations from the wide range of alternatives available in any period, but rather that they would be induced selectively to persist with R&D which had shown itself effective in labour-saving in the past.

Notes

1. For a thorough survey of technology policy, see Stoneman, 1987.
2. The term 'fundamental' research is applied to elements of all basic reserach, its use indicating that the projects described are of an anticipated long-term nature.
3. The importance of such feedback has been shown by von Hippel (1988) and in a study of the machine tool industry by Parkinson (1982).
4. The literature on productivity is vast for a sample of relevant studies, see Kendrick (1973, 1982, 1991), Salter (1966), Caves *et al.* (1982), Diewert (1992) and OECD (1991). But the basic ideas are relatively simple.
5. A more comprehensive range of classification schemes is discussed in Sato and Beckmann (1968), but those analysed here are the most widely used.

References

Abernathy, W.J. and K.B. Clark (1985) 'Innovation: Mapping the winds of creative destruction', *Research Policy* 14, 3–22.

Ahmad, S. (1966) 'On the theory of induced innovation', *Economic Journal* 76, 344–57.

Bjorn-Anderson, N *et al.* (1982) *Information Society. For Richer, For Poorer*, Amsterdam: North-Holland.

Braun, E. and S. MacDonald (1978) *Revolution in Miniature*, Cambridge: Cambridge University Press.

Bush, V. (1945) *Science the Endless Frontier*, Washington: Office for Scientific Research and Development.

Caves, R., L. Christensen and W. Diewert (1982) 'The economic theory of index numbers and the measurement of input, output and productivity', *Econometrica* 50, 1393–414.

Diewert, W. (1992) 'The measurement of productivity', *Bulletin of Economic Research* 44, 163–98.

Dosi, G. (1988) 'Sources, procedures and microeconomic effects of innovation', *Journal of Economic Literature* 26, 1120–71.

Englander, A.S. and A. Mittelstadt (1988) *Total Factor Productivity: macroeconomic and structural aspects of the slowdown.* OECD Economic Studies No. 10, Spring 1988. Paris.

Hacche, G. (1979) *The Theory of Economic Growth*, London: Macmillan.

Hahn, F.H. and R.C.O. Matthews (1964) 'The theory of economic growth: a survey', *Economic Journal* 74, 779–902.

Harrod, R.F. (1984) *Towards a Dynamic Economics*, London: Macmillan.

Hicks, J. (1963) *The Theory of Wages*, London: Macmillan.

Hughes, W. (1971) 'Scale economies and electric power', in W. Capron (ed.) *Technical Change in Regulated Industries*, Washington, DC: Brookings Institution.

Irvine, J. and B.R. Martin (1984) *Foresight in Science*, London: Pinter.

Kaldor, N. (1957) 'A model of economic growth', *Economic Journal* 67, 591–624.

Kaldor, N. and J.A. Mirrlees (1962) 'A new model of economic growth', *Review of Economic Studies* 29, 174–92.

Kendrick, J.W. (1973) *Postwar Productivity Trends in US Manufacturing*, Washington, DC: National Bureau of Economic Research.

Kendrick, J.W. (1982) *Interindustry Differences in Productivity Growth*, Washington, DC: American Enterprises Institute for Public Policy Research.

Kendrick, J.W. (1991) 'Total factor productivity: What it does and does not measure', in OECD, *Technology and Productivity: The Challenge for Economic Policy*, Paris. 149–56.

Kennedy, C. and A. Thirlwall (1972) 'Technical progress', *Economic Journal* 82, 11–72.

Kline, S.J. and N. Rosenberg (1986) 'An overview of innovation', in R. Landau and N. Rosenberg (eds) *The Positive Sum Strategy: Harnessing Technology for Economic Growth*, Washington, DC: National Academy Press.

Kuhn, T.S. (1970) *The Structure of Scientific Revolutions*, 2nd edn, Chicago: University of Chicago Press.

Layard, P.R.G. and A. Walters (1978) *Microeconomic Theory*, New York and London: McGraw-Hill.

Lundvall, B.A. (ed.) (1992) *National Systems of Innovation: Towards a Theory of Innovation and Interactive Learning*, London: Pinter Publishers.

Marquis, D.G. (1988) 'The anatomy of successful innovations', in M.L. Tushman, and W.L. Moore (eds) *Readings in the Management of Innovation*, 2nd edn, Cambridge, MA: Ballinger, 79–88.

Mensch, G.O. (1979) *Stalemate in Technology*, Cambridge MA: Ballinger.

Mowery, D. and N. Rosenberg (1982) 'The influence of market demand upon innovation: A critical review of some recent empirical studies', in N. Rosenberg (ed) *Inside the Black Box*, Cambridge: Cambridge University Press.

National Science Board (1983) *Science Indicators, 1982* Washington DC: National Science Board/National Science Foundation.

Nelson, R.R. (ed.) (1993) *National Systems of Innovation: A Comparative Study* Oxford: Oxford University Press.

Nelson, R.R. and Winter, S. (1982) *An Evolutionary Theory of Economic Change*, Cambridge, MA: Belknap, Harvard.

OECD (1981) *The Measurement of Scientific and Technical Activities* ('Frascati Manual'), Paris: OECD.

OECD (1991) *Technology and Productivity: The Challenge for Economic Policy*, Paris: OECD.

OECD (1992) *Technology and the Economy: The Key Relationships*, Paris: OECD.

Parkinson, S. (1982) *New Product Development in Engineering*, Cambridge: Cambridge University Press.

Pavitt, K. (1984) 'Sectoral patterns of technical change: Towards a taxonomy', *Research Policy* 13, 343–73.

Robinson, J. (1937/8) 'The classification of inventions', *Review of Economic Studies* 5 139–42.

Ronayne, J. (1984) *Science in Government*, London: Edward Arnold.

Rosenberg, N. (1976) 'The direction of technological change: inducement mechanisms and focusing devices', in N. Rosenberg, *Perspectives on Technology*, Cambridge: Cambridge University Press, 108–25.

Rosenberg, N. (1982) 'How exogenous is science?' in N. Rosenberg, *Inside the Black Box: Technology and Economics*, Cambridge: Cambridge University Press, 141–59.

Sahal, D. (1985) 'Technological guideposts and innovation avenues', *Research Policy* 14, 61–82.

Salter, W.E.G. (1966) *Productivity and Technical Change*, Cambridge: Cambridge University Press.

Sato, R. and M. Beckmann (1968) 'Neutral Inventions and production functions', *Review of Economic Studies* 35, 57–66.

Schmookler, J. (1966) *Invention and Economic Growth*, Cambridge, MA: Havard University Press.

Schumpeter, J.A. (1934) *The Theory of Economic Development*, Cambridge, MA: Harvard University Press.

Scott, M. Fg. (1988) *A New View of Economic Growth*, Oxford: Oxford University Press.

Silverberg, G., Dosi, G. and Orsenigo, L. (1988) 'Innovation, Diversity and Diffusion: A Self-organisation model', *Economic Journal* 98, 1032–1054.

Solow, R.M. (1963) *Capital Theory and the Rate of Return*, Amsterdam: North-Holland.

Solow, R.M. (1970) *Growth Theory: An Exposition*, Oxford: Oxford University Press.

Stoneman, P.A. (1987) *The Economic Analysis of Technology Policy*, Oxford: Oxford University Press.

Teece, D.J. (1986) 'Profiting from Technological Innovation', *Research Policy* 15(6). 285–306.

Tushman, M.L. and W.L. Moore (eds) (1988) *Readings in the Management of Innovation*, 2nd edn, Cambridge, MA: Ballinger.

Twiss, B. (1987) *Managing Technological Innovation* 3rd edition, London. Pitman.

Uzawa, H. (1960/1), 'Neutral invention and the stability of growth equilibrium', *Review of Economic Studies* 28, 117–24.

von Hippel, E. (1988) *The Sources of Innovation*, Oxford: Oxford University Press.

von Weiszacker, C.C. (1966) 'Tentative notes on a two-sector model with induced technical progress', *Review of Economic Studies* 33, 245–51.

Williamson, O.E. (1975) *Markets and Hierachies*, New York: The Free Press.

3

Innovation and the economics of demand

Introduction

The ultimate aim of all productive activity is to answer individuals' needs. Exploiting new technology is neither socially useful nor commercially viable unless it meets needs. Users' needs are expressed through their preferences for the properties of services which products offer. These properties correspond to the performance of the product. Preferences form the raw data underpinning *demand* for products (Teubal, 1979).

At a general level, innovation is potentially valuable because it enables society's needs to be met with more success than in the past. Process innovation reduces the resources required to meet needs at a given level and frees resources to be diverted to new uses. This will be reflected in the falling relative prices of existing products. Product innovation improves old products and introduces new ones. To understand the processes by which innovation occurs, it is essential to understand the determinants of the potential and actual demand producers face. Producer firms are the key players in converting ideas and knowledge into usable products (see Chapter 5). Their decisions in turn hinge crucially on their perceptions of market demand.

From the perspective of the firm, process innovation offers the potential of lower production costs (see Chapter 4) and scope for reducing price and/or increasing profit. The extent to which sales, output and profit levels are affected by lower production costs will depend on the sensitivity of quantities demanded to price changes. On the other hand, scale-related process innovation may be induced by exogenous expansion in market demand for existing products. Product innovation offers the firm the potential of influencing market demand by meeting needs in new ways and in a few cases exposing and meeting new needs. Taking advantage of new flexible manufacturing systems (Chapter 4), many modern firms compete by product differentiation and proliferation (Chapter 5). Given that innovation is costly and can only be justified if it offers the potential of a competitive return on investment, the expectation of meeting a market need is essential for business innovation and new perceptions of market need may well act as a prompt to the process.

Users may be either consumers (households and the individuals in them) or producers (firms). Economic theory deals with both. This chapter begins with a review of the conventional, utility-maximising approach to consumer demand for an existing and finite set of known products. This approach is helpful for identifying the dimensions and determinants of market demand which producers must bear in mind when considering cost-reducing process innovation. But the usefulness of basing analysis on a finite set of existing products has to be questioned when there is widespread and continuous product innovation. Later sections develop analytical concepts designed to address demand under product innovation and allow for imperfect knowledge and for learning effects.

In the second part of the chapter, we turn to the demand for producer goods and sketch the basic theory of firms' demand for investment goods and intermediate inputs. This builds on work already covered in Chapter 2 and provides further foundations for Chapters 4 and 5.

Consumer demand

The economic approach to consumer choice

Economists predict how much of a consumer product will be demanded in total by theorising at the level of the individual, then aggregating, on the assumption that each individual acts independently. In the approach most widely used in standard analysis, the amount individuals demand at any price is based on their preferences with respect to all potentially obtainable bundles of goods. If one bundle is preferred to another, it yields the individual a higher level of **utility**. In this context, utility should be thought of as 'happiness' or 'well-being' and not 'usefulness' and the crucial behavioural assumption is that individuals are utility **maximisers**. Given sufficient information about the specification and prices of goods, individuals operating in accordance with this principle make choices about the quantities of products they would like to buy which yields them the maximum utility which can be attained with their finite resources (income or wealth). Which goods are bought, and in what quantities, is analysed in a later section.

Four elements of this approach deserve comment. First, utility maximisation implies *rational* behaviour: individuals knowingly compare all alternative consumption bundles and choose the best (from their point of view), given prices and their income. In undertaking theoretical analysis, this has proved a very helpful abstraction, but has been questioned for its acceptability as a model of how individuals choose (see pp. 87–91).

Second (and one reason for questioning rational behaviour), is the **perfect information** assumption: buyers know all about the good they are purchasing *before* they buy it. Consumers will be **imperfectly** informed at the time of purchase if aspects of the quality of the good can be either discovered only *after* the good is purchased (or a commitment to purchase is irrevocable), or when aspects of quality are intrinsically difficult to discover (Nelson, 1970; Darby and Karni, 1973). Goods for which information is perfect are called **search goods**; given that quality is known beforehand, purchase decisions among different types of good will call for search of what types are available and at what prices. Of goods for which information is imperfect, the first kind are called **experience goods**, for example, any durable whose reliability of performance over time can be discovered only by use over time. Goods of the second kind are called **credence goods** since you often have to believe what you are told about some aspect of quality, or can only check this aspect at great cost. An example might be the capacity of some patent medicine to prolong life.

An implication of imperfect information is that individuals will learn from each other about the performance of products as they are introduced into the market. Consumption may therefore not be based on isolated individual choice, but can be influenced by the experience and opinions of others. Such dynamic learning effects are important to understand the diffusion of new goods and are taken up in a later section.

Finally, consider how utility is generated. When individuals' preferences are expressed in terms of products themselves, it is the 'appleness' of apples or the 'umbrellaness' of umbrellas that generates utility. The more apples we have, the more 'appleness' is made available. In the logic of the theory, that is *all* we know about the link between the quantity of a good and the utility it generates. The approach has proved successful in helping to model many (some very complex) problems in economics. This partially excuses what might seem a shortcoming. But for the sort of problems in which we are particularly interested, the nature of the abstraction can be a barrier to understanding.

Suppose, for example, a new variety of light bulb entered the market. Assuming the new bulb was no cheaper than existing ones, we would have to know details of its specifications and performance to understand whether people thought their utility would be increased if they bought the new bulb. To do this, we could say that goods might be thought of as **bundles of characteristics**: in the case of a light bulb its brightness relative to the power used, its operational life, its size and so on. In the case of an apple, corresponding characteristics would be its nutritional value, juiciness and sweetness. It makes a good deal of sense to think of utility being derived from the characteristics of goods rather than the goods themselves, for it is the characteristics of the product that offer the key to understanding how needs are met. Consumers acquire goods because it is in the nature of consumption that only those goods give access to these characteristics. Our need for the nutrition offered by an apple explains (in part) why we eat it. Our need for a sweet taste on the palate explains (partly) why we sometimes eat apples in preference to shallots.

The word 'characteristics' owes its widespread use in economics to the work of Lancaster (1966, 1971, 1979). It is also used in the literature to refer to aspects of products which include their quality, location, time of delivery and even the amount of information available about them.

Associated with the distinction between goods as goods in their own right and goods as bundles of characteristics is a methodological distinction in the way in which economists have come to think about demand. If utility is viewed as deriving from product characteristics, each good may be identified by its **address** in terms of characteristics. The term 'address' reflects its origins in the spatial approach to modelling variation among product types pioneered by Hotelling (1929), but applies generally in models in which utility is derived from characteristics of any kind. If consumers vary in their preferences for characteristics, each individual can also be identified by an address which specifies his or her preferences in terms of characteristics. The capacity of a product to satisfy a given consumer depends on how well-matched these addresses are at given prices. Work which approaches analysis in this way comprise address models. Knowledge of this approach turns out to be particularly useful in the study of product innovation and demand, since it offers precision in describing what constitutes the innovation and permits analysis of the potential for innovations of different kinds.

The alternative to address models is the **non-address** or **goods-are-goods** approach. This is the approach taken by the standard textbook analysis of consumer demand where tastes or preferences are stated in terms of goods, each one of which is described by a name which identifies it. Analysis is conducted in the framework of a predetermined and finite set of such goods, which makes it difficult to incorporate the effects of innovation since innovation continually expands and changes the structure of the set (Ironmonger, 1973). Eaton and Lipsey (1989) point out that non-address models which attempt to analyse the effects of product differentiation also fail to come to grips with important 'awkward facts' which usually exist in markets where product innovation has given rise to significant product differentiation. For example, to permit aggregation and the derivation of market demand, many non-address models build on the notion of a representative consumer who purchases some of every product variety. Spence (1976) and Dixit and Stiglitz (1977) are pioneering examples. But preferences differ among consumers and each one buys only a subset (often small) of the product varieties actually on offer. To circumvent this difficulty, other non-address models (e.g. Sattinger, 1984; Anderson, de Palma and Thisse, 1988) allow individuals to differ, but implicitly assume all product varieties are equally good substitutes for one another. This conflicts with the observation that some groups of varieties are perceived to be better substitutes for one another than for varieties in other groups.

Since product innovation adds to the variety of product types and its impact may depend upon the fraction of the potential market with a taste or pronounced preference for that type of innovation, models which do not incorportate these 'awkward facts' would seem to be ill-suited for our purpose. On the other hand, it is worth reviewing the textbook non-address approach, partly because it develops certain tools of analysis which have wide application elsewhere and partly because it is wholly relevant for considering the impact on demand of price-reducing process innovation.

Static consumer demand analysis: goods-are-goods approach

Following convention in the economic analysis of demand, we focus initially on search goods in a non-address framework. It is assumed that utility-maximising individuals make decisions subject to their resource constraints and do so independently, allowing simple aggregation. Some goods (like food) and all services are consumed or used up in the period of purchase. Others (like refrigerators, VCRs) generate services to their owner over a number of periods. These are called **consumer durables**. Theory developed in this section can apply to both sorts of goods. To start with we deal with static analysis. Later, we consider how demand for a product might grow through time.

Analysis

An axiom relating to preference structures is that individuals always prefer more of a good to less, other things equal. Thus their utility is positively related to (rises with increases in) the amount of goods they consume. But if we ask about changes in the consumption bundle which keep individuals at a fixed utility level, it is assumed that successive one-unit sacrifices of any one good will only be made in exchange for increasingly large additions to their consumption of other goods.

These assumptions are captured in terms of a 'utility map' made up of contours, called **indifference curves**, representing given levels of utility. From a formal mathematical point of view, these correspond exactly to the isoquants of production theory, except that output levels are measurable in physical units while utility is not. Figure 3.1 is the utility map in relation to two goods, X and Y. The contour U_0 shows all the combinations of quantities of X and Y consumed which will generate the same level of utility U_0. These are consumption bundles between which the individual is said to be indifferent, i.e. no one bundle is preferred to any other on the curve. If any point on the curve is chosen and either X and Y held constant while the other is increased, the new bundle is preferred to the old and the resulting move takes the individual to a higher level of utility. This is true, for example, of the move from A to C where Y remains at Y_A while X increases from X_A to X_C.

Compare now points A and B. The slope at each point on a curve shows how much extra X an individual would have to be offered to compensate him or her (i.e. leaving them at a given level of utility), for the sacrifice of a unit of Y. This amount is larger at B than A, which makes sense since $X_B > X_A$, and $Y_B < Y_A$. Alternatively, moving down the curve, individuals will give up less and less Y to obtain additional units of X. This leads to the statement that the marginal rate of substitution of Y for X diminishes down the indifference curve.

Utility cannot be objectively measured, but for analytical purposes it is sufficient to know that individual utility rises between one indifference curve and any higher

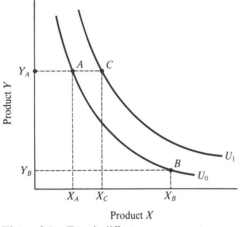

Figure 3.1 Two indifference curves.

one. We often appeal, however, to the additional principle of **diminishing marginal utility**, which states that as consumption of a given good increases, it yields additional utility, but at a diminishing rate.

To maximise utility, the individual must be on the highest indifference curve he or she can reach. Individuals are constrained in their choice by their income or budget for the period. This budget, B, is an amount of dollars. Assume the budget is wholly devoted to purchases of X and/or Y. We can then write:

$$B = P_X X + P_Y Y \qquad (3.1)$$

where P_X and P_Y are the prices per unit, respectively, of goods X and Y. Equation (3.1) is called the **budget constraint** and can be rewritten:

$$Y = B/P_Y - (P_X/P_Y)X \qquad (3.1')$$

When $X = 0$, the budget is spent wholly on Y and the quantity of Y purchased is B/P_Y. Every time purchases of X increase by one unit, the amount spent on Y must decline by (P_X/P_Y), the negative value of the relative price ratio. When $Y = 0$:

$$B/P_Y = (P_X/P_Y)X$$

or

$$B = P_X X$$

i.e.

$$X = B/P_X$$

For any value of B, equation (3.1') can be represented by a straight line such as MN in Figure 3.2. This is called a budget function and has the negative slope $-(P_X/P_Y)$, reflecting the relationship between X and Y captured in (3.1'). If relative prices remain

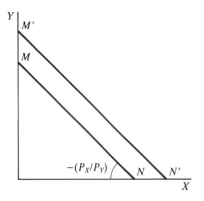

Figure 3.2 Two budget constraint lines.

unchanged, the effect of increasing the budget is to shift the budget function farther from the origin, but without change of slope (see $M'N'$ compared with MN). If relative prices change, the slope of each budget line changes, becoming steeper if P_X rises (or flatter if P_X falls) relative to P_Y. If P_Y were unchanged in absolute terms while P_X rose or fell, the budget line would pivot on a Y-axis intercept such as M or M'. The line would pivot on an X-axis intercept (like N or N') if only P_Y rose or fell. Formally, the budget function is identical to the isocost line for the firm introduced in Chapter 2.

For the individual consumer, two sorts of questions can now be asked: How is utility maximised at given levels of income and prices? What is the impact of allowing income or prices to take different values? In answer to the first question, set B equal to the individual's money income. The individual takes P_X and P_Y as given. This establishes a given budget constraint which can be superimposed on the individual's utility map (Figure 3.3). All points along the budget line MN (and within it, in the

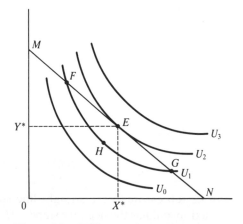

Figure 3.3 Utility maximisation with two products.

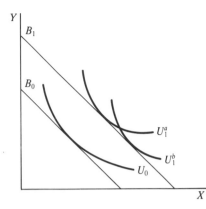

Figure 3.4 The income effect: X as a normal and inferior good.

so-called **opportunity set** OMN) are attainable, but point E is the one which lies on the highest indifference curve which can be reached, representing the highest level of utility U_2 which can be achieved under this budget constraint. Thus E is the utility maximising point and is associated with purchases of Y^* and X^*.

At E the slope of the budget line, $-(P_X/P_Y)$, is equal to the slope of the indifference curve, the marginal rate of substitution of Y for X. This condition must ensure the attainment of a utility maximum. At points like F and G, for example, the slopes are different and it is possible to move up from the lower level of utility U_1 to U_2 by changing the proportions in which X and Y are purchased. The equal-slopes condition is not sufficient to ensure a utility maximum unless, as assumed earlier, the budget is exhausted by purchases of the two goods (see, for example, point H). The analysis here presupposes that individuals spend all of their income for the period on consumption.[1]

In answer to the second question, consider first higher income level. This means B is higher so a budget function of identical slope further from the origin becomes relevant. Compare the higher line B_1 with B_0 in Figure 3.4. A good is defined as *normal* when consumption of it rises with income and *inferior* when consumption falls. If in Figure 3.4 the individual's utility map included curves U_0 and U_1^a, both X and Y would be normal goods for that person. If it included U_0 and U_1^b, X would be normal but Y inferior.

Suppose now the price of one of the goods changes: P_X falls. Two effects must be considered. The first, the **substitution effect**, is unambiguous. It says that if an individual's real standard of living is held at a fixed level and one good becomes less expensive relative to another, individuals will change their consumption patterns in favour of the good which has become relatively cheaper. That this must be so is clear if we interpret a given indifference curve (or utility level) as a given standard of living and recall that a change in relative prices is represented by changing the slope of the budget line touching the indifference curve. In Figure 3.5, P_X has been allowed to fall relative to P_Y and observing the change in the slope of the budget functions just

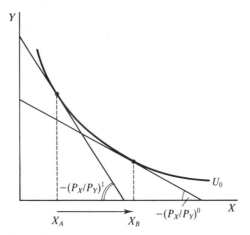

Figure 3.5 Substitution effect: When (P_X/P_Y) falls from $-(P_X/P_Y)^1$ to $-(P_X/P_Y)^0$, substitution effect raises demand for X from X_A to X_B.

touching the given indifference curve U_0, it can be seen that the substitution effect works in favour of X.

But when P_X falls, it is not sufficient just to consider the response to the associated relative price change at a given standard living, i.e. along a given indifference curve. When the price of a good falls, and the money value of income is constant, the buying power of the individual's budget must increase. We should also take account, therefore, of the effect of the lower price on real income, and its effect upon purchases. This is the **income effect component** of the price change.

We noted earlier that a fall in P_X, with P_Y and B constant, causes the budget line to pivot outwards on its vertical intercept. In Figure 3.6, this is shown by rotating

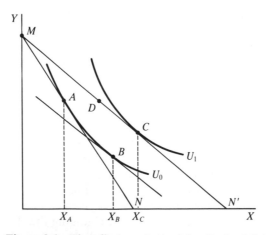

Figure 3.6 The effect on demand for X of a fall in its relative price decomposed into a substitution effect AB and an income effect BC.

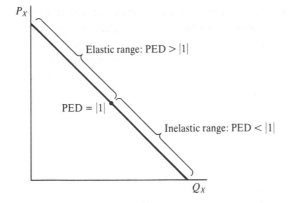

Figure 3.7 Varying price elasticity along a linear demand curve.

the budget function *MN* outwards to *MN′*. At the initially high price for *X*, utility was maximised at *A* and the substitution effect associated with the relative price fall is shown by the movement from *A* to *B*. But because the lower price now makes *MN′* the relevant budget function, *C* is the new utility-maximising point. The movement from *B* to *C* represents the increase in living standards or real-income effect of the price fall. In this case, the income effect has a positive influence on purchases of *X*, since $X_C > X_B$, and reinforces the substitution effect. But if U_1 and *MN′* were tangent at any point left of a line vertically above *B* (at *D*, say), the income effect would be negative and would reduce the positive impact of the substitution effect. For this to be so, *X* would have to be an inferior good for the individual.

This analysis gives rise to the so-called **law of demand** – that whenever the price of a good falls (rises), more (less) of it will be demanded by any individual whose money income is constant. An unspoken but crucial additional assumption is that all other prices have remained constant. Since market demand is seen as the simple sum of individual demands, the implication is that when the price of a good rises (falls), other things being equal, the quantity demanded in total will fall (rise). Figure 3.7 is an example of the standard downward-sloping market demand curve this implies where Q_X measured on the horizontal axis is the total amount of *X* demanded.

Such a curve might be a straight line or curvilinear. The responsiveness or sensitivity of quantities demanded to changes in price along the curve are captured by a measure called the **price elasticity of demand (PED)** where:

$$PED = -[(\text{per cent change in quantity demanded})/$$

$$\text{per cent change in price})]$$

This can be shown to be product of two terms:

$$PED = -[(dQ/dQ)/(dP/P)] = -[(dQ/dP)/(P/Q)]$$

where dQ/dP measures the change in quantity demanded when there is a small change in price. Subscripts to P and Q denoting the identity of the product have been dropped for ease of notation. Minus signs are conventionally used in definitions of the PED since the arithmetic value of the terms for a downward-sloping demand curve must itself always be negative and it aids intuition to convert this value into a positive number. Moving down a linear demand curve, the elasticity falls, since the slope of the curve, dQ/dP, is constant and P/Q by observation falls.

In fact, P/Q must approach infinity near to the vertical axis and approach zero near to the horizontal. The expression for the PED must also fall from near infinity to zero down the demand curve. It can also be shown that the PED is always equal to one at the midpoint of a linear demand curve. As a matter of terminology, the curve is said to be elastic when PED exceeds one and to be inelastic when PED is below one. This is important information because the total revenue from market sales, calculated as price times total sales $(P \cdot Q_X)$, initially rises as price falls from its level at the vertical intercept, but declines below the point at which PED $= 1$. The reason is a matter of logic.

To say that PED > 1 is, by definition, to say that a small proportional fall in price is associated with a greater proportional rise in quantity demanded. Thus total sales revenue earned in the market must rise. But to say that PED < 1 is to say that a small proportional fall in price is associated with a *smaller* proportional rise in quantity demanded, so sales revenue must fall. These relationships become particularly relevant when we consider firms whose past innovations have yielded for them market niches in which the market demand for their products is also the demand which they, individually, face.

The market demand curve shifts outwards whenever a greater quantity is demanded at every price. This will occur, all other things equal:

1. For normal goods when incomes rise.
2. If all individuals acquire a stronger preference for the good. This would be represented on utility maps by a displacement of all the indifference curves in the direction of the favoured good.
3. If population increases. This calls for adding in the demand of more individuals.
4. If there is a rise in the price of a good which consumers regard as a substitute – where goods A and B are defined to be substitutes if a rise in P_A, all other things equal, is associated with a rise in the quantity of B demanded.
5. If there is a fall in the price of a good which consumers regard as a complement – where goods A and B are defined to be complements if a rise in P_A, all other things equal, is associated with a fall in the quantity of B demanded.

For innovating firms, information about market demand is crucial. Knowing the position of the demand curve tells them about the size of the market for existing products and knowing its slope tells them by how much the volume and value of sales will vary if process innovation permits price reductions. This is important information for firms considering expenditure on cost-reducing innovation, since the

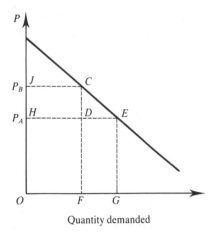

Figure 3.8 Price discrimination.

investment will not be undertaken unless sufficient additional revenue makes it worthwhile.

Knowing the elasticity of the demand curve is also valuable for firms introducing product innovations and wishing to maximise their returns by **price discrimination**. Price discrimination occurs when firms charge one price to one part of the market, and a different price to another. This practice is widespread because firms make more profit if they can charge a high price to some consumers and a low price to others than they would if all consumers paid the same lower price. To see this, look at Figure 3.8 which shows the market demand curve for a monopolist, a firm which is the only one serving the market. If all the firm's customers paid price P_A, the firm's total revenue would be $OHEG$. But if OF of the product could be sold at price P_B and the rest, FG, were sold at price P_A, the firm's total revenue would be $OJCF$ for the first segment and $FDEG$ for the second – $JCDH$ more than the firm would obtain from selling only at the low price. If all units of output were produced at the same unit cost, price discrimination would yield more profit than if all consumers paid the same.

Price discrimination is only possible if the high-price and low-price buyers can be effectively kept apart; otherwise low-price buyers will purchase in order to profit for themselves by selling at a price to the rest of the market somewhere above P_A but below P_B. This is an example of **arbitraging activity**. In the case of new products, however, producers often have the opportunity to engage in a form of price discrimination by exploiting market separation over time and the strong preference of some individuals for novelty.

Returning to Figure 3.8, suppose OF is the size of the market segment comprising individuals who are so anxious to obtain a new product upon its introduction that they will pay a higher price for it than most of the rest of the potential market. Such people may include those with an acute, short-term need (e.g. sufferers from a disease which a new drug promises to cure or alleviate), or those who obtain utility from buying the very latest models of car or equipment, the newest titles in the bookshop, the latest fashions in the couturiers. Suppose sellers try to exploit this strong preference for novelty by charging a relatively high price for the good when it is introduced with the intention of reducing the price at some future date when only a low price will induce individuals in the segment FG to buy. If they wish to do this, they can protect themselves against arbitrage activity by delaying the price reduction until they are confident that most of the individuals in the OF segment have already bought. By the time the good becomes more cheaply available, there is then no-one left prepared to pay P_B. (It is true that people between F and G would be prepared to pay more than P_A, but assuming all of them know the good is available at that price and can obtain it from the seller at that price, arbitrage is impossible. The firm would maximise its revenue by discriminating with great precision between buyers at each point on its demand curve. But this would also be prohibitively costly to achieve.)

The major difficulties with the non-address approach arise not in connection with process but in product innovation. When product innovation occurs (or is considered), it contributes to the differentiation of products in a given industry. But how should we decide *which* industry (or industries) the innovation will enter? And how can we know *what* differentiates one product from another in the industry and whether the differences between some pairs of products is greater than between others? These questions are clearly of importance for understanding the terms on which new products will compete with existing ones and the incentives to undertake product innovation. Models in the address style have been devised to try to provide answers.

Static consumer demand analysis: address models

In this section, two alternatives to modelling demand under conditions of product heterogeneity are presented: the characteristics approach of Lancaster (1966, 1979) and the spatial approach of Hotelling (1929). Each allows for new products to be introduced easily into the analysis; discussion of fully fledged models of product innovation is left until Chapters 5 and 6.

Lancaster's characteristics approach

Characteristics space

In Lancaster's approach, goods may in principle embody any finite number of characteristics, but to illustrate, we will consider for most of this section a product which can be defined in terms of only two characteristics. For concreteness let the product be apples, and the two characteristics juiciness (J) and sweetness (S). Assume that units of objective measurement can be found for each characteristic. To illustrate, Figure 3.9 shows on the vertical axis units of J and on the horizontal units of S. In

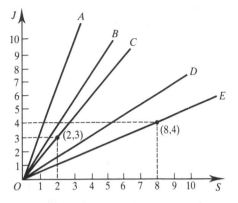

Figure 3.9   Rays of different slope representing, in characteristics space, different varieties of apple.

the quadrant formed by the two axes lies the characteristics space in which various types of apple are represented. In this case the space is two-dimensional, but it may have as many dimensions as there are characteristics, the quantities of each characteristic being measured along each axis.

Representing goods

Pick a type of apple and measure that it offers three units of juiciness ($3J$) and two of sweetness ($2S$). This is shown by point (3, 2) in Figure 3.9. If we cut the apple in half, we have $1.5J$ and $1S$ and if we take two apples of the same kind, $6J$ and $4S$. In each case the ratio is the same: $1.5:1$. This ratio defines this particular type of apple. It is represented in the diagram by the slope of a ray from the origin through (3, 2) and on into the rest of the space. Label it C. Distances along the ray measure the number of apples. Adding to the number of apples increases the distance along the ray.

Now take another type of apple, labelled E, offering $4J$ and $8S$. Although E has more juice per apple than type C, the crucial point is that it is less juicy relative to its sweetness: the ratio is $0.5:1$. This particular bundling of characteristics is represented by the slope of ray OE.

The diagram shows five varieties of apple, $A - E$, each defined by a different ratio.

Defining an industry

An industry is a group of firms which have in common the fact that they produce goods which are close substitutes in consumption. With the apparatus so far presented, we can think of the consumption technology as the description of how goods transfer characteristics to consumers, i.e. the ways in which goods bundle up the characteristics which ultimately generate utility.

Suppose now we took all goods currently produced in an economy and defined them according to their characteristics. Most goods would have several or many characteristics and some groups of goods would turn out to have characteristics in common which were not shared by any other products. Firms producing that group could then be said to comprise an industry. The firms most likely to offer competition to a product innovator could in turn be identified by inspecting the characteristics of their existing and planned product lines.

While some goods have exclusive consumption characteristics which make it fairly easy to define the industries producing them (for example, cement, tyres, water heaters, photographic film), others offer problems. Electronic components, for example, may fit into a wide range of modern goods which provide services as wide-ranging as music reproduction, machine control and espionage. These services in turn could be provided by a range of other means. Nonetheless, the characteristics model does help define industries by telling much more about what it is that makes a good the good that it is in consumption terms than in the non-address approach. This is quite independent of how the good is produced.

Efficiency frontier

The efficiency frontier in this framework is analogous to the budget constraint in our earlier analysis. It shows the maximum amounts of characteristics the consumer can obtain with a given level of expenditure. To derive this frontier, focus again on the two-characteristic case and make three assumptions. First, the individual has already decided what fraction of his or her income to spend on each class of products, one of which might well be apples. Call it the apple budget. Second, it must be possible to buy each product variety in any quantity desired, including small quantities; all goods must be divisible. Third, two goods with different characteristics ratios can be combined in consumption to generate same total quantity of each characteristic as would be yielded by one good.[2]

The first step is to find out how many units of each variety the consumer would obtain by devoting their whole apple budget to buying one variety. This is found by dividing the apple budget by the price per apple in each case and gives a number of units which can be measured off as a distance along each of the rays. These are shown as the points a, b, c, d and e in Figure 3.10.

Now any point on a negatively sloped line between neighbouring rays can be reached by adding together lengths of the two rays. Thus, M between d and e on OD and OE can be reached by adding Oe_1 of OE to e_1M of OD (or, equivalently, Od_1 of OD to d_1M of OE). In terms of consumption, the individual buys $Oe_1 = d_1M$ of variety E and $e_1M = Od_1$ of variety D and combines them to obtain a total characteristics bundle of $J_m + S_m$.

The efficiency frontier comprises line segments exclusively of negative slope. Since the frontier shows the maximum characteristics obtainable for a given outlay, segments can never have a positive slope. Moving in a north-easterly direction up a line of positive slope, more of both characteristics would be obtained indicating that points

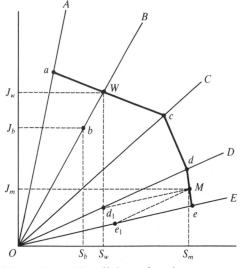

Figure 3.10   The efficiency frontier.

to the south-west on the line could not have yielded maximum characteristics in the first place. The efficient frontier comprises only those points which are as far away from the origin as it is possible to get with the given outlay. This means that some goods can be priced out of the market. In Figure 3.10, the price of variety *B* is so high that the apple budget will purchase *Ob* B-type apples and thus only $J_b + S_b$ characteristics. Point *b* lies within the line segment *ac* and for that reason is inefficient. For the same outlay, consumers combining varieties *A* and *C* could reach points on *ac* which gave them more of both characteristics, for example $J_w + S_{w'}$ at point *W*.

Maximising utility

To see how consumers maximise utility, assume all individuals have preference structures which give rise to indifference curve maps exactly analogous to those found in goods space. Thus, indifference curves in characteristics space have a diminishing marginal rate of substitution, and curves further from the origin represent higher utility levels.

The indifference curve map – an individual's utility function in terms of charac-terisitics – can now be superimposed on the efficiency frontier diagram and the utility maximising choice of consumption found by identifying the point at which the highest indifference curve is reached. In Figure 3.11, indifference curve maps for two individuals are shown. For consumer 1, utility is maximised by purchasing good *B* alone, at point *b*. For consumer 2, utility is maximised at point *m* by buying some *C* and some *D*.

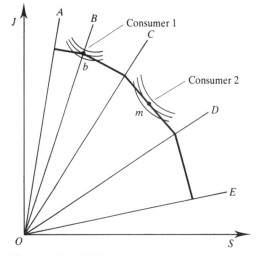

Figure 3.11   Utility maximisation and market segments.

Preference patterns and demand

Different individuals will usually have different preferences over characteristics. How those preferences are distributed has important implications for the product variants which will be in demand. Lancaster (1979) assumes that preferences are uniformly distributed around the frontier. But we have no reason to expect in practice that preferences will always be distributed uniformly (see Eaton and Lipsey's 'awkward facts' earlier). Preferences for certain ratios of characteristics may cluster in one or two parts of characteristics space, while other parts will remain largely unoccupied. When this occurs, it is said that these are **market segments**. Referring back to Figure 3.11, we might imagine consumers were segmented into two sets, each with one or other of the indifference curve maps shown. In that case, there would be no call (at prevailing prices) for variants *A* and *E*. How much of variants *B*, *C* and *D* was demanded would depend on the relative sizes of the two segments and the relative prices of the variants.

Price changes and the demand curve for each variant

When the price of a variant falls, more of each variant can be obtained for the same budgetary outlay and the relevant point on the efficiency frontier moves outwards. Consider the four-variant case shown in Figure 3.12 where the industry produces a good with two characteristics, *X* and *Y*. Assume that preferences are clustered into two segments represented by the two sets of indifference curves shown. For simplicity, all individuals are assumed to allocate a similar budget to purchases of the product.

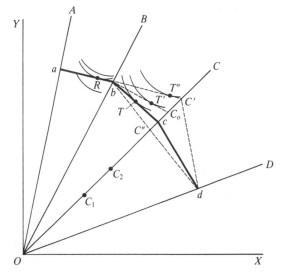

Figure 3.12 Effects for the efficiency frontier and changes in demand of varying the price of variant *C*.

Initially, the efficiency frontier is *abcd* and demand for variants can be found by reference to points *R* and *T*. As the price of *C* falls to P_{co}, individuals in the eastward segment can be expected to buy more of it. As shown, purchases associated with the utility-maximising points *T* and *T'* are, respectively, OC_1 and OC_2. If the price falls to $P_{c'}$, purchasers who have been buying *A* and *B* in the westward segment now find it equally attractive to combine *A* and *C*. If the price falls fractionally below $P_{c'}$, *B* will cease to be purchased at all, because *b* will now lie inside the new line segment from *a* to *OC* (not shown). Purchases of *C* will jump as members of the westward segment defect from *B* to *C* (combined with *A*), and *C* and *A* become neighbours. Note that such jumps become less marked, as the market is less segmented and the more evenly distributed indifference curves are around the frontier. As the price continues to fall, *C* will continue to attract further custom from both segments.

On the other hand, if *C*'s price rises, less of it will be bought until at any price above $P_{c''}$ consumers will buy variants *B* and *D* rather than *B* and *C*. At $P_{c''}$, *C* is priced out of the market and *B* and *D* become neighbours. The demand curve associated with this analysis is shown in Figure 3.13 (Lancaster, 1971: 88). The kinks in the curve indicate critical prices at which demand for *C* jumps as P_c becomes low enough to capture the entire market of variants which had been neighbours of *C* when P_c was higher. As noted above, the more evenly distributed preferences become, the more kinks in the curve are smoothed out.

One lesson from this analysis is that the incentive to undertake process innovation to reduce prices will vary with the number of near neighbours already in the market and the nature of preferences with respect to characteristics. Given the situation

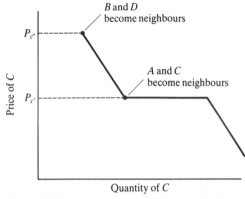

Figure 3.13   Demand curve for variant *C*.

depicted in Figure 3.12, for example, a firm whose price was currently only a little above $P_{c'}$ would face the relatively large incentive of wiping out *B* and capturing all its sales if it reduced the price only a little (assuming *B* could not retaliate effectively). But the potential gains would be less if preferences were more evenly distributed and/or there was a larger range of variants 'near' to *C*. The picture is altered if the same firm produces a number or all of the variants in the industry. There is less incentive then to cut the price of any one variant to reduce the sales of others and the firm is more likely to focus on generating the range of variants best suited to the distibution of preferences in the market, at prices just low enough to discourage other firms from wishing to compete with it. This strategy is discussed in Chapter 5.

Introducing new products

This analytical framework may also be employed to represent product innovations and to identify the demand for them. Innovations can be classified into four main types: first, innovations in which every unit of a product variant is 'packed' with more of each of its characteristics, but the characteristics ratio remains constant; second, innovations in which a new product variant is generated by bundling existing characteristics in a new ratio; third, innovations in which subsets of characteristics are drawn from two or more different product classes to form a new product class. The first corresponds to vertical product differentiation and the second to horizontal product differentiation. The third we shall call complex differentiation of the product. A special case of complex differentiation would occur when a set of characteristics defining one product class was enhanced by the inclusion of one or more characteristics which until then had been incorporated only in other products. A fourth possibility is that an altogether new characteristic might be included in bundles for the first time, but this would be an unusual event. All of these innovations but the first correspond in fairly obvious ways to Schumpeter's description of innovation as 'new combinations'. It is probably reasonable to say, however, that he had more in mind the major sorts of change implied only by the third and fourth types.

We now ask: How does product innovation affect demand? A central point here is that product innovation can *create* demand, in the following sense: with given consumer preferences over characteristics, a new product combines characteristics (and has the potential to meet consumer needs) in ways that existing products did not. Thus even with given income levels, new demand – demand for a new product – now comes into existence. Usually, this will have implications for the demand for other products. We will concentrate on judging the market prospects for a new product. But note, merely capturing new sales is no guarantee of profitability. For that to be the case, we would have to make additional assumptions about price–cost margins related to supply-side issues which are dealt with in Chapters 5 and 6.

Vertical differentiation in product innovation

If vertically differentiating innovation occurred in variant *C*, we could use exactly the same diagram as found in Figure 3.12, which illustrated the effect of a price fall. The reason is that whether a price falls per unit for given quantities of characteristics, or quantities of characteristics rise at a given price, a given budget will buy more of both characteristics in each case in the ratio which defines the product variant.

Although the product is an innovation, it retains characteristics in the same ratio as an existing product variant. It will therefore attract the market share that attached to the existing product, but will add to it in the same way that a price reduction would have increased the market share of that variant. Its market share depends on whether preferences are uniformly distributed, clustered around *OB* exclusively, or clustered in clumps around *OB*, *OA* and *OC*; or how much more of each characteristic the innovation offers.

Horizontal differentiation in product innovation

To analyse this type of innovation continue to assume that all product variants are divisible and combinable without cost. The innovation is represented in Figure 3.14 as a new ray, *ON*, added to existing rays *OA*, *OB*, *OC* and *OD*.

Following the lines of earlier analysis, *N* would make no impression at all on the market if the supplier priced it at any point within the efficiency frontier (such as at n_o). Even if priced at P_n or $P_{n'}$, it would still make no impression if preferences were clustered in the north-west and south-east regions of the diagram as shown. In the case of apples, such clustering would reflect market segmentation between those who strongly preferred 'juicy-unsweet' and 'dry-sweet' fruit. To gain market share, the new product must both fill a gap (have an address similar to those denoting unmet preferences in the market) and do so at a competitive price.

If preferences were spread more evenly around the efficiency frontier, P_n would be the critical price to allow *N* to enter the market and as the price fell (say to $P_{n'}$), its market share would rise. If preferences were clustered as shown, the price would have to be as low as $P_{n''}$ to permit *N* to make any sales and as price fell to $P_{n'''}$, *N* would capture the markets first of *C* and then *A*.

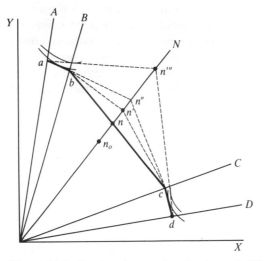

Figure 3.14 Product innovation: horizontal differentiation.

If products are assumed not to be combinable, the efficiency 'frontier' collapses into a set of unconnected points, one on each ray and individuals will maximise utility by purchasing only the single variant which yields for them the highest utility. In Figure 3.15, the individual or group whose preferences are shown chooses variant A before the product innovation arrives. To capture the custom of this individual or group, the supplier of N must price at a level below P_n.

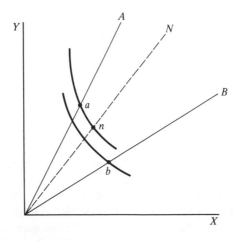

Figure 3.15 A new product variety where products are non-combinable.

Complex product innovation

To represent complex product innovation, we employ a three-dimensional diagram, Figure 3.16. Each axis, X, Y and Z represents a different characteristic. As before, a three-characteristic good may be represented by straight lines, such as OA and OB, along which characteristics X, Y and Z are held in constant proportions to each other – $X_M: Y_M: Z_M$ along OA and $X_N: Y_N: Z_N$ along OB. Goods with four or more characteristics cannot be represented in diagrams drawn on a two-dimensional page. In complex innovations, we might imagine first, adding an extra characteristic dimension represented by an extra axis; second, adding more than one extra characteristic dimensions represented by two or more extra axes; third, removing one characteristic and replacing it with another, which would involve relabelling one of the axes; fourth, removing two or more characteristics and putting others in their place which would involve relabelling two or more axes; or fifth, changing some characteristics and adding others. To represent the most radical complex innovations, one of the new axes would have to relate to a characteristic which had not before been bundled in any product.

As an example, consider a class of products made of plastics. Plastics are a problem for waste disposal because they are very slow to break down in the natural environment; they are essentially non-biodegradeable. Biodegradeability is not a characteristic of plastic products. One complex and radical innovation would be plastics which include the characteristic of biodegradeability found in, say, paper products. Along a new axis we could measure the speed at which a given quantity of the material was absorbed into the natural environment.

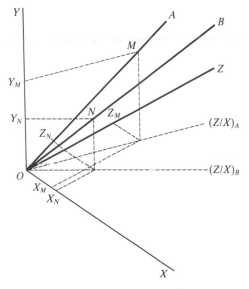

Figure 3.16 A three-characteristic product variant.

As in the analysis of horizontally differentiated innovation, everything will ultimately depend here on whether preferences for the new combinations of characteristics are strong enough to supply a market for the products which offer them at the price at which they are offered. But in this case, there is an extra twist which until now we have put on one side. When new variants are introduced into an existing product class, consumers and potential consumers have to do relatively little learning to understand what the innovation amounts to. But when a new characteristic (or more than one) is introduced into an existing product, it changes the nature of the product in a way which requires more extensive learning before the consumer can evaluate it. It has been argued that the more extensive the learning which has to be done about the product, the less sensitive consumers will be to price. They will be relatively price-insensitive when the first new brand in a product class is introduced, but increasingly price-sensitive as subsequent brands follow (Howard and Moore, 1988).

This point has wider ramifications and should be addressed in the light of issues raised later about rational behaviour with incomplete information. In Lancaster's world, there is implicitly full information. Utility derives from characteristics which are, on his definitions, concrete and observable. The evidence on new goods can always be collected in advance therefore and given an assumed competence in information processing, individuals can define their preferences completely and maximise utility. Making utility derive from characteristics *per se* is equivalent to saying that consumers already know how various characteristics and their quantities will meet their needs. So Lancaster effectively avoids the problems that would arise if utility depended on abstract, unobservable product performance dimensions. Had that been the case, 'consumers – even if able to define utility in terms of the abstract dimensions – would not automatically be able to define their preferences completely in terms of concrete product characteristics' (Teubal, 1979: 273).

We would like to put the issue slightly differently. Some characteristics which generate utility may simply not be objectively measurable, while others, which are, may be perceived differently from one person to another. For example, aesthetic pleasure derived from a musical performance cannot be measured objectively. And while the heat given out by an electric space heater has an unambiguous measure in terms of degrees celsius, different people will feel differently about a given level of heat. For both these reasons, the relationship between a unit of a product through its characteristics to utility cannot have quite the solid objective basis that Lancaster sought. The bundle of characteristics comprising a good are entities which all have some subjective content (Triplett, 1975).

This is an important comment on the whole approach, but it becomes particularly relevant in cases where products are refashioned to meet needs in new ways. Since individuals cannot know with objective certainty how and to what extent their needs will be met by a new product, they will indeed have to learn, partly vicariously through the experience of others and partly by their own experiment. Such dynamic effects are absent in what is essentially a static analysis.

Hotelling's spatial approach

To know how much and what type of product variety there will be in an industry, we have to know a great deal about the costs of production innovation, production conditions in general and the competitive conditions among firms within an industry and between them and potential entrants to the industry. These matters are discussed in detail in Chapters 5 and 6. But to build a bridge to that analysis, let us consider Hotelling's (1929) approach to modelling product variety and the demand curves for specific variants. Even with only the barest description of production conditions, it is possible to derive interesting results. (Waterson (1984: 114–7), is a helpful presentation of the analysis and the treatment presented here owes much to his.)

In the analysis, consumers are imagined to live at equally spaced intervals along a straight road of given length. This road can also be given the interpretation of a continuum of variation in some product characteristic such as the sweetness of cider. At one end would be consumers who most favoured the sweetest cider, at the other those who enjoyed the sourest. The location of each individual on the road, represented by a straight line, is his or her address. In general, however, there may be two, three or many consumers at any one address and addresses might vary in distance from each other. Firms supplying the market make only one product each and each can also be located at an address somewhere on the road. Consumers are assumed to be entirely price-inelastic in their demand and to buy one unit of the product per period from the firm supplying at lowest delivered price. Again, however, we might want to consider price-elastic consumers.

Delivered price to consumers comprises two elements: factory-gate price, P_g, reflecting production costs; and transport costs, $t \cdot D$, where t is the transport cost per km, and D the distance travelled to deliver the good. (Transport costs are here assumed linear in distance, but need not be so. Tirole (1988: 279), for example, uses a quadratic formulation in which transport costs are $t \cdot D^2$. The further a consumer is from the supplier, the higher the delivered price. In terms of product variation, transport costs in location theory can be interpreted as the costs of making alterations to products in order to 'tailor' them to the precise preferences of consumers. This is done, for example, with newspapers which are both zoned according to local interests and tailored according to other specialist interests of readers (Smith, 1980). Stigler (1964) suggests the example of alterations to an 'off-the-peg' suit.

Producers must also be assumed to have scale economies in production. Were each to have constant returns to scale technology at every level of production, there would be no difference between the costs of producing for one consumer or many and a producer would set up at every location where a consumer could be found. This would then render it irrelevant to pursue the analysis further.

Product innovation occurs when some firm starts producing at a new location. Three sets of conditions may bring this about: first, one or more existing single-product firm(s) move(s) from one location to another; second, a new firm arrives to occupy a location which existing firms have left vacant; and third, an existing firm or firms

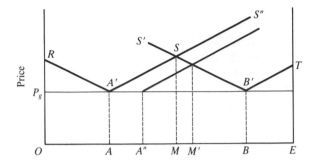

Figure 3.17 Two product varieties in a Hotelling style of spatial location model.

start to produce at a new location while continuing to operate at existing ones. The third of these possibilities relaxes the assumption of single-product firms. A crucial factor in determining whether the first or second case is relevant in any particular application is the size of relocation costs, which in the context of product innovation is equivalent to product development costs. When such costs are negligible or zero, it is reasonable to cast the analysis in terms of choice of location. When they are substantial, it is more plausible to take existing locations as given and to analyse potential changes in product type within that context.

First case

Consider the simplest case of two firms, labelled 1 and 2, each with identical production costs and producing a single variant. P_g is fixed exogenously at the same level for each firm, high enough to exceed marginal costs. Also assume (reasonably enough in the absence of other information) that if the firms are located at the same point, they share market demand equally.

Suppose initially the firms pick different locations. In terms of the cider example, one makes a quite sweet and the other a quite sour drink. These are marked as points A and B on the line OE in Figure 3.17. Both firms charge a factory-gate price of $OP = AA' = BB'$. The schedule of delivery-inclusive prices is shown by the lines $A'R$ and $A'SS''$ for firm 1 and $B'T$ and $B'SS'$ for firm 2. Firm 1 sells to the portion of the market where its price lies below that of firm 2, i.e. over the range OM, with sales totalling OA plus half of AB, since $A'S$ and $B'S$ both have the same slope. Firm 2 has a demand of ME. Under the assumptions, each firm will increase its profit if it increases its sales. Firm 1 has an incentive to relocate to A''. From that address, its sales rise to OM'. By the same token, however, firm 2 has an incentive to move towards firm 1; the incentive for each to move towards the other will only disappear when each is at the same location.

But what will their address be? In principle, it could be anywhere along OE, but again the incentive structure implicit in the model suggests it will be at the half-way

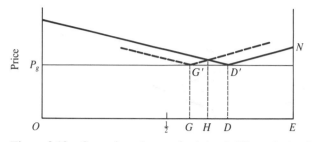

Figure 3.18 Central tendency of minimal differentiation in the Hotelling framework.

point (to see this, refer to Figure 3.18). Suppose we imagine the firms are both located at *D*, to the right of the half-way point. This situation could not persist, for it would be in the interest of one firm to move left towards the half-way point, say to *G*. At *G* the firm that moved would now have a market of *OH*, which is unambiguously greater than the half it had before. Both firms would therefore want to move towards the centre. Once at the centre, neither would have any incentive to move again since, by symmetrical argument, if either moved it would necessarily reduce its market share to less than 50 per cent.

In terms of innovation, this analysis suggests that in a two-firm industry with negligible relocation costs we might expect to find product innovation as the industry settles to its equilibrium configuration, but after that there will be no further change. It also suggests that both firms will produce similar products (Hotelling's principle of minimal differentiation) and that the particular product type chosen will serve best the preferences of consumers with 'middle of the range' tastes. Examples where such a story seems plausible might be a town or region with two newspapers, or a country or region with two airlines. In Australia, the insistence of the Government for many years that the country should be served domestically by only two major airlines led to a situation where the schedules of the two companies became almost identical on many routes.

The neatness of the result disappears if more than two firms are involved (Dasgupta and Maskin, 1986), and as we see below also requires modification if firms make more than one product or face substantial relocation costs. It also seems likely that if consumers were located in clusters at isolated points along the road, there would be an incentive for firms to settle at different locations.

Second case

Suppose relocation costs are substantial. Then location decisions are increasingly likely to be irreversible. Eaton and Lipsey (1978), for example, calculate that firms are likely to stay put when more than half of their fixed costs (costs which do not change with output) are specific to their existing location. Analogously, new product development costs are largely non-recoverable and tend to make firms cling to the

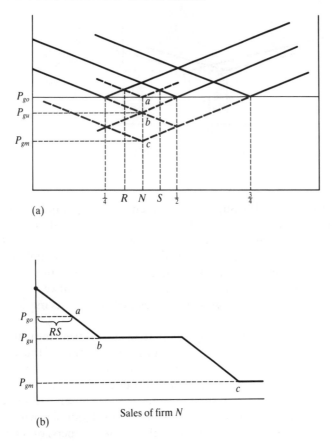

(a)

(b)

Sales of firm *N*

Figure 3.19 (a) The effects of new entry on a pre-existing symmetrical pattern of location; (b) The kinked market demand curve for product *N*.

variants they have generated. When firms make irreversible decisions for such reasons, it can be argued that they are likely to form a symmetrical pattern along the line (Prescott and Visscher, 1977).

Any newcomer to an industry which has already adopted a symmetrical structure will do best by locating exactly half-way between any two adjacent firms. Once there, the entrant has to decide on the factory-gate price it will charge, and this in turn takes us to the derivation of a market demand curve for the new product, assuming all other firms leave their prices unchanged. In Figure 3.19a, existing firms occupy positions 1/4, 1/2 and 3/4 of the way along the line and charge a gate price of P_{go}. The newcomer enters 3/8 of the way along, at *N*. If it also charges P_{go}, it will take a market share proportional to the distance *RS*. If its gate price falls, it will take progressively more of the market – and if it falls below P_{gu}, the firm undercuts completely firms to its left and right. At P_{gm}, the newcomer also undercuts the remaining firm and becomes a monopolist. The information contained in Figure 3.19a gives rise to the demand curve for N shown in Figure 3.19b. As in Lancaster's analysis there are kinks when critical prices are reached, at which N captures the markets of neighbouring suppliers.

Now rule out the possibility that a newcomer would reduce the price to P_{gu}, and take the location of existing firms as fixed. Then it can be shown (Eaton and Lipsey, 1978) that potential new entrants will often be denied the prospect of profitable operation, and will not enter at all. The basic reason for this is that with increasing returns to scale in the production technology, existing firms can be profitable on the basis of existing market shares, while a newcomer would have to drop its price too far in the context of a smaller market share (and hence higher marginal costs) to enable it to be profitable. Issues like this are explored further in Chapter 5.

Third case

In contrast with the Hotelling principle of minimal variation, many individual firms diversify their product range deliberately. One explanation for this is again substantial relocation costs.

Suppose the distance between two adjacent existing brands is so large that, given the prevailing production conditions and transport costs, there is scope for an outsider to move into the gap and make a profit. Existing firms will be reluctant to let this happen, since the newcomer will acquire a market share and hence some of the profit they would otherwise have earned. One defensive strategy might be for the two firms to reduce the price to a level so low that the outsider would be unable to match it and remain profitable. But there are dangers with this strategy. As we shall see in Chapter 5, outsiders might draw on existing resources to bear initial losses and still enter with the intention of competing for the market share. Thus, existing firms might fill the gap themselves in order to deter entry a strategy of pre-emptive proliferation.

Consumers and rational behaviour

The analysis of demand presented in this chapter so far has been built on the usual and fundamental assumption that individuals act 'rationally', i.e. 'choose optimally on the basis of their own preferences and subject to external constraints upon their choices' (Tisdell, 1975). The qualification about 'external constraints' draws attention to the important point that rationality implies **feasibility**; rational individuals will only ever choose to do what is possible. This implies that they know where the line falls between possible and impossible and in the case of rational consumers this means they know their budget and expect from products only the services they were designed to provide. But to choose optimally, consumers must also compare all possible options in terms of the types and quantities of goods they might acquire and then select the bundle which within their budget achieves for them the highest level of utility.

Two sorts of problem arise when an individual deliberately tries to maximise utility and explain why rationality is sometimes said to be 'bounded'. This is apposite in the case of new products. First, information about the alternatives and constraints upon action will usually be incomplete. With reference to feasibility, future and even current incomes are often subject to uncertainty, especially in times of structural change and threatened unemployment. And from many goods (experience and credence goods in particular), we do not know what service to expect. Ignorance about the performance characteristics of goods also makes it logically impossible to compare the levels of utility which could be achieved by buying different types and quantities of goods. Rationality requires that every option but the most superior be rejected, ensuring a utility maximum. But ignorance makes it impossible to know for sure which the superior option actually is.

Even if all relevant information were available, however, there is a second problem. To maximise utility, we must compare every possible option with every other. In this extreme case of perfect information, all goods by construction become search goods, but difficulties arise in determining preferences over different bundles of goods because of the complexity of the task. As Simon (1957) puts it, individuals 'have not the wits to maximise' (p. xxviii). The problem might not appear too striking if applied to a single-period maximisation exercise involving only greengroceries. But first, many important consumption decisions have multiperiod dimensions (accommodation, personal transport, consumer durable purchases); second, many consumption goods have multiprice tariffs (electricity, telephone services, anything bought with a bulk-purchase discount); third, plans to buy products in future must take account of changes in future prices and the expected performance characteristics of goods; fourth, utility derived from one product may be influenced by the availability and price of goods which are complementary to it, e.g. the utility from bread depends for many on the availability of butter and the utility from their joint consumption on the prices of both; fifth, in other cases, it may be technologically impossible to derive utility from a product unless it is combined with others (e.g. speakers generate no utility unless attached to other elements of a sound system, such as a compact disc player), and the amount of utility may depend in complex ways on the particular components purchased and the specific systems built from them; sixth, on the constraint side, the resources available to make purchases depend on the composition and size of expected incomes. With perfect information, we would know everything about all of these things, but Simon's point is that we could not process the information. There is just too much for the human brain to handle simultaneously, too many dimensions in which to work, too many trade-offs to perform. Rationality is bounded.

Conceptually, the problems of ignorance and complexity are separate. But in actual decision-making, they very often appear together and, clearly, processing problems become all the more complex; formidably so, once the information to be processed is uncertain. When individuals are assumed to have all relevant information and to be able to process it successfully, instantaneously and without cost, they are said to have **perfect unbounded** rationality. 'Perfect' refers to their information, 'unbounded' to their capacity for processing it. Their rationality would be unbounded but imperfect if they had to make choices on the basis of uncertain prospects (Tisdell, 1975: 265). Most theory which takes this approach hypothesises that individuals maximise **expected** utility, a probability-weighted average of the utility levels associated with each possible outcome (von Neumann and Morgenstern, 1944; Friedman and Savage, 1948). An individual's expected utility in this case is often derived on the basis of subjective probability weights which initially may not coincide with objective probabilities. If they did not, Bayesian probability theory may be used to show how prior probabilities might logically be adjusted to take account of additional information. The approach implies that individuals learn from experience and adapt their behaviour in the light of what they learn. The stronger rational expectations hypothesis goes even further. Even when consumers are imperfectly informed about products, the hypothesis states that they nonetheless form **rational expectations** about the services they will derive from goods, i.e. they exhibit no systematic bias in their predictions of how well (or poorly) it will meet their needs (Tirole, 1988: 114). This implies that at the time they make decisions, they make full and efficient use of all information that is known about the properties of a new good. Spence (1977) is an exception in assuming consumers overestimate the probability that products will not fail.

The rational expectations approach (Muth, 1961) is an elegant way of formalising the proposition that individuals do as well as they can for themselves, with whatever information is available. But it can be questioned on the grounds that individuals have often been observed to put a disporportionate weight on recently acquired information and so might expect more or less utility from a new product than more distant historical experience might suggest was justified (Spence, 1977).

Both expected utility maximisation in general and optimisation with rational expectations in particular attribute to decision-makers a fabulous capacity to process information. We have already noted Simon's argument from complexity which throws doubt on such capacity. But it is important to note that individual rationality may also be bounded for other reasons. Whenever their decision-making capacity is bounded, it is said that individuals **satisfice** rather than maximise (the term is due to Simon (1955)). Elster (1983: 74–5) suggests that there are two reasons to consider. One argument for satisficing is associated with cases in which decision-makers face problems that have no well-defined solution. A trivial example offered by Elster would be: 'Find the smallest real number which is strictly larger than 1'. But there is also a general argument which applies to all choice situations in which information about all possible options is not freely available.

To maximise utility, individuals must engage in costly search to find out all the options. But how much search? Assuming the additional utility from further search steadily falls as progressively more information is discovered and that the additional disutility of further search is constant or rising, the total utility of search will be maximised when the utility gains from an extra unit of search have fallen to the level of utility losses from extra search. Beyond this point, utility losses from extra search will outweigh any gains, so total utility will be reduced. The central logical problem with this, however, is that we cannot know what the utility gain from any particular bit of search will be until it has been undertaken. So we can never know, until it is too late, whether we should have undertaken it or not.

The general argument has been put by Winter (1964). 'At some level of analysis, all goal-seeking behavior is satisficing behavior. There must be limits to the range of possibilities explored and those limits must be arbitrary in the sense that the decision-maker cannot *know* that they are optimal' (p. 264). The relevance of this argument to consumer demand with product innovation should be apparent. When new products are being produced, consumers will always be unsure whether the products they plan to purchase at current prices will actually meet their needs most effectively within their budget. They cannot try every new product that appears in the market-place as soon as it appears and can only partially remedy this by resort to consumer information. And they cannot be sure that the cost of any experimental purchase will repay the outlay in terms of the extra utility it subsequently yields. Thus they can never know exactly the types and quantities of products they would have to purchase in order to maximise utility. Uncertainty of this kind has been emphasised by Shackle (1955), and characterised as 'radical' by Loasby (1976), 'genuine' by O'Driscoll and Rizzo (1985), 'extended' by Bookstaber and Langsam (1983) and 'structural' by Langlois (1986).

Particularly when product innovation is rapid, continuous and widespread, it is clear that perfect, unbounded rational behaviour of the kind which underlies simple maximising models can only be accepted as an idealised abstraction. But even accepting that point, we do not have to abandon the idea that consumers behave rationally; we could alternatively seek a different definition of what constitutes rational action. Hayek, for example, makes the point that maximising rationality arises from a philosophical tradition which sees **logical consistency** – 'a capacity of deductive reasoning from explicit premises' (1967: 84) – as the criterion for rational action. This is the Cartesian tradition. An alternative tradition is 'evolutionary' rationalism, in which reason is defined by the 'capacity to recognise truth' and rationality is marked by ability to learn from experience, though without necessarily making the most of it, as envisaged in the rational expectations hypothesis. Elsewhere, Hayek (1978) has written eloquently of competition as a process of exploration so it is entirely consistent that he should also see rationality in terms of learning capacity. For Langlois, the same tradition is important, but his view of rationality perhaps broader still: 'the criterion of rationality is to act reasonably, to act appropriately to one's circumstances, to adapt' (1986: 230). It could be argued that it is this 'evolutionary' approach to rationality which underpins the accounts of consumer reactions to product innovation which are found in the literature of management and marketing, to which references are made elsewhere in this chapter.

From the discussion in this section, we recognise the need for caution in applying 'standard' utility-maximising models of demand analysis. Consumer demand analysis, assuming perfect unbounded rationality, makes most sense in a world where the range of products on offer is relatively small and fixed. It remains a plausible approximation when the larger part of expenditures is directed towards a relatively small range of products in which the innovation rate is slow. But when expenditures are spread widely over many product types and when innovation is fast in at least some areas where expenditure is significant, it is hard to escape the conclusion that rationality becomes bounded, so that some account has to be given of how consumers cope and how learning occurs. We turn now to analysis.

Dynamic demand analysis

Adoption and diffusion

Until now we have been essentially concerned with static demand. But when new products arrive in the market, it is not the case that the level of demand is at once established at a stable level from which it never subsequently changes. If the innovation is successful, the quantity of the good demanded per period will rise from a zero level on the date before the product was introduced, at a rate determined by the availability and competitiveness of substitutes and the strength of demand growth.

Two sets of forces are at work here. First, the price of the product may decline because of falling costs resulting from scale economies, learning by doing and the pressure of competition on the supply side. As the price falls, so the quantity demanded increases down any given market demand curve. We concentrate on the supply side and competitive factors behind falling price in Chapter 6. Second, the whole demand curve may shift bodily outwards. This will occur as incomes rise, population grows, and as knowledge about the new product spreads and preferences for having what it offers intensify in its favour. In this chapter, we have already discussed this latter group of factors in selected static models. In this section, we introduce another model, which builds on the standard textbook approach to the demand for homogeneous search goods and use it as the foundation for presenting analysis of the growth of demand.

The growth of demand for a product can be analysed by asking about three groups of households and the relationships between them. The first group is the set of all households in the economy. Within that group there will at any time be a subgroup comprising **potential users** which excludes people who would never plan to acquire any of the good, even if it were free and those who simply do not know about the product. The latter group may become potential users once they have learned about the product through formal and informal advertising (i.e. word of mouth reports of other users).

Within the group of potential users are **actual users**. Sales will increase as the number of actual users increases and as the number of units purchased per user increases. Those who become users and go on using the product are also called **adoptors. Diffusion** of a new product is the spread of the innovation throughout the population and a diffusion curve shows how the innovation spreads over time (see Figure 3.23, discussed in detail later). All diffusion curves have time on the horizontal axis and some fraction on the vertical axis. This fraction might be the proportion of an overall population which has adopted an innovation, or the fraction of potential

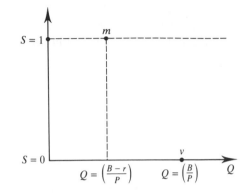

Figure 3.20 The budget constraint for a consumer durable purchase.

users to have become adoptors. If the whole population is regarded as comprising potential adoptors, there is no conflict. But if potential adoptors are regarded as comprising only a subset of the whole population, it is important to ask what determines the size of the potential adoptor group, and to know whether it changes through time as a proportion of the whole population.

A theory of diffusion should include reference to two critical points: first, the conversion of non-potential users into potential users; and second, the conversion of potential users into adoptors. In what follows, we offer a simple microeconomic model of demand for a new consumer durable which allows us to see how the population might be divided into the three groups we have described, and provides the basis for predicting patterns in the diffusion of ownership.[4]

Adoption

Interest focuses on households' decisions to own (or not own) a consumer durable of which, it is assumed, they will only ever acquire at the most one unit. The durable comes in a single size and ownership gives the user access to its services, therefore, in a fixed and unalterable amount per period. It is also assumed that the good can be acquired through a rental market, or that finance can be raised to buy the good, so that the debt servicing flow per period can be regarded as a rental equivalent. The household's budget constraint may then be written:

$$B = PQ + rS \qquad (3.2)$$

where B is the household's budget (or income), assumed to be totally spent in each period, Q the quantity of a composite comprising all goods other than the durable, P a price index for the composite good and r the rental price per period for the durable. S takes the value 1 if the household owns the good, 0 if not.

If a household is not an owner, $S = 0$ and (3.2) implies:

$$Q = (B/P) \qquad (3.3)$$

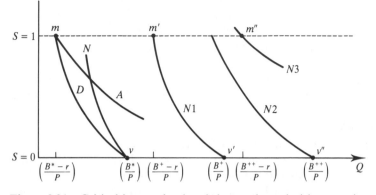

Figure 3.21 Critical income level and the purchase decision: varying income levels and preferences.

i.e. the quantity of the composite good purchased is simply the household budget or income divided by the prices of such goods. If a household is an owner, $S = 1$ and (3.2) implies:

$$Q = [(B - r)/P] \tag{3.4}$$

i.e. the quantity of the composite good purchased is (r/P) less than in (3.3) for given values of B and P, an amount reflecting the fact that r per period is now being spent on the durable rather than the composite of non-durable goods. For given values of B, P and r therefore, the budget constraint in the space of durable goods and composite goods comprises just two points, marked m and v in Figure 3.20.

Indifference curves in this space have the usual shape, except that on this occasion we allow them to have intercepts with the horizontal axis to indicate utility levels associated with non-ownership. Households' preferences between the services of the durable and the composite good generate downward-sloping indifference curves with diminishing marginal rate of substitution. Even though access to the services of the good can be acquired only in discrete and indivisible units, it is possible for consumers to imagine what it would be like to enjoy such services in smaller amounts per period, or for shorter periods of time than the consumption technology in actuality permits.

In Figure 3.21 we show on the left the utility maximising choices of three different households, N, A and D, when each has a given budget B^*. Recalling that households are constrained to choose between m and v, notice that N chooses v (all composite good and no durable) because m would be on a lower indifference curve, A chooses m (a unit of the durable and some of the composite) because v would be on a lower indifference curve and D is indifferent between m and v. By inspection, the shapes of the three households' indifference curve vary; they have different tastes and preferences. Within any given income bracket, therefore, variations in preference might account for differences in choice about ownership, as we would expect.

What would it take to make N adopt the innovation? For N to become an adoptor, it would have to have an indifference curve associated with ownership which lay above the indifference curve associated with non-ownership. To see how this might come about, notice that the horizontal distance between $[(B-r)/P]$ and (B/P) is always (r/P), whatever the value of B. In Figure 3.21, we allow B to rise from B^* to B^+ to B^{++}. When $B = B^+$, N is indifferent between ownership and non-ownership: m' and v' lie on the same indifference curve, labelled $N1$. But when $B = B^{++}$, the indifference curve $N2$ through v'' unambiguously lies below that through m'', $N3$, and N will be an owner.

There are two lessons to learn from this experiment. First, given N's pattern of preferences, there is some income level very close to B^+ at which it would become an adoptor. We call this its **critical income** level. Different households with different patterns of preferences would become adoptors at other income levels. A's critical income level must lie below B^*, for example and D's must lie very close to B^*. Differences in critical income levels are a way of indicating differences among households' preferences at any actual income level.

Second, N would become an adoptor at a higher income level only if its indifference curves became 'flatter' at higher income levels. Recall that the horizontal distance (r/P) is constant at all levels of B. Therefore a perpendicular to $[(B-r)/P]$ can cross the highest attainable indifference curve only if it becomes less steep. Since there is no reason why we should expect indifference curves to behave in this way for all households, we should not expect all households to become adoptors. In fact, if there is *no* finite critical income level at which a household would adopt, we could not regard it as even a potential adoptor.

On the other hand, it is intuitively plausible to believe that indifference curves will become flatter at higher income levels. To see why, consider the slopes of indifference curves at points like v, v' and v''. As we move out from the origin, higher values of B are associated with higher values of Q, the composite good. If the slopes of indifference curves near to the Q-axis become flatter further from the origin, this indicates that, in return for some (small) level of service from the durable, households would be prepared to sacrifice increasingly more of the composite, consistent with maintaining some given level of utility. But as we move out along the axis, we are looking at increasingly high levels of Q. So increasing marginal sacrifices of Q in return for a little of the services of the durable would seem be a reasonable expectation. If the same argument can be applied to all levels of Q between $[(B-r)/P]$ and (B/P), then indifference curves will become flatter at higher income levels and a finite level of critical income can then be established.

The diagram also makes it clear how changes in preference patterns associated with changes in critical income levels may lead to adoption. This is seen most obviously by supposing that N's indifference curves tilted to become the same as A's. N's critical income level would then become the same as A's, somewhat below B^*, which is well below N's previous critical income level near B^+. With income B^*, N with the changed preference pattern would become an owner. Changed preferences suggest the influence of learning, whether from the experience of others or from advertising.

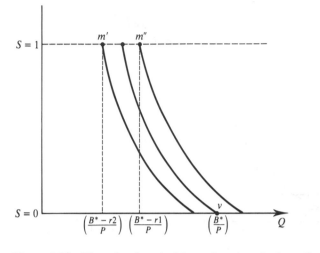

Figure 3.22 The adoption decision: changing the (rental) price.

Finally, consider a fall in the rental price of the durable. Holding B constant at B^* and fixing P, the horizontal distance between $[(B - r)/P)]$ and (B/P) will clearly be reduced (see Figure 3.22 , in which r falls from $r2$ to $r1$.) When $r = r2$, the household will maximise utility as a non-owner at v, preferred to m'. But when r falls to $r1$, the household maximises utility as an owner at m'', preferred to v. With the fall in r, the household's critical income level must therefore also have fallen from a level above B^* to a level below it.

We have used this framework to show the conditions under which a potential adoptor becomes an adoptor and to say what it might mean to be a non-potential adoptor. But there is one other case to consider. Up to this point, we have taken preferences to be well defined. But some households may not even know of the existence of the new consumer durable. In that case and until they have made some evaluation of the product, however intuitive, their preference patterns cannot be said to include the good. Their indifference curves cannot therefore even be drawn. Until their preferences exist, we regard such households as also being non-potential owners.

We now turn to diffusion. Some of the literature in the area (for example, Bonus, 1973) views diffusion as an information spreading process (or set of processes) which constitutes only a part of the explanation for the growth in adoption. Rising incomes and falling prices are economic factors which also help explain the growth of adoption but, in this view, are conceptually separate from diffusion *per se*. Other parts of the literature (see Deaton and Muellbauer, 1980: 370), however, regard all growth in ownership as the result of a diffusion process, to which economic factors are viewed as contributing. We shall adopt the latter usage here.

The purely informational aspects of diffusion may be divided into two elements. At given prices and incomes, **vertical diffusion** occurs as 'households become sufficiently

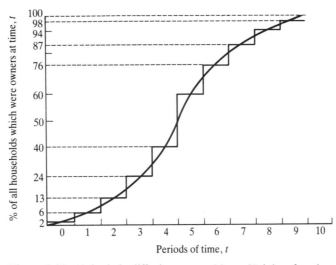

Figure 3.23 A logistic diffusion curve. Note: Height of each step shows average ownership fraction over a period.

aware of the commodity to desire its ownership' (Bonus, 1973: 658). Notice there are two steps here. First, individuals must be informed of the existence and basic nature of the product. Second, they must form preferences on the basis of that information which, for each one of them, will imply a finite value of critical income. Vertical diffusion, therefore, relates to the conversion of non-potential adoptors into potential adoptors. Contrasted with this, **horizontal diffusion** 'induces households that are aware of the good, and potentially interested in its possession, to revise their plans to allow for actual ownership at a lower income' (Bonus, 1973: 658). Horizontal diffusion will be marked, for any household, by a reduction in the level of critical income compared with its level when the household initially became a potential adoptor.

Observed diffusion curves, or growth-of-ownership curves, are usually S-shaped, or sigmoid (see Figure 3.23). In words, the fraction of owners in the population rises first at an accelerating and then at a decelerating rate until all potential owners have adopted. When growth curves are symmetric, i.e. acceleration gives way to deceleration when exactly half the population have become owners, they are called **logistic**. A logistic curve is found by solving an equation of the form:

$$dn(t)/dt = b[n(t)/N(N - n(t))] \qquad (3.5)$$

where $n(t)$ is the number of adoptors at t, N is the population size and b a parameter reflecting the likelihood of adoption. The solution to this differential equation (found by integration, but for detail see van Duijn, 1983) is:

$$n(t) = N\{1/[1 + e^{(-a - b(t))}]\} \qquad (3.6)$$

where a is a constant of integration and positions the curve on the time axis. If growth curves are non-symmetric, or skewed, they look like a cumulated log-normal curve.

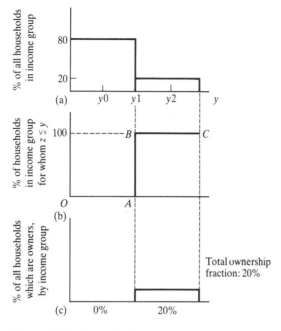

Figure 3.24 Example 1.

To understand why diffusion of demand curves take the shapes they do, we now develop a diagrammatic analysis depicted in Figures 3.24–3.28. In the analysis, we shall denote actual incomes by y and critical incomes by z. Throughout, we shall make the plausible simplifying assumption that the higher a household's income bracket, the greater the probability that a randomly selected household's income will be above its critical income. This implies that the higher the income bracket we observe, the greater the proportion of households in that bracket that have adopted. The framework of the analysis is flexible enough, however, to accommodate cases where this is not so.

We start by examining ownership patterns under three increasingly complex sets of conditions, the last most closely approximating what we actually observe. We may then explore diffusion by allowing the conditions underlying ownership patterns to change. Unless otherwise stated, assume the entire population comprises potential owners.

In Example 1 (shown in Figures 3.24a, b, c), assume all consumers have identical preferences, represented by sets of indifference curves which become increasingly flat at higher income levels. The critical income level for all consumers is $z1 = y1$. The income distribution, in general, shows the proportions of the population in each income bracket and in this example we have divided the population into two groups, of which 80 per cent have an income of $y0$ ($<y1$) and 20 per cent an income of $y2$

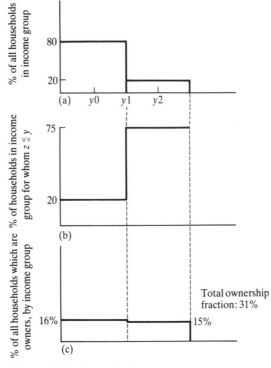

Figure 3.25   Example 2.

($> y1$). Income level $y0$ is at the mid-point of a cell defining an income bracket from 0 to $y1$, and $y2$ at the mid-point of a cell defining the higher income bracket, above $y1$ (see Figure 3.24a). In Figure 3.24b, we show the percentage of households in each income class for whom critical income is equal to or less than their actual income, which by definition must tell us the ownership fraction within that income bracket. For those in the lower income bracket, with income $y0$, this is 0 per cent, and for those in the higher bracket, with income $y1$, 100 per cent. The step function *OABC* is one example of a **quasi-Engel function**. An Engel function shows how the demand for a product rises when incomes rise; a quasi-Engel function shows how ownership fractions in income brackets rise as we move to higher income levels.

To derive the ownership fraction for the population, the proportion of owners in any income bracket must be multiplied by the proportion of the population in the same bracket and the resulting percentages for every bracket added together. Diagrammatically, Figure 3.24c shows the result of multiplying together these fractions for the two income brackets, 0 per cent times 80 per cent yielding 0 per cent, and 100 per cent times 20 per cent yielding 20 per cent. The sum of these two percentages is 20 per cent. Without further analysis, it should be clear that this ownership fraction

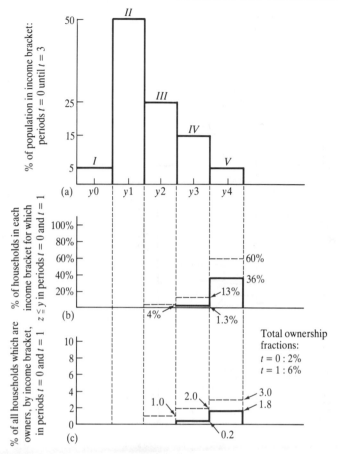

Figure 3.26 Shifting critical incomes and changes in the spread and pattern of ownership: periods 0 and 1.

would rise if either the upper income group grew, or if preferences changed in a way which gave at least some consumers a critical income level of y0 or less.

In Example 2 (shown in Figure 3.25a, b, c) we have left the income distribution unchanged but allowed preferences to be heterogeneous in each income bracket. In the low income bracket, 20 per cent of consumers have critical incomes below y0, and 80 per cent have critical incomes above y0. In the high-income bracket, 75 per cent have critical incomes below y2, and 25 per cent above it. This implies 20 per cent of low-income earners will be owners, comprising 16 per cent of the population, and 75 per cent of high-income earners will be owners, comprising 15 per cent of the population. By allowing even a quite small proportion of the dominant low-income group to become owners, the ownership fraction in the overall population thus becomes much larger: 31 per cent as opposed to 20 per cent. But there is an economic

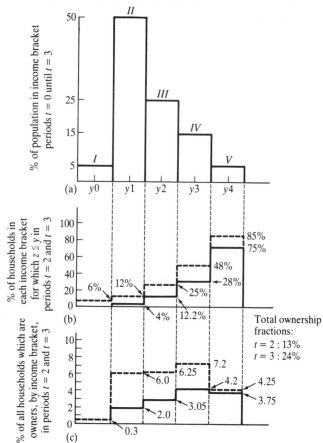

Figure 3.27 Shifting critical incomes and changes in the spread and pattern of ownership: periods 3 and 4.

ingredient missing here which must be borne in mind. If households on low incomes are actually to take ownership, they must be able either to pay for the good outright, or raise a loan on which they can service the debt. In many cases, households in low-income groups will not have the capital to do the former and may find it difficult to persuade lenders (banks, hire purchase companies and the like) to allow them to borrow. We shall assume that some low-income earners can take one of the two routes to ownership, but acknowledge these difficulties as a partial explanation for low-ownership fractions among low-income groups.

In Example 3, we show in Figures 3.26a–3.28a a stylised version of the sort of income distribution most often observed, i.e. one with a log-normal shape. A log-normal distribution is one that is normal in the natural logarithms of the actual values of income. A normal distribution is symmetric and can always be transformed

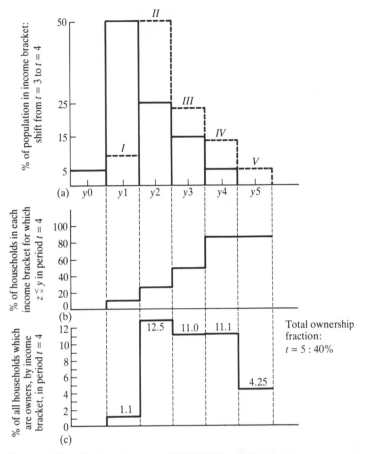

Figure 3.28 Shifting income distribution and changes in the spread and pattern of ownership.

into a distribution with mean zero and standard deviation of 1. We show five income brackets or groups labelled *I, II, ... V.* In Figures 3.26 and 3.27, relating to periods $t = 0$ to $t = 3$ inclusive, incomes are unchanged. But in Figure 3.28, relating to period $t = 4$, all income groups have been shifted upwards. Throughout, the bulk of the population (55 per cent rising to 59 per cent) lies in the two lowest income brackets. It is a characteristic of log-normal distributions that the mode and median both lie below the mean because the distribution is skewed in this way.

Figures 3.26b–3.28b again illustrate the Quasi-Engel function. Between $t = 0$ and $t = 3$ (Figures 3.26 and 3.27) this function shifts continually as the proportion of owner households rises in higher income groups and takes on positive values in the lower income groups for the first time. Only in period $t = 4$ is the quasi-Engel curve made to stabilise, allowing us to observe the effect of a rise in the income distribution.

Figures 3.26c–3.28c are derived from Figures 3.26a–3.28a and 2.26b–3.28b the population ownership fractions by income group and indicates how the total population ownership fraction rises over time from $t = 0$ to $t = 4$. We assume throughout that membership of each of the income groups is constant. This simplifies and gives quantitative precision to the analysis, although in reality income group membership changes over time. We will now use Example 3 to illustrate how diffusion is driven. The diagrams should be read in conjunction with Table 3.1 which lays out the calculations behind the illustrations.

Table 3.1 Calculation of ownership fractions

Period	% Population	% Ownership in group	% Ownership in population
Period t = 0			
Income group			
V	5	36.0	1.8
IV	15	1.3	0.2
I, II, III	Varied	0.0	0.0
		Population ownership %: 2.0	
Period t = 1			
Income group			
V	5	60	3.0
IV	15	13	2.0
III	25	4	1.0
I, II	Varied	0	0.0
		Population ownership %: 6.0	
Period t = 2			
Income group			
V	5	75	3.75
IV	15	28	4.2
III	25	12.2	3.05
II	50	4.0	2.00
I	5	0.0	0.0
		Population ownership %: 13.0	
Period t = 3			
Income group			
V	5	85	4.25
IV	15	48	7.20
III	25	25	6.25
II	50	12	6.00
I	5	6	0.30
		Population ownership %: 24.0	
Period t = 4			
Income group			
V	5	85	4.25
IV	13	85	11.1
III	23	48	11.0
II	50	25	12.5
I	9	12	1.1
		Population ownership %: 39.95	

It should be clear from inspecting the diagrams that the ownership fraction for the population will rise if the quasi-Engel function shifts upwards, reflecting increased ownership proportions in some or all income brackets, as reported in Table 3.1. Given the particular amounts by which we have shifted each step of the function upwards, the population-wide ownership fraction rises from 2 per cent in $t = 0$, to 6 per cent in $t = 1$, and then 13 per cent and 24 per cent in periods $t = 2$ and $t = 3$. When the whole population comprises potential adoptors, such a shift occurs as the result of horizontal diffusion. Horizontal diffusion implies that the whole distribution of critical incomes will shift downwards, reflecting an across-the-population intensification of preferences in favour of the new good. Thus, in every actual income bracket, the proportion of households for whom critical income, z, lies below actual income, y, will increase. Even quite small increases in the height of steps in the low to middle-income brackets may yield substantial additions to the ownership fraction because that is where the bulk of the population's income is found. In proportionate terms, these additions will make their most substantial contribution when the overall ownership fraction is initially low. This is one reason why we would expect the diffusion rate to accelerate in the early stages. But as the quasi-Engel function continues to rise, scope for further additions to new ownership is constrained by existing ownership levels and the growth rate of ownership must necessarily decline. If steps along the function rose particularly quickly in the lower income brackets, we might expect the diffusion curve to be skewed, with the first half of the population becoming owners faster than the second. Bonus argues that refrigerators, cars and vacuum cleaners diffused in West Germany as the result of horizontal diffusion.

In the analysis above, we regarded the entire population as potential adoptors, but as a matter of logic, actual adoption can take place only after a household has first become a potential adoptor. Before any new wave of horizontal diffusion can occur, therefore, it must have been preceded by vertical diffusion throughout at least part of the community. When we observe upward shifts in the quasi-Engel curve, therefore, it must, with a lag, reflect the fact that vertical diffusion has at some stage occurred. The feature of the curve which most accurately reflects the impact of vertical diffusion is its asymptote, i.e. the ownership fraction which the curve approaches in the highest income ranges. Since it is assumed that those with highest incomes will have the greatest probability of adopting, an ownership fraction well below 100 per cent in the highest income bracket would suggest that substantial vertical diffusion has yet to occur. Vangrevelinghe (1965) and Bonus (1973) both conclude (for France and Germany, respectively) that an upper limit to the possible diffusion of washing machines existed for a number of periods, with the latter arguing that this ceiling rose over time according to a logistic curve.

Note also that if the price of the new good falls over time, the quasi-Engel function will again shift upwards since the falling price reduces the level of critical incomes across the board so that, in each income bracket, there will now be more individuals for whom critical income lies below actual income.

For the purposes of illustrating the role of rising incomes in diffusion, we have held the quasi-Engel curve at a constant level in periods $t = 3$ and $t = 4$ but have shifted the whole distribution of actual incomes upwards. (see Figure 3.28) The lowest income bracket, *I*, now has a mid-point for its cell of $y1$ and the highest, *V*, a mid-point of $y5$. We have also adjusted slightly the relative proportions of the income groups from $5:50:25:15:5$ to $9:50:23:13:5$. And for simplicity we have assumed that the ownership fraction for the now higher level of highest incomes remains at 85 per cent. The implications of this, which are quite dramatic, are apparent from Table 3.1. Because the largest of the income groups, *II* and *III*, now have the relatively high-ownership fractions which were formerly associated with smaller groups on higher income levels, additional purchases in the larger groups noticeably accelerate the pace of ownership in the population at large. It is not difficult to grasp intuitively, therefore, that even if the quasi-Engel curve remains fixed (in the form of a step function like those in the diagrams), continuous upward movement in the income distribution will of itself generate diffusion. The path is likely to be sigmoid, since the period of initial acceleration we have illustrated above must be followed by a period of deceleration as the proportion of non-owning households continues to be eroded by the purchasing decisions of adopters.

While we have separated each of the mechanisms driving diffusion for individual treatment, it is usual for them all to make simultaneous contributions. Upon initial introduction of a new good, we would expect the quasi-Engel function to have relatively low and shallow steps until the highest income brackets were reached, but for the middle and then lower segments to rise at the same time as the overall income distribution shifted upwards. As the market widened and competition intensified, we would also expect the price of the good to fall, shifting the quasi-Engel curve even faster up. All these factors would need to be taken into account in determining the exact shape of the diffusion curve, but for the reasons outlined above, we should generally expect a sigmoid of some kind, increasingly compressed laterally, the faster critical incomes fell and the faster actual incomes rose.

Bonus's empirical work suggests that, when diffusion is driven by rising actual incomes alone, the diffusion curve will be symmetric (logistic) if per capita income grows at a constant exponential rate, the whole population comprises potential adopters and the distributions of actual and critical incomes are both log-normal. The curve will again be logistic but steeper if median critical income falls exponentially. If the fraction of potential adopters is also growing, itself in a logistic fashion, the resulting diffusion curve will usually be skewed. In our example, we generated values which constitute the first half of the diffusion curve in Figure 3.23. The example should provide enough guidance for interested readers to generate the rest of the curve by shifting either the quasi-Engel curve, or the income distribution, or both.

Other empirical work on consumer durables by Pyatt (1964), Bain (1964) and Deaton (1975), also find sigmoid ownership growth curves to be characteristic of the pattern of demand over time. And Ironmonger (1973) offers similar findings for non-durables including tea, bananas and ice-cream. As Bain (1964), in his work on televisions, points out, however, observed growth curves will on many occasions have to be interpreted as an envelope of 'short-run' sigmoid diffusion curves. There might be at least two reasons for doing this. The first is that, if they are to be viewed as 'pure' diffusion curves based on informational effects alone, each curve must take as given both the price of the product and the distribution of incomes. For each significant reduction in price and for any significant surge in overall incomes, we should (on this view) start a new curve. The second is that the nature of the product itself changes over time. To take one example, the observed ownership growth curve for micro-computers since their first introduction would include periods before and after the incorporation of built-in screens: 'pre-laptop' and 'post-laptop'. Laptop and non-laptop microcomputers package the characteristics of this type of product in ways which enable them to be separately identified and for each of which a separate ownership growth curve could be observed.

To end this section, we draw attention to the notion of the **product life cycle** (**PLC**). The PLC is sometimes depicted as another sort of sigmoid curve drawn with time on the horizontal axis, but on the vertical axis is the real value of total expenditures per year rather than the percentage of households in the community to have adopted (see, for example, Howard and Moore, 1988: 344). In this construct, it is accepted quite explicitly that innovation in the nature of the product will occur during its lifetime. A PLC starts with the introduction of a new good at the point where it creates a new class of product, such as microcomputers. At this point consumers have to work out what the product is and does, which requires what Howard and Moore call *extensive* problem solving and will appeal, mostly, to 'venturesome' consumers who like to confront this sort of problem. As a general rule, we would expect people of this type to be in a minority and for early sales to be modest. Later, as new brands and product variants are introduced, a substantial portion of the population has learned what goods in this product class do, but now need to engage in limited problem solving to evaluate which of the varieties they should acquire, if any. Assuming a larger proportion of the population has the inclination to sort out 'pros and cons' now they are well defined, this would explain an acceleration in sales. They will probably be encourged to perform this sort of evaluation exercise when they also observe that at this stage the price of the good is tending to fall. Finally, once the prospects for introducing new brands and variants have become exhausted, the good becomes a search good for almost all of the population and sales settle down at the 'market saturation' level.

The point to note with this account of the PLC is that consumers are assumed to vary in their capacity to come to grips with new information and that the sort of information they have to acquire varies with the stage in the PLC. Early on, product identification calls for cognitive skills possessed only by a minority and a willingness to confront the partially unknown. Later, purchasing the new type of good becomes a routine exercise for the few who learned early, is a limited problem of evaluation for the majority and remains an extensive problem of identification for another minority. Towards the end, information is so widespread and reliable, that for most purchasing has become a routine exercise, but for shrinking and vanishingly small minorities, respectively, purchase remains either a limited problem-solving exercise or one which requires extensive learning.

There is no necessary presumption in the PLC that the well-off are most likely to adopt first. But we might expect many of the well-off *to be* well-off because they have shown themselves capable of extensive learning in the past and because they have been successful as risk-takers. Furthermore, we might expect that those who are now well-off are in a relatively strong position to take the risk that a new good will not meet their needs since the proportion of their income at stake in purchasing the good is small compared with that of people whose incomes are lower. In other words, the well-off have (in terms of the proportion of their income) less to lose. There is much in common, therefore, between the earlier analysis and the PLC. The PLC curve also links into the range of technology strategies firms may pursue (Chapters 4 and 5). 'Market leader' firms, for example, specialise in dealing with market conditions where consumers are venturesome and to do so develop particular competence in risk management and customer training. 'Follow-the-leader' firms come into their own when purchasers are mostly limited problem solvers; their strength is in developing incremental changes to products.

Producers' demand for inputs

In Chapter 2 we showed how technological progress in production is represented by an inward shift of isoquants. That implies that at any given level of input prices, there will be a fall in the employment of inputs used in producing any given quantity of output – the exact amounts involved reflecting both the extent of the shift and the factor saving bias of the progress. But in determining the relationship between technological progress and the demand for inputs generally, this is only one part of the story.

The demand for inputs is a *derived* demand: it is built on the demand for output which producers meet at given prices. Each firm has a demand function for inputs and so does each group of firms comprising an industry, and so does the economy as a whole. In this section we examine the input demand functions of the firm and industry. The implications of technological progress for employment at the macro-level are taken up in Chapters 7 and 8.

The demand curve for inputs at the firm level is built on the proposition that inputs are employed up to the point where the return on employing an extra unit of the input is equal to the cost of employing that unit. At the industry level, all constituent firms' input demand curves must be considered – along with the implications for output price of variations in industry production level associated with the supply-side decisions of all firms. The analysis of input demand is intricate, even in the absence of technological change (Layard and Walters, 1978: Chs 7, 9). Once technological change is introduced, it can become quite daunting (Stoneman, 1983: Ch. 11; Dobbs *et al.*, 1987). None the less, one result of performing the analysis is well worth noting in advance: once the scope of the analysis is broadened, it is easy to show that the demand for inputs might well increase as the result of technological progress. Other factors offset the inward shift of isoquants.

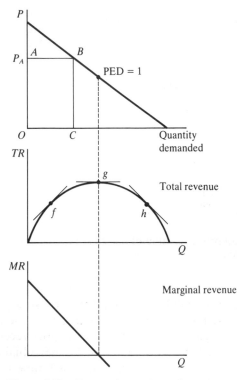

Figure 3.29   Demand curve, total revenue and marginal revenue curves for a firm which must reduce price to increase sales volume.

Input demand in the short run: the firm

For economists, the meaning of the short run is a period during which at least one of the factors of production, or inputs, is fixed. In the long run all inputs are variable. When labour and capital are taken to be the factors of production, capital is usually regarded as fixed in the short run and labour as variable. The addition to output generated by increasing a variable input by one unit, holding all other factor(s) constant, is the marginal (physical) product (MP) of that input – which, as noted in Chapter 2 (p. 39), is usually assumed to fall (eventually) as increasing quantities of the variable input are put to work with the fixed input. These are important conceptual foundations.

Firms produce to sell. The additional sales revenue they receive from selling an extra unit of output is termed **marginal revenue (MR)**, which is constant and equal to the price per unit of the product if all units can be sold for the same price, but must fall if the price falls with increased sales volume. The price received by an

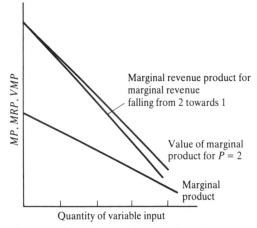

Marginal revenue product for
marginal revenue
falling from 2 towards 1

Value of marginal
product for $P = 2$

Marginal
product

Quantity of variable input

MP, MRP, VMP

Figure 3.30 Marginal (physical) product, value of marginal product and
marginal revenue product curves.

individual firm for the sale of an extra unit will be constant if the firm's output is so
small relative to the total volume of that kind of output produced for the market
that its own output decisions have no impact on market price. The price received by
the firm will fall if, as in Figure 3.29a, the demand curve for the individual firm is
downward sloping, which it will be if it has to reduce the price each time it wishes
to attract additional custom. The area of the rectangle under the firm's output demand
curve at any price, such as $OABC$ in Figure 3.29a, in relation to price P_A, shows its
total revenue at that price. Total revenue rises from zero at the vertical intercept of
the demand curve over the elastic portion of the curve, while sales volume rises at a
faster proportional rate than price per unit falls, and falls over the inelastic portion
(where price per unit is falling at a faster proportionate rate than sales volume is
rising) (see Figure 3.29b). Over a firm's linear demand curve, total revenue rises at a
declining rate until the PED $= |1|$ because, for every successive fall in price, sales
volume increases by a smaller additional proportion. Marginal revenue is the change
in total revenue when sales rise by one unit and is shown by the slope of a tangent
to the total revenue curve (see tangents at f, g, and h in Figure 3.29b). Tangents are
positive but declining until PED $= |1|$, and after that point negative. This is shown
in Figures 3.29b and c.

The additional revenue from employing an extra unit of variable input is marginal
revenue times the marginal product (MP). This is the **marginal revenue product** (**MRP**)
of the input, or in the case of a constant price, **value of the marginal product** (**VMP**).
If price is constant as sales volume increases, marginal product (which falls as more
of the input is applied) will be multiplied at all levels of input use by the same number
and the VMP curve will lie above the MP. If price falls as sales volume increases,
MP will be multiplied by an ever smaller number, the declining level of marginal
revenue, so the curve linking input use to MRP will fall more steeply than the VMP

curve (see Figure 3.30 for illustrative relationships between MP, MRP and VMP curves).

We will now assert that the MRP curve can be thought of as a firm's demand curve for the variable input, by assuming that firms maximise profit.

To see why, suppose that the firm pays the same price per unit for a variable input X, however much or little of the input it uses. Denote this price w_0: w for 'wage rate'. This is also the marginal cost of employing an extra unit of the input. Because the firm is a profit maximiser, it should increase employment of X if the additional revenue from doing so is greater than the additional cost – for then its profit (revenue minus costs) will rise. In Figure 3.31, the horizontal line at height w_0 is the infinitely elastic supply curve for input X: X is supplied in any quantity at the unit price w_0. The MRP curve is taken from Figure 3.30 and for lower levels of X lies above w_0. According to our argument, more X should be employed until it reaches the level X^*.

By a similar argument, the firm should reduce employment of X if MRP lies below w_0 – for then it would reduce its costs by a greater amount than it would lose revenue, again increasing profit. In Figure 3.31, MRP is below w_0 for all levels of X above X^*. The quantity of X employed should thus be cut until X^* is reached.

Putting together the arguments of the last two paragraphs, profit rises as X^* is approached from both below and above. So at X^*, where MRP $= w_0$, profit must be at a maximum. In general, the profit maximising firm will hire the variable factor where MRP $= w$. If the wage rate is above w_0, less of the input than X^* is employed; if below w_0, more. It is in this sense that the MRP curve for X is interpreted as the firm's demand curve curve for X.

Innovation may have an impact on both the MRP curve and the input price. As we saw in Chapter 2, technological progress allows for savings to be achieved in the amount of inputs used per unit of output. This shifts the firm's isoquants inwards and its total product curve upwards. If for every input level the new higher TPC is also steeper than the old lower one, then the MP curve moves bodily outwards; technological progress has raised marginal products at every input and output level.

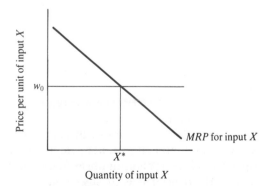

Figure 3.31 Profit maximising input demand decision for variable input X.

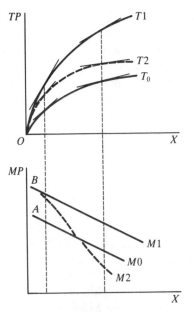

Figure 3.32 Technological progress, shifts in the total product curve and shifts in the marginal product curve.

Compare OT_0 with OT_1 and $AM0$ with $BM1$ in Figure 3.32. This would happen with Hicks-neutral progress, for example, where the marginal products of both labour and capital would be rising at the same proportional rate and hence preserve at a constant value the ratio of the marginal products, which is equal to the marginal rate of technical substitution between capital and labour.

On the other hand, technological progress might raise the marginal product of an input in the lower output ranges, but reduce it in higher ranges. Even though average productivity (output per unit of input at a given output level) would thus rise throughout the TPC, the effect on the marginal product curve crucial for decision-making would be to swivel it, rather than to cause a bodily outward shift. Compare OT_0 with OT_2 and $AM0$ with $BM2$ in Figure 3.32.

The implications of technological progress for the MRP curve are found by again multiplying each value of MP by marginal revenue.

When the firm sells all output at the same price per unit, the firm's marginal revenue is constant and any shift or swivelling in the MP curve will feed through into a corresponding shift or swivel in the MRP curve. When the firm faces a downward sloping demand curve, however, the MRP associated with any given level of input employed might fall. To see this, note that when the TP curve shifts from T_0 to T_1

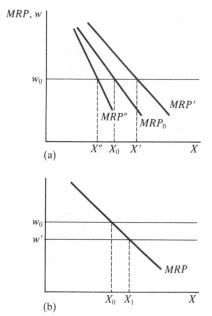

Figure 3.33 Innovation and the demand for a variable input: the firm.

in Figure 3.32, the output produced from each level of input rises as well as the marginal product of the input. To sell the additional output, the firm must reduce price: marginal revenue will fall as a result and may even become negative. If marginal revenue falls by enough, relative to the rise in marginal product, MRP will fall.

Consider now the input supply side. Process and/or product innovation on the part of suppliers can lead to reductions in price per unit of certain inputs and/or improved performance in the production process of the user firm, which would be captured through changes in the MP curve. When price per input unit is reduced, the supply curve for the input slides down relative to any given MRP curve.

The effects of innovation on input hiring and buying can be seen by looking at changes in the profit-maximising decisions firms make. Consider first Figure 3.33a. Here, MRP_0 is the firm's demand curve for X before a technological innovation has occurred, MRP' is a curve after the innovation for a firm selling all output at a given price and MRP'' a curve after innovation for a firm facing a downward-sloping MR curve. At the given input price, w_0, innovation leads to an increase in input demand, from X_0 to X', in the first case and a decline, from X_0 to X'', in the second. In Figure 3.33b, X is taken to be a material input, innovation in producing which has reduced its price from w_0 to w' and increased the quantity demanded.

Input demand in the short run: the industry

The industry demand curve for a variable input is found by adding together the consequences of all decisions made by individual firms. It is unlikely in this process that prices could be treated as constant. Consider two examples.

First, the input price falls because of supplier innovation as shown in Figure 3.33b. While this initially raises demand for X at the firm level, it will be possible to sell the increased output which all firms together now produce only if output prices fall. As we noted in Figure 3.33a, that shifts the MRP curve for every firm inwards. At the firm level, therefore, the quantity of X demanded will rise by less than $(X_1 - X_0)$. And at the industry level the quantity of X demanded will not be X_1 times the number of firms in the industry, but a smaller amount. The amount by which quantity demanded falls short of X_1 times the number for firms will reflect the amount by which output price falls – which is determined by the price elasticity of market demand. The less elastic is market demand, the more price must fall and the less input demand will expand. Indeed, if the MRP curve shifts inwards enough, input demand may contract.

The second example supposes that product innovation and process innovation occur together, the first increasing quantity demanded at any price and the second enhancing productivity in production. In this case the outward shift of the MRP curve shown in Figure 3.33a occurs at the firm level for all firms, reflecting enhanced marginal physical productivity at all levels of X employed. But market price may not fall at all, and may even rise, as increased output is produced – because of the enhanced quality of the product. This will help sustain and reinforce increased input demand.

Input demand in the long run

In the economist's long run, all inputs are variable. When technological progress shifts the firm's isoquants inwards at given input prices, the quantities of all inputs required to produce given output levels will decline – though the relative proportional reduction in input-requirement will vary according to the bias of the progress. But the firm will also expand output: with lower production costs flowing from higher productivity that will be the profit-maximising response at given output prices. This will increase the quantities of all inputs demanded. As noted above however, when all firms expand, market price will fall and the extent to which firms will regard it as worthwhile to purchase more inputs will depend on the price elasticity of market demand. A further factor of importance will be scale economies: the output expansion effect will be smaller, the greater are such economies.

When technological progress in a supplier industry reduces the price of an input we may apply four rules first enunciated by Alfred Marshall (1948) and discussed in Layard and Walters (1978: Ch. 9).

The price elasticity of demand for the input can then be shown to be positively related to:

1. the price elasticity of demand for the product made by the firm;
2. the elasticity of substitution between the input whose price has fallen and other inputs;
3. the elasticity of supply of other inputs;
4. the cost-share of the input.

Intuitively, point (1) says that a falling input price leads to a falling output price, so the demand for the input will depend positively on the price elasticity of demand for output. Point (2) says that when inputs are relatively easy or hard to substitute for each other in producing any given amount of output, a fall in the price of one input leads to large or small shifts towards using it. Point (3) say that when a fall in the price of input *A* causes an increase in demand for output, this leads to an increase in the demand for other inputs and will drive up the prices of other inputs if they are in scarce supply. The faster their prices rise, the faster profitable expansion will be arrested and the less additional demand there will be for input *A*. Point (4) is based on the proposition that the lower the share of an input in a firm's costs, the less a fall in its price will depress the price of the product. While there is a partial truth here, condition (4) must actually be modified to reflect the fact that, when an input's price falls, there will also be a substitution effect in favour of using it, unless production takes a fixed coefficient form.

The upshot of this is that technological progress is likely at given output levels and prices to reduce the quantity demanded of all inputs and will always reduce that for some. The actual quantities involved will depend on the sort of progress made. But this is never the end of the story. Output price will fall and quantity demanded will increase when progress allows costs to fall at constant input prices. Output price will be put under further downward pressure if input prices also fall. Input quantities demanded will rise back towards their pre-innovation levels, though how far this goes depends on the price elasticity of demand for output. If output demand is elastic, post-innovation input demand could ultimately exceed pre-innovation levels. Changing relative input prices will also have implications for the relative proportions in which different inputs are hired. If interinput substitution is easy, demand for any input whose price has fallen relative to those of other inputs should rise quite sharply.

Demand for capital inputs: the investment decision

Many decisions related to innovation are in the nature of **investment** decisions; they involve expenditures now which have beneficial results in the future. This is particularly relevant when we recognise that most firms are in business for the long haul and in every period make decisions which influence their long-term profits, their profits over many periods.

If we think of a firm as a long-run profit maximiser, we have to redefine its maximand to put on commensurable terms all of the annual profits amounts it expects to receive during its life. The very existence of positive rates of interest suggests that most people (including the shareholders of firms in whose interests profits are generated) would prefer to receive $1 today rather than in one year's time; they have to be bribed by the interest payment to induce them to sacrifice access to the $1 for twelve months. But this necessarily implies that $1 not received until next year is worth, in today's terms, less than $1. For example, if $1 grows to $1.15 with interest over a year, because of a 15 per cent annual interest rate, this is equivalent to saying that the present value of $1.15 received in a year's time is $1. Thus $1 received in a year's time has a present value of $[1/1.15] = $0.87. The same example can be extended over any number of periods by assuming that the amount accruing at the end of each year can be reinvested at the same rate as before. The $1 becomes $1.15 after a year; $1.15 becomes worth $1.15 × 1.15 = $1.3225, which is $1 × $(1.15)^2$, after two years; this becomes $1.3225 × 1.15 = $1.5209, which is $1 × $(1.15)^3$, after three years; and, in general, $1 becomes worth $1 × $(1.15)^n$ after n years. Similarly, since $1 received in one year is worth $[1/1.15] today, the same amount received in two years has a present value of $[1/(1.15)^2] or $0.765; $1 received in three years has a present value of $[1/(1.15)^3] or $0.658; and $1 received in n years is today worth $[1/(1.15)^n].

When dealing with amounts spent and received this year with amounts to be spent and received in future years, therefore, like can be compared with like only if every sum is measured in terms of their present values. If the interest rate is r, this can be done by applying a **discount factor**, $[1/(1 + r)^n]$ to any amount received in n years' time. Thus, amounts received and spent in the current year will not be discounted at all, but amounts received and spent in future years will be more and more heavily discounted, i.e. they will be 'scaled down' more and more by the discount factor, the longer into the future we look and the higher n becomes.

Many of the inputs firms acquire last for more than one period. In this case, the question is: Will an additional unit of input add to the long-term value of the business? If it does, it should be acquired; if not, it should not. To know whether it will add to the value of the business, we have to find the **net present value** of putting the unit of input to use in the firm. This can be done by entering initial outlay on the input as a negative amount of expenditure, $-K_0$, then seeing whether the present value of the profits the input generates exceeds or falls short of that outlay. It is easiest to imagine that the unit of input involved is a machine, a 'lump of capital'. In each period, profit is the difference between sales revenue raised by using the machine, $R(t)$, and the costs of other inputs used in operating the machine, $C(t)$. The net present value of investing in additional capital input would then be:

$$NPV = -K_0 + \{[(R(1) - C(1))/(1 + r)] + [(R(2) - C(2))/(1 + r)^2] + \ldots +$$

$$[(R(T) - C(T))/(1 + r)^T]\}$$

where T is the number of periods for which the input contributes to profit and r is assumed constant. Notice that $R(t)$ is the product of price per unit of output $P(t)Q(t)$, and that $C(t)$ is the result of adding together the products of input price and quantity used for all cooperant inputs, i.e. inputs used with capital to produce output.

Firms will add to their stock of capital inputs when the *NPV* for such inputs is positive. Innovation may thus add to the demand for capital inputs by any of the following: (1) reducing the cost of a unit of capital K_0 – the result of cost-saving innovation in the capital goods-making industry; (2) increasing the price per unit at which expected output volumes might be sold, the result of product innovation associated with using the new capital good; (3) increasing sales volume at a given price, which could also be achieved by product innovation; (4) reducing the price per unit of cooperant inputs – the result of process innovation in supplier firms; (5) reducing the units of cooperant inputs required to generate given output flows, the result of process innovation in the firm itself and/or product innovation by its suppliers.[7] As always, there are caveats. On (4) above, a fall in the price of cooperant inputs makes investment look more attractive because it reduces the present value of all costs relative to benefits generated by the project. But if there are substitution possibilities, as noted in previous section, a fall in the price of cooperant inputs relative to that of capital will induce substitution of non-capital for capital inputs. This will tend to counteract any increase in demand for capital goods. On (5), outcomes are actually part of more complex calculations involving decisions on how much firms should spend on innovation. This is discussed in Chapter 5. As discussion there also reveals investors' expectations play an important role.

Given the emphasis already laid upon uncertainty in this book, it should be clear that the values which are assigned to the $R(t)$ and $C(t)$ (and also the $r(t)$) must always be in the nature of guesstimates. One way of incorporating anticipations in a formal way is to assume that decision-makers, maximise the mathematical expectation of *NPV*. To do this, they form probability distributions over $R(1)$, $R(2)$, ..., $R(T)$, $C(1)$, $C(2)$, ..., $C(T)$ (and, in principle, $r(1)$, $r(2)$, ..., $r(T)$), so that for each period t, they assign probability weights to each of the values which $R(t)$, $C(t)$ (and $r(t)$) might take. For any given variable, the products of each of the values and its probability weight are added to give the expected value of that variable in that period. If the probability distribution is symmetric and single-peaked, most weight will be given to values close to the mean and least to those relatively distant from the mean in the two tails of the distribution. Once the expected values have been found, they may be discounted as before. Denoting expected values by the prefix E, and assuming $r(t)$ is expected to be constant, the calculation for each period is then:

$$[ER(t) - EC(t)]/[1 + r(t)]$$

and the terms over all periods are then added to give the *ENPV*.

Decision-makers are classed according to their attitude to risk. **Risk-neutral** decision-makers will be indifferent between any two purchases with identical *ENPV*s. But other decision-makers will be influenced by the shape of the distribution and the expected value. To see how, consider two purchases with the same *ENPV*. The first, A has a distribution in which anticipations are clustered around the mean and only very small probability weights are attached to potential profit outcomes far from the mean. The second, *B* has a distribution with a wider dispersion of anticipations; compared with *A* larger probability weights attach to outcomes relatively distant from the mean. In statistical terms, *B* has a greater standard deviation than *A* and can be thought of as relatively high risk. Decision-makers who prefer *A* to *B* are called **risk-averse**, and those who prefer *B* to *A* **risk-lovers**.

If we think of decision-makers as having utility functions which guide them, or as being guided by the utility functions of the firms' owners, it is useful to characterise attitude to risk in terms of utility functions comprising indifference curves. To be kept at any given level of utility, risk-averse decision-makers will require to be given increases in *ENPV* to compensate them for any increase in riskiness, represented by the standard deviations of the anticipated profit distributions. Utility will be increased if *ENPV* rises at a given level of risk, or risk is reduced at a given level of *ENPV*, or if *ENPV* rises and risk falls. The converse will be true of risk-lovers, for whom utility will be raised when risk rises for any given level of *ENPV.*

The implications of this for the demand for inputs is that in a world of predominantly risk-averse decision-makers and opportunities perceived to be of high-risk, the demand for inputs associated with these opportunities would in general be less than a world in which prospects were perceived to be less risky or in which decision-makers were risk-lovers. Taking the risk attitudes of decision-makers as given and assuming risk-aversion to be dominant, high-risk innovative projects and the inputs associated with them will need to offer very high mean returns, relative to other projects.

A fundamental problem, however, is that the method of maximising expected utility and the value of a firm's assets again encounters the difficulties presented earlier in relation to consumer rationality. Decision-makers confront highly complex alternatives, each surrounded by a degree of uncertainty. Especially, if a firm is contemplating the purchase of new-technology capital designed to generate new products, it may be possible either to enumerate or imagine the technical and market-related problems which contribute to the uncertainty of the investment (or alternatives to it). On the other hand, many capital good purchases are much more straightforward; the technology they embody will often be well-known, advancing only incrementally, and equipment backed by a maintenance service of good reputation. Uncertainty then attaches only to market-related factors such as cyclical demand swings and the availability of cooperant inputs. Orthodox optimising choice models of investment retain their relevance, therefore, but must be treated increasingly as an abstraction the more acute are the problems posed by the complexity of the choice and the uncertainties surrounding each one.

Appendix

In the main body of the text we used an expression for *NPV*, derived by taking discrete observations on revenues and costs expected for each year of the project involved. But it is often analytically more convenient to work with the continuous case, in which we take the dollar return (revenues less costs) earned in each infinitesimally short period $[t, t + dt]$ and add all of their discounted values over the life of the project. Letting $\pi(t)dt$ stand for the profit earned in the interval $[t, t + dt]$, the continuous version if the *NPV* expression given in the text is:

$$NPV = -K_o + \int_0^T e^{-rt}\pi(t)dt \tag{A3.1}$$

where e is a constant 2.71828 .... To see why this should be, consider first an economic interpretation of e.

If \$1 were invested at the rate of 100 per cent p.a., compounded once a year, the value of the \$1 would rise at year end to:

$$\$1 \, (1 + 100\%) = \$2$$

If interest were compounded semiannually, however, the \$1 would grow to \$1.50 after six months (\$1 plus half of 100 per cent \$1) and at the end of year to:

$$\$[1(1 + 50\%)] \, (1 + 50\%) = \$\left(1 + \frac{1}{2}\right)^2 = \$2.25$$

Extending this principle to an arbitrarily high frequency of interest compounding, *m* times per annum, \$1 would grow to:

$$\$\left(1 + \frac{1}{m}\right)^m \tag{A3.2}$$

at the end of the year. Substituting into this expression $m = 3$, $m = 4$, ..., etc., it is easy to confirm that its value converges as *m* rises. In fact, as *m* approaches infinity, the value of the expression converges on the number e $= 2.71828...$. Thus e is the year-end value to which an asset of \$1 will grow if interest at a rate of 100 per cent per annum is compounded continuously.

Now if \$1 is invested at a continuously compounding 100 per cent interest rate for two years, its value at the end of year two must be \$e.e $=$ \$$e^2$, and at the end of *t* year \$$e^t$. Extending the same formula, \$$X$ will grow after *t* years to \$$Xe^t$ if invested at a 100 per cent continuously compounding rate. Finally, if (A3.2) is modified to allow for both these extensions, and the interest rate is set at *any* level, *r*, it will read:

$$\$X\left(1 + \frac{r}{m}\right)^{mt}$$

This can be rewritten:

$$\$X\left[\left(1 + \frac{r}{m}\right)^{m/r}\right]^{rt} = \$X\left[\left(1 + \frac{1}{Z}\right)^Z\right]^{rt}$$

where $Z = \dfrac{m}{r}$.

As *m* approaches infinity, so does *Z* and thus the square-bracketed expression tends to e. Thus with continuous compounding (i.e. with *m* approaching infinity) at an interest rate *r*, \$*X* will grow by the end of *t* to:

$$\$Xe^{rt} \tag{A3.3}$$

This information is directly relevant to discounting exercises. To see why, let *V* be the value to which *X* grows. If there is annual compounding at the rate *r*:

$$V = X(1 + r)^t \tag{A3.4}$$

But then:

$$X = \frac{V}{(1 + r)^t} = V(1 + r)^{-t} \tag{A3.5}$$

Recalling the work in the text, *X* is thus the present value of *V*, where *r* is the discount rate. In a discounting problem, we know (or supply the values of) *V*, *r* and *t* and must find the present value, here denoted *X*.

In the continuously compounding case, from (A3.3):

$$V = Xe^{rt}$$

and so

$$X = \frac{V}{e^{rt}} = Ve^{-rt} \tag{A3.6}$$

where, again, the present value *X* is to be computed from Knowledge of *V*, *r* and *t*.

Now (A3.6) indicates how to find the present value of a single, given sum received at the end of period *t*. Investment exercises involve discounting a stream of such sums.

Returning to (A3.1), we can now see that $e^{-rt}\pi(t)dt$ is the present value of profit earned in the interval $[t, t + dt]$ applying a discount rate *r*. The integral sign is an instruction to add and the limits on the sign, $[0, T]$, tell us to add up all the discounted profit amounts earned in each short interval between the beginning of the project ($t = 0$) and the end ($t = T$). The whole of the right-hand side of (A3.1) is the result of taking this continuously discounted stream of profits and subtracting from it the initial capital outlay.

Notes

1. Readers should not be anxious about this. The basic framework presented here can be extended and modified in many directions and can easily allow for saving to occur by postponing consumption from one period (shown on one axis) to another (shown on the remaining axis).
2. This is the least appealing of the assumptions made in this model. Characteristics of one good can only rarely be obtained by purchasing two other goods and mixing or combining them. Lancaster (1979) offers a related but more technically demanding analysis which takes care of this problem and interested readers are directed to that reference.

3. For an application, see Stoneman's intrafirm diffusion model in Chapter 5.
4. The exposition follows Deaton and Muellbauer (1980), Chapter 13.

References

Anderson, S.P., A. de Palma, and J.F. Thisse (1988) 'A representative consumer theory of the logit model', *International Economic Review* 29.

Bain, A. (1964) *The Growth of TV Ownership in the UK Since the War*, Cambridge: Cambridge University Press.

Bonus, H. (1973) 'Quasi Engel curves, diffusion and the ownership of major consumer durables', *Journal of Political Economy* 655–77.

Bookstaber, R. and J. Langsam (1983) *Coarse Behavior and Extended Uncertainty*, Provo, Utah: Brigham Young University, Photocopy.

Darby, M. and E. Karni (1973) 'Free competition and the optimal amount of fraud', *Journal of Law and Economics* 16, 67–88.

Dasgupta, P. and E. Maskin, (1986), 'The existence of equilibrium in discontinuous games, II: Applications', *Review of Economic Studies* 53, 27–42.

Deaton, A. (1975) 'The structure of demand, 1925–70', *Fontana Economic History of Europe* 6, Section 2.

Deaton, A. and R. Muellbauer (1980) *Economics and Consumer Behaviour*, Cambridge: Cambridge University Press.

Dixit, A. and J. E. Stiglitz (1977) 'Monopolistic competition and optimum product diversity', *American Economic Review* 67, 297–308.

Dobbs, I.M., M.B. Hill and M. Waterson (1987) 'Industrial structure and the employment consequences of technical change', *Oxford Economic Papers* 39, 552–67.

Eaton, B.C. and R.G. Lipsey (1978) 'Freedom of entry and the existence of pure profit', *Economic Journal* 88, 455–69.

Eaton, B.C. and R.G. Lipsey (1989) 'Product differentiation', in R. Schmalensee and R. Willig (eds.) *Handbook of Industrial Organisation*, ch. 12, Amsterdam: North Holland.

Elster, J. (1983) *Explaining Technical Change*, Cambridge, Cambridge University Press.

Friedman, M. and L.J. Savage (1948) 'The utility analysis of choices involving risk', *Journal of Political Economy* 56, 279–304.

Hayek, F.A. (1967) *Studies in Philosophy, Politics and Economics*, Chicago: University of Chicago Press.

Hayek, F.A. (1978) 'Competition as a discovery procedure', *New Studies in Philosophy, Politics, Economics and the History of Ideas*, Ch. 12, Chicago: University of Chicago Press.

Hotelling, H. (1929) 'Stability in competition', *Economic Journal* 39, 41–57.

Howard, J.A. and W.L. Moore (1988) 'Changes in consumer behaviour over the product life cycle', in M.L. Tushman and W.L. Moore (eds) *Readings in the Management of Innovation* 2nd edn, Cambridge, MA: Ballinger Publishing, Ch. 6, 343–51.

Ironmonger, D. (1973) *New Commodities and Consumer Behaviour*, Cambridge: Cambridge University Press.

Lancaster, K. (1971) *Consumer Demand: A New Approach*, New York: Columbia University Press.

Lancaster, K. (1966), 'A new approach to consumer theory', *Journal of Political Economy* 74, 132–57.

Lancaster, K. (1979) *Variety, Equity and Efficiency*, New York: Columbia University Press.

Langlois, R. (1986) *Economics as a Process: Essays in the New Institutional Economics*, Cambridge: Cambridge University Press.

Layard, P.R.G. and A.A. Walters (1978) *Microeconomic Theory*, New York and London: McGraw Hill.

Loasby, B. (1976) *Choice, Complexity and Ignorance*, Cambridge: Cambridge University Press.

Marshall, A. (1948) *Principles of Economics* 8th edn, London: Macmillan, 384–6, 852–3.

Muth, J. (1961) 'Rational expectations and the theory of price movements', *Econometrica* 29; 315–35.

Nelson, P. (1970) 'Information and Consumer Behavior', *Journal of Political Economy*, 78, 311–29.

O'Driscoll, G.P. and J.J. Rizzo (1985) *The Economics of Time and Ignorance*, Oxford: Blackwell.

Prescott, E.C. and M. Visscher (1977) 'Sequential location among firms with foresight', *Bell Journal of Economics* 8, 378–93.

Pyatt, F.G. (1964) *Priority Patterns and the Demand for Household Durable Goods*, Cambridge: Cambridge University Press.

Sattinger, M. (1984) 'Value of an additional firm in monopolistic competition', *Review of Economic Studies*, 43, 217–35.

Savage, L.J. (1954) *Foundations of Statistics*, New York: Wiley.

Shackle, G.L. (1955) *Uncertainty in Economics*, Cambridge, Cambridge University Press.

Simon, H.A. (1955), 'A Behavioral theory of rational choice', *Quarterly Journal of Economics* 69, 99–118. Reprinted in *Models of Man*, Part IV. New York: Wiley, 1957.

Smith, A. (1980) *Goodbye Gutenberg*, Oxford: Oxford University Press.

Spence, M. (1976) 'Product selection, fixed costs and monopolistic competition', *Review of Economics Studies* 43, 217–35.

Spence, J. (1977) 'Non-price competition', *American Economic Review*, 67, 225–259.

Stigler, G.J. (1964) 'A theory of oligopoly', *Journal of Political Economy* 72, 44–61.

Stoneman, P.A. (1983) *The Economic Analysis of Technological Change*, Oxford: Oxford University Press.

Teubal, M. (1979), 'On user needs and need determination: Aspects of the theory of technological innovation', in M.J. Baker (ed.), *Industrial Innovation*, London: Macmillan.

Tirole, J. (1988) *The Theory of Industrial Organisation*, Cambridge, MA: MIT Press.

Tisdell, C. (1975) 'Concepts of rationality in economics', *Philosophy of the Social Sciences* 5, 259–72.

Triplett, J.E. (1975) 'Consumer demand and characteristics of consumption goods', in N. Terleckyi (ed.) *Household Production and Consumption* New York: NBER Studies in Income and Wealth, No. 40.

van Duijn, J. (1983) *The Long Wave in Economic Life*, London: George Allen and Unwin.

Vangrevelinghe, M.G. (1965) 'Projection de la consommation des menages en 1970: Les despenses d'habitation', *Etudes et conjuncture* 20(9), 3–73.

von Neumann, J. and O. Morgenstern, (1944) *Theory of Games and Economic Behavior*, Princeton: Princeton University Press.

Waterson, M. (1984) *Economic Theory of the Industry*, Cambridge, Cambridge University Press.

Winter, M. (1964), 'Economic natural selection and the theory of the firm', *Yale Economic Essays* 4: 225–72.

4

Innovation and production costs

Introduction

In this chapter, we focus on the cost-reducing potential of technological innovation. As motivation, it is taken as axiomatic that producers will always be interested in cutting production costs, either to make themselves more competitive, to raise profit, or both. Cost functions relating production costs to the scale of output are derived and the influence of technological innovation analysed. Unit costs fall at given input prices because productivity increases and we look at how innovation, increased technical efficiency and scale economies interact to bring this about. While the early part of the chapter concentrates on single-output production, the implications for costs of producing two or more products are dealt with later. It is then made explicit that while innovation is a major route to reducing production costs, innovation is costly in itself and we look at the conceptual and empirical underpinnings of input–output and output–cost relationships which might be found in R&D.

An aspect of cost structures dealt with in the last part of the chapter is interfirm variation. Such diversity is central to evolutionary theory. A section here is the first in a series designed to weave evolutionary perspectives into the analysis and we argue that, in terms of that approach, interfirm differences in costs are important for two reasons. First, because they suggest some firms will be more profitable than others and potentially capable of more rapid growth, they provide a basis for selection processes operating on the population of firms and hence for understanding structural changes within (and among) industries. Second, cost variations reflect differences in past production decisions made by firms and, more generally, differences in their history and experience of innovation, leading some to reduce costs more rapidly than others. Given that each firm has its own history, we should expect interfirm cost differentials and the dynamic processes to which they give birth. While standard microeconomic theory concedes that firms may vary, with implications for the nature of market equilibrium outcomes, evolutionary theory sees in such differences the very heart of the economic analysis of change.

121

The cost function

Central to any description of a firm is its cost structure. In this section we consider the cost structure of a single-product firm, assuming throughout that the price per unit of inputs purchased by the firm is exogenously given and unvarying with the rate of input usage. The impact of exogenous technological change is then examined.

Production function, long-run costs and simple progress

Economists distinguish between **fixed** costs, which take a given value at all output levels and cannot be changed during the period of analysis, and **variable** costs whose level alters within the period of analysis as output levels change. Since we are taking price per unit of input as constant, fixed costs relate to inputs which are available to the firm in a fixed quantity for the period, while variable costs relate to inputs which may be varied with production requirements. Economists also distinguish between the **short run**, in which at least one input is in fixed supply and the **long run**, in which all inputs may be varied.

For the purposes of deriving cost curves, we shall assume unless otherwise stated that all inputs are homogeneous, completely divisible and the costs arising from their use variable. The cost curves derived are therefore long-run ones. As a matter of definition, the cost curves of economic theory show how costs vary with scale of output, on the strict assumption that firms minimise costs at all output levels. Both technical and economic efficiency are assumed. Initially (although this is a particular case), we also work with a production function which is such that, as firms expand output at given input prices, they will do so along a ray from the origin, i.e. employing inputs in the same proportions, though in varying amounts.

In Figure 4.1, economic efficiency occurs at points $A–F$. In this example, the price per unit of capital, r, is \$20 and the price per unit of labour, w, \$6. Isocost lines for expenditures ranging from \$100 to \$420 are shown, each dollar amount reflecting the total cost of producing output levels shown on isoquants to which they are tangent. The unbracketed labels on isoquants show output levels before a technological advance and the bracketed ones levels after it. For the purposes of exposition, we have allowed the technological progress shown here to be of a particularly simple kind, increasing output for any given combination of inputs by a factor of 1.2.

The isoquant map has also been drawn to reflect a production function in which there are first increasing then decreasing returns to scale. To see this, note that twice the distance OB is OB'. But output at B is 20 units and double that amount, 40, is achieved at with inputs corresponding to D, which lies well towards the origin compared with B'. This implies increasing returns to scale. Between E and F, the diagram has been drawn to show an equiproportional increase of each input by a factor of 1.4, while output rises by a factor of only 1.2, an obvious indication of decreasing returns to scale. In the case of constant returns-to-scale throughout, equal

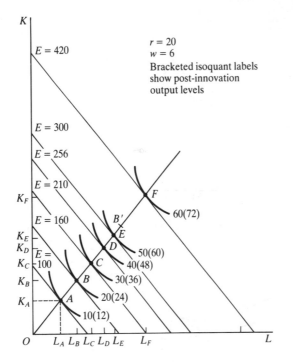

Figure 4.1 Increasing then decreasing returns to scale.

Numerical values associated with each point

| (A) | $L_A = 10$ | $WL_A = 60$ | 100 |
| | $K_A = 2$ | $rK_A = 40$ | |

| (B) | $L_B = 16$ | $wL_B = 96$ | 160 |
| | $K_B = 3.2$ | $rK_B = 64$ | |

| (C) | $L_C = 21$ | $wL_C = 126$ | 210 |
| | $K_C = 4.2$ | $rK_C = 84$ | |

| (D) | $L_D = 25.6$ | $wL_D = 153.6$ | 256 |
| | $K_D = 5.12$ | $rK_D = 102.4$ | |

| (E) | $L_E = 30$ | $wL_D = 180$ | 300 |
| | $K_E = 6.0$ | $rK_D = 120$ | |

| (F) | $L_F = 42$ | $wL_F = 252$ | 420 |
| | $K_F = 8.4$ | $rK_F = 168$ | |

proportional increases in all inputs would at all levels be associated with the same proportional increase in output.

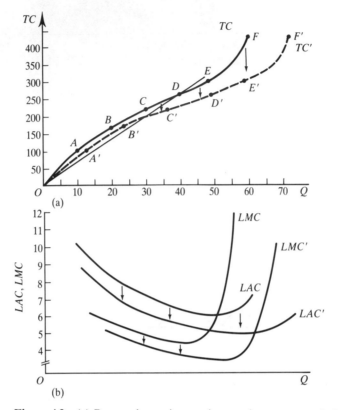

Figure 4.2 (a) Pre- and post-innovation total cost curves derived from Figure 4.1; (b) Pre- and post-innovation long-run average and marginal cost curves derived from Figure 4.2(a).

Table 4.1 shows the total costs TC incurred in producing the pre-innovation and post innovation levels of output, Q_o and Q_N represented in Figure 4.1. From this information we have constructed the pre- and post-innovation TC curves $OABCDEF$ and $OA'B'C'D'E'F'$ shown in Figure 4.2a. Notice that the range of outputs over which total costs rise at a decreasing rate is associated with increasing returns to scale in the production function and that where total costs rise at an increasing rate, there are decreasing returns to scale. In the case of constant returns all along OF, the TC curve would be linear, a ray of constant slope from the origin. As the diagram also shows, the post-innovation curve lies below the pre-innovation curve, so we see that the effect of technological progress has been to allow output at all levels to be produced at lower total cost, or for any total expenditure to yield more output.

In Table 4.1 we also show the long-run **average** and **marginal** costs of producing at each output level, before and after technological progress. **Long-run average cost (LAC)**, is found by dividing TC by output at each level and geometrically would be represented by the slope of a ray to a point on the TC curve, such as OD, in relation

Table 4.1 Calculations of the numerical values used in deriving the LAC and LMC curves in Figure 4.2(b)

Q_o	Q_N	TC	LAC_o	LAC_N	LMC_o^*	LMC_N^*
10	12	100	10	8.3		
					6	5
20	24	160	8	6.7		
					5	4.2
30	36	210	7	5.8		
					4.6	3.8
40	48	256	6.4	5.3		
					4.4	3.7
50	60	300	6	5.0		
					12	10
60	72	420	7	5.8		

*MC = (dTC/dQ)

to an output level of 40 produced with the pre-innovation technology. By inspection, the slopes of such rays would decline along *ABCDEF* as far as *E* (as far as *E'* on the post-innovation *TC* curve), then start to rise again. The same information is found from the arithmetic in Table 4.1, beneath the headings LAC_o and LAC_N long run average costs before and after innovation respectively. The effect of increasing (decreasing) returns to scale is observably to generate declining (rising) long-run *AC* under any given state of technology and hence to yield a downward (upward) slope in the LAC curve linking output per period to *LAC*. This is shown in the curves labelled LAC and LAC' in Figure 4.2b, which are derived from *TC* and *TC'* in Figure 4.2a and plot graphically the information in Table 4.1. The LAC curve is sometimes also called the **scale curve**, because it shows how unit production costs vary with variations in the scale of operation, i.e. plant size, of cost-efficient firms. When the *TC* function is a straight line from the origin, long-run average costs are constant (equal to the slope of the *TC* line) and the LAC curve is horizontal.

Long-run marginal cost (LMC) is found by asking how much *TC* rises when output rises by a small amount, formally (d*TC*/d*Q*), and is represented geometrically by the slope of a tangent to the *TC* curve where the change is taking place. The marginal cost of increasing output from 30 to 40 units under the old technology is shown by the slope of the segment *CD*. Since the slope of the *TC* curve changes all the time, we would look at the slope round about the mid-point of this segment to approximate *LMC*. The arithmetic would be:

$$[(256 - 210)/(40 - 30)] = \lfloor 46/10 \rfloor = \$4.6$$

Marginal costs for pre- and post-innovation technology are shown under LMC_o and LMC_N in Table 4.1 and curves labelled LMC and LMC' in Figure 4.2b have again been derived from *TC* and *TC'* in Figure 4.2a using information found in Table 4.1. If the *TC* function were a ray from the origin, *LMC* would be constant and equal to *LAC* at all points.

As noted above, the effect of increasing then decreasing returns is to make the LAC curve first fall, then rise again. Notice that *LMC* lies below *LAC* where *LAC* is falling and above *LAC* when *LAC* is rising. The logic of this is simple. Consider any average, such as a batsman's average score over a number of innings or a student's average mark over a number assignments. If the next (i.e. marginal) score or mark is below the current average, it will drag the average down; if it is above the current average, the average will rise. Further, the average must be constant when the marginal is equal to it. It follows that, if the average first falls then rises, the marginal must first be below and then above it.

The marginal must be equal to the average at the point where a falling average turns into a rising average, i.e. at its minimum point. This logic is reflected in both of the sets of LAC and LMC curves in Figure 4.2b. In the event of an average remaining constant over some range, the marginal will also be constant and equal to the average. This is because an average can remain at a given value only if marginal additions to the overall total are constant and equal to the prevailing average.

Returns to scale and scale economies in the cost function

In the example in Figure 4.1, the cost-minimising choices of technique *A, B* ... *F* have been assumed to lie on a ray from the origin. This has enabled us to link variations in average costs to variations in returns to scale in the production function. Taking input prices as fixed, we have shown that increasing returns to scale are a sufficient condition for falling *LAC*. The locus of cost-minimising input combinations, or choices of technique, is called the firm's **expansion path**. In the example, the expansion path has been deliberately constructed to be linear. But this is not a general case.

Expansion paths will be linear whenever the production function is homogeneous. A production function is homogeneous if, whenever all inputs are increased by a multiple *m*, output rises by a multiple of *m* raised to some given power. The power defines the degree of homogeneity of the function and in the simplest case when the power is unity, the production function exhibits constant returns to scale. When the power is greater (less) than unity, there are increasing (decreasing) returns to scale throughout the production function.[1]

Diagrammatically, returns to scale can be identified by looking at the levels of output represented on isoquants reached along a ray from the origin representing equal proportional increases in inputs. In the case of linear homogeneity, output would vary in the same proportion as the inputs throughout the production function, i.e. along any given ray. For this to be true of all rays simultaneously, the mrts at intersection points with any given ray must not vary from isoquant to isoquant. In Figure 4.1, the expansion path is linear but the isoquants do not represent a homogeneous production function, since we have demonstrated that it has increasing and decreasing returns to scale over different ranges. Thus homogeneity is a sufficient but not necessary condition for a linear expansion path, given fixed input prices.

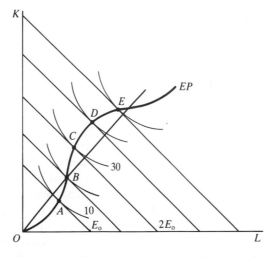

Figure 4.3 Cost minimisation and the expansion path: the general case.

While a linear expansion path occurs in Figure 4.1 despite the non-homogeneity of the production function depicted there, non-homogeneity is very often the reason for a non-linear expansion path. Non-homogeneity will certainly be present if a line from the origin through points of equal mrts is 'wavy', like *OABCDE* in Figure 4.3. With relative input prices constant, *OABCDE* would also be the expansion path if relative input prices were the same as the mrts at points *A* to *E*. When the expansion path becomes non-linear, it is no longer possible directly to relate returns to scale in the production function to falling *LAC*.

In Figure 4.3, for example, it is cost minimising to produce 10 units of output at point *A* and 30 units at point *C*. Total costs (expenditure on inputs) rise only by a factor of 2, so there are clearly falling average costs between *A* and *C*. On the other hand, it is not possible to attribute this directly to increasing returns to scale in the production function, since *C* does not lie on the same ray from the origin as *A*; inputs have not been increased in equal proportions in moving from *A* to *C*.

Bearing this discussion in mind, there would seem to be a case when focusing on cost structures for defining economies of scale in terms directly of the cost function itself rather than in terms of the underlying technology. To do this, recall that when *LMC* lies below *LAC*, *LAC* is falling and when *LMC* is above *LAC*, *LAC* is rising. Now suppose we take as a sign of scale economies the observation that *LAC* are falling. Then we may say scale economies exist in a given output range if average costs exceed marginal costs in that range. Merely because we have redefined scale economies in terms of the cost function does not mean, however, that we should not seek technological reasons for their existence. There are many technological reasons for scale economies and these are identified later.

The impact of progress: variations on a theme

Before we proceed, let us reiterate a central point. However we define our terms, the effect of technological advance will generally be to shift cost curves downwards. This is simply because it increases productivity at given input prices, assuming that firms make the most efficient use of their resources. As we noted in Chapter 2, however, technological progress takes many forms (reflected in how the isoquants shift and change shape), so its precise impact on the shapes of TC, LAC and LMC curves may vary widely. To give one interesting example, we draw on Figure 4.4. In the case of that production function, techniques become increasingly capital intensive (higher capital:labour ratio) as we move to higher output levels produced at given relative input prices. *LAC* falls between *A* and *B*, where it would be unchanged between *A* and *C*. But we could also imagine that, initially, under an older technology, a 20 unit isoquant was tangent to an isocost line of identical slope at *C*, then shifted, because of technological progress, to be tangent to another similarly sloped isocost line at *B*. Suppose the 10 unit isoquant remained unchanged. Then we would have shown the cost reducing effect of labour-saving technological progress restricted to larger scales of output. Under the old technology, the LAC curve for the output range between 10 and 20 units would have been horizontal. With the new technology for producing higher output levels, it would be downward sloping. Readers may wish to experiment for themselves to deal with other cases, and for an extended treatement should consult Ferguson (1969).

Notice also that the cost curves will be shifted downwards if progress in supplier industries reduces the price per unit of firms' non-labour inputs. Its effect on the

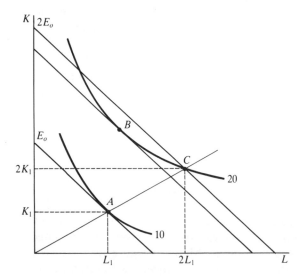

Figure 4.4 Increasing capital-intensity in production at higher output levels.

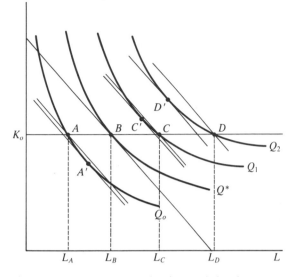

Figure 4.5   Short-run production and the short-run expansion path
ABCD: labour variable and capital fixed.

diagram will be to shift all isocost lines away from the origin, at the same time changing their slopes, except in the freak case where all input prices are reduced in the same proportion. Cost reductions ultimately achieved will reflect reductions in costs per unit of input and induced changes in the proportions in which inputs are employed with each other. Whether such changes are large or small will depend on the curvature of the isoquants, i.e. on the degree of substitutability among inputs which the technology permits. Over time, of course, this itself may be influenced by process innovation.

Short-run and long-run costs

Since above we allowed all inputs to be variable by assumption, we have by definition derived long-run cost curves. An alternative derivation recognises that in the short run at least one input (usually taken to be capital) is fixed in terms of quantity supplied. A (short-run) total product curve for each level of fixed capital input is then derived by allowing variable inputs to increase. In Figure 4.5, capital has been held constant at K_o. If input prices are held constant, the slopes of all isocost lines are identical and points A' to D' mark the economically efficient expansion path of the firm if all inputs are variable. When $K = K_o$, however, the firm's short-run expansion path is along the horizontal from K_o, including points A, B, C and D. The effect of holding K constant is to prevent optimal variations in the input proportions with the result that A, C and D all lie on higher isocost lines than the cost-minimising

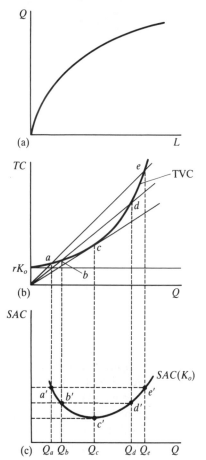

Figure 4.6 Declining marginal product of labour, (a), causes an upward-curving TVC curve in (b). Together with fixed costs rK_0, these factors imply a U-shaped short-run average cost curve in (c).

input combinations shown at A', C' and D'. In other words, the same output is produced at a higher total cost. Only when output is at the level Q^* is K_o the cost-minimising amount of capital to employ and is therefore the optimal scale of production when $K = K_o$

Suppose now that the isoquant map in Figure 4.5 is characterised by constant returns to scale and that $(Q_2 - Q_1) = (Q_1 - Q^*) = (Q^* - Q_0)$. By observation the quantity of additional labour required to move from C to D on the short-run expansion path exceeds that needed to move from B to C. In turn, moving from B to C calls for more labour than moving from A to B. This implies diminishing marginal product of labour along $ABCD$. The same result applies if returns to scale are decreasing throughout the isoquant map. If returns to scale are increasing, the effect

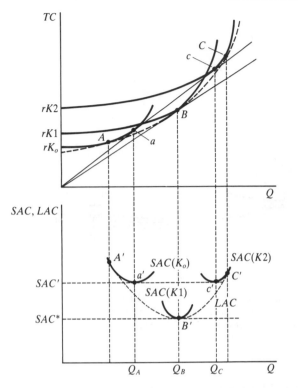

Figure 4.7 Variations in the scale of capital input and the derivation of a U-shaped long-run average cost curve.

of having one factor of production fixed may still be enough to bring about a decreasing marginal product of labour. But if the increasing returns are strong enough, then there could be a range in which the marginal product of labour initially rises.

Suppose MPL falls continuously, as shown in the total product curve in Figure 4.6a. Then as output increases, each increment will require a greater input of labour which, at a given wage per unit, means that the total cost of employing the variable input – **total variable cost (TVC)** – will rise by more at each step. Thus the TVC curve, shown in Figure 4.6b slopes upwards and becomes increasingly steep. To find the total costs of production, we must also add in the cost of capital, rK_o, which is fixed for all output levels. If the TVC curve is added vertically on to rK_o, the slopes of rays to the curve show short-run average costs, plotted for a range of output values in Figure 4.6c to yield the **short-run average cost (SAC)** curve associated with K_o. Readers should confirm for themselves that continually falling MPL is a sufficient condition for SAC ultimately to rise and in the absence of fixed costs, SAC will rise from the lowest output levels; any positive level of fixed costs is sufficient to ensure SAC will initially fall and that they would continue to fall unless MPL were to start declining.

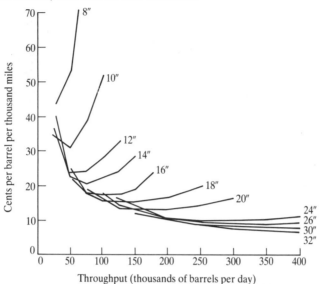

Figure 4.8 Costs per barrel of operating crude oil trunk pipelines. (Reprinted with permission of the publisher from L. Cookenboo Jr (1958) *Crude Oil Pipelines and Competition in the Oil Industry*, Harvard: Harvard Institute for International Development.)

A SAC curve can be derived for each level of fixed capital, as in Figure 4.7. The larger *K* is, the more elevated is the starting point for adding on TVC. Also, the larger *K* is, the higher is the output level at which SAC will be minimised, since the fixed input imposes less and less of a constraint on efficiently producing lower levels of output, the more of the fixed input there is. Furthermore, it is usually found that as plant size increases (i.e. as *K* rises), the minimum level of SAC will itself fall as larger scales of plant allow various economies to be reaped. As drawn SAC(K1) is the curve with the lowest minimum point, *SAC**, with the minimum point on SAC(K2) – *SAC'* – lying well above. This is taken to reflect the existence of diseconomies supposed to set in when plants become very large. Supposing this is the case, an envelope curve drawn to touch each SAC curve at the lowest point possible, given that it must also touch the other curves, is shown as a dashed line which represents the LAC curve. Notice that if diseconomies do not set in, the LAC curve will either continue to slope downwards or will reach a level at which no more scale economies are to be reaped, so the LAC curve becomes horizontal. In the latter case, the point at which scale economies are exhausted is the **minimum efficient scale (MES) of operation.**

A simple but striking example of SAC curves is shown in Figure 4.8. Each SAC curve shows how the unit cost of transporting oil through a pipeline of given diameter varies with the quantity of oil carried. Pipelines of increasing diameter give rise to SAC curves with lower minimum points, reflecting scale economies.

As before, all SAC curves and the LAC curve derived from them are derived on the assumption of given technology. Technological advance will shift the LAC curve downwards as a reflection of cost savings made available at each scale of operation. The LAC might shift downwards throughout only part of its length if technical progress applied only to some plant sizes. In particular, if it is costly to develop new technology, if the ideas can be put to use only by embodiment in new machines and potential user firms are all large, then we might expect progress to be biased to increasing the efficiency of a large-scale plant. This would lead to a lowering of the LAC curve only at higher levels of output, though it might still be efficient for a small scale, old-technology plant to operate (at low output levels) if scale economies in the larger, new technology were so great that large plant short-run average costs rose sharply once output levels fell below those associated with the SAC minimum.

This discussion raises the conceptual difficulty that cost curves are constructed on the assumption that all units of capital input are qualitatively identical, yet, clearly, the new machines are qualitatively different from the old and it is therefore an open question whether a single LAC curve should incorporate both types of plant. This, however, is merely one version of a problem which is actually much more pervasive. As Adam Smith pointed out, it is almost never the case that a larger plant is simply a scaled-up version of a smaller plant. In the oil pipeline example cited above, larger diameter pipes are indeed scaled-up versions of smaller ones. But there are always limits to simple scaling up and beyond a certain point, increasing the production capacity of equipment requires design changes which actually change the nature of the capital. Putting that issue to one side for the moment, however, we can say unambiguously that technological advance will reduce the height of some or all of the LAC curve. We might also expect that if progress is biased towards larger scales of operation, it will raise the MES. This has important implications for industrial structure.

Productivity, technical efficiency and cost

Recall from Chapter 2, that under constant returns to scale and competitive conditions, growth in output comprises the share-weighted contributions of growth in each input and the effect of TFP growth (the 'residual'):

$$(dQ/dt)/Q = a(dK/dt)/K + b(dL/dt)/L + (dT/dt)/T$$

Thus

$$(dT/dt)/T = (dQ/dt)/Q - a(dK/dt)/K - b(dL/dt)/L$$

and since, with CRS, $(a + b) = 1$:

$$(dT/dt)/T = (dQ/dt)/Q - a(dK/dt)/K - (1 - a)(dL/dt)/L$$
$$= (dQ/dt)/Q - a[(dK/dt)/K - (dL/dt)/L]$$
$$- (dL/dt)/L.$$

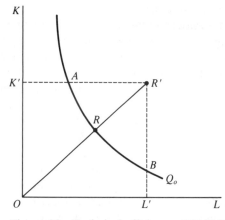

Figure 4.9 Technical efficiency: OR'/OR as a measure of technical efficiency.

But $[(dQ/dt)/Q - (dL/dt)/L]$ is growth in labour productivity. So labour productivity growth derives from total factor productivity growth and the effect of capital deepening (growth in the capital : labour ratio) weighted by the share of capital.

Capital deepening may be a powerful force for raising productivity and as noted already, some economists regard its impact as both central and inseparable from the influence of TFP growth. But assuming the distinction does have conceptual value, what are the components of TFP growth?

As shown in isoquant diagrams in Chapter 2 and the earlier parts of this chapter, technological progress will in many cases reduce the amount of both inputs required to produce a given flow of output and even when innovation leads to a saving on only one input, the total flow of inputs per unit of output will be cut. Thus, technological progress increases productivity. As we have already indicated, this brings about a lowering of the LAC curve, assuming that efficient use is made of any new advance.

But productivity may be raised by two other factors: increased **technical efficiency** (reduced technical inefficiency) and **scale economies**. While progress shifts the LAC curve, reducing technical efficiency allows movements towards the curve, and reaping scale economies permits movements down the curve.

Until now, we have assumed technical efficiency in production. To be technically efficient, firms must know and use existing technological knowledge to its best possible effect, allowing maximum output to be generated from any combination of inputs. In Figure 4.9, we show at point R' production which uses K' and L' of capital and labour to produce an output flow of Q_o when any of the combinations of inputs represented on the Q_o isoquant could have done the job, bearing in mind that no input combination to the south-west of the isoquant would have been technologically feasible. Compared with other points on (and nearer to) the isoquant, R' is technically inefficient. There are potentially several ways in which the extent of ineffiency could be measured (see Farrell, 1957 and Forsund, Lovell and Schmidt, 1980). But for the purposes of simple exposition, consider a ray from the origin to R', OR'. This ray cuts the isoquant on which efficient production by definition occurs at R. An obvious measure of technical inefficiency is the size of the ratio OR'/OR. A similar ratio could be constructed in the same way for any point to the north-east of the isoquant. The larger the ratio, the more technically inefficient production at that point will be.[2]

Total productivity will be raised if a firm moves within the area $AR'B$ towards the isoquant from R': output is Q_o in each case but both inputs fall. Since cost curves are constructed on the assumption that firms are already technically efficient, this implies that firms to the north-east of isoquants will reduce their actual costs as they become less technically inefficient and move from a point above the curve towards a point on it.

The difference between R' and R has been described as **X-ineffiency** (Leibenstein, 1966, 1975).[3] Leibenstein argued that the gap arose in large part because employment contracts could not extract from workers the quantity and type of effort associated with technically efficient performance. Workers are often paid on the basis of work-place attendance rather than through a payment-by-results system. While in principle contracts could be written in enough detail to specify exactly what the employer expected of employees at all times of the day, in practice it would never be possible to write down a description of tasks which ensured efficient performance because external and internal conditions constantly change, and with such change the very description of efficient performance.

Leibenstein's reasoning implicitly rests on the existence of **transaction costs**, costs involved in actually effecting transactions. It was realised by Coase in 1937 that under conditions of uncertainty it would always be costly to gather information about the quantities and quality of inputs required for production, costly to negotiate and set up contracts with suppliers (of labour services as well as other inputs) and costly to enforce contracts. But the lesson Coase drew was that firms existed as institutional devices for minimising such costs. In this view (much extended by Williamson, 1975, 1985), the concept 'the firm' is not defined so much by its technological characteristics as the attributes of the nexus of contracts which determines how it works organisationally (see Chapter 5 for much more on this).

An implication of this work is that productivity increases are closely related to how work is organised and rewarded, i.e. how contracts are written and enforced. This gives an institutional context to the purely abstract analysis of achieving technical and economic efficiency presented so far. One analysis which has pursued these questions in considerable depth is that of **principal and agent** (Grossman and Hart, 1983). Issues in this area arise whenever one person, the principal, hires another, the agent, to act on his behalf, and where the principal is unable to observe or know fully how effectively the agent is performing. In connection with production problems, the principal might be an employer hiring an employee, or a group of shareholders unable to observe directly the performance of a firm's managers. For Leibenstein, under-performance by managers is as much a source of X-inefficiency as slacking by production-line workers.

In an uncertain world, principals and agents are both assumed to strive to maximise expected utility, based on the probability-weighted outcomes of various possible states of the world. Risk is optimally shared when agents' choices of effort levels are such as simultaneously to maximise principals' expected utility. The trouble is that it may be impossible to design compensation (i.e. remuneration) arrangements which simultaneously achieve optimal risk-sharing and optimal incentives to managers to offer effort. For example, if shareholders are risk-neutral and managers risk-averse, making the return to the principal depend partially on profits will do more to optimise risk-sharing than if they receive a flat fee. On the other hand, it is also an implication of this arrangement that managers will have an insufficient incentive to offer the effort required to maximise shareholders' expected utility. Such lack of effort is the key to understanding the source of Leibenstein's notion of X-inefficiency.

Another set of reasons for technical inefficiency has to do with the nature of technological knowledge. The only way to make sense of the assumption that all firms are technically efficient is to say that all firms have free and equal access to all technological knowledge and can use it to equally good effect. This reflects a tradition in economics that technological knowledge is much like general scientific knowledge, expensive to generate but relatively cheap and easy to communicate and transfer. Yet technological knowledge has important tacit elements, acquired only in the actual doing of production and often not articulated in any codified form. In addition, production may have to be done repeatedly before workers become fully skilled in performing their various tasks, singly and as team participants. What this means is that a firm at R could not, even if it wanted to, tell a firm at R' all that it had to do to become efficient. It also means that it is impossible to reach R without producing Q_o per period for several successive periods (or, for fewer periods, producing more than Q_o per period). One reason for the gap thus has to do with the nature of technological knowledge and another with the way in which such knowledge is acquired through **learning by doing (LBD)**.

This discussion raises an interesting conceptual point. As we shall see in a later analysis, economists often represent the effect of learning by doing as a downward shift in the LAC. Now it cannot be denied that LBD will cause a downward shift in actual costs. But the analytical device, the LAC curve, is strictly speaking constructed on the assumption that all firms are already technically efficient, while the very existence of LBD suggests that firms are still finding out how to be technically efficient. If this is how LBD is to be understood, even if only in part, then LBD should be respresented in LAC curve diagrams by movements towards the curve from above it, not by movements in the curve itself.

In the presence of scale economies in the production function, higher levels of productivity and lower average costs will be achieved at higher output levels. Because scale economies are so important for determining industry structure as well as the cost competitiveness of firms, industries and countries, we now devote a section to considering their origins and their connection with innovation.

Economies of scale and technological change

In this section, we examine the sources of scale economies, but with particular reference to their technological origins and the implications for them of innovation (useful references are Pratten, 1971; Scherer, 1980; Hay and Morris, 1991). Economies of scale in producing a single output arise at the level of the plant and at the level of multiplant operations.

Plant level

Scale economies may arise at this level either in relation to the characteristics of physical equipment or in relation to operating costs.

The characteristics of equipment which are relevant here are the **geometric properties** of certain pieces of a plant and **indivisibility**. The geometric properties of interest are those which allow the capacity or rate of operation of plant to expand at a rate faster than the cost of the materials required to achieve that expansion. Such properties include those common to all containers and pipes (recall the pipeline example in Figure 4.8) in which a given proportional increase in surface area will permit a substantially greater proportional increase in volume or carrying capacity. Since cost is directly related to the area of the materials, average costs fall with expanded capacity. The pipeline example noted above is a good example of this and in much engineering design work, it is often assumed that on average a doubling of capacity can be achieved with an increase in costs of only 60 per cent (Chenery, 1949; Hay and Morris, 1991: 31). While technological progress cannot change the laws of physics, it may be able to change the capacity range over which the laws apply, as has been the case, for example, with kilns used in cement industry processes (McBride, 1981). In such cases, the use of a new material or a new method of construction may make it possible to exploit such laws beyond the point formerly possible and increase the MES.

In the case of the cement industry, the capacity of a kiln of given technology is approximately proportional to its volume, while capital costs are roughly proportional to its surface area and rise at about two-thirds the rate at which capacity increases. This means average costs have always initially fallen as scale of output increases, but over the post-war era, the MES increased dramatically from about 250 to 340 thousand tonnes per annum in 1949 to 2,050 thousand tonnes in 1971 (McBride, 1981). The rising MES is a reflection of innovation which has driven cost curves down and simultaneously shifted the minimum point on the LAC outwards.

By indivisibility, we mean that some pieces of equipment, or processes of production have a minimum scale of operation; if they operate at all, they must produce a minimum amount of output. As an example, the vessels and associated plant in a brewery of given design must be filled to a certain point if they are to work at all and this generates a flow of beer which is the minimum scale of operation. The central

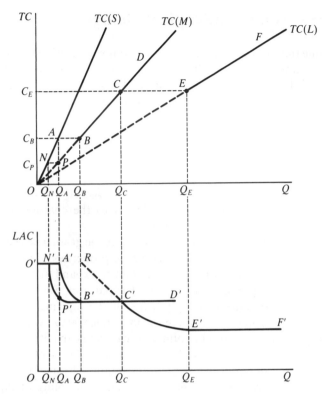

Figure 4.10   Indivisibilities and scale economies. (Adapted with permission of the publisher from A. Koutsoyiannis (1979) *Modern Microeconomics*, London: Macmillan, p. 130.)

point about indivisibility is that the process cannot produce anything less than the amount of output associated with the minimum scale of operation, although it may be possible to expand output above that minimum level without impediment.

In Figure 4.10 (which draws on Koutsoyiannis, 1979: 130), we show the total cost functions associated with three different techniques of production, assumed to be the only three available to the industry. Each could have the same or different capital:labour ratios, but we assume the essential difference lies in their productivity levels (average labour, capital and total productivity). For larger scale techniques, increased productivity may flow from allowing labour to specialise in ways not available with small-scale production methods. These variations in productivity suggest that the homogeneity assumption for both capital and labour has been relaxed.

For small-scale production (everything from one unit upwards), any given proportional expansion of output is achieved by equal proportional increases of each input and total costs increase along ONA, i.e. TC(S). Initially, we assume that there is only one other technique of production known, for which the cost function is labelled TC(M), where '*M*' stands for middle-sized. Under the M-technique, Q_B is the minimum scale of operation. For output levels above Q_B, along *BCD*, there are again constant returns to scale, but total costs rise more slowly with output than under the S-technique because the middle-sized process achieves higher productivity levels. However, because the technique cannot produce less than Q_B, the total cost of producing Q_B or any amount less than Q_B is *CB*. To produce less than Q_B, Q_B itself must be produced and the difference either stored or thrown away. An implicit simplifying assumption here is that there are zero disposal or storage costs. If such costs were positive, they would have to be added. Nonetheless, because the M-technique offers higher productivity, it is more efficient to use it rather than the S-technique to produce any output level above Q_A, because for all output levels between Q_A and Q_B, the total costs of using *M* (i.e. *CB*) are less than the total costs of using *S*. The total cost curve would thus be *OABCD*.

The implications for *LAC* are shown in the lower part of Figure 4.10. For output levels 0–Q_A, *LAC* are constant and equal to the slope of TC(S): see the segment *O'N'A'* (also equal to *LMC*). For output levels above Q_B, *LAC* are lower (equal to the slope of TC(M)) and follow *B'C'D'*. If one more unit than Q_A were produced using the M-technique, average costs would be slightly lower than the height of *O'N'A'* (i.e. $CB/Q_A + 1$) and as further units of output were produced with it, would ultimately fall to the height of *B'C'D'* (CB/Q_B). Since total costs are constant at *CB*, in this range $LMC = 0$. Focusing still on the S- and M-techniques, note that with just these two available, the MES would be Q_B. We now consider two different ways in which technical progress might influence the MES.

Suppose first that a flexibility enhancing innovation made it possible to operate the M-technique at a lower minimum scale, say Q_A. Immediately the total cost curve would no longer be *OABCD* but *ONPBCD* and the corresponding LAC curve *ON'P'B'C'D'*. Progress has lowered the LAC curve over the output range Q_N–Q_B and reduced the MES to Q_A.

Consider, alternatively, the cost curve TC(L), associated with a large-scale technique of yet higher productivity introduced after the other two as the result of technological advance. With this technique, output levels above Q_C should be produced with it rather than the M-technique, because the total cost of producing the minimum output of the L-technique is *CE*, which also applies to any amount less than Q_E, including all amounts between Q_C and Q_E. As before, *LAC* will fall, this time between Q_C and Q_E and the new MES will rise to Q_E. As noted in our earlier analysis, the LAC curve is derived for a given state of technology. But the range *O'A'B'C'* remains relevant even when new technology depresses the LAC curve beyond Q_C because, for output levels below Q_C, the M- and S-techniques generate lower costs. Over Q_B–Q_C, for example, the LAC associated with TC(L) are shown by the dashed line *RC'*.)

Indivisibilities will cause *LAC* to fall whenever it is efficient (or technologically unavoidable) to expand output over some range in which a process is operating either below its minimum efficient scale, or below full capacity when the latter is the level at which unit costs are minimised. This accounts for downward-sloping segments like

$A'B'$ and $C'E'$ in Figure 4.10. But part of the story told above was that at higher output levels, productivity could be progressively raised because of the potential for reaping scale economies within operating costs from the division of labour, or specialisation. This accounts for $E'F'$ being below $B'C'$, and $B'C'$ lying beneath $O'A'$. Such economies arise from the fact that labour is not homogeneous, but varied in its innate capacities and skills.

At low levels of output, every worker has to do all, or a large proportion of the production tasks which have to be undertaken to produce a unit of output. The one-person business is an extreme but not an uncommon example. The Morgan motor car company, which for years made only a dozen vehicles a week, is another. At higher levels of output, however, it is possible to allocate to each member of the work-force a smaller subset of the tasks; their time can be efficiently absorbed doing only a few tasks now that so many units are being made. At the limit, each member of the work-force is given only a single task to do. Economies arise as output levels increase, because workers who are better at doing certain tasks; can be given those they are best at.

Notice that this argument is quite distinct from LBD. The specialisation point relies purely on allocating tasks among workers in a way which maximises the possibilities of benefiting from their innate heterogeneous abilities, a purely static exercise which accounts for the slope in the LAC curve. *LBD* recognises that, over time, doing a task or a set of tasks will enable individuals and teams to do those tasks more effectively, a *dynamic* effect which explains movements towards and of the LAC curve. The two are of course connected. Individuals and teams will learn by doing, whether specialisation is great or small. But if there is an early and substantial division of labour, we might expect that individuals would learn the most efficient way of doing their tasks more quickly than if specialisation were delayed. This argument seems particularly relevant when technological progress has a scale-enhancing bias and indeed partly explains why that bias may come about. But if technological change offers the opportunity of reducing the MES through increased operational flexibility, it may be more important to ensure that individuals retain a wider range of skills and a general ability to cooperate. This is not to say *LBD* then becomes unimportant; it is to suggest that what individuals must learn to do is different.

Another important source of scale economies within operating costs is what Robinson (1958) called **economies of massed reserves**. These economies have much to do with reliability. Supposing that machines break down randomly, the failure of one machine in any given period will affect output less when the total number of machines is large than when it is small. This is because the flow of production can be diverted with less disruption through other machines. Similarly, if the size of the maintenance staff is determined by the requirement that it be able to deal quickly with random breakdowns, the stand-by labour needed to meet this objective increases at a slower proportional rate than that at which the number of machines increases (for further details, see Robinson, 1958 or Hay and Morris, 1991: 32–3). Since one important dimension of technological progress is to increase the reliability of machines (i.e. the probability that they will be working at any given period), reliability advances should increase the output flow and reduce the maintenance costs in relation to any given multimachine operation.

Finally under operating costs, Baumol (1977a) has shown that the average cost of carrying stocks (inventories) of inputs falls with the total number of input units held, which implies inventory costs fall on average with higher output. But for any given output level, average inventory costs fall with the cost of storage and with reductions in the fixed and variable costs of shipping in stock replenishments. Clearly, storage costs will be reduced to nothing if inputs are used as soon as they arrive and this will be possible if managerial and organisational innovations like Just-In-Time methods ensure that input inflows and their use in the production process are exactly coordinated. In addition, innovations in transport and distribution reduce shipping costs over time. Innovations such as containerisation may operate to reduce costs at both small and large scales of operation. Others, such as the bulk transport of raw materials by purpose-designed freight trains, may be effective only for large-scale work.

Multiplant economies

Transport costs have proved to be a particularly important source of scale economies for multiplant operations. (Scherer, 1980, Scherer, Beckenstein, Kaufer and Murphy, 1975: 88–9). In Figure 4.11, the LAC(P) curve in each part of the diagram shows how LAC in any given plant fall when transport costs are omitted. The UTC curve illustrates how unit transport costs might rise with increasing output, though the shape and position of this curve in any particular case will vary with factors, including the weight: value ratio of goods being shipped, the geographic distribution and population density of customers, the structure of transport costs themselves, the pricing system, and the plant size relative to the market served. Although high weight: value ratios and sharply declining customer density away from the plant may lead unit transport costs to rise at an increasing rate, they are most often found to rise at a falling rate. The TLAC curve is found by vertically adding the UTC and LAC(P) curves to give a total LAC curve, which will often have a minimum point. The output of any one plant will be importantly related to the cost-minimising output found on the TLAC curve and the smaller this output is, the more plants a firm is likely to operate.

Comparing Figure 4.11a with 4.11b, the UTC curve has been lowered from UTC(H) to UTC(L) to reflect the impact of innovation which reduces transport costs. The effect is to lower the TLAC curve from TLAC(0) to TLAC(1) and to raise the cost-minimising scale of output in any plant from Q_A to Q_B. As an example, Scherer cites changes in the transport industry in the second half of the nineteenth century, an era of expanding railway networks and falling unit transport costs. When the least-cost scale of production thereupon rose, firms took advantage by building new plants of unprecedented size.

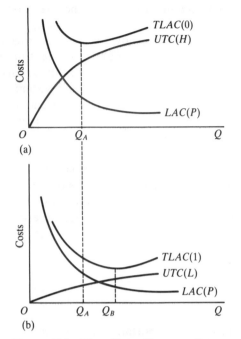

Figure 4.11 The effect of lower unit transport costs on the transport cost-inclusive long-run average cost curve.

The multiproduct cost function

As Hicks (1952) observed, few firms are actually producers of a single product: '... almost every firm does produce a considerable range of different products' (p. 372). He went on to say that firms produce two or more products because there are economies from producing them together, an observation which has been analysed since in greater depth under the rubric of **economies of scope** (Baumol, 1977b, Baumol, Panzar, and Willig, 1982).

Economies of scope are the cost savings which result from producing two or more different products together in one firm, rather than producing each in separate production units. Economies of scope obviously occur where **jointness** in production is an integral part of the production process. Joint production arises when inputs once acquired for producing one good are available for use in producing others without cost (Panzar, 1989: 17). Examples are wheat and straw (both available from the same stalks of a wheat crop), wool and mutton (derived from the same sheep's carcase) and beef and hides (from the same bullock). In cases of jointness like this, intuition suggests that it will be cheaper to produce pairs of items in one firm than in two specialised firms.

But jointness is not the only source of economies of scope; they can also result from the presence of inputs that perhaps because of indivisibilities are easily shared by the production processes of several different outputs (Panzar, 1989: 19). This property of 'shareability' may be viewed as an essentially technological feature; the same piece of capital equipment may, for example, be suitable for producing quite different products. Gun barrel manufacturers have also made bored-metal engine components for motor vehicles. Railway locomotives may haul either freight cars or passenger trains. A given piece of computer hardware may perform any one of a wide range of information-processing tasks which, individually, might be associated with quite different information outputs. This helps explain why some banks (which have traditionally specialised in processing financial data) have diversified into offering other services, like travel advice and bookings, which are also intensive in information storage and transmission.

Economies of scope may also arise in connection with sharing inputs of a less tangible kind. As examples, Teece (1980) has analysed the use of managerial expertise, a successful sales staff and a good financial rating. The first of these provides a possible economic rationale for conglomerate mergers; a management team which has shown itself adept in management decision-making in one area is often viewed as having a general team skill which is transferable to other lines of business. For our purposes, another apposite example might be an R&D facility. The knowledge generated to reduce costs in a firm's core business may turn out to have applications in quite different areas of activity and if that knowledge enables the firm to be competitive in new areas, it may well consider diversifying. These examples are considered again in Chapter 5.

In most cases where scope economies arise from sharing inputs, it is clear that the inputs cannot in some sense have been used to full capacity in producing the single product. This may be because the capacity output of an indivisible input exceeds the size of the market. Thus, the reaping of economies of scope reflects technological factors and the general market conditions in which production takes place (Waterson, 1983).

For analytical purposes, consider an organisation which produces only two outputs. To show the cost conditions faced by such a firm, we need a diagram with three axes (see Figure 4.12). The two axes on the 'floor' of the three-dimensional space illustrated show amounts produced, Q^1 and Q^2, of two products we shall call Good 1 and Good 2. The vertical axis shows the total costs, TC, of producing combinations of the two goods in various quantities and proportions. To find the cost of producing any given combination of quantities, read up from the floor of the diagram to the cost surface, a two-dimensional analogue of the cost curve, and then across to the vertical axis parallel to the floor. For example, the point Z represents the firm's decision to produce amounts of the two goods shown by the co-ordinates Q_z^1 and Q_z^2. The cost of producing this output is found by identifying the point Z' vertically above Z and then reading horizontally across to the point C_z on the vertical axis. The total cost OC_z equals the height of the line ZZ'.

The lines Ma' and Na'' are the edges of the cost surface which run above the axes for Q^1 and Q^2 and show how total costs vary when the firm produces only one of

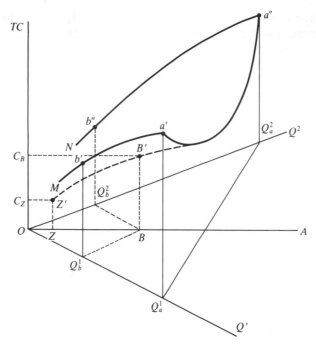

Figure 4.12   The total cost surface in a two-product production process.

the products in any given period. As drawn, total costs increase at a decreasing rate with output for both goods; there are economies of scale in the production of each good taken individually. There is, of course, no necessity for this to be the case; producing either good individually might be associated with increasing, decreasing or constant unit costs or all three, in different ranges of output. This raises the question of how to think about scale effects in the case of multiproduct firms. The solution usually offered (Baumol, 1977b) is that attention should be focused on how costs vary along the cost surface when both (all) outputs are increased in equal proportions. Diagrammatically, this amounts to drawing rays from the origin along the floor of Figure 4.12, such as OA, and observing the curvature of the line vertically above it on the cost surface. Points on the cost surface relate to the minimum costs required under existing technology to produce any given combination of output quantities, as was the case with the simple cost curve.

The particular interest in looking at multiproduct firms, however, is what happens to total costs when the two (or more) outputs are produced in varying proportions. Since we must read across rays to do this, it is said that we are examining the **transray** properties of the cost surface. Suppose we consider all the output proportions on a line (a transray) running across the floor of the diagram between Q_a^1 and Q_a^2. Looking at the corresponding line on the cost surface, $a'a''$, note that it 'dips' down towards the middle from each end. When this happens, that portion of the cost surface is said to be **transray convex**. If it arched upwards, it would be transray concave. What this means economically is that along the transray it is always cheaper to produce a combination of Goods 1 and 2 than to dedicate (i.e. assign specifically) the resources of the firm to producing just Good 1 or Good 2. Cost is minimised when the two goods are produced in the proportions shown by the ray OA.

Movements along the transray from the end-points represent an unambiguous increase in scope in one dimension (two goods produced rather than one) and changes in scope in another dimension (variations in the proportions in which the two goods are produced). In the diagram, economies arise from both effects. It could be argued that the number of products (product range) and the proportions in which they are produced should be the *only* defining elements of scope (Markowski and Jubb, 1989). But scope is nonetheless often taken to allow for changes in both output volume and product range.

As an illustration, output could be produced separately in two small production units in the quantities Q_b^1 and Q_b^2, with associated production costs $b'Q_b^1$ and $b'Q_b^2$. Alternatively, the same quantities could have been produced by a single, larger production unit represented by B on OA, producing the same quantities of the goods jointly at a cost BB'. The cost of producing the two goods separately would be the sum of the two heights $b'Q_b^1$ and $b''Q_b^2$. This is larger than BB'. However, this outcome does not depend on the transray convexity of the cost surface. If there were returns to scale along OA, it would be worthwhile undertaking joint production of the two goods even in the absence of transray convexity, as long as the degree of non-convexity (the amount the transray 'arches') were not too great.

We can now see that technological progress could have a rather wider range of impacts on production than it was possible to show when attention was confined to single-output firms. To start with, however, we hold constant the product range (number of products), scale of output and the proportions in which products are produced and note that some forms of technological progress might simply result in smaller quantities of inputs being required to produce all rates of output of each product. Biases might take several forms. At given input prices, more labour (capital) might be saved, proportionately, than capital (labour) in a similar degree in respect of all products. Proportionally more labour (relative to capital) might be saved in relation to some products than others, or more capital relative to labour. In terms of Figure 4.12, such effects would shift the whole cost surface downwards and by unequal amounts if progress led to greater cost reductions in producing one output rather than the other. These effects are merely the multiproduct extensions of effects already analysed for the one-product firm.

Of novel interest are effects which arise only in the context of multiproduct firms. We divide these impacts into two broad types: those affecting **output capability** and those influencing **response flexibility** (the classification of effects follows that of Markowski and Jubb, 1989). The output capability of a production system relates to the **versatility** of a firm's inputs in generating different sorts of output. With given input quantities, and pieces of equipment which remain unchanged in the number of tasks they perform, technical change may increase versatility in terms of the range of products generated. This might be called 'scope-enhancing' technical progress and would change the cost surface by causing it to be extended into an increased number of output dimensions. Holding the product range constant, technical progress might also enable given equipment to perform more tasks than before, or increase the interinput substitution possibilities in producing any one output. But these effects are just as relevant in relation to single-output firms.

In the case of response flexibility, the issue is not scope *per se* but the ease and speed with which inputs can be switched from producing one output (or output combination) to another, given a firm's production capability. Here, technical progress appears in the form of reduced downtime (and, in general, reduced costs) involved in changing from making one product to another. By extension, response flexibility also refers to the time it takes to extend the scope of production by designing and developing new products and product variants.

Economies of scope can also be shown to have an intimate relationship to **cost complementarity**.[4] Cost complementarity occurs when increases in the output of one product brings with it a reduction in the marginal cost of producing another product. This might occur, for example, when the process of producing one type of good gives rise to a by-product which itself has economic value. Panzar (1989: 21–3) shows that under fairly general conditions a cost function which exhibits cost complementarity is also characterised by economies of scope.

The notion of complementarity, used in a broader sense, is also central to recent work on the characteristics of a **flexible manufacturing system** (**FMS**). A general definition of an FMS is 'a computer-controlled grouping of semi-independent work stations linked by automated materials-handling systems' (Jubb and Markowski, 1988: 6). A fundamental innovation in the FMS is how production is **controlled**. Computers (or microprocessors) collect information from sensing devices on materials-handling equipment and process it to issue commands to other machines, the operations of which they also control. Examples might be production systems comprising **computer-numerically controlled** (**CNC**) machine tools, and programmable equipment used on car assembly lines producing a range of model variants. **Computer-aided design** (**CAD**) facilities assist in speeding the expansion of firms' output capability and can be integrated into **computer-aided manufacturing** (**CAM**) systems.

Now it can be argued that when technological progress acts to reduce the cost of employing any of these computer-driven activities, not only will the level of use of that activity increase, but so will those of other activities in the FMS (Milgrom and Roberts, 1990). The complementarity here is between groups of activities. For example, CAD equipment can generate coded instructions for use in flexible manufacturing equipment. At the same time, increasing and better use of FMS calls for the services of CAD. Suppose technological change allowed the marginal cost of employing CAD equipment to fall. This would encourage increasing levels of use of CAD, but because of the relevance of CAD to FMS, one effect of wider adoption and employment of CAD might also be to reduce the cost of operating flexible manufacturing equipment. Thus falling CAD costs should be associated with increased use of FMS.

As a second effect, increased use of CAD enhances the ease of broadening product lines, i.e. enhances response flexibility in terms of product development and differentiation. But that in turn increases the attractiveness of using manufacturing systems which are themselves more flexible and should increase how much they are employed. A third effect is built on the way in which production equipment now often far outlasts the life cycles of the products it makes. This means that if it is to last long enough to earn a competitive return, the equipment has to be designed to be flexible. Given that CAD is the principal means of exploiting that flexibility, products and product line developments are often designed to take advantage of links between CAD and manufacturing equipment.

All of this is reflected in the observable growth of production processes which look very different from the scale-intensive techniques analysed earlier and are characterised by a degree of flexibility that makes even the smallest of production batches (i.e a single unit) profitable. Warndorf and Merchant (1986), for example, cite a case in which the work of 40 standalone machines could be done instead by a dozen comprising a FMS, with a capability of making 25,000 different part types yearly, of which 70 per cent would be one-off items and half would never be made again. Compared with less flexible arrangements with more product-line dedication of equipment, the number of operators could be reduced by three-quarters. Wright and Bourne (1988), cited in Milgrom and Roberts, report that in a number of aerospace and high-precision industries, 38 per cent of all batches contained 16 units or less, and 8 per cent only one.

Flexibility also shows up in much reduced downtime. Jaikumar (1986) reports that Japanese FMSs have cut downtime to as little as 1–10 per cent in a cross-section of industries. O'Rourke (1988) found that a company making electric controls could switch production among its 725 products and variations with an average changeover time for resetting equipment of six seconds (Milgrom and Roberts, 1990: 511).

While the technological characteristics of FMS and supporting computer-based activities have enormous potential for enhancing the flexibility of manufacturing operations and exploiting economies of scope, it must be added that the nature of the complementarities involved creates heavy demands for effective coordination. FMS will be most effective when, as noted above, it is linked to equipment and product design activities 'upstream' and when it is connected to potential markets by other elements of information technology which gather and transmit information on inventory holdings and specific customer requirements. But then this complex system has to be effectively coordinated within and among organisations. This in turn means that the organisational structures within which the technology is used will themselves become a focus of interest for, given the nature of the coordination problems here, it is no longer clear that the market alone can do the job efficiently. This is a theme to which we return later.

R&D costs

Textbook accounts of firms' cost structures look at all the inputs into production and link the costs of employing them to the final output of the firm. The inputs (or factors of production) are disaggregated to include labour and capital and in more detailed accounts materials and energy as well. But it is unusual, because generally unnecessary for analytical purposes, to examine the separate activities that usually go on in a firm. In a book about innovation, however, it is worthwhile looking more closely at R&D activity and expenditures. There are several reasons for doing this. First, analysis to be presented in due course makes specific assumptions about the structure of innovation costs and it is as well to be prepared. Second, there has been a long-running debate about economies of scale in R&D and firm size, an issue taken up later in the chapter. Third, discussions about input–output relationships in this area quickly run up against a fundamental problem: how to measure the output of R&D. This in itself is worth recognising, since it suggests why hypotheses in the economics of innovation are almost always difficult to test and why the managers of firms often face their thorniest decisions when trying to allocate resources to investment in new knowledge.

The starting point for this discussion is to recognise that on average R&D costs comprise only a relatively modest proportion of firms' overall costs. In a massive survey of data for the United States in the 1970s, Bound *et al.* (1984) found that across all manufacturing, the average R&D to sales ratio for firms with non-zero R&D was 2.7 per cent. The ratio is one widely used measure of research intensity. Of the 2,582 firms included in the survey, only 1,479 claimed to have positive expenditure on R&D, although it is likely that many that said they had zero R&D expenditures did actually have some. The ratio varied widely among industries, however, as would be predicted by reference, for example, to Pavitt's analysis of interindustry patterns of innovation referred to in Chapter 2. In the Bound study, research intensity reached a maximum of 6.1 per cent in office, computing and accounting equipment and a minimum of 0.5 per cent in the food and petroleum refining industries. Across the OECD, manufacturing industries with the highest research intensities were instrumentation, pharmaceuticals and electronics and those with the lowest, wood and furniture, clothing and footwear, paper and printing and food, drink and tobacco (DITAC, 1992).

Distinctions between the concepts of 'research' and 'development' and within each area were discussed in Chapter 2. Here we make the empirical point that within the global figure for research and development for most firms, development expenditures far outweigh research. There are at least two reasons for this. First, much of the work which is usually classified as 'research' generates knowledge which is too non-specific in a technological sense to allow firms which undertook the work to capture or appropriate more than a fraction of the returns from it. The prospects for appropriation are best when new knowledge can be embodied in a product or process which is difficult to imitate. Appropriation problems therefore arise if new knowledge cannot readily be used in commerical products or processes, or if its use could be relatively easily imitated (e.g. through reverse engineering). Firms often perceive that returns from research will be undermined on both of these counts, though there are wide variations from industry to industry. This means in practice that most basic and pure research, which offers the poorest prospect of short- to medium-term competitive commercial returns, is performed in publicly funded institutions such as universities and research institutes.

Second, the development aspect of R&D is simply more demanding of resources. The main reason for this is that research may be regarded as successful if it uncovers *any* new knowledge, regardless of its prospects of useful application. And since knowledge is advancing on so many fronts simultaneously, it is not difficult to find research projects which will incrementally increase the stock of knowledge with a relatively modest expenditure of resources. On the other hand, development by its very nature is directed towards shaping and refining knowledge in very specific ways; it is worth doing only if it generates a product or process of commercial value. This means that many apparently promising avenues are likely to be tried before the way forward is found which both fits with firms' existing capabilities and meets market requirements. Along the way, much new technological knowledge will be discovered, but will also have to be discarded because it will not offer the solution a firm needs.

In this connection, the following findings are useful. In post-war Britain, R&D expenditures have been divided in the proportions 3 per cent to basic research, 22 per cent to applied research and 75 per cent to development (Stoneman, 1983: 8). In 1967, the Charpie Panel (a group of industry, government and academic experts) found technological innovation costs distributed as shown below (U.S. Department of Commerce, 1967):

Research/advanced development/basic invention	5–10%
Engineering and product design	10–20%
Tooling/manufacturing engineering	40–60%
Manufacturing start up	5–15%
Marketing start up	10–25%

Both sets of findings suggest that the research component of R&D, including applied research and design elements, is relatively modest when compared with the development component, when the latter is taken to include tooling/manufacturing engineering and manufacturing start up in the Charpie Panel list.

An alternative set of definitions identifies as 'R&D' the first two items on the list, and the next two 'transition to industrial production'. In these terms, Mansfield *et al.* (1971) found (in a study of fourteen firms in the chemical, electronics and machinery industries in the United States) that 46.2 per cent of technological innovation costs were devoted to R&D, 46 per cent to transition to production and 7.7 per cent to marketing. To use Mansfield's own terminology, R&D can be divided into applied research, 9.5 per cent; specifications, 7.6 per cent; and prototype or plant design and construction, 29.1 per cent, totalling 46.2 per cent. This breakdown might be compared with that found by Kamin, Bijaoui and Horesh (1982) for Israeli data. In a study of thirty-three innovations, they found R&D on the definition in this paragraph accounted for 47 per cent of overall innovation costs. They also found that the R&D percentage increased as firm size fell and rose with increasing complexity in the innovation itself. In analytical work, everything on the Charpie list but for marketing start up tends to be regarded as R&D, even though such work often fails to make it clear that much of what is implicitly included is relatively small-scale, nuts and bolts 'tinkering', essential for getting production lines to operate smoothly but of little account in reshaping the structure of knowledge.

With this background, we now turn to the relationship between inputs and outputs in R&D activity. As before, costs could be divided into fixed and variable and inputs into labour, capital and other. But we shall merely observe here that the largest component of R&D expenditure is usually wage costs. An important question to ask is whether scale and scope economies exist in generating outputs from R&D inputs.

Suppose a satisfactory index of inventive output could be identified. Would we then expect increasing, decreasing or constant returns to scale in the operation of R&D activity? In the Schumpeterian tradition, the answer to this question was that increasing returns might be expected. A more precise interpretation is that average returns per research worker increase with the size of research staff, given firm size and that, for given R&D expenditure, average returns per research worker also rise with the size of the firm. The theoretical elements of the argument are laid out by Fisher and Temin (1973, 1979), Rodriguez (1979) and Kohn and Scott (1982).

First, consider the case of given firm size. If the output value of R&D per research worker rises with the size of the research staff, there must be scale economies. The sources of such economies might be the increased scope for purchasing specialised equipment, permitting more effective experimentation and the synergy arising from larger teams with complementary areas of expertise. Also the larger the R&D staff, the greater the total experience they can accumulate over time will be, so that analogous with the learning by doing and using that goes on in production, the greater will be the extent to which research workers may be able to benefit over time from learning by learning (Stiglitz, 1987). In learning-by-learning, researchers discover that a strategy successful in resolving one problem can also be applied to similar questions and the larger the R&D team, the larger the number of strategies they may discover and the larger the range of associated problems to which each strategy might be applied.

At some stage, however, diseconomies might well set in. In part, this could have to do with the increasing managerial difficulties encountered with coordinating an increasingly expanded, complex and diverse range of projects. Comparing a larger with a smaller R&D department, the larger one must exploit more intensively in any given period the same pool of knowledge related to what the firm already does and/or explore a more diverse range of possibilities. In the first case, it seems unlikely that within any given period innovations of equal value could expand indefinitely at a proportional rate faster than resource input. This is partly because there are limits to usefully stretching knowledge at any point in time and partly because larger R&D departments tend to acquire a bias against more imaginative innovations as they become increasingly large and bureaucratised (see, for example, Cooper, 1964; Jewkes,

Sawers and Stillerman, 1969: Chapter 6). In the second case, co-ordination difficulties become increasingly acute. Even so, it must be remembered that the stock of expertise in the R&D department is a prime example of a shareable input, so economies of scope might be reaped in either case. Even with modestly decreasing returns to scale, therefore, the long-run average costs of the R&D department measured against its proximate output, the innovation flow could decline if scope economies were great enough.

Now consider the implications of increasing firm size. In this case the returns on a given R&D expenditure might rise because larger firms can acquire financial capital on better terms than smaller ones, especially for investments in R&D which are regarded as relatively high risk. Larger firms may also be in a better position to commercially exploit the flow of output from their R&D departments because of their superior marketing and distribution channels (on this, see discussion of complementary assets in Chapter 5).

It would be nice to be able to test whether there are scale and/or scope economies in R&D, but a major difficulty here is how to measure the output of the R&D department. The best measure of output should be the flow of innovations. But these may be either process or product innovations and either varies greatly in size and value, both over time for any given firm or industry and in comparisons among different types of industry. The Japanese electronics giant Sony, for example, brings about 1,000 new products a year to the market, though of these perhaps 30–40 per cent are variations on existing products (Department of Trade and Industry, 1989). In any given year, the Italian textile and clothing industry produces many thousands of 'innovations' in its product lines. But how is each of these innovations to be compared with every other? And how is the flow from firms and industries like these to be compared with the flow from, say, the mining companies, where most advances will take the form of extraction innovation on the processing side? We should separate product from process innovations and identify those which are major departures as opposed to modest modifications. But this always involves subjective judgement and may ignore the crucial difference between innovations of major economic importance but little technological novelty, or of great technological achievement but little economic value.

A different approach to the problem is to focus on patents. This approach continues to be popular among 'economists of a statistical bent ... primarily because of ease of measurement' (Enos, 1989: 4). Numbers of patents can be easily added up and then used in analysis aimed at correlating innovative activity with other measures such as investment or growth. Yet as Scherer (1965) reminds us, a straight count of patents has two serious limitations: first, the propensity to patent an innovation of given quality may vary from firm to firm and from industry to industry; second the quality of underlying inventions varies widely from patent to patent. Scherer also points out, however, that corrections can be attempted, for instance, using dummy variables in empirical work to cope with interindustry differences in the propensity to patent.

Commenting on a compendium of more recent work, Griliches (1984) has reiterated these doubts, adding that analysis is also hampered when the firms under analysis take out only an occasional patent or two. But he concludes that 'something is there, something worth working on and analysing. Patents and patent counts are, after all, one of the few direct quantitative glimpses into the innovation process available to us .... Studies do show a strong cross-sectional relationship between R&D and patents and a weaker, but still statistically significant one between their fluctuations over time. Thus, to a first approximation, one can use patent data as indicators of technological activity in parallel with or in lieu of R&D data' (p. 14). This is not quite the same as saying that patent data are reliable indicators of the output of activity for which R&D is the input, but it suggests that some credence at least might be placed on patents as indicators of innovation activity. (Griliches, 1990, is an up-to-date survey of the whole area.)

If interest is confined to process innovations, the benefit of innovation appears first and foremost in production cost reductions and one index of the output of the innovation process is the percentage cost reduction achieved per period or, better, the present value of cost savings or additional profit. Empirically however, an important difficulty is that the benefits of R&D will occur with a considerable lag and over several, if not many periods. Enos (1958), for example, showed that in the petrochemical industry, average annual cost reductions in the period after the first year when a new process was introduced were three times higher than before. Thus, for input–output purposes, the period relevant for analysis should be quite long, or the benefits should be related to R&D which occurred one or more periods earlier. It is also the case that production costs may be reduced for reasons unconnected, or only indirectly connected with R&D. In any case, R&D undertaken by firms to improve their own production processes constitutes only a minority of all R&D. Scherer (1984) estimates that only 26.2 per cent of all company-financed R&D was directed to process improvement in the United States in the 1970s, with 44.8 per cent being spent on industrial capital goods products, 21.6 per cent on industrial material products and 7.4 per cent on consumer good products.

A final index of R&D performance considered here is the date by which a particular 'problem' is solved. The 'problem' might take the form of a production bottle-neck to be overcome, or a quality improvement required in a product, or, in general, any change to current production arrangements or product characteristics which offers the potential of enhanced performance. Clearly, a solution to the 'problem' is itself an output. But the speed with which success and the timing of the innovation are achieved will often be a crucial additional characteristic in determining its commercial value. Focusing on the timing of the innovation presupposes that the problem is one which has a qualitatively well-defined solution. This sort of approach is thus appropriate to mission-oriented research and to work whose direction is already set in terms of the technological trajectory of a given firm. However, it should be noted that many 'solutions' are only partial, so that the output value, of R&D should be adjusted to reflect its less-than perfect results and that R&D often has quite unforeseen results of value, independent of the particular 'problems' a firm might be trying to solve.

Perhaps unsurprisingly, the evidence on scale economies in R&D is not altogether clear. But if patents are taken as a measure of output and R&D employment as an index of input, Scherer (1965) finds the elasticity of patenting with respect to R&D is unity for most levels of operation, with a suspicion of diminishing returns at the highest;

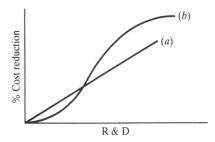

Figure 4.13 Linear (a) and non-linear (b) R&D production functions or innovation possibility functions.

Bound *et al.* (1984) are unable to contradict this result on more recent evidence.

Empirical work on the output from R&D work is now advancing along three fronts: work on patents, work on individual innovations, tracing links of the kind discussed in Chapter 2, and bibliometric work which draws on growing databases of citation indices to identify which lines of research are attracting most attention from other researchers and users (Van Raan, 1988). Empirically based work in the study of innovation still has far to go, but at least the theoretical work discussed in this book suggests appropriate ways of asking questions. We will not pursue empirical studies further here, but are now in a position to conclude this section with two versions of the **invention possibility frontier (IPF)** which offers an abstract representation of input–output relationships in R&D and which is used in theoretical economic models.

The first relates R&D expenditure to the percentage reduction in unit production costs. This has been used, for example, by Nordhaus (1969), Scherer (1972) and Dasgupta and Stiglitz (1980). Here, R&D expenditure or effort is measured on the horizontal axis and percentage cost reductions on the vertical (see Figure 4.13). If there are constant returns to all levels of effort, this version of the IPF will be linear, with a relatively steep slope, indicating relatively easily achieved advances in cost-reducing innovation. If there are increasing returns, the IPF will curve upwards with an increasing slope. Scherer's IPF takes this form over an initial range. If there are decreasing returns, the IPF will have a diminishing slope. Since the horizontal axis shows R&D effort in a given period, the effect of learning by learning over two or more periods would be captured by an upward shift in the IPF.

A second representation of invention possibilities relates to the timing of innovation and is shown in Figure 4.14. Here, the date of the innovation is represented on the vertical axis, while R&D expenditure is measured again along the horizontal axis. Time along the vertical axis is measured from the starting point of research into solving the problem and the downward, negative slope of this version of the IPF reflects the assumption that increasing R&D effort is required to bring forward the date of solution. Often it is assumed that for every increment of time by which success is brought forward, an increasing additional amount of R&D effort will be required. The IPF in this case is often found to become increasingly flat as R&D rises.

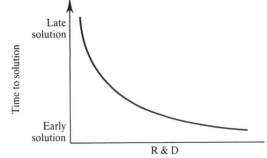

Figure 4.14 R&D and time to solution.

An evolutionary perspective

This section comprises the first part of a series of chapter segments in which we attempt to weave an evolutionary strand of analysis into the overall fabric of the book. In this section, we focus on the evolutionary requirement for variety. Later segments will focus on the adaptive, sequential nature of a firms' decision-making when uncertainty challenges the logical feasibility of profit-maximising behaviour, the mechanisms of selection at the system level, and the structural changes which are generated under the influence of such a selection.

In Chapter 1, we argued that key features of an evolutionary style of argument were persistent, population-wide variety from which a selection process could generate ongoing change at the system level, and an element of ineradicable 'blindness' about outcomes pertaining to forward-looking decisions at the level of the individual entity or organism. Now one of the principal ways in which firms as individual entities could (and in practice do) differ across an industry is in terms of their cost structures. One reason why we see such variety is that firms will often have made decisions under uncertainty in the past and in the ensuing economic conditions, some firms' decisions will have been proved more effective in reducing costs. An evolutionary critique of standard production and cost analysis now follows, then a presentation of evolutionary alternatives providing the foundations for identifying the sources of variety in production performance.

In the orthodox derivation of cost curves, both technical and economic efficiency are built into the derivation. Objections to this approach were canvassed earlier in this chapter but here move to centre stage. Efficient production in standard economic analysis is usually taken to imply that first, relevant decision-makers have perfect information, i.e. knowledge of all alternative techniques of production, how to implement them effectively and of the prices of all inputs on whatever scale they could be hired; second, decision-makers have the capacity to compare the relative merits and disadvantages of all alternatives; and third, the motivations of or pressures upon decision-makers ensure they make appropriate (i.e. cost-minimising) choices.

Evolutionary economists have criticised each of these underlying assumptions, though they are not alone in that. Consider first perfect information about production. The knowledge involved here is often compared with a book of blueprints. The usual implication drawn from this metaphor is that technological knowledge is a matter of public information: 'You can look it up. At least you could if you had the appropriate training' (Nelson and Winter, 1982: 60). Nelson and Winter contest this view. They point out that each firm has its own history of R&D and production experience, has its own secrets and sometimes its own patents. Each has a different knowledge base and different production possibilities on which its cost structure is built.[5]

Nelson and Winter also emphasise that much of each firm's knowledge is **tacit**, a notion which, in general terms has already been encountered. Tacit knowledge cannot be articulated in codified forms such as blueprints and written instructions, which attenuates its public status and makes transferring it difficult and expensive. To reason as if all firms shared the same knowlege base and therefore operate on the same cost curve is in Nelson and Winter's view, implausible. Tacitness in technological knowledge arises for three reasons; first, much operational knowledge cannot be articulated fast enough to talk a newcomer through a task; second, explanations which draw on the full depth of current knowledge cannot be understood by operators lacking certain elements of scientific and technical education; and third, comprehensively detailed explanations often lose coherence in the telling (Nelson and Winter, 1982: 80–2). The more efficient performance of production work requires speed and coping with complex and variable elements, therefore, it is more costly and difficult to instruct individuals in how to perform efficiently. The greater becomes the tacit component in the knowledge which individuals have when they perform.

An implication of this line of argument is that the greater the tacit component of technological knowledge in any particular case, the greater the scope for learning by doing would appear to be. Technical inefficiency (which LBD helps over time to reduce) would therefore seem to reflect, in part, the costs associated with imparting technological knowledge in the first place. Given that costs can be reduced through LBD over time only by additions to cumulative production, firms will therefore also vary in their costs because of differences among them in how much production experience they have had.

Consider, secondly, the assumption that decision-makers have the ability to compare all alternatives. Even if all technological alternatives were completely specified in terms of blueprints, the task of comparison would in many cases be dauntingly large and complex, and defeat the information-processing ability of the decision-maker. These are classical conditions for arguing that the computational limitations of the human brain should cause us to view individuals' capacity to optimise as constrained or bounded. Bounded rationality thus comes into play (see p. 88). But the task of making efficient choices is made all the more difficult if comparisons have to be made between techniques which may never have been used before and when it is recognised that many techniques involve the use of knowledge which is tacit, and so only partially available in codified form. The cost curves of standard economic theory assume that firms operate effectively with the most efficient technique. But these arguments suggest that in many cases decision-makers simply cannot work out what the most efficient technique is.

Finally, incentive structures within firms and the external pressures on them may not be sufficient to drive firms to minimise their production costs. We noted some of the reasons for this earlier in this chapter in considering the difficulties for shareholders in gaining the compliance of managers and the problems faced by employers in inducing efficient performance from employees.

What, then, do the evolutionary economists offer as an alternative vision in this area? Winter (1988) starts by saying that 'fundamentally, business firms are organisations that know how to do things' (p. 175). In regarding the firm as a repository of knowledge about production, the evolutionists have something in common with orthodox textbook accounts. But the obvious difference is that evolutionary economists emphasise 'the inevitability of mistaken decisions in an uncertain world' (Winter, 1988: 172). Firms have different, always inadequate knowledge bases, a differential, always flawed capacity for drawing on their knowledge and yet are confronted with continuous and turbulent change in the economic environment in which they operate. Rather than regarding uniformly efficient performance as the norm, evolutionists are therefore concerned, like biologists, with observed behaviour, and variations in it, much more than what might, hypothetically, be achieved under ideal conditions.

In the context of discussing cost curves, this means evolutionists have little interest in constructs which presuppose perfect knowledge effectively applied, but are concerned more with the costs that firms actually incur. In terms of our earlier analysis this could be interpreted as saying that evolutionists focus on reasons for technical and economic inefficiency. But it is closer to the mark to say they have a different perspective: they do not wish to compare a firms' actual performance with some imagined ideal, but rather to compare the actual performance of each firm with others in the same industry. This is because a central defining characteristic of an evolutionary system is that it contains a mechanism which '"*selects on*" entities present in the system, expanding the relative importance of some and diminishing that of others' (Nelson, 1987: 12). In trying to uncover the workings of such a mechanism, it is mainly important to understand the actual behaviour and performance of entities, not deviations from an 'ideal'.

The 'entities' which interest evolutionists in economic systems vary from author to author, but those emphasised by Nelson and Winter are firms identified in simple models by their techniques of production, and in more complex models additionally by the R&D strategies used to vary production techniques (Nelson, 1987: 14). Techniques of production are a prime example of a concept much used by Nelson and Winter – the **routine**, the term they use for all regular and predictable behaviour patterns of firms (Nelson and Winter, 1982: 14). Like genes in biological evolutionary theory, routines are persistent features of entities, and determine their possible behaviour, though actual behaviour is also determined by the environment. They are also inheritable. This provides a microeconomic foundation for the intertemporal preservation of behaviour patterns, which as in biology is essential to evolutionary explanation. It is crucial for the operation of the theory that routines are also **selectable**, i.e firms with some routines will do better in some environmental conditions than others and as a result increase their relative importance in the industry. Because firms can change their techniques (and their R&D strategies), they are unlike biological phenotypes in the sense that they are not stuck with their genes forever. This makes evolutionary economics more a special case of cultural evolution rather than an attempt merely to mimic biology. But at the same time, *'highly flexible change is not likely to characterise the behavior of individual firms'* (Nelson and Winter, 1982: 135). (My italics.)

For selection to occur, there must be diversity in the first place and for the continuous operation of a selection mechanism, variety generated on a continuous basis. In simple models, diversity arises in relation to the firms' cost structures because of the variety of production techniques they use. It is a part of the evolutionary approach that explanations for the diversity of the firms' actual cost structures lie in the variety of their historical experience.

Costs will vary among firms in an industry for three reasons: first, the diversity of skills and experience which decision-makers and production workers brought to the firm when they joined it; second, the diversity of ways in which members of the firms have subsequently developed their skills and learned to work together; third, the different capital investment decisions firms have made in relation to their skill-base. In any particular firm, the specific ways in which skills and physical capital operate together will constitute its routines of production or production techniques. These routines are unlikely to be flexible because: those engaged in the routine have some evidence or belief that they 'work' and they reflect an often painfully achieved 'truce' or understanding among the parties involved, any alternative to which could effectively be vetoed by one or more of the parties (Nelson and Winter, 1982: 110–11).

Cost structures will nonetheless change in any given firm partly because workers come to perform given skills more effectively and also because the skills required of them change. The latter is the result and reflection of innovation, which appears most obviously in the form of new routines in general and production techniques in particular. Costs will vary among firms partly because they are intrinsically different and undertake production in different ways and partly because these intrinsic differences also lead them to innovate (change their routines) in different ways.

Incorporating innovation in analysis of economic systems is crucial for evolutionists for, without a mechanism which (continuously) introduces novelties, the analysis cannot claim to be evolutionary at all (Nelson, 1987: 12). Says Winter: 'Understanding the ongoing, interrelated processes of change in technology and organisation is the central intellectual problem to be confronted by a theory of the firm' (1988: 172–3). And Lamborghini and Antonelli (1981) describe as the first major commitment of evolutionary theory the requirement to understand '... the circular process which generates technological change and ... is the result of the interaction between the firms system and the world of science and technology' (p. 81).

The ways in which firms may achieve cost-reducing innovation are through: first, formalised search (R&D); second, informal processes of diffusion of information and technolgical capabilities (e.g. via publications, technical associations, watch-and-learn processes, staff transfers); third, LBD and LBU; fourth, the adoption of innovation developed by other industries and embodied in capital goods and other inputs. At this point, we focus on the first and third points.

Routines and R&D

As we saw earlier in the chapter, it is common in the economic theory of innovation to link R&D inputs to inventive and/or innovation outputs through well-defined invention possibility functions. But, unsurprisingly, the evolutionists object to such characterisations on similar grounds to those noted in relation to production functions. If there is uncertainty in establishing the cost-minimising means of producing a flow of outputs with given technology, then a fortiori there will be uncertainty and more of it associated with attempts to change existing techniques for the better. Nelson and Winter argue there are in general two kinds of uncertainty surrounding innovation: first, the precise nature of the innovation arrived at is usually not closely predictable at the start of the work that generates it; second, the consequences of employing the innovation will not be closely predictable until a reasonable amount of actual operating experience with it has been accumulated (Nelson and Winter, 1982: 128–9). Freeman (1974: 226) offers a more detailed taxonomy. This is found in Table 4.2.

Table 4.2 Uncertainty associated with innovation

Nature/degree of uncertainty	Aspect of innovation
True uncertainty	Fundamental research
	Fundamental innovation
Very high degree of uncertainty	Radical product and process innovations
	Especially by outside firms
High degree of uncertainty	Major production innovations
	Radical process innovations within firm
Moderate uncertainty	New 'generations' of established productions
Little uncertainty	Licensed innovations
	Imitation of product innovations
	Modification of products and processes
	Early adoption of established processes
Very little uncertainty	Product differentiation
	Agency for established product innovation
	Late adoption of established process innovation in own establishment
	Minor technical improvements

Source: Freeman (1974: 226).

This classification is far from uncontroversial, as discussion elsewhere in the book suggests and some items bear more directly on production costs than others. But for present purposes, it is sufficient to observe that whatever the innovation, uncertainty is involved.

Despite the uncertainty, however, there might be routines for undertaking R&D as much as production, patterns of firm behaviour in relation to innovation, sufficiently persistent and with sufficient systematic influence on outcomes that they are selectable. Following Newell and Simon (1972), Nelson and Winter call these routines **heuristics**, defined as principles or devices which contribute to reducing the average time and effort devoted to searching for solutions to problems. For example, form a corporate task force comprising a cross-section of individuals with relevant and proven expertise to solve a production problem, or, hire a firm of consultants with a recognised track record to advise on solving a problem and assist in its implementation on a payments-by-results basis, or, organise production along the lines suggested in the 'quality circles' literature. Any of these approaches will probably generate some result or output. The ever-present difficulty is knowing whether any one approach will yield or has yielded the best result achievable, given the alternative ways in which the problem might have been attacked.

Finally, notice that principles which shorten the average search involved in solving problems of corporate survival and profitability are also heuristics. Such principles are also described as **corporate strategy** where 'strategies' can be thought of as the paths a firm might take to achieve its objectives, bearing in mind the threats and opportunities it faces in its environment and the strengths and weaknesses it has brought with it from its history (*cf* the sources of Nelson and Winter's skills).

An important strategy within a strategy is the firm's **technology strategy**, which comprises the principles through which technology might be harnessed to meet the firm's objectives. These might include the offensive ('first to market') strategy – aim to be first to market; the defensive ('follow the leader') strategy – rapidly exploit opportunities opened up by market leaders by going for technological improvements; the imitative ('Me-too') strategy – use established technology to gain market share (Freeman, 1974; Richter, 1983).

Any technology strategy implies a distinctive approach to pursuing innovation and this patterning is taken by Nelson and Winter to be part of the organisational genetic mechanism they see as underlying the evolutionary process (1982: 135).

Learning

Economic historians tend to emphasise the way in which technological knowledge grows out of itself at different rates in different firms, because of interfirm variations in the knowledge bases that firms have at any particular time. (Another way of putting it is to say each firm has its own technological trajectory, a notion discussed in Chapter 2.) This emphasis focuses on knowledge-related, technological factors as an important source of economic diversity and change that has too often been ignored. Such factors help explain why some firms are more successful than others at reducing costs and why some are persistently more successful. It is recognised later that economic mechanisms are just as important; firms which are relatively successful in reducing costs have more profit to reinvest in searching for further advances.

Consider first why change in production costs is continuous and cumulative. Seminal here is Rosenberg's (1976) analysis. This appeals to the notion of **technical imbalance** which arises whenever one or more components of a complex production system 'out-perform' the rest. The result is bottlenecks and other problems. Identifying and resolving such imbalances give rise to compulsive sequences of technical change. Most firm decision-makers are under pressure to undertake actions which offer a short-term pay-off, Rosenberg argues, but the starting point for their efforts will always be the firm's existing range of productive activities. They are naturally led, he says, to search the technological horizon within the framework of those current activities and to attack the most restrictive constraints observed in any one period. But releasing such a constraint often only introduces a new element into the production system, which then creates a new imbalance which almost automatically presents itself as part of a 'problem' to be attacked at the next round. In a sense, this is one example of a 'law of change' at work. It is an early account of how technological 'lock-in', a notion used in analysis later in the book, may also arise.

Rosenberg's analysis identifies cumulative and self-generating elements in technological change in the machine tool and steel industries of the nineteenth and twentieth centuries. Production here involved an interdependent system comprising the cutting tool, the structural or frame elements, transmission components and controls. Every time innovation occurred in one of these four elements, it created the stimulus for change elsewhere, a sequence which proved a highly fruitful source of long term technical change (1976: 112–4).

With all firms in an industry following their own compulsive sequences, some will enjoy relatively rapid advance and quickly falling costs, others slower change. Even if all firms started off with the same production costs, variation would very soon arise. And in the more general (and plausible) case where firms, *ab initio*, have different production costs, the relative levels of firms' costs will change over time. The variety in rates of change will arise because inescapable uncertainty attends all efforts at innovation, so for purely random reasons some firms will in some periods make breakthroughs denied to all others, and firms vary in their experience of production and R&D and how they draw upon that experience to respond to uncertainty.

Complexity, competence and the use of routines

Economics deals with uncertainty in a variety of ways, examples of which will be encountered in later analysis. But one response by evolutionary economists is that the existence of routines (or analogies to them) can best be understood as a means of coping with uncertainty. The foundations of predictable behaviour as a response to uncertainty have been studied by Heiner (1983) and it is to his ideas that we now turn.

Heiner argues that routines can be thought of as behavioural rules which arise because of uncertainties in distinguishing preferred from less-preferred courses of action. By 'preferred' we mean here the course of action which, after the event, is the one which a decision-maker knows he or she would have chosen had it been possible to know in advance and with certainty what the menu of alternatives actually was. Heiner argues that for many decision-makers confronting many decisions, there is a 'gap' between the intrinsic *difficulty* of a problem and the *competence* of the decision-maker to solve it. This immediately implies that there is uncertainty in selecting most preferred alternatives, which will tend to produce errors and surprises.

In the context of this section, the problem managers face (and in standard analysis effortlessly solve) is how to minimise the costs of production. However, it may only be with the benefit of hindsight that managers could say which solutions would have suited their purposes best. At the time of trying to make the decision, they might not even recognise the nature of their problem. For example, while the discussion of flexible manufacturing systems (pp. 146–7) suggested many complementary activities might sometimes need to be adjusted simultaneously to yield optimal results, managers adopting a 'compulsive sequence' approach familiar to them from past experience would operate in a piecemeal fashion that might achieve little.

To achieve generality in the argument, Heiner suggests that the size of the **competence–difficulty (C–D) gap** depends on environmental variables which determine the complexity of the decision, and perceptual variables which determine the decision-makers' competence. In the case of choosing how to produce, an environmental variable which would make the decision complex might be the (as-yet unknown) ability of a potential workforce to deal with different sorts of production method. A perceptual variable would be the technological knowledge and experience of the manager. Uncertainty increases with environmental complexity and falls with decision-makers' perceptual ability.

To put the general ideas to use, suppose that a decision-maker with an existing and familiar repertoire of behaviour is offered the possibility of doing something new, the implications of which are, however, as yet uncertain. There will, objectively, be circumstances in which the new approach (say a production technique) will turn out to have been the best to use and other circumstances in which it will turn out to have been better to use existing techniques. The probability that the right circumstances for using the new technique will arise can be written $P(R)$, and that the 'wrong' (inappropriate) circumstances will occur, $P(W) = 1 - P(R)$. Each of these depends on the environment.

Because of their C–D gaps, decision-makers will not always use the new method when it is appropriate to do so. The conditional probability[7] of a decision-maker using it in the right circumstances is $P(r) < 1$, and in the wrong circumstances $P(w) > 0$. Neither probability is known to the decision-maker. If used in the right circumstances, the new method generates a gain in performance (say, a cost saving) of G compared with what would have been achieved by applying the best existing method. If used in the wrong circumstances, the firm incurs a performance reduction (a cost increase) of L.

Now call the chance of using the new method in the right circumstances relative to using it inappropriately the 'reliability' of the decision-maker's choice, denoted $P(r)/P(w)$. This ratio can be used to show when there is a high enough potential gain from increasing flexibility (i.e. adding new potential methods) to make it worthwhile including a new action, such as a technique, in the repertoire. Extending the menu will be worthwhile when:

$$G \cdot P(r) \cdot P(R) > L \cdot P(w) \cdot (1 - P(R))$$

But this can be rearranged as:

$$P(r)/P(w) > (L/G) \cdot [(1 - P(R)/P(R)]$$

Heiner calls this the **Reliability Condition**. We have already interpreted the reliability ratio on the left-hand side. On the right-hand side is a minimum level which this ratio must attain in order to encourage decision-makers to add to their menu of potential actions. All elements on the right-hand side are determined by environmental factors and, when combined, yield what is defined as a 'tolerance limit', $T(e)$, where e stands for environment.

Inspection of the Reliability Condition at once reveals that for any value of the ratio L/G, $T(e)$ will rise from 0 when $P(R) = 1$ at an increasing rate towards infinity as $P(R)$ falls towards 0. Thus, as the probability of the right circumstances for using a new method declines, decision-makers have to demand of themselves increasing 'reliability' in choosing to use the new action when the right circumstances arise. This means, intuitively, that decision-makers will be reluctant to admit into their repertoire of choices of action potential methods which are appropriate only in unusual circumstances. Conversely, a decision-maker's menu will be limited to actions which are regarded as relatively likely or recurrent.

'A general characteristic of such a repertoire', Heiner concludes, 'is that it excludes actions which will in fact enhance performance under certain conditions, even though these conditions will occur with a positive probability, $P(R) > 0$. We thus have a formal characterisation of the pervasive association of both human and animal behaviour with various connotations of 'rule governed' behaviour such as instincts, habits, *routines*, rules of thumb, administrative procedures ... and so forth' (1983: 567). (My italics)

In other words, the range of responses for dealing with changing environmental conditions is limited to those which are perceived (rightly or wrongly) to be appropriate most of the time, given the incapacity of human decision-makers to judge when conditions calling for 'unusual' courses of action have arisen. This implies the use of rules of thumb or routines rather than the application of exhaustive optimising procedures on a case-by-case basis. Because rule-governed behaviour implies decision-makers will avoid doing things that would, under certain conditions be preferred, the resulting behaviour patterns are not an approximation to performance maximisation or in the case of costs, cost minimisation.

Notes

1. Mathematically, homogeneity of the production function is defined as follows. The production function may be written:

    $$Q = f(K, L)$$

    and for particular base values subscripted with a zero:

    $$Q_0 = f(K_0, L_0)$$

Suppose all inputs are now multiplied by the same factor, m. Output will now rise to a new level, Q_n:

$$Q_n = f(mK_0, mL_0)$$

and if

$$Q_n = m^v \cdot f(K_0, L_0)$$

then the production function is said to be homogeneous of degree v. In the simplest case, where $v = 1$, the function is said to be linear homogeneous and an m-fold increase in all inputs will lead to an m-fold increase in output, i.e. there are constant returns to scale. When $v < 1$, there are decreasing returns to scale and when $v > 1$, increasing returns.

2. In empirical work, the difficulty is to identify points on the isoquant. The practical answer to this question is locally to compare one firm with others in the same industry and to take the most efficient in the industry as the marker. The marker firm is described as using *best practice* technology within the industry. As a more satisfactory guide, we could take the most efficient level achieved anywhere in the world in an industry of this kind – world best practice. But under either approach, it is important to notice that logically this procedure offers no guarantee that we are identifying the absolutely most efficient which could be achieved. 'Best practice' is what it says it is: the best currently being practiced, not the best possible.

3. Leibenstein invented the term X-inefficiency to distinguish the concept from **allocative** efficiency, the term used by economists to signify the allocation of resources among all potential uses in a way which maximises their value to society.

4. Complementarity is a relation suggesting that certain pairs or groups of entities 'go together' in some sense. Consumption goods A and B are said to be complementary if a rise in the price of A leads not only to a fall in the quantity of A demanded but also in the quantity of B. Inputs X and Y are said to be complementary if a rise in the cost per unit of X leads not only to a fall in the quantity of X employed but also a decline in the amount of Y which is used.

5. Nelson and Winter accept that standard theory sometimes allows production possibilities to vary among firms but point out that since such differences are made immutable, interfirm knowledge transfers implicitly become infinitely expensive, which is also implausible (1982: 61).

6. The notion of compulsive sequences has been long used by economic historians and the idea of technical imbalances has appeared, recently, in the work of Hughes (1989: 71–4) described as reverse salients.

7. The conditional probability of using the new technique in the right conditions is the probability that the new technique will be chosen, given that the conditions are appropriate for its use.

References

Baumol, W.J. (1977a) *Economic Theory and Operations Analysis*, Englewood Cliffs NJ: Prentice Hall.

Baumol, W.J. (1977b), 'On the proper cost test for natural monopoly in a multiproduct industry', *American Economic Review* 67 809–22

Baumol, W.J., J.C. Panzar and R.D. Willig (1982) *Contestable Markets and the Theory of Industry Structure*, New York: Harcourt Brace Jovanovich.

Bound, J., C. Cummins, Z. Griliches, B.H. Hall and A. Jaffe (1984) 'Who does R&D and who patents', in Z. Griliches (ed.) *R&D, Patents and Productivity*, ch. 2, Chicago: University of Chicago Press.

Chenery, H. (1949) 'Engineering production function', *Quarterly Journal of Economics* 63, 507–31.

Coase, R.H. (1937), 'The nature of the firm', *Economica*, 4, 386–405.

Cookenboo, L. Jr (1958) *Crude Oil Pipelines and Competition in the Oil Industry*, Harvard: Harvard Institute for International Development.

Cooper, A.C. (1964) 'R&D is more efficient in small companies', *Harvard Business Review* 42, 75–83.

Dasgupta, P. and J.E. Stiglitz (1980), 'Industrial structure and the nature of innovative activity', *Economic Journal* 90, 266–93.

Department of Trade and Industry (1989) *Manufacturing into the late 1990s*, London: HMSO.

DITAC (Department of Industry, Technology and Commerce) (1992) *Australian Science and Innovation Resources Brief 1992*, Canberra: Australian Government Publishing Service.

Enos, J.L. (1958) 'A measure of the rate of technological progress in the petroleum refining industry', *Journal of Industrial Economics* 6, 180.

Enos, J.L. (1989) 'Transfer of technology', *Asia Pacific Economic Literature* 3(1), 3–37.

Farrell, M.J. (1957) 'The measurement of productive efficiency', *Proceedings of the Royal Statistical Society* 120, Part 3, 11–28.

Ferguson, C.E. (1969) *The Neoclassical Theory of Production and Distribution*, Cambridge: Cambridge University Press.

Fisher, F.M and P. Temin (1973) 'Returns to scale in research and development: What does the Schumpeterian Hypothesis imply?', *Journal of Political Economy* 81, 56–70.

Fisher, F.M. and P. Temin (1979) 'The Schumpeterian Hypothesis: Reply', *Journal of Political Economy*, 87, 386–9.

Forsund, F.R., C.A.K. Lovell, and P. Schmidt (1980) 'A summary of frontier production functions and of their relationship to efficiency measurement', *Journal of Econometrics*, 13, 5–25.

Freeman, C. (1974), *The Economics of Industrial Innovation*, Harmondsworth: Penguin.

Griliches, Z. (ed.), (1984) *R&D, Patents and Productivity*, Chicago: University of Chicago Press.

Griliches, Z. (1990) 'Patent statistics as economic indicators', *Journal of Economic Literature* 28, 1661–1707.

Grossman, S.J. and O.D. Hart, (1983) 'An analysis of the principal-agent problem', *Econometrica*, 51, 7–45.

Hay, D. and D. Morris (1991) *Industrial Economics and Organisation: Theory and Evidence*, Oxford: Oxford University Press.

Heiner, R.A. (1983) 'The origin of predictable behavior', *American Economic Review* 73(4), 560–95.

Hicks J.R. (1952) 'Annual Survey of Economic Theory: Monopoly', *Economica*, 3, reprinted in Stigler, G. and Boulding, K. (eds) *Readings in Price Theory*, Chicago: Chicago University Press.

Hughes, T. (1989) *American Genesis: A Century of Invention and Technological Enthusiasm, 1870–1970*, New York: Penguin.

Jaikumar, R. (1986), 'Post industrial manufacturing', *Harvard Business Review* 64(6), 69–76.

Jewkes, J., Sawers D. and R. Stillerman (1969) *The Sources of Innovation*, New York: Norton.

Jubb, C. and S. Markowski (1988) *Flexible Manufacturing Systems: Some Implications for the Theory of Production*, Working Paper 44, Bureau of Industry Economics, Canberra: Australian Government Printing Service.

Kamin, J.Y., I. Bijaoui, and R. Horesh, (1982) Some determinants of cost distributions in the process of technological innovation', *Research Policy* 11, 83–94

Kohn, M. and J.Y. Scott (1982) 'Scale economies in research and development', *Journal of Industrial Economics* 30(3), 239–250.

Koutsoyiannis, A. (1979) *Modern Microeconomics*, London: Macmillan.

Lamborghini, B. and C. Antonelli (1981) 'The impact of electronics on industrial structures and firm strategies, in OECD, Information Computer Communications Policy, 5: *Microelectronics, Productivity and Employment*, Paris.

Leibenstein, H. (1966) 'Allocative efficiency vs X-efficiency', *American Economic Review*, 56, 392–415.

Leibenstein, H. (1975) 'Aspects of the X-efficiency theory of the firm', *Bell Journal of Econmics* 6, 580–606.

Mansfield, E. *et al.* (1971) *Research and Development in the Modern Corporation*, New York: Macmillan.

Markowski, S. and C. Jubb (1989) 'The impact of microelectronics on scale in manufacturing industries', *Australian Journal of Management* 14(2), 171–211.

McBride, M.E. (1981) 'The nature and source of economies of scale in cement production', *Southern Economic Journal* 48, 105–15.

Milgrom, P. and M. Roberts (1990) 'The economics of modern manufacturing: Technology, strategy and organisation', *American Economic Review* 80(3), 511–28.

Nelson, R.R. (1987) *Understanding Technical Change as an Evolutionary Process*, Amsterdam: North-Holland.

Nelson, R.R. and S.G. Winter (1982) *An Evolutionary Theory of Economic Change*, Cambridge, MA: Harvard University Press, Belknap.

Newell, A. and H.A. Simon (1972) *Human Problem Solving*, Englewood Cliffs: Prentice Hall.

Nordhaus, W.D. (1969) *Invention, Growth and Welfare: A Theoretical Treatment of Technological Change*, Cambridge, MA: MIT Press.

O'Rourke, T. (1988) 'A Case for CIM', Lecture at the Conference on Manufacturing, Stanford University, Stanford, 1988.

Panzar, J.C. (1989) 'Technological determinants of firm and industry structure', in R. Schmalensee and R. Willig (eds) *Handbook of Industrial Organisation*, vol. I, Amsterdam: North-Holland.

Pratten, C. (1971) *Economies of Scale in Manufacturing Industry*, D.A.E. Occasional Paper 28, Cambridge: Cambridge University Press.

Richter, P. (1983) *Technological Change and Corporate Strategies: A Review of the Literature*, Lund: Research Policy Institute, University of Lund.

Robinson, E. (1958) *The Structure of Competitive Industry*, Chicago: University of Chicago Press.

Rodriguez, C.A. (1979) 'A comment on Fisher and Temin on the Schumpeterian Hypothesis', *Journal of Political Economy* 87, 383–5.

Rosenberg, N. (1976) *Perspectives on Technology*, Cambridge: Cambridge University Press.

Scherer, F.M. (1965) 'Firm size, market structure, opportunity and the output of patented innovations', *American Economic Review* 55, 1097–23.

Scherer, F.M. (1972) 'Nordhaus' theory of optimal patent life: A geometric reinterpretation' *American Economic Review* June, 422–7.

Scherer, F.M. (1980) *Industrial Market Structure and Economic Performance*, 2nd edn, Chicago: Rand McNally.

Scherer, F.M. (1984) 'Using linked patent and R&D data to measure inter-industry technology flows', in Z. Griliches (ed.) *R&D, Patents and Productivity*, Chicago: University of Chicago Press, Ch. 20, 4178–64.

Scherer, F.M., Beckenstein, A., E. Kaufer and R.D. Murphy (1975) *The Economics of Multi-plant Operation: An International Comparisons Study*, Harvard: Harvard University Press.

Stiglitz, J.E. (1987) 'Learning to learn, localized learning and technological progress', in P. Dasgupta and P. Stoneman (eds) *Economic Policy and Technological Performance*, Oxford: Oxford University Press, Ch. 5.

Stoneman, P.A. (1983) *The Economic Analysis of Technological Change*, Oxford: Oxford University Press.

Teece, D. (1980) 'Economics of scope and the scope of the enterprise', *Journal of Economic Behavior and Organisation* 1, 223–47.

US Department of Commerce (1967) *Technological Innovation*, Washington, DC: US Government Printing Office.

Van Raan, A.F.J. (ed.) (1988) *Handbook of Quantitative Studies of Science and Technology*, Amsterdam: Elsevier Science Publishers.

Warndorf, P.R. and M.E. Merchant (1986) 'Development and future trends in computer-integrated manufacturing in the USA', *International Journal of Technology Management* 1(42), 161–77.

Waterson, M. (1983), 'Economies of scope within market frameworks', *International Journal of Industrial Organisation*, 1, 223–37.

Williamson, O.E. (1975) *Markets and Hierarchies*, New York: The Free Press.

Wiliamson, O.E. (1985) *The Economic Institutions of Capitalism*, New York: The Free Press.

Winter, S.G. (1988) 'Coase, competence and the corporation', *Journal of Law, Economics and Organization*, 4(1), 163–180.

Wright, K. and D. Bourn (1988) *Manufacturing Intelligence*, Reading MA: Addison Wesley.

5

Innovation and the firm

Introduction

The focus of this chapter is the firm, which for simplicity will initially be defined as a decision-making unit engaged in production. It is at the level of the firm that the decisions are made to introduce new technology into production and where much new technology is developed in the pursuit of product and process innovation. To understand the innovation process, therefore, it is important to understand how firms work.

The starting point for the analysis is the simplifying assumption that firms can be viewed as having a clearly defined goal or objective. Most often in economic theory the objective is taken to be short- or long-term profit, but it might also be sales revenue, asset growth or managers' utility. Firms may also have more than one goal. The relevance of innovation to firms is that it offers them the prospect of achieving their objective(s) more effectively. Chapters 3 and 4 have already shown how innovation may enhance market demand and reduce production costs and both of these effects have the potential to raise profits. It follows directly that analysis of the profit-seeking efforts of firms should be able to throw light on how and why innovation occurs. Such analysis must take account of the costly nature of innovation and of the changes that innovation will bring to the structure of the firm.

The first section introduces the construct that is the firm of much standard economic theory and considers the impact on profits of exogenous technological progress and LBD. In the next section, it is recognised that innovation involves costs for the firm. Analysis here focuses first on optimising R&D in one-period models, then on investment choices over many periods. The quantity and timing of R&D undertaken within a firm is considered and the speed at which new technology developed elsewhere might diffuse in the firm after initial adoption. It is also recognised that innovation-related investments may be used strategically, i.e. to alter the competitive conditions under which a firm might confront actual or potential rivals in future periods.

The territory covered by analysis of the firm inevitably impinges to an extent on work at the level of the industry to be dealt with in Chapter 6. This is particularly apparent in the ensuing section on boundaries of the firm and (importantly techno-logical) forces for integration and fragmentation. This section also investigates the notion of a firm's technology strategy, indicating that the notion of 'strategy' in this case has a managerial nuance, giving it a different flavour from that found in the analysis foreshadowed above. The role of entrepreneurship is dealt with in a section of its own.

The chapter concludes with a segment providing an evolutionary perspective on the firm. The focus of attention here is the behavioural assumptions made about firms and the implications of abandoning the notion that firms maximise profit, or indeed anything.

The firm in formal economic analysis

The theoretical construct of the 'the firm' in economics has evolved to meet the requirement that some sort of entity be identified with the tasks of choosing input and production levels and setting prices when market conditions allow. In the simplest economic models, these are the only choice variables, so innovation-related expenditures are simply ignored and the impact of technological change is treated, if at all, as exogenous. As a starting point for the chapter, we consider two polar extremes: first, the firm which is so small relative to its product and input markets that it cannot influence the unit price of its output or the prices of its factors of production; and second, the firm which is the only one in its industry. The first is the firm of so-called 'perfect' competition, the second the monopoly firm. Both are assumed to maximise profit, to have perfect knowledge of all production possibilities and to produce a single product.

To compare the two, consult Figure 5.1. Since perfectly competitive firms cannot influence prices, they have no market power. They are **price-takers**. This implies each firm faces a horizontal demand curve; at the market-determined price it can sell as much or as little as it wishes. Another way of putting it is to say that each firm faces an infinitely high price elasticity of demand. The firms comprise an industry which, in aggregate, faces a demand curve of the usual negative slope. The monopolistic firm, being the only one in the industry, has the same demand curve as its industry. The major difference between the perfectly competitive and monopolistic firm, therefore, is that the former faces an infinitely elastic demand curve, while the latter has a demand curve of less than infinite and often rather low elasticity. Monopolists must cut price if they wish to increase sales volume.

Given that the perfectly competitive firm's demand curve is horizontal, its **total revenue (TR)**, equal to price per unit, P, times quantity sold, Q, increases in direct proportion to Q. That implies that **average revenue (AR)**, equal at any output level to TR/Q, must be constant. **Marginal revenue (MR)**, (dTR/dQ), the slope of the TR function, must also be constant and equal to AR.

Recall from Chapter 3 that TR must first rise and then fall if the demand curve is linear and downward sloping, so in the case of the monopolist, AR must fall continually

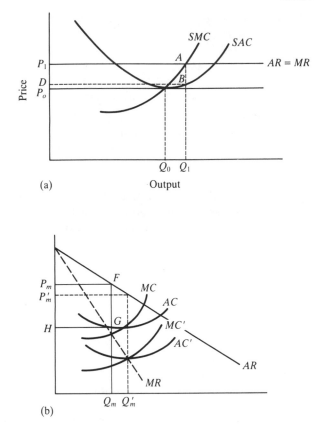

Figure 5.1   (a) The perfectly competitive firm in the short run; (b) the monopolistic firm.

from its intercept on the vertical axis and MR will always lie below it. It is easy to show that when the demand curve is linear, MR will always fall twice as fast as AR. See, for example, Koutsoyiannis, 1979: 51. The precise relationship between price and marginal revenue can be derived as follows:

$$MR = d[P(Q) \cdot Q]/dQ = P + Q[dP(Q)/dQ]$$
$$= P + P/P \cdot Q \cdot dP/dQ$$
$$= P + P(Q/P \cdot dP/dQ)$$
$$= P + P[1/(P/Q \cdot dQ/dP)]$$
$$= P[1 + 1/e]$$

where e is the price elasticity of demand. Because the demand curve has a downward slope, dQ/dP is negative and so, are e and its reciprocal. Another way of writing the same thing is to take the absolute value of e, $|e|$, and re-express the condition:

$$MR = P[1 - 1/|e|]$$

What this says is that when demand is inelastic and $|e|$ is thus less than 1, $P[1 - 1/|e|]$ must be negative, MR negative and TR falling. The intuition is that when demand is inelastic, the price must fall substantially to induce a given proportional increase in sales volume and total revenues will decline. On the other hand, when demand is elastic, a much smaller price cut will increase sales by the same proportion and total revenue will rise. This is reflected in a high (above unity) value of $|e|$ which leads to a positive number for $P[1 - 1/|e|]$.

On the cost side, perfectly competitive firms are assumed to have U-shaped SAC curves and a LAC which is either U-shaped (as in Figure 4.7) or horizontal. In the short run, analysis relates to a SAC curve related to a plant of given size. To maximise profit, each firm chooses to operate where total revenues exceed total costs by the greatest amount. This calls for selecting the output level at which $MC = MR$. Were MC to be less than MR at some output level, increasing production would raise total revenue by more than total costs and so would increase profit. Were MC more than MR at some output level, reducing production would reduce total costs by more than it would reduce total revenue, again increasing profit. Because the SAC curve is U-shaped, the short-run marginal cost (SMC) curve rises to cut the SAC curve from below and, given that the MR curve is horizontal, there will also be a point where the SMC passes through it from beneath. If the firm's cost structure were as shown in Figure 5.1a, and it faced price level P_1, it would produce output Q_1 and make profit $P_1 ABD$, found by subtracting the area under the SAC curve at B – total costs of producing Q_1 – from the area under the AR curve at A, total revenue from selling Q_1. With the same cost structure, the firm's maximum profit would be zero if it faced price level P_o.

Average costs include a return on capital employed by the firm, so 'zero profit' means total revenue, less payments to variable inputs, less what must be paid to the fixed factor (capital) to prevent its owners from transferring it to an alternative use. When profits exceed what the owners of capital require to persuade them to keep their investment in the use made of it by the firm, they are called **excess** or **supernormal profits**, or **economic rent**.

In the short run, the firm might be operating with any one of the SAC curves related to the various plant sizes allowed by the technology. It adjusts to an increase in market price by moving along its SMC curve. If the price rose from P_o to P_1, output would rise from Q_o to Q_1, enabling it to earn an economic rent of $P_1 ABD$. If the price fell below P_o, the firm would make a loss. In the long run, there are no fixed inputs and several further types of adjustment might occur within the firm or around it.

If any firm earns excess profit, this acts as an inducement to it to expand its capacity and to firms outside to enter the industry. Firms which make losses and are unable to adjust will leave. Under the pressure of continuing entry and expansion, the firm will find its price being driven down by the increase in industry-wide productive capacity relative to demand and ultimately only those firms whose SAC curves lie at the lowest point of the LAC curve will be able to survive. In the long-run equilibrium, the firm will produce output associated with the lowest point on its SAC and LAC curves and will earn zero excess profit. Technology (which determines the shape and position of the cost curves) is assumed to remain constant throughout.

In a monopolistic industry (Figure 5.1b), all output is supplied by a single firm. The source of the monopoly might be a legal restriction on entry, unique access to an essential input into production or a substantial barrier to entry such as might be associated with scale economies in the technology, an absolute cost advantage or product differentiation. We consider these barriers at length below, but at this point assume that the monopolist has complete freedom to choose the price it charges, without fear of attracting entry by outsiders. It must, however, bear in mind that the higher the price it selects, the less volume it will be able to sell and that in the price-elastic (upper) region of the demand curve, raising price will bring lower total revenue. As a profit maximiser, its choices are heavily circumscribed; it must produce at the price and output levels where $MC = MR$, i.e. P_m and Q_m. If it does so, it will make profit of $P_m FGH$. Notice from above that when $MC = MR$:

$$MC = P[1 - 1/|e|]$$

which implies

$$(P - MC)/P = 1/|e|$$

Now the proportional price–cost margin shown on the left is a measure of the extent by which the firm can charge a price in excess of its production costs, which is an indication of its market power. According to this formula, perfectly competitive firms, for which e is infinite, have no market power and, as we have seen, will always produce where $MC = P$, since for them, $P = AR = MR$. But the lower the value of e, the greater the price–cost margin and the more opportunity a firm has for profitably exploiting market power.

The intuition of this is that the elasticity will be relatively high if a firm is in a market producing output with close substitutes. Raising its price will then substantially undermine its market position relative to the producers of the substitutes, showing a lack of market power. Conversely, the elasticity will be low if the firm's product has no close substitutes and since, in such cases, price rises will do relatively little to reduce sales, market power is significant.

Notice before we move on why monopoly is often regarded as a problem. In the perfectly competitive industry, firms always produce where the price paid by buyers is equal to the marginal cost of production and in the long-run equilibrium, buyers as a group need to pay no more than the minimum required to induce firms to supply all they require at the market price. In the monopoly case, buyers have to pay a price above the marginal cost of production and are supplied with less output than would be made available by a firm forced to sell at marginal cost.

Exogenous technological progress in the perfectly competitive firm

Under the perfect information and efficient production assumptions of the perfectly competitive model, it makes most sense to think of technological progress as exogenous and applying to all firms in similar measure. If such progress affected fixed costs alone, a possibility in the short run, the SAC curve for each firm would shift down, profits would increase, but the firm would produce the same quantity of output as before. This is because only changes in variable costs affect the structure of marginal costs, so the SMC curve would be unaffected and would intersect the MR curve at the same point as before.

In the long run, all costs are variable and the LMC curve would shift at the same time as the LAC. As we saw in Chapter 4, the LAC curve is likely often to shift down in a way which also takes its minimum point outwards, i.e. the optimum plant size increases. But it was also noted that some types of flexibility-enhancing progress could alleviate constraints imposed by indivisibilities and reduce the optimum plant size. In either case, new supernormal profits would initially be created for existing firms, which would induce newcomers to enter. This would set in motion downward pressure on price. In the new long-term equilibrium, firms would be selling at lower prices. For progress which increases the minimum efficient scale of production, each firm would produce more than before; for progress which reduces the MES, each firm would produce less. Note, however, that the counterintuitive flavour of the latter result rests on the simplifying assumption of strictly one-product firms.

Exogenous technological change and the monopolist

The implications of exogenous technical change for the cost curves of the monopolist are the same as those for the perfect competitor. If progress affects only fixed costs, there will be an increase in the firm's profit margin (price less average costs) and its percentage profit margin (profit margin divided by price). Its profit-maximising price and output will be unchanged, because the MC curve will cut the MR curve at the same point as before. If, on the other hand, variable costs are reduced by progress by a constant amount for all levels of output, marginal cost will fall by the same amount at all output levels and the downward shift in the MC curve will bring about a fall in the profit-maximising price and a rise in output. This is because the new MC curve intersects the MR function lower than before. To see this, compare in Figure 5.1b the post-innovation cost curves AC′ and MC′ with their pre-innovation levels and note that $Q'_m > Q_m$, while $P'_m < P_m$.

It should be clear from inspection of Figure 5.1b that technological progress can be expected to increase the excess of price over average costs. It can be shown formally that the profit margin and proportional profit margin will rise in the case described (Hay and Morris, 1991: 201–3 offer derivations for the analogous case of rising average

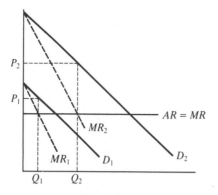

Figure 5.2 Market-expanding product innovation and the monopolistic firm.

costs). In any case, as long as progress depresses the MC curve bodily, the monopoly price will fall and output increase.

Analysis of these and other cases is simplified if it is assumed (quite realistically in many instances) that average and marginal cost curves are horizontal over the relevant range of outputs. This merely invokes the idea that we are focusing on long-run cost curves and that total costs are rising in proportion to output which, assuming constant input prices, would arise from constant returns to scale in the production function.

As an example of the usefulness of assuming constant returns and long run cost curves, consider innovation which shifts the monopolist's demand curve outwards. In general, this would lead to a rise in price and increasing output. That would obviously happen if the slope of the new demand curve were unchanged and the MR schedule derived from it cut a U-shaped MC curve at a higher point than before. But lest the misleading impression be given that it is higher unit costs which cause price to rise, it is easy to observe that, even with horizontal AC and MC curves, the new price will be higher. The case is shown in Figure 5.2 where the new demand curve, D_2 and MR curve, MR_2, are associated with profit-maximising output and price levels Q_2 and P_2, respectively, compared with pre-innovation levels Q_1 and P_1. The magnitude of these effects will also be influenced by simultaneous changes in the slope of the demand curve, but again these will be easier to identify if constant returns are assumed.

The incentive to innovate

Ideas developed above were incorporated in a seminal analysis of innovation undertaken by Arrow (1962), which was designed to identify differing *incentives to innovate* which might confront an innovating firm. The set-up supposes one firm (called, for the purposes of this part of the analysis 'the innovator') generates a process innovation on which a long-term patent is granted and thereby obtains a monopoly in the supply of the new technology. On the demand side, potential users operate in either a perfectly competitive

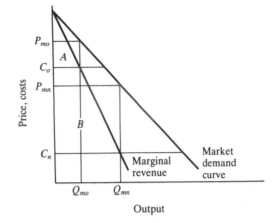

Figure 5.3   The incentives to innovate when a process innovation reduces production costs from C_o to C_n.

or monopolistic product market. Arrow wants to know whether the incentives for the innovator vary with the market conditions for user firms.

The argument is illustrated in Figure 5.3. The monopolistic and competitive industries have identical market demand and cost functions. For both, pre-innovation production costs are represented by the constant average and marginal cost curves marked C_o. The monopoly producer charges price P_{mo}, sells output of Q_{mo} and makes profit represented by the rectangle A. Firms in the competitive industry charge a price equal to C_o and make no excess profit. Putting the innovation to use (by assumption without implementation costs) reduces production costs to the level C_n.

If the innovator is also the producer (i.e. a producer with its own R&D department), post-innovation profit is maximised by selling Q_{mn} at P_{mn} per unit: rectangle B. If the innovator is a specialist supplier of new technology to other firms, Arrow assumes it will let the monopolist use the new process under licence in return for a lump sum payment. The largest lump sum the innovator could negotiate will again be B, though the producer firm should be able to cut into this if it knows the innovator will be unable to find any alternative user and employs this knowledge to put pressure on the supplier. The maximum incentive to innovate in the case of a monopolised producer market is thus $(B - A)$.

In the competitive case, the innovator is assumed to be a firm within the industry which licenses use of the new process by other firms. The maximum total profit that the innovator can earn from firms comprising an industry with the given downward-sloping market demand curve is again B. This is obtained by charging a per unit output royalty fee of $P_{mn} - C_n$. Since the firm was previously earning zero excess profit, the incentive here is B itself, rather than $(B - A)$ and Arrow concludes that competitive product markets therefore tend to encourage innovation more than monopolies do.

While this analysis has been the inspiration for much subsequent analysis, it has been superceded for reasons associated with several shortcomings. For example, the costs of generating the innovation need to be made an integral part of the analysis itself; uncertainty is entirely ignored; costs of implementation and adjustment to new technology are absent; the strategic use of innovation is not discussed. The conclusion of the analysis is also sensitive to the assumption that before the innovation the innovator in perfect competition earned zero excess profit. In a more ambitious analysis, innovation would not take the form of a single episode, but would be a continuous and continuing process in which the innovator could already have been earning excess profit from earlier successes. In that case, the clear advantage of the competitive product market could not be unambiguously established and as shown in the analysis of Kamien and Schwartz (1982), other influences would come into play.

Learning-by-doing and monopoly

We noted earlier that merely by gaining experience through cumulative production, a firm's unit costs will fall over time owing to LBD. In the case of the monopoly firm, an interesting implication of this is that if it performs a multiperiod profit-maximising exercise, taking into account that its costs will fall in future, it will produce more overall than it would have done if it chose output levels on a discrete period-by-period profit-maximising basis. To see this, consider the firm's decisions. Fudenberg and Tirole (1983) argue that in a two-period framework, the firm will charge a price in the first period below that which would maximise its profits at the initial level of costs because by doing so it can increase its sales and, as a result, its longer term opportunities for producing output, learning by doing and reducing future costs. In this story, profit-maximising price falls over time. But Spence (1981) has argued that, with LBD, firms may set a single price associated with the point at which marginal revenue equals the unit cost of production when (almost) all the benefits of LBD have occurred.

In Spence's analysis, total short-run costs comprise one element that simply changes in direct proportion to output and a second component whose value in any period depends on cumulative output to that point. Algebraically, the second component may be written:

$$A(t) = C \cdot z(Q_c(t))Q(t)$$

where $Q_c(t)$ is cumulative output to the beginning of period t, the sum of the outputs per period, $Q(t)$, from $t = 0$; C represents input unit costs and z is a parameter whose value falls from 1 towards a non-negative floor as Q_c increases. In Figure 5.4, the learning curve is shown by the function $z(Q_c(t))$. We denote by $G(Q_o(t))$ the area under the learning curve associated with any selected value of $Q_c(t)$; the area labelled $G(Q_c(4))$ relates to the cumulative output level $Q_c(4)$. If a short period of time were to pass, cumulative output would rise and the addition to the area now under the curve would grow by an amount such as that shown in Figure 5.4 by the cross-hatched area $MNVW$, where WV is an increase in Q_c from $Q_c(4)$ to $Q_c(5)$, equal to output, $Q(4)$. If $Q(4) = WV$

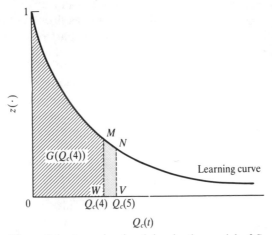

Figure 5.4   Learning by doing in the model of Spence.

is small, period 4 output may be multiplied by $z(Q_c(4))$ to give a good approximation to the area $MNVW$, so we may write:

$$\mathrm{d}G(Q_c(4))/\mathrm{d}t = z(Q_c(4)){\cdot}Q(4)$$

and, in general:

$$\mathrm{d}G(Q_c(t))/\mathrm{d}t = z(Q_c(t)){\cdot}Q(t)$$

But from the definition of $A(t)$ above, this means

$$A(t) = C{\cdot}(\mathrm{d}G(Q_c)/\mathrm{d}t) \tag{5.1}$$

which, if non-learning-related costs are ignored (they make no difference to the qualitative outcome of the argument), is another way of expressing production costs per period. Total production costs from $t = 0$ until a horizon date T are found by adding up all the $A(t)$ over T periods to yield (by integration) $C{\cdot}G(Q_c(T))$, i.e. production cost per unit of output times the area under the learning curve for the whole period $t = 0$ until T. By definition, the marginal cost of increasing output is the increase in total cost incurred as a result. Using the expression for total costs just derived, marginal cost must be the area found by multiplying an increase in cumulative output, Q_c, not by the unit cost of output at the time it is produced, but by the unit cost of output at T. As Spence puts it: 'The firm's true marginal costs at every point of time are equal to its unit costs at the end of the entire period ... That marginal cost does, of course, depend on the rate of output throughout the interval. But the marginal cost is the unit cost at the end, once the learning has occurred ...' (1981: 51).

One implication of this approach is that a profit-maximising firm whose monopoly is entrenched has little motivation to reduce price; the model suggests firms should hold prices constant as costs fall (Lieberman, 1984). We shall see later that if a monopoly firm's position is threatened, there will be a motivation to reduce price. We shall also argue later that learning by doing is a potential source of monopoly. But that argument works best when what the firm learns does not leak out to potential rivals.

Costly innovation in the firm

Once innovation is allowed to involve the firm in explicit costs, the analysis necessarily becomes more complex, but at the same time more rewarding. In the simpler models, optimisation takes place within an essentially static context where firms are viewed as taking much of their environment as given. To use a distinction made by Kamien and Schwartz (1982), these models are to a large extent 'decision theoretic', in the sense that they focus on individual firms and abstract from the simultaneous interfirm interactions which are dealt with in the 'game-theoretic' approach. As Dasgupta (1984) points out, this mostly means that the first sort of model asks a more restrictive set of questions than the second, not that they are actually different approaches. After all, both are based on rational optimisation. But from an expository point of view, it is clearly helpful to start with the more accessible cases.

R&D expenditure on process and product innovation: static analysis under certainty

In Chapter 4 we noted that research intensities varied systematically from industry to industry. But what of firms? What factors influence their research intensities? In this section we analyse that question first for a process innovator, taking the lead of Dasgupta and Stiglitz (1980), and then for the product-innovating firm, following Needham (1975).

The full Dasgupta and Stiglitz analysis of process innovation falls very much into the game-theoretic class of models and is dealt with in Chapter 6. But their characterisation of the firm can be considered independently of industry-wide interactions and is introduced here partly to prepare the ground for the industry-level analysis and partly to generate a useful result analogous to that found for the product innovator. The set-up in the Dasgupta and Stiglitz firm is simple: the firm chooses RD to maximise single-period profit, Π, where:

$$\Pi = [P(Q + Q_R) - C(RD)]Q - RD \qquad (5.2)$$

Here, Q is the firm's output, Q_R the output of all its rivals, and C (constant) unit production costs assumed to fall with increases in RD. Note that price is a function of all industry sales through the demand curve.

To find the conditions characterising a profit maximum, differentiate (5.2) with respect to Q and RD in turn, and set the resulting expression equal to zero.

When $d\Pi/dQ = 0$:

$$C(RD) = [(dP(Q + Q_R)/dQ\cdot Q] + P(Q + Q_R)$$
$$= [(dP/d(Q + Q_R)\cdot d(Q + Q_R)dQ\cdot Q] + P$$

Now suppose the firm believes that it can adjust its production level without provoking any of its rivals to vary theirs. Then if it raises Q by a small amount (dQ), the total of all industry output will rise by the same amount, so that $d(Q + Q_R)/dQ = 1$. Under this assumption:

$$C(RD) = dP/d(Q + Q_R)\cdot Q + P$$
$$= P - (-dP/d(Q + Q_R))\cdot Q$$
$$= P - 1/(Q + Q_R)[P/P\cdot(-dP/d(Q + Q_R)Q\cdot(Q + Q_R)]$$
$$= P - 1/(Q + Q_R)\cdot P[(-dP/d(Q + Q_R)\cdot(Q + Q_R)/P]Q$$
$$= P - 1/(Q + Q_R)\cdot P\cdot e_{inv}\cdot Q$$

where e_{inv} is the inverse elasticity of demand. Thus:

$$C(RD) = P[1 - e_{inv}\cdot Q/(Q + Q_R)]$$

Under certain assumptions about how the firm believes its rivals might react to its *RD* effort, it is shown that:

$$d\Pi/dQ = (dP/dQ)\cdot Q + P(Q + QR) - C(RD)$$

so that when $d\Pi/dQ = 0$

$$C(RD) = P(Q + QR)\ [1 - e_{inv}\cdot Q/(Q + Q_R)] \tag{5.3}$$

where e_{inv} is the inverse elasticity of demand $(-dP/d(Q + Q_R)\cdot(Q + Q_R/P)$ and negative because of the downward slope of the demand curve. Moreover:

$$d\Pi/dRD = -(dC/dRD)Q - 1$$
$$= C'(RD)Q - 1$$

so that when $d\Pi/dRD = 0$:

$$-C'(RD) = 1 \tag{5.4}$$

Together, (5.3) and (5.4) yield the research intensity condition:

$$RD/PQ = [-(RD/C\cdot dC/dRD)]\cdot[1 - Q/(Q + Q_R)\cdot e_{inv}] \tag{5.5}$$

(Stoneman, 1983: 33–4). Here the first term in square brackets is a crucial elasticity, the responsiveness (downwards) of production costs to an increase in R&D.

In Chapter 6 it will be shown that *RD* and market structure are simultaneously determined in the Dasgupta and Stiglitz model, so drawing inferences from (5.5) in isolation is potentially dangerous. However, it is both intuitive and in line with the general conclusions of Dasgupta and Stiglitz that, other things being equal, research intensity will be higher, the larger the responsiveness of production costs to R&D

directed to reducing them. This again suggests a useful line of empirical enquiry into understanding why some firms and industries have higher research intensities; firms which are most effective at converting R&D into lower production costs should, on this account, also be those which have the highest R&D intensities. It is less clear why greater research intensity should always be associated with smaller market shares $Q/(Q + Q_R)$, though it has been hypothesised that any firm's innovative activity will tend to be greater if it has to compete for market share with rivals than if it enjoys a monopoly position. That issue receives further attention later.

The product innovation analysis focuses on the decisions of a firm producing a number of product variants and follows lines developed by Needham (1975). The firm is assumed to maximise its present value, V, the sum of its anticipated stream of profits, discounted continuously from now ($t = 0$) to infinity. In maximising V, the firm allows the number of product variants it makes to vary, certain that expenditures of RD_N are the development costs required to generate one new product variant.

For every new variant the firm introduces, it is assumed that rivals will retaliate after m periods with new, competing products of their own. From $t = 0$ to $t = m$, the innovator enjoys an increase in market share, but after period m will see its share eroded by rivals. The incremental change in V yielded by adding a new product variant is the sum of effects in three phases. First, there are the development costs, $-RD_N$; second, there is the change in (discounted) profits yielded by the innovation-related increased market share before imitation. Third, there is the change in (discounted) profits associated with the new product variant, once it has been imitated.

Taking account of the range of factors influencing profits in each phase, it is possible to derive a useful condition indicating the determinants of the product-innovating firm's research intensity. Assuming that V increases to a single peak value as the number of new products rises, and then declines, it can be shown that:

$$\text{FIRM RESEARCH INTENSITY} = \text{PROMAR } E_{S,n} \int_{0}^{m} e^{-(r+d)t} \cdot dt$$

$$+ E_{S,R} \cdot E_{R,n} \int_{m}^{\infty} e^{-(r+d)t} \cdot dt \qquad (5.6)$$

Firm research intensity is defined as the ratio of total R&D expenditure on new products to the value of the firm's market share. PROMAR is the percentage profit margin of the innovating firm. Equation 5.6 contains three elasticity terms: $E_{S,n}$ is the elasticity of the firm's market share with respect to product innovation in the absence of retaliation, a positive number; $E_{S,R}$ is the firm's market share elasticity with respect to a positive level of rival retaliation, usually a negative number; and $E_{R,n}$ is the elasticity of rivals' response with respect to the firm's product innovation.

Finally, the negative exponent term builds into the condition the firm's discount rate, r, and a depreciation rate, d, to reflect the speed with which product variants become obsolete.

If (5.6) is viewed as a behavioural rule rooted in optimisation, the third of the elasticities, $E_{R,n}$ may be interpreted as the firm's anticipation of its rivals' response. If the firm expects no retaliation, $E_{S,R} \cdot E_{R,n}$ falls to zero and its research intensity will be determined solely on the basis of comparing development costs with additional net revenues (revenues less production costs) which flow from the innovation. If the response is expected to be positive, $E_{S,R} \cdot E_{R,n}$ will be negative and the firm's research intensity will thus be lower than if no retaliation is expected. Research intensity will be lower the earlier a response is expected (i.e. the smaller is m), the greater the response is expected to be (i.e the larger is $E_{R,n}$) and the more damaging to market share (proportionally) any given response would be (i.e. the larger is the (negative) value of $E_{S,R}$).

The analysis underlying (5.6) presupposes a great deal of certainty or predictability in the innovation process. First, each product innovation has both known and identical development costs; second, each innovation has a known (or at least confidently predictable) impact on the firm's market share; and third, the firm is portrayed as knowing (or being able to make firm predictions about) when and how rivals will respond and what impact that will have on its profits. Given the nature of the innovation process, these are strongly simplifying assumptions.

Because of this, the conditions in which the assumptions imply the analysis would be most likely to have relevance are those in which the firm is operating in a settled market, mature in its technology. A major implication of the analysis is that research intensity will vary systematically with the maturity of the market where there are many product variants, declining as the market matures. To see why, recall from (5.6) that the firm's research intensity will be relatively large if, for any PROMAR, $E_{S,n}$ and m are large and $E_{S,R}$ and/or $E_{R,n}$ small. We expect $E_{S,n}$ to be largest in an immature market where there are as yet few product variants and relatively large gaps in the market. In these conditions, a new product should be able to increase the firm's market share by more than if a great many variants had already been introduced.

In general, m will be higher, the longer it takes for rivals to market substitutes. This, in turn, will reflect rivals' imitation costs and, if the innovator has been able to protect the new product through a device such as a patent, the ease or difficulty of inventing around the patent. Rivals' imitation costs are likely to be highest when the industry is immature and least is (widely) known about producing its products. Patent protection will become more difficult to secure when more product variants already exist.

Turning finally to the profit margin, product innovation will confer a degree of monopoly power on individual firms within the industry, which will give them the opportunity to earn monopoly rent, i.e. innovation-related profit. If the number of competing product variants is few and if each firm has focused on producing variants whose characteristics are combined in ways for which there is a strong market preference, each is more likely to earn a higher profit margin, PROMAR, than when the product space has become more crowded and any innovation will have a close substitute.

There are arguments to suggest therefore that, with the increasing maturity of the industry, each firm will face changing incentives to undertake product innovation and may well reduce its product-related research intensity. Evidence in support of this hypothesis can be found in OECD (1988). It is also likely that science-based industries of the kind discussed in Chapter 4 will often be relatively immature, since only recent scientific developments have brought them into existence. It is consistent with the theory here that firms in such industries often have high research intensities.

Adjustment costs and uncertainty in the R&D investment decision

In a simple way, innovation costs have now been incorporated into the analysis of firms' decisions. Missing so far however have been two elements which in reality always characterise investment processes. The first of these is the costs firms must incur to adjust to an optimum, or to move from one optimum to another. In the earlier analysis, optimal levels of R&D investment were identified, but by implication it was assumed that if ever changing conditions called for variations in such levels, those variations could be instantaneously made without cost. Economic analysis has recognised such costs exist and researchers have used them to provide an essential building block in a theory of investment, which is offered as an alternative to the widely-used 'neoclassical' approach pioneered by Jorgenson (1963). We now apply that approach to identify the level of a firm's derived demand for R&D based on, among other things, the demand for output it expects in future.

The second missing element is **uncertainty**. Uncertainty may pertain to technological factors (such as the probable outcome of a research programme) or to market-related factors (such as the responsiveness of potential customers to a new product, or the respite an innovator might enjoy before being imitated). Again, work has been undertaken to tackle uncertainty in R&D investment and two models are presented here, one to show how firms might time their innovations in response to expected technological rivalry (of a rather general kind) and the other to throw light on intrafirm diffusion by bringing adjustment costs and uncertainty together.

Adjustment cost approach

To allow for adjustment costs in the R&D investment function, we draw on the work of Schankerman and Nadiri (1984) which, in turn, builds on Modigliani (1961), Eisner (1978) and Sargent (1978, 1979). It is assumed that firms choose an R&D 'profile', a current investment decision plus a stream of future planned investment, which minimises the present value of all its costs, given expectations about the future price of R&D inputs and the level of output. The firm's stock of knowledge, KN, can be increased, with a lag, by R&D effort. The greater the increase in knowledge required between any two dates, the greater the R&D cost involved and in this case, Schankerman and Nadiri assume that as the level of R&D effort rises to increase KN, the unit (average) cost of R&D inputs rises linearly with it.

To be precise, take t as the base period and write the value of variables planned or expected in t for s periods into the future (the target period), with the subscript

t, s. Thus real R&D investment, planned in t for $t + s$ is $RD_{t,s}$. Let $h(RD_{t,s})$ be the function describing the unit cost of R&D investment and in particular, suppose that $h(\cdot)$ takes the form:

$$h(RD_{t,s}) = P_{t,s}[1 + a \cdot RD_{t,s}] \tag{5.7}$$

where $P_{t,s}$ is the price of R&D inputs expected at t to prevail at $t + s$, and $a > 0$ is a parameter. Thus $h(\cdot)$ rises linearly with $RD_{t,s}$ and total R&D costs $h(\cdot)RD_{t,s}$ will include a term in $RD_{t,s}$ squared and so will rise at an increasing rate with rises in the level of R&D. The rising marginal cost of R&D effort this implies reflects increasing adjustment costs in the R&D department.

Adjustment costs arise whenever one set of production arrangements are substituted for an existing set. In the context of production, the costs relate to increasing the size of a firm's capital stock and possibly changing it qualitatively if technical advance is embodied in new equipment. Internal factors which give rise to adjustment costs include rearranging the physical layout of plant, retraining and redeploying labour and putting greater demands on managerial staff as the productive capacity of the firm increases. External factors include suppliers' demands for a price premium in relation to early deliveries of capital goods and the increasing finance charges which may be attracted at the margin by continuing expansion. In this tradition, it is often assumed that as firms attempt to increase the speed at which they adjust from one level of the capital stock to another, so the adjustment costs will rise (see, for example, Nickell (1978), Chapter 3.) In the Schankerman–Nadiri model, the same assumption is applied to expansion of the firm's knowledge-producing capital, which is why the marginal cost of R&D investment is assumed to rise. Costs involved might include expenses related to searching for, acquiring, installing and commissioning new R&D inputs, perhaps training new R&D technicians and coordinating the whole R&D effort as a component of the firm's activities and as a part of the firm's broader strategy. (See Chapter 2, p. 35; Chapter 4, pp. 159; and this Chapter, p. 204–6.)

We now place this element in the broader context of overall cost minimisation. The firm is assumed to have a production function, exhibiting constant returns to scale in traditional inputs, labour and capital, and to face fixed factor prices for those inputs. Formally, its decision problem may be written:

Choose $RD_{t,s}$ to minimise the sum, over all periods
from the base period t, when $s = 0$, to infinity, of:

$$(1/1 + r)^s \{C(KN_{t,s}, Q_{t,s}, w_{t,s}) + RD_{t,s}h(\cdot)\}$$

subject to:

$$KN_{t,s+L} - KN_{t,s+L-1} = RD_{t,s} - dKN_{t,s+L-1}.$$

In this formulation, it is envisaged that the firm chooses once and for all, at t, the investments it will make in R&D in the current and all future periods. This is its R&D profile. $C(\cdot)$ is the firm's cost function defined over its stock of knowledge, output level and the prices of its variable inputs. Given a constant returns assumption:

$$C(KN, Q, w) = QF(KN, w)$$

Regarding $F(\cdot)$ as separable in its arguments, one assumption which might be made is that it takes the form:

$$F(\cdot) = f(w) - vKN \qquad (v > 0)$$

so that:

$$C(KN, Q, w) = Q[f(w) - vKN]$$

In words, unit production costs rise with increases in input prices and fall (at a rate determined by v) with increases in technological knowledge. The derivative dC/dKN shows the saving in variable costs made by marginally increasing investment in the stock of knowledge. In the constraint condition, L represents the mean gestation lag between R&D outlay planned at t for period $t + s$ and the generation of new knowledge from that R&D. The condition states that increases in the firm's knowledge between the date $t + s + L - 1$ and $t + s + L$ will be equal to the R&D undertaken at $t + s$, less any depreciation in knowledge which might have occurred in the interim.

Detailing the dynamic optimisation exercise involved here is beyond the scope of this book (readers are referred to the original paper by Schankerman and Nadiri, 1984: 318–9, and to Sargent, 1979, Chapter 9). But the basic result is that planned R&D depends on the expected price of R&D inputs and anticipated future output levels. The model is illustrated in Figure 5.5, in which real R&D investment is measured on the horizontal axis and the costs and benefits of R&D on the vertical.

The upward-sloping line labelled $RMC_{t,s}$ shows that in this model the marginal cost of $RD_{t,s}$ rises linearly with $RD_{t,s}$ itself. If the price of R&D investment goods was expected to rise, the whole schedule would shift upwards. The benefit of R&D is to generate cost savings in production and the magnitude of these savings depends on expected output from the time the results of the R&D are put to productive use. The height of the horizontal benefits schedule relevant to $RD_{t,s}$, marked $RB_{t,s}$, reflects the

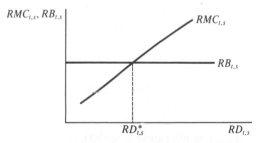

Figure 5.5 Adjustment cost model of investment in R&D. (Reprinted (in adapted form) with permission from M. Schankerman and M. Nadiri (1984) 'Investment in R&D, costs of adjustment and expectations', in Z. Griliches (ed.) *Research and Development, Patents and Productivity*, Chicago: University of Chicago Press. Copyright 1984 by the National Bureau of Economic Research.)

firm's output expectations. If output employing the results of R&D planned at t for $t + s$ was expected to increase, the benefits schedule would shift upwards.

The optimal amount of R&D expenditure, $RD^*_{t,s}$ is found from inspecting the intersection of the two lines. This is where marginal costs are equal to marginal benefits for research planned with the target period $t + s$ in view. Optimally planned R&D expenditure will rise if the expected price of R&D investment goods was to fall and/or expected demand for output were to rise. But these are not the only effects revealed by the analysis.

In particular, a fall in adjustment costs, reflected in a lower value of the parameter a in (5.7), would reduce the overall marginal costs of R&D and shift $RMC_{t,s}$ downwards. This would increase $RD^*_{t,s}$. In addition, if the discount rate fell, the value of future benefits would rise, shifting upwards the $RB_{t,s}$ schedule. And if the effectiveness of new knowledge in reducing variable production costs were to increase, the benefits of R&D would also rise and $RB_{t,s}$ shift upwards. Both of these changes would raise raise optimal R&D investment, other things being equal.

None of these results is particularly surprising, though it must be emphasised that the model from which they spring is open to improvement. As Schankerman and Nadiri (1984: 337) admit, a better model would make the level of output (the level of which depends on the firm's knowledge base) endogenous, proceed from profit maximisation rather than cost minimisation and treat both R&D and physical capital as quasi-fixed assets subject to costs of adjustment. However, its structure does permit empirical tests of how expectations operate in making investment decisions of this kind.

Especially in the context of this book, it is interesting that Schankerman and Nadiri find that hypothesising adaptive expectations works best in predicting actual outcomes, where by 'adaptive' we mean that decision-makers revise single-span forecasts by a fraction of the previous period's forecast error. In the case of R&D input prices, static expectations forecast outcomes reasonably well, where 'static' means that firms are taken to believe future values of exogenous variables will remain at their current levels. The hypothesis of rational expectations works least well, that is the case in which it is assumed the firm forms expectations according to the stochastic processes (presumed to be) generating the exogenous variables. Since the rational expectations hypothesis has been adopted widely as the theoretical route to explaining (rationalising) consistent behaviour in an uncertain and changing world, this result throws some doubt upon the validity of models which take the hypothesis as axiomatic.

Uncertainty and the speed of innovation

In this section, an element of uncertainty is introduced; uncertainty about the point in time at which an innovator might find itself subsequently imitated or, indeed, 'beaten to the gun' by what is portrayed as a 'composite rival', which may be one or many other firms. Bearing in mind the costs and gains of hastening or slowing the pace of innovation in the face of such rivalry, the analysis focuses on the optimal choices firms will then make about their innovation date.

In this analysis (Kamien and Schwartz, 1982: Chapter 4), the subject is a single product or process innovation, to be developed under contract by a specified date T, with no opportunity for the firm to recoup committed funds in the event of a rival innovation appearing before T. The R&D cost function $C_{RD}(T)$ has a form in which total and marginal costs decrease as the completion date is progressively put back and correspondingly increase as T is drawn forward (see Figure 4.14). This means there is always a marginal gain, $C'(T) = dC_{RD}/dT$, to be made from delay, a reduction in development costs. But to find the firm's optimal value of T, T^*, marginal gains have to be compared with marginal losses associated with delay.

The profit-maximising firm will wish to maximise the amount by which expected rewards from introducing the new product/process at T exceeds the costs of doing so. Call this $V(T)$. Now the firm's expected profit stream (abstracting from development costs) if it introduces its new product at T is the sum of three terms. Denoting their total $W(T)$:

$$W(T) = W_o(t) + W_n(t) + W_m(t) \tag{5.8}$$

The first term, $W_o(t)$ represents the present discounted value of all the profits the firm expects from continuing to sell an 'old', pre-innovation product or use an existing process until it introduces 'new' technology at T. In calculating $W_o(t)$, the firm is assumed to make an assessment of the probabilities that its rival will have innovated between now and T and, assuming rival innovation will undermine the profitability of old technology, to reflect that in its judgement of returns. The greater the probability of rival innovation before T, the lower the expected return on old technology.

The second term, $W_n(t)$, represents the capitalised value of what the firm expects to earn from introducing its innovation at T, assuming it is first to market. This sum will include the firm's monopoly rent on innovation from T until rival imitation occurs and the (reduced) return the firm continues to earn thereafter. Here, the value of $W_n(t)$ reflects the firm's assessment of the probability of being imitated at each date after T. The lower the probabilities attributed to early imitation, the greater the expected return on innovation will be. Also, the longer the delay after T until imitation, the greater the expected returns after imitation may be, because of reputation effects building on the demand side and learning occurring in production.

The third term, $W_m(t)$, is the return the firm may expect from its new product/process if it is beaten to the gun, i.e. if the rival innovation appears before T. This in effect makes the firm an imitator and $W_m(t)$ shows the capitalised value of the return to the firm from the new technology after T. Again, the calculation includes an assessment of the probabilities that a rival will introduce the innovation on any date before T. The firm's return on new technology will typically be smaller, the later its innovation date relative to its rival.

Now $V(t)$ is found by subtracting development costs from $W(T)$:

$$V(T) = W(T) - C(T) \tag{5.9}$$

and the idea is to choose T to maximise (5.9). Under some circumstances, Kamien and Schwartz (1982: 125–7, 130–1) show it may not be profitable to develop the innovation at all. But assuming that it is, how does the optimal introduction date T^* vary with pre- and post-innovation returns and the intensity of rivalry?

Consider first the returns, i.e. the incentives to innovate, under any given level of rivalry. For given values of periodic returns on old technology, the optimal planned innovation date T^* will be earlier, the larger the incentives to undertake an offensive, first to market strategy, which are reflected in the levels of profit from innovation. On the other hand, the larger the returns the firm earns on old technology (and which it must sacrifice if it innovates), the greater the incentive to delay introduction of the innovation. This follows since the net gain from innovation is the profit stream from the innovation, minus profits which would in any case have been made by persisting with pre-innovation technology. Given that rival innovation reduces the return on the firm's old technology, however, there is also an incentive to accelerate the innovation date. And the greater this reduction ('loss') is, the greater is the pressure on the firm to introduce the new product/process first.

An increase in the intensity of rivalry is represented as an increase for all t in the firm's assessment of the probability that rivals will innovate in the interval $t, t + 1$, given that they have not done so before. Assume now it is more profitable to be a leader than a follower, and the capitalised profit streams from leading and following are both independent of the lag between innovation and imitation.

Within the context of this model, it can then be shown that the absence of rivalry will favour fast innovation when increased returns are modest, but that if the increased returns are relatively large, the pressure of at least an element of rivalry will be needed to raise the speed of innovation towards its maximum. The first result has a Schumpeterian flavour about it, but is open to the objection (among others) that Kamien and Schwartz abstract in their analysis from the sort of strategic considerations we discuss later. Recent empirical work also suggests the result should be treated with caution (Geroski, 1990).

The second result is a possible theoretical justification for the often-made empirical claim that there is a U-shaped relationship between the intensity of innovation and concentration of production in an industry, which is likely to be determined by the technological influence of scale economies. The intuition behind that claim is that under monopoly there is less threat to a firm's profits on existing products and processes than there would be if there were other firms in the industry. This acts as a discouragement to rapid innovation. On the other hand, in an industry with very many firms, in the limit, a perfectly competitive industry with perfect information and no entry barriers, no firm would have any incentive to spend on R&D, since any improvements it might generate could be imitated so quickly that it would never recoup its outlays. Somewhere in between, there is then perceived to be a structure in which any firm can always pose a threat to its rivals by innovating more rapidly than them, but where there are sufficient 'imperfections' in the market (e.g. imperfect information and adjustment costs giving rise to imitation lags) to allow innovators the opportunity to cover their initial outlays.

Since the U-shaped hypothesis has usually been applied to industry-specific innovation, however, it is not clear that the Kamien and Schwartz analysis can be used to support it. For them, 'rivalry' is a quite general concept and might reflect threats from inside or outside the industry. The possibility of interfirm spill-over effects is also ignored, yet they are often observed. Technological uncertainty relating to the development cost function plays no part, but is everywhere prevalent. The innovation process comprises a continuing sequence of discrete but related innovations and to look at only one at a time gives a very partial view of the competitive forces underlying the process. Finally, to draw conclusions about industry-wide effects we must ultimately use models which incorporate simultaneous interactions among the firms which comprise the industry; treating them on a one-by-one basis simply cannot catch all of the relevant effects.

Diffusion within the firm

This whole section so far has dealt with the generation of new technology within the firm. At this point, we turn to consider how the firm absorbs and diffuses innovations which may well have been developed elsewhere. To do this we use a model of Stoneman (1981) which brings together both uncertainty and adjustment costs in the investment decisions of firms. This treatment offers a possible explanation of another widely recognised empirical observation in the study of innovation, that diffusion occurs according to a sigmoid path.

Stoneman's model depends on three pieces of theory: choice of techniques using mean-variance analysis, adjustment costs and Bayesian learning. Our approach is to rely mostly upon an essentially intuitive account of Stoneman's work which allows us to draw upon a diagrammatic treatment developed here. Formal derivations can be found in the original paper.

The problem

The firm must decide what proportion a_n of given output to make with a new production technique and what proportion $(1 - a_n)$ to make with a pre-existing method. For each period t the firm is portrayed as choosing an optimal value of $a_n(t)$, $a_i^*(t)$ and hence an optimal ratio of the old to new technology, $[a_n^*(t)/(1 - a_n^*(t))]$. How is this optimal ratio chosen, and how will it evolve over time?

Mean-variance approach

To answer the problem, suppose the firm anticipates that the returns to old (o) and new (n) technology at t are normally distributed with means $m_{o,t}$ and $m_{n,t}$ and variances $var_{o,t}$ and $var_{n,t}$, respectively. The additive distributions of returns resulting from using both methods at one time in a heterogeneous capital set-up is characterised by the statistics m_t and var_t, defined by the expressions below, which make use of a_n and $(1 - a_n)$ as weights:

$$m_t = a_n(t)m_{n,t} + (1 - a_n(t))m_{o,t} \qquad (5.10\text{a})$$

$$var_t = a_n(t)^2 \cdot var_{n,t}$$

$$+ (1 - a_n(t))^2 \cdot var_{o,t}$$

$$+ 2 \cdot a_n(t)(1 - a_n(t))cov_{o,n,t} \qquad (5.10\text{b})$$

m_t is the mean and var_t the variance of the distribution of anticipated overall returns to the firm when it uses the two methods at the same time in the proportions a_n: $(1 - a_n)$. For simplicity, abstract from any minor complications introduced by the covariance term.

To show how m_t and var_t may vary with changes in $a_n/(1 - a_n)$, we use a numerical example in which $m_{n,t} = 100$, which exceeds $m_{o,t} = 50$ and $var_{n,t} = 20$, which also exceeds $var_{o,t} = 10$. In words, the mean of the anticipated returns on new technology is higher than that on the old, but because of the relatively high level of uncertainty associated with using new methods, the variance of the distribution for returns on the new technology is also higher. Using the definitions of m_t and var_t given above, it is then a simple matter to calculate the values shown in Table 5.1.

Table 5.1 The mean and variance of overall returns from using old and new technology together when the proportionate use of old and new technology varies: a numerical example.

a_n	m_t	var_t
0.1	55	8.3
0.2	60	7.6
0.3	65	6.7
0.4	70	6.8
0.5	75	7.5
0.6	80	8.8
0.7	85	10.7
0.8	90	13.2
0.9	95	16.3
1.0	100	20.0

On the basis of the information in the table, we may now construct a diagram (Figure 5.6) with m_t on the vertical and var_t on the horizontal axis. The graph of the values in the table is a curve which is the locus of all the combinations of m_t and var_t which arise when the two methods are used in different proportions from 0.1:0.9 up to 100 per cent in the new technology. This curve, labelled TT, can be thought of as an opportunity frontier or transformation function showing the trade-off between mean and variance which the firm can achieve by varying the proportions in which it employs old and new technology. The lowest points on the curve are associated with the lowest values of a_n and those furthest along the curve with highest values of a_n.

The shape of the curve suggests that in the example increasing use of the new technology always brings with it the prospect of a higher overall return, but that once

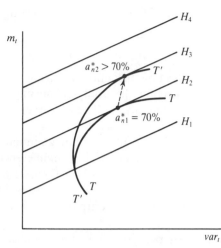

Figure 5.6   Mean–Variance model of investment and intrafirm diffusion.

the extent to which it is used goes beyond a certain critical level, the uncertainty associated with using it increases the variance of prospective returns. Notice also that as a_n increases, m_t rises at a declining rate, while var_t ultimately rises at an increasing rate. The importance of these observations is that decision-makers in firms are often thought to be concerned with the potential variance of the distribution of prospective returns, as a measure of the 'riskiness' of investment, as well as the mean. And the majority are usually regarded as risk-averse, implying that for incurring any increase in risk (any higher level of var_t) they will require an increase in the mean prospect of returns m_t by way of compensation. The next step is therefore to incorporate decision-makers' preferences in a second diagram which allows us to see which point on the transformation curve the firm will choose.

The device used is another version of indifference curves, first introduced in Chapter 3. In this case, the indifference curves may be taken to represent the utility function of the firm's owners or those of its managers, on the assumption that their choices reflect the wishes of the shareholders. As before, any single curve represents a given level of utility and successively higher curves represent higher levels of utility. In some mean-variance analyses, indifference curves are drawn sloping upwards from left to right with increasing slope. This reflects preferences in which successive equal increases in risk require at each stage a larger rise in the expected mean of returns if utility is to be preserved. Stoneman, however, employs a form of the mean-variance utility function which is written:

$$H(m, var) = b_1 m - 0.5 b_2 var - A \tag{5.11}$$

where b_1, $b_2 > 0$, and A stands for the disutility (negative utility) associated with adjustment costs involved in increasing the use of new technology. It is clear that the indifference curves, labelled $H_1, \ldots, H_4$ in Figure 5.6, must be linear since their slope is given by:

$$\mathrm{d}m/d \ var = b_2/2b_1$$

These lines will be steeper, the larger b_2 (reflecting the utility-reducing strength of increased variance) is and the smaller b_1 (reflecting the utility-enhancing power of increasing the mean) is. The effect of A will be to shift any indifference curve downwards by the value which A takes, but for the moment we assume $A = 0$.

The rational firm will want to choose a_n to maximise utility. In diagrammatic terms, this means finding the point on TT which touches the highest indifference curve. Superimposing the indifference curve map (with $A = 0$) on TT in Figure 5.6, we see that a_{n1}^* is the optimal choice of technique. It can be calculated that at this point, the firm would choose to produce about 70 per cent of its output in t with the new technology.

For any transformation function of similar shape, $a_n^*(t)$ will be lower, the steeper the indifference curves, i.e. under preferences, a relatively greater increase in m_t is required to compensate the firm for any rise in var_t. This simply says that the more firms dislike additional risk, the less inclined they will be to substitute relatively high-risk new technology for relatively low-risk old technology. For the purposes of comparison (and for use later), we have also drawn the transformation function $T'T'$ for a case in which $m_{o,t}$ and $var_{o,t}$ are the same as before, but where $m_{n,t}$ is higher (120 rather than 100) and $var_{n,t}$ lower (15 rather than 20). In that case, with indifference curves unchanged, $a^*(t)$ now takes the higher value a_{n2}^* (about 0.85). From this we might conclude that the higher $m_{n,t}$ is relative to $m_{o,t}$ and the lower $var_{n,t}$ is relative to $var_{o,t}$, the greater the proportion of output we should expect to see firms planning to produce using new technology.

But how does this bear upon the question of diffusion? There are two elements to answering that question. First, adjustment costs; suppose the firm plans to purchase new-technology equipment in accordance with the utility-maximising exercise just outlined. Because of adjustment costs, it will not be able to reach the optimum value of a_n^* instantaneously, but while it is producing whatever fraction of output it can with the new technology, it starts to receive information which it did not have before about the returns it might expect from the new equipment. In other words, it learns about the distribution of returns to the new technology by using it.[2]

Stoneman assumes the new technology has true returns normally distributed and constant over time. Firms learn about this distribution in a Bayesian way. This means that they form at the start of each period a view about the distributions on the mean and variance of the returns to the new technology – the prior distributions. And with evidence collected during the period they then amend this view to yield posterior distributions. For the purposes of analysis, however, it is also assumed firms know the variance of the true returns and that uncertainty therefore arises solely in connection with the mean. It is on the distribution of the mean returns that the firm holds a prior distribution and which it amends in the light of its observations. Uncertainty associated with the new technology comprises two elements: the known variance of the true returns (the inherent variance) and the variance of the distribution of the mean. Over time, new information leads to revisions in the distribution of the mean returns and leads to changes in the degree of overall uncertainty associated with using the new technology.

Within this framework, we can now see how diffusion might occur. Initially, at $t = 0$, the firm's beliefs about the potential returns from the new technology lead it to view $a_n^*(0)$ as an optimum. Because of adjustment costs, it fails to reach $a_n^*(0)$ immediately but in the course of using the new technology it acquires information which leads it to revise its view about what the optimum is. Suppose, as seems reasonable, the mean and variance of the distribution of returns to the old technology are known with certainty and that new information from using the new technology both reduces the overall uncertainty associated with it and leads to an upward re-evaluation of the mean of the distribution of true returns. Then the transformation function which the firm believes itself to face will 'uncurl' in an anticlockwise direction. In Figure 5.6 the relative positions of $T'T'$ and TT would represent such an uncurling. As we saw earlier, this would lead to an upward movement in a_n^*.

With positive adjustment costs, however, there will be delays in reaching any given level of a_n^*. Assume: first, the greater the difference between a given level of past use $a_n(t - 1)$ and a current level which is sought $a_n(t)$, the greater will be the adjustment costs in closing the gap in this period, with costs increasing at an increasing rate as the level of current use sought itself rises; second, for any given increase in use, adjustment costs will be lower, the greater the base level $a_n(t - 1)$. Even in the absence of learning effects, it turns out that adjustment costs of this kind are sufficient to ensure that the diffusion of the new technology will occur in a sigmoid pattern if incorporated in the mean-variance model (Stoneman, 1981: 382).

In fact, the time path of diffusion can be represented by a standard logistic curve of the kind derived by Mansfield (1968). He uses a model in which a 'satiation' level of usage reached at the end of diffusion is exogenously determined and proportional changes (reductions) in the gap between initial and final usage are linked positively to the profitability of the new technology and negatively to its uncertainty. Stoneman's model offers an account of a process which endogenously determines the final adoption level and provides microfoundations in learning and adjustment mechanisms to explain the speed of change during the process. He also shows that if there are no adjustment costs (as in the Mansfield approach) and uncertainty is resolved by Bayesian learning, a sigmoid diffusion path cannot be derived. On the other hand, Bayesian learning in the presence of positive adjustment costs may well yield sigmoid diffusion paths.

First, usage of the new technology will rise at an increasing rate if in the initial period planned optimal usage exceeds actual usage and planned optimal usage increases. If, however, it is assumed that the variance of the returns on the old technology is zero, the model also predicts that usage will at some point start rising at a decreasing rate. The required conditions are that planned optimal usage continues to rise, but period zero planned optimal usage is more than twice actual initial usage (Stoneman, 1981: 385). It is also possible to show that the terminal value approached by a_n varies positively with the mean of the distribution of true returns on new technology, a result consonant with Mansfield's predictions about the effect of profitability. The terminal value of a_n is reduced by increases in the mean return to old technology.

Two comments are in order here. First, Stoneman's model offers plausible conditions under which intrafirm diffusion will take a sigmoid path over time, but is unable to rule out the possibility of non-sigmoid diffusion. That is comforting, since we have no reason to believe that all intrafirm diffusion does follow a sigmoid pattern. Second, the model also predicts that if the firm's experience leads it to revise its estimate of mean profitability downwards, then diffusion should come to a halt and perhaps even be reversed if the actual value it attains in some period exceeds what the firm now perceives to be its optimal value.

Strategic innovation investment and entry barriers

In modern analysis, investment in innovation has been recognised for the potential it offers the firm to steal a strategic advantage. What this means is that the firm may use innovation-related investment in an initial period to change the economic conditions under which potential rivals perceive they will have to compete with it in future periods (Schapiro, 1989: 382).

The strategic use of innovation is apparent in the Fudenberg–Tirole (Fudenberg and Tirole, 1983) analysis of LBD noted earlier. There, first-period investment consists of a larger production level than would have been chosen in the absence of learning in order, through experience, to drive down production costs later to a level which gives the firm a competitive advantage. But strategic investment may also occur in relation to cost-reducing R&D (Brander and Spencer, 1983; Spence, 1984), patent licensing (Katz and Schapiro, 1985) and product differentiation (Prescott and Visscher, 1977; Shaked and Sutton, 1982). For a helpful survey, see Schapiro (1989).

An important feature of strategic behaviour is that it should involve investments capable of giving a firm a competitive advantage based on an asymmetry (compared with actual or potential rivals) in terms of costs, market access, production capacity or some other aspect of performance. Such asymmetries spring naturally from capital investments which in future periods become **irreversible** or **sunk**. In future periods, a firm which has acquired assets on a sunk cost basis need not reobtain them. Yet it enjoys the benefits their acquisition bestows, such as lower production costs or superior market access than would have otherwise been available. Asymmetry arises in future periods, because potential rivals will not be able to compete on equal terms unless they make similar investment themselves. The firm which undertook the investment first thus enjoys a **first mover advantage**.

While strategic behaviour is central to the analysis of interaction among two or more rivals in oligopolistic industries (see Chapter 6), it is also relevant to the analysis of a single firm intent on creating or preserving monopoly status. If a firm is first to make a strategic investment (including an element of sunk costs), other firms which might wish to compete with it are faced with the necessity of making similar investments themselves. Compared with the competitive situation, absent from the first mover's investment, any firm which subsequently considers contesting the market will now have to incur an additional cost. In this way, the first mover has created a **barrier to entry**, defined by Stigler (1968) as a cost of production which must be borne by firms seeking to enter an industry, but not borne by firms already in it. Clearly, if entry barriers surrounding any particular firm are substantial, it is in a good position to be the sole supplier to the market: a monopolist. Strategic investment has the capacity to create entry barriers and in turn either provide the conditions for monopoly or the basis for sustaining it.

Strategic behaviour and entry barriers have become closely interwoven, however, for a further and deeper reason. Potential rivals will be deterred from entering a monopolised industry only if they believe the incumbent is committed to contesting the market. The incumbent only has the power to make them hold such a belief if it can threaten to make performance-enhancing investments which are irreversible. Once made, strategic investments change future competitive conditions and indicate a commitment by the incumbent to stay and contest the market. If the incumbent's investments involved no sunk costs, potential rivals would have no reason to believe the incumbent was committed. They could hope to enter the industry and scare the incumbent into selling off some or all of its productive assets, hence destroying the basis for any competitive advantage it might have had. As we shall see later, even sunk-cost investment is not a sufficient condition for guaranteed deterrence, but it implies new entrants would have to bear losses during a post-entry contest.

Established firms which use their incumbency to deter entry are often able to earn supernormal profits, or economic rent. This is reflected in Bain's (1968) definition of barriers. In his view, the height of a barrier reflects the extent to which in the long run the firm can elevate its selling price above the minimum, average cost of production, at the optimal scale of operation, without inducing potential entrants to enter the industry. The highest price a monopolist could charge without attracting entry is called the **limit price**.

While Bain's (and Stigler's) definition goes to the heart of asymmetries which might favour an incumbent firm over a potential entrant, Gilbert (1989) argues that they are 'unnecessarily confining' (p. 477). For example, a firm with technology potentially available on equal terms to all could enter an industry and produce monopoly output, leaving no scope for any other firm to make a profit. But it would be unclear where its cost advantage, if any, was in this case. Instead of focusing on the specific reasons for the difficulty of entry, therefore, Gilbert proposes that 'a barrier to entry is a rent that is derived from incumbency ... it is the additional profit that a firm can earn as a sole consequence of being established in the industry' (p. 478). This quite naturally leads into questions of *how* incumbency allows rent to be earned and *why* entry may be excluded.

We now look at the sources of the rent that both defines barriers to entry and reflects monopoly power, especially as it relates to strategic, innovation-related investment. There is a crucial intersection here between economic and technological considerations. The economic features of monopoly power and the returns to it may be explained by reasons related to innovation. But the specific direction technological change follows may conversely be explained by economic objectives of firms; either their aim to increase profit, or their determination to deter potential entrants. Following a structure pioneered by Bain, we consider in turn investment directed towards entry barriers related to product differentiation, absolute cost advantages and scale economies.

Product differentiation

Empirical work on the sources of monopoly power have tended to conclude that, especially in the case of consumer goods industries, entry barriers related to product differentiation are the most important determinant of firms' ability to earn rent (Bain, 1956; Mann, 1966; Comanor and Wilson, 1967). Standard theoretical analysis focuses on the limit price an incumbent might charge on its existing product variants (resulting from past innovation) to defend its monopoly position. To the extent that limit pricing is successful in deterring entry, this approach suggests that the introduction of new substitute products by new firms will be stifled. And since there is no presumption that the incumbent will continue to invest in product diversification, there is an implication that, once product innovation has created a monopoly, the incumbent firm will manipulate market conditions in a way which inhibits further change.

But this perspective presupposes potential rivals accept the price set by the incumbent, which they might not if they were large enough to stand losses for the duration of a post-entry contest for the market. Further, the analysis starts with the monopoly in place; it says nothing about the process which brought it into being, nor of the innovation strategies (rather than pricing rules) firms might pursue to maintain their monopoly.

A firm's past investments in non-recoverable, product innovation R&D supported by sunk advertising costs are obvious examples of strategic activity to create barriers and a monopoly position. Potential entrants would have to bear their own costs of imitation and undertake a major programme of advertising and/or price discounting to contest the market at a later date. But by then, the first mover might already be so well established that competing profitably could be difficult or impossible.

A further problem for potential rivals is the prevalence of switching costs. Even if customers believe a potential entrant's new product might be a good substitute for that produced by the incumbent monopolist, they may be reluctant to switch, i.e. transfer allegiance, from the incumbent for fear either of utility losses suffered in the course of sampling what might turn out to be a less desirable alternative, or because there are direct costs involved in abandoning existing products. An example of the latter case (cited in Gilbert, 1989: 506) would be the retraining costs associated with changing from one make of software to another.

But rather than rely on switching costs alone, incumbent monopolists may pursue active strategies to maintain their position. Two considered here are **pre-emptive patenting** (Gilbert and Newbery, 1982) and **pre-emptive product proliferation** (Schmalensee, 1978).

Gilbert and Newbery assume that an incumbent monopolist and a number of potential entrants face the same invention possibility function under which time taken to devise a product innovation falls with increases in R&D expenditure. The first firm

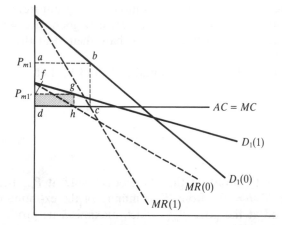

Figure 5.7 An incumbent firm's pre- and post-innovation demand curves and profit if another firm takes out a patent on a substitute product.

to invent acquires a watertight patent. An important feature of the Gilbert and Newbery model is that they assume the monopolist and its rivals compete on equal terms for the patent; there are no barriers to entry in R&D as might spring from the monopolist's previous experience of innovation in the industry. The intensity of competition this implies leads to the conclusion that potential entrants will each spend as much on R&D as they expect to get in profits from winning the patent, but no more, since that would generate an overall loss.

Note here that firms will look at the present value of the post-innovation profit stream and compare it with the present value of R&D expenditures up to the date of patenting. In other words, were the monopolist not to defend itself, all other firms would spend on R&D up to the point where the *PV* of their outlays was equal to the *PV* of their expected post-innovation profits. Given the relationship between R&D expenditure and the date of patenting, this implies some specific date on which the patent is claimed. Call this competitive entry date *T*.

Consider Figure 5.7. The area *abcd* represents the profit per period before innovation, which the monopolist would make if it charged the profit-maximising price P_{m1} for the old product. If the patent for the innovation, a substitute product, went to an outsider, the ex-monopolist's demand curve would shift inwards and flatten out somewhat; compare $D_1(0)$ with $D_1(1)$. Assuming for simplicity constant costs, the monopolist's profit-maximising price would fall to P'_{m1} and its profit per period after the innovation would thus be reduced to *fghd*.

We do not show the monopolist's post-innovation profit if the incumbent took the patent, but we know that one course of action for the firm would be to not produce the new substitute at all, in which case it would continue to make per period profit of *abcd*. If it produced both variants, however, it would set prices to ensure that it maximised profit from doing so and, while the price for the old product might in the post-innovation era be above or below P'_{m1}, we can be sure that in addition to the profit from the old good, it would also make positive profit from the substitute new good. It would thus take *all* industry profits for itself rather than having to share them. But the issue is, when would this be worthwhile?

To answer this question, consider first two magnitudes: V_e and V_p. Let:

$$V_e = a + b$$

and

$$V_p = c + d - e$$

where: $a = PV$ of the monopolist's profit on the old product, sold at P_{m1} per unit, from some initial date 0 until T; $b = PV$ from T to infinity of the ex-monopolist's profit from selling the old good at the price P'_{m1}, which maximises its profit in the industry existing after an outside firm has patented the substitute product and entered; $c = PV$ of the monopolist's profit on the old product, sold at P_{m1} per unit, from date 0 until a short period before T; $d = PV$ of the monopolist's profit from a short time before T to infinity, if it wins the patent; and $e =$ monopolist's R&D required to win the patent a short time before the competitive entry date T. Thus V_e shows the PV of the monopolist's profit from 0 to infinity if it did no R&D and permitted an outsider to enter, with the implication that it would have to share industry profit derived from sales of the old and new goods. V_p shows the PV of the monopolist's profit from 0 to infinity if it spent enough on R&D to ensure it won the patent before the competitive entry date and thus maintained its monopoly. Now, if the monopolist is interested in maximising the PV of its long-term profits, it will choose the course of action which is associated with the larger of the two values, V_e and V_p. It will thus invest enough in R&D to maintain its monopoly position if V_p exceeds V_e, i.e. if:

$$(V_p - V_e) > 0$$

or

$$(c + d - e) - (a + b) > 0$$

or

$$(c - a) + (d - b - e) > 0 \tag{5.12}$$

Suppose we shrink the period between the competitive entry date T and the monopolist's successful patenting date just before it to a minimal length. Then c and a become approximately equal and since all firms face the same innovation possibilities, e approaches the expenditure that outside firms would have to lay out to win the patent: call it e'. But as was argued above, this amount is also the PV of an entrant's profits from producing in the post-innovation industry using the patent. So (5.12) reduces to a condition stating that the monopolist will do enough R&D to win the patent if:

$$(d - b - e') > 0.$$

or

$$d > b + e' \qquad\qquad (5.13)$$

In words, this says that the monopolist will pre-emptively patent if the maximum profit it as the sole firm in the industry can obtain from producing both the old and new products is greater than the industry comprising two firms would earn if an entrant took the patent. It is a common presumption that in a post-entry battle for profits and market share, duopolists will together finish up generating less industry-wide profit than the incumbent would have earned had it retained its monopoly. The Gilbert and Newbery argument thus suggests that incumbent monopolists might quite often be expected to attempt to deter entry in this way.

However, first, it is by no means likely that both incumbent and potential entrants will face the same innovation possibilities. On the one hand, the incumbent will often benefit from learning by learning in its own line of innovation. This would reinforce Gilbert and Newbery's conclusion. On the other, some potential entrants may have technological knowledge developed in connection with other products which has only now become relevant here. That might reverse the Gilbert and Newbery conclusion. Second, patents are rarely watertight. Many innovators do not rely on patents for protection because (a) their innovation cannot be patented, or patented adequately, given the requirements of patent legislation; (b) the time taken to acquire a patent is longer than the period before another round of innovation is forced on the firm by the threat of entry; (c) it is perceived as more effective to rely on secrecy, imitation costs and other forms of protection. Thus the Gilbert and Newberry analysis is most relevant in the (relatively few) industries where patenting is perceived to be effective, such as pharmaceuticals.

The pharmaceutical industry also provides an example of the second sort of strategy, product proliferation If pursued, this strategy suggests much more active innovation in the pursuit of preserving monopoly than is implied in the traditional limit pricing model. In this case, the incumbent may generate such a variety of product differentiates that no segment of the market is left in which a potential entrant could make enough sales to generate even normal profit. The strategy would not be available to the monopolist if it and its rivals had the same constant cost production technology, since the entrant would in that case be able to earn at least a normal return at any positive scale of production. So the workability of the strategy requires that there be increasing returns in the production (and/or marketing) of individual product varieties, at least over some initial range of output levels. We noted in Chapter 4 that economies of scope based on sharing common inputs (e.g. R&D expertise or managerial talent) make this look highly plausible. In addition, potential entrants will be most persuaded that the monopolist will hold to its strategy, even if a rival were to enter, if non-recoverable product development costs were so significant that it would be expensive for the incumbent to 'relocate' its varieties in product space (see discussion in Chapter 3) when contesting the market. These factors form elements of a strategy designed to convince potential entrants of the incumbent's capacity and commitment to stay and defend its position rather than concede segments of the market to a newcomer.

If an incumbent believes product proliferation will protect its monopoly position, it has an incentive to generate product innovations until all potentially profitable segments of its market have been supplied. The threat of entry may be enough to prompt it to do this.

Notice also the way in which a barrier to entry arises here. By construction, the incumbent has no production cost advantage over potential entrants but merely by moving pre-emptively, it can put itself in a position where it leaves only unattractive options to its potential rivals.

Absolute cost advantages

Apparently the most obvious source of monopoly is the advantage one firm may enjoy compared with others in terms of its cost structure. Two examples are shown in Figures 5.8a and 5.8b. In 5.8a, both the incumbent and outside firms face constant long-run costs, but for the incumbent, unit and marginal costs are at level C_1, while potential entrants would have upon entry cost structure C_2. In 5.8b, the incumbent again has an absolute cost advantage, but there are increasing returns and declining average costs for both the incumbent and potential entrants over an initial range of output levels. Suppose potential entrants believe the price set now by the monopolist would persist after entry. If the monopolist then set the price at any level below the unit costs of a potential rival, the new entrant would be prevented from making profit upon entry. The highest such price (the limit price) is just below C_2 in 5.8a and P_L in 5.8b. The incumbent's profits (shaded) in each case reflect the barrier to entry.

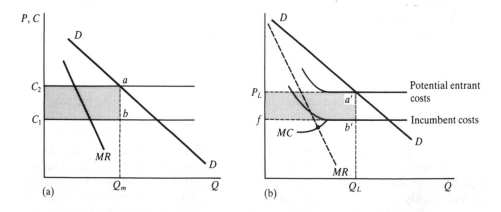

Figure 5.8   (a) Absolute cost advantage in the case of constant costs: the firm with long-run average costs of C_1 has an absolute advantage over the firm with costs of C_2; (b) Absolute cost advantage for an incumbent firm where long-run average costs decline in an initial range of outputs.

Potential entrants may not be deterred, however. If the incumbent maintained its output level, entry would necessarily drive price down and reduce its profits. It could even make a loss. The entrant would certainly make losses upon arrival, but assuming it could stand these, would also be in a position to compete or collude with the first firm for a share of the profits which market conditions in the industry still offered. That said, an incumbent monopolist will always be in a stronger position to deter entry, the lower its costs relative to those of potential entrants. Strategic investment to achieve this might take a number of forms.

The sources of absolute cost advantage may lie in the input prices the incumbent pays relative to those available to potential entrants, quantity constraints on inputs faced by outsiders and the technological knowledge of incumbents compared with outsiders. One form of strategic investment which bears on the first two of these is setting up a long-term contract with suppliers to obtain either bulk discounts on or exclusive access to crucial inputs. Potential entrants would then be at a future disadvantage. An extension of this principle would involve the incumbent in providing financial and/or technical support to a supplier to enable it to undertake innovation to the exclusive benefit of the incumbent. Examples include the arrangements between specialist machine tool suppliers and major users noted in Chapter 2 and the networks of supplier–user relationships widely deployed in Japanese manufacturing. Issues surrounding this sort of relationship are explored further in later analysis on the boundaries of the firm.

One of the most widely cited sources of absolute cost advantage is the possession of a patent on some element of process technology, which could be acquired through strategic investment in R&D. The patent denies potential entrants an essential input, i.e. knowledge about a production process, on terms equal to those enjoyed by the incumbent as patent holder. Further, if the incumbent puts to use the knowledge contained in the patent, it will have elements of know-how gained in development and through LBD which will not be available to other firms which might be licensed to use the patent.

These points are the basis for Gilbert's (1989) observation that, 'A cost disadvantage arising from inefficient production techniques should not be considered a barrier to entry. At a minimum, absolute cost advantages should be qualified to refer to some factor of production that is denied the potential entrant, and but for this omitted factor, the firm would be as efficient as established firms' (p. 493). This brings out an interesting implication of the discussion of technical efficiency earlier in the book. Here, both sets of cost curves reflect technical efficiency in the use of the knowledge each firm actually possesses, rather than knowledge which exists and has ever been used anywhere.

Bearing in mind now strategic issues, consider again the incentives to generate a cost-reducing process innovation for a monopolistic product market. In Arrow's analysis (see pp. 173–5), the innovator was always a monopolist in R&D, but Dasgupta and Stiglitz (1980) show it is important to consider the nature of the market in which the R&D is done, as well as the product market. They consider a number of cases which we shall describe as (1) persistent pure monopoly, (2) inducement to monopoly and (3) monopoly defence. In case (1), the benchmark, the firm in the product market already

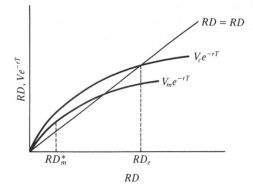

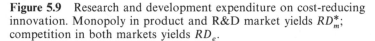

Figure 5.9   Research and development expenditure on cost-reducing innovation. Monopoly in product and R&D market yields RD^*_m; competition in both markets yields RD_e.

holds a patent on existing technology associated with unit costs C_o and is the only firm doing R&D to acquire the patent on new technology, C_n. In case (2), firms using the existing technology are competitive in the product market and there are no barriers to entry giving any one firm an advantage over others in competing to patent C_n, where winning the patent will bestow a monopoly on the successful firm. In case (3), some firm is taken already to have a monopoly in the product market, but to face competitive conditions if it seeks to patent C_n.

Dasgupta and Stiglitz follow Arrow in identifying the areas $(B{-}A)$ and B shown in Figure 5.3 as, respectively, the gross per period incentives for a pure monopolist and for the monopoly winner of a competitive patent race. Call $(B{-}A)$ Π_m and B Π_c. But now, as in the Gilbert and Newbery analysis, firms compare the PV of the expected returns from the patent with the R&D costs of winning it. In the case of the pure monopolist, the PV of the prospective returns from the patent, on the simplifying assumption that it gives protection for ever, is:

$$V_m \cdot e^{-rT}$$

where $V_m = \Pi_m/r$. This expression is derived in detail in the Appendix. The costs of winning the patent are the R&D expenditures required to 'solve' a production 'problem' by the date T, and enter the firm's decision calculus at two points. On the one hand, T is assumed to be related to R&D through an innovation cost function in which T falls, but at a declining rate, with increases in R&D. Increases in R&D therefore reduce T (draw forward the date on which the problem is solved), increasing the value of e^{-rT} and the PV of prospective returns from the patent, as we would expect, since the earlier the patent is won, the greater is the number of years over which it may earn profit for the patent holder. But since T falls at a declining rate as R&D increases, the PV of the patent rises at a declining rate as research effort is stepped up. This is shown in Figure 5.9 by the present value function, labelled $V_m e^{-rT}$.

Taking case (1) as a benchmark, the pure monopolist will maximise the difference between $V_m e^{-rT}$ and its R&D expenditure, RD_m. At this point, assume R&D expenditure constitutes an indivisible, one-off commitment at the outset of the project, so the sort of programme envisaged here is either short and sharp or large and demanding of major sunk inputs to get it going. The implications of spreading expenditure over several periods are considered below. The difference between $V_m \cdot e^{-rT}$ and RD_m is shown by the vertical distance between the present value function and the linear $RD = RD$ function in Figure 5.9 and reaches its maximum for the monopolist where $RD_m = RD_m^*$.

Case (2) shows how and when R&D might be used to create a monopoly. The gross return for holding a patent on C_n is Π_c per period and the *PV* of the return is $\Pi_c / r \cdot e^{-rT}$. The interesting point in the case where competition initially rules in both product market and R&D is that this sum will be set equal to R&D and that if all firms take the actions of other firms as given in determining their own profit-maximising decisions, only one firm will actually do the R&D. The level of R&D for which this is true is shown in Figure 5.9 as RD_e. If any firm were to choose a level of R&D above RD_e, it could never recoup its expenditure; the *PV* of the return on its investment would fall below its initial outlay. If any firm chose a level of R&D below RD_e, it would know that some other firm could choose a slightly higher level, then win the patent. That would put the first firm in the position of knowing that it would receive nothing in return for its initial R&D outlay, which is simply irrational, for the firm could only then make a loss. This is true of all levels of R&D below RD_e and is true of all firms. If one firm, picked randomly, were to commit itself to spending RD_e, therefore, it could be sure of obtaining the patent. The attraction of the profits offered through ownership of the patent suggests that the opportunity will be taken up. But the logic of the argument above suggests that it is rational to choose to spend only RD_e (no more, no less) and that only one firm will do the spending. Success will give that firm a monopoly.

Now, we know $\Pi_c > \Pi_m$, so for similiar demand curves and cost reductions, the curve for $V_c \cdot e^{-rT}$ lies above that for $V_m \cdot e^{-rT}$ and RD_e must therefore exceed RD_m^*. The inducement of acquiring a monopoly through strategic investment in R&D draws out more innovative effort than would occur under an existing monopoly, in which there were barriers to entry in R&D as well as the product market.

Consider now the strategic behaviour of a firm which is an existing product market monopolist, but has no competitive advantage over potential rivals in R&D. This is case (3). We consider two cases here: R&D as a single, upfront commitment and as an initial commitment which is a small fraction of the potential total. Suppose, in the first case, the incumbent's potential rivals took its current R&D zero expenditure as given when forming their own plans. Then the reward for winning the patent would be entry into the industry currently occupied by the monopolist. But as we have discovered, if there is freedom of entry into producing the new process, it will be rational for only one firm to do the R&D and the amount of R&D it does will be equal to the present value of what the winner expects to receive. Entry of the single patent holder into a currently monopolistic industry would turn it into a two-firm industry (a duopoly) and the firm which did the R&D would therefore spend on it just the *PV* of what a duopolist would expect to receive in the industry, call it $V_d \cdot e^{-rT}$.

Although the entrant and the incumbent could in principle collude to generate as much profit as the monopolist alone, we would in general expect the profits of the two firms together, in post-entry competition with each other, to be less than the profit a monopolist with the patent could earn. Potential rivals, who are assumed not to be prepared to take a loss, will spend just $V_d \cdot e^{-rT}$ on R&D. But since $V_d \cdot e^{-rT}$ must be less than the monopolist on its own could earn from the patent, the incumbent has an incentive to spend more than this on R&D to preserve its monopoly. What is more, it knows that if it spends even only a little more than $V_d \cdot e^{-rT}$, it will be guaranteed the patent. 'The reason the monopolist will always pre-empt potential competitors is intuitively clear.... The existing monopolist can always ensure it remains a monopolist by spending a little more on R&D than any potential competitor would find profitable .... It is always in the interests of the monopolist to do so because by remaining a monopolist it can earn a flow of profit in excess of the sum of the duopolists' profits' (Dasgupta and Stiglitz, 1980: 14). [My italics]

Compared with the benchmark case, in which the monopolist faced no competition in R&D, allowing for freedom of entry into R&D would make no difference to the amount of R&D undertaken (and hence the speed of innovation) if RD_m^* were in any case greater than $V_d \cdot e^{-rT}$. But if RD_m^* were less than $V_d \cdot e^{-rT}$, the monopolist's decision to spend more on R&D than $V_d \cdot e^{-rT}$ implies it must increase its R&D to a level above that which would maximise its profits were it completely protected.

Now relax the assumption that all R&D expenditure is committed upfront. Instead, note that in many cases firms undertake research programmes in which only relatively small amounts are committed at the outset. There will still exist one level of programme expenditure which guarantees the patent to the firm undertaking the R&D. But here, once one firm (we assume the monopolist) has made a small commitment, it can announce that it will respond to any subsequent competition in R&D by choosing the level and scheduling of its remaining expenditures such that it can be guaranteed the patent. If other firms' choices are assumed to reflect their belief in the monopolist's threat, they will not find it profitable to respond by doing any R&D at all. Then, however, the monopolist's strategy should be to undertake whatever R&D programme it would have pursued in the absence of competition for the patent.

Reasoning of the kind employed by Dasgupta and Stiglitz has been extended further to take account of sequences of action and reaction among competing firms. That is taken up in a duopolistic framework in Chapter 6. Meanwhile, note that the sharp results derived here depend on there being well-defined R&D functions which make it possible for every firm to know the potential consequences of other firms' decisions. In fact, the results are also robust under uncertainty if all firms' uncertainties are perfectly correlated and all decision-makers risk-neutral, but this seems a rather special case.

Notice, finally, that absolute cost advantages initially created by an incumbent monopolist may be enhanced by subsequent learning effects. Lieberman's (1984) work on chemical processing industries suggests cost reductions through learning occur as quickly through interfirm as intrafirm diffusion. Strategic advantage is most likely to accrue to learning which is specific to the production experience of an incumbent. If rivals could expect, however, to benefit substantially from spill-overs, as Lieberman suggests, LBD offers less as a strategic weapon.

Economies of scale

When there are scale economies over a substantial range of the LAC curve, the size of the market relative to the MES becomes important in identifying the source of monopoly. We concentrate on the implications of a LAC curve sloping downwards throughout the entire output range relevant for meeting market demand. The MC curve lies below LAC at all points.

When LAC fall continuously, it is always less costly for one firm to produce all the output in the industry than for two or more. From Figure 5.10, for example, the average costs incurred by a single firm producing Q^* would be C^* and total costs would be Q^*C^*. But if two firms produced $Q^*/2$ each, the average costs of each would be C', the total costs of each $(Q^*/2) \cdot C'$, and the total cost of producing Q^*, Q^*C', which is greater than Q^*C^*. Since LAC will always be above C^* for any output level below Q^*, the same result applies however the firms divide output between them.

Whenever it is less costly for one firm to produce a given level of output than for two or more firms to produce that level, the cost curve is defined to be **subadditive** at that output level. Clearly, subadditivity is implied by continuously declining average costs over all output ranges, though since it may also occur in cases where there are U-shaped average cost curves, subadditivity does not necessarily imply decreasing LAC everywhere (for an example, see Sharkey, 1982: 5). Further, subadditivity in the cost function at any level of output can be taken to define the existence of **natural monopoly** at that output level (see Sharkey: 1982: 2). In the diagram, the cost function is subadditive

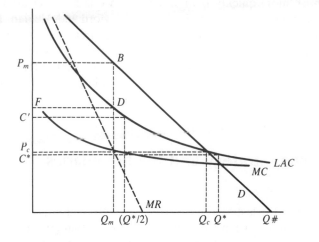

Figure 5.10   Economies of scale and natural monopoly.

for all levels of output shown including, therefore, all output levels from 0 to $Q\#$ which might be required at any price to meet demand in the industry.

Now we already know that a technological trajectory found in a wide range of industries in the nineteenth and twentieth centuries took technological development persistently in the direction of mass production methods aimed at reaping scale economies. A plausible economic reason for this is that monopoly offers rents, most readily earned if a firm can adopt a technology which makes it a natural monopolist. This would encourage investment in innovation aimed at raising the MES and might well have encouraged strategic innovation targeted at creating natural monopolies.

If scale-enhancing innovation involves the firm in R&D, sunk costs are also incurred in achieving a natural monopoly. This is important in the context of a debate over the so-called **contestability** of natural monopolies (Baumol, Panzar and Willig, 1982; Sharkey, 1982). The monopoly would be unable to earn rent if the threat of entry forced it to charge a price equal only to LAC, P_c in Figure 5.10. This is what would happen in a perfectly contestable monopoly. In contestable conditions, a monopoly price above P_c would lead to excess profit which would attract entry and, in any ensuing price war, only one firm (which might not be the initial incumbent) could survive.

But the notion of contestability only makes sense if there are no sunk costs. The incumbent could, however, create an asymmetry by investing strategically in R&D (a sunk cost) to generate proprietary technological knowledge relating to scale economies. This would then create a barrier.

Even in the presence of sunk costs, however, the natural monopolist may have difficulties in sustaining its position if technology is advancing quickly, or if firms in other industries are making similar advances. On the first point, the incumbent's position may be threatened if technological advance is so fast that other firms could invest in superior capital equipment before the incumbent has been able to depreciate its existing plant fully. To defend its position, the incumbent will have at least to be prepared to reduce its price more quickly than when advance is more leisurely and will thus extract a reduced rent (Williamson, 1975; Klein, Crawford and Alchian, 1978; Sharkey, 1982). On the second issue, the monopolist might be threatened at any pace of innovation by what Brunner (1961) has called 'cross entry'. This occurs when a firm making a different product and selling into a different market uses a similar technology. As it makes advances in relation to its own needs, it develops a knowledge base which gives it the capacity to invade other industries.

Innovation, technology strategy and the boundaries of the firm

The notion of strategy used in the last section focused on the formal analysis of how firms might invest deliberately in one period, with the aim of changing the future competitive conditions facing potential rivals. But at a more general level, a firm's strategy can be viewed as a path, or pattern of actions which a firm uses to achieve its objectives. Corporate strategy is sometimes viewed as a deliberate plan of action with a future orientation, but sometimes alternatively as an emergent pattern flowing from the past decisions of firms. An integrated perspective would emphasise the role of a firm's history in conditioning its future planning and feedbacks from outcomes leading to modifications of its strategy (for a brilliant account of the many possible alternatives for an innovating firm see Tom Peters' papers (1990/1)).

In any case, in formulating its corporate strategy the firm will first, consider the threats and opportunities it faces (its business environment) to see what planned actions might be necessary or appropriate; and second, identify its particular strengths and weaknesses to assess its actual capabilities. It may then compare what it might with what it can do to decide what it should do (Twiss, 1987: Chapter 2).

Corporate strategy will typically involve decisions in areas such as finance, marketing and personnel as they relate to a firm's competitiveness. But in the last two decades it has been recognised that the the deployment and development of technology are also of central importance for competitiveness and the notion of technology strategy has emerged in its own right. In aiming to realise the competitive potential of technology, technology strategies complement the other aspects of corporate strategy (Dodgson, 1989).

The formulation of technology strategy is described by Porter (1985) as a multistage process which can be seen as an expanded version of the outline of corporate strategy formulation given above. It involves:

1. Identifying the technologies currently used in the value-adding activities of the firm.
2. Identifying the technologies used elsewhere and currently under development of potential use to the firm.
3. Predicting the evolution of technologies currently or potentially relevant to its needs.
4. Determining which technologies and innovations will have most significance for competitive advantage and industry structure.
5. Assessing the firm's strengths and weaknesses in using and improving relevant technology.
6. Actually choosing a technology strategy.

We noted in Chapter 3, p. 106 and Chapter 4, p. 159 that technology strategies themselves could be classified as 'offensive', 'defensive', 'imitative' and 'dependent' and that this classification could be linked to the product life cycle. But it is possible to identify at least six distinct groups of issues with which technology strategy should deal, implying that a potentially much wider range of strategies could be devised. The areas are: **technology choice** (i.e. which technologies look most promising and how to incorporate them in the firm's products and processes); **level of competence** (i.e. what depth of knowledge to acquire from internal and external sources about the firm's production technologies); **sources of technology** (i.e. whether to obtain new technology from external sources or internal R&D) **R&D investment level** (i.e how much to invest in R&D); **competitive timing** (i.e. whether to attempt to lead or follow in the innovation process); **R&D organisation and policies** (i.e. how to organise laboratories and their staff, how to coordinate R&D with other corporate activities, how to appropriate returns on R&D effort) (Maidique and Patch, 1982; Johnston *et al.*, 1990).

Many of the issues raised by technology strategy have already been discussed in varying degrees. Technology choice was dealt with in relation to demand-side characteristics in Chapter 3 and technological trajectories at various points. Choices about competence levels are driven partly by expected gains from learning by doing and learning. R&D investment levels and the timing of innovation have been covered at length in this chapter and will reappear in Chapter 6.

Issues which receive treatment in this section relate to the sourcing of new technology and, given that new technological ideas are continually being developed in firms, whether or not to diversify to capitalise on the results. These fall, respectively, under sources of technology and R&D organisation and policies in the previous paragraph, though the second involves issues of diversification which are also raised under technology choice. Both of these areas have direct implications for the **boundaries of the firm**, i.e. the scope of the activities in which the firm engages.

In connection with sourcing, the firm which chooses to undertake its own R&D operates, other things being equal, a more extensive range of activities than the firm which buys or licenses new technology developed externally. But why might a firm generate new technology internally when it could, potentially, have acquired it from a specialist supplier through the market? In other words, why is the boundary of its activities defined to include or exclude R&D? Or to put it another way, why is R&D sometimes **vertically integrated** with the rest of the firm's activities, and sometimes not? Vertical integration occurs when intermediate products formerly produced in another sector and sold through the market to a firm start to be produced within the firm itself. In connection with diversification, it is clear that the scope of the firm's activities has in some way changed and entry into new product markets, mergers with other firms and the development of new processes may be included. Diversification therefore implies that innovation is occurring, though sometimes only in the organisation and structure of the firm. But there is more to learn about the connection than we have already encountered.

Once the boundary of the firm itself becomes an issue, we are led to ask more wide-ranging questions about the forms of economic structure most appropriate for coping with the activities and transactions which take place within the innovation process. This issue was first raised in connection with the chain-link framework of analysis in Chapter 2.

External versus *internal sourcing of new technology*

Since the end of the nineteenth century, American corporations have increasingly drawn on in-house rather than external sources for their R&D. 'In-house research [has come] to be the dominant mode for supporting corporate research in America, for small as well as for large organisations. By the 1970s, there were very few stand-alone research organisations, and these typically performed a very limited kind of research … typically where the research objectives are simple and obvious, and where the risks are low.' (Teece, 1988: 258).

In a sense this is surprising. Specialised research laboratories ought to be able to reap economies of scale and scope in undertaking contract work for a wide range of clients. This should generate a comparative advantage for standalone laboratories compared with in-house facilities; standard microeconomic analysis, in other words, suggests that contracting for R&D services from an established low-cost provider would be a superior alternative for a producer to undertaking the research itself (Stigler, 1956). This is a sound argument, but only if contracts written to facilitate such market transactions can be written and implemented effectively and at low cost. The theoretical benchmark where this would be true is the case of perfectly competitive markets.

In such markets, all transactors are price-takers. They may buy and sell goods (including assets) and services at market-determined prices without incurring any costs related to the transaction *per se*. Implicitly, a complete structure of operating markets without cost is assumed to be in place to handle trade in goods and services to be delivered now, at all times into the future and in any state of the world which might arise. Markets closest to the perfectly competitive ideal are most likely to arise when there are many traders on both sides and the good traded is homogeneous and divisible, produced under constant returns to scale, and its characteristics and price well known. There is then no need for search, no scope for traders to negotiate special deals to their individual advantage and no advantage to producing or purchasing large rather than small quantities.

But this is an idealised account of the world in which we live. Markets capable of dealing with all possible sorts of transaction, current and future, certain and uncertain, would be unimaginably costly to set up and run, which is why there are huge gaps in the coverage of futures and contingency markets, markets which deal, respectively, in terms of contracts to deliver goods at future dates and to provide insurance in the event of specified conditions. In the case of many goods and services, moreover, there are only one or a few traders on one or both sides of the market, goods may be heterogeneous, indivisible and even unique, information on them imperfect and production subject to scale economies. These are the conditions under which it becomes necessary (or at least worthwhile) to incur costs associated with the transaction itself; transaction costs which Arrow (1969) has called the 'costs of running the economic system'.

More specifically these costs relate to the written or implicit **contracts** on which individuals must agree, which embody the terms and conditions under which they will trade among themselves. One important aspect of contracts is to assign property rights, rights of ownership which relate to the rights to use an asset, appropriate the returns from it and to change its form or substance. Market analysis has usually assumed property rights underpinning trade are unambiguous and enforceable without cost. But given the innate difficulties of patenting or copyrighting many pieces of new knowledge, the peculiar properties of knowledge often make it difficult for inventors to write contracts which establish ownership rights (intellectual property rights) and appropriate rewards commensurate with its value to users (Arrow, 1962). Moreover, new technological knowledge and artefacts are heterogeneous, often indivisible and unique, information about them highly imperfect and the number of potential traders often few. All of this implies that it will be necessary to incur transaction costs in trading new knowledge and some of the artefacts embodying them. There are transaction costs before the contract is struck, which relate to search, to drafting, negotiation and safeguarding and costs afterwards which include monitoring, haggling to adjust the contract if it is found inadequate and the costs of resolving disputes and enforcing sanctions. These costs turn out to be one way of explaining why firms may choose to do their own R&D.

Transaction cost economics can be traced back to Commons (1934) and Coase (1937) but has been pioneered in the post-war era by Williamson (1975, 1985, 1986, 1989). Williamson's argument is that all transactors in an economy are aware of transaction costs and set out rationally to minimise them. But their rationality is assumed to be bounded, a proposition already familiar from our discussion of the foundations of evolutionary economics. Additionally, they are assumed to behave **opportunistically**. This is in some ways an extension of the conventional notion of rationality. In its strong form, self-interest seeking with guile, we may see opportunism taking the forms of cheating or lying. These sorts of behaviour involve 'going outside the rules' to increase claims on resources. While opportunism does not usually take forms as blatant as this, it always involves 'the incomplete or distorted disclosure of information' (Williamson, 1986: 175). It involves taking advantage of situations in which we can improve its position by deliberately not playing by the rules which exist to govern trade in any particular instance. Clearly, such behaviour is only possible under conditions of uncertainty, i.e. when at least one party is imperfectly informed about potential outcomes. A classic example is entering into a contract for insurance with an insurer without declaring all information relevant to the assessment of risks, in the expectation that this will reduce the premium.

Finally, transaction cost economics argues that the most critical dimension for describing transactions is a condition called **asset specificity**. Asset specificity refers to the degree to which an asset can be redeployed to alternative uses and by alternative users without sacrifice of productive value (Williamson, 1989: 142). The less easily an asset can be redeployed, the more specialised to a task or set of transactions it is and the greater its specificity. There is an obvious relationship here to the idea of sunk costs. Williamson identifies asset specificity in relation to physical assets, human assets, sites, dedicated assets and brand names. To give an example of the first, suppose specialised dies are used to produce particular metal components for downstream use in an engineering process. The dies are assets specific to this activity and this may have implications for the contractual and organisational relationships governing transactions between component manufacturer and users. As an illustration of the second, LBD gives rise to human asset specificity. Individuals acquire expertise specific to the production processes of a particular firm and this may affect the terms on which individuals offer and firms purchase labour with that expertise.

To see why this style of analysis is relevant to transactions which might occur in the course of innovation, consider the following analysis by Teece (1988). Williamson argues in general terms that the occurrence of substantial transaction costs is likely to militate against market-mediated trade and in favour of vertical integration. Teece uses similar arguments to explain why R&D is in many cases integrated with production activities and not contracted out. He sugests there are three types of problem in trying to contract out R&D: specification, disclosure and 'lock-in'. The first of these, arising from the difficulty of specifying fully the characteristics of an as-yet unproduced new product renders competitive bidding for an R&D contract in the industry impossible. This is really the bounded rationality aspect of the issue.

But for a price for the job to be determined, it is not sufficient even to specify problem and desired solution. It is necessary also to spell out conditions which will ensure the producer has unique access to and use of the information it has bought. This is where disclosure issues arise, an element of opportunism.

The supplier (in this case an independent laboratory) generates a solution to a problem which it then passes on to the producer. But those individuals who discovered the solution have memories, so that even if all written record of their work is transferred to the client firm, they are still in a position to sell the information again to a client's rival or to other firms in other industries using similar technology. Since the value of the information to the client resides importantly in his or her unique access to it, the user will be reluctant to contract the work out at any price; it will always fear disclosure by the supplier or its employees, acting opportunistically by selling the information for their own further gain, despite undertakings to the initial user not to do so. The threat of legal action may well not be effective here, though fear of a damaged reputation for trustworthiness might.

The third problem, 'lock-in', is closely aligned with asset specificity. For the user, the problem here is that the very nature of the way in which innovation proceeds may deny it choice among alternative suppliers, once an initial decision has been made. This in turn removes from it an important potential element of sanction in its relationship with the supplier to which it has become committed. To illustrate, suppose the innovation process has already reached the development phase. The final user must decide whether to develop a research idea itself, or contract out the work to a development organisation. If it considers writing a contract with an independent organisation, it will want to include in that contract provisions to terminate the agreement and take the work elsewhere if the initial contractor underperforms in some way. But the client firm's ability to pose this as a threat to the developer is undermined by asset specificity. In this case, the asset specific to the transaction is the tacit knowledge acquired by the developer's staff in the course of bringing the innovation to a commercially implementable form. Possession of such knowledge puts the initial developer at a considerable advantage over potential rivals to whom the work might subsequently be handed and may even give the developer the capacity to produce the good itself. The client is thus 'locked-in' to using the initial developer by the potentially high costs it would have to incur if it tried to terminate the contract (Teece, 1988: 260–1). Since users may be assumed to have enough foresight to realise this, we have another explanation for why R&D work might not be contracted out.

All of the problems discussed above apply to any contract a producer might consider signing with an independent R&D organisation. They apply with particular force to contracts in which a price for the job has to be agreed in advance, a fixed price contract and especially if both parties are either risk-averse or risk-neutral. As an alternative, firms might consider cost-plus contracts, in which the client firm undertakes to cover the R&D firm's costs for the project, plus an agreed percentage as profit. For a client to feel satisfied with such a contract, however, it would have to guard against abuses by engaging in monitoring of the developer's performance, i.e. watching that the contractor did not incur excessive costs. This, in turn, implies setting up an administrative 'watch-dog' structure at considerable cost to itself. The irony is that though a contract has been signed between legally separate corporate entities, an administrative mechanism ultimately has to be invoked which amounts to the equivalent of a vertically integrated organisation! Why, then, bother to operate at arm's length in the first place?

This discussion should have made it clear why firms may very well often have a predisposition to doing their own research and development, rather than contracting it out. But this is only a part of a larger argument for incorporating the range of diverse activities contributing to innovation with a single business.

Teece (1986) argues that 'the successful commercialisation of an innovation requires that . . . know-how . . . be utilised in conjunction with other capabilities or assets. Services such as marketing, competitive manufacturing, and after-sales support are almost always needed. These services are often obtained from *complementary assets* that are specialised' (p. 288). [My italics] The role of such assets varies with whether the rewards to an innovation can be reaped with ease and certainty (conditions of 'tight appropriability'), or whether, as usual, there is doubt on these scores (giving rise to conditions of 'weak appropriability').

There will be less pressure to acquire access to a wide range of specialised complementary assets (thereby expanding the boundaries of the firm) if an innovator can be sure of watertight protection from the legal system through patents or copyright. In this case, the innovator retains ironclad protection of the intellectual property and may appropriate returns effectively by licensing its technology. But this is unusual. More often than not, protection is imperfect. This may not be a serious problem before the dominant design emerges in a new technology and the firm is a small-scale monopolist in the particular version of the innovation it has pioneered. But as the dominant design becomes apparent, two factors bearing on the boundary of the firm will become relevant.

First, an easily imitated common or core technology will emerge. Second, firms will start to encounter the demands of producing efficiently for a mass market. This will call for access to specialised assets needed to deploy its innovative technological knowledge effectively: tooling, equipment and distribution channels. Given the ease with which imitation may occur, an obvious way in which the firm may try to appropriate the return on an innovation is to bring within the boundary of the firm the assets and activities complementary with its new technology. Failure to do so may allow external owners of such assets to appropriate a large part of the returns and this, in turn, would reduce the incentive to the firm to deploy its new knowledge on a large scale.

Diversification

Vertical integration diversifies the range of activities a firm undertakes (and may be called vertical diversification), but it may not increase the diversity of products which the firm brings to the market. But firms clearly do diversify their product range and when they do so, **horizontal diversification** is said to occur. That sort of strategy is considered here. Since it involves the firm moving into product lines which are (for it) new, we are necessarily considering an aspect of product innovation, important aspects of which were covered earlier in the chapter. Here, however, we add two new twists; the effects of allowing for imperfect appropriability and the pursuit of a growth-oriented corporate objective.

Consider first the way in which opportunities for diversification are created. A firm which invests heavily in technology is in reality engaged in two businesses; its primary business which is directed towards satisfying identified market needs and a secondary technological business generating technology of commercial value, but often unrelated directly to corporate objectives (Twiss, 1987: 30). What a business achieves in its secondary business creates, internally, opportunities for its primary business to extend into new areas.

It is often argued that the richer in technological opportunity the firm's environment, the greater the flow of knowledge per dollar of R&D from which the firm might benefit will be and the greater will be the technological push to diversify. But even if a positive relationship were found between R&D and horizontal diversification, this would not necessarily support the hypothesis that causation flows unidirectionally from techno-logical opportunity to diversified firm structure. To make the contrary case, the more diversified a firm, the better positioned it might be to take advantage of advances generated by R&D, which suggests diversification offers an incentive to undertake research (Grabowski, 1968). Whichever hypothesis we might favour, however, neither addresses the issue of why firms exploit such opportunities by horizontal diversification rather than any other means, most obviously by selling or licensing new production technology to other potential producers.

A profit-maximising firm will diversify to make use of an underutilised asset rather than sell it, if it believes it will not realise the full value of the asset when it tries to license its use or sell it in the market. The incentive to diversify rather than sell again lies in imperfect appropriation. If the firm tried to sell knowledge it had gained from R&D, potential purchasers would want to know what they could expect for their money before a deal was struck. But once the seller had conveyed the content of those R&D findings, there would be no incentive for the potential buyer to pay for the information. So the seller would receive nothing, but would lose the potential of making a positive return from exclusive access to the knowledge. Potential sellers of information know this. They may try to acquire property rights to the knowledge through the patent system, but if this proves impossible or offers only limited potential protection, they may well conclude that using the knowledge themselves is the most promising way to maximise returns. The perceived incentives to in-house diversification are reinforced if the firm believes that subsequent learning by doing will further increase its returns, rather than allowing a purchaser of the knowledge to enjoy such gains without having paid in full for them at the time of sale.

There is no guarantee, however, that in-house diversification on this basis offers the best promise of success for the innovation. Some new ideas may be profitably exploitable using knowledge which the firm already possesses. But others might be 'spin-offs' from R&D which would be best exploited by other firms with specialist expertise in a quite different technological area.

A second explanation for diversification lies in the proposition that some firms maximise growth rather than profit (Penrose, 1959; Marris, 1966; Heal and Silberston, 1972; Hay and Morris, 1991: Chapter 10). A firm's growth rate is measured by the proportional rate of expansion of its productive assets or resource base. In the long run, such supply-side expansion only makes sense if sales also grow at a similar rate, so that demand for output keeps capacity fully utilised.

Suppose managers in the firm enjoy a significant degree of immunity from shareholder pressure to maximise profit, for reasons to do with fragmentation in the shareholder body and costs of monitoring and enforcement. They might then pursue growth, because growth brings with it increasing size, which gives the managers perceptions of greater security and professional excellence and offers them the expectation of higher salaries, all of which raise managers' utility. Faster growth through diversification will be easiest to achieve when substantial economies of scope exist.

But the growth rate must reach an upper limit, because first, managerial efficiency will peak then decline as the demands of managing an increasingly complex and diversified empire increase exponentially (the so-called 'Penrose Effect') and second, growth at too fast a rate can only be accommodated by borrowing from banks or raising new equity at a rate so high that it ultimately suppresses share prices and makes the firm the target of a take-over, which it is assumed managers fear.

But even if a modest growth rate is to be maintained, diversification is a necessary corollary. Such diversification can be vertical, but in the long run it will almost inevitably also be horizontal. This is because corporate growth means expanding the asset base and this can only be justified by an associated expansion in sales. It is in the nature of the product life cycle that sales growth accelerates to a peak, then steadily declines through the periods of maturity and decline. So to sustain firm sales growth at a constant rate, the firm must have several products selling simultaneously at different points in their life cycles. And as mature product lines go into decline, new products must be introduced to provide a compensating element of faster growth elsewhere in the firm's product portfolio.

This means that diversification through the introduction of new product lines is a direct implication of the assumption that managers wish to achieve sustained growth in sales, whether or not this conforms to shareholder objectives.

Entrepreneurship

The mainspring of Schumpeter's analysis of innovation is the entrepreneur. For him, the entrepreneur is defined by the function of creativity. In this section, we ask what role the entrepreneur might these days play in the theory of innovation. And in answering that question, we shall see that entrepreneurship cannot in general be automatically equated with the qualities of the *Schumpeterian* entrepreneur. Other authors have constructed the entrepreneur in other images.

To place the entrepreneur in the context of the economic theory of the firm, it is worth referring back to Baumol's (1968) paper 'Entrepreneurship in Economic Theory'. As he points out, the entrepreneur was for long identified as the apex of the hierarchy that determines the behaviour of the firm and was endowed with responsibility for the vitality of the free enterprise system. Yet in contemporary textbooks, references to the entrepreneur were 'scanty and more often ... totally absent. The theoretical firm is entrepreneurless – the Prince of Denmark has been expunged from the discussion of Hamlet' (p. 66).[4]

In essence, the entrepreneur has been read out of the model of the firm in almost all formal theoretical analysis. Certainly in competitive equilibrium analysis, the firm has been set up as a passive calculator that reacts mechanically to changes imposed upon it by fortuitous external developments and over which it exerts no influence. Notice the direct relevance of this to our discussion in Chapter 1 about mechanical and evolutionary systems. The firm in this model is 'essentially an instrument of optimality analysis of well-defined problems which require no entrepreneur for their solutions' (Baumol, 1968: 67).

While Baumol is careful to say such problems are very real and important, the passively calculating mechanical firm is an inadequate or inappropriate conceptual construct to act as the locus for decision-making when problems are not well defined, i.e. when the firm's environment is changing but in uncertain ways, when one firm's decisions affect overall market conditions and invite unpredictable reactions from rivals and when firms perceive their best interests may be served by actively attempting to change their competitive environment. When any or all of the latter conditions prevail, the door is opened to allow a role for the 'clever ruses, ingeneous schemes, brilliant innovations (and) charisma ... of which outstanding entrepreneurship is made' (1968: 67).

This image of the entrepreneur coincides with the picture of a Schumpeterian hero figure whose natural habitat is the turbulent world of disequilibrium and dynamic uncertainty. Indeed, Baumol's point is that in a world of equilibrium, there is no place for the entrepreneur. This merely points to the fact that different authors have viewed the notion of entrepreneurship in different ways. Take, for example, the view of the entrepreneur offered by Walras, generally regarded as the founding father of modern general equilibrium theory. Walras (quoted in Walker (1986) p. 4) considers the entrepreneur exclusively as a person who for profit or loss buys productive services and sells products. There are three things to notice about this definition. First, Walras' entrepreneur is not required to be an innovator. Second, he/she must be a firm owner or else he/she could not bear a loss. And third, the focus on the entrepreneur as an intermediary allows Walras to view the entrepreneur as the instrument of **equilibration**, i.e. propelling the market from any exogenously induced state of disequilibrium into a state of equilibrium.

Schumpeter's *Theory of Economic Development* (1934) has as its first chapter the picture of an economy in equilibrium which owes a great deal to the Walrasian vision. But Schumpeter's own vision, developed in subsequent chapters, was very different. At the level of the industry or economy, Schumpeter viewed the notion of equilibrium as somewhat artificial. Since economies adjusted only gradually to equilibrium when disturbed, it seemed unlikely that they would ever be in equilibrium, given that their technological conditions and the preferences patterns of households were in continuous flux. Secondly, while Walras emphasised the equilibrating role of entrepreneurs, Schumpeter stressed that it was entrepreneurs who initiated the sorts of change which induced disequilibrium.

The first point is relevant to analysis in Chapter 6. Here, consider the second point. The Schumpeterian entrepreneur is motivated by the dream and will to found a private kingdom, the drive to succeed for the joy of success itself and the pleasure of creation (1934: 93–4). Only the first of these directly gives rise to the possibility of pecuniary gain and he quite specifically claims that entrepreneurial profits are in no way a return for risk-taking, since, he argues, the financial risks of innovative investment are borne by lenders of financial capital. This then offers an entirely different picture of the entrepreneur from that envisaged by Walras, on which the orthodox notion of the profit-maximising firm owner, motivated only by the prospect of pecuniary gain, is built. Each of the Schumpeterian entrepreneur's three goals are, if attained, associated with profit, but this is incidental in Schumpeter's vision.

Schumpeter's vision makes most sense when linked to his specific notion of innovation. The function of his entrepreneur is to innovate, but further, 'Schumpeter accustomed economists to thinking of technical change as involving major breaks, giant discontinuities or disruptions with the past. This rather melodramatic conception fitted in well with his charismatic approach to entrepreneurship' (Rosenberg, 1976: 166). In this connection, one of the quotations for which Schumpeter is best remembered is, '(Innovation) is that kind of change arising from within the system which so displaces its equilibrium point that the new one cannot be reached from the old one by infinitesimal steps. Add successively as many mail coaches as you please, you will never get a railway thereby' (1934: 64).

Yet, as we have already discussed in this book, 'technological change is also (and perhaps even more importantly) a continuous stream of innumerable minor adjustments, modifications and adaptations' (Rosenberg, 1976: 166). Since this is how our understanding of the world now compels us to interpret a large element of innovation, the nature of the 'entrepreneurial' function which drives it is clearly somewhat removed from what Schumpeter had in mind. We shall reserve the description of the Schumpeterian entrepreneur for the individual who, principally for the intrinsic creative joy of it, *does* disrupt existing market equilibria by introducing radically new products or techniques of production, or uncovers a new source of raw materials and in so doing, knowingly changes the boundaries and internal structure of industries.[5]

Apart from the rather special meaning entrepreneurship acquires in relation to Schumpeter's vision of innovation, his notion of the entrepreneur is open to question on two other grounds. First, his view that the entrepreneur does not bear financial risk has proved controversial. And second, there is little in his work which indicates what the entrepreneur in a detailed sense actually does; rather as the construct of the orthodox firm serves as the passive calculating machine in general equilibrium systems, so the the Schumpeterian entrepreneur is, in some senses, just another construct, defined by the need in the Schumpeterian system to have an instrument of disequilibration.

On the question of risk-bearing, recall that in Walras' definition the entrepreneur could take a loss. But uncertainty is not given any great role in Walras' analysis, whereas in Schumpeter's world uncertainty is endemic. Every investment decision is risky and someone must bear the risk. Where Schumpeter argued that this risk was borne by lenders, Frank Knight (1921) took the view that it was intrinsic to the notion of entrepreneurship that the entrepreneur was a risk-bearer. With his/her own capital, the entrepreneur would be prepared to pursue investments which the risk-averse would avoid. This allows motivation to be defined in terms of the sort of situation which entrepreneurs seek. Where the risk-averse individual would be put off by the high probability of loss, the entrepreneur is the sort of individual attracted by the prospect of great gain, even though the probability of success is small.

Clearly, prime candidates among situations described in these terms are innovation projects where a new market opportunity might exist for using some technological advance, but where uncertainty about profitability can be resolved only by 'sucking to see'. A weakness of this approach is that it says all entrepreneurs are risk-takers, but cannot say that all who take risk by choice are entrepreneurs. Thus risk-taking can at best, be a necessary condition for entrepreneurship. And, rather as Schumpeter claimed, it might not always be a *sufficient* condition. Depending on the depth and breadth of institutions in the capital market (and, sometimes, government policy), entrepreneurs may be able to acquire at least some finance externally and spread the risk.

It may be argued, as an alternative, that an important part of the risk which entrepreneurs bear relates to the return on human, not financial capital. This view acquires particular force in a modern version of entrepreneurship that occurs within corporations. **Intrapreneurs** are individuals who create and promote innovations while corporate employees. Their prestige and prospects within a corporation will depend upon their success in the highly risky business of championing a new product or idea, often against the resistance of a conservative, risk-averse bureaucratic structure. That they choose to take this path rather than any other, however, marks them out as 'entrepreneurial'.

Individuals who have risked their time, effort (and possibly financial capital) on innovation in the past are, according to Peters' 'Hire Renegades' strategy (Peters, 1990/1), the best people for a corporation to employ if it wishes to succeed through innovation in the future. But the restless energy of such individuals will undoubtedly involve them personally in taking apparently huge risks, 'break a *lot* of china, irritate a *lot* of people' (Peters, 1990/1: 10). How great the risks actually are (to them) will depend on the attitudes and approach of the particular corporation. Firms are faced with a Catch-22 dilemma: keep the intrapreneur and suffer the disruption he/she brings or get rid of him/her and suffer the lack of an innovative edge. Every corporation will judge differently the point at which intrapreneurial disruption becomes too dysfunctional to tolerate any longer.

The second shortcoming of Schumpeter's own presentation is that it is short on the detail of what entrepreneurs do. Different authors have given different answers here. Leibenstein (1978) emphasises the intermediary role identified by Walras, but in a world of uncertainty is particularly concerned with the part the entrepreneur plays in enhancing information flows in the markets for venture capital and management skills. He sees an important role for the entrepreneur in filling 'gaps' that might arise in the network of potential trading connections between innovating firms and their customers. Again in the shadow of Walras, Kirzner (1976) sees the entrepreneur's main job as that of adjusting price when markets are out of equilibrium, a task for which entrepreneurs are especially well fitted because of a special quality which Kirzner identifies as 'alertness' (superior foresight) in relation to profitable opportunities.

From either of these perspectives, a crucial role for the innovator is to collect and process information about the market potential for new products and processes. But this does not (any more than merely risk-taking) define entrepreneurship. Rather an entrepreneur is someone who collects and synthesises information as a basis for the specialised task of 'taking judgmental decisions about the co-ordination of scarce resources' (Casson, 1982: 23).

For Casson, the central function of the entrepreneur is to coordinate. Coordination is defined as a beneficial reallocation of resources, capturing the idea that the entrepreneur is an agent of change, concerned with improving (not perpetuating) the existing allocation. The first point at which entrepreneurs distinguish themselves in connection with innovation is in spotting an opportunity (Kirzner's 'alertness'). Entrepreneurs do not necessarily possess information no-one else does; their advantage lies in their recognising complementaries among certain items of information that others have missed. Another talent of the entrepreneur is to assimilate and make sense of diverse information on preferences, technology, input supply, transport services and government policies which might restrict resource reallocation. And to be informed accurately and early, it is necessary to go to primary sources of information, which tend to be geographically dispersed. So entrepreneurs are often highly mobile.

Coordinating information is also relevant to the various aspects of **market making** (Casson, 1982, Chapter 9 and p. 382), i.e. creating trade among potential transactors. As we saw in the last section, normal market mechanisms may not exist or may fail because of obstacles to trade, including lack of contact between potential buyers and sellers, disagreements over price and specification, costs of transferring ownership and post-sale performance deficiencies. Casson argues that it is an important part of the entrepreneur's function to make markets by overcoming these obstacles. The motivation to do this is that the expected net benefit of creating the market is positive, i.e. despite the costs of setting up the market, the benefits from having the market rather than not are ultimately expected to exceed the set-up costs. This does not provide a complete theory of entrepreneurial activity, however, unless we know how the entrepreneur shares in the benefits. The entrepreneur must be assumed to gain personally from increasing net benefits if this description is to acquire the power to explain why he/she performs these functions and at what level.

That said, these functions are of particular importance when there is a market to be made for a novel product or process and suggest an important role for the entrepreneur to the extent that overcoming difficulties attending trade in innovatory goods and services defines the substance of entrepreneurship. The coordinating role of the entrepreneur can also be seen in a way which addresses a question raised in Chapter 2. There it was noted that a disparate set of activities is involved in the innovation process, each providing an output required elsewhere in the process. To see entrepreneurship as a means of coordinating two sides of the market for a single new product or process, is an oversimplification; it must coordinate and integrate activities which might occur in a number of markets. The entrepreneur becomes someone with a specific talent for bringing these elements together. Certainly this may involve making markets which might not otherwise have existed. But it will also involve internalising some trade and locating it within the boundaries of the firm which the entrepreneur has created.

In a shorthand fashion, all of this activity falls under the rubric of removing obstacles to trade. But this perspective conceals that obstacles arise not only for informational and institutional reasons, but also because of the very different types of people who are engaged in each type of activity. Researchers and businessmen, for example, receive quite different sorts of education and, as groups, exhibit major differences in aims and attitudes, values and desired rewards (Dubinskas, 1985). Twiss (1987) reports that while R&D managers are strongly oriented towards the world of science and technology, marketing managers have an equally strong tendency to pay attention to the world of commerce, with the result that most R&D managers perceive that communication breakdowns between themselves and the marketers is the major barrier to innovation in their company (p. 6).

This point can be generalised; there are several functionally defined professional and technical groups who must contribute effectively if the innovation process is to proceed. Each group tends to have its own view of how the world works, each its own 'culture', with its own way of defining 'problems' and how to resolve them and its own perceptions and misperceptions about the value of the approaches taken by other groups. Left to themselves, these groups objectively find it hard to communicate, because each use their own jargon and structures of thought which are unfamiliar to other groups. Subjectively, they may well also have little sympathy for the perceived motivations of other groups. Some research scientists, for example, are jaundiced at the prospect that their ideas might be used in ways which generate profits for individuals who had nothing to do with generating the science.

Given this, the coordinating role of the entrepreneur implies a skill that goes beyond collecting and synthesising information; he or she must understand a variety of jargons and disciplinary approaches. And beyond the somewhat abstract notion of negotiation lies the skill of gaining the willing cooperation and interaction of groups who are naturally inclined to suspect each others' motives. The act of creation in which the entrepreneur engages is therefore the act of teaming together elements which might not in the normal course of events have seen that any mutual advantage could spring from their cooperation and motivating them to form a whole greater than the sum of their parts.

By way of conclusion on entrepreneurship, we must recognise that entrepreneurs are instruments of change. Whether, however, entrepreneurs are the restless, initiating hero figures we find in Schumpeter, or just persistent tinkerers with a nose for new modifications, they will be of little or no significance to the economic system unless they can channel their vision through successfully operating trading entities – the firms that comprise the system. They must, therefore, either have the coordinating expertise to run a firm which brings innovations into the market or uses them in serving the market or, as intrapreneurs, they must have the drive and ability to convince corporate hierarchies to invest capital in their brainchild. In either case, the capacity to line up people behind their vision and to get them to commit themselves to fulfilling it is crucial. Despite being a social science, this is a perspective which economics often fails to reveal.

An evolutionary perspective on innovation in the firm

Analysis of economic systems focuses on characterising conditions of market and multimarket equilibrium, with a view to seeing how prices are determined and whether prices meet certain criteria relative to costs which ensure that resources are allocated with maximum social benefit. In that context, it is extremely convenient to represent firms as 'optimising machines' since their activities then amount to tackling mathematical problems whose solutions provide the basis of the final equilibrium. This approach owes much to the mechanical vision of the physical universe described in Chapter 1.

In the previous two sections, however, we have seen approaches to analysis which are responses to the perception that firms cannot always be modelled as reading with confidence the nature of their economic environment. Especially when they are engaged in innovation, their relationships with both suppliers and customers are ill-defined contractually and infused with uncertainty and the dangers of opportunistic behaviour. Transaction cost analysis and theories hinging on entrepreneurial behaviour attempt to provide foundations for understanding economic behaviour when setting up the conditions for trade is itself a major problem. Both approaches take us in a direction away from the mechanical analogue; instead of seeing the firm as operating within a well-defined and predictable framework, they emphasise the variety of possible strategies a firm might pursue as it both influences and responds to changes in its economic environment.

When we talked about corporate and technology strategies, we noted that each firm had its own specific strengths and weaknesses, which would influence strategy formulation and that strategy will often be modified in the light of experience. Again entrepreneurship is a concept designed to fill a gap, to offer some sort of device to explain how the economic system can at the microlevel grope to coordinate the activities of disparate and unconnected resource owners on both sides of many markets. As Casson argues, a theory of the entrepreneur looks more likely to be a feature of evolutionary economics than of analysis in a mechanical mould.

That said, transaction cost work and theories which motivate entrepreneurial activity by appeal to the benefits it yields to the entrepreneur both imply some sort of maximising principle at the level of the decision-making unit to complete the model. However, evolutionists wish to abandon the notion that firms optimise at all and argue that the characterisation of firms as maximisers may cease to be appropriate in the context of analysis designed to consider questions other than pure resource allocation.

Evolutionary theory is not concerned so much with the question 'How do we characterise the conditions necessary for an efficient allocation of resources?' as 'How do we characterise the dynamic processes by which firm behaviour patterns and market outcomes are jointly determined over time?' (Nelson and Winter, 1982: 18). In the latter context, it may make little sense to characterise firms as optimising machines for they may often not be in a position to know at the start the consequences of their decisions. Because their decisions involve undertaking R&D whose outcomes in relation to the value of resulting innovations are unknowable, there are aspects of their future which cannot be entered into an optimising calculation.

The response to this problem by evolutionary theorists is (in part) to say that firms which cannot know at the start what is best to do are similar to biological organisms born with a genetic inheritance where it is a matter of luck whether or not they are well-equipped for their environment. Such firms (organisms) only discover which among them has behaviour patterns destined to generate most profit (reflect greatest fitness) in the course of the ensuing competitive selection process. But how, in this context, are firms to be viewed? The answer is that their existence as constructs within the theory derives from the need to have entities which may display the variety of behaviours over which the selection procedure will operate. It is for this reason that Nelson and Winter describe their approach to the firm as 'behavioural'. Their motivation is to have us understand what it is that determines behaviour and it is within the context of the firm as an entity which displays behaviour that this has logically to be done.

An alternative to profit maximisation

To start with, notice that Nelson and Winter (1982) abandon the notion that firms maximise anything. To quote them; 'Possession of a complete, clearly defined objective function is not a necessary condition for business operation in the real world; all that is required is a procedure for determining the action to be taken .... Presumably, if the firms in the world can get along without being entirely clear about their goals, so can the firms in a theoretical model' (p. 57). Firms in a formal competitive equilibrium could not 'get along' in this way, for they must be 'optimizing machines' for the larger theory within which they operate to yield results. But in evolutionary theory the emphasis is on environmental 'pressure on decisions' which allows only those motives to persist which do not depart too much from 'survival requirements' (p. 58). Within the general recognition that survival is the minimum but still vital requirement, it is plausible to assume that 'making money (in some sense) is a dominant business motivation' without representing that as profit maximisation (p. 58).

Nelson and Winter stress simply that firms do what they do; their principal business is to produce and to make some money at it. There are good reasons to believe that they cannot (logically) be maximisers. And if we can release ourselves from a commitment to a larger theoretical framework, which requires that firms be viewed as maximisers, then we have no need to assume they are maximisers. In the context of an evolutionary theoretical framework, no such need arises, any more than in biological evolution we need to assume that individual organisms strive consciously to maximise their reproduction rate. Firms simply display whatever behaviour arises from the procedures they adopt. And in the context of an environment influenced both by other firms' and industries' activity (cf the biotic environment) and changes in technology, tastes and natural resources (cf the abiotic environment described in Stenseth, 1986: 131), the hypothesis is that the firms whose behaviour is best suited to prosper in the environment come to dominate.

The process of selection may be fast or slow, but there is no reason in logic to expect that the profitability (cf biological fitness) of firms with a dominant behaviour reflects the fact that they chose the best way of doing things as part of a maximising exercise. As Alchian (1950) elegantly shows, even in an industry with randomly behaving firms, some will make large profits. But by construction they cannot be profit maximisers, in the sense of making decisions in advance which they anticipate will yield for them more profit than any other decision for them.

From the perspective of analysing the rate of innovation and productivity growth, the issues of interest surround how firms seek and are driven to look for more effective means of production relative to their current practice and relative to the current practice of other firms. As a logical possibility, some sort of natural selection process operating on non-maximising firms might lead to an industry dominated by a firm or firms using techniques identical to those predicted by a model in which firms are viewed as maximisers from the start. But if the argument of natural selection is the basis for our belief in profit-maximisation, then we should deal in terms of that basis itself and not the profit-maximising behaviour it may imply (Jacquemin (1987) p. 13, citing Koopmans (1957), p. 140).

The relationships between individual firms and their environment form the substance of Chapter 6. Here we identify how an individual firm's behaviour may, in an evolutionary view, be modelled, in terms of its production activity at any moment and in attempts to adapt and improve its performance. Look first at the procedures referred to above, the devices individuals and organisations employ to cope with their information-processing constraints and the sorts of uncertainty they confront. We need not delay over this because that ground has already been covered in Chapter 4, in the discussion of routines and skills in production. But we now need to build on that to provide a formal account of how firms innovate and imitate under evolutionary pressure, i.e. *modify* their routines.

The model presented here (Nelson and Winter, 1982: 282–5) manages to capture central conceptual elements of innovation from which we argued in Chapter 1 standard theorising has tended historically to deflect attention: intractable uncertainty, irreversibility (implying path dependence) and heterogeneity. It operates as follows.

There is a probability that a given firm may in any period change its production routines either as a result of innovation or imitation. Whichever of the two leads to the new routine, the new production method will apply to all a firm's capacity without further cost. The conceptualisation of the firm now focuses on two questions: What determines the probability of a firm changing its production techniques in any period? What will these changes look like?

To the first question, Nelson and Winter offer an answer which in its general form is identical, irrespective of whether firms finish up imitating or innovating. The probability that a firm i will change by innovation in period t is written $Pr(d_{i,n,t} = 1)$, and the probability that it will change by imitation $Pr(d_{i,m,t} = 1)$. $Pr(d_{i,n,t} = 0)$ and $Pr(d_{i,m,t} = 0)$ would denote the probability of no change in the firm in t. By construction, $0 < Pr(d_{i,m,t} = 1), Pr(d_{i,n,t} = 1) < 1$, so there is never complete certainty that a firm will change in any given period. This is because for example, $Pr(d_{i,m,t} = 1) = 20$ per cent, means that, on average, firm i will change by innovation once every five periods.

Whether through innovation or imitation, change is the result of search which requires R&D expenditure. The probability of change in any period is modelled as proportional through a scaling parameter a (which applies to all firms in the industry), to R&D expenditures per period by the firm on each kind of R&D. Thus if $R_{i,n,t}$ and $R_{i,m,t}$ are, respectively, the dollar outlays on innovation and imitation R&D by firm i in t:

$$Pr(d_{i,n,t} = 1) = a_n R_{i,n,t}$$
$$Pr(d_{i,m,t} = 1) = a_m R_{i,m,t}$$

Although we do not yet know what the changes to production routines will look like, this approach conceptualises change at the firm level as one in which something of positive value is generated from time to time from search processes. And the more spent on search, the more often something of positive value will be found and applied. For firms doing similar amounts of search, the frequency of change is determined by a_n and a_m. These parameters take values which ensure the probability terms never exceed unity. They vary from industry to industry, reflecting differences in technological opportunity and other features which influence the probability of search success.

To obtain further insights, consider the ratio of R&D expenditures to the value of firm's capital stock at t, $K_{i,t}$. This can be written $r_{i,n}$ in the case of innovation and $r_{i,m}$ for imitation expenditure. Then

$$Pr(d_{i,n,t} = 1) = a_n r_{i,n} K_{i,t}$$
$$Pr(d_{i,m,t} = 1) = a_m r_{i,m} K_{i,t}$$

What this implies is that firms have a probability of changing via innovation or imitation which is sensitive to two components: first, a ratio of R&D expenditures to a measure of firm size (a research intensity ratio) and second, firm size itself.

The intensity ratio can be viewed as a policy or decision rule, similar in many essentials to the often-observed rule that R&D expenditure should be undertaken in proportion to the value of sales (another measure of size). For any two firms of given size (K_i), the firm with the rule reflecting a higher ratio of research to sales will be the one with the higher probability of success. Such rules constitute the basis for continuity in characterising firms over time and hence are the raw material for economic selection processes. Rules might change over time, but it is the hypothesis in this model that while they can be expected to vary from firm to firm (a source of diversity), they will be constant characteristics of firms over time.

The role of firm size reflects the view that between any two firms with identical decisions rules, the larger firm will have a higher probability of changing production routines in any one period. This is because, with identical values of $(R_{i,n}/K_i)$ and $(R_{i,m}/K_i)$, a higher value of K_i must imply research expenditures higher in the same proportion. The probabilities are strictly proportional to K_i, so there are no economies of scale in R&D.

If firms knew what sort of changes were implied by being an innovator or imitator in some period, the uncertainty embodied in the style of search explored thus far might appear relatively innocuous. The only issue would be how often in actuality search would lead to changes in production routine. This is more troublesome than might initially appear. Let us assume that the model captures at least the essence of conditions under which search proceeds. Then it would be the case that interesting uncertainty is reflected in this part of the model because success on average in say, 20 per cent of periods could imply that change occurs in all sorts of actual patterns over time. For example, the same 20 per cent figure would apply to changes which occurred in the first two of ten periods, the last two of ten or two widely spaced periods. This is interesting because the same innovation made earlier can have irreversible effects which preclude success for other innovations whose arrival is delayed and may do so even when subsequent innovations are technically superior (see references to the effects of 'lock-in' in Chapter 6).

The Nelson-Winter model of the firm's innovation behaviour can be adapted to allow for either of two regimes of technological change: **science-based** and **cumulative technology**. In the first, overall potential for advance is envisaged to be determined by events outside the industry which are constantly generating new and more promising technological possibilities. In the second, advance takes place within a given set of technological opportunities, only some of which have yet been discovered. Search proceeds by first examining the characteristics of production routines quite similar to those already in use. But the opportunity set is not envisaged to change as the result of events outside the industry (1982: 283).

The stylised representation of search under each routine involves the firm in sampling from distributions of techniques each defined by a value of the average productivity of capital. Under a science-based regime, firms sample from a log-normal distribution of techniques, the nature of each drawn from the sample being independent of previous draws. The distribution is envisaged to shift upwards over time, with the rate of increase of the mean of the distribution identified as the **rate of growth of**

latent productivity. The more research expenditure a firm undertakes, the more often it is able to draw techniques from the distribution and the more closely, as a result, it is able to track developing technological opportunities. In this characterisation there is no explicit element to capture the presence of learning within the firm, or of attempts to draw on science informed by past and current experience of the technology. All draws from the distribution are independent of each other over time.

Under a cumulative technology regime, the alternative techniques not yet discovered by the firm are characterised by their relationship to the techniques already used by a firm. Nelson and Winter (1982) regard the probability of moving from one technique to another as being related in decreasing fashion to distance away from what is already known, i.e. the closer a previously unknown technique is to one that the firm already knows, the more likely it is to be found. 'Search is "local" in the sense that the probability distribution of what is found is concentrated on techniques close the current one' (Nelson and Winter: 211). In contrast to firms searching under a scientific regime, what firms find when they *do* innovate is directly influenced by what they already know. Since techniques are represented by output: capital ratios, this means that small increments in capital productivity are envisaged as more likely than large ones.

Finally, Nelson and Winter provide a rule which determines how firm-level productivity changes from period to period. Quite simply, firms consider their alternatives and choose the one offering highest productivity. In each period t, they look at their current practice productivity and compare it, if they may imitate, with industry best-practice productivity and, if they may innovate, with the technique they drew from the distribution. A firm will neither innovate nor imitate if it has spent nothing on R&D ($r_{i,n,t} = r_{i,m,t} = 0$). Even if it has undertaken search in both areas, there will be potentially many periods when, because $Pr(d_{i,m,t} = 1)$ and $Pr(d_{i,n,t} = 1)$ lie below unity, no opportunity to imitate or innovate will arise. In this view, rising productivity between any two periods for a firm requires as a necessary condition that the firm both undertake search at positive cost in at least some period and that what it discovers as a result offers higher productivity than it already achieves. Uncertainty arises in the timing of discoveries and (especially) in relation to what will be found.

On the last point, note that the modelling of search processes here is consistent with intractable uncertainty. To model the entire system (industry) in a way which offers the prospect of making predictions, it is a helpful strategy to use the device of giving specific form to the distributions which firms are envisaged as sampling. But there is no presumption that firms from their individual standpoint know what the distribution looks like. As omniscient observers, we might know that firm's probabilities of raising productivity by x per cent are whatever they are by observing the distribution from which the firm samples, but the firm is not presumed to know that.

Whether innovation occurs under a science-based regime or cumulative technology, existing production routines will change. But the fact that such routines exist in the first place is important. Existing routines never work perfectly and observation of production will always suggest how they might be changed. The point to note is that the existing routine defines or frames relevant questions to ask, questions which would not or could not be asked without experience of a prevailing routine. Routines are important for innovation because the hard part of important innovation is in locating the right question; finding the answer is often relatively easy (Nelson and Winter, 1982: 129).

This is crucial to an evolutionary story of innovation. It is consistent with the cumulative technology regime, since questions prompted by prevailing routines are more likely to yield answers in closely related routines than questions posed independently of existing experience. But it can also be made consistent with the science-based regime. In that case, the natural presumption prompted by the image of firms sampling from a random set of techniques is that science generates the techniques independently, which firms then scan. If a firm commissions a research organisation to solve a production problem, attempts to generate a solution will not be independent of its experience. But uncertainty still attends the question of whether and how the production problem will be solved, hence the device of a distribution of potential outcomes.

The stylised account of innovation basically says that what firms spend on search determines how often they will make a discovery which will change their production routines and that the unknown (to them) distribution of production techniques to be sampled determines whether what they find is worth implementing. This account captures the essential idea that the outcome of all search is unknowable in advance.

What also needs emphasis is that all search builds on existing experience. Different firms have different starting points, which accounts for their initial heterogeneity. But for each innovating firm, the outcome of its search is more likely to be shaped by its own experience than that of other firms (for then it would be an imitator). Thus firms retain distinct identities through time.

Equally importantly, there is a basis for **path dependence**. This arises when the probability of an event occurring in a future period is directly influenced by events which took place in an earlier period. If firms adopt solutions which arise as the result of answering questions raised by their existing routines, clearly the specific innovations we observe from a given firm over time will be path-dependent. Even if two firms finish up with identical levels of unit cost, we should usually expect the actual techniques they use to be different.

Appendix

In deriving the expression in the text, it is assumed that the patent bestows monopoly profit, π_m, which is the same in dollar terms for each period, forever. Now, it was shown in the Appendix to Chapter 3 that the PV of a profit stream flowing from now until year T would be:

$$\int_0^T e^{-rt}\pi(t)\,\mathrm{d}t$$

In that case $\pi(t)$ could vary from period to period but, by assumption, we here make it a constant and will denote it π^*.

When profit period is constant for every period into the future, the PV of such a stream is:

$$\int_0^\infty e^{-rt}\pi^* \, dt \tag{A5.1}$$

which is an improper integral and cannot be evaluated.

If we took as the upper limit of the integral some year n, a finite year in the very distant future, we could evaluate (A5.1) by allowing n to approach infinity. First write (A5.1) in the slightly modified form:

$$\int_0^n e^{-rt}\pi^* \, dt$$

This may be re-expressed:

$$\pi^* \int_0^n e^{-rt} \, dt$$

and after integration evaluated as:

$$\pi^*[(1/r)e^{-rt}]_0^n$$

Allowing n now to approach infinity, this expression becomes:

$$\lim_{n \to \infty} [(-\pi^*/r)e^{-rn} - (-\pi^*/r)]$$

$$= \lim_{n \to \infty} [\pi^*/r - (\pi^*/r)e^{-rn}]$$

$$= \frac{\pi^*}{r} \tag{A5.2}$$

This is the expression for the present value of an income stream, flowing forever at a constant rate per period.

In our problem, however, the constant income per period starts to flow only when the patent is won at year T sometime in the future. In this case, it is necessary to consider the expression:

$$\int_T^\infty e^{-rt}\pi^* \, dt$$

to obtain the PV of the profits from the patent.

Adopting the same strategy as before to evaluate this:

$$\lim_{n \to \infty} \int_T^n e^{-rt}\pi^* \mathrm{d}t = \lim_{n \to \infty} [(-\pi^*/r)e^{rn} - (-\pi^*/r)e^{-rT}]$$

$$= \lim_{n \to \infty} [(\pi^*/r)e^{-rT} - (\pi^*/r)e^{-rn}]$$

$$= \frac{\pi^*}{r} e^{-rT} \tag{A5.3}$$

Since π^*/r is the same as $\pi_m/r = V_m$ in the text, this demonstrates that PV of the income flow after T is:

$$V_m e^{-rT}$$

We also have a helpful interpretation of V_m itself.

Notes

1. The technical appendix to Chapter 3 explains the continuous discounting procedure employed to derive present values.
2. Learning about the returns generated by the new technology is conceptually different from LBD and LBU, which have to do with learning how to apply the new technology. This can be seen by recognising that a firm could, in principle, become no better at all in operating the new technology but by observing its contribution to profit in the particular circumstances of the firm would nonetheless increase its knowledge of the distribution of returns associated with the new technology.
3. The relevance of this argument can be seen, for example, in the work of Harley (1973), who explored why wooden ships continued to be built in North America long after new construction methods had been introduced elsewhere.
4. Baumol's observation still remained more or less true quarter of a century later. Layard and Walters (1978: 220–1), however, present a substantive and succinct account of entrepreneurial capacity, arguing that this is a capacity that everyone possesses in some measure, but that it differs from factors of production like labour and capital in that it receives a **residual income**, i.e. is paid on a non-contractual basis. 'The entrepreneur's net reward is the difference between the amount he obtains when *organising* a firm's activities and the amount he could receive by hiring out his services to some other entrepreneur'. [My italics] Layard and Walters stress the organisational or coordinating role of the entrepreneur, and use interfirm variations in entrepreneurial capacity to explain interfirm differences in profitability.
5. See Chapter 2 for the associated discussion found in Abernathy and Clarke 1985.

References

Abernathy, W.J. and K. Clarke (1985) 'Innovation: mapping the winds of creative destruction', *Research Policy* 14, 3–22.

Alchian, A. (1950) 'Uncertainty, evolution and economic theory', *Journal of Political Economy* 58, 211–222.

Arrow, K.J. (1962) *'Economic Welfare and the Allocation of Resources for Invention'*, Washington: NBER.

Arrow, K.J. (1969) 'The organisation of economic activity: Issues pertinent to the choice of market vs non-market allocation, in *The Analysis and Evaluation of Public Expenditure*, Vol. 1, Washington, DC: Government Printing Office.

Bain, J. (1956), *Barriers to New Competition*, Cambridge, MA: Harvard University Press.

Bain, J. (1968) *Industrial Organisation*, New York: Wiley.

Baumol, W.J. (1968) 'Entrepreneurship in economic theory', *American Economic Review* 58, 64–71

Baumol, W.J., J.C. Panzar and R.J. Willig (1982) *Contestable Markets and the Theory of Industry Structure*, New York: Harcourt Brace Jovanovich.

Brander, J. and B. Spencer (1983) 'Strategic commitment with R&D: The symmetric case', *Bell Journal of Economics* 14, 225–235.

Brunner, E. (1961) 'A note on potential competition', *Journal of Industrial Economics* 9, 248–250.

Casson, M. (1982) *The Entrepreneur: An Economic Theory*, Oxford: Martin Robertson.

Coase, R.H. (1937) 'The nature of the firm', *Economica* 4, 386–405.

Comanor, W.S. and T.A. Wilson (1967) 'Advertising market structure and performance', *Review of Economics and Statistics* 49, 423–40.

Commons, J.R. (1934) *Institutional Economics*, Madison: University of Wisconsin Press.

Dasgupta, P. and J.E. Stiglitz (1980) 'Uncertainty, industrial structure, and the speed of R&D', *The Bell Journal of Economics* 11(1), Spring, 1–28.

Dasgupta, P. (1984) 'The theory of technological competition', in J. Mathewson and J.E. Stigilitz (eds) *Modern Approaches to Industrial Economics*, London: Macmillan, 519–47.

Dodgson, M. (ed.) (1989) *Technology Strategy and the Firm: Management and Public Policy*, Harlow: Longman.

Dubinskas, F.A. (1985) 'The culture chasm: Scientists and managers in genetic engineering firms', *Technology Review* 34, May/June, 25–30.

Eisner, R. (1978) *Factors in Business Investment*, Cambridge, MA: NBER General Series, 102.

Fudenberg, D. and J. Tirole (1983) 'Learning by doing and market performance', *Bell Journal Economics* 14, 522–30.

Gaskins, D. (1971) 'Dynamic limit pricing: Optimal pricing under threat of entry', *Journal of Economic Theory* 2, 306–322.

Geroski, P. (1990) 'Innovation, technological opportunity and market structure', *Oxford Economic Papers* 42, 586–602.

Gilbert, R.J. (1989) 'Mobility barriers and the value of incumbency', in R. Schmalensee and R. Willig (eds), *Handbook of Industrial Organisations*, Vol. 1, Amsterdam: North-Holland, ch. 8.

Gilbert, R.J. and D. Newbery (1982) 'Pre-emptive patenting and the persistence of monopoly', *American Economic Review* 74, 514–526.

Grabowski, H.G. (1968) 'The determinants of industrial research and development: a study of the chemical, drug and petroleum industries', *Journal of Political Economy* 76, 292–306.

Harley, C.K. (1973) 'On the persistence of old techniques: the case of North American wooden shipbuilding', *Journal of Economic History*, 372–98.

Hay, D. and D. Morris (1991) *Industrial Economics and Organization*, Oxford: Oxford University Press.

Heal, G. and Z.A. Silberston (1972) 'Alternative managerial objectives: An exploratory note', *Oxford Economic Papers* 24, 137–50.

Jacquemin, A. (1987) *The New Industrial Organisation: Market Forces and Strategic Behaviour,* Oxford: Oxford University Press.

Johnston, R., D. Scott-Kemmis, T. Darling, F. Collyer, D. Roessner and J. Currie (1990) *Technology Strategies in Australian Industry*, Canberra. DITAC/Centre for Technology and Social Change, Wollongong.

Jorgenson, D. (1963) 'Capital theory and investment behaviour', *American Economic Review* 53, 47–56.

Kamien, M. and N. Schwartz (1982) *Market Structure and Innovation*, Cambridge: Cambridge University Press.

Katz, M.L. and C. Schapiro (1985) 'On the licensing of innovations', *Rand Journal of Economics* 16, 505–20.

Kirzner, I. (1976) 'Equilibrium versus market process', in E.G. Dolan (ed.) *The Foundations of Modern Austrian Economics*, Kansas City: Sheed and Ward.

Klein, B., R.G. Crawford and A. Alchian (1978) 'Vertical integration, appropriable rents and the competitive contracting process', *Journal of Law and Economics* 21, 297–326.

Knight, F. (1921) *Risk, Uncertainty and Profit*, Boston: Houghton Mifflin.

Koopmans, T. (1957) *Three Essays on the State of Economic Science*, New York: McGraw-Hill.

Koutsoyiannis, A. (1979) *Modern Microeconomics*, London: Macmillan.

Layard, R. and A.A. Walters (1978) *Microeconomic Theory*, New York: McGraw-Hill.

Leibenstein, H. (1978) *General X-efficiency Theory and Economic Development*, New York: Oxford University Press.

Lieberman, M. (1984) 'The learning curve and pricing in the chemical processing industries', *Rand Journal of Economics* 15(2), 213–28.

Machlup, F. (1967) 'Theories of the firm: Marginalist, behavioral, managerial', *American Economic Review* 57, 1–33.

Mann, H.M. (1966) 'Seller concentration, barriers to entry and rates of return in thirty industries', *Review of Economics and Statistics* 48, 296–307.

Mansfield, E. (1968) *Industrial Research and Technological Innovation*, New York: Norton.

Maidique, M.A. and P. Patch (1982) 'Corporate strategy and technological policy', in M.L. Tushman and W.L. Moore (eds) *Readings on the Management of Innovation*, Boston: Pitman, 273–85.

Marris, R. (1966) *The Economic Theory of Managerial Capitalism*, London: Macmillan.

Modigliani, F. (1961) *The Role of Anticipations and Plans in Economic Behavior and Their Use in Economic Analysis and Forecasting*, Urbana: University of Illinois Press.

Needham, D.C. (1975) 'Market structure and firms' R&D behaviour', *Journal of Industrial Economics* 23, 241–55.

Nelson, R.R. and S. Winter (1982) *An Evolutionary theory of Economic Change*, Cambridge, MA: Belknap Press of Harvard University Press.

Nickell, S.J. (1978) *The Investment Decision of Firms*, Cambridge: Nisbet, Cambridge University Press.

OECD (1988) *Industrial Revival Through Technology*, Paris: OECD.

Penrose, E. (1959) *The Theory of Growth of the Firm*, Oxford: Oxford University Press.

Peters, T. (1990/1), 'Get innovative or get dead', *California Management Review* 33(1) and (2), Parts 1 and 2.

Porter, M.E. (1985) *Competitive Advantage*, New York: Free Press.

Prescott, E. and M. Visscher (1977) 'Sequential locations among firms with foresight', *Bell Journal of Economics* 8, 378–94.

Rosenberg, N. (1976) *Perspectives on Technology*, Cambridge: Cambridge University Press.

Sargent, T.J. (1978) 'Rational expectations, econometric exogeneity, and consumption', *Journal of Political Economy* 86, 673–700.

Sargent, T.J. (1979) *Macroeconomic Theory*, New York: Academic Press.

Schankerman, M. and M.I. Nadiri (1984) 'Investment in R&D, costs of adjustment, and expectations', in Z. Griliches (ed.) *Research and Development, Patents and Productivity*, Chicago: NBER, University of Chicago Press.

Schapiro, C. (1989) 'Theories of oligopoly behavior', in R. Schmalensee and R. Willig (eds) *Handbook of Industrial Organisations*, Vol. 1, Amsterdam: North Holland.

Schmalensee, R. (1978) 'Entry-deterence in the ready-to-eat breakfast cereal industry', *Bell Journal of Economics* 9, 305–27.

Schumpeter, J.A. (1934) *Theory of Economic Development*, Harvard. First published by the Department of Economics of Harvard University: Volume XLVI in the Harvard Economic Studies Series, 1934. First issued as an Oxford University Press paper back, 1961.

Shaked, A. and J. Sutton (1982) 'Relaxing price competition through product differentiation', *Review of Economic Studies*, 49, 3–14.

Sharkey, W.W. (1982) *The Theory of Natural Monopoly*, Cambridge: Cambridge University Press.

Spence, M. (1981) 'The learning curve and competition', *Bell Journal of Economics* 12(1), 49–70.

Spence, M. (1984) 'Cost reduction, competition and industry performance', *Econometrica*, 52, 101–22.

Stenseth, N.C. (1986) 'Darwinian evolution in ecosystems: a survey of some ideas and difficulties together with some possible solutions', in J.L. Casti and A. Karlqvist (eds) *Complexity, Language and Life: Mathematical Approaches*, Berlin: Springer Verlag, Chapter 5, 105–45.

Stigler, G.J. (1956) 'The statistics of monopoly and merger', *Journal of Political Economy* 64, 33–40.

Stigler, G.J. (1968) *The Organisation of Industry*, Homewood: Irwin.

Stoneman, P. (1981) 'Intra-firm diffusion, Bayesian learning and profitability', *Economic Journal* 91 (June), 375–88.

Stoneman, P.A. (1983) *The Economic Analysis of Technological Change*, Oxford: Oxford University Press.

Teece, D. (1986) 'Profiting from technological innovation', *Research Policy* 15(6), 285–305.

Teece, D. (1988) 'The nature of the firm and technological change', in G. Dosi *et al.* (eds) *Technical Change and Economic Theory*, London: Pinter, 256–81.

Tirole, J. (1988) *The Theory of Industrial Organisation*, Cambridge, MA: MIT Press.

Twiss, B. (1987) *Managing Technological Innovation*, 3rd edn, London: Pitman.

Varian, H.R. (1984) *Microeconomic Analysis*, 2nd edn. New York: Norton.

Varian, H.R. (1987) *Intermediate Microeconomics: A Modern Approach*, New York: Norton.

Walker, D.A. (1986) 'Walras theory of the entrepreneur', *De Economist* 134(1), 1–24.

Williamson, O.E. (1975) *Markets and Hierarchies: Analysis and Anti-trust Implications*, New York: Free Press.

Williamson, O.E. (1985) *The Economic Institutions of Capitalism*, New York: Free Press.

Williamson, O.E. (1989) 'Transaction cost economics', in R. Schmalensee and R. Willig (eds) *Handbook of Industrial Organisation*, Amsterdam: North Holland, ch. 3.

Williamson, O.E. (1986) 'The economics of governance: framework and implications', in R.N. Langlors (ed.) *Economics as a Process: Essays in the New Institutional Economics*, Cambridge: Cambridge University Press. Chapter 8, 171–201.

6

Innovation, competition and industry structure

Introduction

All firms must make decisions about the conduct or strategy variables they use to compete with one another: price, capacity, advertising and innovation. The decisions they make reflect the existing competitive environment in which they currently operate and in the longer run help to reshape that environment. At any given moment, the competitive environment is structured to a significant degree by the nature of the technology which firms are already using. As we have now noted, production technology may vary in terms of the scale economies it offers, its specificity in relation to particular products or processes, its maturity and the 'lumpiness' of the capital equipment which has to be used in deploying it. These aspects have implications for the terms on which firms compete with each other within an industry, and for the barriers to entry which potential entrants may face (discussed in Chapter 5).

In this chapter, we focus principally on the interfirm rivalry among profit seeking firms within an industry. An industry is defined as comprising enterprises producing outputs which are closer substitutes for each other in demand than they are for other goods. Such enterprises may form only part of a diversified corporation operating in two or more industries (as discussed in Chapter 5). We adopt the simplifying assumption, unless otherwise stated, that each firm operates only in a single industry. Rivalry in pursuit of profit takes place in terms of price, especially in industries producing a homogeneous output (such as cement or milk) and product differentiation where the product is more heterogeneous (as with domestic appliances, or aerospace components). Innovation forms a part of this rivalry to the extent that productivity-raising process innovation sharpens price competitiveness, while product innovation has a direct bearing on the competitive quality of products and the effectiveness with which firms can capture market segments and/or create market niches. In each case, innovation may be plausibly portrayed as an essential part of the pursuit of profit, though more fundamentally it is also essential to survival if rival firms are engaged in innovation.

Rivalry among profit-seeking firms and innovation are inextricably linked. The competition to survive and succeed drives the generation (through R&D) and diffusion of new process technology and new products. This is true even in the short run. But during any one period, the innovative activity of firms changes the production processes and products which define the structure of the industry and the competitive environment in which future rounds of competition will take place. Thus the innovations introduced under the pressure of one period's competition, themselves help to frame the conditions in which the next period's competition will occur.

Analysis proceeds within the framework of the theory of oligopoly, the theory of interfirm competition designed to deal with industries in which firm numbers are small enough that the behaviour of any one of them affects the market conditions confronting all. Modern oligopoly theory makes extensive use of game theory, in which equilibrium conditions again play an important role, though the equilibrium concepts are defined in somewhat different terms from those found in perfect competition and general equilibrium analysis. This approach enables us to incorporate genuine interdependence into the analysis and can cope, up to a point, with uncertainty and interfirm asymmetries. In addition, the implications of innovation for industry structure are dealt with endogenously. On the other hand, much of the analysis has focused either on one part of the innovation process (R&D) or single episodes of innovation and when it has been extended to examine sequences of innovation episodes, learning effects have been allowed to play little part. Despite that, decision-makers are endowed with unbounded information-processing capacity at each stage in the sequence.

From the innovation perspective, the early parts of the chapter focus on R&D as a competitive weapon, i.e. upon the generation of new technology and products. In later sections, the emphasis is on diffusion, defined first narrowly to refer to a single, well-defined innovation, then more broadly to include the impact of ongoing learning and R&D on the character of the innovation itself. Game theory has a place in this analysis, but it is here that evolutionary theorising looks to be making its most promising contributions. Such models emphasise the processes of change more than equilibrium states, assume significant bounds on rationality and hence attribute a substantial role to learning from experience. How firms learn and what they learn feeds back into the innovation process to determine the trajectory which the technology will take through time and helps to shape changes in industry structure.

Game theory, oligopoly pricing and the influence of technology

The modern literature on innovation and interfirm interaction relies heavily on analytical tools developed in the context of game theory. This is because game theory seems to offer a natural framework in which to consider the classical problem of oligopoly: what happens when profit-maximising firms have to decide on their conduct when the decisions made by any one of them significantly affects the market possibilities facing its rivals. Readers unfamiliar with the game-theoretic approach will find an introduction to the subject in the appendix at the end of this chapter, with a range of references for further reading. The approach taken in the main text is first to illustrate game theory at work in the familiar context of price determination, then to proceed to the less familiar territory in which innovation-related strategies become the centre of attention. Even at the first stage, however, it turns out that the prospects for a game-theoretic equilibrium in prices are affected by innovation, as is the nature of the equilibrium itself.

Games and equilibrium

Games analysed by game theory have rules which define the set of possible courses of action for each player and given nothing but the players' choices of courses of action, determine the outcome. Players in game theory have well-defined preferences, known at the outset and in games of perfect information, knowledge of all the rules and all the consequences of their actions. Game theory can, however, accommodate non-perfect information.

In playing a game, players adopt **strategies**, rules which tell them what action to choose at each and every point of the game, given what information they have. After all players have chosen and played out their strategies, their rewards are their **pay-offs**. In economic games, strategies relate to what are called **conduct variables** in the theory of industrial organisation: prices, output levels, advertising, R&D expenditure, etc. Pay-offs, classically defined in terms of utility or expected utility, often appear in the form of profits, which, after all, give rise to utility for those who receive them.

The challenge confronted by game theory is to predict the strategies each player will adopt. The approach taken is to select a **solution concept**, a concept in terms of which a game-theoretic equilibrium might be defined. Equilibrium here captures the idea of a state of affairs in which players will have no tendency to change their strategies once they are being played. Game theory offers a number of alternative concepts. The simplest, the **dominant strategy equilibrium**, is found in cases where every player's equilibrium strategy is the best possible response to any possible strategy other players might follow. Given that economic situations often fail to offer the possibility of such an equilibrium, widespread use has been made of an alternative concept, the **Nash equilibrium**, a combination of strategies such that no player has any incentive to deviate from his/her strategy, given that the other players do not deviate. This definition has two important implications. First, it embodies the essentially economic idea that people act in accordance with their incentives. Second, it reflects the outcome of strategic patterns of behaviour, in which individuals take account of the impact of their decisions on others and of the reactions which their own decisions might induce.

Having defined the central terms, it is worthwhile restating the reason for deploying game theory in the study of industry interactions, but in the sort of terms which a game theorist might use. Reinganum (1984) puts it this way: 'As students of industrial organisation, we cannot ignore interactions among the agents we study. Positive industrial organisation is the study of business policy and strategy. Modern, non-cooperative game theory is a language of strategy and equilibrium; that is, it provides an equilibrium framework in which to examine individuals' strategic behaviour' (p. 61). That said, we shall need to ask later how appropriate it is to apply game theory to the analysis of innovation.

Equilibrium pricing and Bertrand duopoly

The classical models of oligopoly abstract from every possible complication in order to focus on the central issue of interdependence. The multiplicity of firms is made as small as possible: two; the product of the industry is one-dimensional and homogeneous: water from a mineral spring; the market demand curve is linear; the cost structure is simplicity itself: both firms have zero costs; competition between the firms takes the form of a single encounter in which price and output are determined once and for all by a simultaneous, non-cooperative interaction. In this structure, one could hardly object to the profit-maximisation assumption which is also adopted.

A real problem in the original formulation and presentation of these models was that their authors bestowed upon firms the behaviour 'not of rational economic agents but of imbeciles' (Bacharach, 1976: 71). In the original presentations, equilibrium is the outcome of a series of iterations. The firms are 'imbeciles' because they are never allowed to learn; at every stage in the process of convergence upon an equilibrium, each firm is made to believe that its rival's decision on the value of a strategic variable (such as price) will remain unchanged, irrespective of what the first firm does and despite evidence that, when the first firm has varied its competitive conduct in the past, that has induced a reaction.

In the game-theoretic account of the same situation, the problem of imbecilic, memoryless behaviour is neatly side-stepped. Depending on the strategy chosen, Firm 1 asks itself 'What price will my rival charge? or What output level will it set?', bearing in mind that its rival is asking itself the same question. 'The only solution to this interdependent thought process, in which each firm correctly anticipates its rival's action, is the Nash equilibrium. Anything else implies an error of understanding or calculation on the part of one of the players. There is no period of myopic, dynamic adjustment in which firms are repeatedly surprised ... They immediately play the Nash equilibrium strategy,' (Brander, 1992: 7) The point is that the Nash equilibrium makes sense; it treats the players as rational people who recognise, among other things, the rationality of each other.

Classical oligopoly theory focuses on two different strategies or conduct variables: price and output. In the latter case, the Cournot model, firms choose quantities of output, but the market price is allowed to vary freely until equilibrium occurs. The basic version of this model is outlined in the appendix and elements of it applied in analysis in subsequent sections. Here we take the approach in which firms choose price and sell as much as they can. This was the line followed by Bertrand (1883).

In game-theoretic terms, there are two players who must choose price strategies with a view to attaining their largest pay-offs in profit. Remembering that production costs are zero, the pay-offs are also the sales revenues of the firms. Each firm anticipates the price the other will charge given its own and we assume it does this correctly. In the Bertrand equilibrium each firm charges a price such that its profit is maximised, given the other firm's price. The surprising thing about this equilibrium is that both firms only just cover their production costs, which in the case of a zero cost model means that both firms charge a zero price and make zero profit.

To see why this is so, take as an example the market demand curve used in the appendix for the output strategy case:

$$P(Q) = 210 - Q$$

or

$$Q(P) = 210 - P \qquad (6.1)$$

Assuming two firms, labelled A and B, with respective prices P_a and P_b, the pay-offs to each will depend on the price each one charges relative to the other. If P_a is less than P_b, there is no reason for buyers to purchase any of B's product and A will command the entire market, selling a quantity $Q(P_a) = 210 - P_a$, and making a profit of $P_a \cdot Q(P_a) = P_a(210 - P_a)$. If P_a is greater than $P_b \cdot A$ will by symmetrical argument sell nothing and its profit will be zero. Meanwhile, B will make a profit of $P_b(210 - P_b)$. Now consider what happens when A and B charge the same positive price $P_a = P_b > 0$. Here we have to make an assumption about the distribution of purchasers between them and the most reasonable is that each firm would take half the market, earning profit of $[P_a(210 - P_a)]/2 = [P_b(210 - P_b]/2$.

Now an examination of the pay-off structure makes it clear that it will never be worthwhile for either firm to choose a price which is greater than its rival's or, more accurately, to plan to charge a price greater than that which it correctly anticipates its rival will charge. It would always do better to charge the same price as its rival, since $P_a \cdot Q_a/2$ and $P_b \cdot Q_b/2$ will be positive for any positive price at which any output could be sold. But wait; $P_a = P_b > 0$ cannot be an equilibrium, for it is always in the interests of one of the firms to charge a price just a little below that of its rival. Looked at from the perspective of A, if it thought B would charge price P_{b1}, charging $P_{a1} = P_{b1}$ would yield it profit of $P_{a1}.(210 - Q(P_{a1}))/2$ while charging just below $P_{a1} - -P_{a0}$, say – would bring it $P_{a0}.(210 - Q(P_{a0}))$, which must be larger. It would therefore have an incentive to reduce its price if B's strategy remained unchanged. Symmetrically, if B thought A would charge P_{a1} and not change, it would also have an incentive to cut its price. Thus, by definition, $P_a = P_b > 0$ cannot be a Nash equilibrium, which implies it cannot be a dominant strategy equilibrium.

While it is quite possible for games to have no equilibrium (or many), this game has just one: $P_a = P_b = 0$. When each firm's price is zero, there is no longer an incentive for either firm to cut the price further, given the strategy of the other. It may be objected that neither firm could reduce price below zero (though it could always pay customers to take its product away). But a moment's thought should convince the reader that the same argument we have just used must apply, even when there are positive costs, in which case, given constant unit costs of C, the equilibrium will be $P_a = P_b = C$. Again, neither firm makes any profit. They are the victims of 'cut-throat' competition.

The disturbing feature of this equilibrium is that we, as outside observers, can see that the firms could do better for themselves than this; if they could only agree on a price structure $P_a = P_b > C$ (or > 0 in the original example), they could both make positive profits. The point is that we have been analysing a non-cooperative game in which neither firm is allowed to communicate with the other or to make binding commitments and undertakings about any price it might set. Had we set up the analysis as a cooperative game, we could have allowed for the possibility that the firms might cooperate, or collude in setting a price which gave them both positive profits. When failure to cooperate leads to relatively bad outcomes for players pursuing their own best interests to the hilt, there is said to be a Prisoners' Dilemma situation (see appendix to this chapter).

Collusion

To see how by cooperating the players could have done better than in a Bertrand equilibrium, recall first the assumption in the Bertrand game that the firms divide the market equally between them, so the price that maximises the joint profit of the firms also maximises the profit of each of them. Maintaining the zero-cost assumption for simplicity, the price that achieves this is that which maximises total revenue, or the area of the rectangle under a point on the market demand curve. Total revenue is $P \cdot Q(P) = P \cdot (210 - P) = 210P - P^2$, and maximising this with respect to P, we find that the price which maximises joint profits, at a level of 11,025, is 105. Each firm would then supply 52.5 units of output and make a profit of 5,512.5.

Notice, however, that the logic of the situation facing the players still has not changed. If one of them reduced the price slightly and anticipated no reaction, it would believe it could claim the whole market and, from its individual point of view, do better than it would in the joint profit-maximising case. For example, if A reduced its price from 105 to 100, and B offered no response, A would sell 110 units and make a profit of 11,000 instead of 5,512.5. While colluding therefore offers a much higher pay-off than competing non-cooperatively, the collusive outcome will be threatened if ever one of the players comes to believe it could renege on a pricing agreement without provoking a price cutting war in which its profits would be reduced to zero.

In many countries, explicit collusive agreements have been made illegal because, as anticompetitive devices, they are seen as impeding the working of the market to achieve economic efficiency. There is a central problem here, however, for the efficient regulation of competition. High levels of profit may arise either from the operation of anti-competitive arrangements among firms in an industry or from the competitive success of one firm compared with its rivals, based on greater efficiency and most probably innovation. Regulators who look only at profits and not at the reasons for them are likely to condemn some highly successful innovative firms in the mistaken belief that high profit can spring only from anticompetitive behaviour. If this happens, the entire economic system is in danger of losing its dynamism. Innovative firms oriented to continuous productivity and product performance improvement will see that any success they have is likely to be misinterpreted as the fruit of anticompetitive arrangements and that they are as likely to be penalised as rewarded for their innovative efforts. They will therefore be induced to dilute their innovative effort, or to move offshore.

In addition to the legal framework, purely economic reasons also play an important role in determining how easy it is for collusive behaviour to survive. In general, collusive pricing agreements will be endangered whenever one player believes it to be in its best interests to reduce a price. When information is good and all firms identical in product and processing technology, it is hard to see why any one firm should believe its unilateral action would not attract reprisals. But often information is imperfect and firms diverse in their characteristics and these factors may offer scope for individual firms to break away.

Technology and the maintenance of collusion

Stigler (1964) pioneered arguments related to imperfect information. He asked whether a secret price cutter could escape detection, assuming that that firm's market share would observably increase as a result. If the firms are in a homogeneous-good market with similar costs, their relative shares will vary if customers switch from one firm to another. Each firm will expect some variation due to essentially random switching of this kind and a secret price cutter will escape detection so long as the increase in its market share cannot be distinguished from the impact of those random effects. What Stigler showed was that the fewer the firms in the industry, the easier it was to distinguish systematic increases in market share from random ones. Bearing in mind that high levels of industry concentration often arise because of technologically determined scale economies, the nature of the technology can often create conditions conducive to maintaining collusive agreements. The same point may be made in relation to coordination costs. The fewer the firms in an industry, the easier it should be to set up a collusive agreement in the first place and subsequently to monitor, police and enforce it.

Interfirm diversity in costs and changes in technology may, however, undermine the potential for long-term collusion. If different firms use technology with differing levels of technical efficiency, some firms will have higher costs than others. Particularly when industry-wide demand falls away in the downswing of a cycle, higher cost firms may be tempted to depart from pricing agreements, reducing prices in an effort to increase their total revenues. It has been argued, however, that when economic downturns are severe and prolonged, firms will be more than usually aware of the penalties of a price-cutting war and may tend to cling together (Clarke, 1985: 61). However, such behaviour may well require the implicit approval of government regulation agencies and even the support of the financial institutions (Swann, O'Brien, Maunder and Howe, 1974).

Innovation and the undermining of collusion

Collusion is also less likely to persist (or even become established) if an industry is experiencing rapid technical innovation. If the technology is industry-specific, firms may be reluctant to enter price-fixing agreements, on the grounds that such collusion will only impede their flexibility to cut price if they employ a new, low-cost process or set whatever price they think is appropriate in introducing a new product. Furthermore, given the tacit and cumulative nature of technological knowledge, the production activity of firms will be different from each other and different in potentially unidentifiable ways. This may make coordination doubly costly and difficult to achieve (Clarke, 1985: 59). If the technology is used in many industries, individual firms already in any one industry may wish to retain the option of cutting price if a new entry threatens. Price collusion among incumbents aimed at creating monopoly profits is in any case unlikely to survive if the only consequence of their efforts is to attract a new entry. These arguments suggest collusion will be least prevalent where innovation is most rapid, especially in new and developing industries. This in turn suggests that an emphasis on changing the technology may in itself be supportive of competitive pricing practices.

Particularly when technological change was introduced, the discussion above departed from the strict confines of static analysis built into the game-theoretic framework we started out with. To close this section, we return to a strictly static framework to show how product differentiation, the result of product innovation, may be used by firms to avoid cut-throat competition, an issue canvassed by Shaked and Sutton (1982).

Differentiated products

Suppose the demand functions for each of two firms A and B reflect a continuous, negative relationship between quantities demanded and changes in the firm's own price and a continuous, positive relationship between quantities demanded from one firm and the price changes by the other. In this case, a fall in P_b would cut into the sales of A but would not reduce them at once to zero and a rise in P_b would cause customers to switch from B to A, but not to desert B altogether. This describes a case in which the output of the industry is not homogeneous; the two firms produce goods which meet similar needs, but which are not perfect substitutes. The more sensitive is the volume of a firm's sales to changes in its rival's price, the closer are the two goods as substitutes. As an example of a duopoly with differentiated products, consider a version of the case analysed by Rasmusen (1989: 267–9). The two demand functions are specified as follows.

$$Q_a = 36 - 3P_a + P_b \tag{6.2a}$$

$$Q_b = 36 - 3P_b + P_a \tag{6.2b}$$

Again returning to the simple zero-cost case, the pay-off for firm A is:

$$\Pi_a = P_a(36 - 3P_a + P_b)$$
$$= 36P_a - 3P_a^2 - P_a \cdot P_b \tag{6.3a}$$

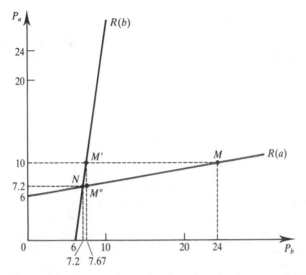

Figure 6.1   Bertrand reaction functions in the case of differentiated products.

and symmetrically B's pay-off is:

$$\Pi_b = 36P_b - 3P_b^2 - P_b \cdot P_a \tag{6.3b}$$

When P_a is set to maximise Π_a:

$$d\Pi_a/dP_a = 36 - 6P_a + P_b = 0$$

and

$$P_a = 6 + P_b/6 \tag{6.4a}$$

By identical argument, Π_b is maximised when

$$P_b = 6 + P_a/6 \tag{6.4b}$$

Now (6.4a) and (6.4b) are **reaction functions**, equations which show the pay-off-maximising strategy for each of the firms, given a strategy chosen by a rival. As Figure 6.1 shows, each function can be drawn on a diagram with P_a and P_b as axes (and in this simple case are both linear). $R(a)$, A's reaction function, shows for any value of P_b the price strategy A will choose to maximise its pay-off; $R(b)$ shows B's pay-off-maximising strategy for any value of P_a. Were B to set $P_b = 24$, for example, it can be seen by reading across from point M on $R(a)$ that A's best response would be $P_a = 10$. The same conclusion is equally easily reached by plugging $P_b = 24$ into (6.4a).

Notice, however, if A sets $P_a = 10$, B's best response is $P_b = 7.67$ (see (6.4b) for the arithmetic), which can also be seen by inspecting the coordinates of point M' on $R(b)$. If A sets $P_a = 10$, therefore, B has an incentive to deviate from its initial choice of $P_b = 24$ and reduce P_b to 7.67. Thus the strategy combination ($P_a = 10$, $P_b = 24$) cannot be an equilibrium. But neither is the strategy combination ($P_a = 10$, $P_b = 7.67$), for with $P_b = 7.67$, A would maximise its pay-off by setting $P_a = 7.28$ (see point M″ and (6.4a)). In fact, the only strategy combination in which neither firm would have an incentive to deviate, given that the other did not change its strategy, would be at the intersection of the reaction curves, point N. In the simple example given here (where reaction functions are symmetrical), the equilibrium strategies can be found by setting $P_a = P_b$ and solving either (6.4a) or (6.4b) to yield:

$$P_a^* = P_b^* = 7.2 \tag{6.5}$$

Substituting back into (6.2a) and (6.2b), we find that at this price each firm would sell 21.6 units of output and make a profit of 155.52.

Two points should be noticed about this. First, if the firms colluded, they could as before make more profit than this. Even if interest is confined only to cases in which $P_a = P_b$, each firm could earn as much as 162 by charging a price of 9. Second and more obviously, a significant implication of allowing the firms to produce differentiated (as opposed to homogeneous) products is that in the Nash equilibrium each now makes positive profits, where with the homogeneous goods case they made none. There is therefore an inducement to differentiate products when price competition is endogenous, which is not evident in models where price is set exogenously. This result should be compared with the case in the Hotelling model of Chapter 3, which predicted minimal product differentiation.

In a model which brings both sides of the story together, d'Aspremont, Gabszewicz and Thisse (1979) allow firms simultaneously to choose their locations in a linear city model of product space and subsequently to choose their prices. In the duopoly case, the two firms locate at opposite ends of the city. In this maximal differentiation case, 'each firm locates far from its rival in order not to trigger a low price from the rival, and thus price competition is softened' (Tirole, 1988: 281). Like the Hotelling model, however, this analysis abstracts from costs of product differentiation and persists in a static form of analysis. It is now time to incorporate innovation costs in the game-theoretic analysis of technological competition and to start moving towards a dynamic approach.

Interindustry variations in R&D intensity: the game-theoretic approach to technological competition

Research intensity and endogenous market structure: a static analysis

It is now time to put the game-theoretic framework to work, analysing how firms use investment in new, cost-saving process technology to compete with each other. Because game-theoretic methods are available to us, we can ask how much R&D

will be undertaken, under simplifying assumptions about invention possibilities, at the industry level, when interdependence among firms' strategies is taken into account. More profound effects than those we have considered until now also arise, since strategies which influence costs in each firm must also have implications for the structure of the industry at large and in particular, how many firms will be found in the equilibrium state of the industry under given demand conditions. Work performed in this framework also allows us to draw into the analysis determination of the structure of the industry (in terms of the number of firms) simultaneously with determination of the industry-wide research intensity ratio.

Static game theory analysis of the first kind conflates the co-determination of R&D instensity and industry structure into a single timeless event, in which the basic exogenous data are now demand-side elasticities and innovational opportunity. This highly stylised approach ignores dynamics and uncertainty, but generates insights which empirical work has suggested are of considerable robustness.

In what follows, we draw first upon important articles by Dasgupta and Stiglitz (1980a and b) and Dasgupta (1986). The simplifying assumptions made for the analysis are:

1. The game is 'static', in the sense of involving the simultaneous selection of strategies by all players on a 'one-off' basis.
2. Players (firms) are identical in terms of their behaviour, profit maximisation and their production and research capabilities.
3. Strategies relate to decisions about output and R&D expenditure and are chosen non-cooperatively.
4. Firms make their decisions using so-called Cournot conjectures about their rivals' reactions, i.e. they conjecture that any change in strategy variables on their own part will induce no response from other firms. Another way of putting this is to say that the players have zero conjectural variation with respect to output and R&D; they conjecture a zero change in rivals' responses to their own actions.
5. R&D expenditures give rise, with certainty, to cost-reducing process innovations by a continuous range of innovation possibilities; if RD is R&D expenditure and C unit production costs, $C(RD)$ falls as RD rises but at a declining rate.
6. The industry faces a downward-sloping demand function, $P(Q)$, where Q is total output of the homogeneous commodity produced in the industry. The specific characteristics of $C(RD)$ vary from industry to industry; in some industries a given increase in R&D will reduce production costs by more than in others.

To provide a sharper characterisation of their results, Dasgupta and Stiglitz give particular forms to the innovation possibility function $C(RD)$ and the market-demand function. The first is written:

$$C(RD) = b \cdot RD^{-a} \qquad a, b > 0 \tag{6.6}$$

and the second:

$$P(Q) = s \cdot Q^{-e} \qquad e, s > 0 \tag{6.7}$$

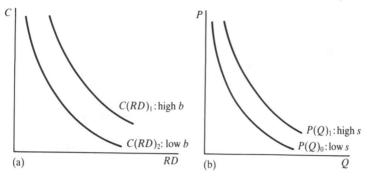

Figure 6.2 (a) The innovation possibility function: a relationship between research and development expenditures (*RD*) and production costs. Lower values of *b* indicate increasing ease in exploiting new knowledge. (b) The industry demand curve: varying the size of the market.

For given values of *a* and *b* in (6.6) and *e* and *s* in (6.7), each of these functions can be represented by a downward sloping curve (see Figures 6.2a and 6.2b). The larger is the value of *b* in (6.6) and *s* in (6.7), the further from the origin the curve will be. Since *b* and *s* determine the position of the curves, they are shift parameters.

It can be seen that $C(RD)$ and $P(Q)$ slope downwards and become increasingly 'flat'.[1] To illustrate what happens to the curves if *a* or *e* take different values, we have in Figure 6.3 set *b* and *s* to unity, so that (6.6) and (6.7) take the forms:

$$C(RD) = RD^{-a} \qquad\qquad (6.6')$$

Note: *e* is the inverse price elasticity of demand, denoted e_{inv} from page 243 onwards.

Figure 6.3 Illustrative examples of variations in the elasticity parameters of the innovation possibility and industry demand functions. Higher values of *a* reflect larger proportional reductions in production costs for given increases in R&D; higher *e* at lower price elasticity.

and

$$P(Q) = Q^{-e} \tag{6.7'}$$

Then, as a or e rises, the curves rotate in clockwise direction, all intersecting at the same point.

We now give an economic interpretation to these parameters. First, the lower b is in (6.6), the lower the unit production costs achieved for any R&D outlay will be. A given level of R&D outlay may be expected to have greater results if the R&D undertaken with these dollars is linked to a relatively rich underlying scientific base. Thus, b is taken to represent that base and the lower b is, the richer that *base* is purported to be for any given industry. Second, the higher s is in (6.7), the greater the volume of market demand at any price level will be. It is thus natural to interpret s as market size.

Third, the exponent a is an elasticity measure which Dasgupta (1986: 530) interprets as an index of innovational opportunities. To see why it is an elasticity, take the natural logarithms of (6.6) and differentiate:

$$\ln C(RD) = \ln b - a \cdot \ln RD$$

so that:

$$a = -(\text{d} \ln C(RD)/\text{d} \ln RD)$$

$$= -(\text{d}C(RD)/\text{d}RD \cdot RD/C(RD)).$$

(To confirm the last step, consult any introductory text on mathematical methods in economics). The last bracketed expression is the elasticity of (reduction in) unit production costs with respect to R&D expenditure. For higher values of a, Figure 6.3 shows that given proportional increases in R&D will be associated with increasingly large reductions in production costs. The greater the innovational opportunities to use new knowledge to reduce production costs, the higher this elasticity will be.

Finally, notice that (6.7) implies:

$$P(Q)^{1/e} = s^{1/e} \cdot Q^{-1} \tag{6.7''}$$

so that:

$$1/e \cdot \ln P(Q) = 1/e \cdot \ln s - \ln Q$$

and

$$-(\text{d} \ln Q/\text{d} \ln P) = -(\text{d}Q/\text{d}P \cdot P/Q) = 1/e$$

But $-(\text{d}Q/\text{d}P \cdot P/Q)$ is the expression for the price elasticity of demand, so in this formulation, e stands for the inverse elasticity of demand, $-(\text{d}P/\text{d}Q \cdot Q/P)$, which we write e_{inv}. The higher the absolute value of e found in (6.7), the higher e_{inv} and the lower the price elasticity of market demand, as usually defined.

To examine the relationship between R&D and market structure, suppose that the industry is in a Nash–Cournot equilibrium (see the appendix). Given that all firms are identical in form and behavioural characteristics, the equilibrium is also symmetric. Dasgupta and Stiglitz (1980a) show in a technical appendix that such an equibrium exists given certain restrictions on the values of a, e_{inv} and n. There is no guarantee, however, that equilibria will always be realised, even if in principle their existence can be demonstrated. At the equilibrium, each firm i has chosen output, Q_i, and R&D expenditure, RD_i, with a view to maximising its profit: total revenue less production and R&D costs. In algebraic notation, each firm i maximises:

$$[P(Q_i + Q_R) - C(RD_i)]Q_i - RD_i \tag{6.8}$$

where Q_R is the total output of all firms other than i (its rivals) so that price P is shown as a function of $(Q_i + Q_R) = Q$.

Now, to find the conditions characterising the maximum of II_i, firm i's profit, differentiate (6.8) with respect to Q_i and RD_i in turn and set the resulting expression to zero. We showed in Chapter 5 that:

$$C(RD_i) = P(Q)[\ 1 - e_{inv} \cdot Q_i/Q] \tag{6.9}$$

Moreover:

$$-C'(RD_i) = 1 \tag{6.10}$$

Because the analysis is restricted to a symmetric equilibrium, every firm will produce the same output Q^*/n^*, where the starring convention is used to indicate equilibrium values and where n^* is to be determined. But if $Q_i^* = Q^*/n^*$, $n^* = Q^*/Q_i^*$, so that at the equilibrium, (6.9) can be simplified to read:

$$C(RD^*) = P(Q^*)[1 - e_{inv}/n^*] \tag{6.11}$$

where the symmetry of the equilibrium has allowed us to drop i subscripts. By the same reasoning, (6.10) can be rewritten:

$$-C'(RD^*)\ Q^*/n^* = 1 \tag{6.12}$$

When barriers to entry prevent any short run change in the number of firms in the industry n is exogenous. Dasgupta and Stiglitz show that when (6.6) and (6.7) are combined with (6.11) and (6.12) for a given value of n, R&D per firm and for the industry increases with market size and with the cost reduction elasticity, a. If b is higher, firm and industry R&D are higher if market demand is price inelastic, but lower if demand is elastic. Within a range required to ensure equilibrium exists, the impact of exogenous variations in n may also be observed. As n rises (i.e. as inter-firm competition increases), each firm spends less on R&D but the industry total of R&D rises because there are more firms. There is an important implication here for costs. Since each firm does less R&D as n rises, the unit production costs of each firm are higher than they would be if there were fewer firms, each undertaking more cost-reducing innovation. On the other hand, the equilibrium of industry increases with n and product price falls – as would be expected with increasing competition.

In the longer run, however, the number of firms in the industry should itself be treated as a variable and endogenised in the analysis.

Under conditions of free entry, we would expect firms to continue to be attracted to the industry until profits, as defined in (6.8) were driven to a low enough level to no longer act as a magnet to newcomers. To ease the exposition, it is assumed that all firms make just enough revenue to cover production and R&D costs and since all firms are the same, this means all make zero profit and that:

$$[P(Q^*) - C(RD^*)]Q^* = n^*RD^* \tag{6.13}$$

i.e. industry total revenue less industry total costs is equal to industry outlays on R&D.

Studying innovation, a central issue of interest is why industries may vary in their R&D activity, a telling index of which is the industry level of research intensity, here denoted Z:

$$Z = n \cdot RD/P(Q)Q$$

Given the symmetry assumption, this index will also reflect the amount each firm will, in equilibrium, choose to devote to R&D as a proportion of sales. What we now show is that this index of R&D activity is linked to basic conditions characterising demand for the product and opportunities for technological innovation.

To do this, substitute the expression for $C(RD^*)$ given in (6.11) into (6.13). Then:

$$[P(Q^*) - P(Q^*)(1 - e_{inv}/n^*)]Q^* = n^*RD^*.$$

Dividing through by $P(Q^*)Q^*$:

$$1 - (1 - e_{inv}/n^*) = n^*RD^*/P(Q^*)Q^*$$

or

$$n^*RD^*/P(Q^*)Q^* = e_{inv}(Q^*)/n^*$$

Thus equilibrium research intensity is:

$$Z^* = e_{inv}(Q^*)/n^* \tag{6.14}$$

In Figure 6.4, values for Z^* are measured on the vertical axis and for e_{inv} on the horizontal. Increasingly low values of e_{inv} correspond to values of the PED approaching infinity and increasingly high values of e_{inv} correspond to values of the PED approaching zero. From (6.14), increases in $e_{inv}(Q^*)$ will be associated with increases in Z^* by a multiple $1/n^*$, with the increase in Z^* being greater, the smaller n^* is. The relationship between Z^* and $e_{inv}(Q^*)$ may be drawn as a family of rays from the origin, whose slopes vary with n^*. The larger n^*, the less steep the slope of a ray will be. In Figure 6.4, $n^* = 1 \ldots 5$.

In words, (6.14) says that in equilibrium, industry research intensity rises, with any given number of firms, the less price-elastic is the industry demand curve. This conforms well with intuition. The higher the price elasticity of demand (i.e. the lower is e_{inv}), the more firms in the industry face competition from substitutes produced by other industries and the less they can therefore rely on the differentiated nature of

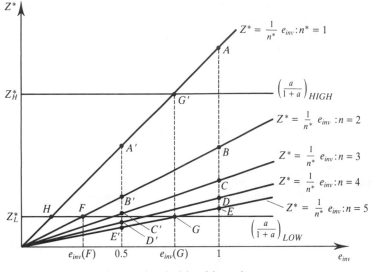

Figure 6.4 caption area:

Figure 6.4 The simultaneous determination of equilibrium industry research intensity, Z^*, and industry concentration, $1/n^*$, in the Dasgupta–Stiglitz model of industrial structure and innovative activity.

their products to protect them from competitive forces. This implies that firms will make less profit (which could have been spent on R&D) than in industries where there are fewer good substitutes and profits are likely to be greater.

Now Z^* can be expressed in another way (Dasgupta and Stiglitz, 1980a: 276), using (6.12), namely:

$$Z^* = a(RD^*)/[1 + a(RD^*)] \qquad (6.15)$$

where a is the parameter discussed above, showing the elasticity of unit cost of production with respect to R&D expenditure, evaluated here at the equilibrium. What this says is that different industries with different demand elasticities would have identical research intensities if they faced the same level of innovation opportunity, that is, could reduce production costs, in equilibrium, by the same proportion when they raised R&D expenditures by the same small fraction. This would be true of points G, F and H in Figure 6.4. Inspection of those points also reveals that for industries facing the same innovation opportunities in equilibrium, there will be more firms in an industry, the lower is the price elasticity of demand.

An implication of what we have done so far arises from combining (6.14) and (6.15) to give:

$$n^* = e_{inv}(Q^*)[1 + a(RD^*)/a(RD^*)] \qquad (6.16)$$

This shows endogenous determination of n^* will ultimately rest on the values at equilibrium of two elasticities, describing essential aspects of market demand and opportunities for technological innovation. Now $(1/n^*)$ can be regarded as an index of the **degree of concentration**, with small values of the reciprocal associated with many firms and low concentration and large values (approaching unity in the limit) associated with few firms and high concentration. So (6.16) suggests that this potentially important element of market structure flows from the nature of market demand and the possibilities for reducing production costs through R&D. How intensive such activity will be is simultaneously determined in the model.

We now present four key propositions predicting how R&D intensity in equilibrium might vary between one industry and another.

1. Comparing industries which all have the same price elasticity of demand, $1/e_{inv}$, research intensity, Z^*, will be proportional to the degree of concentration, $1/n^*$ in each industry.

   This proposition is merely putting equation (6.14) into words. If $e_{inv} = 1$, $Z^* = 1/n^*$; if $e_{inv} = 2$, $Z^* = 2(1/n^*)$; if $e_{inv} = 0.5$, $Z^* = 0.5(1/n^*)$. In the diagram, points A, B, C, D and E show how Z^* varies with $1/n^*$ when $e_{inv} = 1$, and points A', B', C', D' and E' how Z^* varies with $(1/n^*)$ when $e_{inv} = 0.5$. Another way of putting the point is to say that if we compared industries facing the same price elasticities of demand, we would expect them to vary in terms of market size and the R&D technology available to them. For industries where e_{inv} was the same in equilibrium, Z^* and n^* could thus vary among industries since their specific values are determined by parameters in (6.6) and (6.7). But this proposition predicts that, if the assumptions of the model applied, the ratio of Z^* and $(1/n^*)$ would be constant. *For industries of given price elasticity, equilibrium research intensity is expected to be greater where equilibrium concentration is greater.* As noted above, however, this can only be true because higher levels of equilibrium innovation opportunity allow it to be so. Thus equilibrium levels of Z and $1/n$ are determined simultaneously by exogenously given innovation opportunities and market demand elasticity.

2. *For industries of given levels of concentration in equilibrium, those with relatively price-inelastic demand (higher e_{inv}) will be characterised by higher levels of research intensity.*

   This can be checked in the diagram by comparing the levels of Z^* associated with points such as B (for a lower price elasticity) with B' (for a higher price elasticity). It is important to remember here, from (6.16), that n^* is itself endogenously determined by a and e_{inv}. If industries of similar concentration level have varying levels of R&D intensity, it is because, there must be differences among them in both price elasticity and innovation opportunities. For Z^* to be higher, $a(RD^*)$ must also be higher. But if $a(RD^*)$ is higher n^* can be constant only if $e_{inv}(Q^*)$ is also higher – since higher levels of a (RD^*) yield lower levels of $(1 + a/a)$ in (6.16).

3. *Industries with a given equilibrium elasticity of cost reduction, a(RD*) but facing different price elasticities of demand, will have the same level of equilibrium research intensity, but different levels of concentration.*

To illustrate this proposition we focus on the horizontal line $(a/1 + a)(\text{LOW})$. That line is evidently associated with a given level of Z^*, $Z^*(L)$, but crosses all of the rays relating $Z^*(L)$ to $1/n^*$. For the relatively high price elasticity of demand found at $e_{inv}(F)$, $Z^*(L)$ is associated with a duopoly, while for the lower price elasticity found at $e_{inv}(G)$, $Z^*(L)$ is associated with an industry of five firms.

Before proceeding to the final proposition, we refer back to equations (6.11) and (6.16). Substituting (6.16) into (6.11):

$$P(Q^*)[1 - \{e_{inv}(Q^*)/(e_{inv}(Q^*)\cdot(1 + a(RD^*)/a(RD^*)\}]$$

$$= C(RD^*)$$

implying

$$P(Q^*)(1/1 + a(RD^*) = C(RD^*)$$

or

$$P(Q^*)/C(RD^*) = 1 + a(RD^*) \tag{6.17}$$

The ratio of price to production costs is often taken as a measure of **monopoly power** and the fourth proposition incoporates this feature in the analysis.

4. Industries with the same price elasticity of demand, but *varying innovational opportunities, vary predictably in their equilibrium concentration levels and research intensities,* but *higher concentration may be associated with high or low monopoly profits,* depending on the value of the price elasticity.

The first part of this proposition draws in part on the analysis arising from (6.15). From Figure 6.4, it is also clear when e_{inv} is held constant and $a(RD^*)$ is allowed to rise, there is a fall in the equilibrium number of firms. To see this compare points D, C and B, for example. The result that research intensity is directly and positively related to exogenously determined innovation opportunities (for industries of similar price elasticity) is of great importance and reflected consistently in empirical findings.

From (6.17) we note that a higher level of $a(RD^*)$ a will be associated with greater monopoly power, reflected in the ratio of price to production costs. So when price elasticity is held constant among industries, we would always expect to see greater innovation opportunities, and hence research intensity, associated with smaller equilibrium numbers of firms and higher price–cost margins. This would appear to conform to the Schumpeterian idea that innovative activity may be encouraged by industry structures in which firms are few and monopoly power is substantial. On the other hand, it appears from Figure 6.4 that a given level of concentration may be associated with either high or low price–cost margin (compare *G'* with *H*, and *A'*) and that a given margin might arise at any of a large number of concentration levels (compare *H* with *F*, and *G*). In each, different combinations of price–cost margin and concentration arise from variations in the price elasticity of demand. As Dasgupta (1986) notes, however, the range of values over which these relationships hold may be more restricted than we have depicted.

Quite apart from any general objections which might be raised against using game theory to deal with innovation in the first place (see pp. 263–6), it is clear that the formulation of technological competition used here begs many questions.

1. No interfirm spill-over effects are allowed for. No one firm can learn from any other and no firm is allowed even to sell its knowledge to others.
2. Innovation, of which R&D is a part, is a dynamic process in which firms make their decisions sequentially to gain first-mover advantages, or to delay until it is possible to learn from the experience of others. To model the game as one in which strategies are all played simultaneously, immediately abstracts from these elements.
3. Firms vary widely within a given industry in both their production and research capabilities and to assume they are identical is to ignore all of the implications of diversity.
4. Choosing output as a strategy variable has the advantage of yielding tractable analysis but leaves unaddressed of the issues raised when firms use price cutting as a weapon.
5. Technological and commercial uncertainty are absent.
6. Costs of introducing and using new technology are ignored.

This is a long list and suggests that we should be cautious in attributing to any conclusions greater generality than they deserve. But the model has set the agenda for all subsequent research in the area and in subsequent sections we shall be able to see that, while other insights can be gleaned from responding to these criticisms, it has proved a solid foundation on which to build.

Research intensity and endogenous market structure: allowing for 'spill-overs'

An important feature of the innovation process noted in Chapter 2 but omitted from the analysis so far is an increase in any one firm's R&D leads to a reduction in its own costs and has the potential to reduce the costs of other firms in the same industry, influencing the foundations of industry structure in another way.[2] These external effects occur when labour (particularly managers and engineers) transfer from firm to firm and through industrial espionage, innocent informal contacts, licensing agreements, reverse engineering and so on. In any of these ways the results of costly

R&D in one firm become known to rival firms so they benefit in terms of lower unit production outlays. To formalise this, we can envisage a pool of technological knowledge at the industrial level growing as the result of all of the R&D being done in the industry. Not all firms need be involved and some may be involved in joint projects. Each firm's unit costs, C_i, are then related to its own R&D expenditure, RD_i, and to the sum of all industry spending on R&D (including its own), denoted M. So:

$$C_i = C_i(RD_i, M) \tag{6.18}$$

where C_i falls, but at a decreasing rate, with both RD_i and M.

We have noted elsewhere the importance of appropriability in the economics of innovation. Firms undertake costly R&D only if they expect to enjoy returns on their investment large enough and/or for long enough to justify their original outlay. But if the results of the R&D can be easily imitated, other firms will quickly be able to follow where they have led and erode the potential monopoly profits which the innovator had hoped to earn. If imitation is hard, the rewards of R&D are more easily appropriable than if imitation is easy. To extend the model of the previous section to incorporate interfirm spill-over effects, we draw on the work of Levin and Reiss (1984).

Appropriability depends mainly on the ease with which innovators can be imitated. Imitation will be more difficult to achieve if the innovation can be effectively patented, guarded by secrecy or protected by learning effects. In a static model (which abstracts from dynamic learning) appropriability can be viewed as having three aspects: technological, structural and behavioural. Cost function (6.18) captures the first of these dimensions. To the extent that C_i is elastic with additions to the pool of industry-wide R&D (holding RD_i constant), it can be inferred that imitation without cost is relatively easy or that, for technological reasons, the returns to R&D are relatively inappropriable. Discussion of the other dimensions is postponed until the rest of the model has been presented.

The market-demand function is here generalised to include the impact of advertising, AD, assumed positive. Each firm i maximises profit:

$$\Pi_i = [P(Q, AD) - C_i(RD_i, M)]Q_i - RD_i - AD_i \tag{6.19}$$

Firms are assumed to entertain **zero conjectural variations (ZCV)** with respect to output and advertising. This implies $dQ/dQ_i = dAD/dAD_i = 1$; industry-wide totals change only by the same amount as the variable changes in firm i. But the conjectural variation with respect to R&D expenditure is left unspecified, leaving it to empirical testing to reveal what the firms' beliefs actually are. The derivative dM/dRD_i, denoted m_i, represents the extent to which firm i believes industry-wide R&D spending will change when it varies its own R&D expenditure by a small amount.

Following lines of analysis identical to those in the last section, it is possible to derive the following equation:

$$Z^*/[1 - (Z^* + W^*)] = -[(C'(RD^*) \cdot RD^*/C) + 1/n^*(C'(M^*) \cdot M^*/C)m] \tag{6.20}$$

On the left-hand side, Z^* is the ratio of R&D outlays to industry sales and $[1 - (Z^* + W^*)]$ the share of sales revenue devoted neither to R&D nor advertising, i.e. the ratio of production costs alone to revenue. The total expression shows the ratio of industry R&D expenditure to total production costs, which may be taken as an alternative measure of research intensity. To compare results in terms of this measure with those in terms of Z^* found in the last section, note that Z^* and W^* are fractions whose sum cannot exceed unity, so $Z^*/[1 - (Z^* + W^*)]$ must always be greater than Z^* and must increase at an increasing rate as Z^* rises.

On the right-hand side, let $[-(C'RD^*/C)]$ be denoted $a\#$. This is the elasticity of reduction in unit production costs with respect to a firm's R&D, holding industry-wide R&D constant. It is analogous with the elasticity a, encountered in the previous section. The reciprocal $1/n^*$ represents the equilibrium market share of each firm and m is the conjectural variation parameter. Now $[-(C'(M^*).M/C)]$ denoted h, is the elasticity of reduction in any firm's unit production costs with respect to industry-wide R&D, holding that firm's R&D constant. Then:

$$Z^*/[1 - (Z^* + W^*)] = a\# + 1/n^* \cdot hm \qquad (6.20')$$

As in the previous section, industry-wide research intensity rises with the innovational opportunity associated with its own R&D, here $a\#$. But each firm also benefits from the expanding pool of industry-wide knowlege (to which its own R&D effort contributes). Appropriability issues naturally arise.

In the terminology of Levin and Reiss (1984) the technological element of appropriability reflects the intrinsic level of difficulty with which the results of R&D may be imitated. When h is high imitation is easy and when h is low, imitation hard. Each firm finds appropriating the rewards from its own R&D more difficult the higher is h. But because all firms benefit from each others' work, higher h industries will also be higher research intensity industries, for any given level of conjectural variation and industry structure. More recent analysis (Cohen and Levinthal, 1989, 1990) gives further insight into this point. When firms undertake R&D they generate their own innovations but also enhance their capacity to identify, assimilate and use new knowledge being generated elsewhere. To the extent that spillovers reduce the ability of an innovating firm to appropriate the resulting profits for itself, there is a disincentive to undertake R&D. But because the activity of undertaking R&D in-house increases a firm's absorptive capacity, firm-level R&D will be encouraged when spillovers from other firms are large because increasing R&D will put each firm in a better position to learn from its rivals and appropriate rewards from their work.

The extent to which research intensity varies between high and low h industries depends in part on how each firm expects its rivals to respond to its initiatives, what Levin and Reiss call the behavioural dimension of appropriability. Even if each firm believes its rivals will cut back on the R&D to take a 'free ride' on its own efforts, research intensity will still increase with h, but only so long as m is positive (Nelson, 1959). It will be negative if each firm believes its rivals will cut their total R&D by more than it planned, in equilibrium, to raise its own.

Levin and Reiss identify a third dimension of appropriability as structural. Whatever benefits each firm believes it will reap from extending the common pool of knowledge will be 'weighted' by the size of the firm relative to the industry. Using the example offered by Levin and Reiss (1984: 181–2), suppose each firm entertains ZCV so that $m = 1$. Then a 1 per cent increase in any one firm's R&D will be equivalent to a $1/n$ per cent rise in industry-wide R&D in a symmetric equilibrium. Bearing in mind that the elasticity h shows by how much production costs will fall in any firm when industry-wide R&D rises by 1 per cent, it is clear that with given industry size, a monopolist's costs would fall h per cent while an oligopolist's would fall by only (h/n) per cent. This is another mechanism for seeing why there might be a positive connection between increased industry concentration and higher levels of research intensity, though it must be borne in mind that causation from structure to the conduct variable, research and development is not a claim of the model since the number of firms is itself endogenously determined.

Dynamic interactions: an introduction

The outcomes we have been examining are associated with long-run equilibrium states, i.e. states in which, implicitly, all decision-makers have made all the adjustments, which leaves them with no incentive for deviation. Since the equilibrium is the outcome of a simultaneous-move game in terms of a 'one-shot' strategy, research and devolopment, and R&D has immediate, costless and predictable implications for production costs, there is no scope in the framework of the model for considering the path to equilibrium, or any processes of adjustment which might have been involved.

This abstraction would therefore seem to be most appropriate for considering the 'mature' state of an industry. In the mature industry, the number of firms has settled to reflect stable levels of the basic parameters relating to market and innovation opportunity.

But the structure of an industry usually varies over time as it matures. To understand what is happening, we need to proceed to analysis which allows us to explore the dynamics of industry-level interactions.

Consider some of the questions that arise:

1. Can the dynamic issues addressed at the firm level by Kamien and Schwartz (see Chapter 5) be incorporated in a genuinely interactive framework? If so, an element of uncertainty can be incorporated.
2. The only equilibria so far discussed have been symmetric. This offers the advantage of tractability but the disadvantage of ignoring a very obvious reality, that all firms are different. Could interfirm diversity in any one period help explain changes in the technology and/or industry structure over time? One way of dealing with this could be to incorporate various forms of 'asymmetry' into the gaming framework, in particular in relation to informational advantages of 'first

movers' or cost asymmetries associated with expenditures sunk into R&D. Another could be to invoke the evolutionary approach of building the whole analysis on asymmetries – diversity among firms – without invoking the structuring devices of game theory.

3. Incorporating asymmetry can give rise to rather strong predictions that monopoly must result from technological competition (see Chapter 5 for detailed discussion). In fact, innovation may not generate monopoly if the innovation is only one of a sequence, or if the rewards to any single episode of innovation are imperfectly appropriable. These issues need to be canvassed.

4. All of the analysis in this chapter has been based on some notion of equilibrium. Yet it is a central claim of the Schumpeterian tradition that innovating activity generates and sustains processes which are associated with disequilibrium in economic systems and which may not ultimately lead to equilibrium states or paths. We must ask whether the equilibrium style of analysis is appropriate to analysing innovation-driving dynamics and if not what might take its place.

5. Diffusion is a further issue which the simultaneous-move game cannot address. The whole process of diffusion becomes an issue once it is recognised that dynamic interaction is likely to involve both the spread of new technology to firms striving to keep up and the development of new technology as firms compete.

To address these issues we first turn to dynamic game theory. However, we shall argue that in a complex dynamic context, the more ambitious examples of the game theoretic approach implicitly demand of decision-makers a capacity to collect and process information far in excess of what seems reasonable. If we take only half seriously the notion of bounded rationality, there therefore seems to be a case for considering adaptive, sequential models of evolution in which firms do not have to be characterised as profit maximisers. This, in turn, leads us to the evolutionary framework.

Dynamic games

Identical firms and stochastic patent races

To introduce time and uncertainty into the analysis, consider a game in which identical firms compete in a race to patent an invention. The formulation of their invention prospects should look familiar from the work of Kamien and Schwartz. Investment of RD_i at time $t=0$ buys for firm i some probability of success by a specified date. The success date t_i^* is a random variable related to RD_i through a hazard rate $H_i = H(RD_i)$ defined so that:

$$Pr\{t_i^*(RD_i) < t\} = 1 - e^{(H_i(RD_i)t)} \qquad (6.21)$$

In words, this says that the probability, Pr, of firm i succeeding at or before any given date t is an exponential function of the hazard rate, $H_i(t)$, which shows the

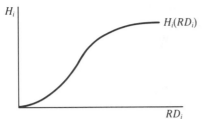

Figure 6.5 A stochastic innovation production function: as firm i R&D increases, the probability of success by time t, assuming no prior success, rises at an increasing then decreasing rate.

conditional probability density of success at t, given no success to date. Another way of thinking of $H(RD_i)$ is as a stochastic **innovation production function (IPF)** which shows for every date t how the conditional probability of success will vary with research effort. It is assumed that as RD_i inputs increase at an equiproportional rate, this IPF will first show increasing then decreasing returns to scale (see Figure 6.5). For any given level of the choice variable, RD_i, a corresponding value of H_i can be found. And for any given value of H_i, allowing t to rise (i.e. considering the probabilities of success at even later dates) has the effect of increasing the product $H_i(RD_i)t$. So $e^{(-H_i(RD_i)t)}$ falls and $(1 - e^{(-H_i(RD_i)t)})$ rises. This effect is shown for a 'high' and a 'low' level of H_i along the two curves A and B in Figure 6.6. Notice that every such curve must in the limit approach a ceiling value of 1 as t grows increasingly large. Comparing points a and b in the same diagram, it is also clear that for any date t, the probability of success increases with H_i, as we would expect, since higher levels of H_i flow from increased research input.

Now the **hazard rate** $H_i(t)$ can be represented as the product of a **hazard function**, $u(t)$, say and a **hazard parameter** h. The advantage of using the exponential distribution is that the expected time until success for firm i, $E(t_i^*)$, is then $1/h(RD_i)$ and the expected

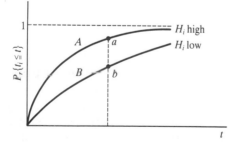

Figure 6.6 Time and the probability of success: as more time is spent on research and development at a given rate per period, the probability of success in the next period increases.

time to invention, is (given the symmetry of the firms) $1/nh(RD)$, for an industry of n firms.

In its most basic form, introducing time and uncertainty actually adds rather little to the analysis. The patent race applies to a single episode of innovation and the game is based upon the assumption that all players move simultaneously. Analysis focuses on a symmetric Nash equilibrium in R&D strategies. Initially, patent protection is also assumed perfect.

Under these conditions, it can be shown (Loury, 1979; Lee and Wilde, 1980; Dasgupta and Stiglitz, 1980b; Reinganum, 1984, 1989) that aggregate industry investment in R&D always increases with the number of firms in the industry and hence must always hasten the date of first success. On the other hand, the amount of investment per firm may rise or fall, depending on how the investment is undertaken. If it takes the form of a lump sum committed to a given scale of laboratory work at $t = 0$, then the amount invested by each firm falls with increasing numbers of firms; if it takes the form of a flow of periodic outlays supporting a chosen level of research intensity, halted at the moment innovation somewhere occurs, then the rate of investment per firm rises along with the number of contestants. In both cases, increasing the number of firms reduces the probability of success for any one player, so reducing the benefits expected by each player from its R&D and hastening the date of first success. Because the success date is drawn forward, adding new players reduces any firm's total expected cost flows when its outlays occur on a periodic basis, but has no effect on its costs if committed as a lump sum. When changes in net expected benefits (benefits less costs) are considered, incentives to invest are raised in the first case but reduced in the second.

As we saw in an earlier section, non-cooperative equilibria may have quite different characteristics from collusive or cooperative outcomes. In this case, the firms could, for example, engage in a joint venture, investing cooperatively and sharing the rewards (equally) among themselves (Tirole, 1988: 413–14). Assume that each firm's pay-off first rises then falls with increases in its own R&D. Then the combined profits of the industry will be greater and aggregate R&D less when firms join an equal-shares joint venture than when they act non-cooperatively. This indicates that failure to cooperate leads each firm to ignore the reduction its own R&D imposes on the value of its rivals' expected profits, so all firms invest too much. Or to put it another way, there is excessive duplication of effort because of a failure to communicate, providing another example of the Prisoners' Dilemma.

One of the worrying simplifications made in the analysis of this section so far is of perfect patent protection. Yet the protection offered by a patent will diminish over time for two reasons; first, the owner may be unable to maintain complete proprietary rights over the information contained in it; second, new information may appear which causes the patent to be superseded, wholly or in part. To be precise, Pakes and Schankerman (1984) find on European data that the decay rate in revenues appropriable from patents usually lies between 18 and 36 per cent per annum, with an average of 25 per cent. What difference does this make?

To answer this question, Reinganum (1982) sets up a patent race analysis in the form of a differential game, a game played in continuous time and solved using dynamic optimisation methods.[3] Here we note only the important result that the degree of appropriability is an influential ingredient in determining the relationship between industrial structure and innovation. For example, while increasing the number of firms in an industry reduces to zero the R&D undertaken when rewards are wholly inappropriable, there always remains an incentive to innovate when rewards are fully appropriable and even when the number of firms is very large, some R&D will still be done. That said, however, Reinganum's conclusion (1989: 865) is that once patent protection becomes imperfect and simple extreme cases are ignored, this approach can only indicate that outcomes will depend on the specific nature of institutions and the processes which determine the relative pay-offs to innovators and imitators.

This discussion also shows, however, is that even with a substantial jump in the ambitiousness of analytical technique, we can move only a few steps closer towards a persuasive portrayal of the innovation process and even then find that significant questions remain unanswered. In particular, innovation has been modelled as a single and discrete episode when we know it to comprise a sequence of connected episodes. Interest has continued to focus on symmetric equilibria, implying that firms start with identical credentials for the race, whereas we know that history bestows upon different firms potentially useful experience, but in varying degrees. Even when firms start off on equal terms, Flaherty (1980) has shown that they may finish up following quite different paths, despite the absence of uncertainty. And although the analysis has had a dynamic form, we are left with the feeling that we have learned little more than from the static models. In one way that is a comfort; it suggests consistency. But in another it is a concern; Should there not be more to learn about innovation dynamics if we model the process dynamically than if we hold to a static abstraction?

This line of questioning leads inevitably to the frontier at which the most productive research seems to be underway; dynamic games with asymmetry.

Interfirm asymmetry

Asymmetry among firms in games of technological competition may arise in a number of ways. In Chapter 5 we explored the implications of an asymmetry based on one firm's incumbency compared with the non-incumbent position of potential entrants or challengers. In this chapter we shall have little more to say about that, therefore, but focus instead on asymmetries which arise among firms which are either already all incumbents, or are competing for a place in a new industry where incumbency is not yet an issue.

Asymmetries will be divided into two kinds: those which relate to the incentives facing intrinsically similar (though not necessarily identical) firms and those which mark the firms as being intrinsically different in ways which affect their innovation performance. The implications of asymmetry can in principle be explored in the context of single episodes of innovation (Gilbert and Newbery (1982) and the stochastic racing model of incumbency due to Reinganum (1983)). But more interesting results which incorporate the idea of continuous innovation can be found by looking at work which has dealt with a sequence of patents. Here, we report on the findings of Vickers (1986) on process innovation and Beath, Katsoulacos and Ulph (1987) on product innovation. In each case, the authors seek conditions which reveal when the same firm will always hold the technological lead and those in which the lead will change hands, a pattern of 'action–reaction'.

If the plausible assumption were made that the sequence of patents involved here was technologically linked, the analysis could in principle be used to offer insights into the process of diffusion, broadly defined to encompass incremental advances in the technology. But it must be said that this is not the purpose for which the analysis was designed and given that it is confined to a maximum of two firms, it would imply that diffusion could occur over only the most limited range of potential users.

Asymmetric incentives and patent sequences

We approach the Vickers (1986) analysis from the angle of the now familiar model of Cournot duopoly in the market for a homogeneous product. The market-demand curve is assumed linear and described by the simple function $P = A - Q$. Of the two firms, one (L) has low unit production costs C, and the other (H) has high costs, $C + b$. A new, infinitely long-lived patent offers the prospect of reducing costs to a level $C - d$. What are the incentives for each firm to invest in acquiring the patent and what implications will acquiring it have for the industry structure?

The incentive to either firm is defined as the difference between its profit if it takes the patent and its pay-off if it loses. By 'investment in acquiring the patent' (usually thought of as R&D), we mean something rather stylised, namely the amount a firm would bid to buy the patent if it already existed and were put up for auction. The winner must pay the maximum that its rival would have paid to have the patent. The loser does not forego its bid. This formulation offers enhanced tractability in identifying equilibria in sequential games, but because of its deterministic form is inappropriate for innovation where substantial uncertainty remains. The stochastic racing models considered above are more appropriate then.

That said, there are in a single-period Cournot equilibrium, only three possible cases, depending on the relative values of b, the initial cost disadvantage of H; d, the superiority of the new technology; and $(A - c)$, the margin between unit cost and the highest price per unit the market would bear. In the first case, d is 'large' (i.e. greater than $(A - c)$), implying a cost reduction so great that whichever firm won the patent it could charge a monopoly price below C. In this 'drastic innovation' case, representing rapid technical progress, the incentive to both firms is the same; if it wins, it earns the monopoly profit; if it loses it earns zero. There is therefore no asymmetry in incentives but one firm is assured a monopoly.

In the second case, the relative sizes of b and d allow L to become a monopolist if it wins (H being unprepared to supply at the new monopoly price), but for L to remain active if H wins. In this case, L has the greater incentive to win and converts the industry into a monopoly. But the third case is most interesting. Here, whichever firm wins the patent, *both* remain active. Vickers calls this 'action-reaction.'

The setting is that the values of both b and d are 'small' enough to ensure that the sum $(2b + d)$ falls below $(A - C)$. The steeper the demand curve and the more modest unit costs, the wider the range of values which b and d may take and still fall within this case. As the analysis proceeds, however, we shall see that it is crucial to action–reaction that the industry joint profits if H wins exceed those if L wins. For that to occur, it can be shown that more severe limits must be put on the 'smallness' required of b and d. One could characterise it as a case of slow progress and slight cost differentials.

To examine the implications of this for a sequence of innovations, suppose the game takes the form a sequence of T patent auctions where T is the first, $T - 1$ the second, '2' the penultimate and '1' the last. At the start of each period t, a patent t is auctioned, giving access for the successful bidder to cost level $C(t)$. Upon payment of the bid, the firm becomes technologically superior to its rival and its costs fall. Thus:

$$C(T) > C(T-1) > \ldots > C(t + 1) > C(t) > C(t - 1) > \ldots > C(2) > C(1)$$

Notice, however, that while each firm may well be drawing on the same body of processing technology in successive periods, this characterisation contains no presumption that a firm's research success in one period will give it any advantage in further research on future occasions. This is the sense in which asymmetry derives from incentives alone and not from the intrinsic capabilities of the firms.

Current profits for the firms depend on the technology levels each achieved after their most recent patent win. Net of R&D outlays, the single-period profit of a firm with cost level $C(s)$, when its rival has a cost level of $C(t)$, is denoted $\Pi(s, t)$. Profit rises with improvements in the firm's own technology and falls with improvements in its rival's technology. By assumption, both firms make non-negative profits throughout. The single period joint profit of the firms is:

$$j(s, t) = \Pi(s, t) + \Pi(t, s) \tag{6.22}$$

Each firm maximises the sum of its profits over all periods, minus its R&D expenses. To understand how the incentives of each firm affect their behaviour we need to look at each stage in the game at the firms' pay-offs for the **subgame** following the acquisition (or non-acquisition) of a patent, i.e. for what is left of the whole game after a firm or its rival has won (or lost) a stage. (The approach is suggested by Selten's, 1975, notion of subgame perfection in which strategies must be maximising for entire games as well as for each subgame within it.)

Before a patent race at date t (call it patent t), L will have costs $C(t + 1)$, having won the previous patent, and H costs $C(t + k)$, where its level of technology is that of k periods ago, $k > 1$. If H now won the patent, its pay-off for the remainder of the game (including R&D outlays) could be written as a value function $V(t, t + 1)$ where, as before, the first argument denotes the patent on which this firm's costs are based and the second that for rival costs. But this would not be its incentive to acquire the patent since, even if L won, H would make a non-negative profit. If L won, H's pay-off would be $V(t + k, t)$. So H's incentive to bid for patent t, $G_h(t)$ is:

$$G_h(t) = V(t, t + 1) - V(t + k, t) \qquad (6.23)$$

Given that the competition in R&D is constructed as an auction, H wins if $G_h(t)$ exceeds L's incentive:

$$G_l(t) + V(t, t + k) - V(t + 1, t) \qquad (6.24)$$

There are asymmetric incentives whenever $G_h(t)$ and $G_l(t)$ are unequal:

$$G_h(t) > (G_l(t)$$

if

$$[V(t, t + 1) - V(t + k, t)] > [V(t, t + k) - V(t + 1, t)]$$

or

$$[V(t, t + 1) + V(t + 1, t)] > [V(t, t + k) + V(t + k, t)] \qquad (6.25)$$

But the terms in square brackets in (6.25) on the left-handside, are the industry profits for the post-patent subgame after t if H wins the patent and, on the right-hand side, the corresponding industry profits if L wins. If H wins, its costs fall to $C(t)$ from $C(t + k)$, above the level $C(t + 1)$ at which L had been operating as the winner of the last patent and at which it continues to operate for at least this period if H wins. If L wins, its costs fall to $C(t)$ from $C(t + 1)$ and its rival's costs remain at their previous high level, $C(t + k)$. Call these, respectively, $J(t, t + 1)$ and $J(t, t + k)$. Then firm H has the greater incentive to win and thus in this framework does win if $J(t, t + 1) > J(t, t + k)$, i.e. if the industry subgame profits from H's winning are greater than they would be from L's. Vickers refers to this as the **patent allocation rule (PAR)**.

Since the PAR is defined in terms of value functions, we can apply it to any stage of the sequence and, if we know the value functions, predict which firm will win a patent. The simplest case is for the last auction when subgame and single-period profits from patent 1 coincide, so that:

$$V(1, k) = \Pi(1, k)$$
$$\text{for } k > 1$$
$$V(k, 1) = \Pi(k, 1)$$

The first of these shows the value of the patent to the winner if its rival has costs $C(k)$, and the second shows the value of the patent to the loser, given that the winner has costs $C(1)$. Here, the PAR says H wins if $J(1, 2) > J(1, 1 + k)$. But this is equivalent to the single-period condition $j(1, 2) > j(1, 1 + k)$; H will have the incentive to put in the larger bid and will win if the profits the industry makes are larger than the industry profits after a win by L. Recall, however, that single-period industry profits are larger when H wins in the Cournot case we explored above. If we assumed that the competition were taking place in an industry with that structure, then the last patent race would have to be won by H.

For every other race, the value functions relate to longer subgames and are more complex. In general:

$$V(t, t + k) = \Pi(t, t + k) + \max[V(t - 1, t + k) + V(t + k, t - 1)$$
$$- V(t - 1, t), V(t, t - 1)] \qquad (6.26)$$

is the value to a winning firm in the post-t subgame if its rival has costs $C(t + k)$. In (6.26), $\Pi(t, t + k)$ is the current-period profit from t. In the square brackets we show the maximum value of future profits viewed from the day of the auction, conditional upon the current position of the two players. If this firm won the next auction ($t - 1$) as well, the value of its profits would be $V(t-1, t + k)$ minus the costs of its winning bid, $[V(t - 1, t) - V(t + k, t - 1)]$, equal to the maximum the other firm would have been prepared to pay for ($t - 1$). If this firm lost, its value function would simply be $V(t, t- 1)$. Analogously:

$$V(t + k, t) = \Pi(t + k, t) + \max[V(t - 1, t) + V(t, t - 1) - V(t - 1, t + k),$$
$$V(t + K, t - 1)] \qquad (6.27)$$

(see Beath, Katsoulacos and Ulph, 1987: 38).

The value functions for the last patent can be used with (6.26), (6.27) and the PAR to determine recursively which firm wins each auction. One perspective on this is that without further specific assumptions to structure the enquiry the pattern of success and failure will turn out to be highly complex. But, if we assume that in each period the industry achieves a slow progress, slight cost-differential Cournot equilibrium, then we can suppose that $J(t, t + 1) > J(t, t + k)$ for an arbitrary sequence of patent auctions leading to the final one. Then in each case we can predict that the currently higher cost firm will win the next auction because it is prepared to outbid its rival. The intuition behind the result is that if L won, only L's costs would be reduced and since the reduction in this case would be modest, shared-industry profits would rise by only a small amount, offering only a small incentive to L. But if H won, there would be a larger cost cut (by $b + d$ rather than just d), shared-industry profits would rise by more and H as a result always has a larger incentive. It can therefore always outbid L (Beath, Katsoulacos and Ulph, 1987: 33, footnote 2).

Notice two important points about this analysis. First, the action–reaction case is one in which we can see an example to counter some of the worryingly strong results in Chapter 5, where monopoly seems to follow inevitably from technological competition. But it is not enough simply to incorporate successive episodes of innovation; even then, persistent monopoly may be an outcome. The initial details of the market structure and the pace of technical progress matter, which leads to the second point.

Vickers argues that as behaviour in the product market becomes more price competitive, it becomes increasingly unlikely that the Cournot-derived assumption needed for action–reaction will hold. In the case, for example, of cut-throat price competition (Bertrand type of behaviour), the low-cost firm would always set its price just below the cost level of H, denying it the opportunity to earn positive profit. In that event, a necessary condition exists for increasing dominance in the sense that the low-cost firm in any period will always win the next patent. Our intuition here is that when the low-cost firm acts in this way, industry profits going solely to *L* increase as the gap between the least-cost technologies of the two firms widens and this gives *L* a greater incentive to win the next patent.

The net result of the analysis is a paradox. Bertrand competition is good for consumers in the short run, because it leads to lower prices than are found in the corresponding Cournot equilibrium. But Bertrand competition is bad for consumers, in the sense that the dominant firm might choose to set its price only fractionally below that of the higher cost firm, despite repeated cost reductions. In the Cournot competition, however, action–reaction would lead to steadily falling prices.

Does the same sort of conclusion arise in the case of product innovation? Beath *et al.* (1987) examine this question in a framework modelled closely on that of Vickers. But their approach is to characterise a Bertrand equilibrium in a market with differentiated products and to show that with product innovation such competition can lead to either persistent dominance (as with process innovation) or to action–reaction. The details of the proof are not given here, but it is important to give a flavour of the work to complement both the process innovation case and to expose an aspect of competition in product innovation which was not raised earlier (See also Chapters 3 and 5).

In their model, Beath *et al.* consider vertically differentiated products. In this case, all consumers agree on the most preferred mix of characteristics. So, for example, for two laptop computers of given size, everyone would prefer the machine with greater power (translated as processing speed, memory capacity, etc.). At each auction, firms bid for a patent which would give them the know-how to produce a good of any quality up to the maximum quality level specified. The technological progress giving rise to the know-how is exogenous. Let $q0$ stand for the quality level of some default quality good available at a zero price which represents the consumer's option of not buying either of the two goods under analysis. And let $\Pi(r, s)$ stand for the profit of a firm, *H*, producing a good of high-quality level qr while its rival, *L*, produces one of low-quality level qs. Then assumptions may be made which imply Bertrand equilibrium profit functions for the high-quality and low-quality firms, $\Pi(r, s)$ and $\Pi(s, r)$ respectively. From these may be derived (by vertical addition) the industry profit function (see Figure 6.7 which is Beath, Katsoulacos and Ulph's (1987) Figure 1, p. 37). On the horizontal axis, increasing quality is measured from left to right.

In particular, note from Figure 6.7 that all profits disappear if both firms produce the same good (point *A*); H is always more profitable than *L*; increasing the quality of the low-quality good, making it a closer quality substitute for the high-quality good, reduces the profits of *H*; increasing the quality of the low-quality good first raises *L*'s profits because higher quality eases its competitive position *vis-à-vis* zero price default goods, but reduces them again as its good becomes an increasingly close substitute for the high-quality good. The net effect is that industry profits peak before *L*'s (compare points *B* and *C*). Furthermore, though this is not immediately apparent from the diagram, both firms' profits are assumed to increase if there is an increase

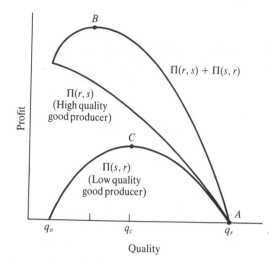

Figure 6.7 Profit functions for high- and low quality good producers and for the industry. (Reproduced with the permission of Blackwell Publishers from J. Beath, Y. Katsoulacos and D. Ulph (1987) 'Sequential product innovation and industry evolution', *Economic Journal* 97(Conference): 37.)

in the quality of H's good. And for any quality level chosen by H, L's best response, is a strictly increasing function of the quality of H's good (L's best response to H employing qr, for example, is qc).

For industries in which these assumptions hold (and they may not always) it is possible to find a condition for action–reaction in a Bertrand competition. This condition is twofold. First, technical change must be rapid enough to ensure that neither firm can ever make the best response to a rival's newly introduced product, i.e. neither firm already holds a patent which allows it to offer a product of the quality that would give it maximum possible profit, given the other firm's quality level. To give an example, in Figure 6.7, L cannot respond to H producing at qr by employing qc; it is constrained to choose a quality level below qc. Second, suppose that at the time of each auction the relative quality levels of the products of each firm are such that the profit of a firm employing the latest, top-quality patent would decrease with increases in the quality of its rival's output and that the joint profits of the industry would increase with an increase in the quality of the product currently produced by the low-quality producer. In this case, there is action–reaction. Beath, Katsoulacos and Ulph also find a necessary (and this time, sufficient) condition for the high-quality firm to win every auction. In essence, the condition is that technical progress should be extremely slow. That is to be compared with the process innovation case, where sufficiently rapid progress will ensure the winner of a patent will always secure monopoly power and render the sequential structure irrelevant.

Intrinsic asymmetries

While asymmetric incentives have turned out to be potentially important, the sort of asymmetries that would appear most obvious relate to intrinsic characteristics of individual firms: the relative sizes and qualities of their knowledge bases, their efficiency in undertaking R&D and their impatience for results, reflected in their discount rates. The previous section showed that even if we ignored these sources of asymmetry, there were conditions in which two (and in general more) firms could survive a succession of stages in a technological competition. That analysis presupposed each firm knew the outcome of R&D at each stages, which, in principle, might be regarded as a strength rather than a weakness, since its predictions did not have to rely on any appeal to uncertainty. Nonetheless, the absence of uncertainty limits the scope of the appropriate applicability of such analysis and in this section we return to a stochastic formulation.

We have noted before the significance of first-mover advantages. In the context of asymmetric games, both Fudenberg *et al.* (1983) and Harris and Vickers (1985) have shown that if one firm enters a two-firm patent race before the other, the learning advantage which this gives the first over its rival may often secure the patent for it. Suppose, for example, that a firm can always increase its relevant knowledge base in a predictable way by spending more per period on R&D though the marginal cost of learning will usually rise. At the same time, imagine that the greater the firm's experience (knowlege base) at any moment, the higher the probability that it will make the discovery needed to secure the patent in the next period. Then if the patent bestows a profitable monopoly patent, but neither firm has positive expected profits if they both persist with the costly race, we might expect the late entrant with little accumulated knowledge to drop out first or logically not even to enter it. This is the pre-emption argument used before in connecton with monopoly in Chapter 5.

If the short period of time by which the first mover beats the late entrant to the gun is denoted ε, we understand why this is called the ε pre-emption result (Dasgupta and Stiglitz, 1980b). It depends, however, upon the first mover being able to credibly threaten a potential late entrant with an increase in the speed of its R&D sufficient to ensure that it will secure the patent. If the first mover is well informed about potential latecomers' plans and can react quickly if they enter, it can always speed up and, given its existing headstart, stay in the lead. What is more, so long as expected profits remain positive (as in this model they would), there is always an incentive to remain in the lead. Since potential latecomers should thus regard the threat as credible, the first mover should be able to proceed at a relatively leisurely pace through its research programme; given the increasing marginal costs of acquiring knowledge, it would not be rational to rush to discovery.

But suppose now that the first mover can only gauge the level of its rival's knowledge with a lag. Then, assuming that it started first, there is now the danger that it might be overtaken – **leapfrogged** – without knowing it, if it proceeded at the leisurely pace described above. And once the latecomer took the lead, the probability of its winning the race would rise above that of the first mover and could make it unprofitable for the first mover to continue. The existence of such information lags may therefore have two effects: one encouraging latecomers to enter on the grounds that they now have a chance to win, the other driving the first mover to invest at a faster rate than it would have done in the absence of the lags. It can also be shown, however, that competition only generates this faster investment rate in learning if the latecomer's accumulated experience is close enough to its own for the first mover to consider it a real threat. One element missing from this analysis is complementary assets. As Teece (1986) argues, a first mover may also lose out to a 'fast second' if the later arrival is better equipped with distribution channels and the capacity to generate new versions of the innovation.

In a version of leapfrogging which incorporates part of this story, Park (1984), Judd (1985), Grossman and Shapiro (1987) and Harris and Vickers (1987) set up a multistage innovation race in which a firm must make an intermediate discovery at Stage 1 before aiming for a patent or other equivalent prize available only after success in Stage 2. Analogous with the information lag model, research effort is intensified when the accumulated knowledge of the latecomer approaches that of the first mover.

While these models have an air of reality about them that was missing where firms were assumed symmetric and, importantly, tell us why there might be competition in R&D, the stylisation chosen to describe firms' acquisition and use of knowledge has much more regularity about it than is usually characteristic of the innovation processes we observe. Firms may not be able to gamble on catching up with a first mover in a particular race by embarking on a research programme with that aim in view. But they will gain new knowledge which might have value to them in other ways, which could take them to the lead in a quite different race, or which could lead them to become first movers in a race initiated by their own efforts. The ever-present danger of formalising technological competition is that it may lead us to forget the messiness and serendipity of it all.

Queries about game theory

Developments in game theory have been a (perhaps the) major catalyst in infusing the analysis of industrial organisation with new life since the Second World War. As we have seen, game theory, which allows us to view decision-makers as rational rather than as imbeciles incapable of learning, can be adopted in many ways to address a wide range of interesting problems, and in the context of industry economics, provides an analytical framework for considering the endogenous determination of industry structure along with strategic variables. These are major steps forward, or at least appear to be. In this section, however, we draw attention to doubts which are now being voiced about the whole approach and specific questions about the usefulness of game theory in modelling innovation.

First, **rationality**. The downside of portraying players as rational rather than imbecilic is that decision-makers are now called upon to be *too* rational. Partly this is because game theory equilibria depend on the ability of each player to think through all their rivals' decision process. Thus each player must be assumed to believe in all other players' rationality and to be able to process all of the implications of all other players' plans. This criticism acquires particular force when games take place over a sequence of steps (as with patent sequences). It seems logical to model the sequence as repeats of a single game and to define each player's strategy as a rule indicating what to do at each point, depending on the actions other players had taken at previous stages. But then, even with a game as relatively simple as the Prisoners' Dilemma, working forwards through five rounds of repeats will give rise to a set of over two billion strategies for each player (Sugden, 1986). It overstrains credulity completely to imagine any individual coping with the challenge of effectively processing so many alternatives.

Two possible responses to this point are that many games may be single-stage events and that an alternative approach to multistage games, backward induction, offers a helpful escape route. The problem with the first response is the abstraction of optimising choice reflecting rational behaviour actually makes most sense when individuals do the same thing repeatedly and so by trial and error work out what are the best solutions for them. Brander (1992) points out that situations represented by many games in industrial organisation fail this test and so to associate rationality, implicitly, with experience makes little sense. For example, it is implausible to model as a game based on rationality a one-off decision about whether to license or sell-off a particular new technology. A player can hardly be expected to take full account of other players' thought processes when neither he/she nor they may have been in the situation before.

Backward induction was introduced in the models of Vickers and Beath *et al.* In general it calls for all players to envisage themselves at the end of the game and then work backwards to decide the rational strategies each would play in the final period, the last but one, the antepenultimate and so on. The backward induction approach has the advantage of offering a way around the impenetrable multiplicity of strategies found by reasoning forwards and suggests a way of dealing with a second major problem in game theory, **multiple equilibria**.

Particularly in dynamic and repeated game models, there can easily be a whole range of Nash equilibria (Friedman, 1971) and this has been as true of various attempts to model R&D as efforts to analyse other questions in industrial organisation. This might be regarded as an advantage in some circumstances. But as Kreps and Spence (1985) remark, formal non-cooperative game theory fails to offer the analyst any reason to choose one of these equilibria than any other. What is more, the power of a theory may be judged by its capacity to rule possibilities out; a theory which offers too many possibilities explains rather little.

Backward induction seems to offer a solution here; the method at least rules out solutions that rest on players making non-credible threats and restricts the numbers of plausible equilibria to those characterised by credible strategies alone. This is one example of the sort of refinements which game theorists apply to try to restrict candidate equilibria to a subset meeting plausible additional criteria. The credibility criterion gives rise to 'subgame perfection' which require of equilibrium strategies that they individually maximise for the whole game and each stage (subgame) within it (Selten, 1975).

Unfortunately, subgame perfection as an equilibrium concept fails always to provide unique solutions when information is asymmetric, i.e. when sellers in a market know more about a good or service than buyers. It is certainly true with product innovations that this will very often be the case, but the point has wide-ranging relevance.

Attempts to remedy this by introducing further refinements run foul of another objection: 'particularising' theory (Brander, 1992: 10–11). This means that a plausible game-theoretic model can be constructed to explain *any* business practice we observe. But since we then have a particular theory for every observed practice, it becomes unclear obscure how much generality the theory has or, indeed, whether it is a theory at all in the sense of abstracting from particulars.

There are other difficulties too. Game-theoretic analysis takes the number and identity of players as given through any given game. But the identities of the firms in a technological competition are likely to change as the contest proceeds. Some firms will go bankrupt, some will enter from outside the industry and others set up business from scratch when the competition is well under way. It is unclear that game theory can cope with this degree of discontinuity in areas as structurally fundamental as these. How can the strategies of firms present at the outset be modelled in a way which reflects their expected responses to the strategies of other players which will not even exist from some time to come and are therefore, at best, ill-defined?

Again the analysis has become increasingly intricate and complex as uncertainty, asymmetry and sequential effects have been combined, additional insights have been confined to particular cases in which convenient parameter values happen to yield unique and transparent results.[4] It is often not made clear how sensitive particular results are to such choices of parameter value, but it is widely recognised that the nature of equilibria 'can be fundamentally altered by apparently small changes in the specification of the game, such as minor changes in the ordering of moves, in the specification of strategy spaces, or in the specification of uncertainty', (Brander, 1992: 10–11).

Despite all the technical sophistication of game-theoretic models, another criticism is that in one way they are too simple; they often focus in only one strategic variable at a time (Kreps and Spence, 1985). As we noted in Chapter 5, firms make decisions about R&D interdependently with other investment choices and technology policy is only a part of (and interdependent with) firm's overall corporate strategies. Models which fail to recognise this are bound to be missing something.

Finally, there are very few game-theoretic models in which learning ever takes place. This is particularly serious for innovation games, in which it is a reasonable assumption that firm's knowledge about technology is cumulative. As Kreps and Spence (1985) point out, the equilibria in many-period games often hold together because firms believe certain actions will provoke reactions from rivals which they would prefer to avoid. But in this formulation, firms never look backwards to learn from the past. To allow for this possibility, players may be endowed with incomplete information and learning then appears in the game as the resolution of their uncertainty through the unfolding of events. The resulting analysis is necessarily highly complex and other work has attempted to simplify matters by examining learning problems in which intellectually limited agents interact (Lipman, 1991).

Little of this work has yet shown any prospect of throwing further light on the nature of technological competition. This may be because game theory is essentially tidy while innovation is inherently messy. As we move towards accounts of diffusion where learning effects become of central importance we turn to other modes of analysis, including evolutionary ones, to frame the argument.

Diffusion, competition and evolution

In this latter part of the chapter, we analyse with a strong (but not exclusively) evolutionary flavour the diffusion of innovation.

In this sort of work, the unit of analysis is an innovation or a set or sequence of related innovations. The diffusion process may be thought of as taking place within a given industry but, recognising that process innovations may produce a variety of goods, it may equally be viewed as occurring across several industries simultaneously. When innovation has implications for two or more industries, it opens the door to the possibility that a firm hitherto confined to one industry may attempt to enter another, or that already diversified firms will use new technology in several markets. Implications of those possibilities were analysed in various parts of Chapter 5 but here we ignore those aspects and pick up others.

Analytically, the simplest case of diffusion relates to a single, discrete innovation which, implicitly, is supplanting an existing product or products. But more often than not there are competing innovations from the outset and interesting questions relate to which one will come to dominate. Taking one step further, diffusion can be understood to involve several processes simultaneously; increasingly widespread use of a most efficient technique, imitation and innovation building sequentially and incrementally on existing models, but within a given trajectory. Finally, diffusion may be viewed as the process by which an entirely new technological trajectory establishes itself. Each of these is considered in turn.

Diffusion of a single innovation

In orthodox economic models, technical and economic efficiency are assumed for all firms. This implies that once a new efficiency-enhancing process or product has been developed, it will at once be put to use, with equal maximum effect by all firms. As we have argued throughout the book, this is a most misleading picture.

If we confine interest to a single, well-defined advance (a new process embodied in a piece of capital equipment, say), it is invariably observed that some firms will start using it before others and laggards may not follow sometimes, for many years, if ever (Griliches, 1957; Salter, 1966; Nasbeth and Ray, 1974; Davies, 1979). In Chapter 5, diffusion within firms was considered as a separate issue. Here, implicitly, it is assumed that each firm adopts 100 per cent or not at all.

As we noted earlier, a common empirical observation is that innovations spread among potential users according to a sigmoid pattern over time. Any theory of diffusion should therefore be capable of generating a sigmoid path under plausible conditions. Several types of theory offer this possibility in relation to a single innovation and we consider them before proceeding to accounts of diffusion which also allow for developments in the innovation itself as part of the process.

Much of the work in the area views the diffusion process as a pure demand phenomenon; the pattern and rate of diffusion are made to depend on the characteristics and decisions of potential users without regard to developments on the supply-side of the market. A pioneering example of research in this style is Mansfield (1968). Here, the underlying theoretical framework suggests the existence of a fixed potential number of users. The proportion of non-users to adopt in any period is hypothesised to be determined by the (constant) return on investing in the innovation, the (also constant) cost of installation and the proportion already using it. The last of these points to the foundation stone of Mansfield's reasoning that delayed adoption (retardation) reflects differences in the uncertainty firms attach to future profit streams, which, in turn, arises from differences in the rate at which firms learn from existing users' experience. From somewhat casually justified foundations, Mansfield derives an 'epidemic' equation for $N(t)$, the number of adopters at t for each period. He also concludes that diffusion will be speediest in industries where expected profits are highest and installation costs lowest.

One of the more serious shortcomings of the Mansfield model (discussed in relation to the intrafirm analysis of Chapter 5) is its inconsistency with the plausible Bayesian approach to learning. Jensen (1982) and Stoneman (1980) allow firms to learn in precisely this way. In these models, it is assumed that firms may differ in their initial assessment of the value of adopting an innovation at fixed cost. Because their starting points vary, they take differing periods of time to learn enough to convince them that investment will be worthwhile. Under certain assumptions about the distribution of these initial beliefs, the sigmoid curve again emerges. For each firm, the probability of adoption on or before a specified date increases with the firm's initial strength of belief in the profitability of the innovation, the number of subsequent observations which tend to confirm this belief, the rate of return and the discount rate. As in Mansfield, information is acquired without cost. If search is costly and firms learn of only modest profits as they sample adoptions which would otherwise have occurred might be discouraged (McCardle, 1985).

An alternative way of attacking diffusion associated with David (1969) and Davies (1979) uses the critical level notion we encountered in relation to critical income in Chapter 3. This is the so-called **probit approach**. A 'stimulate variable' – here firm size, S_i – is observed to vary across firms. Adoption occurs when the value of the variable for any given firm comes into equality with a critical level S_c. For a given distribution of firm sizes, diffusion occurs as S_c falls over time. The diffusion path can be found if we know the distribution of the S_i and the rate at which S_c falls. The economic reasons for the diffusion path taking the specific form that it does can be found if we know the shape of the distribution and why S_c falls at the rate it does.

In a modified version of David's approach, Stoneman and Ireland (1983), assume we know the number of potential users of a new process will be N. Following their approach let $D(t)$ be the proportion of potential user firms operating the new technology at time t. This fraction is related to S_c through a cumulative distribution function $F(S_i)$ over firm sizes. For any S_i, $F(S_i)$ shows the proportion of all firms of size S_i or smaller. As S_i reaches the size of the largest firm, $F(S_i)$ converges on 1, since all firms ranked from the smallest up are now accounted for. If S_c has a high starting level then falls, and given that firm i adopts only when S_c has fallen to its size level S_i, the fraction $F(S_c)$ shows the proportion of firms yet to adopt and the fraction $(1 - F(S_c))$ the proportion already to have become users, D.

The diffusion path is defined by the pattern of adoption over time; the way in which D increases from period to period until $(1 - F(S_c)) = 1$. Take the distribution of firm sizes as given. It is, then, the way S_c falls which determines the diffusion path. Suppose:

$$S_c = \mathrm{h}(p/w) \tag{6.28}$$

where h is a constant, P is the purchase price of the new process and w the unit cost of other inputs. This says that the lower P is relative to w, the lower is S_c thus the higher is D. The simple economic mechanism, founded on relative prices, which drives the model is that the higher w is relative to P, the greater the cost savings to be made by adoption and the smaller the firms which find it desirable to adopt. Assume, for simplicity, that each user, irrespective of size, buys only one unit and never needs to replace it. Then the total number of units in use at period t will be DN, the total potential times the fraction to have adopted. Denote this x. Then as (P/w) falls, S_c also falls, D rises and along with it x. Thus x, the cumulative total of units in use at t (which can never fall) rises either because P falls, or because w rises, or both together.

Suppose first w is constant at w(o). Then $S_c = (\mathrm{h}/\mathrm{w}(o))P$ and, given the argument above:

$$x = f((\mathrm{h}/\mathrm{w}(o))P) \qquad df/\mathrm{d}P < 0 \tag{6.29}$$

which may be inverted to yield:

$$P = g(x) \qquad \mathrm{d}g/\mathrm{d}x < 0 \tag{6.30}$$

This is a form of demand function, which says that for given costs of all other inputs, the purchase price of the innovation will have to be reduced each time sales of the technology are increased by a further unit. On the other hand, even if P is held constant S_c will still fall and x rise if w rises. For x to rise at a given level of P, the whole $g(x)$ function must shift. When P is fixed by assumption, the rate at which w rises over time determines, in conjunction with the shape of $F(S_i)$, the diffusion path.

As an example, suppose the distribution of firm sizes among potential users is log-logistic. The accuracy of this assumption would need to be tested for any case to which the model was applied empirically, but may well be a good approximation in a significant number of cases. If so, $F(S_i)$ takes the particular form:

$$F(S_i) = 1/\{1 + \exp\left[-(\log S_i - a)/b\right]\} \tag{6.31}$$

where a is the mean of the distribution and b a parameter related to the variance. Then it can be shown that the corresponding form of $g(x)$ will be:

$$g(x) = (\mathrm{w(o)}/\mathrm{h})\, e^a [x/(N-x)]^{-b} \tag{6.32}$$

It is clear that $\mathrm{d}g/\mathrm{d}x < 0$, as required, since w(o), h, a and b are all positive constants and with N also given, any rise in x also increases $[x/(N-x)]$ (the ratio of adopters to non-adopters) and hence implies a fall in $g(x)$, and thus a lower price so long as $w = \mathrm{w(o)}$. We saw above that for P to be constant, w must rise. If:

$$w(t) = \mathrm{w(o)} \cdot e^{ut} \tag{6.33}$$

so that all other input costs rise at a constant proportional rate of u per period, then with P constant, S_c will fall at a rate of u per cent per period. With that information, it can be shown that D follows a cumulative logisitic path by setting:

$$-b(\mathrm{d}\log/\mathrm{d}t)\cdot[x/(N-x)] = -u \tag{6.34}$$

and integrating with respect to time.

One objection to this approach is that the ceiling level N should itself be determined within the model. Another is that none of the firms analysed is allowed to take into account the impact of other firms' adoption decisions on its own profits. Reinganum (1981a, b) addresses the latter problem in a game-theoretic model, in which firms are identical and in which learning about rivals' experiences has no role to play. Implementation is assumed to be a lengthy and costly business and the adoption date for a firm is defined to be the date at which this process is complete. Diffusion, defined by the spread of a adoption dates, reflects the different adoption-date choices firms make, assuming that for each firm adjustment costs rise quickly as the implementation period is increasingly foreshortened, but that a cost-minimising adjustment period exists. Firms make their choices irreversibly at the moment a cost-reducing, capital-embodied new process becomes available, taking account of the potential profits for themselves and the impact of their decisions upon their rivals. Reinganum shows that the resulting Nash equilibrium is asymmetric, implying that interfirm variations in dates of first operating the new process will be observed. The pattern of diffusion is significantly altered if firms are not irreversibly committed from the outset and can respond to news of rivals' decisions without incurring prohibitive costs in changing their adjustment paths. To counter threats of pre-emption, firms will bring forward their adoption dates and the diffusion process will be speeded up (Fudenberg and Tirole, 1985).

A characteristic of both the probit and game-theoretic approaches is that they implicitly describe diffusion as an equilibrium phenomenon. Yet no account is given of conditions on the supply-side of the market where the innovation is being generated. We therefore know nothing of the basis on which the price of the innovation is being built, or how the interplay between adopters and potential adopters on one side and suppliers on the other may influence the equilibrium price and the associated diffusion path.

Silverberg *et al.* (1988) discussed below analyse the wide range of demand- and supply-side influences at work when the innovation is itself evolving along a new technological trajectory. But in the case of a single invariant innovation, Stoneman and Ireland (1983), analyse a sequence of market equilibria in which the supplying industry is allowed to be either monopolistic or oligopolistic. In the monopoly case, the supplier takes equation (6.32) as its demand curve (i.e. users' other input costs are constant) and benefits from no technological advance itself in capital goods production. At given levels of experience, its marginal production costs are positive (and could be rising) and there is a well-defined minimum-efficient scale of production. Learning economies shift all cost curves down as experience increases.

If the monopolist maximises the present value of future profits, a zero discount rate (no impatience) implies that the supplier will do best to produce at the same rate each period, that associated with MES and so diffusion cannot be sigmoid and with a non-zero discount rate, diffusion will not be sigmoid if there are no learning economies. Both a positive discount rate and learning are required to produce the sigmoid path and even then, in some cases may not.

In the oligopolistic case, the cost of users' other inputs is allowed now to rise over time at a constant proportional rate and suppliers' costs are permitted to fall through the influence of technological advance, but are set to be proportional to output. One implication of this set up is that the time path of diffusion cannot be traced as in the monopoly case, only steady-state equilibrium paths, on which quantities of the new capital supplied and demanded expand at equal proportional rates. Supplier firms are assumed to choose their optimal output paths, taking as given the output paths of competitors, which they also assume to be optimal and which they correctly anticipate. From given output decisions, price can be determined through the inverse demand function, and costs through the cost function and hence profits over time, the present value of which firms maximise.

Among the many results which can be derived in this framework, Stoneman and Ireland show that on steady-state paths: first, accumulated sales will, in each period, be greater, the larger the number of producers and/or users of the new capital good; second, prices and price–cost margins will be lower, the larger the number of producers; third, the diffusion speed is invariant with respect to the number of producers and/or users. One implication of these results is that monopolisation through, say, patents will reduce the level of usage of a new technology in all periods.

Two missing elements from this story are worth noting: *differences between innovations* and the *role of expectations*. On the first of these, Davies (1979) makes the important point that the sigmoid diffusion curve for a simple innovation will usually be asymmetric (and hence non-logistic), while the curve for more 'complex' innovations is usually symmetric. The difference reflects the relative ease of learning about simple innovations and hence the rapidity with which they 'take off' compared with more complex innovations which require more learning by both producers and users. Davies' analysis also suggests that innovations which are relatively labour-intensive will diffuse most rapidly.

On the question of expectations, casual empiricism suggests that potential users often put off adoption in the expectation either that price will fall or quality improve if they wait. A familiar example from recent history would be the microcomputer, but we noted when discussing intertemporal price discrimination in Chapter 3 that the point has wide relevance. While waiting, potential users sacrifice access to the innovation, but Rosenberg (1976) argues that for any given current price and technology, the probability of delay will increase, the lower expected future price and the more technological improvements are anticipated.

In an extension of their earlier work, Ireland and Stoneman (1986) point out that Rosenberg ignores the impact that expectations might make on current prices and has nothing to say about the end-point of the diffusion process. They consider a product innovation and focus on two aspects of expectations: those about the potential appearance of a new product which would render the current innovation obsolete; and the way in which forecasts of future price are generated from existing information.

In the case of a monopoly supplier, diffusion terminates when unit costs cease to fall, whether expectations are myopic or perfectly foresighted, assuming the product has not been rendered obsolete. But ownership or use of the product will be less at all times under perfect foresight, As to technological expectations, an increased expectation of obsolescence reduces usage along the diffusion path, compared with what it would have been otherwise, under both forms of price expectation. Assuming myopic expectations, sigmoid diffusion is possible but not certain. In the case of oligopoly, equilibrium sales per period increase with the number of suppliers under perfect foresight. As the number of suppliers becomes infinitely large, the perfect foresight path looks increasingly like the monopoly path with myopic price expectations. If myopia prevails on both sides of the market, sales under oligopoly supply exceed those under monopoly.

Despite the wide range of considerations incorporated, the analysis so far ignores two important realities. First, diffusion usually involves at least two and usually families of distinct variants of the same innovation (Rothwell, 1990). Second, the diffusion of an innovation, especially when defined to involve changes in the innovation itself, is likely to interact with changes in market structure, in particular the number and relative sizes of firms. These leads are followed up in the remainder of the chapter.

Competing innovations and path dependence

When two or more variants of a new technology arrive at the same time in the market, diffusion of the innovation involves a competition among the alternatives. From an economic and technological point of view, the magnitude of long-term benefits from the innovation may depend on which of the variants comes to dominate. The Vickers and Beath, Katsoulacos and Ulph analysis presented earlier offers insights into this question, but because of the absence of uncertainty in that approach, an important dimension of the problem was never raised. Here, as a direct opposite, we recognise that essentially random events fairly early in the diffusion process can direct future technological developments into particular channels and have implications for the long-term technological structure of the economic system (David, 1985; Arthur, Ermoliev and Kaniovski, 1987, Arthur, 1988, 1989). This sort of work throws new light on the claims of evolutionists that technological change is largely cumulative; once a direction has been established, it tends to be pursued even when apparently superior pathways might be available.

Path dependence and lock-in are central to the analysis in this section and provide it with strong evolutionary credentials. Path dependence arises in a process (here diffusion) when outcomes in one period depend on events during the transitions that led to it, rather than being predetermined and predictable from conditions characterising the system at the outset. Path dependency tends to suggest the operation of lock-in, a set of conditions which make it either impossible or for some other reason highly unattractive to move from one period to the next in more than a very narrow range of ways. Lock-in may arise because of:

1. increasing returns to scale in knowledge, i.e. the costs of increasing output by X per cent rise by less than X per cent if the knowledge input into production is through previous learning already part of a firm's knowledge base and so does not need to be acquired anew;
2. the costs of moving out of the 'rut', i.e. the cost of acquiring new technological knowledge is costly compared to reusing existing knowledge;
3. existing complementarities, i.e. existing production knowledge is usually a specific asset with complementary assets have been built up (skills, supplier relationships, market reputation, etc.). Abandoning one approach implies abandoning other assets too.

Lock-in has the technological consequence of confining innovation in many cases to a narrow corridor of developments. Economically, it will in the short run favour firms with particular sorts of experience over those which lack it. In the longer run, however, those same firms emay be threatened by outsiders whose technological experience is entirely different, but for whom there may be increasing returns to scale and existing complementarities to be exploited by launching into a new area.

A relatively simple but striking way of showing how technology may be directed by essentially random factors has been developed. (Arthur, Ermoliev and Kamiovski, 1987; Arthur, 1988, 1989).

This analysis seeks to identify how structure emerges in systems characterised by random events and applies the approach to tracing the emergence of a dominant technology. To give the simplest example of how the approach works, consider the experiment of tossing a coin. Then the structure of the experiment could be viewed as any long-run fixed pattern to emerge in the proportion of heads to tails. According to the 'Law of Large Numbers', there is a 100 per cent probability that with a fair coin, the proportion of heads will settle down eventually to an expected value of 0.5. This is because the law states that repeated random variables that are independent of the previous ones (and clearly the event 'heads' on any given toss is always independent of previous tosses) have long-term averages, observed here to be very close to 50 per cent of the total, that must approach their expected values.

In the case of the diffusion of a new technology, the increments analogous to each toss of the coin, i.e. successive adoptions, are *not* independent of each other. For a wide range of reasons, the more any one variant has already been adopted, the more likely that variant will be taken up the next time an adoption occurs. The reasons for the relative advantage gained by greater existing market penetration include:

1. Greater price reductions that scale economies in production may have brought about (if the technology is embodied in a product);
2. Greater improvements inperformance generated by cumulative learning by using.
3. Greater beneficial network externalities generated by the larger group of users.
4. An enhanced awareness of the nature of the more widely used variant in the minds of potential adopters.
5. A more developed structure of complementary support, such as maintenance services.

Under these circumstances, Arthur *et al.* argue, there will be increasing returns to adoption: the probability of adoption rises with the market share of the variant.

To model the emergence of structure from random events, Arthur employs Polya-type path dependent processes (Polya and Eggenberger, 1923). To understand such a process, think of an urn containing two balls of different colour, red and white. Randomly choose one ball, replace it, then add to the urn a further ball of the same colour. Next time, randomly choose a ball and again replace it, along with another ball of the same colour. This process has increments that are clearly path dependent, since at any one time, the probability that the next ball added is red (or white) equals the proportion red (or white) at that point. Polya proved that the proportion of red balls to white would settle down to a given level, with a probability of one, but that the level itself was a random variable, i.e. unpredictable at the outset. It is absolutely certain that structure (a fixed proportion of red to white) will emerge, but absolutely uncertain what the details of the structure (the value of the percentage) will be. The level at which it settles always turn out to depend on early random movements.

A shortcoming of this version of the Polya process is that it requires a special type of path dependence, in which the probability of adding a red ball exactly equals the proportion of red balls in the urn. For general use, we might wish to consider cases in which the probability of an increment of a particular kind was a function of the proportions of all alternatives. In such non-linear Polya processes, Arthur, Emoliev and Kaniovski (1987), show that stochastic motions dominate early on and 'select' from the structures which are possible.

As an example of the simpler, special case, Arthur (1989) sets up an experiment in which the potential market for a new technology is divided into two equally sized segments, groups Type R and Type S. Type R prefers variant A, Type S, variant B. For R-type individuals, the returns to adopting A and B are, respectively, $[a(R) + rn(A)]$ and $[b(R) + rn(B)]$, and for S-type individuals, $[a(S) + sn(A)]$ and $[b(S) + sn(B)]$, where $a(R) > b(R)$ and $b(S) > a(S)$. Parameters r and s are positive, and $n(A)$ and $n(B)$ are the numbers of adopters of variants A and B at any given moment. The return to either type of individual from using either variant rises with the extent to which any given variant has already been adopted.

The factor which determines the proportions in which A and B are used is the sequence in which the two types of adopter make their adoption decisions. This is assumed to be purely random. If adoption decisions were made in a strict sequence of R, S, R, ... (or S, R, S, ...), both variants would remain in use. But if adoption decisions were made, purely by chance at some point, in a sequence such as S, R, S, R, R, R, ... this could well be enough to raise the level of $n(A)$ high enough to put $[a(S) + sn(A)]$ above $[b(S) + sn(B)]$ and cause S-type individuals to switch from then on from B to A. Since R-type individuals in any case prefer A, that would spell the end for variant B, locking the future development of the technology into a path determined by the characteristics of A. The chance element involved in the selection of a dominant technology here makes the analysis deeply evolutionary in spirit.

In principle, variant B could stage a come-back if $b(R)$ and $b(S)$ both rose relatively quickly. But notice, it is not enough for $b(R)$ and $b(S)$ to rise relative to $a(R)$ and $a(S)$; they must rise faster than that to overtake the impact of increasing returns to adoption captured by the terms $rn(A)$ and $sn(A)$. Particularly if B has lost its market, it will be hard for development of B to proceed quickly enough for it to break back in. Yet this offers the potential for inefficiency; in some cases B, had it survived, might have improved more rapidly and offered greater overall benefits than A. The same pure chance that structures the technology (i.e. 100 per cent to A) may also prevent society enjoying the greater benefits that might have accrued had chance selected differently.

The example here is suggestive and captures an observable element of truth about actual histories of technology. It simplifies matters, however, not only by ignoring more general forms of the non-linear Polya process, but also by reducing the emphasis of factors which economists would recognise as important. First, the example involves what Arthur describes as an unsponsored technology, one that is open to all and in relation to which agents are simple consumers who act directly or indirectly as developers of them (1989: 117). The alternative is to consider sponsored technology in which particular firms use variants strategically in competing with each other. We have considered such competition in depth.

Second, the example tends to suggest that lock-in is irreversible, a proposition which should perhaps be recast in terms of adjustment costs. Arthur himself recognises this (1988: 13) by asserting that any particular structure is locked-in 'to a degree measurable by the minimum cost to changeover'. He explores this somewhat informally when linking the probability of exit from lock-in to its various sources. Changing the technological structure will be relatively difficult if positive feedbacks arise from learning effects associated with a now-dominant variant. This is because the advantages of learning relating to one variant are neither reversible nor fully transferrable to other variants.

On the other hand, if coordination effects are the source of lock-in, it may sometimes be rather easier to reposition the system. Coordination effects arise when all users of a technology agree that it would be to their mutual advantage to standardise the way it is used. If a technological standard is embodied in equipment, then switching will be costly, and may be costly enough to prevent change. For example, changing the standard for road transport from driving on the left-hand to the right-hand side would be costly in terms of altering the production of steering assembly units. But changing the standard for maximum amplification on sound reproduction equipment would merely call upon users to modify and control their use of existing technology. This would involve very little cost so that switching from loud to quiet variants of the technology would be easy. Such a change could be achieved by fiat. Or, as Farrell and Saloner (1985, 1986) show, every user will decide independently to switch, so long as all are certain the others will prefer the alternative. In the event of uncertainty, the change would not occur if no individual would be willing to take the gamble of switching for fear that the others might not follow.

The potential strength of coordination effects is well reflected in two studies of historical events which did lead to lock-in. They seem to explain how the the QWERTY typewriter keyboard and alternating current became locked-in, the first of these (like FORTRAN, the programming language and the US colour television system) also preventing alternative superior variants from making any impact later (David, 1985; David and Bunn, 1987). Lock-in through learning seems to have occurred in nuclear reactor technology, and in the steam *versus* petrol car competition of the 1890s.

Evolving technology and changing industry structure

Fisher's 'fundamental equation of natural selection'

The starting point for the evolutionary approach to relationships between innovation and industry structure is to assume there are arbitrarily many firms at the outset of a competitive process. Changing structure in the industry then reflects the varying fortunes of the firms as they strive to increase profit through the employment of different production methods, to imitate and innovate. It is this process which defines and directs, in its broadest sense, the diffusion of new technology.

As a precursor to discussing the process, we first emphasise first an analytical device which has been central to evolutionary thinking about these issues: Fisher's equation from the theory of natural selection.

First (following Nelson and Winter, 1982; 160–1) suppose the economic environment to be simply represented by the prices which each firm may obtain for its product. Clearly, the price any given firm charges will be determined (in important part) by the routines the firm employs. More efficient production routines will be associated with lower unit costs and hence, for a given level of profitability, lower prices.

Second, let a firm's fitness be represented by its profitability. How profitable a firm is will depend on the price:cost ratio of any given firm, given the (weighted) average price of products, i.e. where it stands relative to the average.

Third, which firms come to dominate depends on how profitable any firm's routine is relative to the average, since a high level of profitability allows large-scale investment and rapid growth.

In other words, which firms come to dominate depends on which are most profitable relative to the average. This in turn depends on which have lowest unit costs relative to the average. At the same time that average is not exogenous to the industry, but determined within it as a weighted average of what all individual firms do. The course of the competition is captured by identifying where each firm stands relative to the average. If it is relatively competitive, its share in the market will grow, simultaneously influencing the average itself. If it is relatively uncompetitive, its share will decline.

This mechanism is captured by an equation which has become a touchstone of evolutionary economics:

$$\mathrm{d}f_i/\mathrm{d}t = A(E_i - E\#)f_i \quad i = 1, \ldots, n; \ A > 0 \tag{6.35}$$

where f_i is the market share of firm i, $\mathrm{d}f_i/\mathrm{d}t$ the change in firm i's market share over a short period of time, E_i a measure of performance of firm i, $E\#$ an industry-wide weighted average of that measure, $\Sigma_i f_i E_i$ and A an adjustment parameter. In its basic form, this equation was first introduced by R.A. Fisher in his mathematical formulation of natural selection, with E_i referring to the reproductive fitness of a species in a population of interacting species, f_i the proportion of the population belonging to the species and $E\#$ the average fitness of the population. In population biology, 'fitness' refers to the capacity of a species to reproduce itself. In economics, fitness has sometimes been taken (by Nelson and Winter, for example) to be represented by profitability. But elsewhere in the literature fitness has been represented by a firm's price relative to the average, its delivery lag relative to the average (Silverberg, Dosi and Orsenigo, 1988), or its unit costs relative to the average (Iwai, 1984a, b; Metcalfe, 1986).

To interpret the equation notice first that A is positive and constant by construction while f_i, market share, must take a positive value for any firm currently in the industry. Thus if E_i is greater than E, the whole right-hand side must be positive which means $\mathrm{d}f_i/\mathrm{d}t$ will also be positive. The meaning of a positive value of $\mathrm{d}f_i/\mathrm{d}t$ is that in this period the firm's market share f_i, is increasing. On the other hand, if E_i is less than $E\#$, the difference term $(E_i - E\#)$ will be negative, the right-hand side negative, $\mathrm{d}f_i/\mathrm{d}t$ negative and the firm's market share f_i falling. The speed at which market share rises or falls in any period will be greater the greater the size of market share at the beginning of the period, the greater the difference between E_i and $E\#$, and the greater the adjustment parameter, A.

In grasping how the equation works, it is also important to recognise that if df_i/dt is positive in any period, the weight of E_i in calculating the weighted average $E\# = \Sigma f_i E_i$ will have increased. This will act to reduce the difference between E_i and $E\#$ compared with what it would have been if $E\#$ were constant and to slow down the rate at which the market share of i is increasing. One clear result, proved initially by Fisher and replicated in an economic context more recently (see pp. 280–2), assumes that at some point in time there are many values of E_i (say, a variety of unit cost levels across firms), but that each E_i remains constant throughout time, i.e. firms vary in performance among themselves, but their individual performance characteristics never change. Intuitively, it can be seen that if every firm starts off with an equal market share, the one with the highest E_i will initially increase its share fastest, but this will also drive up the value of E. The values of any given E_i will remain above the average as long as other firms with lower E_i, remain to drag the average down. This means the firm with the highest E_i will continue to see its share increase, but at an increasingly slow rate as the E_i value of the superior firm comes to dominate the weighted average calculation and $E\#$ approaches E_i. If all other firms disappear, the industry and the superior firm become identical, $E\#$ becomes E_i and so df_i/dt falls to zero with $f_i = 100$ per cent.

Assuming the firm with the highest E_i is the firm with the most efficient version of a technology, the increasing dominance of this firm (betokening changing market structure) will simultaneously see the increased diffusion of its technique at the expense of all inferior versions. But in this case there is no change to the variants of technology in use.

In the next section, we look at a model in which a Fisher-style equation is actually derived from economic assumptions to provide the basis for embedding economic selection in other processes of imitation and innovation. The technological trajectory here is at most implicit. So in a subsequent section we consider how purely random factors can 'select' one technological variant over another in giving explicit direction to a technological trajectory. That approach, however, abstracts largely from economic influences and consequences, especially in relation to industry structure. To remedy that, we report on the findings of simulations run by Nelson and Winter. In the final section, we examine a model in which firms may move from one trajectory to another. Here, E_i and $E\#$ comprise two elements of performance and in which the difference terms $(E_i - E\#)$ are influenced by investment in capital embodying new technology and the rate at which firms learn to use new technology. Since the E_i vary over time in this case, the outcome is less predictable than in the straightforward Fisher-style, constant E_i case.

Selection, imitation and innovation along a given technological trajectory

Contrary to what would be predicted by theories resting on assumptions of perfect information and zero adjustment costs, Iwai (1984a) has observed that 'establishments with a remarkably wide range of productivities co-exist in an industry, and this wide

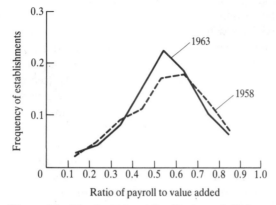

Figure 6.8   The frequency distribution of efficiency in metal stampings industry. (Reprinted with permission from K. Iwai (1984) 'Schumpeterian dynamics: an evolutionary model of innovation and initiation', *Journal of Economic Behaviour and Organization* 5(2), published by Elsevier Science Publishers.)

dispersion of productivities has no tendency to disappear over time' (p. 161). Figure 6.8 (Iwai, 1984a: 161) shows how the ratio of payroll to value added, an index of the reciprocal of labour productivity, is typically distributed. The picture is, of course, a snapshot at a particular moment in time. The question is: What forces are at work over time to generate such a distribution and maintain its general shape?

One answer is to provide an analysis of how innovation continuously disturbs the tendency of imitation to bring about the uniform application of a most efficient technique and hence to provide a picture of an industry continually in disequilibrium. The interesting conclusion is that while innovation is a major force for disturbance, we need impose only very simple assumptions about economic behaviour to generate regularity in the distribution. The analysis in effect addresses the question of diffusion, interpreted widely as the development of a technology along a technological trajectory through a sequence of incremental advances, though no account is taken of the costs of either innovating or imitating.

Consider an industry in which production methods in use can be represented by unit cost levels C_i, where C_n is the unit cost of the best practice method so that:

$$C_n < C_{n-1} < \ldots < C_i < \ldots C_1 \qquad i = 1, \ldots, n$$

The state of the technology in the industry is, at any moment, represented by the relative frequency distribution of the C_i. But over time firms will strive to find better production methods and in the processes will:

1.   Change the shape of the distribution as they abandon a relatively high value of C_i for a lower one, somewhere down to C_n. This is imitation.

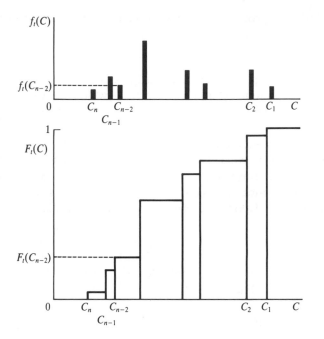

Figure 6.9 The state of technology: relative frequency distribution $f_t(C)$ and cumulative frequency function $F_t(C)$ for industry unit costs. (Reprinted with permission from K. Iwai (1984) 'Schumpeterian dynamics: an evolutionary model of innovation and initiation', *Journal of Economic Behavior and Organization* 5(2), published by Elsevier Science Publishers.)

2. Change the position of the distribution as they introduce entirely new production methods, $C_{n+j}(j = 1, \ldots, N)$, for which $C_{n+j} < C_n$. This is innovation.

It is changes in the state of the technology, so defined, which define the evolution of the technology.

Figure 6.9 illustrates the state of technology, first in terms of a relative frequency distribution (in which $\Sigma f_t(C_i) = 1$) and below it in terms of a cumulative frequency function $F_t(C)$. In the upper diagram, $f_t(C_i)$ represents the relative frequency (fraction of the total) of firms with unit costs of C_i at time t. In the lower diagram, $F_t(C_i)$ represents the fraction of all firms with costs of C_i or less, at t. As a convention, $F_t(C) = 0$ for $C < C_n$ and $F_t(C) = 1$ for $C \geq C_1$. Thus, the fraction firms with costs higher than C_i must be $(1 - F_t(C_i))$.

The analysis incorporates the impact of interfirm growth rate differences, so a description of the changing state of technology has to take account of the changing weight attached to the importance of each technique as changes occur in the size of firms using each technique. To allow for this, the relative frequency function $f_t(C_i)$ is paired with a capacity share function, $s_t(C_i)$. The capacity share function is defined as the fraction of total industry productive capacity which uses production methods with unit costs C_i:

$$s_t(C_i) \equiv k_t(C_i)/K_t$$

Analogously, the cumulative frequency function $F_t(C_i)$ is used in tandem with a cumulative capacity share function of unit costs $S_t(C_i)$, which shows, at t, the proportion of total industry productive capacity using production methods with costs of C_i or less.

A crucial ingredient is a simple account of how firms grow, which in turn is directly related to their investment in new capacity. Iwai assumes the industry is 'perfectly competitive' in the sense that all firms make an identical product and are price takers. When a firm imitates or innovates successfully its costs fall, profits increase and capital investment is stimulated. Taking the firm's profit margin to be:

$$\frac{P(t) - C_i}{P(t)}$$

assume $P(t)$ and C_i are close enough together for the ratio to be accurately approximated by $(\ln P(t) - \ln C)$.[5] Then:

$$\frac{\mathrm{d}k_t(C_i)/\mathrm{d}t}{k_t(C_i)} = \gamma(\ln P(t) - \ln C_i) + X \tag{6.36}$$

where the left-hand side is the rate of capacity growth of a firm with unit costs C_i; γ is a positive constant indicating that the higher the profit rate, the faster (other things being equal) a firm will invest to expand capacity; and $X > 0$ summarises effects on investment such as the interest rate, 'animal spirits', etc.

The analysis now proceeds in three stages. First, the evolution of technology – the changing relative importance of each production method – is traced in the absence of imitation or innovation. Such an evolution occurs because initially lower cost firms grow faster than higher cost firms. Second, the effects of imitation are considered. Third, innovation is introduced.

Stage 1: Economic selection

In the absence of imitation or innovation, the proportion of firms with any given cost level, C_i, remains unchanged. Initially low-cost firms remain as efficient forever as at the outset. Initially high-cost firms are forever inefficient. This means each $f_t(C_i)$ and $F_t(C_i)$ is invariant over time. But the state of technology changes for more efficient firms grow at a faster rate than the less efficient can be expected to grow. The mechanism that makes this so, relatively fast investment by relatively profitable firms, is the basis for an economic selection process which promises, like its biological equivalent, to lead to domination by the most fit.

To see why this is so, consider the capacity share function for firms with costs C_i:

$$s_t(C_i) = \frac{k_t(C_i)}{K_t}$$

Taking natural logs and differentiating with respect to time:

$$\frac{\mathrm{d}\ln s_t(C_i)}{\mathrm{d}t} = \frac{\mathrm{d}\ln k_t(C_i)}{\mathrm{d}t} - \frac{\mathrm{d}\ln K_t}{\mathrm{d}t}$$

or:

$$\frac{\mathrm{d}s_t(C_i)/\mathrm{d}t}{s_t(C_i)} = \frac{\mathrm{d}k_t(C_i)/\mathrm{d}t}{k_t(C_i)} - \frac{\mathrm{d}K_t/\mathrm{d}t}{K_t}$$

Now K_t is the sum of all the different amounts of productive capacity, k_t with different cost levels, C_i, $i = 1, \ldots, n$.

Thus:

$$K_t = \sum_{i=1}^{n} k_t(C_i)$$

and

$$\frac{\mathrm{d}K_t}{\mathrm{d}t} = \sum_{i=1}^{n} \frac{\mathrm{d}k_t(C_i)}{\mathrm{d}t}$$

Thus

$$\frac{\mathrm{d}K_t/\mathrm{d}t}{K_t} = \frac{\mathrm{d}k_t(C_l)/\mathrm{d}t + \ldots + \mathrm{d}k_t(C_n)/\mathrm{d}t}{K_t}$$

$$= \frac{\mathrm{d}k_t(C_1)/\mathrm{d}t}{K_t} + \ldots + \frac{\mathrm{d}k_t(C_n)/\mathrm{d}t}{K_t}$$

$$= \frac{\mathrm{d}k_t(C_1)/\mathrm{d}t}{k_t(C_1)}\, \frac{k_t(C_1)}{K_t} + \ldots + \frac{\mathrm{d}k_t(C_n)/\mathrm{d}t}{k_t(C_n)}\, \frac{k_t(C_n)}{K_t}$$

$$= \sum_{i=1}^{n} \frac{\mathrm{d}k_t(C_i)/\mathrm{d}t}{k_t(C_i)}\, s_t(C_i)$$

This means

$$(\mathrm{d}s_t(C_i)/\mathrm{d}t)/(s_t(C_i)) = [(\mathrm{d}k_t(C_i)/\mathrm{d}t)/k_t(C_i)]$$

$$- \sum_{i=1}^{n} (\mathrm{d}k_t(C_i)/\mathrm{d}t)/(k_t(C_i)\cdot s_t(C_i)$$

Now recalling the hypothesis that:

$$\frac{\mathrm{d}k_t(C_i)/\mathrm{d}t}{\mathrm{d}k_t(C_i)} = \gamma\,(\ln P(t) - \ln C_i) + X$$

and substituting this into the right-hand side of the expression for $(\mathrm{d}s_t(C_i)/\mathrm{d}t)/(s_t(C_i))$, we obtain

$$\frac{ds_t(C_i)/dt}{s_t(C_i)} = -\gamma\,(\ln C_i - \ln C \#(t))$$

where

$$\ln C \#(t) = \sum_{i=1}^{n} s_t(C_i)\ln C_i$$

which is the industry-wide average unit cost at time t. Since $(ds_t(C_i)/dt)/(s_t(C_i))$ shows the growth rate at t in capacity share of production methods with unit costs C_i, this result indicates that the growth rate will be positive when C_i is below the industry average and increasingly fast, the further below it is. The growth rate will be negative (declining share) when C_i is above the average and declining most rapidly the further above the average it is. That at once suggests that the lowest C_i, i.e. C_n, will ultimately come to dominate.

To see that more precisely, consider how average unit costs will fall over time. We already know that $\ln C \#(t)$ is the weighted geometric average of existing unit costs, where the weights are their corresponding capacity shares, $s_t(C_i)$, which of course change through time. To find the growth rate of this average (expected to be negative), we simply differentiate with respect to time:

$$\frac{d\ln C \#(t)}{dt} = \frac{dC \#(t)/dt}{C \#(t)} = \sum_{i=1}^{n} \ln C_i\; ds_t(C_i)/dt$$

Notice that the $\ln C_i$ are retained as constants, since they are fixed throughout by construction, but are multipliers of the $s_t(C_i)$ which do change through time. Using the result that:

$$ds_t(C_i)/dt = -\gamma(\ln C_i - \ln C \#(t))s_t(C_i)$$

we can substitute for $ds_t(C_i)/dt$ and derive (Iwai, 1984b: 329):

$$\frac{dC \#(t)/dt}{C \#(t)} = -\gamma \sum_{i=1}^{n} (\ln C_i - \ln C \#(t))^2 s_t(C_i) \tag{6.37}$$

which is easily recognised as a version of the 'fundamental equation of natural selection' which we have called Fisher's equation (see the previous section). Clearly, the expression on the right-hand side is negative, which confirms industry average unit costs will, in this model, fall over time. The terms covered by the summation sign constitute an expression measuring the (share weighted) variance of the (logarithmic values of) unit costs in the industry. Thus the larger the dispersion of unit costs at any time, the faster industry average unit costs will fall. This conveys the important insight that 'progress', the rate of decline of average unit costs across the industry, is best served by variety. The greater the diversity of experiments (production methods) being tried, the more opportunity there is for the system to 'select' the more successful and to achieve system-wide advance. (This point has been made in the context of a very similar analysis by Metcalfe, 1986.)

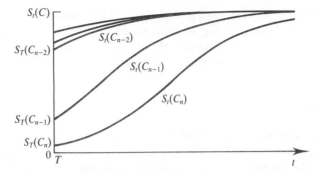

Figure 6.10   The evolution of relative shares for firms with varying unit costs. (Reprinted with permission from K. Iwai (1984) 'Schumpeterian dynamics, Part II: technological progress, firm growth and economic selection', *Journal of Economic Behavior and Organization* 5, published by Elsevier Science Publishers.)

Average costs will continue to fall while the shares of firms without the least-cost technique remain non-negligible. As the share of least-cost firms approaches 100 per cent, $s_t(C_n)$ approaches 1 and all other $s_t(C_i)$, $i \neq n$, become trivially small. That means all terms under the summation can be ignored but for $[(\ln C_n - \ln C \#(t))^2 \cdot s_t(C_n)]$.

However, the effect of the growing share of least-cost firms is also to drive $\ln C \#(t)$ down towards $\ln C_n$, so the variance term in this case approaches zero. Ultimately therefore, average costs stop falling when, but only when the least-cost firms have come to dominate. In brief, the process of capacity growth represents the force which tends to amass productive capacity in the hands of a few technologically advanced firms and leads to the emergence of the 'fittest' as the dominant group.

While the proportion of firms with best practice technology $f_t(C_n)$ remains constant, the share of industry capacity using best practice technology must increase until that share approaches 100 per cent. Iwai shows that the share of industry capacity produced with costs of C_i or less evolves according to the equation:

$$dS_t(C_i)/dt = (\gamma\delta)S_t(C_i)[1 - S_t(C_i)] \quad i = 1, \dots, n$$

which has an explicit solution showing the value of this share at any time t:

$$S_t(C_i) = \{1 + (1 - S_T(C_i) - 1) \exp[(\gamma\delta)(t - T)]\}\{\cdot\}^{-1} \tag{6.38}$$

where $T \leq t$ is a given initial time. In these equations, δ is a parameter representing the difference between average unit costs which lie above and include C_{i-1} and the average of those which include and lie below C_i. A diagram showing how the capacity shares, $S_t(C_i)$ change relative to each other is found in Figure 6.10 (see Iwai, 1984b: Figure 2, p. 331). Notice that the equation:

$$dS_t(C_i)/dt = S_t(C_i)[1 - S_t(C_i)]$$

would in any case generate a sigmoid growth path in $S_t(C_i)$. The product of parameters $(\gamma\delta)$ represents the effect of firms growing at different rates. Through γ, the more sensitive are firm's investment responses to profitability, the more quickly cumulative shares will change. Through δ, the more dispersed unit costs are, the faster shares will change.

Stage 2: Imitation

The patterns of change established under differential growth rates are predictable and clear-cut, although this depends upon investment in new capital working according to a particularly simple mechanism and firms operating as price-takers in conditions where firms might well be expected to influence price. But of central interest here is the robustness of these patterns under imitation and innovation.

Suppose, as does Iwai, that ease of imitation is affected by the number of firms using a given production method and the size of those firms. His simple imitation hypothesis is then that the probability of a firm with unit cost C_i imitating during a period Δt, a production method with unit cost $C < C_i$ will be:

$$\mu s_t(C) \, \Delta t$$

where $\mu > 0$ is an imitation parameter. In words, the probability that a firm will copy a particular production method is proportional to the fraction of industry capacity using that method in that period. The hypothesis leads to the conclusion that in any period Δt, the relative frequency of firms with unit costs of C_i or less $S_t(C_i)$ will change by an amount:

$$(mS_t(C_i)\Delta t) \, (1 - S_t(C_i))$$

The first term represents the probability that any firm with costs higher than C_i would have of imitating any one of the production methods with costs C_i or less, the result of adding $ms_t(C_n)\Delta t$, $ms_t(C_{n-1})\Delta t$ and so on up to $ms_t(C_i)\Delta t$. The second term represents the relative frequency of all firms whose costs actually exceed C_i.

The change in $S_t(C_i)$ can also be written:

$$S_{t+\Delta t}(C_i) - S_t(C_i)$$

creating an equality from them, dividing through by Δt and letting Δt approach zero:

$$dS_t(C_i)/dt = mS_t(C_i)(1 - S_t(C_i)) \tag{6.39}$$

This equation describes the evolution of cumulative shares, on the assumption that all firms retain an identical market share throughout a process of change driven by imitation alone. If differential firm growth is also introduced we must add the effects captured by economic selection in the equation:

$$dS_t(C_i)/dt = (\gamma\delta)S_t(C_i)[1 - S_t(C_i)]$$

The two sets of effects can be added, as long as time in the model is assumed continuous and yield:

$$dS_t(C_i)/dt = (\mu + \gamma\delta)(S_t(C_i)[1 - S_t(C_i)]$$

which implies the cumulative share of productive capacity of costs C_i or less, at t, will be (Iwai, 1984b: 333):

$$S_t(C_i) = \{1 + (1/S_T(C_i) - 1)\exp[(\mu + \gamma\delta)(t - T)]\}^{-1} \qquad (6.40)$$

Again a logistic growth path has emerged, but one in which shares change more rapidly because $(\mu + \gamma\delta) > (\gamma\delta)$ and the most efficient method comes to dominate more quickly.

The evolution traced here springs from tendencies which bear upon best-practice technology use in two different ways. As in the pure differential growth case, firms which start with best-practice technology initially grow faster and share with other firms, allowing best practice to start becoming more dominant.

But here, the growth of best-practice firms attracts the attention of potential imitators and the larger the most efficient firms become, the greater the probability they will be imitated. This 'dissipates the advantage of low cost production methods among all firms' (Iwai, 1984b: 334). This time the proportion of firms with lowest costs, $F_t(C_n)$, grows as well. In the final analysis, the most efficient production method comes to dominate but is widely used by all firms, not used exclusively by those lucky enough to have known about it at the outset. Thus: 'The human force of imitation thus has the power to overcome the blind force of economic selection,' (Iwai, 1984b: 335)

What Iwai means by this is that imitation – the 'Lamarckian' mechanism – allows the initially 'unfit' to be able to survive by acquiring the characteristics of other firms observed to be doing better. By imitation, a human activity involving learning, the initially 'unfit' can become 'fit' (i.e. low-cost producers) and survive. This contrasts with a 'Darwinian' vision in which the initially 'unfit' remain unfit and lose out, ultimately failing to survive, as the 'fit' remaining fit, come to dominate.

In each case, diversity remains only as long as these processes work themselves out and in the limiting case where imitation is very easy because information about best practice is easy to obtain, it is possible to argue that the neoclassical vision of uniformly efficient firms, all using best practice, might not be a bad approximation after all. A principal source of longer term diversity might be either information imperfection itself, or difficulties firms encounter in putting information effectively to work in their own enterprises: 'imitation costs'. But for Iwai, the key to persistent diversity again lies in innovation.

Stage 3: Innovation

To consider the impact of innovation, Iwai retains the capacity growth rule (or 'investment function'), and the imitation hypothesis, but now brings in a potential cost-reduction function, $C(t) = e^{-\lambda t}$, in which λ represents the potential impact of invention on cost reduction. His innovation hypothesis is that every firm has an equal and constant probability v of successful innovation at every point in time. Size does not provide the firm with any advantage in the probability of its innovative success.

Under these assumptions, the state of technology changes over time according to the equations:

$$dS_t^*(C)/dt = (\mu + \delta\gamma)(S_t^*(C)(1 - S_t(C)) + v(1 - S_t^*(C)) \qquad (6.41)$$

$$dF_t^*(C)/dt = \mu S_t^*(C)(1 - F_t^*(C)) + v(1 - F_t^*(C) \qquad (6.42)$$

where the stars indicate we are dealing with expected or average values of the functions over time.

These equations can be solved explicitly to yield expressions for S_t^* and F_t^*, for all t and C_i, determining the state of technology over time. These expressions can be recast as functions of the cost gap, $Z \equiv \ln C_i - \ln C(t)$, where $C(t)$ is the cost level associated with the most recent innovation.

In the long run, it turns out (under Iwai's assumptions) that the development of an industry's technology can be characterised by a **statistically stable distribution of cost gaps**; the cumulative frequency distribution of the cost gaps is found to have a sigmoid form. The existence of the cost gaps reflects the fact that the industry is in technological disequilibrium, in the sense that most firms are at any one moment catching up with best practice. The important general point is that the dispersion (once established at some level as a long-term average) never disappears; a spectrum of productive methods with diverse unit costs remains forever in the industry.

The long-run average density of cost gaps generated here constitutes a distribution whose shape corresponds quite closely to the empirically based distributions of productivities noted earlier. The analysis thus provides one possible theoretical story to support an important empirical observation which is often ignored by economic theory.

To make interindustry comparisons, we also want to know the impact on the state of technology of variations in the forces of economic selection ($\delta\gamma$), imitation (μ), innovation (v) and invention (λ). Again, given the assumptions used by Iwai, it can be shown that increases in $\delta\gamma$, μ and v tend to reduce the dispersion among cost gaps, while an increase in λ tends to widen it (1984b: 341–2).

There is an interesting point of comparison here with the Dasgupta–Stiglitz analysis of R&D performed in a game-theoretic framework. There, we discovered that in industries with a relatively high elasticity of cost reduction with respect to innovation, we should expect R&D intensity to be greatest. Here, that elasiticity is represented by λ. Iwai has no account of R&D expenditures, but putting the two analyses together, the prediction emerges that in industries with the highest R&D: sales ratios, we should also expect to find the widest disparities, other things being equal between average and best-practice technology.

In Iwai's story, innovation alone explains the persistence of the dispersion; because of innovation operating continuously over time new sources of dispersion are always being born. The forces of economic selection and imitation can thus be thwarted. Moreover, the exact form of the distribution of cost gaps as a long-run average, can be found from knowledge of the parameters embodied in the hypotheses about capacity expansion, imitation, innovation and invention.

But Iwai's picture is also rather stark. First, dispersion could persist without innovation as long as best-practice firms grew relatively slowly and less-efficient firms failed to imitate successfully.

Second, the patterns depicted look as if they might depend upon the parameters being uniform across the industry and over time. Simulation exercises reported later suggest however this suspicion is ill-founded.

Third and more worryingly, the investment mechanism central to the whole mechanism of firm growth is very crudely modelled and there is no place in the analysis for learning effects beyond allowing firms to recognise that more efficient production techniques exist elsewhere.

Fourth, any notion of how prices are determined or fifth how industry-wide output grows is absent from the model. Metcalfe (1981) contains an attempt to respond to that sort of challenge.

Market structure and evolving technology

Changes in industry structure are at best left implicit in the Iwai analysis, but the interdependence between structure and innovation, so clearly indentified in the static analysis of Dasgupta and Stiglitz, are brought to the fore in Nelson and Winter (1982) Chapters 12–14.

In what we regard as a 'rock bottom' evolutionary model, Nelson and Winter (1982: 283–5) consider a 'science-based' industry, with exogenously driven productivity growth; assume all firms make an identical product and choose output as their conduct variable. Capital in any period is the result of previous periods' investment decisions and output is determined in each firm as the product of its capital stock and the (average capital) productivity of the technique it uses. Industry output is the sum of individual firms' outputs and price is determined by industry outputs given a standard market-demand function. Each firm's investment in capital reflects first, the need to make good depreciation, and secondly the joint influence of three factors on desired expansion or contraction. Investment is non-decreasing in the firm's price–cost margin (a measure of its market power) and non-increasing in its market share; the greater its market share, the more the firm fears further expansion will spoil its market by reducing total sales revenue. Overall profitability constrains the firm's ability to finance its investment.

The investment function is the major channel for achieving intertemporal adjustment within the industry. Given the factors which influence investment, it is clear that interfirm differences in investment-determined capacity and output growth will reflect interfirm variations in the influence of R&D outlays on costs and profits. The route by which R&D increases productivity is characterised by the two-stage random process described in Chapter 5.

It is here that we find the evolutionary essence of the model. 'Firms do not know, *ex ante*, whether it pays to try to be an innovator or an imitator, or what levels of R&D expenditure might be appropriate. Indeed, the answer to this question for any single firm depends on the choices made by other firms, and reality does not contain any provisions for firms to test out their policies before adopting them.' Nelson and Winter, 1982: 286).

Simulations

In the first set of simulations, ten different sets of initial conditions are explored. There are two financing regimes: under an 'easy-money' assumption, firms can borrow up to 2.5 times their net profits; under a 'tight-money' regime, borrowings are limited to a matching of their profits. Each regime is applied to five different market-structure assumptions defined by the number of (equal-sized) firms: two, four, eight, sixteen and thirty-two firms. All start with the same level of productivity; half spend on R&D for both innovation and imitation; half spend only on imitative R&D. The larger the number of firms, the larger is the initial capital stock and the lower the price.

Nelson and Winter can now ask a question not broached by Iwai, for whom the number of firms in the industry was arbitrary: How does the industry structure influence productivity-related performance? They find that best-practice productivity is insensitive to industry structure (and to total industry innovative R&D), largely because, in this case, the driving force of technological advance is exogenously determined; this will be contrasted with the endogenous case below. On the other hand, average productivity is markedly lower when industry structure is more fragmented and consequently the gap between average productivity and best-practice (the focus of Iwai's work) is greater too. It is not, as the Schumpeterian argument would have it, that best-practice technology evolves more slowly when there are many firms. Rather, the gap is wider because with larger numbers of firms, capital is more fragmented, reducing the scope for applying individual successes.

The other side of the story is to ask what happens to industry structure itself as the technology evolves. Initially concentrated industries remain concentrated; less concentrated industries become more so. The main reason for this is that R&D in innovation turns out on average to be unprofitable in the case considered here. Concentration increases as unsuccessful innovators decline. The role of failure in innovation cannot be ignored. In the most ambitious evolutionary model we consider in the final section, it will again be found that innovation can impose penalties from which firms may never recover.

In a second set of simulations, Nelson and Winter explore the implications of allowing critical parameters to vary. We focus here on varying the pace at which productivity rises and the difficulty of imitation. Comparing here just the four and sixteen firm cases, the more concentrated industry showed little change in relative firm shares whatever parameter settings were chosen, mainly because all of them had numerous R&D successes. But in the sixteen firm industry, concentration always increased more over time when productivity growth was relatively high, and if imitation was relatively difficult.

The final simulation results cited here replace the assumption of exogenously driven productivity growth with the cumulative-technology case, in which innovative R&D success for a firm is centred on its existing technique. As in the previous case, relatively fast innovation combined with hard imitation tends to lead to increasing industry concentration. But in this case, best-practice productivity and industry-average productivity are both influenced negatively by what Nelson and Winter call 'aggressive competitive behaviour'. What they mean is that once success brings a firm a degree of growth, it actively chooses to press its advantage by investing heavily in new capacity. The alternative would be to exercise restraint in expanding. In a variety of situations, the effect of aggressive competitive behaviour is to undermine the position of innovators. The reason for this is that imitation can bring an imitator a productivity level as high as that of an innovator. But because the imitator has not incurred innovative R&D costs, it enjoys higher profit. With this profit, it can expand aggressively if it wishes, cutting innovators' market share and, with it, the capacity to undertake R&D on a scale which could let them hit back. The 'fast second' strategy thus allows a successful imitator to outgrow all of the firms around it.

The negative impact of this strategy on innovative R&D has limited influence on industry-best practice in science-based industries where exogenous forces are constantly forcing the frontiers of productivity achievement forward. But in cumulative technology cases, both best practice and average productivity are lower when firms are aggressively competitive than when they exercise restraint.

Moving on to a new trajectory: implications for industry productivity growth and the pattern of diffusion

The most radical and Schumpeterian of the cases occurs when a new technological trajectory becomes available to an industry and firms must make decisions about when to abandon an existing trajectory and move on to the new one. The implications of this question are considered along lines established by Silverberg, Dosi and Orsenigo (1988).

Intractable uncertainty arises in the analysis from the fact that when the new technology becomes available, the benefits from adopting it depend on the speed at which a firm learns to use it effectively and this cannot be known in advance. Path dependence arises from the fact that once one or more firms have started to adopt the new technology, other firms face changed prospects compared with those which existed in any previous period. In particular, spill-over effects (learning 'leaks') from first movers can enhance the net benefits enjoyed by late-comers. So when and whether a firm adopts depends upon what other firms have already done. Heterogeneity could arise from many sources in the model, but interest is focused on interfirm variation in expectations with respect to the development potential of the new technology, rivals' reactions and the prospects of appropriating quasi-rents.

The factors underlying intractable uncertainty ensure individual decision-makers act with an essential element of 'blindness' and the actual paths of development observed depend for their initial impetus and for the specifics of their subsequent evolution upon the heterogeneity among firms. If every firm held identical views about the future, no firm would switch to the new technology at all. The views they hold determines in part the path that then evolves. Analysis of patterns at the system level proceeds by observing how each individual firms, acts within the evolving industrial framework, to whose development it is simultaneously contributing. System-level patterns over time are derived by observing how the aggregate of firms' actions changes at each successive moment in history. But the acts of each firm at any moment are influenced by its position relative to the rest of the population (as it perceives it) in the previous period. This, of course, only serves to change the characteristics of the population in this period and induce further changes at the individual level.

It is this which gives the Silverberg, Dosi and Orsenigo model its fundamental evolutionary character. System-level (population average) characteristics are explicitly generated from the interactive behaviour of individual members of the population acting blindly under fundamental uncertainty. This in turn gives an evolutionary structure to the economic history generated here, a history which basically tells how a new technology diffuses through an industry. Little is said about market structure, but the data generated would allow that to be traced if we wished. It is endogenous, in line with the thrust of this chapter.

The starting point of the model is a form of the Fisher equation:

$$df_i/dt = \alpha(E_i - E\#)f_i \quad i = 1, \ldots n; \alpha > 0$$

in which $E_i = -\ln P_i - dd_i$, and $E\# = \Sigma f_i E_i$, where the subscript i indicates the identity of the firm, P is price and dd the current delay or lag in delivering orders. Price and delivery lag are thus taken as the measures of fitness or competitiveness in this case.

If expanded, the equation reads:

$$df_i/dt = \alpha[(-\ln P_i - \Sigma f_i \ln P_i) + (-dd_i - \Sigma f_i dd_i)]f_i$$
$$= \alpha[(-\ln P_i - P\#) + (-dd_i - dd\#)]f_i \quad (6.43)$$

where variables modified with a '#' are share-weighted averages across the industry. If the logarithms of price reflects a principal focus on relative price ratios such as (P_i/P_j), the logarithm of which is $\ln P_i - \ln P_j$. For E_i to exceed $E\#$ (an indication that the firm is relatively competitive), P_i and dd_i must lie below the industry averages. When E_i exceeds $E\#$, the market share of firm i grows. If P_i and dd_i are both above industry-average levels, $E\#$ exceeds E_i and the firm's market share falls.

If all the E_i were constant, the industry would ultimately become dominated by the firm with the lowest E_i value. But the model is designed to allow the E_i to change over time in complex ways in response to the strategies of the firms and feedbacks from the rest of the system. Thus the evolution of market structure is determined by the n Fisher equations:

$$df_1/dt = \alpha(E_1 - E\#)f_1$$
$$df_2/dt = \alpha(E_2 - E\#)f_2 \quad (6.44)$$
$$\vdots$$
$$df_n/dt = \alpha(E_n - E\#)f_n$$

all operating simultaneously to codetermine period-by-period changes in market shares $f_1, f_2, \ldots, f_n$. But the outcome is unpredictable at the outset and will depend upon how each of the E_i changes in relation to changes in $E\#$, to which, of course, changes in all the E_i contribute.

Letting lower case p stand for the logarithm of price, Silverberg, Dasi and Orsenigo propose that price changes according to the equation:

$$\mathrm{d}p_i/\mathrm{d}t = \beta(p_{ci} - p_i) + \gamma(E_i - E\#) \tag{6.45}$$

where p_{ci} is firm i's mark-up price, based on its unit costs. The greater the monopoly power of firm i within the prevailing structure of the industry, the higher p_{ci} may be assumed to be and the first part of the equation says that the further below this level a firm's current price, the faster the price will rise. On the other hand, the higher production costs are, the higher p_i becomes, the less competitive the firm's price and once it rises above the average price for the industry, the relative price element of $(E_i - E\#)$ will become negative and tend to drive p_i down.

Firm i's **delivery delay**, dd_i, will rise if output increases more slowly than the stock of unsatisfied orders which reflects importantly the growth rate of demand-set exogenously. If this happens, dd_i will ultimately rise above the industry average, the firm's market share will fall and the rate at which new orders arrive will slow. If firms are to avoid loss of market share through lack of competitiveness on delivery dates, they must raise output. In this model, output is simply the product of the existing capital stock K_i and its level of capacity utilisation, u_i:

$$Q_i = u_i K_i \tag{6.46}$$

The further behind an 'industry-wide standard level' a firm is with its deliveries, the faster u_i is assumed to adjust upwards. But there is clearly a limit to the output increases which can be achieved by working the existing plant harder and output can be raised on a sustained basis only by increasing the capital stock.

We have so far learned that in the Silverberg, Dosi and Orsenigo vision, the dynamics of changing market share will be driven partly by interfirm variation in unit production costs (according to Iwai), reflected in prices and also by the rate at which the capital stock expands.

Net investment in Silverberg, Dosi and Orsenigo's terms is the difference in any period between total capital installed and the quantity of equipment scrapped. They hypothesise that the state of business confidence or pessimism primarily determines the rate of net investment, but that net investment, per period will be faster the greater the gap between actual and desired levels of capacity utilisation. All capital installed in period t is vintage t capital. Scrapping rates are determined by the application of a payback rule, which indicates the 'useful life' of a machine. Total capital investment in a period is derived arithmetrically from knowledge of the other two elements.

The investment model provides a foundation for deriving unit operating costs, $C_i(t)$, which comprise prime and overhead costs. **Prime** unit costs are the product of the nominal wage and the average quantity of labour used per unit of output. Labour used per unit of output varies with the vintage of capital with which labour is employed

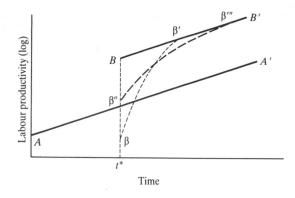

Figure 6.11 Labour productivity growth paths for old and new technology.

and for each vintage t' the labour-output coefficient is denoted $a_i(t')$. Weighting each coefficient by the proportion of a firm's capital investment in that vintage, the average labour used per unit of output is then calculated as a weighted average over all vintages still in use, and denoted a_i. Changes in the average reflect changes in the weights of different vintages as old (high labour output) machines are replaced by new (low labour output) equipment. Clearly, a_i will fall over time. Unit **overhead** costs are set to be proportional to prime costs. Average unit costs will decline while inputs per unit of output fall more quickly than nominal wages rise.

The lower $a_i(t')$, the higher (average) labour productivity associated with that vintage t' will be and the lower unit costs will become for each vintage compared with previous vintages. This will be true however fast wages rise, as long as labour working with all vintages is paid the same wage at any given time. Each vintage has benefits from an increment in technical advance and this advance will be incorporated automatically in the aggregate capital stock as the continual decline in production costs draws scrapping dates forward and new, higher productivity capital replaces old lower productivity machines. The process will be hastened when net investment is faster. What we may now ask is what will happen when firms are confronted with an entirely new technology.

The choice faced by firms is illustrated in Figure 6.11. Until t^*, firms using best-practice techniques in an existing technology enjoy labour-productivity growth following the path AA', which represents a technological trajectory. At t^* a new technology becomes available which, if used with maximum effectiveness, allows labour productivity to rise along the trajectory BB'. But a technology is used to maximum effect only when labour has acquired the specific expertise and experience necessary to operate the equipment to its full potential. Firms are assumed to have done this along AA', and in this sense the existing technology is mature. But for the new technology, many skills have yet to be acquired in operating the innovatory equipment, so realised productivity will follow a path more like $\beta\beta'$, or $\beta''\beta'''$, full potential productivity at any moment adjusted for the skill level, $SKL_i(t)$, where $0 < SKL_i(t) < 1$.

Now assume that firms do not know how fast potential labour productivity will grow along the new trajectory, nor how quickly their skills in using the new technology will increase, i.e. their **learning rate**. But assume firms know the current productivity they could realise with the new technology (full-potential productivity times skill level) and hence current unit operating costs with the new technology and a basis for making investment decisions.

To plot the dynamics of the system, assumptions must be made about how fast skills will grow and about the expectations firms have about future developments.

Firms are assumed to have a level of skill derived from a publicly available base of knowledge SKL_{pub}, and from internally generated learning SKL_{int}. Even if a firm has not yet adopted the new technology, it will have the generally available skill base and that even non-adopters acquire new skills and expertise at the rate publicly available knowledge grows as knowledge leaks from users and elsewhere. Public knowledge increases at a rate governed by the difference between average internal skill level and the existing level of public knowledge. The higher the average base of internal skill compared to public knowledge, the faster public knowledge rises.

If a firm has already adopted, it will know some things other firms do not, so that for firm i:

$$SKL_i = SKL_{int,i} + SKL_{pub} > SKL_{pub}; \quad 0 < SKL_i < 1 \qquad (6.47)$$

SKL_{pub} provides a floor level of skill to which internal learning adds. Internal learning of course occurs only if the firm produces with the new technology. The notion of learning by doing is captured by writing:

$$dSKL_{int,i}/dt = \sigma[Q_i(t)/Q_{ci}(t) + k)]\, SKL_{int,i}(1 - SKL_{int,i}) \qquad (6.48)$$

where $Q_i(t)$ is current production at t, $Q_{ci}(t)$ cumulative production at t using the new technology, and k is a constant proportional to the capital stock. The same equation can be written:

$$\frac{dSKL_{int,i}/dt}{SKL_{int,i}(t)} = \sigma[Q_i(t)/(Q_{ci}(t) + k)]\,(1 - SKL_{int,i}(t)) \qquad (6.49)$$

which makes clear that the proportional growth rate of internally generated skills will, for any current rate of output, be slower, the greater the cumulative output already produced and, as also reflected in $[(1 - SKL_{int,i})$, the more learning already done. Similarly, skills will be growing proportionately more slowly, the greater the capital stock already invested (and learned from) in the new technology and the smaller σ, which represents a speed of learning effect.

The first form of the learning equation implies that with the passage of time $SKL_{int,i}(t)$ rises at a declining rate.[6] To see this, Note 5 (at the end of this chapter) provides a simple example of how the first part of the expression on the right-hand side generates a function which has the standard shape for a learning curve. But this effect is also modified by the term $SKL_{int,i}(1 - SKL_{int,i})$ Interpretation of the impact of this term is eased by recognising that equations of the form:

$$dx(t)/dt = b \cdot x(t) [1 - x(t)]$$

can be represented by a graph for $x(t)$ which is a 'logistic growth curve'. Here the specific version of that general form is:

$$dSKL_{int,i}/dt = \sigma \, SKL_{int,i}(t) [1 - SKL_{int,i}(t)]$$

but adjusted by the inclusion of the term $[Q_i(t)/(Q_{ci}(t) + k)]$, which itself varies with time. The net effect of these two influences is for $SKL_{int,i}(t)$ to rise over time, but at a declining rate. The numerical example of Note 5 (at the end of this chapter) is extended in Note 6 (at the end of this chapter) to illustrate this.[7]

Now combine this mechanism with an account of expectations. To do this, let C_1 and C_2 represent respectively unit costs under the old and new technologies. Then make the following assumptions.

Each firm knows what its current costs with the new technology, C_2/SKL_i, would be. Since realised productivity is a *fraction* SKL_i of potential productivity, realised unit costs must be a multiple $(1/SKL_i)$ of the unit costs associated with the technology used to its full potential (e.g. for a firm with skill level $SKL_i = 0.25$, four times as many inputs will be used per unit of output than when the technology is mature and so unit costs will be $(1/0.25) =$ four times as high.) No firm knows the current values of $SKL_i(t)$ and potential productivity separately nor their prospective growth rates.

The firm's judgements about the future development of costs can be captured in the notion of an *anticipation bonus*, X_i, which exceeds unity in value while the firm believes there is any scope for increasing productivity in future. To reflect the expected improvement, C_2 is divided by X_i. X_i is higher: the greater the expected development potential of the new technology; the greater perceived appropriation prospects (i.e. the greater are anticipated internal learning levels); the less likely it is believed that rivals will respond.

The price per unit of capital embodying new technology, P_{K2}, is initially greater than the old, P_{K1} – but P_{K2} falls over time.

Unit operating costs of the new technology, C_2, are lower than those of the old, C_1, when each is working at maximum potential efficiency.

Firms now compare the capital purchase price differentials and the difference between the unit cost of operating the old technology and that of the new technology adjusted for skill level and anticipation bonus. They invest if:

$$\frac{P_{K2} - P_{K1}}{C_1 - (C_2/SKL_i \cdot X_i)} \leqslant b_i$$

where b_i is the required pay-back period chosen by firm i. Thus, suppose $P_2 = 150 > P_1 = 100$, $C_1 = 80 > C_2 = 40$, $SKL_i = 0.3$ and $b_i = 10$ (periods). Then for a firm to invest in new technology capital, X_i must take a value of at least

1.67, i.e. the firm must evaluate the productivity prospects of new technology at a level 67 per cent above its current realised value. If $X_i = 2$, the left-hand side becomes 3.85, so the condition is satisfied with a wide margin: the firm expects investing in a unit of the new technology to pay for itself in 3.85, periods as against its target of 10. If all firms adopt similar pay-back criteria, this indicates that firms with the most optimistic expectations about the new technology, highest X_i, will invest first and probably most. Firms for which $X_i < 1.67$ would not invest at all, at this point.

However, this is a dynamic model. As time passes P_{K2} falls, so that even if nothing else changed, firms with $X_i < 1.67$ would gradually adopt. But what is essential is that for every firm SKL_i will rise with the passage of time. Even if they have not adopted, firms still using the old technology learn about the new one from the experience of early adopters. As SKL_i rises, for given X_i, the left-hand side falls, so again more firms now become adopters.

Simulations

The properties of the diffusion process are explored by allowing certain parameters characterising the system to vary, then simulating the evolution of the system with computerised experimental runs. For the sort of model Silverberg, Dosi and Orsenigo describe, comprising a set of differential-difference equations with age-dependent effects[8], there is little choice but to proceed in this way since in general little is known about the mathematical properties of such systems. The problem is which parameters should be varied and what values should be allowed to take? The initial number of firms in the industry is itself a parameter and for each firm in every experiment all parameters can be allowed to vary. To throw light upon the properties of the system, however, we would like to find parameters and give different values to them such that differences in outcome are thrown up which, because of the choices made, indicate something worthwhile about how it works.

Silver, Dosi and Orsenigo's choice is to characterise initial interfirm heterogeneity solely by variations in X_i. Among firms, this ranges between values of 1.0 and 3.33, clustering around 1.33. For comparative purposes over a series of three experiments, all other parameters are applied uniformly to all firms.

In all experiments, market demand and nominal wage growth are exogenously fixed and if operated to their full potential, both advance steadily at a rate which raises productivity at a constant rate. The new technology is assumed potentially 100 per cent more efficient. The industry initially has ten firms, all enjoying an equal market share.

Interfirm variations in X_i at the outset (with at least one X_i 'high enough') ensures at least one firm chooses to adopt the new technology immediately. This sets in motion the dynamics of the diffusion of the new technology. If all firms were identical and had the same X_i, Silverberg, Dosi and Orsenigo's simulations predict no firm would ever innovate. Not all of the interconnected mechanisms are spelled out by Silverberg, Dosi and Orsenigo, but the following are worth noting:

1. On introducing new technology, average productivity (across all vintages of both technologies) for any firm tends to dip initially. This is because all firms have limited skills at the outset, which means realised productivity with new-technology capital will often be relatively low.This effect is likely to be most marked for first movers, who adopt when skill levels are at their lowest. Industry average productivity growth will also tend to be temporarily slowed, compared with the rate which could have been achieved by keeping to the old technology. First, movers often find their average productivity below industry average. Notice: initially low realised productivity is not a discouragement to first movers because as their high X_i attest they expect (with greater optimism than other firms) to make gains in future.

2. As the experience of early adopters increases their internal skills, their average realised productivity starts to rise. But as they continue to invest in new capital, industry average productivity also rises. Because the industry average is weighed down by the performance of non-adopters, fast-learning early adopters see their average productivity rise above the industry average.

3. As the experience of early adopters leaks out, an increasingly high productivity platform is created off which later adopters can launch themselves. For them too there will be costs incurred as they learn by doing and, to catch up the first movers, they must do as much production as early adopters so their internal learning rate can gather momentum. But if the scope for learning by first movers is limited and much publicly available knowledge has leaked out, later adopters sometimes catch up.

4. The movements in productivity noted in (2) and (3) above influence competitiveness directly, by affecting the unit-cost level of firms and indirectly though delivery lags. When a firm's productivity falls below the industry average, its unit costs will rise above the industry average which, with a given mark-up, will tend to drive its price above the industry average. At the same time, its delivery delays may lengthen relative to industry average. These influences will cause first movers to lose market share.

5. Whether first movers can regain market share depends on how fast their productivity rises relative to the industry average. For given learning effects, first movers' productivity gains will be most rapid if they introduce new-technology capital quickly to replace the old. New-technology capital will progressively replace the old anyway; that is the message of the vintage model. Net expansion in new technology capital will be fastest when existing levels of capacity utilisation exceed the desired level. This is most likely to be the case when delivery lags lengthen relative to the industry average as initially for first movers. As first movers speed up investment in new-technology capital, their initial loss of competitiveness could be reversed.

6. The firm's competitiveness relative to the industry average is critical for market share. The central result of Silverberg, Dosi and Orsenigo's simulations is that this will depend importantly on the rate of internal learning. To see this, they allow σ to take a low and a high value. When σ is low, first movers, whose high

X_i indicates they expected to do well, actually bear relatively heavy development (learning) costs, lose market share and at the end of the day have a smaller market share than almost all other firms. The reason is that other firms with lower X_i and later adoption dates, start from a higher base of skills before the first movers have been able to appropriate the gains which would have accrued to their innovating activity if their rivals had persisted with the older technology. When internal learning is slow (and especially if 'leaks' are substantial), it pays to wait. But none of the firms knew this would be the case in advance.

When σ is high, the optimistic expectations of first movers are borne out by their actual experience. This is reinforced, the fewer leaks there are into public learning. Fast learning quickly drives down their unit costs, increases profits, releasing financing constraints on investment and allowing them to raise output, cut delivery delays and generally become more competitive. Firms which delay entry never catch up and mostly retain only their initial share in what is, however, a growing market. Again, none of the firms knew in advance that this would happen.

7. What makes the model distinctively evolutionary is that firms do not know in advance whether they will learn quickly or slowly and whether it will pay in the long run to have been a first mover or to have waited. Firms adopt early because they believe they can benefit more than their rivals, but they cannot know that in advance. They may not turn out to have been right.

In the above paragraphs, we have tried to capture some of the forces of change at work in determining the evolving structure of the industry. This reveals the pattern of change underlying diffusion, but has not indicated what the diffusion curve for the new technology might look like. This is easily derived. One might observe either the percentage of firms which have adopted the market share of adopters or, perhaps most importantly, the proportion of overall productive capacity embodied in the new technology. In each case the curve is S-shaped. As a measure of the speed of diffusion, Silverberg, Dosi and Orsenigo look at the time taken for the new technology to increase its share in total capacity from 10 per cent to 90 per cent and find that this increases, but at a decreasing rate with increases in the rates of internal and public knowledge accumulation.

The appeal of the model is that the simulations lay bare how the structure of the industry evolves. But the ultimate messages of the exercise are:

1. Heterogeneity (represented here by variation in X_i) is required to get the diffusion process underway.
2. The actual firms which maximise market share in the long run vary with the internal learning rate assumed, relative to the initial structure of expectations.
3. Faster internal and public skill acquisition speeds diffusion along a sigmoid path.

Message (1) suggests that analysis which ignores interfirm diversity will not be able to focus on the trigger for the diffusion process. On the other hand, Silverberg, Dosi and Orsenigo do not report on the implications of diversity deriving from sources other than X_i, nor upon allowing the variation among X_i to change.

Message (2) says that final outcomes relating to who wins and who loses will always be unpredictable if firms do not know how quickly they will learn. This is an important lesson for individual firms in the competition, although the blow might be softened if some firms start with a larger relevant knowledge base than others, giving them a first-mover advantage, and some or all firms know from other experience how fast they are likely to learn. Such information will be increasingly unreliable, the more 'removed' from existing technology the new one is.

But notice what message (3) does not say. Silverberg, Dosi and Orsenigo offer no analysis of the kind found in Nelson and Winter, in which indices of market structure are calculated. Of course, they in principle could be, but is conceivable that whether first movers win or lose, the final market structure over all firms could be quite similar. What determines this and how that relates to the diffusion rate, we are not told.

Message (3) says that despite the wide variation in possible patterns of structural change, the comforting sigmoid diffusion path is likely to emerge. But it would be nice to know how robust that result is to admitting variation in other parameters and/or to allowing the X_i, for example, themselves to evolve. Since Silverberg, Dosi and Orsenigo focus on a process innovation and set demand growth at an exogenously constant rate, it is also unclear how well this result would stand up to product innovation over the new trajectory.

Appendix

Game theory: an introductory sketch

This appendix is meant to be no more than the briefest introduction to the large and complex body of technical literature on game theory, but it is designed to be sufficient to allow readers to make sense of arguments in the text which rely on this style of analysis. For a more extensive but accessible introduction, readers are recommended to consult Rasmusen (1989), to which this sketch owes a considerable debt. Bacharach (1976) is another readable introduction. Standard works of reference in the area include von Neumann and Morgenstern (1944), Luce and Raiffa (1957) and Shubik (1982). Particularly useful in relation to oligopoloy analysis are Friedman (1977), Tirole (1988) especially Chapter 11, Fudenberg and Tirole (1989).

First define common terms found in setting up a game-theoretic analysis. An **action** by player i, denoted a_i, is a choice 'he' ('she' or 'they', since players can be collectives and groups of many kinds) can make. The set from which choices may be made is the **action set**, A_i. A player's strategy, s_i is a rule which tells what action to choose at any point in the game, given his/her information set. A strategy is a complete set of instructions which tells a player what to do at every moment in the game. Strategies may be **pure** or **mixed**. A pure strategy is a choice of a given action with certainty (e.g produce 100 cars per day). A mixed strategy is one in which the player applies

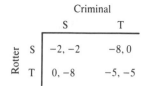

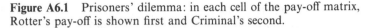

Figure A6.1 Prisoners' dilemma: in each cell of the pay-off matrix, Rotter's pay-off is shown first and Criminal's second.

a randomising rule such as 'produce 100 units per day with a probability of 0.7 and 0 units with a probability of 0.3'. The pay-off to player i, Π_i, is the utility or expected utility which he/she receives after all players have chosen and played out their strategies. It is a function of the ordered set of strategies of all the players, the strategy combination $s = (s_1, \ldots s_n)$.

Given the strategies and pay-offs of all players, the game has a structure, in relation to which it is possible to ask what the outcome of the game will be. To illustrate, consider an example of what is called the **normal-form** representation of a game between two players.[9] Criminal (C) and Rotter (R) have strategies which we will, for the moment, simply label S and T. The pay-off to any strategy followed by C depends on that followed by R, and *vice versa*. If R follows strategy S, his payoff is -2 if C also follows S and -8 if C follows T. In the normal-form matrix shown in Figure A6.1, these are the numbers shown as the first of the pair in the top left cell and the first in the top right. Numbers showing the pay-off to Rotter always come first, so the numbers 0 and -5 in the lower row show Rotter's pay-offs from strategy T if Criminal chose, respectively, S and T. Numbers showing Criminal's pay-offs are always shown second in any pair. So, looking at the first column, C's pay-off from S is -2 when R also chooses S, and -8 when R chooses T. C's pay-offs from T are 0 and -5.

The question now is: Can we predict which strategies each player will chosse? To answer that question, we seek a **game theory equilibrium**, defined as a strategy combination, $s^* = (s_1^*, \ldots, s_n^*)$, comprising a best strategy for each of the players in the game. Given the way in which game theory equilibrium has been defined, notice first that the equilibrium itself comprises a set of rules – the players' strategies. Second, the sense in which those strategies can be defined as best strategies depends on the type of **solution concept** adopted. The solution concept is, in essence, the central organising device in game theory: it is itself a rule that defines an equilibrium. Given all the sets of strategies available to each player, and all the pay-offs generated by their interactions, the solution concept is a rule which determines, definitionally, when some particular strategy combination (or combinations) may be viewed as constituting an equilibrium.

The most obvious example of a solution concept is the **dominant strategy equilibrium**. In this case, the strategy combination comprises each player's **dominant stategy**, where a dominant strategy is in turn defined to be the strictly best response to any strategies the other players might choose. This can be illustrated by reference to our example. Starting (arbitrarily) with Rotter, suppose he picks stategy *S*. Then Criminal's best response is *T*, since $0 > -2$. Criminal would again respond with *T* if Rotter himself picked *T*. So whatever choice Rotter made, *T* would be the dominant, and *S* the dominated strategy for Criminal. Turning now to Criminal, if he chose *S*, Rotter's best response would be *T* $(0 > -2)$ and if he chose *T*, Rotter would again do best to pick *T* himself (-5 being less negative than -8). Clearly, *T* is the dominant strategy for both Criminal and Rotter, so *T, T* is the dominant strategy equilibrium.

There are several points worth noting about this particular example. First, it illustrates what is known as the **sure-thing principle** – a principle of rational choice that requires that if one action is preferable to another in every state of the world, that is the one which should be chosen. If the players are regarded as rational, they will also regard each other as rational. Knowing all the pay-offs, Rotter knows that whatever he chooses, Criminal will pick *T* and so can reject the possibility that Criminal might choose *S*. Rotter is thus driven to choose his own strategy on the assumption that Criminal will pick *T*. An identical argument works analogously for Criminal. Second, while *T, T* is an equilibrium of the game, it appears to be a paradoxical one. If the players had chosen *S, S* instead of *T, T*, both would have done better and in terms of the combined pay-offs, *T, T* is actually the worst strategy combination.

The reason the dominant equilibrium in this case can turn out so unsatisfactorily is that the set-up of the problem is a **non-cooperative** game, i.e. a game in which the players cannot make binding commitments before declaring their strategies. Such commitments can be made only if the players are allowed to communicate with each other. If they are not allowed to, they must fall back on the sure-thing principle. In the absence of communication, Rotter will not pick *S* (even though *S, S* yields less disutility for him than *T, T*) because if Criminal is rational he will respond with *T* which would give a pay-off of -8 to Rotter, a worse result than Rotter would get from any response by Criminal to Rotter choosing *T*. For the same reasons, Criminal will not pick *S* either. Were the game **cooperative**, however, Rotter and Criminal could get together and agree to a binding commitment that each would follow strategy *S*.

A game with this structure of pay-offs is called the Prisoners' Dilemma. It takes its name from a story in which Rotter and Criminal have been arrested on suspicion of a serious crime. They are placed in separate cells with no possibility of communication. Each has a choice of strategy: he may remain silent (*S*), or tell (*T*) all that happened, including evidence against the other. The pay-off information in the thieves' hands is that if one confesses while the other remains silent, he who tells is allowed to go free as a reward for securing the conviction of the other. In that case, the prisoner who remained silent but is condemned out of the mouth of the first will receive a maximum sentence of eight years in gaol. If both tell, each will be given credit for admitting guilt and can expect a less-than-maximum sentence of five years. If neither tells, each knows that it will be possible for the police to secure convictions only on a less serious offence and that both will be sentenced to two

He

		Ballet	Football
	Ballet	2, 1	−1, −1
She	Football	−1, −1	1, 2

Figure A6.2 Battle of the sexes: in each cell of the matrix, Her pay-off is shown first and His second.

years imprisonment. The point of the story is that, denied the possibility of cooperating, both prisoners will be much worse off in the dominant strategy equilibrium of the game than they would have been if they could have struck a pact to remain silent. Nonetheless, T, T is the dominant strategy equilibrium and the only plausible outcome.

While the Prisoners' Dilemma has important implications for economics since it suggests that cooperation, or the intervention of some superior agency, like government, may be able to generate unambiguous improvements, the example given above is relatively unusual in having a dominant strategy equilibrium in the first place. The most widely used alternative is the **Nash equilibrium** (Nash, 1951). Aumann (1985) has said that 'Nash equilibrium embodies the most important and fundamental idea of economics, that people act in accordance with their incentives' (p. 43) so it is not surprising that economists have taken up this particular solution concept with such enthusiasm. In terms of what we have already learned, it also has the advantage that all dominant strategy equilibria are Nash equilibria, though the converse is not true.

In a dominant strategy equilibrium, each player's equilibrium strategy has to be the best possible response to any possible strategy other players might follow. A strategy combination is a Nash equilibrium if no player has any incentive to deviate from his strategy, given that the other players do not deviate. Wordings of the definition vary: this version Rasmusen's (1989: 33). Thus a Nash strategy need only be a best response to other Nash strategies, not to all possible strategies. We illustrate the idea of a Nash equilibrium first with a game called Battle of the Sexes.

In the Battle of the Sexes, the strategies are two entertainment venues which a loving couple, He and She, have the choice of attending. He derives more utility from Football than Ballet, She greater utility from Ballet than Football, but each derives positive utility from going to either venue together and negative utility (disutility) from being separated. The pay-offs are shown in Figure A6.2. Notice first that there is no dominant strategy equilibrium in this game which illustrates the very general point that, for any equilibruim concept selected, a game may have one, more than one or no equilibria. This game has no dominant strategy equilibrium because if She picks Football, His highest pay-off is from choosing Football too, while if She picks Ballet, His pay-off is maximised from Ballet also. Thus His pay-off-maximising strategy varies with Her choice, as Her pay-off-maximising strategy would vary with His. For a dominant strategy equilibrium to exist, however, each player must pick the same strategy, whatever strategy the other(s) follow.

But while there is no dominant strategy equilibrium here, there are two Nash equilibria: *F*, *F* and *B*, *B*. To see this, note that the way of finding a Nash equilibrium is to postulate some strategy combination and then ask whether each player's strategy is a best response to the other's strategies. Suppose, for example, He somewhat altruistically chose Ballet and She, in a similar frame of mind, chose Football. Given Her choice of *F*, His best response is *F*, not *B*, and given His choice of *B*, Her best response is also *B*. So neither player's strategy is the best response to the other's choice and the postulated strategy combination cannot therefore be a Nash equilibrium. If He chose *F* and She *B*, this again is not a Nash equilibrium strategy combination since, given His choice, Her best response is not *B* but *F*, and given Her choice, His best response is *B*. If either chooses Football, the best response of the other is Football, in the sense that, given the choice of one of them, Football is the best response of the other, so there is no incentive to deviate. The same argument applies to the joint choice of Ballet. And this establishes *F*, *F* and *B*, *B* as Nash equilibria.

One of the difficulties raised by game theory is that when multiple equilibria occur, as in this example, additional criteria are needed, or further structure has to be introduced into the problem to allow a choice to be made between them. As Rasmusen (1989: 35) points, out, one additional element of structure which would lead to a resolution here is knowledge of who moves first. If either one of the players bought one ticket in advance, knowledge of this act by the other would be enough to induce the other to follow suit.

Nash equilibrium in a Cournot oligopoly

In the theory of oligopoly, the players' strategies will be conduct variables such as price, output, advertising expenditures, number of product variants of the Nash equilibrium is that for a two-firm oligopoly, a duopoly, in which the businesses produce identical products and, given the interactive effects of their choices, each chooses output levels with a view to maximising profit. For the simplest illustrative exposition, we assume zero production costs and linear demand curves.

Denote the sales volumes of the two firms, A and B, as Q_a and Q_b, total quantity sold as $(Q_a + Q_b)$ and the demand function relating market price per unit of sales to quantity sold:

$$P(Q_a + Q_b) = 210 - Q_a - Q_b \tag{A6.1}$$

The pay-offs are in this case the firms' profits which, with zero costs, are simply the value of sales for each firm:

$$\Pi_a = P \cdot Q_a = (210 - Q_a - Q_b)Q_a$$
$$= 210Q_a - Q_a^2 - Q_aQ_b \tag{A6.2a}$$
$$\Pi_b = P \cdot Q_b = 210Q_b - Q_b^2 - Q_aQ_b \tag{A6.2b}$$

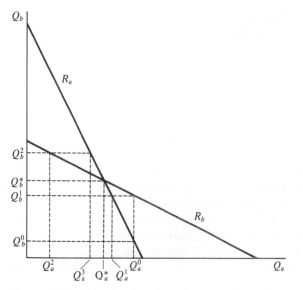

Figure A6.3   Reaction functions in a two-player Cournot oligopoly game.

The best responses of each firm in this case are the pay-off (i.e. profit) maximising output choices each firm makes, given the output level of the other firm. The best response function, also known in this literature as the **reaction functions**, are found by maximising Π_a with respect to Q_a and Π_b with respect to Q_b, yielding:

$$Q_a = 105 - Q_b/2 \tag{A6.3a}$$

and

$$Q_b = 105 - Q_a/2 \tag{A6.3b}$$

With these simple linear equations, we can find the best response of each player to any choice of strategy made by the other. The minimum value for firm A output is zero and occurs in response to B producing 210 units of output; its maximum value is 105, in response to B producing nothing. Similarly, B's output must also lie somewhere between 0 and 105. The two reaction functions, R_a and R_b, are shown in Figure A6.3. Where the functions intersect there is a Nash equilibrium.

To see why this is so consider the strategy combination (Q_a^0, Q_b^0). With that combination, A maximises its pay-off given B's strategy, but B has an incentive to deviate: given Q_a^0, B would increase (in fact, maximise its pay-off by following strategy Q_b^1. But with Q_b^1, Q_a^0 is no longer a best response for A; its best response would be Q_a^1. So neither the strategy combination (Q_a^0, Q_b^0) nor (Q_a^0, Q_b^1) can be Nash equilibria. Again, if we look at (Q_a^2, Q_b^2), we see that Q_a^3, not Q_a^2, is A's best response to Q_b^2, so that A has an incentive to deviate. Only where R_a and R_b intersect is it true that Q_b, with a value of Q_b^*, is B's best response to a value for Q_a, Q_a^*, which is simultaneously

A's best response to B. In these conditions, there is no incentive to deviate.

At the equilibrium, $Q_a = Q_a^* = Q_b^* = Q_b$, so we may write:

$$Q_a = 105 - Q_b/2 = Q_b \tag{A6.4a}$$

and

$$Q_b = 105 - Q_a/2 = Q_a \tag{A6.4b}$$

Solving, we find that $Q_a^* = Q_b^* = 70$, and substituting into the demand function discover that $P = 70$ also, so that each firm's pay-off in the equilibrium will be 4900.

This analysis offers a game-theoretic solution to a very old problem: How duopolists choose values for conduct variables with a view to maximising profit when the decision made by either one of them significantly affects the market possibilities facing the other. In the version in which output is taken as the conduct variable, the classical solution to this problem was offered by Cournot (1838). But in order to obtain a solution (the same as that offered above), Cournot made the ultimately indefensible assumption that each producer assumed the decision of the other would remain unchanged, whatever changes the first might make and however irrational it might seem for the other not to change. As Bacharach (1976: 71) elegantly puts it:

> 'They learn nothing, clinging in spite of overwhelming counterevidence to their expectations of zero reactions. In forming their hypotheses in the first place, they fail to notice the glaring contradiction in them that would be apparent if they tried for a moment putting themselves in the other's shoes... Cournot ... failed to come to terms with the problem of rational duopolistic decisions: what is good for me is good for you; I cannot therefore attribute *mechanical* reactions to you when I myself am searching for an *optimal* rule. Game theory does come to terms with this puzzle. It succeeds in cutting a hard old analytical knot and clearly expressing the essentials of the problem, whose symmetry of minds, the source of the problem, it highlights.'

These basic foundations can be built upon in many ways. These are games with many players, with so-called mixed strategies (when probability weights are attached to any of the two or more strategies any player might follow), with imperfect information and with many steps. Modern game theory extends to cover all of these possibilities and uses a variety of equilibrium concepts to deal with them. The reader is referred to the works cited at the beginning of the appendix to follow these developments through.

Notes

1. $C'(RD) = \mathrm{d}C/\mathrm{d}RD = -ab \cdot RD^{(-a-1)}$

    $P'(Q) = \mathrm{d}P\mathrm{d}Q = -es \cdot Q^{(-e-1)}$

2. It also has the potential to reduce the costs of firms in other industries, but this is an effect which is left until Chapter 7.
3. For a general account of dynamic optimisation methods see Intriligator (1971), and for a discussion of its use in differential games see Bagchi (1984).
4. See, for example the Reinganum analysis of appropriability, the analytically tractable but necessarily special hazard-rate distributions used in stochastic racing models, and the one-product firms of Beath Katsoulacos and Ulph.
5. Suppose $P = 10$. Let $C_i = 9, 7.5$ and 5. Simple metal arithmetic reveals that $(p - C_i)/p$ will then yield, respectively, 0.1, 0.25 and 0.5. The corresponding results for $\ln P - \ln C_i$ are 0.105, 0.288 and 0.693. The approximation diverges from the true value by only 5 per cent when the profit margin is 10 per cent, by 15 per cent for a margin of 25 per cent and 39 per cent for a 50 per cent margin.
6. To take a simple example, ignore k (which makes no qualitative difference to the outcome) and set $\sigma = 1$. Then suppose zero output growth, production per period of 10 units and an initial skill level $SKL_{int,i}(0) = 0.1$. Then over a succession of periods, the term $\sigma(Q_i(t)/Q_{ci}(t))$ evolves as follows:

t	$Q_i(t)$	$Q_{ci}(t)$	$[Q_i(t)/Q_{ci}(t)]\sigma$
0	10	10	1.0
1	10	20	0.5
2	10	30	0.3
3	10	40	0.25
4	10	50	0.2
:	:	:	:
9	10	100	0.1
:	:	:	:
99	10	1000	0.01

   Diagrammatically $\sigma[.]$ is approaching the origin at an ever slowing speed as cumulative production builds up over time.
7. Extending the example in Note 6, suppose $SKL_{int,i}(0)$, the initial value is 0.1. Then $SKL_{int,i}(1 - SKL_{int,i}) = 0.09$, and with $SKL[.] = 1$ in this period, $SKL_{int,i} = 0.99$ also. This means $SKL_{int,i}$, will rise to 0.19 by the start of period 1, so that in that period, $SKL_{int,i}(1 - SKL_{int,i})$ will be 0.154. This is the value by which $\sigma[.] = 0.5$ must be multiplied to a yield value for $S_{int,i}$ in period 1 of 0.077, implying that $SKL_{int,i}$ itself will rise to 0.267. Repeating this procedure, we find $SKL_{int,i}(t)$ rises from 0.1 to 0.387 by period 4, but that in each period the amount of increase declines:

t	$SKL_{int,i}$	$dSKL_{int,i}/dt$
0	0.1	
		0.09
1	0.19	
		0.077
2	0.267	
		0.065
3	0.332	
		0.055
4	0.387	

8. A differential equation has as its dependent variable a term which is a time differential, such as $f_i(t)$; it becomes a differential–difference equation when dependent on differences, such as $(E_i - E\#)$; and age-dependent effects arise through the vintage model of capital which makes unit costs for any firm (which in turn influence competitiveness and market share) dependent on the capital investment history of the firm.

9. The alternative type of representation is called **extensive form** and makes explicit more informtion about the game than the summarised description found in the normal.

References

Arrow, K.J. and S. Honkapohja (1985) *Frontiers of Economics*, Ch. 1. Oxford: Blackwell.
Arthur, W.B. (1988) 'Self-reinforcing mechanisms in economics', in D. Pines (ed.) *The Economy as an Evolving Complex System*, Reading, MA: Addison Wesley, 9–31.
Arthur W.B. (1989) 'Competing technologies, lock-in and competition', *Economic Journal*, 99 116–24.
Arthur, W.B., Y.U. Ermoliev and Y.M. Kaniovski (1987) 'Path dependent processes and the emergence of macro-structure', *European Journal of Operational Research* 30, 294–303.
Aumann, R. (1985) 'What is game theory trying to accomplish?' in K.J. Arrow and S. Honkapohja (eds) *Frontiers of Economics*, Oxford: Blackwell.
Bacharach, M. (1976) *Economics and the Theory of Games*, London: Macmillan.
Bagchi, A. (1984) *Stackelberg Differential Games in Economic Models*, Berlin: Springer Verlag.
Beath J., Y. Katsoulacos and D. Ulph (1987) 'Sequential product innovation and industry evolution', *Economic Journal* 97, (Conference), 32–43.
Bertrand, J. (1983) 'Recherches sur la theorie mathematique de la richesse', *Journal des savants* 48, 499–508.
Brander, J. (1992) 'Recent developments in industrial organisation', in *Papers and Proceedings of the 1992 Conference of Industry Economics*, ANU, Canberra, Occasional Paper 8, Bureau of Industry Economics.
Clarke, R. (1985) *Industrial Economics*, Oxford: Blackwell.
Cohen, W.M. and D.A. Levinthal (1989) 'Innovation and learning: the two faces of R&D', *Economic Journal* 99, 569–96.
Cohen, W.M. and D.A. Levinthal (1990) 'The implications of spillovers for R&D investment and welfare: a new perspective', in *Advances in Applied Microeconomics*, 29–45. Greenwich, NY: JAI Press.
Cournot, A. A. (1838) *Researches into the Mathematical Principles of the Theory of Wealth*, English edition of *Researches sur les principles mathematique de la theorie des richesses*, New York: Kelley.
d'Aspremont, C., J. Gabszewicz and J. Thisse (1979) 'On Hotelling's "Stability of Competition"', *Econometrica* 47(5), 1145–50.
Dasgupta, P. (1986) 'The theory of technological competition', in J. Mathewson and J.E. Stiglitz (eds) *Modern Approaches to Industrial Economics*, London: Macmillan, 519–47.
Dasgupta, P. and J.E. Stiglitz (1980a) 'Industrial structure and the nature of innovation activity', *Economic Journal* 90, 266–93.
Dasgupta, P. and J.E. Stiglitz (1980b) 'Uncertainty, industrial structure and the speed of R&D', *Bell Journal of Economics* 11(1), 1–28.
David, P.A., (1969) 'A contribution to the theory of diffusion', Stanford Center for Research in Economic Growth, Memorandum, Stanford University.
David, P.A. (1985) 'Clio and the economics of QWERTY', *American Economic Review* (Papers and Proceedings) 75, 332–7.
David, P.A. and J. Bunn (1987) 'The battle of the systems and the evolutionary dynamics of Dnetwork technology rivalries', Stanford Center for Research in Economic Growth, Memorandum, Stanford University.
Davies, S.J. (1979) *The Diffusion of Process Innovations*, Cambridge: Cambridge University Press.
Farrell, J. and G. Saloner (1985) 'Standardisations, compatibility and innovation', *Rand Journal of Economics* 16, 70–83.

Farrell, J. and G. Saloner (1986) 'Installed base compatibility', *American Economic Review* 76, 940–55.

Flaherty, M.T. (1980) 'Industry structure and cost reducing investment', *Econometrica* 48, 1187–1209

Friedman, J. (1971) 'A noncooperative equilibrium for supergames', *Review of Economic Studies* 38, 1–12.

Friedman, J. (1977) *Oligopoly and the Theory of Games*, Amsterdam: North-Holland.

Fudenberg, D., R. Gilbert, J. Stiglitz and J. Tirole (1983) 'Preemption, leapfrogging and competition in patent races', *European Economic Review*, 22, 3–31.

Fudenberg, D. and E.J. Tirole (1985) 'Preemption and rent-equalisation in the adoption of new technology', *Review of Economic Studies* 52, 383–401.

Fudenberg, D. and E.J. Tirole (1989) 'Non-cooperative game theory for industrial organisation: An introduction and overview', in R. Schmalensee and R. Willig (eds) *Handbook of Industrial Organisation*, ch. 5, Amsterdam: North-Holland.

Gilbert, R. and D. Newbery (1982) 'Pre-emptive patenting and the persistence of monopoly', *American Economic Review* 72, 514–26.

Griliches, Z. (1957) 'Hybrid corn: an exploration in the economics of technological change', *Econometrica* 25, 501–22.

Grossman, G. and C. Shapiro (1978) 'Dynamic R&D competition', *Economic Journal* 97, 372–87.

Harris, C. and J. Vickers (1985) 'Perfect equilibrium in a model of a race', *Review of Economic Studies*, 52, 1–22.

Ireland, N. and P. Stoneman (1986), 'Technological diffusion, expectations and welfare', *Oxford Economic Papers* 38, 283–304.

Iwai, K. (1984a) 'Schumpeterian dynamics: An evolutionary model of innovation and imitation', *Journal of Economic Behaviour and Organisation* 5(2), 159–90.

Iwai, K. (1948b) 'Schumpeterian dynamics: Part II: Technological progress, firm growth and economic selection', *Journal of Economic Behaviour and Organisation* 5(3), 321–51.

Jensen, R. (1982) 'Adoption and diffusion of an innovation of uncertain profitability', *Journal of Economic Theory* 27, 182–93.

Kreps, D. and A.M. Spence (1985) 'Modelling the role of history in industrial organisation and competition' in G. Feiwel (ed.) *Issues in Contemporary Microeconomics and Welfare*, ch. 10, London: Macmillan.

Lee, T. and L. L. Wilde (1980) 'Market structue and innovation: A reformulation', *Quarterly Journal of Economics* 94, 429–36.

Levin, R.C. and P.C. Reiss (1984) 'Tests of a Schumpeterian model of R&D and market structure', in Z. Griliches (ed.) *R&D, Patents and Productivity* Chicago: NBER/University of Chicago Press.

Lipman, B. L. (1991) 'How to decide how to decide how to ...: Modelling limited rationality', *Econometrica* 59(4), 1105–25.

Loury, G. C. (1979) 'Market structure and innovation', *Quarterly Journal of Economics* 93, 395–410

Luce, R. D. and H. Raiffa, (1957) *Games and Decisions: Introduction and Critical Survey*, New York: Wiley.

Mansfield, E. (1968) *Industrial Research and Technological Innovation*, New York: Norton.

McCardle, K. F. (1985) 'Information acquisition and the adoption of new technology', *Management Science* 31 1372–89.

Metcalfe, J. S. (1981) 'Impulse and diffusion in the study of technological change' *Futures* 13, 347–59.

Metcalfe, J. S. (1986) 'Technological innovation and the competitive process', in P.H. Hall (ed.) *Technology, Innovation and Economic Policy*, Oxford: Philip Allan.

Nasbeth, L. and G.F. Ray (1974) *The Diffusion of New Industrial Processes: An International Study*, Cambridge: Cambridge University Press.

Nash, J. F. (1951) 'Non-cooperative games', *Annals of Mathematics* 54, 86–295.

Nelson, R. and S. Winter(1982) *An Evolutionary Theory of Economic Change*, Cambridge, MA: Harvard Univesity Press, Belknap.

Nelson, R.R. (1959) 'The simple economics of basic scientific research', *Journal of Political Economy* 67, 297–306.

Park, J. (1984) 'Innovation competition under certainty', PhD dissertation, Northwestern University, (cited in Reinganum, 1989, p 907.)

Polya, C. and F. Eggenberger (1923) 'Ueber die Statistik verketteter Vorgaenge', *Z. Angew. Math Mech.* 3, 279–89.

Pakes, A. and M. Schankerman (1984) 'The rate of obsolescence of patents, research gestation lags, and the private rate of return to research resources', in Z. Griliches (ed) *R&D Patents and Productivity*, Chicago: National Bureau of Economic Research and University of Chicago Press.

Rasmusen, E. (1989) *Games and Information: An introduction to Game Theory*, Oxford Blackwell.

Reinganum, J. F. (1981a) 'On the diffusion of new technology: A game theoretic approach', *Review of Economic Studies* 48, 395–405.

Reinganum, J. F. (1981b) 'Market structure and the diffusion of new technology', *Bell Journal of Economics* 12, 618–24.

Reinganum, J. (1982) 'A dynamic game of R&D: Patent protection and competitive behaviour', *Econometrica* 50, 671–88.

Reinganum, J. (1983) 'Uncertain innovation and the persistance of monopoloy', *AER* 73, 741–48.

Reinganum, J. (1984) 'Practical implications of game theoretic models of R&D', *AER (Papers and Proceedings* 74(2), 61–6.

Reinganum, J. (1989) 'The timing of innovation: Research, devlopment and diffusion', in R. Schmalensee and R. Willig (eds.) *Handbook of Industrial Organisation*, ch. 14, Amsterdam: North-Holland.

Rosenberg, N. (1976) 'On technological expectations', *Economic Journal* 86, 523–35.

Rothwell, R. (1992) 'Successful industrial innovation: Critical factors for the 1990s', *R&D Management* 22(3), 221–39.

Salter, W.E.G. (1966) *Productivity and Technical Change*, Cambridge: Cambridge University Press.

Selten, R. (1975) 'Reexamination of the perfectness concept for equiulibrium points in extensive games', *International Journal of Game Theory* 4(1), 25–55.

Shaked, A. and J. Sutton (1982) 'Relaxing price competition through product differentiation', *Review of Economic Studies* 49(1), 3–14.

Shubik, M. (1982) *Game Theory in the Social Sciences: Concepts and Solutions*, Cambridge, MA: MIT Press.

Silverberg, G., G. Dosi and L. Orsenigo (1988) 'Innovation, diversity and diffusion: a self-organisation model', *Economic Journal* 98, 1032–54.

Stigler, G. (1964) 'A Theory of oligopoly', *Journal of Political Economy* 72, 44–61.

Stoneman, P. (1980) 'The rate of imitation, learning and profitability', *Economic Letters* 6, 179–83.

Stoneman, P. and N. J. Ireland (1983) 'The role of supply factors in the diffusion of new process technology', *Economic Journal (Supplement)* 66–77.

Sugden, R. (1986) *The Economics of Rights, Cooperation and Welfare*, Oxford: Blackwell.

Swann, D., D.P. O'Brien, W.P. Maunder and W.S. Howe (1974) *Competition in British Industry*, London: Allen and Unwin.

Teece, D. J. (1986) 'Profiting from technological innovation', *Research Policy* 15(16), 285–305.

Tirole, J. (1988) *The Theory of Industrial Organisation*, Cambridge, MA: MIT Press.

Vickers, J. (1986) 'The evolution of market structure when there is a sequence of innovations', *Journal of Industrial Economics* 35(1), 1–12.

von Neumann, J. and O. Morgenstern (1944) *The Theory of Games and Economic Behaviour*, New York: Wiley.

7

Innovation and long-run economic growth

Introduction

This is the first of two chapters devoted to the impact of innovation on the aggregate or national economy. In this chapter attention focuses on long-run growth theory, traditionally the arena in which analysis of technological progress has been found. The fluctuations in economic activity described as the business cycle have tended to become the subject of a separate body of literature and are dealt with in Chapter 8. But the division between long-run theory dominated by the supply-side and short-run theory dominated by demand-side considerations is somewhat arbitrary. The long run, after all, is nothing but a sequence of short runs and what happens in any short run must have implications for the longer run.

Economic growth with endogenous cycles is itself a growth area in contemporary analysis and is introduced towards the end of the chapter. But leading up to that point, we start with growth model which has dominated work in the area in the post-war era, the so-called neoclassical growth model of Solow (1956) and Swan (1956). It is in the context of that model that technological progress was discovered to be the key to achieving long-run sustained growth in real income per head. In one sense, however, that proved a paradox for economic theory; technological progress was central to understanding long-term growth, yet at that time technological change remained 'the "*terra incognita*" of modern economics' (Schmookler, 1966: 3).

Economists have since done a great deal to map out the territory, though many questions remain. In this chapter, we trace the results of attempts to endogenise both the bias (direction) and pace of innovation in aggregate growth models, taking account of the new generation of growth modellers who appeared in the 1980s led by Paul Romer. Endogenous research and development, formal education and various forms of dynamic learning have now been introduced into growth models – a major leap forward when compared with the exogenous progress approach which characterised much earlier analysis. Another feature of Solow's model was that it had only one, all-purpose good available for both consumption and investment. This enabled him to avoid both the problems and benefits which arise in multisectoral treatments. These are also dealt with here.

In a final section, much of the smoothness and equilibrium tendency that is a feature of neoclassical analysis is abandoned. Growth is either cyclic or jerky, driven by bursts of innovation which dramatically punctuate economic history, as in the Schumpeterian vision and take the economic system off along new paths, subject to continuous changes in structure. The sources of these revolutions in technology and economic structure remain very much in Schmookler's '*terra incognita*'.

Theory of long-term economic growth

Economics provides us with a wide range of models of long-term economic growth.[1] Indeed, the analysis of growth has preoccupied economists since its earliest days.[2] But the model which serves as the foundation for almost all modern analysis – some have called it the 'workhorse' model – can be attributed to Robert Solow (1956) and Trevor Swan (1956).

Solow's contribution is regarded as so important that he was awarded the Nobel Prize for Economics, in large measure in recognition of it. In its citation, the prize selection committee commented: 'Every long term report ... for any country has used a Solow-type analysis' (Nordhaus and Samuelson, 1989: 855). Swan, independently constructed a very similar model at about the same time. The model presented here is not identical to either Solow or Swan, but incorporates their ideas in an expositionally accessible approach used by Jones (1975). In conformity with widespread usage we shall call it the **neoclassical growth model (NGM)**.

The NGM belongs to a class of models which comprise growth theory. This may seem like a statement of the self-evident, but as Hicks (1965) has said, growth theory is a label conventionally attached to only a part of the economic theory that addresses the analysis of economic growth. In this usage, it relates to long-run, **steady-state growth (SSG)**, i.e. the analysis of paths along which all variables defined in the model grow at the same proportional rate and in which conditions are sought to determine how economies might converge to such paths. Another commonly used term for SSG is **balanced** growth, which captures the idea that both supply-side and demand-side variables are growing at the same rate.

The rationale for focusing on balanced growth is discussed helpfully in both Dixit (1976: 7–10) and Hacche (1979: 20–8). But the basic idea is that it provides a useful benchmark for analysing dynamics, rather like competitive equilibrium in comparative statics. Analysis has to start somewhere. And one obvious way of structuring enquiry is to take it as a first working hypothesis that dynamic economic systems tend towards balanced growth paths. We can then ask what growth along such paths would look like and what it would take to ensure that economies always tended towards balanced growth after any shock. A technical advantage of this approach is that the formal techniques for analysing balanced growth are also reasonably well established and the results derived from their use well defined and transparent. A theoretical implication of the approach is that when all prices and quantities are taken to be changing at a constant rate, a logically credible setting has been created for decision-takers to make correct forecasts about factors which underlie equilibrium paths through time, or paths which converge on equilibrium. Furthermore, observation has led many economists to agree that in the long run economic systems actually tend to be stable; forces which drive economies along seem to propel them ultimately towards balanced growth rather than self-destruction (Solow, 1988).

The test of whether the approach is justified lies ultimately in its success in explaining historical observation. Although the NGM is so stripped down that it has the status of a 'fable' (Solow, 1970), it has proved surprisingly effective in identifying the major sources of long-term economic growth. As Solow has emphasised, however, the NGM is a good place to start on the analysis of growth, but not the place to finish. Some of the puzzles it has left unexplained are being tackled within more ambitious versions of the SSG approach. But, much current interest also lies in questioning the balanced approach itself. Before we can proceed to those questions, however, we need to look at the NGM and its extensions first.

The bedrock NGM

The setting for the analysis is a one-good, perfectly competitive, closed economy in which, under given technology, homogeneous labour, L, combines with homogeneous capital, K, to produce output, Q, through a constant returns to scale aggregate production function:

$$Q = F(K, L) \tag{7.1}$$

The marginal products of capital and labour are both positive and declining. By virtue of constant returns, increasing both K and L by a given multiple implies Q will also rise by the same multiple. Letting that multiple be $1/L$:

$$Q/L = f(K/L, 1)$$

or

$$q = f(k) \tag{7.1'}$$

where lower case letters are used to indicate that output and capital are being written in per worker form. To simplify exposition, we invoke conditions under which (7.1 '), sometimes called the intensive form of the aggregate production function, is structured so that $q = 0$ when $k = 0$; y rises continuously with k, but at a declining rate; as k approaches infinity, associated increases in q become vanishingly small. These conditions are consistent with the assumptions underlying (7.1) and are reflected in Figure 7.1.

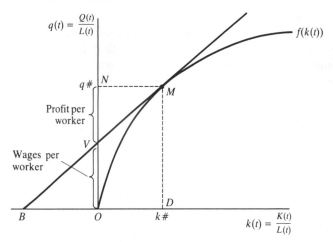

Figure 7.1   The intensive form of the aggregate production function and the distribution of income.

Notice some of the implications of this set-up:

1. With technology given and constant returns to scale, output (and real income) per worker can rise only as the result increasing capital per worker, i.e. capital deepening. In terms of the diagram, q can rise as the result only of moves along the (intensive) production function. Moves from inside or below $f(k)$ towards it would imply initial technical inefficiency. This is outlawed by the perfect competition assumption. Moves of $f(k)$ call for technological progress, which at this stage is assumed absent.

2. The slope of a ray to $f(k)$ at any point is $(Q/L)/(K/L) = (Q/K)$, the average product of capital, or the inverse of the capital: output ratio. As K/L rises, Q/K falls and K/Q rises.

3. The slope of a tangent to $f(k)$ at any point (such as VM at M) is $d(Q/L)/d((K/L) = dQ/dK$, the marginal productivity or return on capital which under perfect competition is equal to the real interest rate, r. As K/L rises, this falls. This intuition here is that capital projects are undertaken in descending order of expected rate of return. As long as the labour force growth rate is non-negative, the capital stock must expand if K/L is to rise. But such expansion necessarily involves investing in projects offering successively lower rates of return.

4. The slope of the tangent VM is also NV/MN. This particular tangent is associated with the capital: labour ratio $k\#$ equal to OD, which equals MN. Thus the real interest rate, r, can be expressed as the ratio NV/OD, or $NV/k\#$, implying that NV equals $r \cdot k\#$, or profits per worker. Under constant returns to scale and perfect competition, each input is paid its marginal product and the total payments made to the inputs exactly account for the value of output. What is left of output per worker after profits have been distributed must be paid out as wages per worker. In the diagram, output per worker $q\# = ON$, and $ON - NV = OV$, where OV

is therefore wages per worker. As we move upwards along $f(k)$, wages per worker rise (intuitively, each worker has more capital to work with and so becomes more productive) and profits per worker fall.

5. With wages per worker rising and profits per worker falling along $f(k)$, we would also expect the ratio of wage rate : profit (or rental) rate to be rising. That this is indeed the case can be seen by noting that the slope of MV, the rental rate, is also OV/OB, or the ratio of the wage rate to OB. Thus OB itself must be the wage : rent ratio, and unambiguously rises as we move upwards along $f(k)$.

It is clear from (1) that if we are to understand why real income per worker increases, we must first understand why capital deepening occurs. To do this, assume that the labour force grows at the same rate as the population, a rate exogenously determined at the constant positive value n. Then, arithmetically, for K/L to rise, K must rise at a rate faster than n. If K grows at the same rate, (K/L) is constant. If K grows more slowly than n, K/L falls.

What then determines how fast K grows? In answering this question, we shall be concerned centrally with changes over time and so as a matter of notation, start to indicate explicitly which variables are time-dependent. It is assumed that capital does not depreciate so that every expenditure on capital stock, gross investment, also constitutes net investment, additions to the capital stock. Investment in any period $I(t)$, is equal to the increase in capital stock, $dK(t)/dt$. In the bedrock NGM, aggregate-planned investment is set equal to aggregate-planned saving:

$$I(t) = S(t) \qquad (7.2)$$

Out of any flow of income per period, $Q(t)$, individuals as a group choose to spend a fraction up to 100 per cent on goods and services used in that period, consumption, denoted $C(t)$ and to put the remainder aside as savings. The amount they decide to save in aggregate is assumed in the NGM to be determined by a fixed proportional saving function:

$$S(t) = sQ(t), \; 0 < s < 1 \qquad (7.3)$$

It is this amount $S(t)$ which is automatically invested.[3]

The increase in capital stock – investment – per worker is therefore determined by savings per worker, $S(t)/L(t)$. By simple expansion:

$$S(t)/L(t) = S(t)/Q(t) \cdot Q(t)/L(t)$$

which, recalling (7.3), can be written $sq(t)$ or $sf(k)$. Bearing in mind that the labour force is growing, the level of saving and thus investment per worker, might not be sufficient to keep capital growing at the same rate as labour and thus keep $K(t)/L(t) = k(t)$ constant. To keep $k(t)$ exactly constant, $I(t)/L(t)$ must be at the level $nk(t)$.

The reason for this is that $nk(t) = n(K(t)/L(t))$, so that if $I(t)/L(t) = n(K(t)/L(t))$, then $[I(t)/L(t) \cdot L(t)/K(t)] = n$, or $I(t)/K(t) = n$. But $I(t)/K(t)$ is the proportional growth rate for $K(t)$. And if this is n, then both $K(t)$ and $L(t)$ are growing at the same rate, so $k(t)$ is constant. Thus if saving (and investment) per worker is greater (less) than $nk(t)$, $k(t)$ will be increasing (declining).

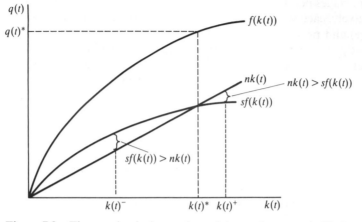

Figure 7.2   The neoclassical growth model: steady-state equilibrium occurs where $k(t) = k(t)*$ and $q(t) = q(t)*$. Here saving and investment per worker are exactly the amounts required to keep the capital–labour ratio at constant level.

In Figure 7.2, we show two functions in addition to $f(k(t))$. First, the saving per worker function, $sf(k(t))$, is derived by scaling down $f(k(t))$ by the exogenously fixed fraction s for every value of $k(t)$. Second the $nk(t)$ function is found by multiplying each value of $k(t)$ by the parameter n. Since the $sf(k(t))$ function is a scaled down image of $f(k(t))$, it must rise continuously but at a declining rate: like output and income per worker, saving per worker (measured on the vertical axis) rises with $k(t)$. Since n is a positive constant, $nk(t)$ is linear and upward sloping; the higher $k(t)$, the greater the investment per worker required per period to keep it constant (also measured on the vertical axis). For any positive values of n and s, the two functions must cross at some point because of their shapes. At the level of $k(t)$ where the two intersect, $sf(k(t)) = nk(t)$; investment per worker is exactly what is required to keep $k(t)$ constant, so $k(t)$ at this point, denoted $k(t)*$, will neither rise nor fall. This means capital and labour must both be growing at the proportional rate n and, given constant returns to scale, that implies output and real income are also growing at the rate n, yielding a level of output and real income per head of $q(t)*$. The values $k(t)*$ and $q(t)*$ are associated with growth paths of $K(t)$, $L(t)$ and $Q(t)$ which constitute a steady-state growth path for the economy.

At the end of the penultimate paragraph we argued that if saving (and investment) per worker exceeded (fell below) $nk(t)$, then $k(t)$ would rise (fall). This in fact is the verbal form of the equation of motion for this growth model which we may now write down explicitly:

$$dk(t)/dt = sf(k(t)) - nk(t) \tag{7.4}$$

In terms of the diagram, we can see that if $k(t)$ were to take a value below $k(t)*$, say $k(t)-$, $sf(k(t))$ would be above $nk(t)$, so that from (7.4), $dk(t)/dt$ would be positive, i.e.

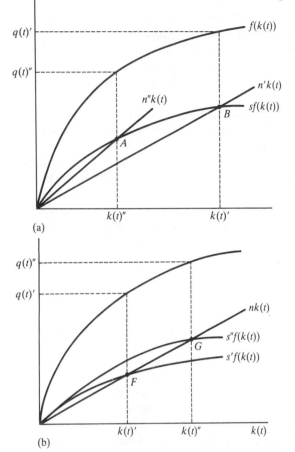

Figure 7.3 (a) Steady-state growth in the NGM and different growth rates of the labour force: $n'' > n'$; (b) Steady-state growth in the NGM and different saving ratios: $s'' > s'$.

$k(t)$ would be rising. By symmetrical argument, if $k(t)$ were $k(t)+$, $dk(t)/dt$ would be negative and $k(t)$ falling. The NGM also has the property of long-run stability; whatever the initial value of $k(t)$, the dynamics of the system will always tend to take it towards steady state.

The strong predictions of the bedrock NGM are that the long-run SSG rate of output growth is determined by the growth rate of population and the labour force n and that the level of output, real income and consumption per worker depends on how much is saved and invested per head, given n. We consider these in turn.

Labour force growth rate

For any given value of the saving ratio s, a relatively high (low) labour force growth rate will be associated with a relatively high (low) output growth rate. But a high labour force growth rate, given s, will also be associated with a low level of income per head. In Figure 7.3a, this can be seen by comparing the SSG paths associated with points A and B. At A, labour force growth rate n'' is fast compared with n', that at B. But at B, with the relatively slow labour force growth rate, the capital:labour ratio $k(t)'$ is higher than that at A and as a result real income per head, $q(t)'$, is also higher.

Since the major purpose of stimulating economic growth is to raise real income per head, it is of little comfort that a higher n brings faster overall output growth, since it also depresses the amount of income each individual on average receives. In addition, the wage rate, reflecting the marginal product of labour and average labour productivity Q/L, both fall as n rises, as can be confirmed by referring back to Figure 7.1 and superimposing a new tangent to $f(k(t))$ to the left and down from M. The intuition here is that as labour inputs arrive at an accelerated rate with no change in the proportion of incomes invested, so diminishing marginal returns from labour become increasingly severe.

Saving ratio

Taking n as given, a higher saving ratio s will yield a higher capital:labour ratio and hence a higher level of real income per head. To see this, compare the SSG paths at F and G in Figure 7.3b associated with, respectively, the low saving ratio s' and the higher one s''. At both F and G in Figure 7.3b, however, labour, capital and output are growing at the same proportional rate n. Thus the higher saving ratio and resulting increase in investment per worker do nothing in the long run to raise the growth rate. All the same, it may take many years to move from a point like F to a higher level steady state like G. And since real income per head $q(t)''$ is greater than $q(t)'$, income must grow at a faster rate than n during the period of transition.

The conventional wisdom that faster output growth can be achieved by increasing investment per worker on the basis of a higher saving ratio is borne out while the economy is moving from a lower to a higher level of output per head, but no longer. In the long run, the gain is purely in terms of higher real incomes per head.

Consumption and optimal growth

While the level of real income per head is a good general guide to the standard of living a country has achieved, the benefits of growth can only be felt in any period by the level of consumption that individuals on average enjoy. Consumption is the difference between income and saving, and consumption per person thus shown in the diagrams by the vertical distance between the $f(k(t))$ and $sf(k(t))$ functions. In SSG, consumption per head is constant, but must increase if $k(t)$ is approaching $k(t)^*$ from below and fall if $k(t)$ is falling towards $k(t)^*$.

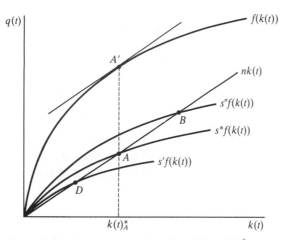

Figure 7.4 Optimal growth: when $k(t) = k(t)_A^*$, consumption per head is maximised.

Suppose now we wished to find the SSG path associated with maximum consumption per head. Taking the labour force growth rate as given, it is easy to see which path that will be. In steady state, the $sf(k(t))$ and $nk(t)$ lines intersect. Steady-state consumption per head (the distance between $f(k(t))$ and $sf(k(t))$ in steady state) is at a maximum where the distance between $f(k(t))$ and $nk(t)$ is also at its greatest. The point on $f(k(t))$ furthest above $nk(t)$ is the point whose tangent has an identical slope to $nk(t)$, i.e. A' in Figure 7.4, where consumption per worker is $A'A$. When consumption per head is maximised, therefore, the slope of $f(k(t))$, the real rate of return on capital, is equal to the labour force growth rate n, a result which is often called the Golden Rule of Accumulation (Phelps, 1961). By assumption, the saving ratio is exogenously determined and it would be a miracle if it took the value s^* which in the diagram allows the $sf(k(t))$ function to cross $nk(t)$ at A. It could equally well be s' (SSG at D) or s'' (SSG at B). But if the saving ratio could be manipulated by governments through the taxation system, the Golden Rule gives a degree of guidance on the sort of ratio they should seek to achieve.

So far we have said nothing about technological progress. But we are now ready to incorporate it. This will allow us to see how to achieve both faster growth rates of output in the long run and continuous increases in real income and consumption per head.

Exogenous technological advance in the NGM

The effect of technological advance, efficiently deployed, is to shift upwards the intensive form of the aggregate production function which we have been using. This is because with any given level of capital per worker, technological advance raises the productivity of at least one and usually both inputs and hence raises the level of output per worker which can be produced. If technological advance is continuous, any given level of $k(t)$ will thus be associated with continually rising real incomes per worker. Notice that with a given saving ratio the upward shift in the $f(k(t))$ function will also increase saving and investment per worker, $sf(k(t))$ for each level of $k(t)$. The proportion of income per worker saved and invested remains the same, but since incomes are rising, the amount saved per worker and in aggregate increases. The same is also true of consumption.

To obtain greater precision in the analysis we shall however slightly modify the details of the approach used so far. To capture the idea that the effect of technological progress is to shift the production function upwards, advance is represented by a purely time-dependent factor augmentation term. Algebraically:

$$Q(t) = F(a(t)K(t), b(t)L(t)) \qquad (7.5)$$

where $a(t)$ and $b(t)$ are positive numbers and $a(t)K(t)$ and $b(t)L(t)$ are effective capital and labour inputs or capital and labour measured in efficiency units. In the simple but important purely labour augmenting case, $a(t)$ is set to equal one and $[db(t)/dt]/b(t)$ assumed to be constant at the exogenous rate m.

To consider the implications of such advance, work in terms of capital and output per effective unit of labour, $K(t)/b(t)L(t)$ and $Q(t)/b(t)L(t)$, respectively, denoted $k_{eff}(t)$ and $q_{eff}(t)$. Now by construction, labour augmenting technological progress at rate m has exactly the same effect on output as allowing the flow of labour inputs to grow at that rate. When progress is purely labour augmenting, its total impact is therefore equivalent to an acceleration in the growth rate of labour inputs from its natural rate n to the higher rate of $(m + n)$. When, in effect, labour is growing at the rate $(m + n)$, capital must also grow at the rate $(m + n)$ if $k_{eff}(t)$ is to be constant. If capital is growing at this rate, then output will also grow at the rate $(m + n)$ and $q_{eff}(t)$ will also be constant.

For $k_{eff}(t)$ to be constant, saving and investment per effective worker $sf(k_{eff}(t))$ must be equal to the investment required per effective worker to keep $k_{eff}(t)$ constant, which in this case is $(m + n)k_{eff}(t)$, since the work-force is now effectively growing at the rate $(m + n)$, not just n. Refer now to Figure 7.5, in which distances along the axes now measure capital and output per effective worker and where the $f(k(t))$, $sf(k(t))$ and $nk(t)$ functions found in earlier diagrams have been relabelled to show output and savings per effective worker and the investment per effective worker required to keep capital per effective worker constant. From this it is clear that if saving and investment per effective worker were above (below) $(m + n)k_{eff}(t)$, then $k_{eff}(t)$ would rise (fall) until the two converged (assuming, as in the earlier analysis that the functions are 'well behaved').

In its structure, the analysis is identical to that of the NGM without technological progress. But its implications are dramatically different. At the steady state values for $k_{eff}(t)$ and $q_{eff}(t)$, capital and output are both growing, not at rate n but $(m + n)$, the growth rate of effective labour. Thus, in steady state, the ratio of capital to actual

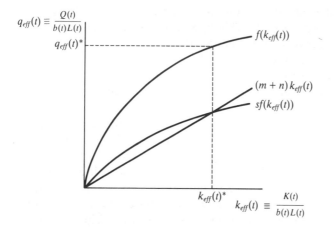

Figure 7.5   Steady-state growth in the NGM with pure labour-augmenting technological progress.

labour is growing at rate m, and output and real income per head are also growing at rate m. For our purposes, this is the central and most significant conclusion to be drawn from elementary growth theory; in the long run *only* technological progress will allow real output to grow at a rate faster than that of the labour force. The faster the rate of technological progress, the faster output and real per capita incomes rise.

Since saving is by assumption a constant fraction of income, aggregate saving per period will rise at the same rate as income, $m + n$, and saving per worker will rise at that rate, minus the growth rate of the actual labour force, i.e. $(m + n) - n = m$. By symmetrical argument, consumption per worker will also rise at the rate m. As before, a rise in the saving ratio during the transition to a new steady state will raise the growth rate above its steady-state value of $(m + n)$, but in the long run can only raise income per head to a higher steady-state level.

At least this degree of modification to the bedrock NGM was required if it was to pass the test of offering a plausible explanation for observed facts. We know that both output per worker and the capital:output ratio have exhibited a long-run upward trend in industrialised economies. In the steady state of the bedrock model, absent technological progress, both are constant. But by introducing only the simplest possible representation of technological progress, this anomaly is removed; both ratios would rise through time in the steady state, at rate m.

Issues for analysis

1. Purely labour augmenting exogenous technological progress (equivalent to Harrod-neutral progress) is consistent with SSG, as we have shown. It turns out,

however, to be the *only* form of progress consistent with SSG in a growth model of this kind (Uzawa, 1960–1). This finding limits the value of SSG models as representations of reality (Hahn and Matthews, 1964: 53) and leaves us to puzzle over why the finding should be so (Solow, 1970: 35).

We need, therefore, to ask whether there is any good reason to expect progress to be Harrod-neutral and find that leads us into considering the **endogenous theory of bias**.

2. The pace of technological progress in the long run determines the speed at which real incomes per head grow. While endogenising the bias of progress is important, it is also vital to endogenise its speed. Possible ways of doing this include recognising first, the implications of static and dynamic scale economies associated with innovation; second, the role of education and training in supporting the generation and diffusion of new technology; third, the influence of the R&D 'sector'; and fourth, the part that capital investment plays in promoting diffusion.

3. By construction, the bedrock NGM is a one-good model. It is impossible to analyse within it the relationships between economic growth and structural change. Growth models with two or more sectors are, significantly more demanding analytically than the one-sector NGM so far considered. But issues raised by changing structure are too important to ignore. They also allow us to consider another empirical hypothesis due to Kuznets, linking growth to the distribution of income.

4. The bedrock NGM also assumes a closed economy. It is thus impossible to use it to explain how international trade in goods, services and knowledge may influence growth and how technical change may influence trade. This is a particularly serious omission in a world of globalised production, foreign investment on the large scale and technology transfer across international borders.

5. Hints above suggest that it might be too restrictive to confine attention to a method of analysis moulded by the notion of steady state, one in which equiproportional growth rates of variables gives rise to an essentially linear vision of expansion. Evolutionary economists studying economic growth have wished not only to endogenise technical progress, but also to address the non-linear nature of growth pointing to sigmoid diffusion patterns, waves of varying length and causal connections between regularly observed business cycles and economic growth rates.

6. While growth models can incorporate an element of fluctuation, the main body of literature which deals with short- and medium-term fluctuations relates to macroeconomic theory, where the demand-side has a larger role to play.

The cues supplied by points (1), (2), (3) and (5) are the starting points for the remaining sections of this chapter. Technological progress in short- and medium-term macroeconomic analysis is dealt with in Chapter 8 and international trade and innovation in Chapter 9.

Endogenised bias

It can be shown rigorously that, if technological progress is not purely labour augmenting, advance is incompatible with SSG in the widely used one-sector model typified by the NGM (Uzawa, 1960–1, Hacche, 1979). Whether this is serious or not rather depends on whether actual economies, in which progress observably occurs, do tend to SSG paths and whether there is any good reason for believing progress might actually take that form.

If actual economies offer no evidence of a long-run tendency to SSG, then the methodological approach of orthodox growth theory should be questioned.[4] But assuming for the moment that sufficient reason exists to support working with SSG paths, it would be very comforting if Harrod-neutral technological progress could be given some economic rationale. In this section, a key result is to provide conditions under which Harrod-neutral technical progress would be endogenously generated.

In the analysis, we explore the implications of the **invention possibility frontier (IPF)** devised by Kennedy (1964) and von Weizsacker (1966) and used by Drandakis and Phelps (1966) and Samuelson (1965). We follow here the approach of Jones (1975). Hacche (1979) offers a useful comparison of Kennedy's analysis with that of Hicks (1963) and Ahmad (1966). The central idea here is that producers can influence the factor-saving characteristics of technological progress and that they do so by allocating their R&D among alternative projects in a way designed to minimise overall costs.

First, recall (7.5):

$$Q(t) = F(a(t)K(t), b(t)L(t))$$

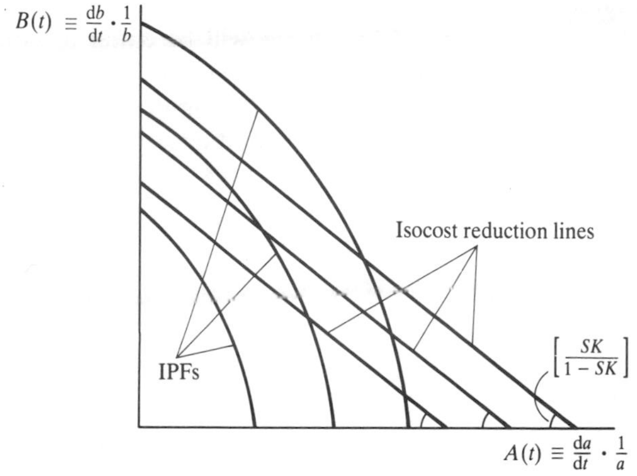

Figure 7.6 Invention possibility frontiers and isocost reduction lines in a model of endogenised bias.

where $da(t)/dt \cdot 1/a(t)$, written $A(t)$, represents the rate of capital augmentation and $db(t)/dt \cdot 1/b(t)$, or $B(t)$, the rate of labour augmentation. At any given moment t, an exogenously given amount of R&D effort yields progress which is either purely labour augmenting, purely capital augmenting or some combination of the two. As R&D effort rises, the faster will be the technological progress achieved, so that for any given $A(t)$, the higher $B(t)$, and for any given $B(t)$, the higher $A(t)$. But at the heart of the analysis is the notion of a trade-off between $A(t)$ and $B(t)$ for any given level of R&D effort. The proposition is that opportunities for innovation occur in a way which has a particular implication; an increased rate of labour augmentation can, from any initial level, be achieved only at the cost of reducing the rate of capital augmentation and *vice versa*. This means that for any given level of R&D, an IPF drawn between axes measuring $A(t)$ and $B(t)$ will slope downwards from left to right. But there is more. Decreasing marginal returns to R&D in obtaining technological advance augmenting either one of the inputs are also assumed. $A(t)$ declines at an increasing marginal rate as $B(t)$ rises and *vice versa*. All of this is depicted in Figure 7.6, which shows a family of IPFs. As noted above, higher IPFs will be associated with the potential for achieving faster technological advance.

The foundation of the analysis is to assume the existence of a continuous range of possibilities for achieving combinations of labour- and capital-augmenting technical progress which, moreover, exist in a form which implies an IPF which is concave, as shown. The problem now is: How will firms divide their R&D between projects in such a way that the combination of $A(t)$ and $B(t)$ which they achieve will serve their purposes best?

To answer this question, assume that firms are always motivated by the desire to minimise unit production costs, implying maximising the rate of cost reduction. Now the speed of reduction of unit costs will depend on the rates of factor augmentation and the relative importance of each input in the production process. Assuming constant returns, the shares of capital and labour in total output will be the same as their respective shares in total costs. The sum of the shares will be equal to either total costs or total output. Denoting unit costs by C, capital's share SK and labour's share $(1 - SK)$, the rate of unit cost reduction is the share-weighted sum of the cost reductions obtained from each source of factor augmentation:

$$dC(t)/dt \cdot 1/C(t) = \gamma(t) = SK \cdot A(t) + (1 - SK) \cdot B(t) \qquad (7.6)$$

It is at once evident that for any given value of $\gamma(t)$, we can rearrange this to generate a linear function in $A(t)$ and $B(t)$:

$$A(t) = \gamma(t)/SK - [(1 - SK)/SK] \cdot B(t) \qquad (7.6')$$

or

$$B(t) = \gamma(t)/(1 - SK) - [SK/(1 - SK)] \cdot A(t) \qquad (7.6'')$$

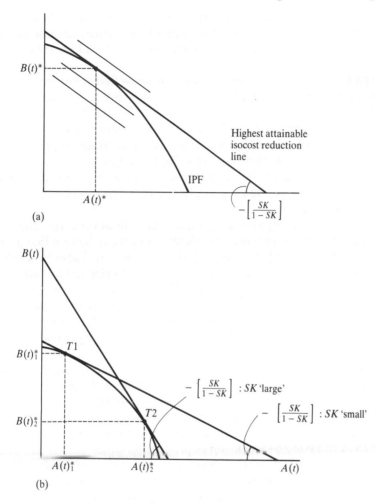

Figure 7.7   (a) An optimal combination of labour- and capital-augmenting technological progress; (b) A relatively large capital share encourages a bias towards capital-augmenting technological progress; a smaller capital share is associated with progress biased towards labour-augmentation.

Call such a function an **isocost reduction line**. Each such line shows, for given relative shares, the combinations of rates of capital- and labour-augmenting technological change which yield a given rate of cost reduction. Working with (7.6″) the slope of each line will be $dB(t)/dA(t) = -[SK/(1 - SK)]$, the ratio of the relative shares (see Figure 7.6). When $A(t) = 0$, i.e. when technological progress is purely labour augmenting, $B(t)$, the rate of labour-augmenting technological progress will be $(\gamma(t)/(1 - SK)$.

Since there is in principle a large number of possible values for $\gamma(t)$, there will also be a family of isocost reduction lines, all parallel to each other, because the relative shares are given. The higher is any given line, the greater will be the rate of cost reduction which it represents.

With a given IPF, the objective of all firms will be to find the point on that IPF which allows them to reach the highest isocost reduction line. At such a point, the slope of the IPF, which shows the marginal rate at which additional labour augmentation can be achieved by switching R&D resources from projects which would achieve further capital augmentation, will be equal to the slope of the isocost reduction lines, the ratio of the relative shares. Such a tangency point will imply how R&D effort should be allocated among projects to achieve an optimal combination of labour- and capital-augmenting progress. In Figure 7.7a, the optimal combination is denoted $A^*(t)$ and $B^*(t)$.

An interesting and intuitively appealing implication falls at once from this analysis. From the derivation of the isocost reduction lines above it can be seen that if capital's share SK is small, the slope of the lines, $-[SK/(1 - SK)]$, will also be small in the sense that, if drawn between a vertical axis for $B(t)$ and horizontal for $A(t)$, the lines will be relatively flat. If, on the other hand, SK is large, the lines will be relatively steep. For any given IPF, this means that the tangency between it and the highest attainable isocost reduction line must occur further up the IPF when SK is small than when it is large. In Figue 7.7b, a low SK yields the tangency $T1$ with associated values $A^*(t)1$ and $B^*(t)1$ and a high SK yields tangency $T2$ with associated values $A^*(t)2$ and $B^*(t)2$. This suggests that firms will tend to concentrate their resources on developing labour-augmenting advances when labour's share is relatively large (i.e. SK low), but when labour's share is relatively small, they will instead tend to concentrate on developing capital-augmenting progress.

That prediction is consistent with Hicks' (1963) hypothesis that innovation will tend to be directed to saving on any factor of production which has become relatively more expensive to purchase. Salter (1966) however contended that firms were interested in reducing total costs, and that even if the costs of only one input were to rise, any factor-saving innovation would be welcome, irrespective of whether it economised more on labour or capital.

We now state, but do not prove, that in a neoclassical type of growth model with a constant savings ratio and innovation induced as we have described above, a unique equilibrium SSG path exists, characterised by purely labour-augmenting technological progress (see Samuelson (1965), Drandakis and Phelps (1966) and Hacche (1979)). We also state that from any initial (equilibrium) position, the economy will converge upon that SSG path, subject to the condition that the elasticity of substitution is less than one. An intuitive argument (due originally to Solow) then shows relatively easily that an economy will tend to a path on which technological progress is purely labour augmenting. (For details see Jones, 1975.)

In terms of the diagrams, it has to be shown that wherever the economy starts on the IPF, it must move ultimately to the point where the IPF intersects the vertical axis, for at that point, $A(t)$ is zero and the value taken by $B(t)$ is the rate of purely labour-augmenting technical advance. If we were to start at any point along the IPF other than this, it is required that compared with its initial level, capital's share in output must fall. The argument consists in showing why, in this model, that would happen.

The model predicts first that if technological progress is induced by the mechanism outlined by Kennedy and von Weizsacker, the form taken by technological progress in SSG will be Harrod-neutral (i.e. labour augmenting). Harrod-neutrality is no longer an assumption that has to be made to achieve SSG, but a prediction of what will be found when SSG occurs. It also predicts that if equilibrium growth is characterised by a form of technological progress which is not initially Harrod-neutral, then so long as the elasticity of substitution in production is less than one, the economy will tend towards a SSG path along which, when attained, technological progress will be Harrod-neutral.

What these results seem to imply is that it might not be so troublesome after all that technical progress must be Harrod-neutral to be consistent with SSG. And that in turn provides some justification in theory for using the SSG method of dynamic analysis even when technical progress is present. But two sorts of caveat are in order.

First, the IPF and firms' behaviour. The position of the IPF and hence the pace of technological change remain exogenous. Might the results not be affected if both bias and pace of technological change were simultaneously endogenised?

Why should the IPF be continuous or concave? There are no obvious laws to suggest that a continuous range of innovation possibilities exists to await discovery, or that such possibilities as there are imply further savings in one factor can be achieved only at the cost of increasing marginal reductions in the saving on other factors.

The firms in this analysis maximise the current rate of progress; they respond to today's cost ratio with no regard to how that ratio might change in future. This implies they are surprisingly myopic, particularly when we recall that a rationale for SSG was that unfolding events should be consistent with firms' expectations of events.

Second, there are supplementary conditions not directly related to the IPF: (a) the saving ratio is required to be constant to obtain these results, but observably fluctuates in the short run and in the longer run will be subject to demographic and other factors; (b) the elasticity of substitution required to fall below unity has been found, empirically, to take a wide range of values some close to or above unity. This suggests that the stability result presented above would be in danger.

One reason why it has often seemed attractive to discount the importance of these objections is that in SSG, when $A(t)$ has fallen to zero, the shares of capital and labour become constant. It has been said that the wage share of income has tended to vary so little in the long run that it merits description as one the Great Ratios of contemporary economics (Drandakis and Phelps, 1966: 823). The Kennedy/von Weizsacker account of induced bias offered here provides a plausible explanation for this apparent fact (for evidence, see for example, Zarembka (1970)). However, this is somewhat incidental to our main concerns and Solow (1958) is among those to have expressed doubt about the constant wage-share proposition in the first place.

Endogenised pace of technological progress

Static increasing returns

In many cases, scale economies are closely related to technological progress and as Adam Smith first thought of them, were inseparable from it. As we noted earlier in the book, however, increasing returns to scale may be an important cause of productivity growth, even with given technology.

Interest in growth with increasing returns was rekindled in the 1980s when it was realised that theory developed to analyse product diversity (Dixit and Stiglitz, 1977) could be applied to consider the impact of increasing specialisation in production (Ethier, 1982; Romer, 1987). The setting for Romer's argument is that output of final consumption goods in a closed economy is a function of labour and a range of specialised intermediate inputs produced by monopolistically competitive firms. In this form of market, all of the assumptions of perfect competition but one are preserved. There is still freedom of entry and exit, perfect information and certainty and a large number of firms small relative to the size of the market. But each firm now has a degree of market power reflected in a downward slope in the firm-level demand curve it faces – not the horizontal demand curve of the perfectly competitive firm (Chamberlin, 1933; Robinson, 1933). The intermediate inputs in the model are produced from a primary resource which can be expanded over time by using output for investment rather than consumption. If the primary resource were interpreted as labour, investment would take the form of education and training to increase the effective labour-force over time.

The productivity-raising impact of specialisation is captured by adopting a form of production function for the final good, from which it follows that, even when the quantities of labour and intermediate inputs are held constant, output will rise with the range of different inputs. The degree of specialisation is limited in any period by the presence of fixed and variable costs in producing intermediate inputs. This ensures that the cost functions for producing intermediate inputs are U-shaped and allows the fixed supply of the primary resource in any period to determine the number of specialised firms. Investment increases the supply of the primary resource and induces a corresponding increase in the range of intermediate products. This sustains growth. The growth rate increases in this model if saving and investment increase, because the range of intermediate products can increase more rapidly as a result and increased specialisation will have an enhanced productivity-raising impact. Despite the absence of technological change, these effects will make it look as if the economy is experiencing exogenous, labour-augmenting advance which, as we have shown, is in its pure form consistent with SSG.

Dynamic increasing returns: LBD and learning by learning in economic growth

As we have noted elsewhere, LBD can also be regarded as a form of increasing returns. A striking, early attempt to endogenise the rate of technological progress through

LBD is found in Arrow (1962),[2] Levhari (1966a, b) and Sheshinski (1967). The approach is illustrated in terms of Arrow's (1962) analysis. Recalling (7.5) again, technological progress is endogenised through the coefficient $b(t)$, the efficiency index of labour, increases in which show the rate of labour augmenting advance. Arrow's learning function makes $b(t)$ increase with the total of cumulative gross investment which has ever occurred in the economy, the integral of investment per period to date:

$$b(t) = z\left[\int_{-\infty}^{t} I(t)\mathrm{d}t \right]; \qquad z' > 0 \tag{7.8}$$

If we assume capital does not depreciate, cumulative gross investment becomes the current capital stock and (7.8) can be written:

$$b(t) = z \cdot K(t); \qquad z' > 0 \tag{7.9}$$

If $b(t)$ has constant elasticity with respect to $K(t)$, (7.9) may be given the specific form:

$$b(t) \, c \cdot K^m \tag{7.10}$$

where c is an arbitrary constant and m the elasticity, by assumption less than unity in value.

What are the ideas behind this formulation? Essentially, we are back to spillover effects again. Every act of physical investment in an economy generates not only a new machine but also new knowledge: firms making the new capital learn as they produce; firms undertaking the investment learn by using; firms not currently investing learn from the experience of others. All this new knowledge itself becomes an input into production throughout the economy, and owing to the *irreversibility* of learning, can be viewed as a by-product of all investment ever to have occurred. This process enhances the effectiveness of physical inputs globally, and because the effectiveness of inputs is enhanced at the same time as the aggregate capital stock increases, a doubling of all inputs can yield a more than doubling of aggregate output, that is, increasing returns at the macro-level.

It is possible in this style of model still to assume constant returns at the micro-level if firms take the state of technological knowledge as given when making their production decisions. This is a reasonable assumption to make if we believe firms will discount any link between their individual investment decisions and the impact this will have at the macro-level on economy-wide learning.

Firms are least likely to take such links into account if they are unable to lay any proprietary claim to the new knowledge generated from their capital investment and hence unable to appropriate any rewards from it. This will be the case when all such knowledge is public knowledge, the assumption implicit in Arrow's analysis and reflecting a tradition going back to Marshall (1920) and Young (1928) focusing on increasing returns external to the firm.

If knowledge is wholly public, it can be viewed as a public good – a good which is non-rivalrous and non-excludable. Rival goods are those whose use by one individual or firm precludes use by any other – such as raw material inputs. By contrast, non-rival goods may be used simultaneously by two or more individuals or firms. All forms of knowledge, including scientific and technological, are examples. Excludable goods (either rival or non-rival) are those in which it is possible to establish clear property rights allowing owners to exclude others from using the good and, by implication, to charge others for using it. Non-excludable goods are those in which it is impossible or prohibitively expensive to establish and enforce property rights.

The knowledge generated in Arrow's model is non-rivalrous and non-excludable, and firms may treat it as a public good (Shaw, 1992; 614). Given constant returns to scale in physical inputs at the micro-level, competitive equilibrium can thus co-exist with increasing returns at the macro-level. Increasing returns internal to the firm imply that, if inputs are paid their marginal products, total factor payment will exceed total output. This makes the achievement of equilibrium impossible. But if increasing returns are external to the firm, equilibrium can occur because only labour and capital are actually compensated financially (Shaw, 1992). With this in mind, we may turn to the characteristics of Arrow's growing economy with learning by doing. Suppose the economy's production function takes the Cobb-Douglas form:

$$Q(t) = K(t)^a [b(t)L(t)]^{1-a} \tag{7.11}$$

Then, given Arrow's learning function (7.10), it can be shown that in SSG, the growth rate itself will be $(n/1 - m)$, where n is the labour force growth rate. Since $m < 1$, SSG with learning is faster than SSG without it and that the greater the elasticity m, the faster SSG will be. Simple manipulation also reveals that output per head grows at the rate $(m/1 - m)n$ (Hacche, 1979: 143).

Arrow's work set an important precedent, but more recently Stiglitz (1987) has obtained a richer menu of results in a model which divides learning effects into two: first, LBD, productivity increases resulting from production and hence linked to output; and second, learning by learning which reflects the belief that 'experience in learning may increase one's productivity in learning. One learns to learn ... in the process of learning itself' (p. 130).

To obtain a preliminary result, assume first that technological progress is purely labour augmenting at a rate $B(t)$, endogenously determined by the ratio of capital to effective labour, $k_{eff}(t)$. The higher $k_{eff}(t)$, the greater $B(t)$. Arguments for this hypothesis might be that a high $k_{eff}(t)$ implies a fast investment rate relative to labour-force growth, bringing embodied new technology into production at a rate which implies increasing productivity potential or, a high $k_{eff}(t)$ suggests high value, possibly hi-tech capital equipment, the introduction of which stimulates the labour working with it to perform with greater enthusiasm. Algebraically the hypothesis may be expressed:

$$B(t) = B(k_{eff}(t)) \qquad dB/dk_{eff}(t) > 0 \tag{7.12}$$

To this, an assumption must be added about saving and investment. Rather than taking the saving ratio s as a constant, Stiglitz, with plausible intuition, argues that when output and thus income increases relatively rapidly, it is easier to save. The the

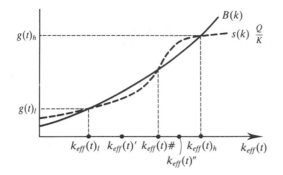

Figure 7.8 Steady-state growth path possibilities in a model where the saving ratio depends on the rate of technological progress. (Adapted with permission of the publisher from J.E. Stiglitz (1987) 'Learning to learn, localised learning and technological progress', in P. Dasgupta and P. Stoneman (eds) *Economic Policy and Technological Performance*, Cambridge: Cambridge University Press.)

saving rate might be expected to increase with the growth rate of output and income per head, which we know from earlier analysis depends on the rate of labour-augmenting technological progress:

$$s = s(B(t)(k_{eff}(t))) \qquad (7.13)$$

Assuming finally that the labour force is constant ($n=0$), SSG will occur when $(dK(t)/dt)/K(t)$ equals the growth rate of effective labour, $B(t)$. But $dK(t)/dt$ is (absent depreciation) equal to aggregate savings per period. So in SSG:

$$(dK(t)/dt)/K(t) = sQ(t)/K(t) = [s(B(t)(k_{eff}(t)))]\cdot[Q(t)/K(t)] = B(t) \qquad (7.14)$$

To analyse the implications of this, Figure 7.8 has $k_{eff}(t)$ on the horizontal axis and $B(t)$, sQ/K and the growth rate of income per head on the vertical. From (7.12), $B(t)$ rises with $k_{eff}(t)$ and this relationship is shown by the solid line $B(k)$. Now sQ/K comprises two components. From earlier work on the NGM, recall that as K/L rises, Q/K falls. But by assumption here, as rising K/L causes growth in Q/L through raising $B(t)$, s will rise. The combination of these effects could easily cause sQ/K to rise (and/or fall) at varying rates with changes in $k_{eff}(t)$, leading the sQ/K function to criss-cross $B(k)$. One possible configuration of sQ/K is shown by the dotted line in Figure 7.8.

In Fig 7.8, $k_{eff}(t)$ will rise towards $k_{eff}(t)h$ from any point below it but above $k_{eff}(t)\#$ and fall towards $k_{eff}(t)_l$ from points above it but below $k_{eff}(t)\#$. At $k_{eff}(t)''$, for example, sQ/K exceeds $B(k)$, so from (7.14), $(dK(t)/dt)/K(t)$ must be positive, i.e. $k_{eff}(t)$ must be rising, given that labour inputs are constant. At $k_{eff}(t)'$, $B(k)$ exceeds sQ/K, and the converse is true. This suggests one way in which countries may become caught in a 'low-level equilibrium trap', characterised in Figure 7.8 by $k_{eff}(t)_l$ and its associated growth rate of output per head, $g(t)l$. If $k_{\text{eff}}(t)$, despite investment effort to boost it, is not raised above $k_{eff}(t)\#$, it will always slip back towards $k_{\text{eff}}(t)_l$. At that level, $k_{\text{eff}}(t)$ is so low that labour-augmenting progress and the growth of per capita incomes are relatively slow and the savings ratio as a result also depressed, which only reinforces a low investment rate. On the other hand, if $k_{\text{eff}}(t)$ could be raised only fractionally above $k_{\text{eff}}(t)\#$, which would call for a 'big push' if $k_{\text{eff}}(t)$ were low to start with, it would continue to move upwards to the high-level equilibrium $[k_{\text{eff}}(t)_h, g((t)_h]$ from then on.

As in the NGM with simple technological progress, advance is exogenous and purely labour augmenting. But in the Solow-type model, a strong implied prediction is that the growth rates of income per head of all countries (with similar labour-force growth rates) should converge in the long run since all economies should be able to tap into new technology on more or less equal terms and benefit from it to a more or less similar extent. This is not what has been observed (Lucas, 1988) and in recent times, an increasing amount of effort has been devoted to trying to explain why (Dowrick and Gemmell, 1991). The basic Stiglitz model outlined above gives a hint at the sort of factors which might impede convergence, since countries might be divided among those with low and those with high-level equilibria. And only massive investment by the former group could place those countries irreversibly on paths to high-level growth.

But the same general style of set-up can also be used to frame a richer analysis which brings in learning effects directly. Before, $B(t)$ was related to $k_{\text{eff}}(t)$ alone. Now assume that for any given level of $k_{\text{eff}}(t)$, $B(t)$ will be faster, the greater is the learning capacity, J, of the economy. Learning capacity itself increases with $k_{\text{eff}}(t)$, but the speed at which it may grow over time depends on the level at which it starts. An economy with a low historic level of $k_{\text{eff}}(t)$ will have had little opportunity to develop general experience of how to learn, so its learning capacity will be restricted [low $J(k_{\text{eff}}(t))$] and this in turn implies that the economy will be slow to learn how to make best use of any increase in investment which raises $k_{\text{eff}}(t)$. This has two implications.

First, as before, there may be more than one equilibrium and a modest increase in investment may not be enough to allow a country to vault irreversibly from a low-level trap. On any SSG path, real incomes per head would again rise at the rate of technological progress, but that rate itself is now determined by the learning capacity of the economy which, in turn, is low if $k_{\text{eff}}(t)$ is low, higher if $k_{\text{eff}}(t)$ higher. But, second, even if large-scale capital investment were to raise $k_{\text{eff}}(t)$ significantly, a limited learning capacity related to the previously low level of $k_{\text{eff}}(t)$ would prevent output and income per head from rising very quickly. Supposing the saving rate is still to be linked to per capita income growth, the slow response of labour productivity growth could prevent domestic savings from rising enough to support continued large-scale investment. The slow learning phenomenon could then prevent the country from ever enjoying faster growth in real incomes per head.

Finally, the rate of progress and hence growth rate of income per head can be linked both to learning by learning and LBD. To do this, set:

$$B(t) = \left(\frac{L}{Q}\right) \cdot m(J, k_{\text{eff}})Q \tag{7.15}$$

so that the rate of technological change is proportional now to the output level. For any given output level, technical change will be faster and output per head growing faster, the greater capital intensity and learning capacity. Increases in output level have two contrary effects. First, they tend to raise the rate of productivity growth through LBD by increasingly large amounts, the larger the initial learning capacity of the economy, reflected in the size of $m(J, k_{\text{eff}})$. But second, labour requirements per unit of output are included to capture the idea that as (L/Q) falls, the scope for further improvements may become increasingly limited and the pace at which labour can be augmented therefore falls.

This formulation can be simplified by recalling that L is constant in this model, so choosing units to make $L = 1$, (7.15) may be rewritten $B(t) = m(J, k_{\text{eff}})$. In steady state, the growth rates of capital and effective labour must as before be equal and recalling (7.16):

$$B(t) = sQ/K = m(J, k_{\text{eff}}) \tag{7.16}$$

The growth rate of incomes per head will be greater in steady state, the more able an economy is to exploit potential gains from LBD as a consequence of previous experience having raised its general learning capacity. This result coincides nicely with the prediction, at the industry level, of the evolutionary diffusion model discussed in Chapter 6. The higher the productivity growth generated, the greater the profits for reinvestment and so the higher the rate of capital accumulation.

Since (7.16) is identical to (7.14), the same argument as before can be used to predict that economies might not be able to reach high-level equilibria and become trapped at low growth rates of per capita income. In either case however, the degree of capital intensity and general learning capacity achieved in the past will have a great influence on the productivity growth rate the economy can hope to sustain in the future. While arguments in the past have tended to emphasise the need for a big push to raise the capital : labour ratio, Stiglitz stresses the learning implications of changes in technique which increased investment should bring. It is less clear how a country which reaches a high-level equilibrium growth path might slip off it and start to grow more slowly, as appears to have happened with Britain.

Human capital accumulation

In contrast to the 'by-product' nature of LBD, knowledge which is potentially valuable for increasing the productive capacity of labour can also be acquired as the consequence of decisions to invest in human capital (Schultz, 1961, Becker, 1975). This was studied in the context of growth models by Uzawa (1965) under the assumption that the labour force was divided into 'productive' and 'educational' groups and that $B(t)$ increased at a decreasing marginal rate with the proportion of the total labour force in the educating group (for a formally identical model relating to R&D, see next section). Uzawa's analysis has now been generalised by Lucas (1988).

The idea of these models is not to endogenise technological progress (its rate is exogenously given), but to show how investment decisions for human and physical capital can influence the effectiveness of labour in deploying new technological knowledge.

Lucas uses a general form of the Cobb-Douglas production function in which first, the effective work-force is made to reflect individuals' skill levels and the proportion of their non-leisure time devoted to production, given that there is an alternative use of time: investing in human capital. Second, the contribution of inputs to producing output is influenced positively by a factor, the average level of skill across all workers, which is taken to reflect the beneficial externality arising from individual decisions to add to their human capital. Taking an individual's human capital stock, h, to be his/her general skill level, Lucas assumes h grows at a proportional growth rate which is linear in the fraction of non-leisure time devoted to enhancing it.

Lucas is able to show that if $[(dh/dt)/h]^*$ is the growth rate of human capital accumulation on a balanced, competitive equilibrium growth path, real per capita consumption will grow at a rate faster than that by a factor which is positively related to the size of the beneficial economy-wide externalities reaped from individuals' decisions to invest in raising their skills. In the spirit of Stiglitz, he also discovers that an economy beginning with a low level of human and physical capital will remain permanently below an initially better-endowed economy.

It is important to note that the optimising foundations which Lucas gives to investment decisions in this model also allow him to identify the determinants of $[(dh/dt)/dt]$ on a balanced growth path. It will rise with the effectiveness of investment in human capital and fall with the discount rate. The latter factor establishes a link between 'thrift and growth, since the higher the discount rate, the lower we would expect saving and investment rates to be in all forms of capital and hence the slower the long-run growth rate of consumption per head. However, because of the externality, some of the gains from increased human capital enjoyed by society will not be connected by individuals to the sacrifices they made to acquire it on an individual basis. Thus there will be a tendency for individuals to invest less in formal skill enhancement than is socially desirable. This, in turn, provides an important rationale for subsidising education.

Research and development

The most straightforward way of incorporating R&D in formal growth models is to stick with the NGM formulation and again to assume that technological progress takes a pure, labour-augmenting form. Suppose, following Phelps (1966), that the economy can be viewed as having two sectors, One, which we shall call the Research Sector, generates new technological knowledge. The other produces a final consumption good. The labour force is divided between the two sectors, so that $L(F)/L$ is the exogenously determined proportion u engaged in final production and $L(R)/L$ the remaining fraction $(1 - u)$ involved in R&D. Taking account of labour-augmenting progress, the size of the effective labour force in final production is $b(t)u(t)L(t)$, the ratio of capital to effective labour is $K(t):b(t)u(t)L(t)$, denoted $k_{eff}(F)$, and final good output per effective worker rises at a decreasing marginal rate with increases in $k_{eff}(F)$.

The impact of work in the R&D sector is shown through changes in $b(t)$ generated via a technological function which makes the instantaneous rise in $b(t)$, $db(t)/dt$, depend positively on levels already achieved (cf. learning by learning) and on the labour force dedicated to R&D. Labour alone is used to increase knowledge through R&D. Diminishing marginal returns are associated with increased R&D effort in any period. With these assumptions, Phelps derives a version of the equation of motion taking the form:

$$dk(t)/dt = sb(t)u(t)\cdot f(k_{eff}(F)) - nk(t) \qquad (7.17)$$

where $b(t)$ grows at a constant proportional rate, m.

In SSG in this model, the technical progress rate $B(t)$ turns out to be exactly the same as the growth rate of labour n, implying that both actual capital and output grow at a rate $(n + m) = (n + B(t)) = 2n$.

The analysis abstracts from a number of potentially important complications. First, both labour and non-labour inputs are used in R&D, though it cannot be denied that much R&D is very labour intensive. It is because R&D output has been keyed to labour input alone, however, that Phelps can obtain the simple result that output grows at twice the rate of labour-force growth. Second, the division of the labour force between 'researchers' and 'producers' is to a large extent the result of economic decisions undertaken at the microlevel with a view to maximising expected returns. Making it constant by assumption clears the way for analysis, but side-steps the observation that the fractions u and $(1 - u)$ actually vary over time. From a theoretical standpoint, endogenising technical progress satisfactorily requires invoking economic explanations for variations in $L(R):L(F)$. Third, the technological function adopted by Phelps appears to be motivated partly by the need to ensure that SSG results can be obtained. In this spirit, it is constructed to imply that R&D effort will not be concentrated in some periods more than in others. Yet the 'bunching' of R&D that this outlaws can often be a feature of discovery processes; a single breakthrough will sometimes allow a whole series of connected advances suddenly to be made. Finally, it is unclear how the implicit underlying structure of perfectly competitive equilibrium in the NGM could be consistent with externalities associated with R&D, the benefits which imitators often gain from the costs incurred by innovators. Implicitly such external effects are absent here.

It is criticisms of this kind which motivated Romer (1986) to reformulate the whole question in a general way. Romer's review of international evidence on rising per capita incomes suggests that real output and income per head do not converge on zero growth rates, but have an upward trend strong enough in the long run to demand explanation. On data from Maddison (1979), he shows that the average US annual compound growth rate of real per capita GDP grew almost uninterruptedly from

0.58 per cent in 1800–40 to 2.47 per cent in 1960–78, slowing slightly over the period 1920–60. On a trend test for eleven countries (United Kingdom, France, Denmark, United States, Germany, Sweden, Italy, Australia, Norway, Japan and Canada), the null hypothesis of a non-positive trend is rejected at the 5 per cent level in five nations and at the 10 per cent level in eight. Observations stretch back to 1770 in the United Kingdom and France, and start most recently (in 1870) in Japan and Canada.

The essence of his first explanation for these observations is that economy-wide, productivity-raising benefits spill-over from individual firms' private investments in new knowledge, which they employ with fixed quantities of all other inputs. Such benefits bring about increases in the marginal product of aggregate knowledge and offset the limitations on growth imposed by the labour supply.

The explanation owes much to Arrow's work on growth and his approach is in some ways a special case in a class of models inspired by that example (Stern, 1991).

But in an alternative approach Romer (1990) follows lines laid down by Uzawa (1965) (echoed in Phelps' work, above), Shell (1973) and Lucas (1988). Here, technological advance has its origins in a sector which produces productivity-raising ideas. A crucial endogenous variable then becomes the amount of resources devoted to that sector. The model incorporates important strands of analysis dealt with in this book and has also provided a foundation for major advances in the analysis of international trade and growth (see pp. 392–8). We focus on it here.

Romer's model is based on three premises: first, technological change lies at the heart of economic growth; second, technological change arises mostly because of intentional profit-seeking actions taken by decision-makers responding to market incentives; third instructions for transforming raw materials are different from other economic goods in the sense that, once created, no extra cost has to be incurred in using them repeatedly.

Romer's approach is a significant advance on earlier growth models. First, it recognises and gives separate attention to the various elements of innovation process: producing new knowlege, embodying it in new producer goods (capital) and deploying new capital in generating final output. Second, it makes the incorporation of knowledge a matter of economic and technological concern: research is explained in terms of profit-maximising behaviour. Third, it reflects the fact that the creation of new knowledge is invariably associated with monopolistic tendencies. Fourth, it provides a basis for understanding how beneficial externalities in the innovation process can lead to unbounded growth. Here the key insight is that new technological knowledge has two roles to play, each with potentially different appropriability characteristics. On the one hand, new knowledge may be incorporated in a patented design for a new product, in which connection the owner of the design has property rights over its use in production and can exclude other potential users from reaping returns on it. On the other, the inventor of a new design cannot prevent other inventors rfrom using his or her knowledge, revealed in the design, in their research work.

The benefits which arise from the use of the knowledge in other products are non-excludable and constitute the beneficial externalities or overspill effects of the original invention. These may be very extensive and in Romer's account are the mainspring of a growing economy. But because some of the benefits *are* excludable, it becomes possible to explain research as a profit-maximising activity in a way earlier models were unable to do.

We now sketch the model itself. The framework is as follows.

A closed economy comprising three sectors: the research sector producing new technological knowledge in the form of designs for new producer durables, the intermediate goods sector which produces a range of producer durables and the final goods sector.

Technological knowledge, denoted Ω, is measured in terms of the number of designs extant and each new design thus adds 1 to the current value of Ω. Producer durables comprise a set $\{X\} = \{x_1, x_2, \dots x_\Omega \dots x(\infty)\}$, where x is the output level and the numbers $i = 1, 2, \dots \infty$ label the goods. Within the set, $x(\Omega + 1) \dots x(\infty)$ take zero values until further new knowledge has been generated.

Final output Q is produced with a Cobb-Douglas production function:

$$Q = H_Q^a \cdot L^b \sum_{i=1}^{\infty} x_i^{(1-a-b)} \tag{7.18}$$

where H_Q is human capital in producing Q. The aggregate labour force L is assumed constant, as is overall human capital, H, of which H_Q forms one part.

In (7.18), designs are treated as discrete, indivisible objects but if problems of indivisibility and uncertainty are ignored, the index i on x can be treated as a continuous variable and (7.18) rewritten:

$$Q = H_Q^a \cdot L^b \int_0^{\infty} x(i)^{(1-a-b)} \, di \tag{7.18'}$$

In either case, the function is homogeneous of degree one, allowing output in the final goods sector to be described in terms of a single, price-taking firm.

In the intermediate goods sector, each producer durable is produced by a different firm which has bid successfully for (i.e. purchased) the patent on the design for the good and thereafter manufactures it exclusively. Inputs into production are the design and capital goods converted from output sacrificed from consumption on a one-for-one basis. As a simplifying assumption, labour inputs are set at zero. Given its monopoly position on design i, Firm i faces a downward sloping demand curve along which $x(i)$ units of i are at any point rented at a rate of $P(i)$ per unit per period. Assuming no depreciation, the value of a unit of good i is the PDV of the rental income stream it generates.

In the final goods sector, the representative firm's profit, expressed in units of output, is:

$$\int_0^{\infty} [H_Q^a \cdot L^b \cdot x(i)^{(1-a-b)} - P(i) \, x(i)] \, di \tag{7.19}$$

To maximise this with respect to the quantities of each producer durable hired, (7.19) must be differentiated with respect to $x(i)$ and set equal to zero, which after rearrangement implies an (inverse) aggregate demand function for durables:

$$P(i) = (1 - a - b) \cdot H_Q^a \cdot L^b \cdot x(i)^{(-a-b)} \tag{7.20}$$

For given values of H_Q and L this is a constant elasticity demand curve for each i which the monopoly producer of each durable takes as given in setting its profit-maximising output level and price.

Each firm will already have invested in acquiring the design for the durable, but this is a sunk cost. In making its forward looking choices, it takes as given H_Q, L and r, the interest rate on loans measured in units of current output, to choose an output level x to maximise at every date its revenue less variable cost. Its revenue, $P(x)x$ is its flow of rental from final goods producers and from (7.20) equal to $(1 - a - b) H_Q^a \cdot L^b \cdot x^{(-a-b)}$.

To make each unit of the durable, J units of output are sacrificed from consumption. Variable costs thus total rJx, implying a constant marginal cost of rJ. Each monopolist's price, $RJ/(1 - a - b)$ is a mark-up over marginal cost determined by the elasticity of demand.

Total capital K, the aggregate of producer durables in use, is found by multiplying the quantities of each type of capital employed in production by the output foregone in producing each unit.

$$K = J \int_{i=1}^{\infty} x(i) \tag{7.21}$$

The aggregate K changes according to the accounting rule:

$$dK(t)/dt = Q(t) - C(t) \tag{7.22}$$

where $C(t)$ is consumption.

Research sector output comprises increases in technological knowledge, $d\Omega/dt$ and is generated with inputs of existing knowledge and human capital located in the sector. If researcher m has an amount of human capital H_m and access to a portion Ω_m of the total stock of knowledge implicit in previous designs, the production rate of new designs by m will be $z \cdot H_m \cdot \Omega_m$, where z is a productivity parameter. All researchers are assumed to have free access to all knowledge Ω at any given time. Thus over all researchers:

$$d\Omega/dt = z \cdot H_\Omega \cdot \Omega \tag{7.23}$$

where H_Ω is total human capital in research.

Implicit in this formulation are two further and crucial assumptions. First, devoting more human capital to research leads to an increase in the rate of production of new designs, since $[d(d\Omega/dt)/dH_\Omega] = z\Omega > 0$. Second, adding to the stock of knowledge, Ω, yields growth in the marginal productivity of human capital in research at a rate constant and proportional to Ω itself. This is so because the marginal productivity of H_Ω, $d\Omega/dH_\Omega$, is rising at the rate (d/dt) $(d\Omega/dH_\Omega)$, which from (7.23) is $z\cdot\Omega$. As noted earlier, this rising productivity in research reflects beneficial spill-overs. It also has the effect of preventing the returns to human capital from falling and hence prevents migration from research to manufacturing as Ω grows (see comments on (7.27) below). This in turn prevents any slowing in the flow of new ideas, the fuel for the growth process.[6]

The market for designs is competitive, so the price for designs is bidden up by potential users until it is equal to the present value of the net revenue that a monopolist expects to extract from it. In a formulation taken from Grossman and Helpman (1989). Romer then shows that at every point in time the excess of revenue over marginal cost must be just sufficient to cover the interest cost on the initial investment in the design.

Thus:

$$\Pi(t) = r(t)\, P_\Omega \tag{7.24}$$

where $\Pi(t)$ is monopolist's profit, and P_Ω the cost of producing a new design. This condition determines whether a new design will be produced or not, i.e. depending on whether its costs will be covered or not.

Finally, consumers are endowed with fixed quantities of labour and human capital, own the existing durable goods producing firms and an implication of their intertemporal maximising behaviour used in the analysis is that consumption grows at the rate $(r - d)/s$, where d is the subjective discount rate and s is the intertemporal rate of substitution.

Results

If Ω is fixed:

$$Q = (H_Q\cdot\Omega)^a\cdot(L\cdot\Omega)^b\cdot K^{(1-a-b)}\cdot J^{(a+b-1)}$$

$$= H_Q^a\cdot L^b\cdot\Omega\cdot x\cdot \#^{(1-a-b)} \tag{7.25}$$

where the symmetry of the model implies that all existing durables will be supplied at the same level, $x\#$ The model behaves like the NGM with labour- and human capital-augmenting technical change.

If Ω grows at an exogenously specified exponential rate, the economy converges on a balanced growth path on which the rate of supply of durables and the ratio of K to Ω would be constant. Since both K and Ω are growing, human capital wage in final output will also rise, reflecting increased research productivity implied by equation (7.23).

To identify the characteristics of the model, in this case solve the equilibrium conditions along the balanced growth path. Using the implications of the monopoly pricing problem, (7.20) and (7.25), it can be shown that:

$$P_\Omega = [(a+b)/r](1-a-b)\, H_Q^a\cdot L^b\cdot x\cdot\#(1-a-b) \tag{7.26}$$

In equilibrium, the return on human capital in both research and manufacturing wH must be the same as the marginal productivity of human capital in each sector otherwise it would pay some units of human capital to relocate. The wage in the research sector is simply all the income generated there $P_\Omega \cdot z \cdot \Omega$ and to equalise returns to human capital in both sectors, $H_Q = H - H_\Omega$ must be chosen so that wH and $P_\Omega \cdot z \cdot \Omega$ both equal the marginal product of human capital in the final goods sector:

$$a \cdot H_Q^{(a-1)} \cdot L^b \cdot \Omega \cdot x \#^{(1-a-b)} \tag{7.27}$$

It is clear from (2.27) that the marginal product of H_Q grows in proportion to Ω. As noted on page 337, rising productivity of human capital in the research sector, implicit in (7.23), is essential to prevent human capital from migrating to manufacturing. This in turn is vital to ensure that the research engine of growth is maintained and that sustained, non-slowing can persist.

Together (7.26) and (7.27) imply:

$$H_Q = (1/z)r\{a/[(1 - a - b)(a + b)]\} \tag{7.28}$$

Now, from (7.23), recall that Ω grows at the exponential rate $z \cdot H_\Omega$ when $H_\Omega = H - H_Q$ is fixed. If r is fixed, $x\#$ is also fixed (an implication of monopoly pricing). And from (7.25), Q grows at the same rate as Ω if L, H_Q and $x\#$ are fixed. If $x\#$ is fixed, K and Ω grow at the same rate, since total capital usage is $\Omega \cdot x \# J$. Let g stand for the common growth rate of Ω, K and Q. Then:

$$g = (dQ/dt)/Q = (dK/dt)/K = (d\Omega/dt)/\Omega = z \cdot H_\Omega$$

which, together with (7.28) implies:

$$g = z \cdot H_\Omega = zH - [a/(1 - a - b)(a + b)]r \tag{7.29}$$

Equation (7.29) clearly predicts that, along balanced growth paths, countries with greater stocks of human capital will experience faster rates of economic growth. It also suggests that economic growth will be faster, the greater is the productivity of human capital employed in research. Although Romer approaches the analysis in a different way from Stiglitz (1987) and Lucas (1988), his results re-affirm the central importance of human capital and its productivity in understanding why growth rates differ.

Like Lucas's model, Romer's also predicts that the interest rate has a role to play – again related to human capital. In both cases, it may be noted that a higher interest rate implies a higher opportunity cost of investing in education to acquire human capital and hence tends to discourage investment in it. But part of the intuition behind (7.29) lies in realising that the opportunity cost of human capital in research is the wage it could earn in manufacturing. The return to human capital in research is the stream of net revenue that a design generates in future. If r is higher, the PDV of that stream is lower, so less human capital will be attracted to that sector and the growth rate will suffer.

It is less easy to understand why neither L nor J appear in (7.29). Higher L should increase monopolists' demand, lower J should reduce their costs, each encouraging higher output levels, $x\#$. This, in turn, should raise the return to human capital in research, attract more of it to research, and increase research output. But in general, higher L and lower J will also raise returns on human capital in final goods production, offering a counter-attraction there. And in this model, the two effects cancel each other, something which cannot be expected to be true in general. The correct inference, as Romer points out (1990: S94) is that implications of changes in L and J are ambiguous.

Romer's modelling of economic growth has made a significant impact, but is not without its critics. Among questions raised are the following:

1. Romer relies on an aggregate production function in which knowledge and physical capital make separate and distinct contributions to output. But so much new knowledge is embodied in new capital that it may make little sense to separate the knowledge from the equipment and more sense to focus on the act of investment in physical capital, a notion which was central to Kaldor's technical progress function and has more recently been taken up again by Scott (1989), discussed below.
2. The model emphasises the important benefits of increasing the stock of human capital but ignores the resource costs of education and training, and the dynamics of a transition from a low-growth to a high-growth economy built on expanding human capital. The lesson from Stiglitz's (1987) analysis is that a major increase in human capital in the past might explain internationally high growth rates for long afterwards. But while the historic costs of increasing human capital for faster-growth nations must now be viewed as bygones, nations wishing to increase human capital now also need guidance on the optimal resource investment to make on human capital and time horizons before positive results can be expected. In addition, such analysis needs to consider whether some sorts of human capital should be preferred to others and on what grounds.
3. It may be difficult to identify a knowledge-producing sector in real economies, which makes it hard to undertake empirical work with Romer's approach. (Stern, 1991: 127)
4. Firms in Romer's world decide what resources to devote to creating new knowledge, but new knowledge then diffuses to other firms completely without cost; there are no implementation or imitation costs (Schmitz, 1989).
5. Relatedly, assuming that all researchers have free access to all knowledge at all times ignores the costs, gradualness and imperfections of learning processes.

Embodiment and diffusion

Much new technical knowledge can obtained only by purchasing the new machines in which they are embodied. The age structure of the aggregate capital stock, in addition to its size, may well have a bearing on economic performance. The larger the proportion of relatively new capital, the more influential on overall productivity, the higher productivity new machines will be and so the greater average productivity should be.

We would expect that an increase in the rate of investment in new machines, those of most recent 'vintage' should, through the effect of increasing the proportion of all machines which are new, also raise productivity and hence growth. It is an important element of vintage models, which examine the implications of varying the age structure of capital, that at any one moment several or many vintages of capital will coexist. If new technological ideas can be obtained only by buying machines which embody them, the diffusion of a new idea depends on the rate at which new-technology machines supplant old-technology machines in the overall aggregate.

Solow (1960) experimented with a model of growth incorporating a vintage capital structure and found, somewhat to his surprise, that it fitted the facts of observed growth no better than models in which capital had been treated as a homogeneous lump subject to exogenous technological advance. Denison (1985) also concluded that there was no explanatory value in the embodiment idea. But perhaps the most thorough examination of the issue was conducted at the theoretical level by Phelps (1962). He discovered that if embodied and disembodied progress were introduced into a neoclassical style of growth model with vintage capital, output in SSG would expand at the rate $n + (m + d)/(1 - a)$, where n is the constant growth rate of labour, m the rate of embodied technical progress, d the rate of disembodied progress and $(1 - a)$ the share in total income earned by labour. This confirms our expectation that an increase in the exogenous rate of technical progress will raise the steady-state growth rate. But the growth rate is found independently of the investment rate and suggests, in line with the findings of Solow and Denison, that reducing the average age of capital by increasing the investment rate will make no difference.

Responding to this sort of conclusion, Solow has commented: 'I do not know if that finding should be described as a paradox, but it was at least a puzzle' (1988: 315). However, the solution may not be too hard to find. The Solow and Phelps results are findings based upon a comparison of steady-state growth paths. We have already noted that in the transition from a low investment to high investment steady-state path, real output per head can rise, even in the absence of technological progress. One possible implication of this is that if technological progress at a given rate is embodied, output growth will accelerate if investment speeds up at least in the medium term, i.e. until the new SSG path has been reached. Solow draws attention to this when citing Wolff (1987).

Wolff calculates the average growth rate of total factor productivity and various measures of the speed of investment and across countries, he finds a strong, positive correlation between them. His interpretation is that this provides confirmation of the embodiment hypothesis:

> 'If we suppose that all these countries had access to roughly the same pool of technological innovations, then it appears that the ones that invested fastest were best able to take advantage of the knowledge available. That is certainly one reasonable interpretation and it is one I like'

says Solow (1988: 315).

Investment and the diffusion of new technology could be linked in either of two directions; the rate of investment in certain types of new capital good could encourage innovation in the production of those goods, and the embodiment of new technology in capital goods could induce firms to purchase new-technology machines. Scott's analysis (helpfully summarised in Scott, 1992) takes the first of these as its cue.

He argues that investment should be defined as the cost of changing economic arrangements, hopefully for the better. Decisions to change such arrangements are made in the light of current and expected future conditions. But the shape of the future depends largely on unknown changes that others will make. Thus investment opportunities emerge mostly from the existing situation. Current economic conditions change continuously *because of* investment – giving rise all the time to new investment opportunities. The source of these opportunities, says Scott, is 'not just the progress of science, or R&D expenditures, as some seem to believe ... but they are just one form of investment, and all forms of investment can give rise to further investment opportunities' (1992: 625).

The fact the investment creates and reveals further investment opportunities suggests benefits accrue to the economy at large which are not appropriated by the investor. This he calls the *learning externality* of investment. Scott measures this externality as the difference between the return to a *business* on increasing its investment rate at the margin (marginal private return) and the return to the *economy* (marginal social return). The latter is substantially larger (in the UK and USA), Scott calculates because it includes the effects of extra opportunities created for other businesses when one business invests at a faster rate (1989, Chapters 7, 15). As his measure for return on capital, Scott subtracts the growth rate in quality-adjusted, (effective) labour employment from the output growth rate.

In his growth model, Scott (1989) uses the device of investment programme contours (IPCs) which show how varying levels of investment per unit of output relate to growth in output and quality-adjusted labour employment. It is assumed that firms' gross investment is financed by their own gross savings, that managers seek to maximise the value of firms to their owners and that savings and investment will be pursued to the point where the marginal return on investment equals the owners' rate of discount. Owners formulate savings plans with a significant regard for future generations. With this framework, values for major growth variables are endogenously determined, including the growth rates of output capacity, quality-adjusted employment, the investment: output ratio, the wage share and the return on capital.

Scott deliberately abstracts from explicit inclusion of a term for technological progress in his analysis, not because he believes it unimportant (quite the contrary), but because he wishes to capture its impact through the gross measure of investment. In its most basic form, his growth equation links the rate of output growth to the rate of gross investment, its efficiency (cf Wolff) reflecting the speed of learning, or the quality of the project selection process and the rate of growth of employment. When applied to a set of international growth data, Scott finds the contribution of physical investment on average exceeds that of quality-adjusted employment, though the relative contributions vary greatly between countries and periods. When he adds a constant to allow for any element of technological progress not already included, he finds the impact insignificantly different from zero.

Models which focus on R&D emphasise the generation of new technology to the exclusion of considering its diffusion. But the rate of diffusion is logically at least as important (and empirically probably more so) in explaining the speed at which economies benefit from new knowledge. Another way of endogenising the pace of innovation, therefore and to take account of points (1) and (4) on p. 339 is to consider the lessons of the vintage capital models of diffusion pioneered by Solow (1960), Phelps (1962) and Salter (1966), and the more recent work of Stoneman (1983), and Schmitz (1989).

Suppose, to take the alternative starting point, that the demand for new capital goods is driven by firms' desire to acquire the technology they embody. Imagining that capital markets work well enough to yield the savings required to support planned investment, can we say anything about the determinants of the pace of capacity expansion? If so, that should throw new light on the mechanisms by which technical advance might be translated into aggregate growth.

When a new process is introduced, two classes of firm will be interested in investing; first, those which need to buy new equipment to use the new process: users; second, those who produce the capital goods embodying the new process, who need to increase their own capital stock to meet the derived demand from users (Stoneman, 1983: 212–15). It is then possible to argue that with a fixed capital:output ratio in the capital goods industry and demand growth in the user industry following a sigmoid path, investment per period will initially surge as both classes of firm build up their capital stocks, then fall away as the investment of producers and growth of usage decline. This story would be consistent with an initial surge of growth of output gradually falling back to some steady-state level, but it takes no account of repeated episodes of innovation over a succession of periods, as might arise in a technological competition of the kind explored by Vickers and Beath, Katsoulacos and Ulph (Chapter 6 of this book).

Stoneman shows that with a succession of innovations, each diffusing logistically, the consequence of all firms investing only to implement new technology will be a more or less constant aggregate investment rate. This rate will be faster, the more capital intensive the innovations and the more slowly the newest techniques render existing ones obsolete.

To link this to growth, assume savings per head are sufficient to maintain a given ratio of capital to effective labour. With purely labour-augmenting technological progress, this would yield a steady-state growth path and the growth rate of output would be equal to the sum of labour-force growth and the rate of progress. The result would be the same as for the simple neoclassical model, but the mechanism is different.

If there were a sudden burst of new opportunities from one innovation a year, say, to one per month this would breed a surge in planned investment, calling for a burst of new savings. In the earlier NGM, technological progress could fall like manna from heaven upon the capital stock and raise output per head by enough, at any initially given savings ratio, to generate the savings required to cover the new investment. In this case, however, it is not as clear how the transition from one SSG path to another would work since firms would respond to the new opportunities by planning investment, but the income to generate new savings at the given savings ratio would not be created until the investment, which requires more saving in the first place, had actually been undertaken. It is likely in cases such as these that the real interest would rise, as firms attempted to induce households in increase their savings. But that could slow down the diffusion rate compared with that which would have been observed at a constant interest rate.

While sequences and bursts of innovation can thus be allowed for, it is not clear that spill-over effects are being fully dealt with. In particular, interindustry spill-overs are ignored. This ignores the point that industrialisation has been historically characterised by the introduction of a relatively small number of broadly similar production processes to a large number of industries (Rosenberg, 1976: 15)

In an analysis which seeks to take account of this, Schmitz (1989) argues that spill-overs will depend on the number of entrepreneurs who set up to diffuse (imitate) existing industry knowledge in any period and the degree of similarity of technologies over industries (technology convergence). The growth rate of consumption in his model is positively related to the proportion of individuals who become entrepreneurs, and the rate at which industry knowledge grows, itself a positive function of the economy's communications infrastructure. Entrepreneurial participation depends on the exogenously determined factors of financial incentives, a view which forms the centrepiece of Baumol's (1990) historical analysis discussed later (see pp. 364–6) and technological integration achieved through the communications infrastructure.

Verdoorn's law

One of the most widely cited empirical regularities in the literature of economic dynamics is the positive relation often found between the growth rate of labour productivity and that of output. The relation has been found to apply both in intercountry studies (Verdoorn, 1949, Kaldor, 1966, Cripps and Tarling, 1973) and interindustry work (Salter, 1966; Metcalfe and Hall, 1983). Others, like Rowthorn (1975) point out that the strength of the relationship may depend to an uncomfortable extent on the impact of special cases.

Nonetheless, the ground we have covered in this section suggests that we might expect such a relationship to arise for theoretical reasons. In various guises, Verdoorn, Salter (1966), Thirlwall (1980) and Vaciago (1975) all suggest that increasing returns may explain the relationship, a point incorporated explicitly in the Romer style of analysis above. Kaldor offers supplementary arguments (a shortage of labour and the slow pace of export market growth) to explain why rapid output growth was impeded and scale economies thus not exploited in British manufacturing. Salter and Thirlwall, like Stiglitz, argue that faster output growth is causally related to the pace of technological progress and add the possibility that in sectors experiencing rapid output growth, capital deepening may also occur at a faster rate.

The magnitude of interest in this analysis is the 'Verdoorn Elasticity' defined:

$$V = \{[(\mathrm{d}(Q/L)/\mathrm{d}t)/(Q/L)]/[(\mathrm{d}Q/\mathrm{d}t)/Q]\}$$

which shows the ratio of the proportionate growth rate of labour productivity to the growth rate of output, the elasticity of labour productivity with respect to output. Now it can be shown (Thirlwall, 1980) that, if the production function takes the dynamic form:

$$Q(t) = e^{T(t)} \cdot K^a \cdot L^b$$

(where T is the rate of disembodied technical progress, and a and b the output elasticities of capital and labour), another way of expressing the Verdoorn Elasticity is:

$$V = 1 - 1/\{b + [a(\mathrm{d}K/\mathrm{d}t)/K \cdot L/(\mathrm{d}L/\mathrm{d}t)] + [T \cdot L/(\mathrm{d}L/\mathrm{d}t)]\} \qquad (7.30)$$

If the input growth rates $(\mathrm{d}K/\mathrm{d}t)/K$ and $(\mathrm{d}L/\mathrm{d}t)/L$ are exogenously determined, it can be concluded unambiguously that V will be higher, the greater are scale economies, represented by $(a + b)$, the rate of technical progress T and the growth rate of capital inputs. V will be lower, the higher the labour force growth rate. However, as Boulier (1984) points out, the input growth rates (reflecting the profit-maximising input hiring decisions of firms) are not exogenously determined; they are influenced by scale economies and the rate of technological progress. When a model incorporating profit-maximising input hiring decisions is constructed, it is possible to show that variations in the level of V in no way necessarily imply corresponding variations in any of the factors identified above.

To show this, Boulier relies on a model of a profit-maximising monopolist, facing a demand curve of price elasticity of demand below unity, shifting outwards annually a constant rate of D per cent. The supply elasticity of labour to the firm, with respect to the wage rate is positive and the Kaldor labour shortage hypothesis is included by letting the firm's share of the labour force fall at the given wage rate if demand for labour by other firms grows. The labour force grows at a constant exogenous rate. It is then possible to determine the path of wages through time in terms of the parameters of the model and with that information to discover the corresponding paths for the firm's labour and capital hiring decisions and the growth rate of labour productivity.

As Boulier's paper reveals, the expressions involved are much messier than Thirlwall's. Given our work in Chapter 6, it is hard to believe that extending the analysis to oligopolistic industries and/or several sectors would simplify the results. However, it is possible to conclude that productivity growth is enhanced when there are substantial economies of scale and the firm is able to exploit these fully because of a high growth rate of labour supply, due to either a rapid growth rate in the economically active population and or a low growth rate of demand by other firms. Productivity growth is also positively related to the growth rate of demand if returns to scale or the output elasticity of capital are relatively large or if the wage elasticity of labour supply is relatively small (Boulier, 1984: 263).

When Boulier takes the final step of finding V in terms of the parameters of the model, all clarity disappears. V depends in such a complicated way on all of the parameters (a, b, T, D, labour force growth and elasticities), as well as the growth rate of capital costs, that it is impossible to know, in general, whether V would rise or fall if any one of the parameters changed. A moment's reflection should convince readers that this is not a perverse finding; the general relationship between output growth and productivity growth when everything is allowed to be variable (which is what we must assume when taking empirical observations) could be influenced by almost anything. And as we have noted throughout the book, changes in the technology of production in particular have the capacity to alter demand- and supply-side relationships fundamentally and the nature of economic equilibria in input and product markets.

Thus it is reasonable to conclude that V will depend in a complex way on the characteristics of the production function, factor supply and output demand and that little weight should be attached to inferences about the nature of technological progress, the extent of scale economies or the labour-supply elasticities derived from comparing V in one country with that in another, or in one industry with that in another (Boulier, 1984: 265).

Such caution is consistent with many findings elsewhere in the book, which imply that we have to be extremely careful before making specific economic predictions about the effects of technological progress, or inferring that observed economic changes have technological origins of a specific and obvious kind.

Many sectors and structural change

One of the most obvious ways in which the analysis so far has abstracted from the complexities of real economies is in its assumption that the whole system can be treated as if it were a single sector producing one good. In this section, we first indicate how the analysis can be extended to many sectors, but note that the innovation process can be incorporated only in the most stylised way in the multisectoral growth models we yet have. In a second part, we focus on another famous empirical claim, that income inequality varies in a predictable and interesting way with long-run growth in incomes per head. The two parts are linked because intersectoral movements in resources yield changes in income inequatity.

A considerable literature exists on two-sector growth models, with or without technological progress and readers are referred to Hacche (1979: Chapter 6), for an introduction. In the interests of brevity, however, we move here directly to a model which can incorporate any number of sectors. This is the so-called linear production model pioneered by Leontief (1941, 1953) and von Neumann (1945).

In the von Neumann model, the central focus is that goods produce goods. What we have called production processes (such as tanning or shoemaking), von Neumann calls **activities**. Any activity, j, requires $a(i, j)$ units of input i per unit of the activity at one point of time. Units of measurement of the activity are essentially arbitrary.

By the end of the production period, $b(i, j)$ is the quantity of commodity i which has been produced by a unit of the activity j. With n commodities and m activities in the economy, $A = [a(i, j)]$ and $B = [b(i, j)]$ will be $n \times m$ matrices:

$$A = \begin{bmatrix} a(1, 1) & a(1, 2) \dots a(1, m) \\ a(2, 1) & \dots \\ \dots \\ a(n, 1) & \dots a(n,m) \end{bmatrix}$$

$$B = \begin{bmatrix} b(1, 1) & b(1, 2) \dots b(1, m) \\ b(2, 1) & \dots \\ \dots \\ \dots \\ b(n, 1) & \dots b(n,m) \end{bmatrix}$$

In von Neumann's original formulation, every commodity was used as an input or produced as an output in every production process, which is clearly unrealistic, but modifying it in the interests of greater realism (see Kemeny, Morgenstern and Thompson, 1956) has not prevented progress being made in using the approach. Outputs include, therefore every input which might be needed as an input into next period's production.

Another distinctive feature of the von Neumann approach is that labour 'plays the role of a farm animal' (Sinclair, 1983: 293). Labour is itself a part of the overall productive process taking food, shelter, clothing and so on as inputs, and converting them into the output of services labour provides as productive inputs in activities throughout the economy. Consumption is not explicitly treated, though Morishima (1965) has since modified the approach to incorporate it. From our point of view, however, the most serious omission is that the set of possible technological relationships captured in the values of the $a(i, j)$ and $b(i, j)$ coefficients is taken to be invariant over time.

For analysis of the model, readers are referred to Champernonwne (1945–6), Sinclair (1983) and Takayama (1974). But the basic results are that, if competitive economic behaviour and equilibrium conditions are imposed on the von Neumann economy, a balanced growth equilibrium will exist at which the growth rate is maximised at a rate g^*, equal to the lowest possible interest rate (cf the Golden Rule). But balance applies only to goods in relation to each other; if the population grows at a rate faster than g^*, unemployment will grow continuously. This possibility can be ruled out with certainty only if wages along the balanced growth path are at a level low enough (cf Malthus) to ensure population will not expand at a rate faster than g^*.

Along the balanced growth path, all profits are saved and all activities expand at a rate determined by the ratio of investment to capital which, in this model turns out to be also the rate of profit, total profit divided by the capital stock.

To adapt this approach for our purposes, we first take the simplifying step of reducing the number of activities available for producing each good to one, and abstract from joint output. The $a(i, j)$ are now interpreted as the fixed amount of *current* input i required to produce a unit of output j, and the $b(i, j)$ denote the quantity of the ith good *invested* in the jth industry in order to increase output of that industry by one unit. $A = [a(i, j)]$ and $B = [b(i, j)]$ are again the corresponding $n \times m$ coefficient matrices. It is easy to show (Takayama, 1974: 507, for example) that the total demand for good i in period t, $q_i(t)$ comprises three elements:

1. Demand as a current input into all industries:

$$\sum_{j=1}^{n} a(i, j) \, q_j(t)$$

2. Investment demand by all industries:

$$\sum_{j=1}^{n} b(i, j) \, [q_j(t + 1) - q_j(t)]$$

3. Final (mainly consumption) demand:

$$c_j(t)$$

where $q_j(t)$ is the total output of good j in period t. In matrix form we may then write:

$$q(t) = A{\cdot}q(t) + B{\cdot}[(q(t + 1) - q(t)] + c(t) \tag{7.31}$$

where $q(t)$, $q(t + 1)$ and $c(t)$ are n-vectors, i.e. lists with n elements. That (7.31) describes a system in motion can be seen by rewriting it in the form:

$$q(t + 1) = [I + B^{-1}(I - A)]{\cdot}q(t) - B^{-1}c(t) \tag{7.32}$$

where I is the n-dimensional identity matrix, a matrix with ones running down the diagonal and zeroes elsewhere. If (7.32) is simplified by setting $c(t) = 0$ for all t, we are left with the **closed, dynamic Leontief** system:

$$q(t + 1) = M{\cdot}q(t) \tag{7.33}$$

where $M = [I + B^{-1}(I - A)]$. To describe the evolution of the system, (7.32) should be run forward through time. But there is a potential problem here; starting from some initial output and stock vectors, the stock of at least one good might become negative at some point in the future, rendering any further motion economically meaningless (even though mathematically unexceptionable). Technically, the problem is one of so-called 'causal indeterminacy' and whether it arises or not in any specific case depends on the specific characteristics of the technology described in the A and B matrices.

Certain 'relative stability' conditions were discovered by Solow and Samuelson (1953) which ensure the system is causally determined, and these have since been generalised by others. In the **static, open Leontief** system:

$$q = (I - A)^{-1} \cdot c$$

finding a unique, economically meaningful solution depends on the so-called Hawkins–Simon conditions which require any industry or subgroup of industries to be capable of producing just enough to meet its own requirements for production and the requirements of all other industries in the economy (see Takayama, 1974: 359–66). The relative stability conditions for the dynamic system are much less transparent in their economic implications and on the basis of other findings by Hawkins (1948), there is a worry that they might fail to be met. For an expanding system, there can be no more than one economically meaningful solution consistent with balanced growth. Instability, in the form of continuously growing unemployment, would result from 'lack of a sufficient degree of linkage or "coupling" between the different branches of the economy in terms of the input requirements of each branch from its own output relative to the requirements of all other branches' (Harris, 1982).

While vital to an understanding of multisectoral growth analysis, a major defect of both the von Neumann and Leontief system models is that technology described in the *A* and *B* matrices is taken as fixed throughout. We must turn to the work of Pasinetti (1981) to remedy that. (Harris, 1982, is a most useful review of Pasinetti's analysis and we draw on it here.) Pasinetti converts the input–output scheme considered above into a model of vertically integrated sectors. The main benefit of this is that all the analytically useful structural relations and equilibrium conditions in the economy can as a result be expressed in terms of physical quantities of labour. The theoretical problems he wants to discuss can be considered without reference to intermediate use of commodities, yet, should the implications for the intermediate structure of the economy need to be brought out, this is possible through the use of a special matrix of his own devising.

Equilibrium prevails in the system under three conditions; first, that the labour demands of all sectors other than households (which supplies labour) must be equal to total labour supply; second, full-capacity utilisation of capital; third, a capital accumulation condition which requires investment to be allocated among sectors in proportions compatible with the exogenously determined rate of capacity growth in each. Notice that the first condition, requiring full employment, amounts to satisfying the Hawkins–Simon condition as applied to the household sector supplying labour services, bearing in mind that 'households' are viewed as fully incorporated into productive activity (Harris 1982: 31–2).

Enter, now, technological change. In Pasinetti's world, advance occurs at an exogenously determined, constant rate in each sector. But from sector to sector the rate varies. So an important foundation for uneven growth is laid. The rate of change of labour productivity differs among sectors, giving rise to the potential for differential growth rates of output and employment, the very stuff of structural change, i.e. change over time in the proportions of output and employment accounted for by each sector. Linked to productivity growth rate differentials are intersectoral variations in the growth rates of consumer demand. And for completeness, technological change is defined broadly to encompass process innovation and the introduction of new products.

It must be said at once that the processes which drive technological progress are not incorporated in the model. Both technological progress and the determinants of consumer preference are taken to be beyond economic analysis, despite our demonstration in many parts of this book that the innovation process is, to an important degree, economically driven. Nonetheless, the implications of Pasinetti's approach are profound. Obviously, the matrices of technology coefficients can no longer be taken as given (except in the short term). But the effect of building in changes in the technological structure and patterns of consumption is to alter fundamentally the theoretical vision of a growing economic system.

In almost all of the economic growth analysis discussed so far, it has been implicitly assumed that the price mechanism would always work to ensure that labour is fully employed. SSG paths, with or without technological progress, are also full employment equilibrium paths. In addition, capital is fully employed and investment occurs at just the rate required to keep the growing labour force employed under the prevailing technology. While the Keynesian–neo-Keynesian tradition has always emphasised the possibility of unemployment in a growing economy, Pasinetti shows how that concern should spring automatically from the implications of differential technological progress across sectors.

In Pasinetti's world, the equilibrium conditions in each period are different from each other; changes in technology and consumption patterns are continuous and occur at different rates across a large number of sectors. Any possible equilibrium is always under threat. For orthodox neoclassical analysis, the constantly changing technological structure would pose no real problem; perfect information, foresight, or rational expectations, combined with zero transaction and adjustment costs would allow markets through the price mechanism to work efficiently to take the economy from one equilibrium to another. But for Pasinetti, prices do not play this active, constructive, signalling and ultimately directing role; rather they 'play an entirely passive role ... mirroring and adjusting to the changes taking place in production' (Harris, 1982: 40) and the changes in production costs to which these give rise.

Pasinetti does not appeal to the price mechanism as the means of maintaining equilibrium because in his view technology and preferences change through a learning process focused on a relatively narrow range of alternatives related to specific experience (cf 'local' learning emphasised by Stiglitz, 1987, and Nelson and Winter, 1982.) While this view is not translated into a formal foundation for the changing technology coefficients (which change at constant exogenous rates), it is used in deriving the evolution of consumers' demand patterns and an implication that saturation levels will ultimately be reached for every class of consumer goods.

In this world of patchy knowledge and localised experiential learning, it makes little sense to think in orthodox neoclassical terms of production and preference functions, each comprising a wide range of potential and mainly untried alternatives known to and understood by all relevant decision-makers. Yet we have to think in those terms if applying the orthodox-optimising techniques used to demonstrate the efficient operation of the price mechanism. Denied the price mechanism as a means of achieving or maintaining equilibrium, Pasinetti devises an idea to analyse the characteristics of a system in ongoing equilibrium on the assumption that it is achievable. He calls this device the 'natural economic system', within which framework and with the assistance of vertically integrated sectors, he is able to show how it is possible to have a pure labour-value theory of price. Since, however, it is unclear how Pasinetti believes an economy could ever reach the equilibrium path he describes, or what sort of interpretation might be given to his 'natural' system, we shall not pursue the implications of that line of reasoning here.

Rather we draw attention to the implications he raises for unemployment if the economy were to develop as he generally describes it. If saturation levels are reached in all classes of consumption, consumer demand will in total tend to grow at a declining rate relative to growth in labour productivity and income per head. This 'stagnation' or 'underconsumption' will tend to create unemployment at a greater rate, the more its bias towards labour saving. This tendency will be offset, however, by the creation of new sectors and job opportunities by product innovation, and the extent to which rising income per hour leads to an increased propensity, at the margin, for the employed to take leisure and for the participation rate to decline.

As should be clear, the 'Luddite' claim that technological progress destroys jobs would, in this framework, seem to be potentially true in relation to relatively slowly growing or actually shrinking sectors, but quite possibly be invalid at the aggregate level if overall growth was being driven by product and process innovation generating the creation and growth of new sectors. The specifics of Pasinetti's model lead him to conclude that there is a persistent tendency towards unemployment. This should be viewed as an assertion about the short-run implications of consumer saturation in existing product classes, though the short run may last for an uncomfortably long time for the unemployed themselves. Clearly, fast enough product innovation across a wide enough range would go a long way towards reversing this conclusion in the longer run. But the implications of that logic cannot be carried forward in Pasinetti's model unless a theory of product (and process) innovation is incorporated.

The preoccupation with the tendency of innovation-driven growth to create unemployment is of venerable pedigree, having first been explored by Ricardo (in whose tradition Pasinetti has developed many of his ideas) and later by Marx. A recent contribution on the subject is Katsoulacos (1986).

Pasinetti's approach contains elements with an obvious evolutionary flavour, in particular, learning and it implications. But to the extent that evolutionary models are about the innovation process, Pasinetti can be criticised for treating as exogenous the innovation process driving technological progress. Reference to Chapters 5 and 6 should make it clear that this implies Pasinetti's approach also misses much that recent advances at the industry level of analysis have shown to be important. In particular, while the technological structure is allowed to change, there is no account of how the structure of industry changes, other than as a direct reflection of the changing technology, taken to occur exogenously. This means that the Pasinetti approach cannot shed light on the important interactions between industry structure and technological change, which form so much of the substance of dynamic competition from which growth and structural change result.

The Kuznets hypothesis: growth and income distribution

One of the most popular empirical hypotheses in the study of long-run growth is that as real incomes per head rise from their lowest levels, so the distribution of income will become more unequal at a later stage, however, becoming more equal again. The hypothesis has been named after Kuznets (1955) who first speculated on the existence of the relationship, having surveyed the historical experience of the United States, England and Germany. We consider the hypothesis here because, a logical explanation for its operation can most effectively be mounted on a two-sector vision of the economy, a special case of multisectoral growth.

The term 'income distribution' may be taken to refer to the *functional* distribution, showing the relative shares in income received by each factor of production, or the *personal* distribution, which shows the proportions of total income received by individuals or households grouped according to the income brackets which they occupy. The latter is the focus of interest in the Kuznets hypothesis. There is considerable literature on the various concepts and measures which might be used to judge the degree of inequality present in a given distribution of incomes (Atkinson, 1970; Fields, 1980). Kuznets himself inspected changes over time in the income shares received by households in the highest and lowest quintiles of the distribution. But most measures since have been linked in some way to the **Lorenz Curve** which, starting with the poorest households and working upwards cumulatively, shows what proportion of total incomes goes to the poorest, 1 per cent, 2 per cent .... 10 per cent .... 50 per cent ... 99 per cent of the population. A widely used measure derived directly from the Lorenz Curve is the **Gini coefficient**, which, roughly summarises the extent to which the Lorenz Curve departs from the line it would follow if income were distributed perfectly equally.

Since Kuznets' paper was first published, a vast amount of research has been carried out to discover how robust the relationship might be empirically. Since the relationship arises from historical experience, the only ultimately acceptable tests of the hypothesis call for an international comparison of single-country histories. In the early days of the research, such data were not readily available for large samples and work proceeded on the basis of cross-section analysis which, up to a point, gave qualified support to the idea. But cross-section studies can give rise to misleading inferences about historical experience in any one of the countries, and as better time series data have appeared on individual countries, it has become clear that evidence for the Kuznets hypothesis is rather mixed.

To see why this is so, consider the theoretical reasons why the relationship might arise. This is most easily understood by assuming a **dualistic** (i.e. two-sector) structure for all countries. The basis for the dualism is often taken to be technological, but may be derived from other sources (Dixit (1973) provides a useful discussion). If it were technological, we could imagine one sector using low and the other high productivity methods. Label these sectors, respectively, 'Lo' and 'Hi'. Now suppose wages (and other incomes) in Lo are lower than in Hi, but that in each sector, everyone receives the same income. And imagine that early in its development, a country's technology is dominated by the low-productivity technique but that, over time, domestic and foreign investment in the high-productivity technique allows the output potential of Hi to grow.

If all of the population initially derived its income from employment in Lo, incomes per head in the country would be low, but there would be no inequality, since all would be receiving the same income. If the prospect of a higher wage in Hi encouraged the work-force to start to relocate there from Lo, average income per head would start to rise. But the first migrants would now be receiving a high wage, while the large majority left in Lo would continue to receive the low wage associated with the low-productivity technique. Clearly, inequality now exists in the distribution of income. Arithmetically, it is not hard to show that the income share of the poorest X per cent of the population will continue to fall until $(1 - X)$ per cent of the population has shifted from Lo to Hi.

While this is a crude measure of inequality, using it reveals that inequality will rise continually at the same time as income per head is increasing. Nobody is becoming absolutely poorer, merely that an increasingly large fraction of the population is becoming absolutely better off, while a continuously shrinking fraction remains on the same income as before. Once the fraction of the population in Hi exceeds $(1 - X)$ per cent, further migration will now raise incomes per head again, but the poorest X per cent will now include some individuals who receive the higher wage, so the income share of the poorest 20 per cent will start to rise. This was the prediction of the Kuznets hypothesis.

In any real economy, this simple story would have to be amended in various ways. In particular, productivity might be rising in both sectors. Even so, migration from Lo to Hi would still yield the same relationship so long as the productivity level in Hi remained above that in Lo (see Lydall, 1979: Ch. 12 for a good exposition of this possibility). Governments often intervene to ameliorate growing inequality with redistributive policies (taxing Hi and subsidising Lo). But what impact would that then have on growth? In actuality, productivity levels in some countries have converged, labour markets have tended to reduce wage differentials and governments do redistribute incomes. It should not be surprising therefore that the Kuznets relationship has not always been found to operate.

Disequilibrium, non-linearity and evolutionary accounts of growth

Consider the question posed by Richard Day (1984), who has been at the forefront of research into adaptation, adjustment and the implications of complexity and uncertainty. Day's central question is: 'Are economies ... best understood as equilibrium or as disequilibrium processes?' (1984: 59). While this issue has been discussed at length in the economic literature, the practice of emphasising equilibrium analysis, certainly in growth theory, tends to suggest that the discipline believes understanding is best to be achieved by following the equilibrium route. The other part of the story, however, is that in setting up disequilibrium models 'there is a bewildering range of possibilities to choose from, and often a seemingly slight difference in assumptions can lead to a major difference in results' (Dixit, 1976: 174). Without suitable criteria to allow choice among these alternatives, there is a strong (and practically relevant) case for persisting with a tried and tested research method.

But does the equilibrium method hold out best hope of understanding technological innovation and its impact on the economic system? One answer might be that innovation-related factors which have the potential to generate disequilibrium, like indivisibilities and uncertainty, are important but only 'at the micro level and over short periods of time' (Romer, 1990 S82), and so can be ignored in long-run, aggregate analysis. Another response could be that Day's question points us towards the wrong issue. Mensch (1986), for example, argues we might want to recognise, with Schumpeter himself, that innovation disturbs existing equilibria, but would do better to emphasise that the ensuing disequilibrium is entirely consistent with continuity within the economic system, on which the analysis should focus. Both of these answers play down the importance of disequilibrium and if accepted allow us to focus on other matters related to understanding how innovation transforms the economy.

A widely accepted view of how to interpret Schumpeter's vision of market dynamics is, to be sure, as a continuously evolving process, but also as one whose disequilibrium character is central to an understanding of how it works. When all markets are in equilibrium, firms in each industry make just enough profit to discourage them from moving elsewhere and no more. This is **normal** profit, yielding a normal rate of return. In Schumpeter's market dynamics, change is driven by decision-makers' responses to the prospect of making **supernormal** profits from innovation. Innovation drives growth and supernormal profits derived from innovation are a sign of markets not in equilibrium. Incorporating disequilibrium dynamics thus seems to flow naturally from efforts to give a Schumpeterian flavour to growth analysis.

Growth modelling has probably gone furthest in response to Schumpeter's vision in relation to his insistence that economic development is non-linear. In particular, he argued that innovation-driven growth (to him 'development', because of the structural transformations to which it was inseparably linked) did not 'proceed evenly as a tree grows, but as it were jerkily ... [with] ... characteristic ups and downs' (Schumpter, 1934: 223). These ups and downs are **cycles**, generated by the specifics of the innovation process as Schumpeter perceived it and, given that the prime role of innovation was to fuel growth, a by-product of growth itself (Elster, 1983: 123), linked indissolubly to it. The specific view to which Schumpeter subscribed was a 'bunching' in technical innovations: 'new combinations are not ... evenly distributed through time ... but appear, if at all, discontinuously in groups or swarms' (1934: 223).

In Schumpeter's schema, a boom occurs with the appearance of swarm of innovations. Innovations are the result of entrepreneurs' activity, so the question becomes (1934: 228): 'Why do entrepreneurs appear, not continuously ... but in clusters?' A possible answer (Baumol, 1990, Schmitz, 1989) is that entrepreneurial activity responds to financial incentives, so that when (after a change in the tax regime, for example) incentives increase, so does entrepreneurship. But Schumpeter offers a quite different line of argument.

Because innovation in Schumpeter's vision always calls for major, discontinuous leaps in technology and organisation and because booms are generated from conditions of initial stagnation, the start of the boom has to rely on the efforts of a few, specially gifted pioneers. But once the pioneers have broken through, it is easier for others to follow and with the 'progressive lightening of the task continually more people can and will become entrepreneurs' until entrepreneurial profit is eliminated (Schumpeter, 1934: 229). Schumpeter also observes that every boom starts in only one or a few sectors but that as pioneers prove successful in those areas, their example spurs others on in different industries, and may facilitate innovation elsewhere (though not necessarily at the same rate). Innovation-driven development is thus non-linear in two respects; it is 'jerky' through time and it affects some parts of the economy disproportionately.

In the disturbance caused by the factors driving the boom, however, lie the seeds of depression. On one hand, the demand of new entrepreneurs for inputs into production drives up factor prices for them and all other firms. On the other, the supposition that entrepreneurs appear *en masse* in the boom is mirrored in the claim that their products all appear together. Having their origin in one or a narrow range of sectors, the products will also be similar to one another. So revenues fall under the pressure of price competition. With rising costs and falling receipts, collapse would be immediate were it not for credit institutions giving support to long-established business clients. While such support may stave off crisis, however, depression cannot ultimately be avoided.

Van Duijn (1983) has noted that this version of Schumpeter's theory seems to be associated with the seven to eleven year business cycle familiar to nineteenth century economists. Schumpeter, he argues, saw this as an investment cycle in which investment was induced by innovative activity (p. 101). As we have seen, this is the sort of idea exploited more recently by Stoneman (1983) and Scott (1989), though neither attempts to craft a model of cyclical growth from it. In his later work, Schumpeter (1939) applied the relationship between innovation and cyclical fluctuations to all cycles and offered a more elaborate description of the cycle comprising now four stages: prosperity, recession, depression and recovery.

Schumpeter's theory of cyclic growth can, therefore, also be used to explain long swings or waves in economic growth identified, among others, by Kondratieff (1926), Rostow (1975) and Mensch (1979). Whether these authors' observations (which by no means all coincide) can be accepted as genuine patterns remains a matter of controversy. And just as controversial is the claim that the Schumpeterian account of bunching in innovation might explain such patterns. Monetary factors, wars, infrastructural investment and rigidities in agricultural production have all been used to provide alternative explanations (van Duijn, 1983: 68–70, provides a brief review). More important for our purposes is the general proposition that growth is intrinsically cyclical or 'wavy', since that view is inconsistent with SSG and implies non-linear change (as compared with the linear expansion associated with equiproportional growth in all variables).

In this connection, Arrow (1988) has observed that cycles, and even chaotic behaviour, can be generated by the same differential equations which were used in the past to characterise equilibrium dynamics. The question has been considered in depth by Day (1982, 1983) and Kelsey (1988). Whether we characterise the economy in terms of equilibrium or disequilibrium processes of change, there is a growing awareness that we should look out for non-linear dynamic patterns.

Non-linear disequilibrium growth does not have to be identified with evolutionary analysis. But if an evolutionary perspective is adopted to modelling growth and development, non-linearity and disequilibrium naturally emerge. To illustrate what has been achieved in this framework, we present two models which explore a similar question in different ways, yielding different insights. The question is: What pattern of growth emerges when new technology is supplanting old in an economy? For evolutionists, the interest here lies not so much in final equilibrium states which might not ultimately be reached but in the (disequilibrium) process of adjustment on the way. Assume that such transitions take relatively long periods of time and may follow each other in an overlapping sequence which rarely, if ever, allows any given substitution to be fully completed. If this is a plausible assumption, we have every right to be at least as interested in the nature of the transition as the end-point. That is what we now consider.

Nelson and Winter

Nelson and Winter (1974) and Nelson, Winter and Schuette (1976) present a version of an evolutionary growth model in which micro-level diversity is the basis for macro-level growth. It is introduced by taking as a starting point a world with the hundred different techniques in use for producing a homogeneous output. Each technique characterises a different firm. Techniques in use change importantly as the result of firms' R&D activity, in accordance with routines of the kind discussed in Chapter 4.

The key idea in the model is that the state of the economy in any one period bears the seeds of its condition in the following period or, to be more precise, determines the probability distribution of its next-period condition. For analytical purposes, it is assumed that the condition of the economy prior to period t has no influence on the transition probabilities between t and $t + 1$ (Nelson and Winter, 1982: 19). This is a surprisingly strong simplifying economic assumption but is introduced so analysis may draw on the large body of theorems related to Markov processes, a tool used widely in statistical modelling to describe a sequence of events, the probability of each of which is dependent only on the event immediately preceding it. Markov processes can thus be used to describe in terms of the transition probabilities of moving from one state to another, the evolutionary path followed by variables in a system such as that used to model an economy.

This is a highly complex model, which does not lend itself readily to analysis. Nelson and Winter's response is two-fold. First, they run a large number of simulations based on various parameter values and report that their evolutionary model is 'quite capable of generating aggregate time series with characteristics corresponding to those of economic growth in the United States' between 1909 and 1949. Comparing their efforts with those of Solow, who used an aggregate production function approach to describe the same data, they declare the contest a tie (1982: 226). It is not clear, however, how much importance should be attached to simulation runs which proved successful when others, not presented, were less so. And it may also be said that if a substantially more complex explanation can do no better than the elegantly simple (if imperfect) aggregate production function, then why favour it? This leads us to Nelson and Winter's second response: a substantial simplification of their model which allows the mechanisms at work to be more clearly identified. We consider two forms of simplification.

The first version springs from Nelson (1968) characterising 'the great development traverse' for a country gradually substituting modern technology for traditional (Nelson and Winter, 1982: 237–40). There are just two, fixed-coefficient, constant returns techniques, old and new, denoted $T(O)$ and $T(N)$. Growth in use of $T(N)$ relative to $T(O)$ constitutes the selection process in this case. Microlevel considerations are largely subsumed by aggregating over all firms using a particular technique.

Both $T(O)$ and $T(N)$ offer identical levels of output per unit of capital, but labour productivity for $T(N)$ exceeds that of $T(O)$, suggesting pure labour-saving advance. The aggregate labour:output ratio, (L/Y), is found by weighting the ratios for $T(O)$ and $T(N)$, $l(O)$ and $l(N)$, by the proportions of the overall capital stock embodying each of the techniques:

$$(L/Q) = l(O)\cdot[K(O)/K] + l(N)\cdot[K(N)/K]$$

or setting $l(N) = \phi\cdot l(O)$, where $\phi < 1$ to show that $l(N) < l(O)$:

$$(L/Q) = l(O)\cdot[K(O)/K] + \phi\cdot l(O)\cdot[K(N)/K] \tag{7.34}$$

Although Nelson and Winter's main interest is in the disequilibrium traverse, their analytical strategy is to define the characteristics of equilibrium with $T(O)$ only and to assume that the economy will move towards a new equilibrium in which fixed quantities of old and new technology capital coexist, or in which there is only $T(N)$. Equilibrium is characterised by zero supernormal profit; at the outset, all firms using $T(O)$ make just normal profit, implying:

$$PQ(O) = wL(O) - rK(O)$$

or zero net revenues (gross revenues after subtracting wages and the cost of capital services). The crucial assumption governing economic expansion is that investment in any form of capital is directly proportional to the net revenue offered per unit of that capital:

$$[dK(i)/dt]/K(i) = m[PQ(i)/K(i) - wL(i)/K(i) - rK(i)/K(i)] \tag{7.35}$$

where $i = O, N$ and m is a constant, showing the proportion of net revenues invested in capital of type i. This is a stark characterisation of investment indeed and as the sole transition mechanism to capture the dynamics of growth, abstracts from the richer menu of feedback and other effects incorporated in the work of Silverberg, Dosi and Orsenigo. But it may be defensible as a first approximation at the aggregate level, though a fully specified model would at least endogenise m.

Under this specification, $T(O)$ capital stocks will never increase, since net revenues on $K(O)$ are zero, but will remain positive for a substantial period i.e. until replacement investment ceases. The condition for $T(N)$ capital stocks to increase is that net revenues per unit of $T(N)$ capital are positive. Now, by assumption, the capital : output ratios for both $T(O)$ and $T(N)$ are the same. Setting this equal to one, the investment function for $T(N)$ capital can be rewritten:

$$[dK(N)/dt]/dK(N) = m(P - wl(N) - r) \qquad (7.35')$$

If the product is used as the good in terms of which to measure relative prices, P will remain constant throughout. Investment in $T(N)$ capital will be stimulated in the first place because unit production costs with $T(N)$ will be lower than those with $T(O)$ because $l(N) < l(O)$. If r is taken to be parametric, net revenue from $T(N)$ capital can fall to zero, signifying a new equilibrium with no further expansion in $K(N)$, only if w rises. On the assumption that the aggregate labour-supply curve (linking labour supply to wage rate) slopes upwards and does not shift, this is the mechanism which Nelson and Winter invoke.

To characterise the traverse, focus on the expression showing the difference between the proportionate growth rates in $T(O)$ and $T(N)$ capital stocks:

$$[dK(N)/dt]/K(N) - [dK(O)/dt]/K(O) = m(P - wl(N - r)$$
$$- m(P - wl(O) - r)$$
$$= mw(1 - v)l(O) \qquad (7.36)$$

Since $K(O)$ is constant, any growth in $K(N)$ relative to $K(O)$ also implies growth in the ratio of $T(N)$ capital to overall capital, $K(N)/K$. The instantaneous growth rate of this ratio will be greater, the larger m, i.e. the larger the fraction of new revenue invested in new capital, the larger w and the smaller ϕ (i.e. the greater is the extent by which $T(N)$ raises labour productivity compared with $T(O)$).

Nelson (1968) showed that if the wage rate were constant, $K(N)/K$ would evolve in a model of this kind according to the equation:

$$[K(N)/K](t) = 1/\{1 + e^{-ct} [K(O)/K(N)] \#\} \qquad (7.37)$$

where $[K(O)/K(N)] \#$ is the initial value of the ratio, at some arbitrarily early stage of the traverse when $K(N)$ has become positive and $c = mw(1 - v)l(O)$. This equation traces out a sigmoid logistic curve, a path that would also be followed by the proportion of overall output produced using $T(N)$, and by aggregate output per worker. As we noted above, Nelson and Winter rely on rising w to re-establish equilibrium. The implication of this will be that the rate of takeover of $T(N)$ will be hastened throughout the traverse, compared with the constant-wage case.

Implicit in the analysis is a strong Schumpeterian flavour: over the traverse the share of capital in income will lie above the level found in equilibrium. Nelson and

Winter's model incorporates an element which helps us to understand how the transition from $T(O)$ to $T(N)$ is driven by the promise of higher returns.

In Nelson (1968) it is shown that:

$$S_K = r/P + [(dK/dt)/K]/mP$$

where S_K is capital's actual share in income at any period. In this expression, r/P is the rate of return on capital in the initial and final equilibria and the rest of the right-hand side thus represents the return generated out of equilibrium as supernormal profit. Notice that supernormal profit will be larger, the higher $[(dK/dt)/K]$, i.e. in the early stages of the traverse before the logistic curve reaches its inflection point. It will be smaller, the larger m, which makes sense, given that the larger the proportion of profit invested in new capital, the more difficult it will be increase returns at the same rate.

In a second analytical model, selection occurs over many (not two) techniques. The framework could be applied to a single-output economy employing many techniques, but is more appropriate for industry analysis and there are few new insights here to add to those already discussed in Chapter 6 in relation to Iwai's work which in many ways takes its cue from this model. But it is of interest to note that the analysis contains one of the first explicit references to Fisher's fundamental theorem of natural selection (1982: 243), an analogy to which we drew attention in Chapter 6.

Nelson and Winter's work falls squarely into a tradition of gradual evolution: firms which cannot and do not optimise from the start, adjust relatively slowly to changes in their economic environment changing product demand and factor-supply conditions. At the same time, they envisage the speed at which the environment changes to be great enough to ensure that the selection process is unable to dispense with all the techniques (routines) which are unsuited for any given environmental state. Thus efficient and inefficient firms may coexist for long periods and by definition the markets and economies in which they operate are in disequilibrium.

Despite the unsettled state in which the economy is viewed as operating, pattern and design can be discerned throughout. To understand the subtleties of these patterns, it is necessary to get 'inside' the simulations, which is far from easy (but see Nelson and Winter, 1982: 230–2 for a discussion) and not always satisfactory. The analytic models give a stark representation of the patterns, but are abstracted from so much detail that their evolutionary character is to a significant degree diluted.

Other approches to evolutionary analysis have emphasised different aspects of the biological analogy and of Schumpeter's vision. In particular, Nelson and Winter have little to say about cyclical patterns, and their emphasis on gradual change steers them away from the sorts of major discontinuity stressed by Schumpeter. It is to these aspects we now turn.

Goodwin and cyclic growth

When growth is cyclic, major economic variables rise and fall in a regular pattern around a trend. Much growth theory (and all theory based on steady states) implicitly takes the view that cycles constitute short-run deviations from the trend which deserve separate explanation based largely on demand-side considerations. These are taken to be the province of the short- and medium-term aggregate analysis which constitutes national income analysis, or more succinctly, macroeconomics (see Chapter 8). Growth theory sees its work as explaining the trend, implying that explanations for the trend and cycles around it can legitimately be separated. But the two are in fact linked. Investment, which we have seen plays such an important role in explaining the expansion in productive capacity on the supply-side, is also one of the most volatile elements of aggregate demand, and often at the source of macroeconomic fluctuations. This is true even with given technology, but the prospects of profiting from newly embodied technology can be an important and unpredictable source of new capital demand.

Goodwin's (1967) model derives growth from a simple profit-driven investment function, but also shows that real wages and the wage share will fluctuate in a cyclical fashion as a result of the impact of capital investment on employment. Contrast this proposition with the allegation discussed earlier that the wage share was one of the great economic constants. The evolutionary credentials of the analysis are restricted to little more than a formal similarity between Goodwin's central equations and Volterra–Lotka equations used in the so-called predator–prey model, describing the cyclical growth of competing species of fish. Nonetheless, the model has been used in a genuinely evolutionary fashion to examine the implications of innovation for growth cycles.

In the basic model, disembodied technical progress raises labour productivity $\alpha = Q/L$, at a constant exogenous rate $(\mathrm{d}\alpha/\mathrm{d}t)/\alpha$; the labour supply N grows at a constant rate n; homogeneous output is produced with labour employed L and capital K; all wages are consumed and all profits saved and invested; the capital:output ratio v is a constant. The employment rate, L/N is denoted η, and the rate of (real) wage inflation $(\mathrm{d}w/\mathrm{d}t)/w$ is assumed to rise linearly with η as full employment is approached, so that in that region:

$$(\mathrm{d}w/\mathrm{d}t)/w = -m + h\eta \tag{7.38}$$

where m and h are parameters. When η is sufficiently low, the wage rate will fall.

Consider $\eta = L/N$ first. By definition $L = Q/(Q/L) = Q/\alpha$, so the employment rate grows according to:

$$\mathrm{d}/\mathrm{d}t \ln \eta = \mathrm{d}/\mathrm{d}t \ln Q - \mathrm{d}/\mathrm{d}t \ln \alpha - \mathrm{d}/\mathrm{d}t \ln N$$

or:

$$(\mathrm{d}\eta/\mathrm{d}t)/\eta = (\mathrm{d}Q/\mathrm{d}t)/Q - (\mathrm{d}\alpha/\mathrm{d}t)/\alpha - n \tag{7.39}$$

The employment rate grows at the growth rate of real output, less the productivity raising effect of technical progress and the growth rate of labour supply.

Given the assumed constancy of $v = K/Q$, Q must grow at the same rate as K. Since labour's share in income is $wL/Q = w/\alpha$, capital's share is $(1 - w/\alpha)$ and the total amount of profit saved and invested is $(1 - w/\alpha)Q$. Denoting w/α as u, the growth rate of K is $[(1 - u)Q/K] = [(1 - u)/v]$. Since this is also the growth rate of output:

$$(d\eta/dt)/\eta = [(1 - u)/v] - (d\alpha/dt)/\alpha - n$$

$$= 1/v - (d\alpha/dt)/\alpha - n - (1/v)u \qquad (7.40)$$

Turning now to the share of labour:

$$u = w/\alpha$$

so that:

$$(du/dt)/u = (dw/dt)/w - (d\alpha/dt)/\alpha$$

But because of (7.38) this may be rewritten:

$$(du/dt)/u = - [(d\alpha/dt)/\alpha + m] + h\eta \qquad (7.41)$$

Together, (7.40) and (7.41) constitute a dynamic system. In the steady state of the system, $(d\eta/dt)/\eta = (du/dt)/u = 0$, which from (7.40) implies a steady-state value for u:

$$u^* = 1 - v[(d\alpha/dt)/\alpha + n) \qquad (7.42)$$

and that for η:

$$\eta^* = [(d\alpha/dt)/\alpha + m]/h \qquad (7.43)$$

Reference back to (7.39) also reveals that the SSG rate for Q when $(d\eta/dt)/\eta = 0$ must be $(d\alpha/dt)/\eta + n$.

If the economy modelled here were ever to start at a point away from (η^*, u^*), it would cycle indefinitely around this central point (see Figure 7.9). Starting at a point like A, investment in new capital is raising the employment rate and wage rate and wage share both rise as full employment is approached. But rising wages increasingly undermine profits until, at B, investment slows as a result to the point where the employment rate starts to fall. Falling employment in due course leads to a fall in the labour share (beyond C). But falling labour share implies rising capital share and renewed investment which, by D, is rapid enough to start driving up the employment ratio again. Over time, therefore, we see both wage share and the employment rate following a regular cyclical pattern.

The Goodwin model has the advantage of endogenising cycles within the growth process, but depends for the striking clarity of its results on assumptions which should certainly be open to modification. In particular in a growth model, we should question the 'all wages consumed, all profits invested' assumption, and, associated with that, the implications of allowing technology to be embodied in new capital and only gradually diffused by investment.[7] As has been noted elsewhere, it is precisely because of lags in the investment response to external stimuli that cycles are often generated. If the stimulus were the opportunity offered by innovation, Silverberg's (1984) application of the Goodwin model would become relevant.

Here, labour productivity is taken to be constant so that:

$$(d\eta/dt)/\eta = [(1 - u)/v] - n$$

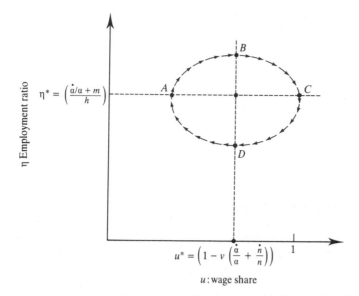

Figure 7.9 Cyclic change in the Goodwin model: fluctuations in wage share and employment ratio.

or

$$(d\eta/dt) = (1/v)\eta - (u/v)\eta - n\eta$$

$$= (1/v)\eta - (\alpha/wv)\eta - n\eta$$

$$= (1/v - n)\eta - (1/\alpha v)\eta w$$

$$= A\eta - B\eta w \tag{7.44}$$

As before:

$$dw/dt = -mw + h\eta w$$

And in steady state $\eta = m/h$ and $w = A/B$.

Now in an initial situation of near equilibrium using only old-technology capital, denoted '1', new-technology capital, denoted '2' is introduced which can produce both final consumption goods and itself, but not old machines. Assuming a uniform wage rate, and employing obvious notation to distinguish between sectors:

$$(dw/dt)/w = -m + h(\eta 1 + \eta 2) \tag{7.45}$$

and with each sector expanding in proportion to its profits:

$$(d\eta i/dt)/\eta i = Ai - Bi \cdot w, \ i = 1, 2 \tag{7.46}$$

Allen's (1975, 1976) work on interacting populations in biology may then be applied to interpret the new technology as a mutant species, the selective potential or potential evolutionary superiority of which can be determined by examining the characteristics of (7.45) and (7.46) at the stationary point $\eta 1 = m/h$, $w = A1/B1$, $\eta 2 = 0$. With $\eta 2 = 0$, the new technology has yet to make its mark. In this framework, it can be shown that the new technology will prove superior to the old (i.e. will be favoured by selection) if it leads to an increase in the ratio $A/B = \alpha(1 - nv)$.

To interpret this condition, suppose first that $n = 0$. Then $\alpha(1 - nv) = \alpha$: new technology will be selected as long as it raises labour productivity. If the labour force is growing ($n > 0$), new technology raising v will depress the value of A/B unless labour productivity not only rises but also rises fast enough to offer compensating gains. Finally, if capital per worker, αv, is viewed as standing for the degree of mechanisation, M, then $A/B = \alpha - nM$, and a new technology which raises M by an increment must compensate with an incremental gain in labour productivity larger by a multiple of n. This model predicts technological progress will generally lead to increases in labour productivity while being neutral to or slightly biased against increases in the capital:output ratio, depending on the rate of growth of labour.

As for the effect of innovation on Goodwin cycles, Silverberg performs simulations which offer a robust prediction for the relationship between productivity and wage rate growth. Productivity will rise to a peak well into the relatively long period during which new technology substitutes for old. But wage rate growth will lag behind for more than half the period of substitution, accelerating as productivity growth peaks, remaining above productivity growth for a while thereafter, only then to collapse. On the way up, wage growth follows a fluctuating path along which Goodwinian cycles gradually disappear, only to reappear after the final collapse when the transition is complete. Corresponding to the experience of wages, profits take most of the benefits of higher productivity in the earlier parts of the transition, but are doubly squeezed when productivity growth falls away and wage growth persists.

There are elements of this story which seem consistent with the Kondratieff cycle. 'If we consider economic history to be a sequence of major "paradigmatic" innovations (the steam engine, iron and steel, electrical power, the internal combustion engine, mass production, electronic communications) followed by improvements and "mopping up" ... then this picture is not all that far-fetched.' (Silverberg, 1984: 200).

Evolution as punctuated equilibrium

In the first chapter of this book, we noted the contrast between those who see evolution as a gradual process of continuous incremental change and those who view it in terms of 'relatively long periods of stability (equilibrium), punctuated by compact periods of qualitative, metamorphic change (revolution)' (Gersick, 1991: 12). In the former view, systems can accommodate almost any change, at any time, if it is small enough and large changes result from the accumulation of small ones. Thus, in the technology, 'major innovations are made possible by numerous minor innovations'

(Sahal, 1981: 37). But in the latter, the emphasis is reversed: 'Radical advances in the manipulation or understanding of physical processes are usually the *beginning not the end* of a prolonged process of improvements and modifications' (Mokyr, 1990: 352).

Both Nelson and Winter and Silverberg model in the gradualist tradition and have nothing to say about the origins of the new technologies whose diffusion they map. Even when Nelson and Winter make innovation partially reflect economic influences (as in their more complex models), they do so in relation to R&D expenditure which, by construction, has the capacity to take technological knowledge forward in only small steps. The radical new insights on which R&D might build remain exogenously determined. The non-linear models we have looked at say little or nothing about the origins of these insights, the mechanisms which draw them into productive use, or the uncertainties surrounding the emergence of a dominant form for the new technology. The last of these issues was dealt with in Chapter 6, especially in relation to the work of Arthur. We close this section by considering the remaining issues.

Knowing about the origins of radical innovation is clearly important and taking the punctuationist perspective, analytically at the centre of understanding history. Mokyr (1990: 351–2) argues that the economic history of technology is much like that traced in biology by Gould: a dynamic pattern of long periods of stagnation or very slow change punctuated by sudden outbursts like the Industrial Revolution. In an analogy with biology, Mokyr puts special store by the technoeconomic equivalent of the rare macromutations (or 'hopeful monsters') which, if successful, result in the generation of a new species. To achieve discontinuous jumps in the technology, macroinventions are needed. The chief importance of such inventions is that they raise the marginal product of developmental effort and thus lead to a sequence of further improvements.

Such a picture would be consistent with the SSG vision of growth with technological progress if for the long periods of equilibrium, improvement occurred at a constant, gradual rate. Between jumps, it could also be consistent with either the Nelson and Winter or cyclic visions, if the macroinvention created non-linear waves of change. But taking an even longer view, the punctuationist approach implies jerky, non-linear progress in economic growth and none of the earlier growth analysis we performed explicitly allowed for this.

Mokyr argues that we know little about the causes of macroinventions. But two major non-economic hypotheses exist to explain how the inertia of an equilibrium period is broken. In science, Kuhn (1970) has argued that when an existing paradigm gives rise to a severe and sufficient crisis (i.e. fails badly enough), ideas from revolutionary thinkers, ignored when things were working 'well enough', can gain acceptance. Crisis in the old is thus a necessary condition for taking on board the new. Revolutionary thinkers, he observes are almost always either very young or very new to the field whose paradigm they change (p. 90). The same argument may well be transferable to technology (Jewkes, Stillerman and Sawers, 1969). An alternative trigger of change is suggested by Levinson (1978) and Gersick (1991) who argue that acute awareness of passing time may stimulate members operating within a system to break existing inertia for themselves.

Within economics, however, the principal agent of such change is seen to be the entrepreneur. Day (1984) echoes Mokyr when he asks: 'Do we know any analytical representation of what happens in [those] shaded domains where things that once were no longer are, and where somehow something new emerges which was not there before?' (p. 74). His own answer is that a force he calls 'creative intelligence' has to be relied upon to achieve 'the surge of economic development from form to form' (p. 74). It was, he argues, Schumpeter's special contribution to have seen the analytical need for such a force, beyond economic rationality and routine adaptive behaviour, if radically new technology were to be brought to life.

In Chapter 5, it will be recalled we argued that 'the entrepreneur' often turns out to be a convenient analytical device, rather like Walras' auctioneer in equilibrium adjustment stories, to fill a gap. Somehow, an explanation has to be provided for how the economy works when decision-makers are assumed boundedly rational, transactions imperfectly coordinated and the potential for instability great. It is 'the entrepreneur' who creates the mechanisms that make the operation of the economic system possible though it might be more accurate to say the entrepreneur is the main mechanism. Given that major technological innovation makes rationality bounded, undermines coordination and generates instability, it is inevitable that the entrepreneur should be identified with creating the mechanisms which put new ideas to use in the economic system. But this is ultimately somewhat unsatisfactory, for it remains unclear why entrepreneurship sometimes plays an effective creative role and sometimes does not.

In response to this challenge, Baumol (1990) argues that entrepreneurs are economic animals like everyone else. There is a number of tasks to which they could allocate their time and effort: Schumpeterian ('productive') ones like introducing a new good, a new product, opening a new market, finding new sources of supply or reorganising an industry, and 'unproductive' ones, often involving rent-seeking or speculation. If entrepreneurs are defined to be people who are ingenious and creative in finding ways to add to their own wealth, power and prestige (p. 897), they will allocate effort among tasks in whatever way maximises this combined objective. Baumol's hypothesis is that it is variations in the reward structure in the economy (its set of rules) that determines how the economic impact of entrepreneurs will vary from one point in history to another. Implicit in this hypothesis is the belief that the objectives of entrepreneurs vary only modestly from time to time and place to place. They always have enough in common to suggest that variations in socio-economic environment mostly determine how entrepreneurs act.

To illustrate his theory, Baumol draws on evidence from ancient Rome, medieval China, and middle ages and renaissance Europe. In Rome, wealth was most honourably acquired through landholding, usury and political payments, while those who engaged in commerce to exploit technology suffered an associated loss in prestige. In China, enterprise was actively discouraged by the imperial officialdom, in whose service the greatest rewards were to be earned. In France and England during the later middle ages, however, increasingly widespread use of the new water-driven mill technology was encouraged by the possibility of acquiring monopoly rights in operation, an option pursued vigorously by the monks, among others.

What are the implications? Baumol points out that the water mill was invented in the first century BC, well known to the Romans, but not in general use until the fifth or sixth century AD and even then only to grind grain. But rather than the Romans, it was the landlords of the middle ages who proved really enterprising in applying it to olive crushing, timber sawing, metal hammering, coin milling, treating woollens and using it to operate the bellows of blast furnaces. It is at least plausible, Baumol argues, that improved rewards to milling-related activity accounted for the robustness of the industrial revolution of the twelfth and thirteenth centuries and for more imaginative range of its use compared with Roman times. As for China, its contributions to technology are numerous: paper, water wheels, gunpowder, water clocks and perhaps the compass. Yet none of this led to a flowering of industry. In the modern United States, he adds finally, rent seeking via litigation, takeovers and tax evasion and avoidance seem to pose the prime threat to productive entrepreneurship.

None of Baumol's argument could ever be tested with full-scientific rigour (as he concedes). But it is at the least highly suggestive and indicates how wide ranging the connections are not only between the economic system and technology, but also the legal, cultural and social environment in which they operate. If we accept the punctuationist view that macroinventions must logically precede periods of gradual incremental improvement and the general proposition that only entrepreneurs can bring macroinventions into economic use, Baumol's hypothesis amounts to saying that the rules prevailing in a previous period of stability will have an important bearing on determining if and when that stability is disrupted.

It is easy to imagine how a reward structure which benefits a governing elite might be perpetuated by that elite, with the simultaneous effect of discouraging disruptions which might threaten their power. This appears to be an important part of China's story, reinforced by the mandarins' determination to protect the country from outside influence through trade. But how could a reward structure which has been consistent with stable if gradual change also encourage major change, even if its effects are only temporarily destabilising? There is clearly the potential for deep conflict here, but observation of history suggests that when the need for change is felt urgently enough, revolutions may occur or the democratic process throw up major shifts in opinion about the reward structure a country wants. Sometimes, though not necessarily, the new prescriptions of the day will encourage entrepreneurs to switch from rent seeking to more productive activity. Alternatively, a country may find itself subject to outside influences which operate despite the rules, such as waves of immigrant entrepreneurs who are relatively insensitive to their new country's reward structure, or the introduction of new technology through invasion or trade.

This is straying far away from economics but that seems to be inevitable if we want to say anything at all about the sources of major innovation. Contemporary developments in this area, stimulated by the collapse of Communism behind the Iron Curtain, have focused increasingly on the institutions required to generate growth, implying of course that major institutional innovation is required if the benefits of technological innovation are to be widely felt and enjoyed. Analysis of this subject would take us deep into the study of comparative economic systems and we leave that for readers to explore for themselves.

Notes

1. For surveys of modern growth theory see Hahn and Matthews (1964), Burmeister and Dobell (1970), Jones (1975), Hacche (1979), Dixit (1976) and Scott (1989).
2. For a modern treatment of the classical theories of Quesnay, Adam Smith, Malthus, Ricardo and Marx, see Eltis (1984).
3. This assumption is far from 'neoclassical' in itself despite the name of the model. 'Neoclassical' work would call for a choice-theoretic analysis of intertemporal consumption and saving behaviour such as that which underlies the life cycle model of consumption (Friedman, 1957; Modigliani, 1986).
4. See later references to the more recent work of Romer (1986, 1987) for an example of analysis which does not rely on the SSG method.
5. Hacche (1979: 142–7) offers a clear analytical summary of the model.
6. To give a simple numerical example if the level of $\Omega(t)$ at $t = 0$, $\Omega(0)$, were set at 100, and $z \cdot H_\Omega = 0.1$, Ω would rise by 10 in the ensuing period and $\Omega(1)$ would be 110. But if $\Omega(1) = 110$, Ω would in the next period rise by $0.1 \cdot 110 = 11$, so $\Omega(2)$ would be 121. And so on, with Ω rising each period by a larger absolute amount than in the previous period, at the constant proportional growth rate of 10 per cent.
7. Desai (1984) has argued that Goodwin's structure is far from robust, mathematically. Even quite small changes in the parameters could radically alter the properties of the system, with the result that (η^*, u^*) would cease to be a centre and instead become a focus. Silverberg (1984: 195), citing Medio (1975), considers this to be of secondary importance, however, arguing that a centre can be thought of as embedded in a family of differential hequations undergoing a Hopf bifurcations as the transitional system between a stable focus and stable limit cycle. The results obtained for the stationary point of the centre can then be generalised to structurally stable and economically relevant cases.

References

Ahmad, S. (1966) 'On the theory of induced invention', *Economic Journal* 76, 344–57.

Allen, P.M. (1975) 'Darwinian evolution and predator-prey ecology', *Bulletin of Mathematical Biology* 37, 389–405.

Allen, P.M. (1976) 'Evolution, population dynamics and stability', *Proceedings of the National Academy of Sciences USA* 73, 655–9.

Arrow, K.J. (1962) 'The economic implications of learning by doing', *Review of Economic Studies* 29, 155–73.

Arrow, K.J. (1988) 'Summary: workshop on the economy as an evolving complex system, in D. Pines (ed.) *The Economy as an Evolving Complex System*, SFI Studies in the Sciences of Complexity, Reading, MA: Addision-Wesley. 275–81.

Atkinson, A. (1970) 'On the measurement of inequality', *Journal of Economic Theory* 2, 244–63.

Baumol, W.J. (1990) 'Entrepreneurship: Productive, unproductive and destructive', *Journal of Political Economy* 98(5), 893–921.

Becker, G.J. (1975) *Human Capital* 2nd edn, New York: National Bureau of Economic Research.

Boulier, B.L. (1984) 'What lies behind Verdoon's Law?', *Oxford Economic Papers* 36, 259–67.

Burmeister, E. and A. Dobell (1970) *Mathematical Theories of Economic Growth*, London: Macmillan.

Chamberlin, E.H. (1933) *The Theory of Monopolistic Competition*, Harvard: Harvard University Press.

Champernonwne, D.G. (1945–6) 'A note on J. von Neumann's article on "A Model of Economic Equilibrium"', *Review of Economic Studies* XIII(1), 10–18.

Cripps, T.F. and R.J. Tarling, (1973) *Growth in Advanced Capitalist Economies*, Cambridge: Cambridge University Press.

Day, R.H. (1982) 'Irregular growth cycles', *American Economic Review* 72, 406–414.

Day, R.H. (1983) 'The emergence of chaos from classical economic growth', *Quarterly Journal of Economics* 98, 201–213.

Day, R.H. (1984) 'Disequilibrium economic dynamics: A post-Schumpeterian contribution', *Journal of Economic Behavior and Organisation* 5, 57–76.

Desai, M. (1984) 'An econometric model of the share of wages in national income: UK 1855–1965', in R.M. Goodwin, M. Kruger, and A. Vercelli (eds) *Non-linear Models of Fluctuating Growth*, Berlin: Springer-Verlag. 252–77.

Denison, E. (1985) *Trends in United States Economic Growth*, Washington: Brookings.

Dixit, A. (1976) *The Theory of Equilibrium Growth*, Oxford: Oxford University Press.

Dixit, A. (1973) 'Models of dual economies', in J. Mirrlees, and N. Stern, (eds) *Models of Economic Growth*, London: Macmillan 325–52.

Dixit, A. and J.E. Stiglitz, (1977) 'Monopolistic competition and optimum product diversity', *American Economic Review* 67, 297–308.

Dorwick, S. and N. Gemmell (1991) 'Industrialisation, catching up and economic growth: a comparative study across the world's capitalist economies', *Economic Journal* 101: 263–75.

Drandakis, E.M. and E.S. Phelps, (1966) 'A Model of induced invention, growth and distribution', *Economic Journal* 76, 823–40.

Elster, J. (1983) *Explaining Technical Change*, Cambridge: Cambridge University Press.

Eltis, W.A. (1984) *The Classical Theory of Economic Growth*, London: Macmillan.

Ethier, W.J. (1982) 'National and international returns to scale in the modern theory of international trade', *American Economic Review* 72: 389–405.

Fields, G.S. (1980), *Poverty, Inequality and Development*, Cambridge: Cambridge University Press.

Friedman, M. (1957) *A Theory of the Consumption Function*, Princeton: Princeton University Press.

Gersick, C.J.G. (1991) 'Revolutionary change theories: A multilevel exploration of the punctuated equilibrium paradigm', *Academy of Management Review* 16(1), 10–36.

Goodwin, R. (1967) 'A growth cycle', in C. Feinstein, (ed.) *Socialism, Capitalism and Economic Growth*, London: Cambridge University Press. 54–8.

Grossman, G. and E. Helpman (1989), 'Product development and international trade', *Journal of Political Economy* 97(6): 1261–83.

Hacche, G. (1979) *The Theory of Economic Growth: An Introduction*, London: Macmillan.

Hahn, F.H. and R.C.O. Matthews, (1964) 'The theory of economic growth: A survey', *Economic Journal*, 74, 779–902.

Harris, D.J. (1982), 'Structural change and economic growth: A review article', *Contributions to Political Economy* 1, 24–45.

Hawkins, D. (1948), 'Some conditions of macroeconomic stability', *Econometrica* 16: 309–22.

Hicks, J.R. (1963) *The Theory of Wages*, 2nd edn, London: Macmillan.

Hicks, J.R. (1965) *Capital and Growth*, Oxford: Clarendon Press.

Jewkes, J., R. Stillerman, and D. Sawers (1969) *The Sources of Invention*, 2nd edn, New York: Norton.

Jones, H.G. (1975) *An Introduction to Modern Theories of Economic Growth*, London: Nelson.

Kaldor, N. (1966) *Causes of the Slow Rate of Economic Growth of the United Kingdom*, Cambridge: Cambridge University Press.

Katsoulacos, Y.S. (1986) *The Employment Effect of Technical Change: A Theoretical Study of*

New Technology and the Labour Market, Brighton: Wheatsheaf.

Kelsey, D. (1988) 'The economics of chaos or the chaos of economics', *Oxford Economic Papers* 40: 1–31.

Kemeny, J.G., O. Morgenstern and G.J. Thompson (1956) 'A generalisation of the von Neumann model of an expanding economy', *Econometrica* 24: 115–35.

Kennedy, C. (1964) 'Induced bias in innovation and the theory of distribution', *Economic Journal* 74, 541–7.

Kondratieff, N.D. (1926) 'Die Langen Wellen der Konjunktur', *Archiv fur Sozialwissenschaft und Sozialpolitik* 56, 573–609.

Kuhn, T.S. (1970) *The Structure of Scientific Revolutions*, 2nd edn, Chicago: University of Chicago Press.

Kuznets, S. (1955) 'Economic growth and income inequality', *American Economic Review* 45, 1–28.

Leontief, W. (1941) *The Structure of the American Economy, 1919–1939*, New York: Oxford University Press.

Leontief, W. (ed.) (1953) *Studies in the Structure of the American Economy*, New York: Oxford University Press.

Levinson, D.J. (1978) *The Seasons of a Man's Life*, New York. Knopf.

Levhari, D. (1966a) 'Further implications of "learning by doing"', *Review of Economic Studies* 33: 31–9.

Levhari, D. (1966b) 'Extensions of "Arrow's learning by doing"', *Review of Economic Studies* 33: 117–32.

Lucas, R.E. (1988) 'On the mechanics of economic development', *Journal of Monetary Economics* 22, 3–42.

Lydall, H. (1979) *A Theory of Income Distribution*, Oxford: Oxford University Press.

Maddison, A. (1979) 'Per capita output in the long run', *Kyklos*, 32(1–2), 412–29.

Marshall, A. (1920) *Principles of Economics*, 8th edn, London: Macmillan.

Medio, A. (1975) *Non-Linear Models of Economic Fluctuations*, unpublished PhD thesis, University of Cambridge.

Mensch, G. (1986) 'Comment', in R. Day and G. Eliasson (eds) *The Dynamics of Market Economies*, Amsterdam, North-Holland, 194–7.

Mensch, G. (1979) *Stalemate in Technology*, Cambridge, MA: Ballinger.

Metcalfe, J.S. (1981) 'Impulse and diffusion in the study of technological change', *Futures* 13, 347–59.

Metcalfe, J.S. and P.H. Hall (1983), 'The Verdoorn Law and the Salter Mechanism: A note on Australian manufacturing industry', *Australian Economic Papers*, (Dec.) 364–73.

Modigliani, F. (1986) 'Life Cycle, Individual Thrift and the Wealth of Nations', *American Economic Review* 76: 297–313.

Mokyr, J. (1990) 'Punctuated equilibria and technological progress', *American Economic Review* 80(2), May, 350–4.

Morishima, M. (1965) *Equilibrium, Stability and Growth*, Oxford: Oxford University Press.

Nelson, R.R. (1968) 'A "Diffusion" model of international productivity differences in manufacturing industry', *American Economic Review* 58, 1219–48.

Nelson, R.R. and S. Winter (1974) 'Neoclassical vs. Evolutionary Theories of Economic Growth: Critique and Prospectus', *Economic Journal* 84: 886–905.

Nelson, R.R. and S. Winter (1982) *An Evolutionary Theory of Economic Change*, Cambridge, MA: Belknap Press of Harvard University Press.

Nelson, R.R., S. Winter and H.L. Schuette (1976) 'Technical Change in an Evolutionary Model', *Quarterly Journal of Economics* 90: 90–118.

Nordhaus, W.D. (1969) *Invention, Growth and Welfare: A Theoretical Treatment of Technological Change*, Cambridge, MA: MIT Press.

Nordhaus, W.D. and P.A. Samuelson (1989) *Economics*, 13th edn, New York: McGraw-Hill.

Pasinetti, L. (1981) *Structural Change and Economic Growth*, Cambridge: Cambridge University Press.

Phelps, E.S. (1961) 'The golden rule of accumulation: a fable for growthmen', *American Economic Review* 51: 638–43.

Phelps, E. (1962) 'The new view of investment: A neoclassical analysis', *Quarterly Journal of Economics* 548–67.

Phelps, E. (1966) 'Models of technical progress and the golden rule of research', *Review of Economic Studies* 133–45.

Robinson, J. (1933) *The Economics of Imperfect Competition*, London: Macmillan.

Romer, P. (1986) 'Increasing returns and long run growth', *Journal of Political Economy*, 94, 1002–37.

Romer, P. (1987) 'Growth based on increasing returns due to specialisation', *American Economic Review* Papers and Proceedings, 56–62.

Romer, P. (1990) 'Endogenous technological change', *Journal of Political Economy* 98(5), S71–S102.

Rosenberg, N. (1976) *Perspectives on Technology*, New York: Cambridge University Press.

Rostow, W. (1975), 'Kondratieff, Schumpeter and Kuznets: trend periods revisited', *Journal of Economic History*, 35, 719–53.

Rowthorn, R.E. (1975) 'What remains of Kaldor's Law?', *Economic Journal* 85, 10–14.

Sahal, D. (1981) *Patterns of Technological Innovation*, Reading: Adison Wesley.

Salter, W.E.G. (1966) *Productivity and Technical Change*, 2nd edn, Cambridge: Cambridge University Press.

Samuelson, P.A. (1965) 'A theory of induced innovation along Kennedy-Weizsacker lines', *Review of Economics and Statistics* 47, 343–56.

Schmitz, J.A. (1989) 'Imitation, entrepreneurship and long run growth', *Journal of Political Economy* 97(3), 721–39.

Schultz, T.W. (1961) 'Investment in human capital', *American Economic Review* 51: 1–17.

Schmookler, J. (1966) *Invention and Economic Growth*, Cambridge, MA: Harvard University Press.

Schumpeter, J.A. (1934) *The Theory of Economic Development*, Cambridge, MA: Harvard University Press.

Schumpeter, J.A. (1939) *Business Cycles: A Theoretical, Historical and Statistical Analysis of the Capitalist Process*, New York: McGraw-Hill.

Scott, M. Fg. (1989) *A New View of Economic Growth*, Oxford: Oxford University Press.

Scott, M. Fg. (1992) 'Policy implications of "A New View of Economic Growth"', *Economic Journal* 102: 622–32.

Shaw, G.K. (1992) 'Policy implications of endogenous growth theory', *Economic Journal* 102: 611–21.

Shell, K. (1973) 'Inventive activity, industrial organisation and economic growth', in J. Mirrlees and N. Stern (eds) *Models of Economic Growth*, London: Macmillan 77–97.

Sheshinski, E. (1967) 'Optimal accumulation with learning by doing', in K. Shell (ed.), *Essays on the Theory of Optimal Economic Growth*, Cambridge, MA: MIT Press.

Silverberg, G. (1984) 'Embodied technical progess in a dynamic economic model. The self-organisation paradigm', in R M. Goodwin, M. Kruger and A. Vercelli (eds) *Non-linear Models of Fluctuating Growth*, Berlin: Springer-Verlag.

Sinclair, P.J.N. (1983) *The Foundations of Macroeconomic and Monetary Theory*, Oxford: Oxford University Press.

Solow, R.M. (1956) 'A contribution to the theory of economic growth', *Quarterly Journal of Economics*, 70, 65–94.

Solow, R.M. (1958) 'A skeptical note on the constancy of relative shares', *American Economic Review* 48, 618–31.

Solow, R.M. (1960), 'Investment and technical progess', in Mathematical Methods in Social

Sciences, in K.J. Arrow, S. Karlin and P. Suppes (ed.) Stanford, CA: Stanford University Press.

Solow, R.M. (1970) *Growth Theory, and Exposition*, Oxford: Oxford University Press.

Solow, R.M. (1988) 'Growth theory and after', *American Economic Review* 78(3), 307–17.

Solow, R.M. and P.A. Samuelson (1953) 'Balanced growth under constant returns to scale', *Econometrica* 21: 412–24.

Stern, N. (1991) 'The determinants of growth', *Economic Journal* 101, 121–33.

Stiglitz, J.E. (1987) 'Learning to learn, localized learning and technological progress', in P. Dasgupta and P. Stoneman (eds) *Economic Policy and Technological Performance*, ch. 5 Cambridge: Cambridge University Press.

Stoneman, P.A. (1983) *The Economic Analysis of Technological Change*, Oxford: Oxford University Press.

Swan, T.W. (1956) 'Economic growth and capital accumulation', *Economic Record* 32, 334–61.

Takayama, A. (1974) *Mathematical Economics*, Hinsdale: Dryden.

Thirlwall, A.P. (1980), 'Rowthorn's interpretation of Verdoorn's Law', *Economic Journal*, June, 386–88.

Uzawa, H. (1960–1) 'Neutral inventions and the stability of growth equilibrium', *Review of Economic Studies* 117–24.

Uzawa, H. (1965) 'Optimum technical change in an aggregative model of economic growth', *International Economic Review* 6, 18–31.

Vaciago, G. (1975) Increasing returns and growth on advanced economies: A re-evaluation', *Oxford Economics Papers* (July), 232–39.

van Duijn, J.J. (1983) *The Long Wave in Economic Life*, London: Allen and Unwin.

Verdoorn, P.J. (1949) 'Fattori che regoleno lo sviluppo della produttivita del lavoro', *L'Industria*. Translated by G. and A. Thirlwall.

von Neumann, J. (1945) 'A model of general economic equilibrium', *Review of Economic Studies* 13: 1–9.

von Weizsacker, C.C. (1966) 'Tentative notes on a two-sector model with induced technical progress', *Review of Economic Studies* 33: 245–51.

Wolff, E. (1987) 'Capital formation and long term productivity growth', Working Paper C.V. Starr Center for Applied Economics, New York University.

Young, A. (1928) 'Increasing returns and economic progress', *Economic Journal* 38: 527–42.

Zarembka, P. (1970) 'On the empirical relevance of the CES production function', *Review of Economic Statistics* 51, 47–53.

8

Technological progress and medium-term macroeconomics

Introduction

While it was shown in Chapter 7 that cycles could be embedded in long-term growth models, the analysis of causes and characteristics of business cycles has usually been regarded as the province of short- and medium-term macroeconomic analysis, largely divorced from implications for longer term trends. At the same time, macroeconomics has largely ignored the impact of changing technology, taking the view that technology advances so slowly that its effects can be put aside for the purposes of focusing on economic movements over periods of perhaps only five to seven years at a time.

But recently there has been a change. First, the centre of attention in most macroeconomic exercises is employment and unemployment. And since changing technology may clearly have employment implications, work has been undertaken to identify the medium-term consequences of innovation for employment in a standard macroeconomic framework. By doing this, the technology–employment link can be explored in a framework designed to deal with system-wide effects. Second, some observed characteristics of the business cycle are a puzzle in terms of accepted macroeconomic theorising and the Real Business Cycle school has appealed to technology shocks as a new source of explanation. As a platform for discussing these developments, we first present a miniature general equilibrium model of the aggregate economy following the lines of Sinclair (1983). More detailed analysis of the employment implications of various types of technological progress is presented on pages 377–80.

A macroeconomic framework

In this presentation, Figure 8.1 is the key.[2] In that diagram, all axes represent positive quantities. Quadrant II depicts the market for a composite good, quadrant III the aggregate production function, quadrant IV the labour market and quadrant I a

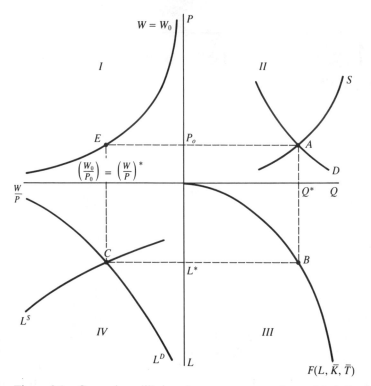

Figure 8.1 General equilibrium in a macroeconomic model, defined by points A, B, C, E. (Figures 8.1–8.3 are reprinted with permission in adapted form from P.J.N. Sinclair (1983) *The Foundations of Macroeconomic and Monetary Theory*, Oxford: Oxford University Press.)

graph of the relationship between the price level and the real wage at various levels of the money wage.

Starting in quadrant III, $F(L, \bar{K}, \bar{T})$ is an aggregate production function, in which the capital stock and level of technology are taken as fixed. Aggregate output of the homogeneous good Q increases at a decreasing marginal rate with increasing inputs of labour L. The slope of the function at any point represents the marginal product of labour $dQ/dL = $ MPL.

For the purposes of simple analysis, it is assumed that labour is homogeneous and hired by profit-maximising firms in perfectly competitive goods and labour markets. Labour is hired up to the point at which the real wage, (W/P) is equal to the MPL. In quadrant IV, the demand-for-labour curve, L^D, is shown as an inverse relationship between the real wage and labour employed, since higher levels of employment will be associated with lower MPL and to be persuaded to hire an extra unit of labour, firms will have to be offered the inducement of lower real wage costs. For real wages to be lower, the nominal wage must rise less quickly than prices; firms hire more labour because the price per unit they receive for increasing sales has increased more than the money cost per unit they have to incur to employ more labour.

The MPL in quadrant III will rise at any given level of L if there is either an increase in the capital stock (releasing a fixed input constraint) or technological progress (which raises the productivity of all inputs). This will shift the production function out in an easterly direction and because the MPL is now higher for each level of L, the L^D curve will shift westwards; firms are now prepared to incur higher real wage costs to secure each extra unit of labour.

On the supply-side of the labour market, the L^S-curve shows a positive relationship between the real wage and utility-maximising households' willingness to sell their labour services to firms. Given the meaning of the real wage, households offer increasing labour to firms when the buying power of the money wage rises, i.e. when money wages rise more quickly than prices. The slope of the L^S curve reflects the sum of two elements, the influence of real wages on (already employed) individuals' decisions about how much labour to offer, and the impact of real wages on whether to enter the labour force at all, with implications for the aggregate participation rate. The position of the curve is determined by individuals' preferences between devoting their time to non-income-earning pursuits ('leisure') and to earning income to purchase goods. A shift in community preferences towards leisure-taking, for example, would reduce the amount of labour offered at any real wage rate and shift the L^S curve in a northerly direction towards the W/P axis. It is also influenced by the size of the population, an increase in which would result in more labour being offered at every wage rate.

In the labour market, the real wage $(W/P)^*$ is that associated with equilibrium employment L^*. This is also called the full-employment level. Should less labour be hired than L^*, there is unemployment. Much of the debate in macroeconomics surrounds the origins and resolution of unemployment. An important part of the logical foundation for the debate can be seen in the simple fact that both L^D and L^S curves are drawn with respect to the real wage, the price variable which would, in a perfectly informed and flexible world, rapidly equilibrate the labour market and counteract any tendency to unemployment. But the real wage is a ratio comprising two elements: the money wage and the general level of goods prices. These are determined in two different but related markets and whether both goods and labour markets are simultaneously in equilibrium depends on the controversial question of how they interact.

Before we turn to analysis of that question, we need to complete the description of the model. In quadrant I, the rectangular hyperbola shown indicates how W/P will rise when P is allowed to decline relative to a given money wage W_0. Other members of a family of such curves may be derived by allowing W to vary. When $W > W_0$, the curve is higher, when $W < W_0$, lower. The relationship here is purely mathematical: no economics is involved.

In quadrant II, the downward-sloping curve labelled D is the aggregate demand curve for a homogeneous, all-purpose final good produced in the economy. The curve is derived from a household utility-maximising exercise of the kind presented in

Chapter 3 of this book. Households are assumed identical and the curve results from aggregating over all their decisions. Households decide on their demand for the all-purpose good simultaneously with decisions on how much time to devote to leisure as against income-earning employment and on the size of nominal money holdings. As usual, there is a budget constraint and assuming the all-purpose good is normal, more of it will be demanded at any price if real incomes increase – shifting the demand curve outwards. The demand curve will also shift upon a change of preferences: outwards if preferences strengthen for purchasing the good, inwards if they weaken.[3] The curve labelled S (for supply) is the representative competitive firm's marginal cost curve. Its upward slope reflects the output-expanding response of firms to an increase in the price level at any given money wage. A higher price reduces the real wage and encourages increased use of the only variable input, labour. S is in fact derived by allowing P to take a range of values; in quadrant I we are seeking, at any given money wage, associated levels of the real wage; tracing through the L^D curve in quadrant IV to find the employment level for each real wage; and through the production function in quadrant III to determine the associated aggregate output level.

A rise in the money wage at any given price raises the real wage and leads firms to contract output; S shifts inwards. An increase in the capital stock or improved technology induces firms to produce more output at any price level, given the money wage; S shifts outwards.

Sources of unemployment

In Figure 8.1 the economy is in general equilibrium. The equilibrium price level P_o in the goods market combines with the money wage W_o to generate a real wage (W_o/P_o) consistent with equilibrium (full) employment in the labour market. Unemployment may arise in two ways. To see how, an important assumption will be made about the working of markets, namely that when a market is out of equilibrium, the *short side dominates.*[4] This means that when the market price is above its equilibrium level and the quantity suppliers offer exceeds the quantity buyers demand, the quantity actually traded in the market is the amount read off the demand curve at that price level. When the market price is below the equilibrium level, the quantity buyers demand exceeds the quantity suppliers offer and the quantity actually traded is found by reading off the supply curve. To put it another way, in the first case suppliers are rationed; they can sell just the amount buyers wish to buy at that price and no more. This has an important implication: sellers in the market can only earn income from the market at a level generated by their rationed level of sales. To the extent that sellers in one market are buyers in others, rationing in one market can have spill-over effects elsewhere. In the second case, there is rationing on the demand-side; at the prevailing price, potential buyers are limited in what they can obtain.

The importance of this assumption is related to the fact that we are now performing short-run analysis. In the short run, we can no longer depend on the price mechanism to ensure equilibrium is maintained in markets at all times. For a range of reasons

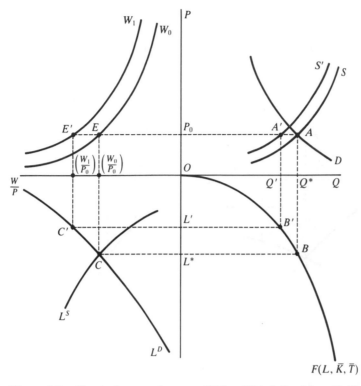

Figure 8.2 Classical unemployment $OL^* - OL'$, defined by A', B', C', E'.

associated with transaction costs in altering prices, fear of losing custom, imperfect information and institutional arrangements which hold prices (especially wages) fixed for periods of time, it is plausible to assume that prices will adjust only with a lag when out-of-equilibrium conditions emerge. A simplified representation of this proposition is to say that, in the short run, prices are fixed. But in that case, an assumption is needed to indicate how trade proceeds out of equilibrium. That is where the short-side domination assumption is brought to bear.

In so-called classical unemployment (Sinclair, 1983: 219–20), the problem is traced to the labour market (Figure 8.2). The real wage is too high. To illustrate, the money wage in Figure 8.2 is at a level $W_1 > W_0$ which, with the price level set still at its previous equilibrium level, generates a real wage (W_1/P_0) incompatible with full employment. Assuming firms continue to hire labour to the point where MPL equals the real wage (i.e. they remain on the L^D curve), they will hire L' of labour, produce Q' output and be located at point A' on the supply curve S' which lies to the left of supply curve S because the real wage is higher. The classical prescription for raising employment back to its equilibrium level was to reduce money wages to W_o. Indeed, with excess supply in the labour market, it was predicted that market forces would

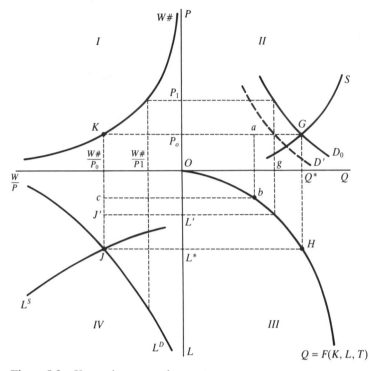

Figure 8.3 Keynesian unemployment.

bring the money wage down, with a resulting outward shift in the supply curve along the given demand curve.

But there is much evidence that money wages are downward-sticky; for the same reason that money wages might in the first place have risen, monopolistic behaviour by trade unions acts on behalf the majority of their members who would not lose their jobs if wages rose and stayed up. In this case, technological progress may (but not necessarily) help, since it will shift the aggregate production function outwards, raise the value or increase the effectiveness of marginal units of labour and make it worthwhile to pay more of them the (now higher) wage. Increased investment in capital will have the same effect. In both cases, the goods market supply curve shifts outwards too.[5] Notice that efforts to shift the demand curve for goods outwards by expansionary monetary or fiscal policy are doomed in this perspective, since the short-side in the goods market is the supply-side, and moving the demand curve away from it will do nothing to induce firms to hire more labour.

While the classical economists provide a supply-side perspective on unemployment, the Keynesians trace the source of the problem to defects in the price mechanism in the labour and goods markets (Sinclair, 1983: 220–2). In the Keynesian tradition, the money wage is often taken to be fixed which is plausible, at least in the short run. We set $W = W \#$, a constant. Refer now to Figure 8.3. Suppose equilibrium throughout the system would occur with the demand-for-goods curve at level D_o, goods price at P_o, and the real wage at $(W\#/P_o)$. The points G, H, J and K trace out the equilibrium. Keynesian unemployment can now be seen to arise for two sorts of reason, both related to 'demand deficiency'.

Suppose first the demand-for-goods curve shifted inwards to D' but the price level was unchanged. Then at P_o, supplier firms would be rationed in the goods market, since only Og units of the commodity would now be in demand. Bearing in mind that firms are also constrained to pay $(W\#/P_o)$, they will employ L' labour to meet this demand, operating off their demand-for-labour curve at J'. But this also means they will generate less wage income than before, with the result that demand will be depressed yet further, shifting the demand curve inwards again (to a level not shown). This will again reduce employment, creating a vicious downward circle that will ultimately converge on a low-level unemployment equilibrium such as that depicted by the points K, a, b and c. In this case, improved technology which saves any labour will merely reduce the employment associated with producing the low-level equilibrium output and so increase the unemployment rate itself. The only solution is to shift the demand-for-goods curve out again.

A second route by which demand-deficiency unemployment might arise is a price shock. Suppose that from the initial equilibrium $KGHJ$, the price rose from P_o to P_1, chosen deliberately to reduce the amount of goods demanded once again to Og. This time the real wage will be reduced to $(W\#/P_1)$ and the labour market must operate on a vertical dropped from that point on the W/P axis. But other than that, the rest of the story is essentially the same. The price stays at its new higher level, employment and wage income fall, the demand-for-goods curve shifts in, inducing firms to cut supply and employment again and so on. Again, technological progress will only amplify the unemployment problem.

Technological change and unemployment: a more detailed analysis

The relationship between technological progress and unemployment in macro-economic models has been analysed in depth by Sinclair (1981), Heffernan (1981) and Hall and Heffernan (1985). Sinclair investigates the impact of disembodied progress on a closed economy under four different assumptions about wages (see below). On the supply-side, a single output is generated from capital and labour through a constant elasticity of substitution production function, in which technological change may be pure labour or capital augmenting, or Hicks-neutral. On the demand-side, expenditures are positively related to real income, usually taken to capture households' consumption behaviour, negatively to the interest rate (principally a reflection of firms' investment decisions) and positively to the real value (buying power or price-deflated level) of the nominal money stock, suggesting a role for wealth, of which real money balances form an element. Given that the economy is closed, national expenditure (aggregate demand) is equal to national output and the real flow of incomes which producing it generates.

The interest rate is determined in the financial markets and is positively related to the price level and real income or expenditure. If one or both of these rise, the value of transactions per period increases. And because of money's unique capacity to act as the universally accepted medium for making transactions, increases in either price or real income lead to a rise in the community's desire to hold their financial wealth in the form of the non-interest-bearing asset, money, rather than interest-bearing assets generically described as 'bonds'. Assuming the nominal money supply to be fixed exogenously, an increase in the demand to hold money must lead to a rise in its 'price', the interest rate on bonds.

Given this structure, the price level and aggregate demand will be negatively related to each other. A rise in the price level would reduce the buying power of a given nominal stock of money, i.e. reduce the value of real balances and cut back expenditures, both directly through reducing wealth and indirectly by putting upward pressure on the interest rate in financial markets, which in turn would reduce interest-sensitive expenditures in the goods market.

In this model, there is always a negative relationship between the real wage and employment. This is guaranteed by Sinclair's assumption that producers are never rationed; they are always on their demand curve for labour and supply curve for the product. In addition, interest focuses on cases in which the real wage is either at or above its equilibrium level; employment is always less than or equal to the supply of labour, but the possibility of excess demand for labour is ruled out. Given that, the impact of technological change on the demand for labour can be found by varying technology parameters in the production function to reflect the forms of progress assumed.

Sinclair's first wage assumption is a fixed real wage. Here demand for labour will *rise* if progress is purely capital augmenting or Hicks-neutral and may *fall* if it is purely labour augmenting (Harrod-neutral). It will rise under Harrod-neutrality only if the elasticity of substitution between capital and labour in the production function exceeds the profit share. Second, assume that the 'Great Ratio' hypothesis (see p. 325) is correct and take labour's share of national income as fixed. Then Hicks-neutral progress leaves labour demand unaffected, capital-augmenting advance raises it and labour-augmenting change reduces it (in each case equiproportionately). Third, make the Keynesian assumption of a fixed money wage. Here, Hicks-neutral progress leads to an increase (decrease) in labour demand if aggregate demand in the goods market is price elastic (inelastic); purely labour-augmenting progress brings about an increase in labour demand if the profit share is less than the substitution elasticity and aggregate demand is sufficiently price elastic, and a decrease if the profit share exceeds the substitution elasticity; purely capital-augmenting progress brings a rise (fall) in labour demand if the price elasticity of aggregate demand exceeds (lies below) the substitution elasticity. Finally, assume the money wage does not rise and the real wage does not fall (i.e. real wages could rise because of falling prices). Here the demand for labour is less likely to fall than in the pure, fixed-money wage case and will be more likely to rise the more readily workers perceive the real wage gains implied by a price fall and the lower the rise in real wage accompanying technological change.

The implications for unemployment require a further assumption to link the demand for labour to the number of employees in work, a fall in which indicates a rise in unemployment. If, for example, every employee were constrained to be employed for a constant, uniform number of hours per year, $\bar{H}$, and L is interpreted as the total volume of hours demanded, then the ratio $L/\bar{H}$ would equal the number of individuals in work. When technological change takes L up or down, this ratio must move in the same direction and unemployment in the opposite one.

More generally, however, we might expect the individual's hours of work per period to be negatively related to the real wage, for which there is empirical evidence (Morishima and Saito, 1972; Stern, 1976). When the real wage is fixed by construction, the implications of this relationship are irrelevant; from the labour demand results above, we may infer that technological progress cuts unemployment when it is Hicks-neutral or purely capital augmenting, but raises it when progress is Harrod-netural and the profit share exceeds the substitution elasticity.

With the wage share fixed, Hicks-neutral and purely capital-augmenting progress again reduce unemployment, but this time Harrod-neutral advance unambiguously increases it. In the case of a fixed-money wage, negative employment implications of technological progress through the demand for labour noted above are muted by the way in which rising real wages induce a fall in hours of work. Unemployment may certainly fall under any of the forms of technological progress considered, but the conclusion is ambiguous. It depends on the specific values of the substitution elasticity, the price elasticity of aggregate demand, the real wage elasticity of hours of work per employee and the profit share. The same is also true of Sinclair's fourth wage case.

The ambiguity of some of these results can be removed by varying the structure of the model. As we saw earlier, if rationing is assumed through a short-side domination hypothesis, Keynesian unemployment may emerge, as firms find themselves rationed in the goods market. This imposes a binding constraint on production and technological progress would then (nearly) always tend to raise unemployment. The issue then becomes to determine which model is more plausible or defensible in terms of the evidence. And this is a matter which itself remains unresolved.

In other dimensions, varying the assumptions only introduces further ambiguity. If two sectors rather than one are allowed for, an additional set of considerations becomes the elasticity of substitution in consumption between the goods produced by the two sectors, quite apart from the relative rates and forms of progress in each sector (Heffernan, 1981; Hall and Heffernan, 1985). If the benefits of technological change can be obtained only through investment in new capital, i.e. it is embodied, new jobs will be created to instal it and if jobs have to be redefined for labour to be integrated with new capital, there may be an increase in employment in training. These factors will offset any Pasinetti-type of tendency for changes in the structure of production to destroy jobs. Introducing *trade* implies that producers should never face any sales constraint from limitations of domestic demand, but at the same time requires a flexible exchange rate to preserve competitiveness and jobs if more rapid technological advance abroad threatens the markets of local firms.

The specifics of the technological change are also potentially important. To the extent that unemployment reflects individuals' decisions to leave a previous job to search for something better, new information technology which makes more job information available more accessibly should reduce the time individuals spend out of work and the numbers between jobs at any moment. Improved communications and computer technology also facilitate more flexible employment practices, including work from home and more self-employment (Toffler, 1980; Hall, 1988). Improvements in household consumption technology (Lancaster, 1966; Gershuny, 1983) free up time which may be used either for more leisure or earning additional income. This might partially explain the rising proportion of women in the labour force. And technological advances in easing and speeding financial transactions may help to reduce the demand for money and, for any given money supply, reduce the 'price' of money, the interest rate. This, in turn, could encourage job-creating investment.

The conclusions of this analysis are an important reminder that the links between technological change, employment and unemployment are anything but unambiguous and predictable, especially in the short and medium term. Once a variety of potential forms of progress is allowed for and a range of assumptions about labour market behaviour considered, almost anything can happen. That said, observed values of the parameters determining the results in this model suggest some outcomes are more likely than others. Steeply rising labour costs relative to capital, make it likely that innovation will have a labour-augmenting bias. The threat of rising unemployment then has much to do with how fast real wages grow. If real wages are fixed, labour-augmenting progress will almost certainly favour employment, since the profit share seems to fall well short of the substitution elasticity. But the faster real wages grow on the back of rising productivity, the greater the danger that technological progress will destroy jobs.

Technological progress and the business cycle

The analysis above deals with the unemployment consequences of innovation, but makes no pretence of explaining systematic patterns of fluctuation in unemployment over time, i.e. cycles. This question has been addressed by the Real Business Cycle theorists (Long and Plosser, 1983 and King, Plosser and Rebelo, 1988) and is discussed in surveys of recent advances in macroeconomic analysis (Hall and Taylor, 1991; Mankiw, 1991). The interesting thing about this work is that until recently, 'shocks' to the macroeconomy from technological advance were never included in short- and medium-run analysis. Shocks were seen as arising principally on the demand-side, either in abrupt and substantial changes in business expectations, leading to major fluctuations in capital investment, or unanticipated movements in the demand for

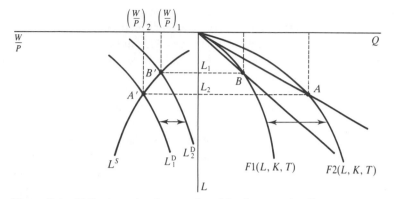

Figure 8.4 Shifts in technology and real business cycle effects on employment.

exports, or unpredictable shifts in the demand for money or from new settings for monetary and fiscal policy. Any of these perturbations could lead to fluctuations in aggregate expenditures at given prices and theories abound on why such fluctuations might take on a roughly regular cyclic appearance.

But macroeconomic theorists in the classical tradition, the New Classical economists, have argued that if all individuals act rationally to make the best use of available information in pursuing their own economic interests, many of these theories are incompatible with microeconomic analysis rooted in optimising behaviour, or imply the existence of disequilibrium for implausibly long periods of time (Lucas and Rapping, 1969; Lucas, 1972; Sargent and Wallace, 1975). One way of escaping this impasse is to suppose that technological shocks on the supply-side are responsible for short- to medium-run fluctuations. The analysis can be carried off entirely within an optimising equilibrium framework and has the additional advantage of explaining an observed empirical regularity which is not always consistent with other stories: procyclical variation in average labour productivity.

To see the thrust of the argument, let the aggregate production function shift between $F1(K, L, T)$ and $F2(K, L, T)$ in Figure 8.4. The source of this shift is assumed to be technological shocks, which may either enhance or reduce input productivity. Given our earlier analysis of how this reflects into the labour market, the L^D curve will also shift, between L_1^D and L_2^D. If the labour market is in equilibrium at all times, employment will vary between a high of L_2 (with equilibrium at A') and a low of L_1 (equilibrium at B') and the real wage will shift in the range $(W/P)_1$ to $(W/P)_2$. Rays from the origin to a production function have a slope representing average labour productivity and comparing points A and B corresponding to A' and B' in the labour market, labour productivity is clearly higher on $F2$ than $F1$. Average labour productivity is procyclical, since it is at its highest when employment and output are at their highest and lowest when they are at their lowest.

For this story to fit other observed facts of the business cycle, real wages must vary over a relatively small range as employment fluctuates, which calls for the L^S curve to be relatively real wage elastic (as drawn). This in turn implies that individuals need to suffer only a relatively small reduction in wages as recession approaches to be prepared, voluntarily, to divert their time from current, wage-earning employment to other non-wage earning activities. Suggestions might include a long holiday to recover from the rigours of intensive work during the boom, non-earning activities which are nonetheless valued relatively highly at the margin by the individuals involved (such as repairs and maintenance on the home, given that tradespersons are expensive to hire but that expected capital gains from improvements may be substantial) and currently non-earning activities which take the form of investment in human capital, offering the promise of higher earnings in future.

For technology shocks to explain business cycles, it must also be true that such shocks are fairly regularly spaced and substantial in their immediate effects on employment. Neither of these implicit assumptions looks very plausible, for though it may be the case that technological change on occasion constitutes the impulse for a cycle, there is a great deal of evidence that other shocks (see above) also set cycles in motion and that technological change is often very slow to make its impact felt (recall Silverberg's simulations as an illustration).

Nonetheless, the arrival of technological change in the analysis of medium-term macroeconomic fluctuations is long overdue. It certainly deserves to be considered as one potential influence on cycles and empirical work suggests that it may at times have been important in explaining episodes of high unemployment (Parkin, 1991). As even the Real Business Cycle school itself admits, however, it would be foolish to attribute all cyclical fluctuations to purely technological factors. And there are other ways in which the procyclicity of labour productivity can be explained.

Notes

1. For another authoritative presentation of modern macroeconomic analysis see Stevenson, Muscatelli and Gregory (1988).
2. Figures 8.1, 8.2 and 8.3 correspond to Sinclair (1983) Figures 7.1, 7.6 and 7.7.
3. A more complete account of the demand side in the aggregate goods market is given on pages 377–8 where it is acknowledged that variations in the price level also affect the interest rate and so influence firms' (and household) expenditures which are interest-rate insensitive. See also Stevenson, Muscatelli and Gregory (1988), Chapter 1.
4. The foundations for work in this tradition may be found in Clower (1970), Muellbauer and Portes (1978) and Malinvaud (1979).
5. Note that P has been held constant at P_o, partly for expositional ease, but more importantly because one of the central observations of modern macroeconomics is that prices are in general slow to adjust. Slow adjustment may well reflect the cost sellers incur in changing their prices: reprinting and circulating price lists and catalogues and, if variations are frequent, loss of customer allegiance (Mankiw, 1991). If P is allowed to be flexible, an outward shift in the aggregate supply curve S will (with a given, downward-sloping demand curve) be associated with lower levels of P. This encourages increased goods purchases

along the given demand curve, but also puts upward pressure on real wages. While higher real wages reduce employment along the labour demand curve, the higher MPL at every employment level shifts L^D outwards which encourages employment. The final outcome depends on the labour saving bias of technological progress and substitutability of labour for capital. As real wages rise, there should also be a positive income effect in demand which shifts the aggregate demand curve outwards, counteracting the downward movement in P initially induced by the shifting supply curve. Allowing for full-price flexibility is at the heart of neoclassical analysis considered later in the chapter.

References

Clower, R. (1970) 'The Keynesian counter-revolution: A theoretical appraisal', in R. Clower, (ed.), *Monetary Theory*, New York: Penguin, 270–97.

Gershuny, J. (1983) *Social Innovation and the Division of Labour*, Oxford: Oxford University Press.

Hall, P.H. (1988) 'Telecommuting, work from home and economic change', in C. Tisdell and P. Maitra (eds) *Technological Change, Development and the Environment*, London: Routledge, 239–59.

Hall, P.H. and S.A. Heffernan (1985) 'More on the employment effects of innovation', *Journal of Development Economics* 17, 151–62.

Hall, R. and J. Taylor (1991) *Macroeconomics*, 3rd edn, New York: Norton.

Heffernan, S.A. (1981) *Technological Unemployment*, D. Phil dissertation, Oxford University.

King, R.G., C. I. Plosser and S.T. Rebelo (1988) 'Production, growth and business cycles: I. The basic Neoclassical model', *Journal of Monetary Economics* 21: 195–232.

King, R.G., C.I. Plosser and S.T. Rebelo (1988) 'Production, growth and business cycles: II. New directions', *Journal of Monetary Economics* 21: 309–41.

Lancaster, K. (1966) 'A new approach to consumer theory', *Journal of Political Economy*, 74, 132–57.

Long, J. and C. Plosser (1983) 'Real business cycles', *Journal of Political Economy* 91: 39–69.

Lucas, R.E. (1972) 'Expectations and the neutrality of money', *Journal of Economic Theory* 4: 103–4.

Lucas, R.E. and L. Rapping (1969) 'Real wages, employment and inflation', *Journal of Political Economy* 77: 721–54.

Malinvaud, E. (1979) *The Theory of Unemployment Reconsidered*, Oxford: Blackwell.

Mankiw, G. (1991) 'A quick refresher course on macroeconomics', *Journal of Economic Literature* 28: 1645–60.

Morishima, M. and M. Saito (1972) 'A dynamic analysis of the American economy 1900–1952, in H. Morishima *et al.* (eds) *The Working of Econometric Models*, Cambridge: Cambridge University Press. 3–69.

Muellbauer, J. and R. Portes (1978) 'Macroeconomic models with quantity rationing', *Economic Journal* 88, 788–821.

Parkin, M. (1991) 'The Great Depression: A 'Real' Explanation', mimeo, Department of Economics, University of Western Ontario.

Sargent, T.J. and N. Wallace (1973) '"Rational" expectations, the optimal monetary instrument and the optimal money supply rule', *Journal of Political Economy* 83: 241–77.

Sinclair, P.J.N. (1981) 'When will technical progress destroy jobs?', *Oxford Economic Papers* 31: 1–18.

Sinclair, P.J.N. (1983) *The Foundations of Macroeconomic and Monetary Theory* Oxford: Oxford University Press.

Stern, N. (1976) 'On the specification of models of optimum income taxation', *Journal of Public Economics* 6: 123–62.

Stevenson, A., V. Muscatelli and M. Gregory (1988) *Macroeconomic Theory and Stabilisation Policy*, Hemel Hempstead: Philip Allan.
Toffler, A. (1980) *The Third Wave*, New York: Murrow.

9

The international dimension: trade, technology and growth

One of the major simplifying assumptions made in presenting the macroeconomic implications of innovation was that the economy was *closed*. This, however, abstracts from the potential of international trade to influence economic activity in any one country partly by opening up global markets for its products and partly by giving a country access to technological developments abroad. Furthermore, many of the current debates in the economics of innovation are ultimately inseparable from international trade; questions relating to the role of **multinational corporations (MNCs)**, the issue of so-called 'globalisation' of production and the nature of technology transfer. Many of these issues lend themselves to economic analysis and our purpose here is to provide a conceptual framework in which to conduct that analysis.

Basis of international trade: a static framework

The rationale for trade among countries is logically identical to that for trade among individuals or firms; with given resources, each can achieve a higher level of utility or welfare for itself, its members or its owners than without trade. It is a fundamental tenet of economic analysis that with good information and motivated only by self-interest, decision-makers will always exhaust all opportunities to gain from trade.

The most widely-analysed basis for trade is **comparative advantage**. This principle is most easily explained in terms of two countries, A and Z, each capable of producing two goods which we shall call food (F) and manufactures (M). Each good requires the same physical inputs for its production, the inputs are in fixed supply but fully employed or utilised and in the absence of trade, the price per unit of each good is equal to the unit production cost. In general, we might expect one country to be able to produce a given good at a lower cost than the other country; that is certainly what we observe. Were A to produce F more cheaply than Z, we should then say that A had an absolute advantage in producing F. But a comparative advantage is different.

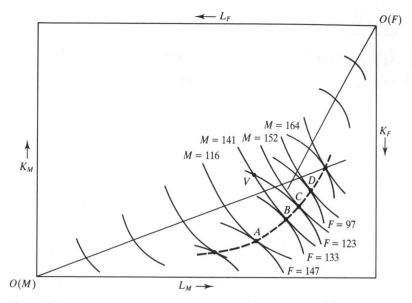

Figure 9.1 An Edgeworth Box comprising two isoquant maps relating to the production of goods *F* and *M* in a single economy.

Suppose both countries use a general purpose input, *J*, to produce each good and have equal resources of *J*, 1,000 units. Irrespective of volumes produced, A uses 2*J* per unit of *F* and 4*J* per unit of *M*; Z uses 4*J* per unit of *F* and 10*J* per unit of *M*. A has therefore an absolute advantage in producing both *F* and *M*, but looking at the international comparison between input:output ratios for each good, we find that for *F* the ratio is 2:4 = 0.5, while for *M* it is 4:10 = 0.4. Since *A* uses less input per unit of output than *Z* in producing *M* compared with *F*, this shows that A has a comparatively greater advantage in producing *M* than *F*. The principle of comparative advantage says that countries should specialise in producing the goods where they have comparative advantage, as A does with *M*. This will enable them to do better than they could have done in the absence of trade. Appendix 1 contains another numerical example and a diagrammatic analysis.

To move in the direction of greater generality, let commodities *M* and *F* be produced by A and Z using two inputs, labour (*L*) and capital (*K*), under perfectly competitive market conditions and constant returns to scale technology. The industry producing *M* is the more labour intensive. Under these assumptions, two isoquant maps with origins *O*(*M*) and *O*(*F*) can be superimposed, with that for *F* upside-down in relation to that for *M* to form an Edgeworth Box of the kind shown in Figure 9.1. The lengths of the side of the box represent the total amounts of *L* and *K* available to the economy and any point in the box (or along its sides) shows a possible allocation of resources between *M* and *F*. The relative labour intensity of *M* compared with *F* is reflected in the positions of the isoquant maps relative to the axes and points *A*, *B*, *C* and *D*

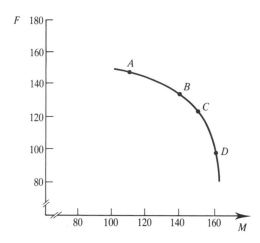

Figure 9.2   Production possibility frontier: points *A*, *B*, *C*, *D* correspond to points *A*, *B*, *C*, *D* in Figure 9.1.

represent four of the infinite number of tangencies between *M* and *F* isoquants within the box.

These tangency points represent allocations of *L* and *K* to *M* and *F* which are efficient in the sense that it is not possible to increase output of one of the commodities from any one of them without reducing output of the other. They should be compared with non-tangency points like *V* from which *L* and *K* could be reallocated in ways which would take the economy to any tangency between (and including) *B* and *C*, at which the same total inputs would generate more total output. The tangency points comprise an efficiency locus which Edgeworth called the 'contract curve'. If new axes are now drawn as Figure 9.2 to measure quantities of *M* and *F*, points on the efficiency locus can be represented in this new space, bearing in mind that each point on the locus formed by the tangencies of the isoquants shows how much *M* and *F* are being produced. The new curve is the **production possibility frontier (ppf)**. It shows all the combinations of *M* and *F* which can be produced when efficient use is made of the economy's resources.

The ppf bows outwards from the origin under CRS if the industries vary in their labour intensity, or if both have similarly shaped isoquants, if at least one industry experiences decreasing returns to scale not outweighed by increasing returns in the other. When CRS prevail, the shape of the ppf reflects the fact that, as output in either industry is reduced, the inputs released become available in proportions not optimal for producing additional units of output in the other industry. For every equal increase in *F* to be achieved, therefore, increasing amounts of inputs have to be withdrawn from *M* and the opportunity cost in terms of lost output of *M* correspondingly mounts. Similarly, for every equal increase in *M*, increasing quantities of inputs have to be withdrawn from *F* and the opportunity cost in terms of lost

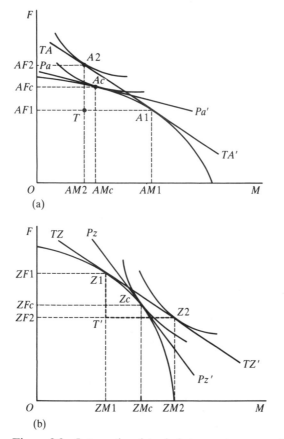

Figure 9.3   International trade between two countries and the welfare gains generated (a) Country A; (b) Country Z.

output of F also increases. The intuition behind the impact of decreasing returns to scale should be self-evident.

The particular point on the ppf where the economy should produce (implying some particular allocation of resources between industries and some specific output combination) is that at which consumer welfare is maximised. Suppose that consumers' preferences can be summarised in a **community indifference curve (CIC)** map. This map can be thought of as that of a 'representative' consumer, or will accurately reflect all consumers' preferences if all have identical tastes. In Figure 9.3, we show, at points Ac and Zc on each country's ppf, the domestically produced combination of M and F at which the highest CIC is reached before trade. A produces and consumes AFc of F and AMc of M; Z ZFc of F and ZMc of M. In a perfectly competitve economy, the relative price ratio represented by the slope of the tangent at such points (see Pa–Pa' and Pz–Pz') is that associated with the allocation of resources which maximises welfare.

Scope for trade is indicated by observing the difference between the pretrade, domestic price ratios. If the countries agreed to trade with each other at an international price ratio, the **terms of trade (TOT)**, somewhere between their respective domestic price ratios, both would gain. To see this, suppose the countries agreed to trade at TOT shown by the slope (the same for A and Z) of lines $TA-TA'$ and $TZ-TZ'$. Then each would produce at the point on its ppf to which the TOT line was tangent and export and import along the TOT line until it reached its highest CIC. At $A2$ and $Z2$, A and Z are on the highest attainable CICs A consuming $AM2$ of M and $AF2$ of F, Z $ZM2$ of M and $ZF2$ of F. In each case, the CIC reached lies unambiguously above that associated with the closed economy optimum and generates greater welfare.

In the case of A, the country specialises, but incompletely, in M, producing $AM1 > AMc$ and exporting what it does not consume $(AM2 - AM1) = (T - A1)$. In return, at the TOT shown by the slope of $TA-TA'$ it imports $(AF1 - AF2) = (T - A2)$. Z, by contrast, specialises in F, producing at $Z1$, exporting $(T' - Z1)$ of F to pay for its imports of M from A, $ZM1-ZM2$. Since A's exports are Z's imports, and Z's exports A's imports and both face the same international TOT, the trade triangles $A2TA1$ and $Z1T'Z2$ must be identical.

A complete analysis also calls for showing how the terms of trade are themselves determined. This is dealt with in Appendix 2.

Impact of exogenous changes in technology

When a country experiences economic growth, its production possibilities expand; the ppf shifts outwards. It shifts outwards either because of an increase in the quantity of inputs, or because of technological progress which allows given quantities of inputs to produce more output. When the ppf shifts outwards, it enables the country to reach a higher TOT line (delineating trade possibilities) than before. The results of the shift will be reflected in both production and consumption effects. The first shows how the structure of production changes with growth, the second how consumption patterns respond to changing real income levels. A classic treatment is Findlay and Grubert (1959). For more recent analyses of this area, see Findlay (1985), Chaciolades (1978) and Meier (1980).

Given our interest in technological change, we ignore factor increases as a source of growth, though the analysis of their production effects follows very similar lines to that of advances in technology. To proceed we must establish some terminology. To do this, look at Figure 9.4 which relates to country A alone. The terminology relies on holding the TOT constant and, starting at the initial production point $A1$, tracing changes in the structure of production when the ppf shifts outwards with progress. Depending on how the ppf shifts, its new tangency with a TOT line of constant slope might lie on an extension of the ray $OA1$ (e.g. at J), above it (e.g. at H) or below (e.g at R). Furthermore, if $A1$ is taken as the origin for new axes (shown as dashed lines), other possibilities are that new tangencies might lie to the left of the vertical (e.g. at G) or below the horizontal (e.g at S).

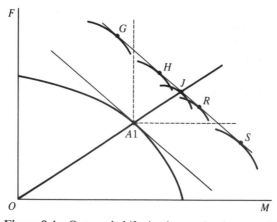

Figure 9.4 Outward shifts in the production possibility frontier. At given terms of trade and with *M* the exported good, the production effect of a shift from *A*1 to *J* is neutral, to *R* is export-biased, to H is import-biased, to *S* is ultra-export-biased, and to *G* is ultra-import-biased.

Recall now that country A exports commodity *M*. Bearing this in mind, production effects are classified as neutral, if they involve a movement along an extension of the ray *OA*1, export-biased, if they fall anywhere in the segment between the extended ray and the dashed new horizontal axis, import-biased, if they fall anywhere in the segment between the extended ray and the new vertical axis, ultra export-biased, if the post-shift tangency lies below the new horizontal axis or ultra import-biased, if the post-shift tangency is to the left of the new vertical. Neutrality implies that production of the exportable, *M* and the importable, *F*, expand at equal proportional rates with progress; export bias, that production of *M* grows at a faster rate than *F*; ultra export-bias, that production of *M* grows at the expense of *F*; import-bias that production of *F* grows faster than M; ultra import-bias that *F* grows at the expense of *M*.

With this terminology, it is now relatively straightforward to present the implications of technological progress on comparative costs. Six cases are considered: technological progress might occur in either of the two industries *M* or *F*, and in one of three forms, Hicks-neutral, labour-saving or capital-saving.

When progress is neutral and occurs in *M* alone, the ppf shifts outwards in a way which implies an ultra export-bias. The nature of the production effect is found by holding the terms of trade (relative prices of *M* and *F*) constant and therefore comparing points of identical slope on the pre- and post-innovation ppfs (Bhagwati, 1959). Any directly eastward movement from the pre- to post-innovation ppf, however, involves in this case moving from a point with a relatively steep to a relatively flatter tangent. The reason for this is that the tangent represents the relative cost ratio and this ratio will fall as the result of innovation in *M* alone at given input prices. Thus post-innovation production at the given commodity price ratio will occur below and to the south-east of the pre-innovation point. Only if there were increasing returns to scale, by assumption ruled out, this might not be so. Innovation in M raises the marginal return on factors producing M and draws resources away from the production of F. Although innovation tends to depress the price of M relative to F, the pre-existing commodity price ratio will be maintained at the new production point as more of the labour-intensive good is produced and the price of labour rises relative to that of capital. An analogous line of reasoning may be employed to show that if neutral progress occurs in producing F, ultra import-bias will result.

When progress is labour-saving in M alone, producing M again becomes cheaper, output of M rises and resources again relocate from F with the prospect of a higher return elsewhere. With innovation releasing more labour than before at any output level and M absorbing it as the relatively labour-intensive industry, production growth is even more ultra export-biased than when progress is neutral.

When progress is labour-saving in F alone, any outcome is possible. As always, innovation has the effect of reducing costs in F, which tends to raise output of F. But since this progress is labour-saving in the relatively capital-intensive sector, the factor-saving effect of innovation will be to release labour which will at given factor prices flow to M, the industry which uses it more intensively. Since labour-saving innovation increases the labour supply relative to capital, it will also tend to depress the wage:rent ratio (increase the cost of capital relative to labour) and reduce the rate at which F will grow relative to M. The more labour-saving the innovation, the lower the rate of expansion of F relative to M. Although (with very little labour saved) production growth might have an ultra import-bias as in the neutral progress case, it might also (with large-scale labour-saving) induce export or even ultra export-bias.

We now merely state as extensions of the above the two last cases: with a capital-saving innovation in M, production growth might be of any kind, but with capital-saving innovation in F, an ultra import-bias will occur.

To complete the picture, consider also the consumption effects of growth. If consumption demand for M and F rise at the same rate, the consumption effect is said to be neutral; if demand for M outstrips that for F, consumption growth is said to be export-biased; and if that for F is faster than that for M, it is import-biased.

The offer curve of a country will also shift when the ppf shifts (see Apendix 2). The direction of the offer curve shift will depend on the nature of the production and consumption biases, the extent of the offer curve shift on the size of the biases and the amount of growth. Taking account of the consequential effects which then follow for the terms of trade and volumes of goods traded, the impact on international trade patterns can be derived. On the simplifying assumption that there is positive real output growth in only one country, the nature of the overall bias in growth in that country can be summarised by the contents of the cells in Table 9.1 (taken from Meier, 1968: 38).

To interpret the data contained in the table, consider the example of either neutral or labour-saving progress in the relatively labour-intensive industry. In those cases, we know the production effect will be ultra export-biased (UX), but we can now see that its ultimate overall effect must also take account of the nature of the consumption

Table 9.1 Export and import bias in the trading patterns of an open, growing economy.

Type of consumption effect	Type of production effect				
	N	*X*	*M*	*UM*	*UX*
N	N	X	M or UM	UM	X or UX
X	X	X	Not UX	UM	X or UX
M	M or UM	Not UX	M or UM	UM	Not UM

Key: N = neutral, X = export-biased, M = import-biased, UM = ultra import-biased, UX = ultra export-biased.

effect associated with higher incomes. While neutral and export-biased consumption effects will combine with the UX production effect to generate export or ultra export-bias, the most that can be said, is that, if the consumption effect is import-biased, the overall effect will not be ultra import-biased. Readers should experiment with other findings above to test their understanding.

The particulars of progress determine how one country's cost advantage will develop relative to another's and, combined with consumption effects, how the terms and volumes of trade and the domestic structure of production, will be affected as a result. We should not however expect technological progress to occur in the same sector and in the same form over long periods of time in every country in the world. In a given economy, a labour-saving advance in *M* might well give way over time to more rapid capital-saving advance in *F*, with significant implications for the reallocation of productive resources throughout the economy and the bias of growth. (Compare the UX and UM columns in Table 9.1.) Such a reallocation would reflect the shift in comparative advantage which changes in the nature of technological progress brought in its wake.

This general point stands out from the details of the analysis we have conducted. An important consequence of technological progress is that it is central to determining how comparative advantage changes, along with changes in the availability of factors, and thus how structural change is driven in open, growing economies as they continuously reallocate their resources among sectors to reap the full benefits of where their comparative advantage at any moment lies.

But once it is recognised that technological progress is not after all exogenous, the further message is that countries have it in their own power to determine their comparative advantage and all that follows from it. We now turn to models which attempt to explain trade patterns from this standpoint.

Innovation, trade and growth

The analysis in this section has so far shown how comparative advantage creates opportunities for trade with given technology and factor supplies and that this in turn allows countries to achieve higher levels of income per head than would be possible without trade. With advances in technology, a country's domestic production possibilities expand, in all probability changing the pattern of trade. We have explored the implications of such advances for domestic production and consumption and for international trade patterns. But we have done so by taking technological change to be exogenous, assuming all markets to be perfectly competitive, and adopting a comparative static approach to analysing change.

Bearing in mind that technological change is always mostly endogenous, that it is usually associated with monopoly power and that innovation-driven growth is a dynamic process, the approach we have followed until now is therefore a considerable methodological simplification. Importantly, this approach also encourages us to think of the links between growth and trade as unidirectional; technological advance exogenously determines growth and changes in domestic production patterns and international differences in domestic production conditions provide the basis for changing trading opportunities. But international trade can also influence growth. Grossman and Helpman (1990) identify four major features of the world economy which are important to understand growth in particular countries.

1. Since new technological knowledge is an input into high-tech products, countries richly endowed with the human capital which gives them a comparative advantage in undertaking R&D will also specialise in producing and exporting high-tech goods. This will influence both the pace and nature of their economic growth.
2. The size of the world market may offer sales prospects which justify local R&D which would not have occurred on the basis of prospective domestic sales alone. To the extent that new knowledge promotes growth (as analysed in Romer (1990)) increases, trade opportunities feed back into economic expansion. Scale effects should also enhance the prospects of gains from LBD.
3. International differences in growth will partially reflect the initial knowledge and human capital endowments of each country; see (1) above, but these bases of comparative advantage are continuously changing. Human capital changes due to education; technological knowledge deepens and broadens with innovation. Such changes may flow from domestic investment or result, in the case of technological knowledge, from international overspill effects from R&D under- taken in other countries. The global implications of such changes depend upon whether the benefits of deploying new knowledge are contained principally within the boundaries of the countries which generated it, or whether it is difficult to exclude other countries from benefiting. In the course of these changes occurring, technology gaps will open up between one country and another. But, at least in those technologies where non-excludable benefits are significant, international diffusion can be relatively rapid and the gaps may be closed, bringing growth in train.
4. Participation in world capital markets offers a greater range of opportunities for financing investment in the generation of new knowledge and its use in manufacturing.

Grossman and Helpman (1989, 1990, 1991) have explored the implications of knowledge creation for growth and trade. They endogenise R&D by making it a costly activity incorporated in a general equilibrium analysis, which determines factor prices and hence the market conditions which help determine how expensive it is to generate new knowledge. In some cases, R&D output is new designs (enhancing product variety) produced with primary inputs like Romer; in others, quality improvements to an unchanged range of products flow from industry specific patent races, each aimed at developing the next generation of product. Research success bestows on users of the new knowledge a degree of market power (the power to price above marginal cost). But with free entry assumed in the sector producing the knowledge in the first place, equilibrium expected returns in the R&D industry will be forced to the level of the opportunity cost of capital. Spill-overs are allowed to take one of two forms: producing new designs increases the overall stock of knowledge and generating a patentable blueprint; in the quality improvement case, a research firm may fail to secure a patent in a race at period t but is equipped now to enter the next race at $t + 1$.

In a rock-bottom model which neglects much of the detail described above, Grossman and Helpman (1990) present a version of their analysis which exposes two of the central features of concern to them: first, determination of the growth rate by the allocation of resources to knowledge-creating activity and second, the critical role of spill-overs in sustaining long-run growth. In this version, land R and labour L, available in fixed supplies, combine to produce output in two sectors $i = 1, 2$ through a CRS, neoclassical production function:

$$Q_i = KF_i(R_i, L_i) \tag{9.1}$$

K is the domestic stock of knowledge at a given time and increases in proportion to the manufacturing experience of one of the sectors, say sector 1:

$$dK(t)/dt = \beta Q_1 \tag{9.2}$$

This reminds us that manufacturing firms produce both their physical outputs and knowledge, but in this case the knowledge generated is restricted to LBD. Assume that the benefits are wholly external to the firms where they arise and raise productivity in *both* sectors. Consumers maximise a homothetic, intertemporal utility function. With a function of this kind, the slopes of all indifference curves are parallel along a ray from the origin.

Consider a small open economy comprising small profit-maximising firms that ignore their own contributions to future knowledge and enjoy no spill-over benefits of knowledge from abroad. The economy faces given relative prices P_1/P_2. As LBD shifts the country's ppf outwards, output in each sector will rise by the identical proportion permitted by the increase in knowledge. Since R and L are given in aggregate and LBD augments their productivity levels equiproportionally in each sector, R_i and L_i will not change as the result of factor growth or intersectoral transfers. Thus:

$$dQ_i/dt = dK/dt \cdot F_i(R_i, L_i)$$
$$= \beta Q_1 \cdot F_i(R_i, L_i)$$

and

$$(dQ_1/dt)/Q_1 = \beta F_1(R_1, L_1) \qquad\qquad (9.3)$$

which is the growth rate common to both sectors.

It is at once clear from (9.3) that the faster LBD occurs (the higher β is), the higher the growth rate will be. The growth rate will also be raised if there is an increase in the supply of the input used intensively in the knowledge-generating sector in this country alone. If the analysis is extended to two countries, each with an explicit R&D activity generating domestic (but still no international) spill-overs, it can be shown that world growth will accelerate when each country's effective labour force grows by the same proportion. Moreover, the higher the long-run world growth rate, the larger the effective labour force of the country with comparative advantage in R&D, but may be slowed if the effective labour force is growing more quickly in the country with comparative disadvantage in R&D.

Now introducing positive international spill-overs, it is easy to see how trade might influence growth. Increases in knowledge dK/dt are a function of output of good 1 in *all* countries. And any one country would enjoy the benefits of technological progress abroad.

As we have noted elsewhere, however, it is usually necessary for a country to invest in resources to capture spill-over benefits. In their 1991 paper, Grossman and Helpman explore the implications of this in the context of a model of the product cycle (see Chapter 3 in this book), featuring endogenous innovation and technology transfer. The international dimensions of the product cycle were analysed by Vernon (1966). In Vernon's framework, the product cycle has three phases. In the first, the product is new and still intensive in its use of research and skilled labour inputs. Costs are high, sales low and many technical difficulties remain. In these conditions, it is rational to undertake both R&D and production in a country at the industrialised centre or in the North, as it was later styled, since such countries have comparative advantage in knowledge-intensive production and the frequent adaptations and modifications needed at this point are most effectively achieved if skills and production are in proximity.

In the second (growth) phase, the solution of technical teething problems and increasing receptiveness in the market allow costs and price to fall and lead entrepreneurs both to seek export markets and possibly to consider production abroad as a means of discouraging foreign firms from profiting by imitation. If they produce abroad, they will look for locations which also offer promising markets close by. In Vernon's third phase, 'maturity', sales growth will have levelled off as the market becomes saturated and peripheral countries (the South) acquire comparative advantage in production by offering relatively cheap labour to work in the now-routine and standardised production lines for the good. The upshot is that 'interregional trade in manufactured goods involves exchange of the latest, innovative goods, produced only in the North, for older more established goods, produced predominantly or entirely in the South' (Grossman and Helpman, 1991: 1214).

Formal attempts to model Vernon's description date back to Krugman (1979), with extensions by Dollar (1986) and Jensen and Thursby (1987). In Krugman's work, the rates of introduction of new products in the North and technology transfer to the South are exogenous, while the extensions have striven to endogenise one or both rates. In Grossman and Helpman (1991) endogenously determined steady-state values are sought for both product innovation and imitation rates.

In their analysis, the North has a substantial absolute and comparative advantage in developing and marketing new products. Innovation and imitation (through reverse-engineering) are resource-costly learning activities in which a single input, labour, is used to create 'blueprints' for producing a particular variety of good. Partly appropriable benefits from using the blueprint in production spill-over into general technological knowledge. Firms in both locations act as profit-maximising Bertrand competitors, Southern wages are below Northern and the innovation productivity of Northerners far exceeds that in the South. These conditions ensure that all innovation occurs in the North and all imitation in the South.

Southerners and Northerners compete in the markets in which each product variant is sold and in conformity with Vernon's vision, Southern firms are always able to use their low-wage cost advantage to price variants at a level which gives them the world market, once successful imitation has occurred. How much imitation occurs depends crucially on expected profitability; imitation occurs only if the present value of profits from manufacturing a variant is at least equal to the costs of imitation. These costs will be lower and (for any given distribution of profit streams) the imitation rate higher, the higher labour productivity is in imitation research work. This productivity level itself rises with the stock of disembodied knowledge, which grows with spill-overs from previous imitation experience and with the number of varieties previously imitated.

Northerners undertake a similar comparison of expected benefits and costs, but, in addition to factoring in their innovation research costs have to account for the probability that any new product developed will be targeted for imitation by Southerners. There are therefore conflicting forces at work, but Grossman and Helpman (1991) show that, within the specifications of their model, trade will speed growth in both regions. Trade increases the expected value of innovators' profit streams above the levels which they would have enjoyed in a no-trade world, even though the probability of imitation rises over time and will ultimately put an end to their monopoly profits.

Other results of the analysis are that increasing Northerner's research-labour productivity would lead to a reduced rate of imitation (in SSG), while rising imitation-labour productivity in the South leads to an increase; size (in terms of labour force) is also important. A larger Southern labour force is (in SSG) associated with faster technology transfer and a rise in Southern wages relative to Northern (contrary to Krugman's earlier results). A larger Northern labour force reduces the imitation rate, but may or may not affect the innovation rate, depending on how far Southern wages are below Northern.

While this analysis takes international spill-overs of technological knowledge as given, Siebert (1991) discusses the range of cases when spill-overs do or do not occur. Far from the findings of Grossman and Helpman, spill-overs might be negligible and the whole process of innovation only contribute to the domestic knowledge base. While it is implausible that this should happen for very long, it might happen for long enough to give a country a first-mover advantage and set in motion the process of establishing it as a 'growth pole' (Myrdal, 1957).

Another way of saying that spill-overs are negligible is to describe knowledge capital as immobile, attracting mobile factors (in particular physical capital) to it. Although it may seem improbable that knowledge should be immobile, Klodt (1991) has argued that this will be the case when R&D interacts with production through a circular process (see p. 250 of this book) in which R&D feeds off LBD, which can occur only in production itself. The aero industry is an example. While much has been made of the global nature of modern industry, it is interesting that a large proportion of R&D continues to be undertaken by MNCs in the country regarded as their base.

In some industries such as electronics and computers, R&D can be undertaken without feedback from production and such activity is potentially more mobile. This observation provides the basis for modifying Vernon's original vision; as skilled labour inputs accumulate with education around the world, it becomes potentially sensible to undertake some types of R&D away from existing industrialised centres. Comparative advantage in undertaking R&D may also shift internationally, as it has from the United States in areas where knowledge capital is mobile.

Clearly, there is a link here to Lucas' work (p. 332). Countries which invest heavily in education can create the basis for comparative advantage in undertaking research in research-mobile industries. This will contribute to their growth potential and will help them towards long-term higher growth rates through learning by learning effects of the kind explored by Stiglitz (pp. 328–31).

Grossman and Helpman (1989) show why MNCs might be expected to emerge. They assume that headquarters administrative services are produced with human capital alone, but that manufacturing uses these services, together with unskilled labour. New products are produced in the country containing the headquarters. If differences in international factor endowments are large enough, MNCs will at some point emerge and over time there will usually be a rise in the number of products manufactured and output and employment levels of subsidiaries.

Other traditions have attempted to explain the existence of MNCs differently (Caves, 1982). Scale economies in the theory of multiplant operation can readily be extended to explain the common ownership of plants in two or more countries. Alternatively, the transaction costs approach of Williamson can be applied. The potential for opportunistic behaviour and uncertainty, for example, creates appropriation problems for an innovator in one country which might consider licensing producers elsewhere to deploy new technology in return for a fee. This might prompt the innovator to buy into the firms instead and become an MNC. The MNC is then the profit-maximising solution when transaction costs are included.

MNCs have attracted substantial criticism over the years, but they are a major organisational vehicle for effecting the transfer of technology internationally (Caves *et al.* 1983; ESCAP, 1984). The main reasons usually given for this are that owing to the high costs and riskiness of developing new technology, only very large companies can afford to undertake R&D and only by hosting a subsidiary of such firms can countries gain ready access to the proprietary knowledge corporations generate; when large companies transfer technology internationally, foreign investment, involving ownership of assets in another country, is their preferred way of proceeding. Thus countries risk never acquiring up-to-date technology in many areas unless they host a subsidiary of an MNC.

That said, Pavitt (1985) notes that local reverse engineering, following the import of final products, led to half of the major innovative imitations of foreign technology in Canada between 1960 and 1979; 280 innovations were studied. That suggests MNC investment may be no more important than local ingenuity in acquiring, absorbing and adapting internationally sourced technology. The reverse engineering skills of the Japanese and Koreans are well known and have laid the local foundations for enterprises which subsequently became multinationals.

Appendix 1

To see an illustration of comparative advantage, look now at Figure A9.1. The lines *bd* and *ef* represent the production possibilities for Z and A, respectively. With a single, general purpose input and fixed input–output ratios for each production process, A could produce a maximum of 500*F* or 250*M*, Z a maximum of 250*F* or 100*M*. Assuming the divisibility and intersectoral mobility of the input, for each unit of *M* sacrificed, A can always produce an extra 2*F* and Z another 2.5*F*. This is just another way of seeing why A has comparative advantage in producing *M* and Z the comparative advantage in *F*. The implication of mobility is that all points on *bd* and *ef* are attainable. The implication of each country having a different comparative advantage is that *bd* and *ef* have different slopes: 2.5:1 and 2:1, respectively. These slopes represent the rates at which *M* can be bought at the cost of *F* (and *vice versa*) in the absence of trade in each country.

Suppose the countries agree to trade *F* for *M* and *M* for *F* at a ratio somewhere between the pretrade rates, say 2.25:1, although there is no necessity at all for the actual rate to be the average of the pretrade ratios. It will be determined by the interaction of supply- and demand-side factors, as always. Then Z could specialise in producing *F* at point *b* and trade along the dashed line *bg*, and A in producing *M* at point *f*, and trade along *fh*. For each country, the opportunities for consumption would no longer be constrained by domestic production possibilities, the areas *Obd* and *Oef*, but would now lie beyond, on the dashed lines. If consumption preferences are summarised in the form of community indifference curves, tangencies at *g*(*o*) and *g*(1) would show how national welfare would be raised in Z, and those at *h*(*o*) and *h*(1) in A. A would export *h*(1)–*u* of *M* for *f*–*u* of imported *F*, and Z export *v*–*g*(1) of *F* for *b*–*v* of imported *M*.

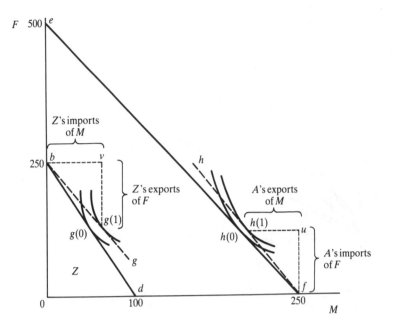

Figure A9.1 Comparative advantage and the gains from trade: the case of two countries, two goods and linear production possibility frontiers with a single, general purpose input.

Anything less than complete specialisation in this simple example would yield smaller gains from trade. But while the example clearly illustrates how the principle of comparative advantage works, it is also too simple an account of production; only one input is considered, the input:output relationship is fixed for all output levels in any country (i.e. a fixed coefficient technology) and the technology, which determines the values of the coefficients, is unvarying through time.

Appendix 2

To show how the TOT are themselves determined, turn to Figure A9.2. On the vertical axis we show quantities of F exported by Z to A and imported by A from Z; on the horizontal, quantities of M exported by A to Z and imported by Z from A. The slopes of the three rays OT', OT'' and OT''' represent different terms of trade. Moving in an anticlockwise direction, the TOT improve from the point of view of A, since the increasing slopes of the rays indicate that for each unit of M exported A will receive more F in return. Moving in a clockwise direction, Z receives increasing quantities of M per unit of F exported, i.e. Z's TOT improve. Given the terms of trade represented on each ray, we can identify at points like V', E and V'' the quantities of M which A is prepared to offer as exports and at points like W', E and W'', the

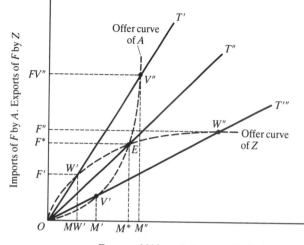

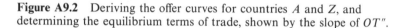

Figure A9.2 Deriving the offer curves for countries *A* and *Z*, and determining the equilibrium terms of trade, shown by the slope of *OT"*.

quantities of *F* which *Z* offers as exports. The curves *OV'EV"* and *OW'EW"* are described as the offer curves of A and Z, respectively.

It will be realised that each point on an offer curve merely conveys information found in the ppf-CIC diagrams in a different fashion. If the absolute value of the slope of *OT"* in Figure A9.2, for example, were the same as that of *TA–TA'* in Figure 9.3 (p. 388), the quantity *OM** offered for export by A would be identical to the quantity *AM2–AM1* shown as the export element of A's trade triangle. The offer curve is derived by allowing TOT lines like *TA–TA'* to rotate around the ppf and finding for each case the trades that A would undertake to reach its highest CIC. The same can, of course, also be said for Z. It is crucial to understand this, since it reveals that the position and shape of each country's offer curve depends on the shapes and positions of their ppfs and CICs. When any country's ppf (or CICs) shifts, so will its offer curve.

Notice, too, that as A's TOT improve, its offers of *M* increase from *M'* to *M** and then *M"*, but at a decreasing rate, reflecting from the outward-bowed shape of the ppf the increasing opportunity cost of specialising further in the production of *M*, the more of it the country produces. As Z's TOT improve, its offers of *F* increase from *F'* to *F** and *F"*, again rising at a falling rate.

Where the offer curves intersect, at *E*, the TOT represented by the slope of *OT"* are those at which A is prepared to trade exactly the same quantities of *M* for *F* as Z is prepared to trade *F* for *M*. This would not be true of any other TOT. If the TOT were the slope of *OT'*, for example, A would be willing to offer *OM"* of *M* in return for imports of *OFV"* of *F*, but Z would be prepared to offer only *OF'* of *F* (much less than OFV'') in return for OMW' of M. This state of affairs should, of course, at once set in motion market adjustments in which A attempted to induce Z to increase its exports of F above OF' by offering more M per unit of F in return, i.e. shifting the TOT in Z's favour, rotating the TOT rays in a clockwise direction. While traders are well informed and can and do respond to market incentives, the TOT will always converge on their equilibrium level, the slope of OT''.

References

Bhagwati, J. (1959) 'Growth, terms of trade and comparative advantage', *Economia Internazionale*, August, 412–14.

Caves, R.E. (1982) *Multinational Enterprise and Economic Analysis*, Cambridge: Cambridge University Press.

Caves, R.E. *et al.* (1983) 'The imperfect market for technology licences', *Oxford Bulletin of Economics and Statistics* 45.

Chaciolades, M. (1978) *International Trade Theory and Policy*, Tokyo: McGraw-Hill.

Dollar, D. (1986) 'Technological innovation, capital mobility and the product cycle in North-South trade', *American Economic Review* 76, 177–90.

ESCAP (1984) *Costs and Conditions of Technology Transfer Through Transnational Corporations*, ESCAP/UNCTC Publications Series B, No.3., Bangkok.

Findlay, R. and H. Grubert (1959) 'Factor intensities, technological progress and the terms of trade', February, 111–21.

Findlay, R. (1984) 'Growth and development in trade models', in R. Jones and P. Kenen (eds) *Handbook of International Economics Vol. 1*, Amsterdam: North-Holland, 187–236.

Grossman, G. and E. Helpman (1989) 'Product development and international trade', *Journal of Political Economy* 97(6), 1261–83.

Grossman, G. and E. Helpman (1990) 'Trade, innovation and growth', *American Economic Review* (Papers and Proceedings), 80(2), 86–91.

Grossman, G. and E. Helpman (1991) 'Endogenous product cycles', *Economic Journal* 101 (September), 1214–29.

Jensen, R. and M. Thursby (1987) 'A decision-theoretical model of innovation, technology transfer and trade', *Review of Economic Studies* 54: 631–47.

Klodt, H. (1991) 'Comparative advantage and prospective structural adjustment in Eastern Europe', Kiel Working Paper 477, Kiel.

Krugman, P.R. (1979) 'A model of innovation, technology transfer, and the world distribution of income', *Journal of Political Economy* 87: 253–66.

Meier, G.M. (1968) *The International Economics of Development*, New York: Harper Row.

Meier, G.M. (1980) *International Economics, The Theory of Policy*, London: Oxford University Press.

Myrdal, G. (1957) *Economic Theory and Underdeveloped Regions.*, London: Duckworth.

Pavitt, K. (1985) *International Patterns of Technological Accumulation*, Sussex: Science Policy Research Unit.

Romer, P. (1990) 'Endogenous technological change', *Journal of Political Economy* 98(5): S71–S102.

Siebert, H. (1991) 'A Schumpeterian model of growth in the world economy: Some notes on a new paradigm in international economics', *Weltwirtschaftliches Archiv* 127(4), 800–13.

Vernon, R. (1966) 'International investment and international trade in the product cycle', *Quarterly Journal of Economics* 80, 190–207.

10
Conclusion

By some standards, this is a relatively long book. But it has touched only briefly on the large body of empirical observations available in the area and has had little to say, directly, about policy. The omissions are deliberate, since a thorough analysis of all historical data in the area and a discussion of all policy implications would have made the book quite unmanageable. One reason why the book is long is that it has focused on the *economic* analysis of innovation but at the same time aimed to be accessible to non-economists. This has called for presenting tools and concepts used in economics generally. Secondly, economic analysis usually takes as exogenous fundamental data relating to preferences and technology; the technology of production is part of the framework within which economic analysis is conducted. To understand how economists deal with issues of technology change, therefore, it is always necessary first to describe generally the setting in which the change is to occur. It would have made little sense in Chapter 9 to talk about the influence of innovation on international comparative advantage, for example, unless the basis for international trade had first been laid out.

Since the technology frames all economic analysis, it should not be surprising that when technology is allowed to change, almost anything can happen, particularly since technological change involves changes to both the nature of goods and services and the ways in which they are produced. This is another reason for the length of the book. The greater the precision required in predicting the potential implications of technological innovation, the more we must specify what sort of innovation is occurring and what is being assumed about other elements of the economic system. This was apparent, for example, in the analysis of connections between technological progress and employment (Chapters 3, 7 and 8). The ambiguities noted should be a caution to those who believe that the connection is either obvious or simple, but a more general lesson is that whenever the economic effects of technological change are considered, analysis will usually involve working systematically through a range of possibilities.

That said, one of the most important insights in modern economics is a single clear prediction: that technological progress and the processes of innovation which drive it are central to achieving sustained, long-run economic growth (Chapter 7 and, in an international context, Chapter 9). Although the specific processes involved here remain controversial (see, for example, the difference in approach of Romer (1990) and Scott (1989)), the intuitive basis for the proposition in a single-output world is clear; once technical efficiency is achieved and scale economies are exhausted, only productivity-raising innovation can increase the output derived from given quantities of inputs. And when inputs are themselves growing, real output and income per head will reach a plateau unless technological progress permits inputs to become ever more effective in producing output over time. This in turn suggests a central role for learning of many kinds and implies the importance of human capital identified in 'New' Growth Theory.

With product innovation, there is also the possibility (Chapters 3 and 7) of qualitative improvement in final output itself, which may involve packing more of the same characteristics into each unit of an existing product or changing the characteristics themselves. Such changes involve effectively deploying knowledge to generate new designs, but may not imply using up physical inputs at any faster rate than before. Output value may increase merely by the more ingenious application of knowledge.

While innovation is central to achieving long-term growth, the growth-theoretic analysis of technological progress tends to conceal more than it reveals about the inherent messiness, turbulence and unpredictability of the innovation process (foreshadowed in Chapter 2). The origins of radical invention, rooted in acts of technological creation, remain largely beyond the reach of economic explanation and not all that happens in the innovation process is economically driven. Furthermore, although economic incentives can be invoked to explain when an invention will be most vigorously applied and developed, random (and sometimes trivial) factors may determine the particular form which the innovation will take (Chapters 6 and 7).

Across space, industries vary substantially in their patterns of innovation and nations around the world also differ widely. Across time, the same industry may at one time be active in innovation and at another investing very little. The same may be true over history of individual countries. Across both time and space, spill-over effects are all the time at work, so that knowledge developed for use in reaching Mars assists the designers of non-stick saucepans, skills acquired in one firm heading for bankruptcy are applied to help another on the path to success and techniques used to enrich dry-land farmers in Australia appear years later in the repertoire of Mongolians.

The astonishing diversity of the processes and phenomena associated with innovation suggests that the idea of a unified theory to explain it all may be a pipedream (though see Dosi *et al.* (1988), OECD (1992), Lundvall (1992) and Nelson (1993) for the most recent efforts). Just as economists have resigned themselves to working with a suite of oligopoly models rather than a single model to accommodate all possibilities, students of innovation may have to be satisfied with a set of approaches, each with its comparative advantage in dealing with a particular type of issue. A major purpose of this book, however, has been to show how using economics can throw at least some light on the ways in which decision-making, driven by economic incentives, can shape the innovation process. Unless it is claimed that the pattern of technological outcomes is entirely unconnected with economic decision-makers' efforts to shape it, there must be a logical case for proceeding in this way. On the other hand it is easy to think of reasons why economic analysis can offer only imperfect and incomplete insights. We treat these in two groups, one broadly concerned with units of analysis and the other with methodological approach.

Units of analysis

The process of innovation cuts across and redefines the boundaries of units of analysis routinely used in economics in particular firms and industries (Lundvall, 1992, considers this at length). Analysis (Chapter 5) which tries to explain the boundaries of firms and the shifting structure of industries goes some way towards dealing with these problems. But while one part of economics recognises the reshaping power of technological change, other parts of economic analysis addressing innovation (most of the game-theoretic modelling of technological competition, for example) appear to ignore it. Another perspective on the same point is to note that the technological trajectory as a unit of analysis in studying innovation is not necessarily anchored to an economic unit of analysis. The evolution of a common approach to dealing with production problems may take place across many industries, as, for example, the widespread application of flexible manufacturing techniques suggests. This means that diffusion and evolution in a technology cannot be understood by reference to industry-specific analysis alone.

A further point is that economics has tended to view firms in two ways, either in support of a model which allows the price mechanism to coordinate all activity, where firms engage in cash-based transactions to trade goods and services with unaffiliated parties, or, in recognition that internal administrative mechanisms often supplant the price system as the device for coordinating activities within organisations, firms are viewed alternatively as large, integrated bureaucratic corporations. It is difficult to model anything but purely exogenous innovation in the first vision and neither approach exhausts the range of organisational options. This is particularly worrying in dealing with technological innovation.

In addition to the options already noted, there are, for example, small entrepreneurial firms which rely on affiliations with the venture capital market and/or with large, multidivisional corporations for financial and other forms of support and which specialise in generating new products and processes (Friar and Horwitch, 1985). Alternatively, firms may perceive that their interests in pursuing innovation are best served by establishing some form of strategic alliance. Teece (1989) points out in detail that such alliances are not organisational forms (like different sorts of firm) but 'rather denote the exchange or transactional context between and among organisations' (p. 29). Two good examples of strategic alliances are consortia (alliances, like Airbus Industrie in Europe, designed to achieve a specific mission) and joint ventures. The latter provide the vehicle for organising collaborative R&D activity and with various operational and equity arrangements are flexible enough to overcome the problems of potential opportunism which we argued (Chapter 5) helped explain integration. The economics behind assessing the relative merits of organisational forms and contractual arrangements as they influence innovation is one of the most intriguing areas of research currently unfolding.

An associated research programme challenges the notion of the industry as the principal multifirm focus for analysing technological innovation. Strategic alliances take analysis beyond the boundaries of the single firm and imply cooperative rather than competitive behaviour. Cooperative interfirm behaviour has usually been treated by economics in the context of oligopolistic collusion, a concept related to industry forms in which competition is the norm (Jorde and Teece, 1990). But more recently a different notion of the group, the network, has emerged as an alternative unit of analysis and this, by construction, is driven by cooperation. Again, research in this area is active.

In its emphasis on competition, economics has tended to adopt units of analysis consistent with a vision of separate competing entities. But as the economics of innovation reveals, there may often be good reason for innovating entities to cooperate, up to a point at least. The cross-firm, cross-industry links which emerge are now being recognised in economics, but may also call for new units of analysis in economics, more closely aligned with flows in the system supporting change in the technology (Chapter 2).

Economic methods: equilibrium and evolutionary modelling

Economics has also appeared to offer a less than persuasive analysis of innovation because of its use of equilibrium (and often static equilibrium) methods. Given the disequilibrium and disequilibrating character of innovation, the essential dynamics of the innovation process and the unpredictability of its path, it appears questionable whether static or even dynamic equilibrium methods are appropriate. The increasing dissatisfaction with subtle and complex game-theoretic equilibrium solutions was canvassed in Chapter 6. This discomfort with equilibrium methods led economists of the evolutionary school, including Arthur, Dosi, Iwai, Metcalfe, Nelson, Orsenigo, Silverberg and Winter, to try a different approach. In that approach, taking its economic cue from Schumpeter, equilibrium is a state towards which an economic system might or might not tend but the focus is in any case on the process of change rather than the implications of some hypothesised final set of conditions.

The approach is spawning its own research programme and it is still too early to judge whether it will remain outside the mainstream of economics, be absorbed by it or subsume it. From what has been presented in the book, we offer the following speculations. First, the demonstrable importance of history in understanding any current state will increasingly be acknowledged in dynamic analysis of all kinds. While evolutionists speak repeatedly of lock-in effects and path dependency, similar effects can be found (but not with those labels) in the work of Stiglitz (learning by learning), Lucas (Chapter 7) and some of the work on pre-emptive patenting (Chapter 6). Since it is empirically observable that success builds on success in innovation, the need to explain the facts must ultimately force all types of theory in the area to take account of history.

Second, evolutionists rely heavily on simple rules, often with just a single parameter, to capture economic behaviour, even though they may be building highly complex systems of equations from such rules. These rules might be used (as with the work of Iwai and Metcalfe noted in Chapter 6) to derive general results such as the economic equivalent of the Fisher equation. Or (as with Nelson and Winter and Silverberg, Dosi and Orsenigo in Chapters 6 and 7), they might be used as the basis for simulation exercises. The general justification for invoking rule-based behaviour may be found in the discussion of routines and rules of thumb (Chapter 4), but the specific causal links between that sort of discussion and variations in actual parameter values is often only imperfectly forged. (Compare, for example, the discussion of non-optimising behaviour in the early parts of Nelson and Winter (1982) and the models they present later in the book.) It is unclear, in other words, that the evolutionists have a microeconomic foundation for their work well enough developed to challenge the tight, axiomatic framework provided by the rationality hypothesis used to underpin optimisation exercises in economics.

Third, the analytical value of simulation exercises remains controversial, though it has to be recognised that complex systems of differential–difference equations are often not susceptible to analysis in any other way. And the result of such analysis is to map in detail precisely the turbulence and messiness of processes of change which much formal analysis tends to disguise. But, it might be argued that the whole purpose of modelling is to abstract from unnecessary complexity and that for many purposes, it is unimportant or irrelevant to know the details of process. Thus, when Nelson and Winter declare a tie in the contest between their growth model and Solow's (Chapter 7), we might want to ask whether all the extra effort involved in laying out and running their many-sector model was worthwhile.

This controversy is unlikely to be resolved satisfactorily at a general level; conclusions will depend importantly on the specific objectives which the analysis is designed to pursue. If we want to know which specific form of a process innovation will triumph in a technological contest, for example, it will be relevant to take account of path-dependent effects, especially learning, which become clear only if the competition is itself analysed as a process. On the other hand, if we want to know the long-term impact of a given form of technological progress on an economy under well-specified conditions, much can be learned merely by analysing steady-state paths.

Fourth, it is unclear how much weight to place on the explanatory power of simulation models. Evolutionary research will need to develop criteria to choose among different simulation models generating similar evolutionary paths. It will also need to address the findings from chaos theory (mentioned briefly in Chapter 7) that even the slightest of variations in initial conditions can breed vast variations between the evolutionary paths which flow from them. Without well-defined foundations for identifying why the initial conditions are as they are, the predictive power of evolutionary modelling will always be subject to arbitrariness.

In conclusion, evolutionary economics, in some ways purposely designed to look at the issues of innovation in economic systems, has done much to expose the nature of the messiness of the process, rooted in the diversity of firms, path-dependent effects and the fundamental uncertainty associated with decision-making when outcomes cannot be known (Chapter 1). Some of its emphases are now echoed in mainstream work, where the importance of history, irreversibilities in investment and the difficulties posed by uncertainty are increasingly recognised. Indeed, it is harder to sustain a clear distinction between 'orthodox' economics and other traditions now than it was when Nelson and Winter wrote their book in 1982.

But while it has illustrated on problems of time and uncertainty often ignored in the mainstream, it remains unclear whether its own analysis of systems incorporating innovation has established a clear edge over other modern theoretical work on firms, industries and the domestic and international economies. Game theory has become bogged down, perhaps, but has shown the crucial role of strategy, in technological competition which tends to be underplayed by evolutionists. Growth theory floundered for a while on endogenising technological progress, but has renewed itself in the 1980s and 1990s precisely by exploiting the insight that new technological knowledge has widespread beneficial externalities. Modern macroeconomics has started to address the employment implications of innovation. Evolutionists cannot claim a monopoly of wisdom in the area, but will also have to get used to imitation and innovative adaptation of their ideas in other parts of the discipline.

Survey of findings

Despite our reservations, the number and breadth of results reported in this book are encouraging. They shed light on the process and will help to shape empirical research and policy formation in the future. What has been learned? A selective survey, confined to ten major points, follows.

First, innovation is costly. Research (and more so development) absorb human and other resources (Chapter 4). Acquiring new technology developed elsewhere involves purchasing new capital equipment or paying licence fees. Learning to use new technology absorbs time and effort which could have been productive in other uses. Putting an innovation to use now, while older technology is still available, involves sacrificing profit which the older technology could have earned. The immediate implication is that innovation is a subject suitable for economic analysis, which is concerned with the allocation of scarce resources among competing uses. In that analysis, prospective benefits must be compared with costs; innovation investment will occur only if those undertaking it believe future returns will at least compensate them for costs incurred. Choices among innovation alternatives will reflect firms' beliefs about the relative magnitudes of returns offered.

As analysis in Chapter 5 suggested, R&D expenditure at the firm level should rise with a fall in the price of inputs into R&D or the interest rate, or a rise in the cost-reducing effectiveness of R&D or demand for the output of firms using new knowledge. The speed of innovation will involve comparing the present value of profits from existing products and processes with those from innovations, given the R&D costs and expected dates of imitation. The aggregate rate of technological advance may also be related to the interest (discount) rate, reflecting the long-term incentives for human capital to locate in R&D activity (Chapter 7). In all of these and many other cases, the quantity and nature of innovative activity reflects the balancing of benefits against costs.

Second, significant sunk costs are involved in innovation. The implication of this is that R&D can be used strategically to create an entry barrier and provides an important part of the explanation why monopoly power tends to flow from innovation (Chapter 5). Profit-seeking firms are motivated to undertake R&D to earn rents associated with the asymmetric advantage it creates and the opportunity it may provide to sustain the advantage through learning by doing.

While innovation is a necessary, though not sufficient, condition for establishing or retaining a competitive edge, case-by-case analysis is required to determine the level of deterrence against entry and associated returns which innovation will yield. Other firms may not have the relevant knowledge and know-how and the financial strength to attempt to undermine an incumbent's first-mover advantage in a post-innovation competition. Precise information about cost conditions, the pace of innovation and firms' internal learning rates relative to their rivals are needed to judge whether action–reaction will occur or, more generally, which firms will come to dominate (if any) (Chapter 6).

Third, new technology varies widely in the way it influences production costs and sales revenues (Chapters 2, 3 and 4). Since these impacts are at the heart of determining the return on R&D, one implication is that R&D intensity also varies widely among firms and industries, reaching highest levels, all things being equal, where an additional R&D dollar has the greatest effect on cost reduction or sales growth (Chapters 5 and 6). This may be taken to reflect the differential impact of innovational opportunity. Another implication is that it may be possible to classify industries according to whether they characteristically undertake R&D themselves or merely diffuse new technology developed by suppliers. This in turn may signpost technological bases for interindustry relationships which might in some cases lead to interfirm integration.

Fourth, firms vary widely in their experience of production, the knowledge base they have built upon it, their imitative and innovative behaviour and in the expectations they entertain about future prospects. Such variations account for the variety of technology strategies firms adopt. Evolutionists see this variety as the trigger for the diffusion of new technology and argue that only very general assumptions about the distributions of behavioural characteristics are needed to generate observed patterns of intraindustry performance indices (Chapter 6).

Fifth, technological knowledge is cumulative; success breeds success. One implication is that the direction of innovation is often strongly guided by what is known by firms already engaged in production. Firms are much more likely to innovate in the neighbourhood of existing practice than to take leaps in the dark. Technology tends to develop along reasonably well established trajectories shaped by what is already known at each point in time. A further implication is that a firm, industry or economy may be able to sustain a competitive edge indefinitely through learning-by-learning effects based on a greater breadth of experience acquired in earlier periods (Chapter 7).

Sixth, spill-over effects allow imitators to benefit from the efforts of an innovator. Although this may undermine the advantage to be gained by first movers, depending on the relative learning rates of innovator *versus* imitator and discourage innovation, from a macroeconomic viewpoint, spill-overs provide the basis for a non-convexity which offers the prospect of unbounded growth (Chapter 7). Globally, spill-over effects help shape the international pattern of trade (Chapter 9).

Seventh, R&D simultaneously draws on the profits of firms in an industry and influences their future costs and product characteristics. Under competitive entry conditions, firms in an innovating industry are driven to use any potential profit on cost-reducing or product-enhancing R&D and in the long run, industry structure and innovative activity are co-determined endogenously by basic technological and market conditions. Industry concentration and research intensity are ultimately determined by opportunities for technological advance, market size and price elasticities of demand. This insight is common to both the game-theoretic and evolutionary styles of analysis. Feedbacks between the basic conditions, innovation strategies and industry performance shape the evolution of each industry.

Eighth, product innovation is a major means of creating entry barriers and may also be used to soften the blow of price competition (Chapters 5 and 6). Theory suggests R&D for product innovation will be at its greatest in young industries, though other explanations would have to be sought for the observation that some mature industries rejuvenate themselves through massive programmes of expenditure on product innovation. Sunk costs help to determine how many product varieties will be generated and under varying conditions firms may choose to produce variants almost identical or as unalike as possible (Chapter 3).

Ninth, the implications of innovation for employment and unemployment are ambiguous. In the grandiose vision of Pasinetti, the employment-creating effects of product innovation tend to be outweighed by the employment destroying effects of increased productivity through process innovation. In the short run, almost all forms of cost-cutting process innovation will reduce employment, but in the longer run the increased competitiveness of production may well lead to new jobs which will absorb some of, all or more than all of the employment initially destroyed. Inter-industry effects are also potentially important and much will depend on both the nature of the advance and the flexibility of wages (Chapter 8).

Tenth, innovation is the ultimate force for reshaping economic structures of all kinds. To accommodate it, firms grow and fragment, integrate and diversify; industries are born, grow and are transformed, economies experience continuous structural change and in international trade develop and exploit new forms of comparative advantage. Yet, as we noted in our first point, innovation is also importantly economically driven. As yet we have no complete map of all the connections between economic forces and changing products and production technology. While the area is no longer an unknown territory, there is ample opportunity for further exploration.

References

Dosi, G. *et al.* (1988) *Technical Change and Economic Theory*, London: Pinter.

Friar, J. and M. Horwitch (1985) 'The emergence of technology strategy: a new dimension of strategic management', *Technology in Society* 7: 143–78.

Jorde, T.M. and D.J. Teece (1990) 'Innovation and cooperation: implications for competition and antitrust', *Journal of Economic Perspectives* 4(3): 75–96.

Lundvall, B.A. (ed.) (1992) *National Systems of Innovation: Towards a Theory of Innovation and Interactive Learning*, London: Pinter.

Nelson, R.R. (ed.) (1993) *National Systems of Innovation: A Comparative Study*, Oxford: Oxford University Press.

Nelson, R.R. and S. Winter (1982) *An Evolutionary Theory of Economic Change*, Cambridge, MA: Belknap Press of Harvard University Press.

OECD (1992) *Technology and the Economy: The Key Relationships*, Paris: OECD.

Romer, P. (1990) 'Endogenous technological change', *Journal of Political Economy* 98(5): S71–S102.

Scott, M.Fg. (1989) *A New View of Economic Growth*, Oxford: Oxford University Press.

Teece, D.J. (1989) 'Innovation and the organisation of industry', unpublished working paper, Center for Research in Management, University of California at Berkeley.

Index